Programming SQL Server 2005

Other resources from O'Reilly

Related titles Database in Depth   SQL Cookbook™
Learning SQL on SQL   SQL in a Nutshell
  Server 2005   SQL Pocket Guide
Learning SQL

oreilly.com *oreilly.com* is more than a complete catalog of O'Reilly books. You'll also find links to news, events, articles, weblogs, sample chapters, and code examples.

oreillynet.com is the essential portal for developers interested in open and emerging technologies, including new platforms, programming languages, and operating systems.

Conferences O'Reilly brings diverse innovators together to nurture the ideas that spark revolutionary industries. We specialize in documenting the latest tools and systems, translating the innovator's knowledge into useful skills for those in the trenches. Visit *conferences.oreilly.com* for our upcoming events.

Safari Bookshelf (*safari.oreilly.com*) is the premier online reference library for programmers and IT professionals. Conduct searches across more than 1,000 books. Subscribers can zero in on answers to time-critical questions in a matter of seconds. Read the books on your Bookshelf from cover to cover or simply flip to the page you need. Try it today for free.

Programming SQL Server 2005

Bill Hamilton

Beijing · Cambridge · Farnham · Köln · Sebastopol · Tokyo

Programming SQL Server 2005
by Bill Hamilton

Copyright © 2006 O'Reilly Media, Inc. All rights reserved.
Printed in the United States of America.

Published by O'Reilly Media, Inc., 1005 Gravenstein Highway North, Sebastopol, CA 95472.

O'Reilly books may be purchased for educational, business, or sales promotional use. Online editions
are also available for most titles (*safari.oreilly.com*). For more information, contact our
corporate/institutional sales department: (800) 998-9938 or *corporate@oreilly.com*.

Editor: Jeff Pepper	**Cover Designer:** Karen Montgomery
Production Editor: Adam Witwer	**Interior Designer:** David Futato
Production Services: Argosy Publishing	**Illustrators:** Robert Romano, Jessamyn Read, and Lesley Borash

Printing History:

February 2006:   First Edition.

ISBN: 978-0-596-00479-8
[LSI]   [2011-04-15]

Table of Contents

Preface

You don't have to be an experienced SQL Server 2005 programmer to use this book; it is designed for users of all levels. You also do not need any experience with SQL Server 2000, as programming SQL Server 2005 is different in nearly every way from programming SQL Server 2000. You do need an understanding of fundamental relational database concepts. Basic knowledge of T-SQL also helps.

The goal of this book is to introduce all facets of programming SQL Server 2005 to developers. This book can be used either as a primer by developers with little or no experience with SQL Server, as a ramp-up to the new programming models for SQL Server 2005 for more experienced SQL Server developers, or as background and primer to specific concepts.

The code in this book is available for download on the O'Reilly web site (*http://www. oreilly.com/catalog/progsqlsvr*), so you don't need to retype it to follow the examples. Only code that is important to illustrate specific concepts is listed in this book, but enough code is presented to let you use the book without loading the actual code. The book does not list user interface code or code generated automatically by Visual Studio .NET.

What You Need to Use This Book

To run the samples in this book, you need a computer running Windows 2000 SP4 or later, Microsoft .NET Framework 2.0 (installed with SQL Server 2005), and SQL Server 2005—Developer, Standard, or Enterprise Edition.

Most of the examples in this book use C# code and Visual Studio 2005. It is easiest to use Visual Studio 2005 to compile and execute the examples in the book. However, you can compile the samples in this book by using the C# command-line compiler (*csc.exe*) included with the .NET Framework.

Some of the examples in this book require the AdventureWorks sample database, which ships with SQL Server 2005 but is not installed automatically. Follow the product documentation to install the AdventureWorks database during the SQL Server 2005 installation or to install it in an existing installation. Other examples in this book require a database called ProgrammingSqlServer2005 that you should create—this new database is used to minimize the impact of the examples on the AdventureWorks database installation.

Conventions Used in This Book

The following typographical conventions are used in this book:

Plain text
> Indicates menu titles, menu options, menu buttons, and keyboard accelerators (such as Alt and Ctrl)

Italic
> Indicates new terms, URLs, email addresses, filenames, file extensions, path-names, directories, and Unix utilities

`Constant width`
> Indicates commands, options, switches, variables, attributes, keys, functions, types, classes, namespaces, methods, modules, properties, parameters, values, objects, events, event handlers, XML tags, HTML tags, macros, databases, the contents of files, or the output from commands

`Constant width italic`
> Shows text that should be replaced with user-supplied values

Code
> Indicates source code—either C# or T-SQL

 This icon signifies a tip, suggestion, or general note.

 This icon indicates a warning or caution.

How to Contact Us

Please address comments and questions concerning this book to the publisher:

> O'Reilly Media, Inc.
> 1005 Gravenstein Highway North
> Sebastopol, CA 95472

(800) 998-9938 (in the United States or Canada)
(707) 829-0515 (international or local)
(707) 829-0104 (fax)

We have a web page for this book, where we list errata, examples, and any additional information. You can access this page at:

http://www.oreilly.com/catalog/progsqlsvr

To comment or ask technical questions about this book, send email to:

bookquestions@oreilly.com

For more information about our books, conferences, Resource Centers, and the O'Reilly Network, see our web site at:

http://www.oreilly.com

Safari® Enabled

 When you see a Safari® Enabled icon on the cover of your favorite technology book, that means the book is available online through the O'Reilly Network Safari Bookshelf.

Safari offers a solution that's better than e-books. It's a virtual library that lets you easily search thousands of top tech books, cut and paste code samples, download chapters, and find quick answers when you need the most accurate, current information. Try it for free at *http://safari.oreilly.com*.

Acknowledgments

This book wouldn't have been possible without the help of many people. I'd like to thank my editors Jeff Pepper, Ralph Davis, and Jonathan Gennick for making this book better. Thanks to reviewers Louis Davidson, Vyas Kondreddi, Deac Lancaster, Alex Lim, and Josh Sackett for providing valuable technical feedback. I'd like to thank the production team—Adam Witwer, Nancy Kotari, and Bill McManus—for putting everything together. I'd also like to thank Jan Shanahan at Microsoft for promptly and patiently answering questions while SQL Server 2005 evolved. Of course, none of this would be necessary without the SQL Server 2005 team at Microsoft—you built a great piece of software. Finally, thank you, Molly, my friends, and my family—you are what matter most.

CHAPTER 1

Introduction

Microsoft SQL Server 2005 is the latest relational database server product from Microsoft, updating Microsoft SQL Server 2000. SQL Server 2005 adds new functionality and improves the performance, reliability, programmability, and usability of SQL Server 2000.

This book describes and shows how to program SQL Server 2005. Generally, the discussions cover the entire topic, because most aspects of programming SQL Server 2005 are new. Examples include using .NET Framework Common Language Runtime (CLR) assemblies to create SQL Server objects, such as stored procedures and triggers, and using SQL Server Management Objects (SMO) to programmatically create, modify, delete, and manage databases, tables, and other SQL Server objects. In the case of Transact-SQL (T-SQL) and ADO.NET 2.0, only enhancements are described and demonstrated. The SQL Server Analysis Services (SSAS) coverage provides a broad introduction to SSAS that should help you to understand what SSAS is, what its key parts are, and how to get started with SSAS programming—the topic is simply too large to do more than that here.

From a programming perspective, new SQL Server 2005 features include the following:

Tools and utilities
> A new IDE called SQL Server Management Studio for managing SQL Server topologies, databases, and objects; and a collection of new tools for tuning, profiling, and developing SQL Server 2005 solutions.

Data types
> New support for storing and working with native XML data and large binary data.

T-SQL enhancements
> New support for Data Definition Language (DDL) triggers, event notifications, bulk operations, recursive queries, and distributed queries, and introduction of new operators.

Programmability enhancements

New support for developing database objects such as stored procedures, triggers, and user-defined functions using .NET programming languages. SQL Native Client (SQLNCLI) combines and replaces the native OLE DB provider for SQL Server and the ODBC provider with a single standalone API. SQLXML 4.0 enhances SQLXML 3.0 with support for new SQL Server 2005 XML data capabilities and SQLNCLI.

XML support

New support for the xml data type used to natively store XML fragments and documents and for manipulating xml data type instances with XML Query Language (XQuery) and XML Data Manipulation Language (DML).

Native XML web services

New support lets SQL Server accept SOAP requests so that you can execute queries without a middle-tier application server such as Internet Information Server (IIS).

SQL Management Objects (SMO)

Extends and supersedes Distributed Management Objects (DMO) for configuring and managing all aspects of SQL Server instances.

SQL Server Integration Services (SSIS)

A new technology for building data integration solutions and workflow solutions. SSIS replaces Data Transformation Services (DTS) introduced in SQL Server 2000.

SQL Server Reporting Services (SSRS)

A server-based reporting technology that supports authoring, distributing, managing, and accessing reports. SSRS was introduced in SQL Server 2000 and has been significantly enhanced in SQL Server 2005.

SQL Server Notification Services

A new built-in technology for building applications that creates and sends messages to subscribers according to a schedule or in response to events.

SQL Server Service Broker

A new technology for building scalable, loosely coupled, distributed applications using message-based communications.

Replication Management Objects (RMO)

Extends and supersedes the DMO replication capabilities for configuring and managing all aspects of SQL Server replication.

SQL Server Agent

Automates administrative tasks by running jobs, monitoring SQL Server, and processing alerts. SQL Server 2005 introduces new SMO classes for creating and managing SQL Server Agent.

SQL Server Mobile Edition
> Provides relational database functionality for mobile devices in a compact footprint with a programming model consistent with SQL Server 2005. Update to SQL Server 2000 Windows CE Edition 2.0.

Contents of This Book

This book is organized into 20 chapters (plus this introduction, and an appendix), each of which focuses on a SQL Server 2005 programming topic. In some cases, more than one chapter is used to cover different aspects of a single topic. Each chapter contains code samples showing you how to program SQL Server 2005. Code samples are written in C# and compiled using the Visual Studio 2005 development environment. To give you an overview of this book's contents, the following list summarizes each chapter:

Chapter 2, *Tools and Utilities*
> This chapter provides an overview of new and enhanced tools and command-line utilities in SQL Server 2005. This chapter describes:
>
> - SQL Server Management Studio, the new IDE for managing SQL Server 2005 objects
> - SQL Server Configuration Manager, used to manage SQL Server 2005 services
> - SQL Server Surface Area Configuration Manager, used to manage the available features, services, and remote connectivity of a SQL Server 2005 instance for security purposes
> - Database Engine Tuning Advisor, used to improve query processing without requiring a detailed understanding of the database structure or how query processing actually occurs
> - SQL Server Profiler, used to monitor query processing for auditing, debugging, and tuning purposes
> - SQL Server Business Intelligence Development Studio, used to develop SQL Server 2005 solutions—Analysis Services, Integration Services, and Reporting Services—with an IDE similar to that of Visual Studio 2005
> - Visual Studio .NET 2005, used for developing CLR routines and solutions for programmatically administering SQL Server 2005
> - The new command-prompt utilities included with SQL Server 2005

Chapter 3, *T-SQL Enhancements*
> This chapter describes the new SQL Server 2005 data types that handle XML and large binary data; enhancements to the T-SQL programming language; new DDL triggers; and new catalog views that replace information schema views in SQL Server 2005 as a mechanism to retrieve metadata about SQL Server objects.

Chapter 4, *Introduction to Common Language Runtime (CLR) Integration*
SQL Server 2005 hosts the .NET Framework CLR in the Database Engine. This arrangement lets you create database objects such as stored procedures, functions, and triggers in programming languages supported by the CLR; you are no longer limited to creating these objects in T-SQL. This chapter introduces programming, testing, debugging, deploying, and securing CLR routines.

Chapter 5, *Programming SQL Server CLR Routines*
This chapter shows how to program the different types of CLR routines—scalar-valued functions, table-valued functions, stored procedures, user-defined aggregate functions, user-defined types, and both DML and DDL triggers.

Chapter 6, *.NET Client-Side Programming*
SQL Server 2005 introduces SQL Native Client (SQLNCLI). It replaces the OLE DB provider for SQL Server and the ODBC provider with a single standalone API that combines their functionality into a single DLL. SQL Server 2005 also introduces SQLXML 4.0, which provides client-side functionality for developing applications that access XML data from SQL Server, process that data, and return the data back to the server. SQLXML 4.0 enhances the functionality of SQLXML 3.0 with support for new XML and web services functionality. This chapter describes SQLNCLI and SQLXML 4.0 programming.

Chapter 7, *XML Data*
SQL Server 2005 introduces native support for XML data storage and processing. Most significantly, a new xml data type stores typed (having an XML schema) and untyped XML fragments and documents. You can manipulate xml data type instances using either XQuery or XML DML. SQL Server also lets you map relational data to XML data, making it easy to work with a mix of data types. This chapter discusses programmatically creating and manipulating xml data type instances and mapping XML data to relational data.

Chapter 8, *Native XML Web Services*
SQL Server 2005 supports native web services, so you can send SOAP messages directly to SQL Server 2005 to execute T-SQL statements, stored procedures, and scalar-valued user-defined functions (UDFs). This chapter shows how to create and manage HTTP endpoints, expose web service methods, work with SOAP request and response messages, work with SOAP sessions, and monitor SOAP requests for performance.

Chapter 9, *SQL Server Management Objects (SMO)*
SQL Server 2005 introduces SQL Management Objects (SMO)—a collection of namespaces used for programmatically managing all aspects of SQL Server 2005. SMO supersedes the database management functionality of SQL DMO used to manage SQL Server 2000. This chapter describes the SMO object model and shows how to create a simple SMO application.

Chapter 10, *SQL Server Management Objects (SMO) Instance Classes, Part 1*
SMO contains a class hierarchy that matches the SQL Server database hierarchy. This chapter describes the SMO classes used to administer database objects that store and access data, such as tables, indexes, triggers, and stored procedures. It also shows how to use the SMO classes programmatically to administer these objects. In addition, it shows how to subscribe to SMO events and handle exceptions.

Chapter 11, *SQL Server Management Objects (SMO) Instance Classes, Part 2*
SMO contains classes for administering database objects that do not store or access data, such as data and log files, logins, users, roles, and .NET Framework assemblies. This chapter describes how to use these classes programmatically.

Chapter 12, *SQL Server Management Objects (SMO) Utility Classes*
SMO utility classes are used to perform tasks that are independent of a SQL Server instance. These classes include scripting, backup and restore, transfer, mail, and tracing classes. This chapter shows how to use these classes programmatically.

Chapter 13, *Programming Windows Management Instrumentation (WMI)*
WMI can be used to manage SQL Server services, network settings, and server alias settings. This chapter describes the classes that you use to access WMI and shows you how to program these classes.

Chapter 14, *SQL Server Reporting Services (SSRS)*
SSRS provides a reporting environment that runs on top of IIS. You can build reports from any data source—for example, relational, multidimensional, or XML—that can be accessed using a .NET managed data provider, OLE DB provider, or ODBC provider. Reports can be accessed through a parameterized URL or by using the report viewer control in either a Windows Forms or Web Forms application. This chapter shows you how to build, configure, access, and incorporate reports into your applications.

Chapter 15, *SQL Server Integration Services (SSIS)*
SSIS is a platform for building data-integration and workflow solutions in which you can merge data from different data sources, populate data warehouses, standardize data, and perform administrative operations such as backing up, loading, and copying data. This chapter provides an overview of SSIS and demonstrates SSIS managed-code programming.

Chapter 16, *SQL Server Agent*
SQL Server Agent automates administrative tasks by running jobs, monitoring SQL Server, and processing alerts. SMO contains classes used to manage all aspects of SQL Server Agent. This chapter describes SQL Server Agent and the SMO class hierarchy for SQL Server Agent and shows how to programmatically create and manage SQL Server Agent objects.

Chapter 17, *Service Broker*

Service Broker is a technology that helps you build scalable, loosely coupled database applications. Service Broker provides a message-based communications platform that is used to integrate independent applications and components. SMO contains classes used to manage all aspects of Service Broker. This chapter describes Service Broker and the SMO class hierarchy for Service Broker and shows how to programmatically create and use a Service Broker service.

Chapter 18, *Notification Services*

Notification Services is a programming framework for creating applications that generate and send messages to subscribers on a variety of devices, either according to a schedule or in response to events. Notification Services is integrated into SQL Server 2005 rather than being distributed as a download component, as was the case with SQL Server 2000. SMO contains classes used to administer all aspects of Notification Services. This chapter describes Notification Services and the SMO class hierarchy for Notification Services and shows how to programmatically create and manage Notification Services objects.

Chapter 19, *Replication*

Replication copies and distributes data and database objects between databases and provides a mechanism to keep the data synchronized. SQL Server 2005 introduces SQL Server Replication Management Objects (RMO), a collection of namespaces used to program all aspects of SQL Server 2005 replication. RMO replaces the replication management capabilities of SQL DMO, used to manage replication in SQL Server 2000. This chapter describes the RMO object model and shows you how to program replication using RMO classes.

Chapter 20, *SQL Server Analysis Services (SSAS)*

SSAS provides online analytical processing (OLAP) and data-mining functionality using a combination of client- and server-side components. This chapter describes SSAS, shows how to programmatically query data and metadata, and explains how to programmatically administer SSAS instances and objects.

Chapter 21, *SQL Server Mobile Edition*

SQL Server Mobile Edition lets you run relational database applications on mobile devices by providing relational database functionality in a compact footprint with a programming model consistent with SQL Server 2005. SQL Server Mobile is an update to SQL Server Windows CE. This chapter describes SQL Server Mobile, shows how to create and manage databases and database objects, and explains how to read, update, and synchronize data programmatically.

Appendix, ADO.NET 2.0

ADO.NET 2.0 is a collection of classes that lets .NET applications consistently access data stored in a wide variety of data sources. ADO.NET is used to retrieve, manipulate, and update data stored in supported data sources including SQL Server, Oracle, and data sources exposed through OLE DB. ADO.NET 2.0 is an update to ADO.NET introduced with Visual Studio .NET 2002. This appendix describes new functionality, support, and features of ADO.NET 2.0.

What's Not in This Book

This book is not a reference, although some reference material is included where it helps explain concepts. Detailed reference information is available in Microsoft SQL Server 2005 Books Online, which is installed by default with SQL Server 2005 and accessed by selecting Start → All Programs → Microsoft SQL Server 2005 → Documentation and Tutorials → SQL Server Books Online. This book does not cover SQL Server 2005 administration or migrating from SQL Server 2000 to SQL Server 2005.

CHAPTER 2

Tools and Utilities

SQL Server 2005 introduces new and enhanced tools and command-line utilities. This chapter provides an overview of those tools and utilities. It focuses on new features and enhancements, and information most relevant to programming SQL Server and programmatically administering SQL Server. For detailed information about these tools and utilities, see Microsoft SQL Server 2005 Books Online.

SQL Server Management Studio

SQL Server Management Studio is an integrated environment for accessing, configuring, managing, and administering SQL Server and for developing SQL Server objects. Management Studio works with all SQL Server components, including Report Services, Data Transformation Services, SQL Server Mobile, and Notification Services.

SQL Server Management Studio combines the features of Enterprise Manager, Query Analyzer, and Analysis Manager in SQL Server 2000 and adds new functionality.

Launch SQL Server Management Studio by selecting Start → All Programs → Microsoft SQL Server 2005 → SQL Server Management Studio from the taskbar. The Connect to Server dialog box opens, prompting you for server information and credentials. Fill in the required information and click the Connect button. Figure 2-1 shows SQL Server Management Studio.

SQL Server Management Studio displays two panes by default:

- Object Explorer
- Document (initially a single Summary Page)

These and other windows can be added using the View menu. The various windows are described in the following subsections.

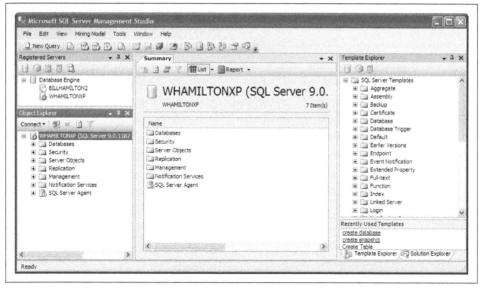

Figure 2-1. SQL Server Management Studio

Registered Servers

The Registered Servers window lists servers that you have previously registered, optionally organized into server groups—a hierarchical structure used to help manage registered servers. A registered server preserves connection information and lets you easily determine whether the servers are running, access Object Explorer and Query Editor for the servers, and provide user-friendly names together with detailed descriptions for the servers.

The toolbar below the main menu lets you switch between the five types of registered servers that you can manage (listed in order from left to right):

Database Engine
> Stores, processes, and secures data

Analysis Services
> Online analytical processing (OLAP) and data-mining functionality

Reporting Services
> Web-enabled reports that connect to a variety of data and content sources, publish reports in various formats, and manage security and subscriptions

SQL Server Mobile
> Relational-database functionality in a compact footprint suitable for mobile devices with a programming model consistent with SQL Server 2005

Integration Services

Packages that extract, transform, and load (ETL) data for use by data integration solutions and data warehousing

You can also switch the type of registered server by using the View → Registered Server Types menu item.

The Registered Servers context menu has the options described in Table 2-1.

Table 2-1. Registered Server context menu items

Menu Item	Description
Connect	Adds the selected server to the Object Explorer window.
Start	Starts the selected SQL Server instance.
Stop	Stops the selected SQL Server instance.
Pause	Pauses the selected SQL Server instance. A paused instance lets connected users complete tasks but does not allow new connections.
Resume	Resumes the paused SQL Server instance.
Restart	Restarts the selected SQL Server instance.
Start/Stop Service and Change Accounts	Lets you configure the SQL Server service.
SQL Server Configuration Manager	Opens SQL Server Configuration Manager (described later in this chapter).
New	Lets you create a new server group or register a server.
Edit	Lets you configure either a server group or a registered server.
Update Local Server Registration	Automatically registers all local server instances.
Move To	Moves a registered server to another server group.
Delete	Removes a registered server.
Import	Imports a previously exported server information file.
Export	Exports registered server information to a file for either a single server or a group of servers.
Previously Registered Servers	Imports servers registered by SQL Server 2000.

Object Explorer

Object Explorer connects to Database Engine, Analysis Services, Integration Services, Reporting Services, and SQL Server Mobile instances. It organizes all objects on the database instance into a tree hierarchy and lets you manage them. Object Explorer is visible by default. Select View → Object Explorer if it is not visible.

The toolbar at the top of the Object Explorer window has five buttons (described from left to right):

Connect

Connects a server instance to Object Explorer. Click the Connect button and select a server type from the drop-down menu. The Connect to Server dialog box opens, prompting for server information and credentials. Fill in the required information and click the Connect button in the dialog box. Alternatively, you can right-click a server name in the Registered Servers window and select Connect → Object Explorer from the context menu. You can also double-click a server instance in the Registered Servers window to connect it to Object Browser.

Disconnect

Disconnects a server instance from Object Explorer. Select the server instance to disconnect and click the Disconnect button.

Stop

Stops the current Object Explorer action.

Refresh

Refreshes a tree node. Alternatively, you can right-click the node and select Refresh from the context menu, or select View → Refresh from the SQL Server Management Studio menu. Object Explorer items do not automatically refresh, to improve performance and to conserve system resources.

Filter

Returns a subset of items in a folder. When you click the Filter button, the Object Explorer Filter Settings dialog is displayed, as shown in Figure 2-2. The Filter button is enabled only when an object type (folder) node is selected in Object Explorer—it is not enabled when a specific object, such as a server instance, database, or table, is selected.

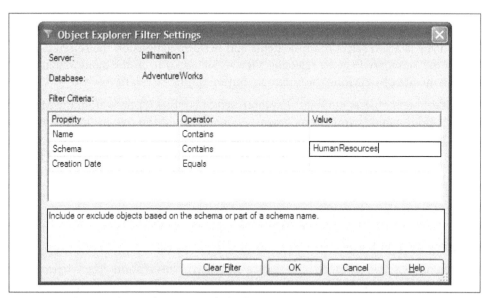

Figure 2-2. Object Explorer Filter Settings dialog box

The dialog box in Figure 2-2 is displayed when you select the Tables node of the AdventureWorks database and click the Filter button. Setting the Schema to HumanResources in the filter criteria limits the tables displayed in the Tables node of the AdventureWorks database to those in the HumanResources schema, as shown in Figure 2-3.

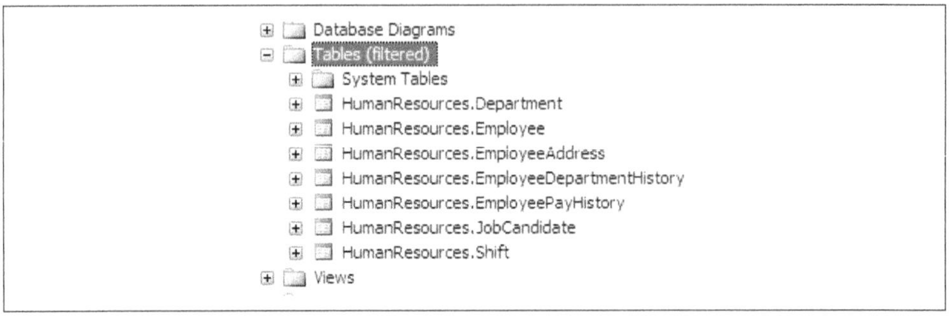

Figure 2-3. Filtered table node

The word "filtered" is displayed in parentheses to indicate that the table list is filtered. Also, when the Tables node is filtered, the Filter button on the Object Explorer toolbar is depressed. To clear the filter, click the Filter button and then click the Clear Filter button in the Object Explorer Filter Settings dialog box. You can also right-click the filtered node and select Filter → Remove Filter from the context menu.

Only one item can be selected at a time in the Object Explorer tree view. The Summary Page lets you select multiple items and perform actions on the selected group. Open the Summary Page by selecting View → Summary from the main Management Studio menu or by clicking the Summary button on the Standard toolbar.

To hide system objects in Object Explorer, select Tools → Options from the Management Studio menu, select Environment → General from the tree in the left panel of the Options dialog box, and then check the Hide System objects in Object Explorer checkbox. You must restart SQL Server Management Studio for the changes to take effect.

The following subsections describe the types of nodes in Object Explorer and the activities that you can perform at each type of node.

Database server instance

The database server instance represents a SQL Server installation. The context menu for the database server instance lets you connect to and disconnect from a server, register a new server, create a query, manage the SQL Server service for the instance, refresh the tree hierarchy, and manage the properties for the server.

Databases node

The Databases node contains system databases, database snapshots, and user databases. Database snapshots are new in SQL Server 2005 and let you create a read-only static view of a database. Create a snapshot by using the CREATE DATABASE T-SQL statement with the AS SNAPSHOT clause.

Figure 2-4 shows the hierarchy of objects under the Databases node.

From the Databases node you can create a new database, attach a database by selecting its database files, or restore a database, file, or file group.

You can create a query from a named database node. Right-click on the database node and select New Query from the context menu to launch Query Editor. Query Editor opens a code pane in which you can enter T-SQL statements. After you execute the statement by selecting Query → Execute from the main menu, by right-clicking in the Query Editor code pane and selecting Execute from the context menu, or by pressing F5, two additional tabs are displayed:

Results
> Displays the result of a query

Messages
> Displays information and error messages

Query Editor is shown in Figure 2-5.

Query Designer is a visual tool that lets you design SELECT, INSERT, UPDATE, and DELETE DML statements. After you open Query Editor, you can launch Query Designer either by selecting Query → Design Query in Editor from the SQL Server Management Studio menu or by right-clicking the Query Editor code pane and selecting Design Query in Editor from context menu. The Add Table dialog box is displayed, letting you select tables to query; you can also add or remove tables while you are designing the query. Once you click the Close button, Query Designer shows three panes—diagram, criteria, and SQL—as shown in Figure 2-6.

You can create the query by using the three panes at the same time. Right-click in the diagram area (top pane) to open a context menu that lets you change the query type, add tables, and change the grouping of results. Relationships are created automatically if they exist in the database. You can also drag one or more columns from one table to another to create relationships between tables. Select columns to display in the query by using the checkboxes next to the column names.

Once you have completed the query design, click the OK button to transfer the generated T-SQL to Query Editor, where you can execute the query. Select the T-SQL in Query Editor, open Query Designer, and the selected T-SQL will be parsed automatically into a diagram.

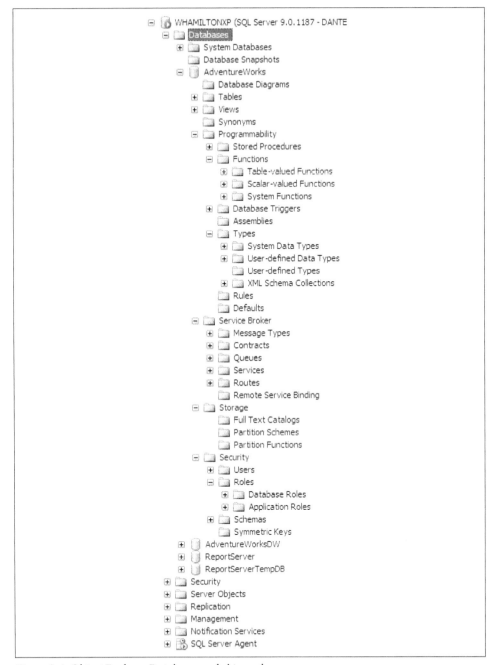

Figure 2-4. Object Explorer Databases node hierarchy

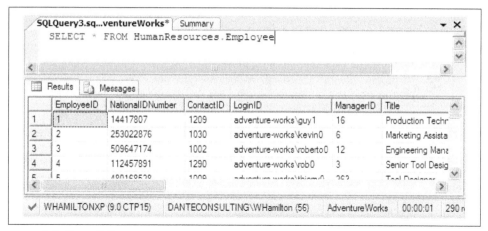

Figure 2-5. Query Editor

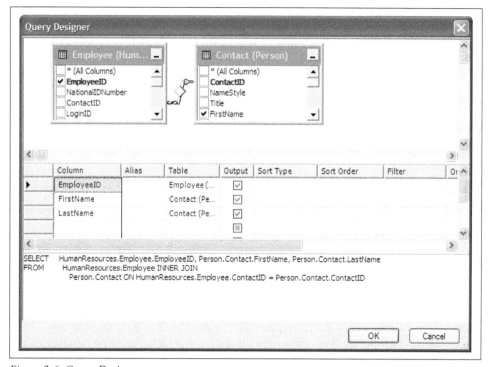

Figure 2-6. Query Designer

You can create database diagrams from the Database Diagrams node (refer to Figure 2-4). Select New Database Diagram from the context menu to launch Database Diagram Designer, a visual tool that lets you create, edit, and delete tables, columns, indexes, constraints, and relationships. You can automatically create one or more diagrams for an existing database—SQL Server keeps diagrams synchronized with the database. Figure 2-7 shows part of a database diagram for the AdventureWorks database.

 If you are creating a diagram for the first time in a database, you are prompted with "This database does not have one or more of the support objects required to use database diagramming. Do you wish to create them?" You must click Yes to create database diagrams.

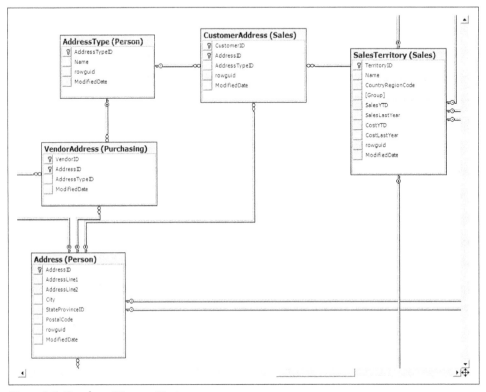

Figure 2-7. Database Diagram Designer

You can also create a new table or edit an existing table by using Table Designer. Select New Table or Modify, respectively, from the Table context menu. Table Designer has two panes. The upper pane is a grid in which each row describes a column in the table. The lower pane shows additional column properties for the column selected in the upper grid. Figure 2-8 shows Table Designer for the Person. Contact table in the AdventureWorks database.

You can use Table Designer to modify indexes, constraints, and relationships by selecting the appropriate option from the context menu.

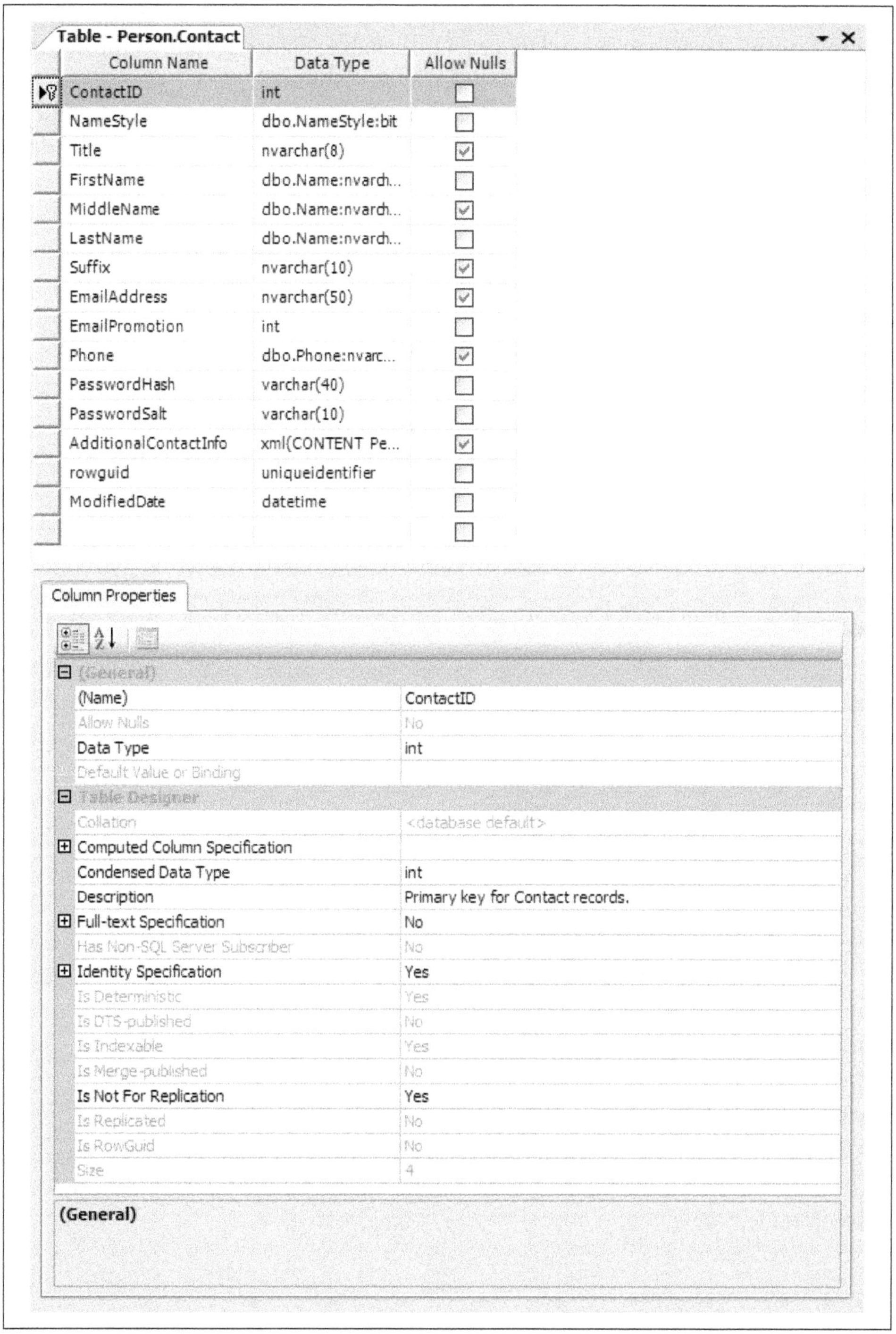

Figure 2-8. Table Designer

You can view and modify data in the table by selecting Open Table from the table's context menu. This brings up a data grid for the table. Figure 2-9 shows the data grid for the Person.Contact table in the AdventureWorks database.

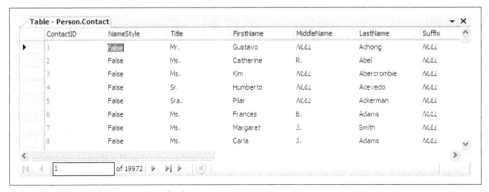

Figure 2-9. Table data viewer and editor

Other nodes in the Databases hierarchy allow you to create, manage, and drop the objects within the node as well as perform other object-specific tasks.

Security node

The Security node lets you manage server logins, server roles, and credentials. Figure 2-10 shows the hierarchy of objects under the Security node.

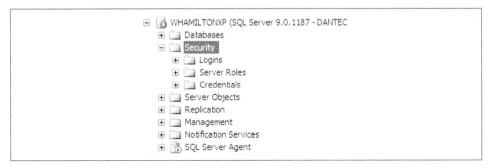

Figure 2-10. Object Explorer Security node hierarchy

Server Objects node

The Server Objects node lets you manage backup devices, endpoints, linked servers, and server DDL triggers. Figure 2-11 shows the hierarchy of objects under the Server Objects node.

Figure 2-11. Object Explorer Server Objects node hierarchy

Replication node

The Replication node lets you manage local publications and subscriptions. Figure 2-12 shows the hierarchy of objects under the Replication node.

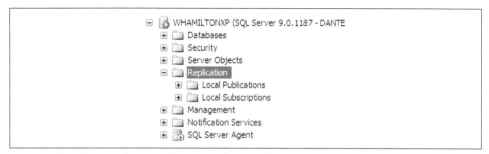

Figure 2-12. Object Explorer Replication node hierarchy

Management node

The Management node lets you manage maintenance plans, server logs, Database Mail, the Distributed Transaction Coordinator, Full-Text Search, and legacy objects. It also provides access to Activity Monitor, which provides information about processes and locks. Figure 2-13 shows the hierarchy of objects under the Management node.

Notification Services node

The Notification Services node lets you manage Notification Services instances.

SQL Server Agent node

The SQL Server Agent node lets you manage jobs, alerts, operators, and proxies and provides access to SQL Server Agent error logs and the SQL Server Agent Job Activity Monitor. Figure 2-14 shows the hierarchy of objects under the SQL Server Agent node.

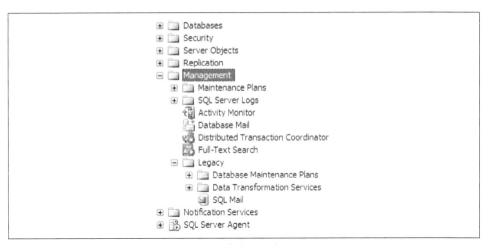

Figure 2-13. Object Explorer Management node hierarchy

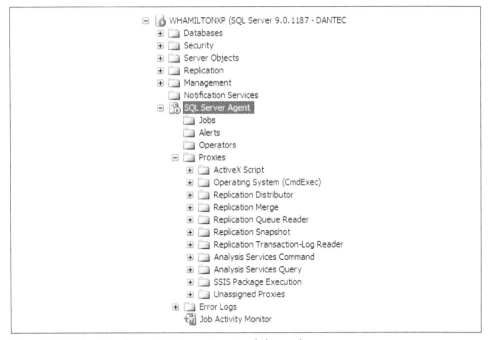

Figure 2-14. Object Explorer SQL Server Agent node hierarchy

Template Explorer

Script templates contain T-SQL statements for performing a variety of common tasks. Open Template Explorer by selecting View → Template Explorer from the main menu or by clicking the Template Explorer button on the Standard toolbar. Figure 2-15 shows the Template Explorer window.

Figure 2-15. Template Explorer

Template Explorer uses a tree structure to organize templates into folders. The bottom of the window saves a list of recently used templates.

The toolbar at the top of the Template Explorer window has three buttons that let you select templates for Database Engine, Analysis Server, or SQL Server Mobile, respectively.

Templates are parameterized to help you customize the code. Parameter definitions follow the format *<parameter_name, data_type, value>*, with values as follows:

parameter_name
> The name of the parameter

data_type
> The data type of the parameter

value
> The value used to replace every instance of the parameter in the script

The create database template (from the Database folder) follows:

```
-- ================================================
-- Create database template
-- ================================================
USE master
GO

-- Drop the database if it already exists
IF  EXISTS (
    SELECT name
        FROM sys.databases
        WHERE name = N'<Database_Name, sysname, Database_Name>'
)
DROP DATABASE <Database_Name, sysname, Database_Name>
GO

CREATE DATABASE <Database_Name, sysname, Database_Name>
GO
```

This script has a single parameter, <Database_Name, sysname, Database_Name>. To replace the parameter, select Query → Specify Values for Template Parameters from the main menu, or click the corresponding button on the SQL Editor toolbar. This displays the Specify Values for Template Parameters dialog box, shown in Figure 2-16.

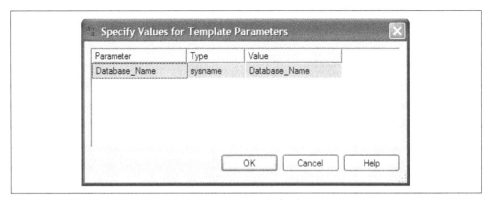

Figure 2-16. Specify Values for Template Parameters dialog box

Replace the value of the Database_Name parameter with the value ProgrammingSqlServer2005 and click the OK button. The script is updated for the parameter value as follows:

```
-- =================================================
-- Create database template
-- =================================================
USE master
GO

-- Drop the database if it already exists
IF  EXISTS (
    SELECT name
        FROM sys.databases
        WHERE name = N'ProgrammingSqlServer2005'
)
DROP DATABASE ProgrammingSqlServer2005
GO

CREATE DATABASE ProgrammingSqlServer2005
GO
```

Note that once you set a parameter value, it is permanently replaced and can no longer be accessed.

You can create custom templates in Template Explorer, as well. Follow these steps:

1. Select the node in which you want to create the template.
2. Right-click in the Template Explorer window and select New → Template from the context menu.
3. Enter the name for the new template.
4. Right-click the template and select Edit from the context menu (or double-click the template). Complete the required information in the Connect to Database Engine dialog box and click the Connect button.
5. Create the script. Insert parameters using the *<parameter_name, data_type, value>* syntax described earlier in this section. You can leave blank *data_type* and *value* (i.e., <myParameter, , >).
6. Save the template by selecting File → Save from the main menu or by clicking the Save button on the Standard toolbar.

Solution Explorer

The Solution Explorer window of SQL Server Management Studio lets you view and manage items associated with a script project. Open Solution Explorer by selecting View → Solution Explorer from the main menu.

SQL Server Management Studio lets you create three types of projects—SQL Server Scripts, Analysis Services Scripts, and SQL Server Mobile Scripts. You can group multiple projects into a solution. A project contains *items*—connection information, queries, scripts (sets of T-SQL statements stored in a file), and miscellaneous files relevant to the project. Solution Explorer lets you open each item in an appropriate editor. The property window located by default in the window below the Solution Explorer window lets you view and manage item properties.

SQL Server Configuration Manager

SQL Server 2005 runs as a collection of services—application types that run in the system background. SQL Server Configuration Manager is a Microsoft Management Console (MMC) snap-in that lets you start, stop, pause, resume, restart, and configure services, including:

- SQL Server
- SQL Server Agent
- SQL Server Analysis Services
- SQL Server Browser
- SQL Server Full-Text Search
- SQL Server Integration Services
- SQL Server Reporting Services

Start SQL Server Configuration Manager by selecting Start → All Programs → Microsoft SQL Server 2005 → Configuration Tools → SQL Server Configuration Manager from the taskbar. Figure 2-17 shows SQL Server Configuration Manager.

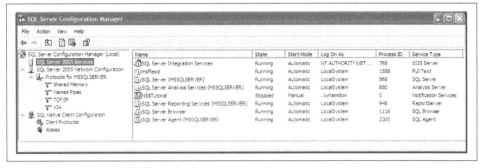

Figure 2-17. SQL Server Configuration Manager

In addition to managing services, SQL Server Management Studio lets you manage server and client network protocols—you can enable or disable protocols and force protocol encryption—and manage server aliases.

SQL Server Configuration Manager combines the functionality of the following: Server Network Utility, Client Network Utility, and Service Manager from SQL Server 2000.

SQL Server Surface Area Configuration

SQL Server Surface Area Configuration lets you enable, disable, start, and stop features, services, and remote connectivity of SQL Server 2005 installations—this helps to secure both local and remote systems.

Start SQL Server Surface Area Configuration Manager by selecting Start → All Programs → Microsoft SQL Server → Configuration Tools → SQL Server Surface Area Configuration from the taskbar.

The sac.exe command-line utility imports Microsoft SQL Server 2005 surface settings so that you can apply them to other SQL Server instances. The utility is in the *C:\Program Files\Microsoft SQL Server\90\Shared* directory (assuming that you installed SQL Server to the default directory).

Database Engine Tuning Advisor

Database Engine Tuning Advisor (DTA) helps you improve query processing without requiring you to understand the database structure or how SQL Server processes queries. DTA helps you select and create an optimal set of indexes, indexed views, and partitions. It analyzes a *workload*—a set of T-SQL statements that runs against the database—against the implementation of one or more databases and recommends changes to the database that reduce the estimated workload cost of the query optimizer. These modifications include adding, deleting, or modifying clustered indexes, nonclustered indexes, indexed views, and partitions.

You launch Database Engine Tuning Advisor in one of three ways:

* Select Start → All Programs → Microsoft SQL Server 2005 → Performance Tools → Database Engine Tuning Advisor from the taskbar.
* From the SQL Server Management Studio menu, select Tools → Database Engine Tuning Advisor.
* Run the command-line tool dta.exe.

SQL Server Profiler

SQL Trace captures database-engine events in real time to a trace file. Traces are based on event class instances that you choose to monitor. Trace information is used to monitor and assess performance, audit activity, and debug SQL statements and stored procedures. Traces are usually managed and accessed through SQL Server Profiler, a graphical user interface to SQL Trace.

SQL Server Profiler lets you create and manage traces, create trace templates, and replay trace results. With SQL Server Profiler, you can monitor how queries are resolved and capture SQL Server events from the Database Engine or Analysis Services to a trace file for analysis. You can later replay the trace events to help diagnose problems.

You launch SQL Server Profiler in one of three ways:

- Select Start → All Programs → Microsoft SQL Server 2005 → Performance Tools → SQL Server Profiler from the taskbar.
- From SQL Server Management Studio, select Tools → SQL Server Profiler.
- Run the command-line tool `profiler90.exe`.

SQL Server Management Objects (SMO) provides classes that can be used to create and manage traces for SQL Server or Analysis Server. They are discussed in detail in Chapter 12.

SQL Server Business Intelligence Development Studio

SQL Server Business Intelligence Development Studio is a development IDE—similar to Visual Studio 2005—for developing Analysis Services, Integration Services, and Reporting Services projects. Business Intelligence (BI) Development Studio lets you develop these projects independently of the server and organize groups of projects into solutions. BI Development Studio lets you deploy projects to testing, staging, and production servers.

 BI Development Studio functionality is added to Visual Studio 2005 on computers where Visual Studio 2005 is installed.

Launch BI Development Studio by selecting Start → All Programs → Microsoft SQL Server → SQL Server Business Intelligence Development Studio from the taskbar. BI Development Studio has five main windows:

Designer
 Designs and creates objects in the project; provides a code view and design view of each object appropriate to the object type.

Solution Explorer
 Manages projects in the solution.

Properties
 Views and modifies properties of an object.

Toolbox
 Contains controls available for an object. Controls are often available only in the design view.

Output

Displays output, debugging, error, and other information during compilation and execution of the solution.

Figure 2-18 shows the BI Development Studio with a sample Analysis Services project loaded.

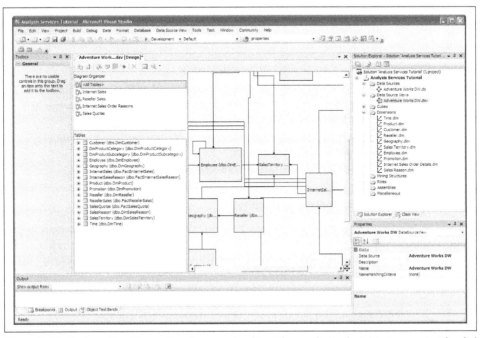

Figure 2-18. Business Intelligence Development Studio with sample Analysis Services project loaded

Visual Studio 2005

SQL Server 2005 hosts the .NET Common Language Runtime (CLR) in the Database Engine. This lets you create database objects such as functions, stored procedures, triggers, user-defined data types, and user-defined aggregate functions in programming languages supported by the CLR. Visual Studio 2005 supports CLR integration into SQL Server with a new project type named SQL Server Project. Once the compiled assembly for a SQL Server project is registered with SQL Server, the database objects in the assembly can be used the same way as if they had been created using T-SQL. Chapters 4 and 5 discuss SQL Server 2005 CLR integration and programming database objects using Visual Studio 2005.

New Command-Line Utilities

SQL Server 2005 introduces the new command-line utilities described in Table 2-2.

Table 2-2. New SQL Server command-line utilities

Utility	Description
sqlcmd	Executes T-SQL statements, system procedures, and script files from the command prompt. The sqlcmd utility is described further later in this section.
sqlwb	Launches SQL Server Management Studio from the command prompt.
profiler90	Launches SQL Server Profiler from the command prompt.
dta	Launches Database Engine Tuning Advisor from the command prompt.
dtexec	Used to configure and execute an SSIS package loaded from a database, the SSIS package store, or the file system.
dtutil	Used to manage and verify existence of an SSIS package stored in the SQL Server msdb database, the SSIS package store, or the file system.
tablediff	Used to compare the data in two tables for nonconvergence.

SQL Server command-line tool (sqlcmd utility)

The SQL Server command-line tool lets you execute T-SQL statements, system procedures, and script files from the command prompt. The sqlcmd utility replaces the osql and isql utilities. sqlcmd uses OLE DB to communicate with the SQL Server Database Engine instead of using ODBC or DB-Library APIs.

Regular command mode in SQL Server Management Studio uses the .NET SqlClient provider for execution in regular and command mode, whereas sqlcmd uses the OLE DB provider. As a result, it is possible to get different results when executing the same query, because different default options might apply.

The following example connects to the default instance of SQL Server and executes a query against the AdventureWorks database. Open a Command Prompt dialog box (Start → All Programs → Accessories → Command Prompt) and execute the following command:

```
sqlcmd -q "SELECT TOP 3 ContactID, FirstName, LastName FROM
    AdventureWorks.Person.Contact"
```

The console output is shown in Figure 2-19.

The -q switch executes the specified query. The -? switch returns information about all switches for the sqlcmd utility. For a complete overview of the sqlcmd utility and its switches, see Microsoft SQL Server 2005 Books Online.

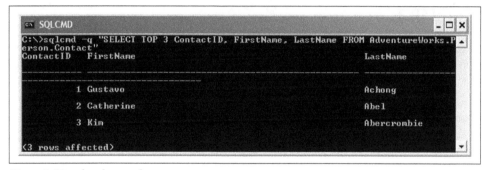

Figure 2-19. sqlcmd example

Alternatively, you can start sqlcmd and execute the preceding query in a batch with the following commands:

```
sqlcmd
SELECT TOP 3 ContactID, FirstName, LastName FROM AdventureWorks.Person.Contact"
GO
```

Figure 2-20 shows the sqlcmd batch.

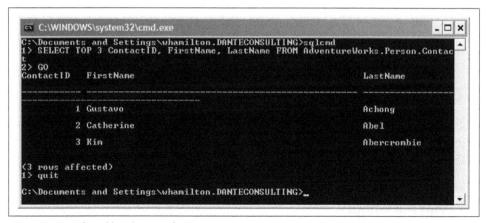

Figure 2-20. SqlCmd batch example

The QUIT or EXIT command exits sqlcmd batch mode.

T-SQL Enhancements

SQL Server 2005 extends the T-SQL language in several significant ways:

- New XML and large object data types
- New and enhanced language capabilities, including support for recursive queries and improved error handling
- Data Definition Language (DDL) triggers
- Catalog views to access metadata

This chapter discusses these enhancements and changes.

New Data Types

SQL Server 2005 introduces the xml data type and *large value data types*. The xml data type supports storing XML documents and fragments in the database. Large value data types—varchar(max), nvarchar(max), and varbinary(max)—extend the storage capacity of varchar, nvarchar, and varbinary data types up to 2^{31} bytes of data.

The xml Data Type

The built-in xml data type stores XML documents and fragments natively as a column, variable, parameter, or function return type. A schema can be associated with an xml data type to validate each instance of the type—the XML instance is then *typed*. An XML instance without a schema is *untyped*. xml data types can be manipulated using XQuery and XML DML. Columns of xml data type can be indexed.

Chapter 7 provides an in-depth look at support for XML data in SQL Server 2005.

Large Value Data Types

SQL Server 2000 has varchar, nvarchar, and varbinary variable-length data types:

varchar

Variable-length non-Unicode data with a maximum length of 8,000 bytes

nvarchar

Variable-length Unicode data with a maximum length of 4,000 bytes

varbinary

Variable-length binary data with a maximum length of 8,000 bytes

SQL Server 2005 introduces large value data types—varchar(max), nvarchar(max), and varbinary(max). You use the max specifier to extend the storage capability of varchar, nvarchar, and varbinary data types to 2^{31} bytes in the varchar and varbinary data types and to 2^{30} bytes of Unicode data in the nvarchar data type.

In earlier versions of SQL Server, you specified these types as varchar(*n*), nvarchar(*n*), and varbinary(*n*), where *n* is an integer specifying the in-row storage limit for large character, Unicode, and binary data—up to 8000 bytes for varchar and varbinary and 4000 bytes for nvarchar. If you needed to store more data, you had to use the large object (LOB) data types—text, ntext, and image—with reduced functionality.

In SQL Server 2005, use varchar(max), nvarchar(max), and varbinary(max) instead of the text, ntext, and image data types, which are slated to be deprecated in a future version of SQL Server.

Large value data types behave in the same way as their smaller counterparts. They are supported for the cursor FETCH statement, for chunked updates through the .WRITE clause, after trigger references in inserted and deleted tables, and with built-in string functions such as LEN and SUBSTR. Large value data types also do not suffer from some of the restrictions of LOB types—they can be used as variables in batches and scripts, for example.

Use the .WRITE clause in an UPDATE statement to modify part of the value stored in a varchar(max), nvarchar(max), or varbinary(max) column in a table or a view. The .WRITE clause syntax is as follows:

```
.WRITE (expression, @Offset, @Length)
```

The .WRITE clause replaces a section of the value in a large value data type column starting at *@Offset* for *@Length* units with the value *expression*.

The following example demonstrates the .WRITE clause. First create a table with a single varchar(max) column and add a row to it using the following statement:

```
USE ProgrammingSqlServer2005

CREATE TABLE WriteMethodDemoTable(
  ID int,
  varcharMaxCol varchar(max)
)
```

```
INSERT INTO WriteMethodDemoTable (ID, varcharMaxCol)
  VALUES (1, 'Imagine this is a very long non-Unicode string.')

INSERT INTO WriteMethodDemoTable (ID, varcharMaxCol)
  VALUES (2, 'Imagine this is another very long non-Unicode string.')
```

Next, query the table, execute the .WRITE clause, and requery the table using the following statement:

```
SELECT * FROM WriteMethodDemoTable

UPDATE WriteMethodDemoTable
SET varcharMaxCol .WRITE('n incredibly', 17, 5)
WHERE ID = 1

SELECT * FROM WriteMethodDemoTable
```

Results are shown in Figure 3-1.

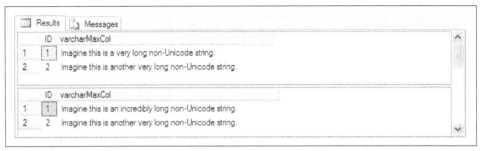

Figure 3-1. Results from .WRITE clause example

For more information about the .WRITE clause, see Microsoft SQL Server 2005 Books Online.

T-SQL Language Enhancements

SQL Server 2005 includes significant enhancements to the T-SQL language:

- The enhanced TOP clause supports using an expression to specify the number of rows or percent of rows returned in the result set.
- The new TABLESAMPLE clause returns a random sample of rows from the result set.
- The new OUTPUT clause returns a result set containing the rows affected by an INSERT, UPDATE, or DELETE statement.
- Common table expressions (CTEs) let you create a temporary named result set from a query, which simplifies tasks such as recursive queries.
- New SOME, ANY, and ALL operators compare the values in a column with a scalar value.

- The new `PIVOT` operator rotates a table, turning unique values in column rows into multiple columns in the result set, while the new `UNPIVOT` operator turns multiple columns in a result set into rows.
- The new `APPLY` operator invokes a table-valued function for each row in a result set.
- The new `EXECUTE  AS` clause defines the user execution context of T-SQL statements.
- The new `ROW_NUMBER( )`, `DENSE_RANK( )`, and `NTILE( )` ranking functions are added to the `RANK` function that exists in SQL Server 2000.
- New support for structured exception handling using `TRY...CATCH` blocks.

This section details these enhancements.

TOP

The `TOP` clause limits the number of rows returned in a result set. SQL Server 2005 enhances the `TOP` clause to allow an expression to be used as the argument to the `TOP` clause instead of just a constant as was the case in SQL Server 2000. The `TOP` clause can be used in `SELECT`, `INSERT`, `UPDATE`, and `DELETE` statements.

The `TOP` clause syntax is:

```
TOP (expression) [PERCENT] [ WITH TIES ]
```

where:

expression
> Specifies the number of rows to return or the percentage of rows in the result set to return. Parentheses are required around the expression if it is not a constant.

`PERCENT`
> Specifies that the query should return a percent of rows from all rows processed rather than a specific number of rows.

`WITH TIES`
> Specifies that additional rows having the same `ORDER  BY` clause column values as the last row of the result set should be returned if they exist even though this causes the number of rows returned to be greater than specified by *expression*. (An example will clarify this shortly.)

The following query shows the enhanced functionality by returning the 10 products with the highest list price from the `Product` table in `AdventureWorks`. A variable is used to specify the number of rows.

```
USE AdventureWorks

DECLARE @n int;
SET @n = 10;
```

```
SELECT TOP(@n)
  ProductID, Name, ProductNumber, ListPrice
FROM Production.Product
ORDER BY ListPrice DESC
```

Results are shown in Figure 3-2.

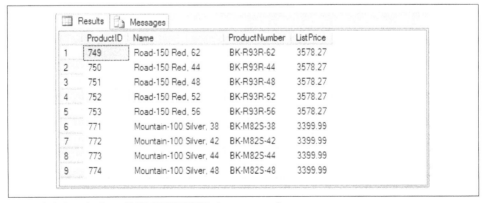

Figure 3-2. Results from TOP clause example

The following example shows the effect of the WITH TIES clause:

```
USE AdventureWorks

SELECT TOP(6) WITH TIES
  ProductID, Name, ProductNumber, ListPrice
FROM AdventureWorks.Production.Product
ORDER BY ListPrice DESC
```

Results are shown in Figure 3-3.

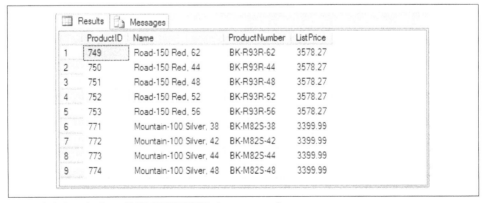

Figure 3-3. Results from TOP WITH TIES clause example

Although six rows were specified in the TOP clause, the WITH TIES clause causes the SELECT TOP statement to return an additional three rows having the same ListPrice as the value in the last row of the SELECT TOP statement without the WITH TIES clause.

TABLESAMPLE

The TABLESAMPLE clause returns a random, representative sample of the table expressed as either an approximate number of rows or a percentage of the total rows. Unlike the TOP clause, TABLESAMPLE returns a result set containing a sampling of rows from all rows processed by the query.

The TABLESAMPLE clause syntax is:

```
TABLESAMPLE [SYSTEM] (sample_number [PERCENT | ROWS])
  [REPEATABLE (repeat_seed)]
```

where:

SYSTEM

An ANSI SQL keyword that specifies a database server–dependent sampling method. Although other databases support additional sampling methods that are database server–independent (e.g., DB2 supports BERNOULLI), SYSTEM is the only method supported by SQL Server 2005 and the default value if not specified.

sample_number [PERCENT | ROWS]

A numeric expression that specifies the number of rows to return or the percentage of rows in the result set to return.

REPEATABLE (repeat_seed)

The seed used to select rows to be returned in the sample. REPEATABLE indicates that the selected sample can be returned more than once. If the same seed is used, the same rows will be returned each time the query is run as long as no changes have been made to the data in the table.

The following example returns a sample result set containing the top 10 percent of rows from the Contact table:

```
SELECT ContactID, Title, FirstName, MiddleName, LastName
FROM Person.Contact
TABLESAMPLE (10 PERCENT)
```

The sample of rows is different every time. Adding the REPEATABLE clause as shown in the next code sample returns the same sample result set each time as long as no changes are made to the data in the table:

```
SELECT ContactID, Title, FirstName, MiddleName, LastName
FROM Person.Contact
TABLESAMPLE (10 PERCENT)
REPEATABLE (5)
```

The `TABLESAMPLE` clause cannot be used with views or in an inline table-valued function.

OUTPUT

The `OUTPUT` clause returns information about rows affected by an `INSERT`, `UPDATE`, or `DELETE` statement. This result set can be returned to the calling application and used for requirements such as archiving or logging.

The syntax of the `OUTPUT` clause is:

```
<OUTPUT_CLAUSE> ::=
{
    OUTPUT <dml_select_list> [ ,...n ]
    INTO @table_variable
}
<dml_select_list> ::=
{ <column_name> | scalar_expression }

<column_name> ::=
{ DELETED | INSERTED | from_table_name } . { * | column_name }
```

where:

@table_variable

> A table variable into which the result set is inserted. The table variable must have the same number of columns as the `OUTPUT` result set, excluding identity and computed columns (which must be skipped).

<dml_select_list>

> An explicit column reference (*column_name*) or a combination of symbols and operators that evaluates to a single value (*scalar_expression*).

<column_name>

> An explicit column reference.
>
> Qualify the column with the `DELETED` or `INSERTED` keyword if it references the table being modified.
>
> *from_table_name* specifies the table used to provide criteria for the update or delete operation.

As an example, you can use the following steps to delete several rows from a table while using the `OUTPUT` clause to write the deleted values into a `Log` table variable:

1. In a new database named `ProgrammingSqlServer2005`, create a table called `OutputTest` and add three rows to it:

```
USE ProgrammingSqlServer2005

CREATE TABLE OutputTest
(
    ID int NOT NULL,
    Description varchar(max) NOT NULL,
)
```

```
INSERT INTO OutputTest (ID, Description) VALUES (1, 'row 1')
INSERT INTO OutputTest (ID, Description) VALUES (2, 'row 2')
INSERT INTO OutputTest (ID, Description) VALUES (3, 'row 3')
```

2. Execute the following query to delete the row with ID = 1 from the OutputTest
table. Use the OUTPUT clause to write the deleted row to the @DeleteLog table
variable.

```
DECLARE @DeleteLog AS TABLE (LogID INT, LogEntry VARCHAR(MAX))

DELETE OutputTest
OUTPUT DELETED.ID, DELETED.Description INTO @DeleteLog
WHERE ID = 1

SELECT * FROM @DeleteLog
```

The last line in the query displays the log result set in the @DeleteLog table variable after the row is deleted from the OutputTest table, as shown in Figure 3-4.

Figure 3-4. Results from OUTPUT clause example

When the OUTPUT clause is used for an UPDATE command, both a DELETED and INSERTED
table are available—the DELETED table contains the values before the update and the
INSERTED table contains the values after the update.

Common Table Expressions (CTEs)

A *common table expression* (CTE) is a temporary named result set derived from a
simple query within the scope of a SELECT, INSERT, DELETE, UPDATE, or CREATE VIEW
statement. A CTE can reference itself to create a *recursive CTE*. A CTE is not stored
and lasts only for the duration of its containing query.

The CTE syntax is:

```
[WITH <common_table_expression> [ , ...n]]

<common_table_expression>::=
  expression_name [(column_name [ , ...n])]
  AS
  (query_definition)
```

where:

expression_name
  Specifies the name of the CTE.

column_name

Specifies the column name in the CTE, unique within the definition. The number of column names must match the number of columns returned by the CTE query *query_definition*. The list of column names is optional if distinct names are returned for all columns in the CTE query.

query_definition

Specifies the SELECT statement that populates the CTE.

The following query uses a CTE to display the number of employees directly reporting to each manager in the Employee table in AdventureWorks:

```
USE AdventureWorks;

WITH ManagerEmployees(ManagerID, EmployeesPerManager) AS
(
  SELECT ManagerID, COUNT(*)
  FROM HumanResources.Employee
  GROUP BY ManagerID
)
SELECT ManagerID, EmployeesPerManager
FROM ManagerEmployees
ORDER BY ManagerID
```

The query returns the results partially shown in Figure 3-5.

	ManagerID	EmployeesPerManager
1	NULL	1
2	3	7
3	6	8
4	7	6
5	12	1
6	14	6

Figure 3-5. Results from CTE example

Although this example can be accomplished without a CTE, it is useful to illustrate the basic syntax of a CTE.

> The WITH clause requires that the statement preceding it be terminated with a semicolon (;).

The next example uses a recursive CTE to return a list of employees and their managers:

```
USE AdventureWorks;

WITH DirectReports(
    ManagerID, EmployeeID, Title, FirstName, LastName, EmployeeLevel) AS
(
    SELECT e.ManagerID, e.EmployeeID, e.Title, c.FirstName, c.LastName,
        0 AS EmployeeLevel
    FROM HumanResources.Employee e
    JOIN Person.Contact AS c ON e.ContactID = c.ContactID
    WHERE ManagerID IS NULL

    UNION ALL

    SELECT e.ManagerID, e.EmployeeID, e.Title, c.FirstName, c.LastName,
        EmployeeLevel + 1
    FROM HumanResources.Employee e
        INNER JOIN DirectReports d ON e.ManagerID = d.EmployeeID
        JOIN Person.Contact AS c ON e.ContactID = c.ContactID
)
SELECT *
FROM DirectReports
```

The query returns the results shown in Figure 3-6.

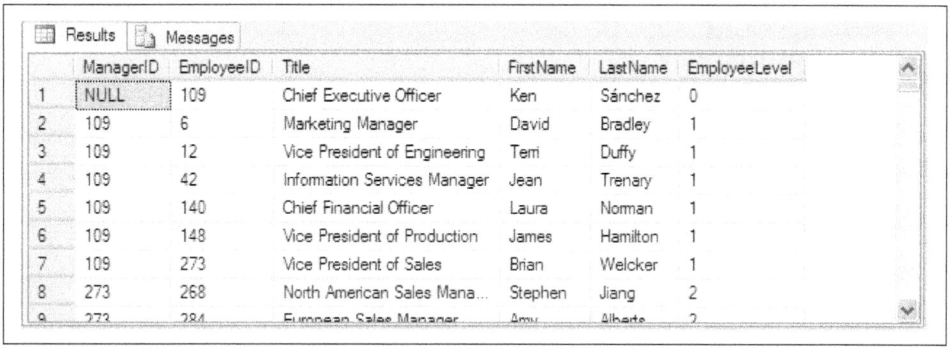

	ManagerID	EmployeeID	Title	FirstName	LastName	EmployeeLevel
1	NULL	109	Chief Executive Officer	Ken	Sánchez	0
2	109	6	Marketing Manager	David	Bradley	1
3	109	12	Vice President of Engineering	Terri	Duffy	1
4	109	42	Information Services Manager	Jean	Trenary	1
5	109	140	Chief Financial Officer	Laura	Norman	1
6	109	148	Vice President of Production	James	Hamilton	1
7	109	273	Vice President of Sales	Brian	Welcker	1
8	273	268	North American Sales Mana...	Stephen	Jiang	2

Figure 3-6. Results from recursive CTE example

A recursive CTE must contain at least two CTE query definitions—an *anchor member* and a *recursive member*. The UNION ALL operator combines the anchor member with the recursive member.

The first SELECT statement retrieves all top-level employees—that is, employees without a manager (ManagerID IS NULL). The second SELECT statement after the UNION ALL operator recursively retrieves the employees for each manager (employee) until all employee records have been processed.

Finally, the last SELECT statement retrieves all the records from the recursive CTE, which is named DirectReports.

You can limit the number of recursions by specifying a MAXRECURSION query hint. The following example adds this hint to the query in the previous example, limiting the result set to the first three levels of employees—the anchor set and two recursions:

```
USE AdventureWorks;

WITH DirectReports(
    ManagerID, EmployeeID, Title, FirstName, LastName, EmployeeLevel) AS
(
    SELECT e.ManagerID, e.EmployeeID, e.Title, c.FirstName, c.LastName,
        0 AS EmployeeLevel
    FROM HumanResources.Employee e
    JOIN Person.Contact AS c ON e.ContactID = c.ContactID
    WHERE ManagerID IS NULL

    UNION ALL

    SELECT e.ManagerID, e.EmployeeID, e.Title, c.FirstName, c.LastName,
        EmployeeLevel + 1
    FROM HumanResources.Employee e
        INNER JOIN DirectReports d ON e.ManagerID = d.EmployeeID
        JOIN Person.Contact AS c ON e.ContactID = c.ContactID
)
SELECT *
FROM DirectReports
OPTION (MAXRECURSION 2)
```

The query results are a subset of the result set in the previous example, and are limited to an EmployeeLevel of 0, 1, or 2. The error message shown in Figure 3-7 is also displayed, indicating that the recursive query was stopped before it completed:

Figure 3-7. Message from MAXRECURSION clause in recursive CTE example

SOME and ANY

The SOME and ANY operators are used in a WHERE clause to compare a scalar value with a single-column result set of values. A row is returned if the scalar comparison with the single-column result set has at least one match. SOME and ANY are semantically equivalent.

The syntax of the SOME and ANY operators is:

```
<scalar_expression> { = | <> | != | > | >= | !> | < | <= | !<}
    {SOME | ANY} {subquery}
```

where:

<scalar_expression>
 A T-SQL expression.

{ = | <> | != | > | >= | !> | < | <= | !<}
 A comparison operator.

<subquery>
 A query that returns a single-column result set. The data type of the column must match that of the scalar expression.

The following query returns from the Person.Address table in AdventureWorks all the employee addresses that are in Canada:

```
USE AdventureWorks

SELECT AddressLine1, City
FROM Person.Address
WHERE StateProvinceID = ANY
  (SELECT StateProvinceID
   FROM Person.StateProvince
   WHERE CountryRegionCode = 'CA')
```

Partial results are shown in Figure 3-8.

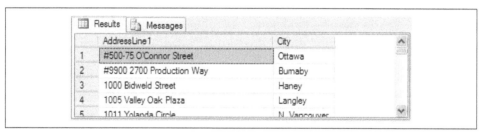

Figure 3-8. Results from ANY clause example

ALL

Use the ALL operator in a WHERE clause to compare a scalar value with a single-column result set. A row is returned if the scalar comparison to the single-column result set is true for all values in the column.

The syntax of the ALL operator is:

```
<scalar_expression> { = | <> | != | > | >= | !> | < | <= | !<}
    {SOME | ANY} {subquery}
```

where:

<scalar_expression>
 A T-SQL Server expression.

{ = | <> | != | > | >= | !> | < | <= | !<}
 A comparison operator.

<subquery>

A query that returns a single column. The data type of the column must be implicitly convertible to the data type of the scalar expression.

The following query returns all the employee addresses that are not in Canada:

```
USE AdventureWorks

SELECT AddressLine1, City
FROM Person.Address
WHERE StateProvinceID != ALL
  (SELECT StateProvinceID
   FROM Person.StateProvince
   WHERE CountryRegionCode = 'CA')
```

Partial results are shown in Figure 3-9.

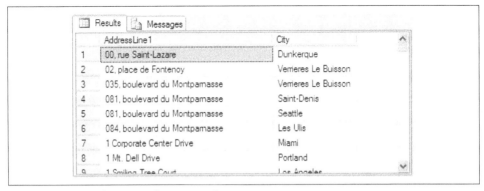

Figure 3-9. Results from ALL clause example

PIVOT and UNPIVOT

The PIVOT and UNPIVOT operators manipulate a table-valued expression into another table. These operators are essentially opposites of each other—PIVOT takes rows and puts them into columns, whereas UNPIVOT takes columns and puts them into rows.

PIVOT rotates unique values in one column into multiple columns in a result set.

The syntax of the PIVOT operator is:

```
<pivoted_table> ::=
    table_source PIVOT <pivot_clause> table_alias

<pivot_clause> ::=
    ( aggregate_function ( value_column )
       FOR pivot_column
         IN ( <column_list>)
    )

<column_list> ::=
    column_name [, ...]
```

where:

table_source
> The table, view, or derived table to use in the T-SQL statement.

table_alias
> An alias for *table_source*—this is required for PIVOT operators.

aggregate_function
> A system- or user-defined aggregate function. COUNT(*) is not allowed.

value_column
> The column containing the pivoted value.

pivot_column
> The column containing the values into which the *value_column* aggregate values are grouped. These values are the pivot columns.

<column_list>
> The pivot column names of the output table.

The following example sums the total orders by each employee in AdventureWorks for the years 2002, 2003, and 2004; pivots the total amount by year; and sorts the result set by employee ID:

```
USE AdventureWorks

SELECT EmployeeID, [2002] Y2002, [2003] Y2003, [2004] Y2004
FROM
  (SELECT YEAR(OrderDate) OrderYear, EmployeeID, TotalDue
  FROM Purchasing.PurchaseOrderHeader) poh
PIVOT
(
  SUM(TotalDue)
  FOR OrderYear IN
  ([2002], [2003], [2004])
) pvt
ORDER BY EmployeeID
```

Partial results are shown in Figure 3-10.

The PIVOT operator specifies the aggregate function, in this case SUM(TotalDue), and the column to pivot on, in this case OrderYear. The column list specifies that pivot columns 2002, 2003, and 2004 are displayed.

UNPIVOT does the opposite of PIVOT, rotating multiple column values into rows in a result set. The only difference is that NULL column values do not create rows in the UNPIVOT result set.

The following is the syntax of the UNPIVOT operator:

```
<unpivoted_table> ::=
    table_source UNPIVOT <unpivot_clause> table_alias

<unpivot_clause> ::=
```

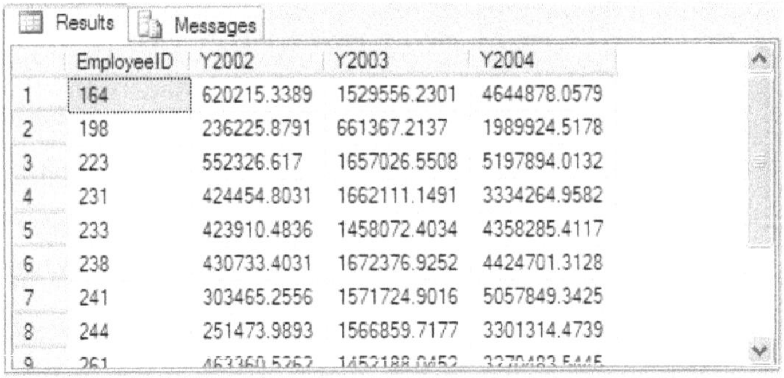

	EmployeeID	Y2002	Y2003	Y2004
1	164	620215.3389	1529556.2301	4644878.0579
2	198	236225.8791	661367.2137	1989924.5178
3	223	552326.617	1657026.5508	5197894.0132
4	231	424454.8031	1662111.1491	3334264.9582
5	233	423910.4836	1458072.4034	4358285.4117
6	238	430733.4031	1672376.9252	4424701.3128
7	241	303465.2556	1571724.9016	5057849.3425
8	244	251473.9893	1566859.7177	3301314.4739
9	261	[illegible]	[illegible]	[illegible]

Figure 3-10. Results from PIVOT operator example

```
    ( value_column FOR pivot_column IN ( <column_list> ) )

<column_list> ::=
     column_name [, ...]
```

The arguments are the same as those for the PIVOT operator.

The following example unpivots the results from the previous example:

```
USE AdventureWorks

SELECT EmployeeID, OrderYear, TotalDue
FROM
(
  SELECT EmployeeID, [2002] Y2002, [2003] Y2003, [2004] Y2004
  FROM
    (SELECT YEAR(OrderDate) OrderYear, EmployeeID, TotalDue
    FROM Purchasing.PurchaseOrderHeader) poh
  PIVOT
  (
    SUM(TotalDue)
    FOR OrderYear IN
    ([2002], [2003], [2004])
  ) pvt
) pvtTable
UNPIVOT
  (
    TotalDue FOR OrderYear IN (Y2002, Y2003, Y2004)
  ) unpvt
ORDER BY EmployeeID, OrderYear
```

The unpivot code added to the previous example is in bold. Partial results are shown in Figure 3-11.

The UNPIVOT operator clause specifies the value to unpivot, in this case TotalDue, and the column to unpivot on, in this case OrderYear. As expected, the results match the pivoted column values in the previous example.

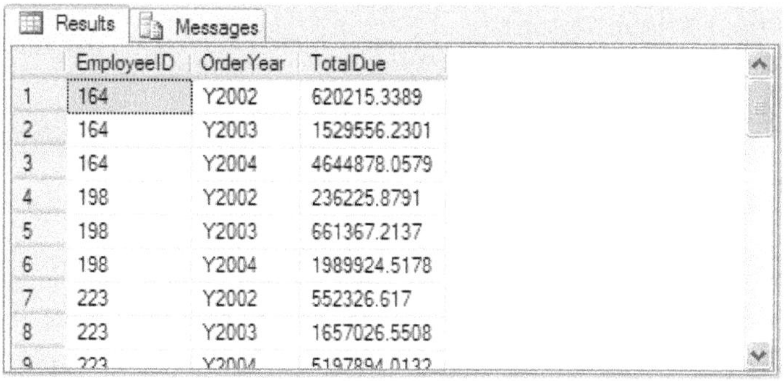

	EmployeeID	OrderYear	TotalDue
1	164	Y2002	620215.3389
2	164	Y2003	1529556.2301
3	164	Y2004	4644878.0579
4	198	Y2002	236225.8791
5	198	Y2003	661367.2137
6	198	Y2004	1989924.5178
7	223	Y2002	552326.617
8	223	Y2003	1657026.5508
9	223	Y2004	5197894.0132

Figure 3-11. Results from UNPIVOT operator example

APPLY

The APPLY operator invokes a table-valued function for each row returned by an outer table expression of a query. The table-valued function is evaluated for each row in the result set and can take its parameters from the row.

There are two forms of the APPLY operator—CROSS and OUTER. CROSS APPLY returns only the rows from the outer table where the table-value function returns a result set. OUTER APPLY returns all rows, returning NULL values for rows where the table-valued function does not return a result set.

The syntax for the APPLY operator is:

```
{CROSS | OUTER} APPLY {table_value_function}
```

where:

table_value_function
: Specifies the name of a table-valued function

Let's walk through an example using the APPLY operator to return sales order detail records from AdventureWorks for a sales order header where the order quantity is at least the minimum quantity specified. You can do this using a traditional JOIN. However, this example uses the APPLY operator and the following table-valued function:

```
USE AdventureWorks
GO

CREATE FUNCTION tvfnGetOrderDetails
  (@salesOrderID [int], @minOrderQuantity [smallint])
RETURNS TABLE
AS
RETURN
(
    SELECT *
    FROM Sales.SalesOrderDetail
    WHERE
```

```
      SalesOrderID = @salesOrderID AND
      OrderQty > @minOrderQuantity
)
```

 You must add a GO command after the USE statement, because the CREATE FUNCTION must be the first statement in a query batch.

The following CROSS APPLY query returns the SalesOrderID and OrderDate from the SalesOrderHeader together with the ProductID for lines where more than one item was ordered:

```
USE AdventureWorks

SELECT soh.SalesOrderID, soh.OrderDate,
  sod.ProductID, sod.OrderQty
FROM Sales.SalesOrderHeader soh
CROSS APPLY
  tvfnGetOrderDetails(soh.SalesOrderID, 1) sod
ORDER BY soh.SalesOrderID, sod.ProductID
```

Partial results are shown in Figure 3-12.

	SalesOrderID	OrderDate	ProductID	OrderQty
1	43659	2001-07-01 00:00:00.000	709	6
2	43659	2001-07-01 00:00:00.000	711	4
3	43659	2001-07-01 00:00:00.000	712	2
4	43659	2001-07-01 00:00:00.000	714	3
5	43659	2001-07-01 00:00:00.000	773	2
6	43659	2001-07-01 00:00:00.000	777	3
7	43661	2001-07-01 00:00:00.000	708	5
8	43661	2001-07-01 00:00:00.000	711	2

Figure 3-12. Results from CROSS APPLY operator example

The result set contains only sales order detail rows where more than one item is ordered. Sales order 43660 does not have any detail lines with more than one item ordered, so the CROSS APPLY operator does not return a row for that order.

Change the query to use the OUTER APPLY operator:

```
USE AdventureWorks

SELECT soh.SalesOrderID, soh.OrderDate, sod.ProductID, sod.OrderQty
FROM Sales.SalesOrderHeader soh
OUTER APPLY tvfnGetOrderDetails(soh.SalesOrderID, 1) sod
ORDER BY soh.SalesOrderID
```

The results are similar to those returned using the CROSS APPLY operator, except that order 43660 is now included in the result set, with NULL values for the two columns from the table-value function. Partial results are shown in Figure 3-13.

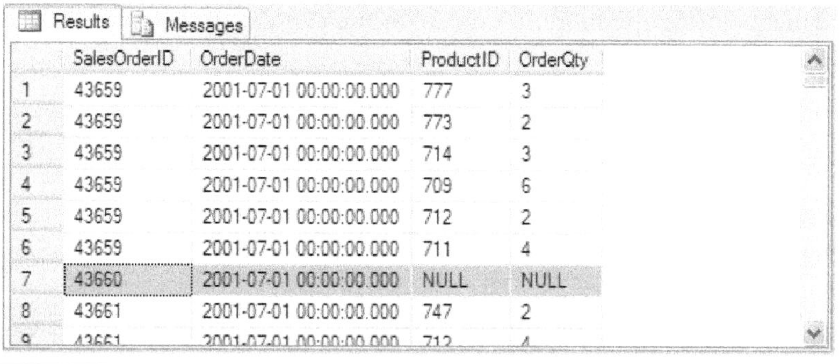

	SalesOrderID	OrderDate	ProductID	OrderQty
1	43659	2001-07-01 00:00:00.000	777	3
2	43659	2001-07-01 00:00:00.000	773	2
3	43659	2001-07-01 00:00:00.000	714	3
4	43659	2001-07-01 00:00:00.000	709	6
5	43659	2001-07-01 00:00:00.000	712	2
6	43659	2001-07-01 00:00:00.000	711	4
7	43660	2001-07-01 00:00:00.000	NULL	NULL
8	43661	2001-07-01 00:00:00.000	747	2
9	43661	2001-07-01 00:00:00.000	712	4

Figure 3-13. Results from OUTER APPLY operator example

EXECUTE AS

SQL Server 2005 lets you define the execution context of the following user-defined modules: functions, stored procedures, queues, and triggers (both DML and DDL). You do this by specifying the EXECUTE AS clause in the CREATE and ALTER statements for the module. Specifying the execution context lets you control the user account that SQL Server uses to validate permissions on objects referenced by the modules.

The syntax of the EXECUTE AS clause is given next for each of the categories items for which you can define the execution context:

Functions, stored procedures, and DML triggers:

```
EXECUTE AS { CALLER | SELF | OWNER | 'user_name' }
```

DDL triggers with database scope:

```
EXECUTE AS { CALLER | SELF | 'user_name' }
```

DDL triggers with server scope:

```
EXECUTE AS { CALLER | SELF | 'login_name' }
```

Queues:

```
EXECUTE AS { SELF | OWNER | 'user_name' }
```

where:

CALLER
> Statements inside the module execute in the context of the caller of the module. CALLER is the default for all modules except for queues for which the CALLER context is not valid.

SELF

Statements inside the module execute in the context of the person creating or altering the module. SELF is the default for queues.

OWNER

Statements inside the module execute in the context of the current owner of the module.

'user_name'

Statements inside the module execute in the context of the user specified in 'user_name'.

'login_name'

Statements inside the module execute in the context of the SQL Server login specified in 'login_name'.

For more information about specifying execution context, see Microsoft SQL Server 2005 Books Online.

New Ranking Functions

SQL Server 2005 introduces three new ranking functions: ROW_NUMBER(), DENSE_RANK(), and NTILE(). This is in addition to the RANK() function available in SQL Server 2000.

ROW_NUMBER()

The ROW_NUMBER() function returns the number of a row within a result set starting with 1 for the first row. The ROW_NUMBER() function does not execute until after a WHERE clause is used to select the subset of data.

The ROW_NUMBER() function syntax is:

```
ROW_NUMBER() OVER ([<partition_by_clause>] <order_by_clause>)
```

where:

<partition_by_clause>

Divides the result set into groups to which the ROW_NUMBER() function is applied. The function is applied to each partition separately; computation restarts for each partition.

<order_by_clause>

Specifies the order in which the sequential ROW_NUMBER() values are assigned.

The following example returns the row number for each contact in AdventureWorks based on the LastName and FirstName:

```
USE AdventureWorks

SELECT ROW_NUMBER() OVER(ORDER BY LastName, FirstName),
  ContactID, FirstName, LastName
FROM Person.Contact
```

Partial results are shown in Figure 3-14.

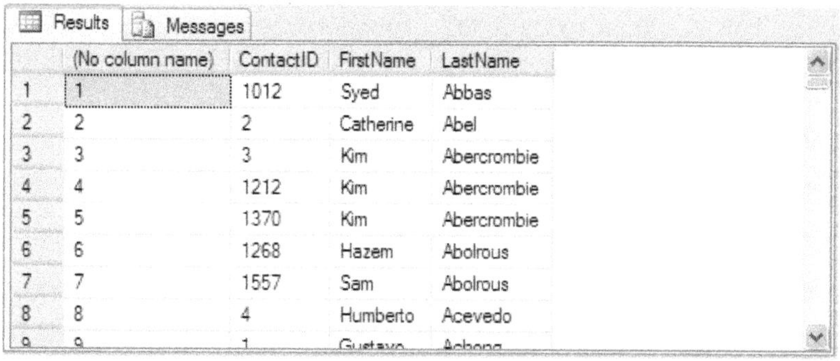

	(No column name)	ContactID	FirstName	LastName
1	1	1012	Syed	Abbas
2	2	2	Catherine	Abel
3	3	3	Kim	Abercrombie
4	4	1212	Kim	Abercrombie
5	5	1370	Kim	Abercrombie
6	6	1268	Hazem	Abolrous
7	7	1557	Sam	Abolrous
8	8	4	Humberto	Acevedo

Figure 3-14. Results from ROW_NUMBER() function example

The following example uses the `PARTITION BY` clause to rank the same result set within each manager:

```
USE AdventureWorks

SELECT ManagerID, ROW_NUMBER( )
  OVER(PARTITION BY ManagerID ORDER BY LastName, FirstName),
  e.ContactID, FirstName, LastName
FROM HumanResources.Employee e
LEFT JOIN Person.Contact c
  ON e.ContactID = c.ContactID
```

Partial results are shown in Figure 3-15.

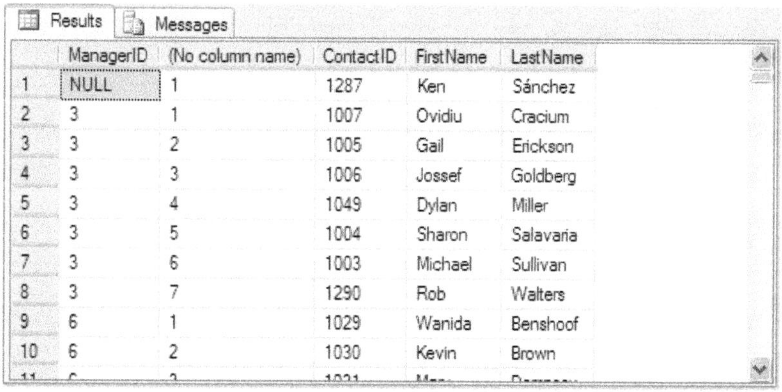

	ManagerID	(No column name)	ContactID	FirstName	LastName
1	NULL	1	1287	Ken	Sánchez
2	3	1	1007	Ovidiu	Cracium
3	3	2	1005	Gail	Erickson
4	3	3	1006	Jossef	Goldberg
5	3	4	1049	Dylan	Miller
6	3	5	1004	Sharon	Salavaria
7	3	6	1003	Michael	Sullivan
8	3	7	1290	Rob	Walters
9	6	1	1029	Wanida	Benshoof
10	6	2	1030	Kevin	Brown

Figure 3-15. Results from PARTITION BY clause example

The row numbers now restart at 1 for each manager. The employees are sorted by last name and then first name for each manager group.

DENSE_RANK( )

The `DENSE_RANK( )` function returns the rank of rows in a result set without gaps in the ranking. This is similar to the `RANK( )` function except that in cases where more than one row receives the same ranking, the next rank value is the rank of the tied group plus 1 rather than the next row number.

The `DENSE_RANK( )` function syntax is:

```
DENSE_RANK( ) OVER ([<partition_by_clause>] <order_by_clause>)
```

where:

<partition_by_clause>
: Divides the result set into groups to which the `ROW_NUMBER( )` function is applied. The function is applied to each partition separately; computation restarts for each partition.

<order_by_clause>
: Specifies the order in which the sequential `DENSE_RANK( )` values are assigned.

The following example shows the difference between `DENSE_RANK( )` and the `RANK( )` function by ranking contacts in `AdventureWorks` based on last name:

```
USE AdventureWorks

SELECT
  DENSE_RANK( ) OVER(ORDER BY LastName) DenseRank,
  RANK( ) OVER(ORDER BY LastName) Rank,
  ContactID, FirstName, LastName
FROM Person.Contact
```

Partial results are shown in Figure 3-16.

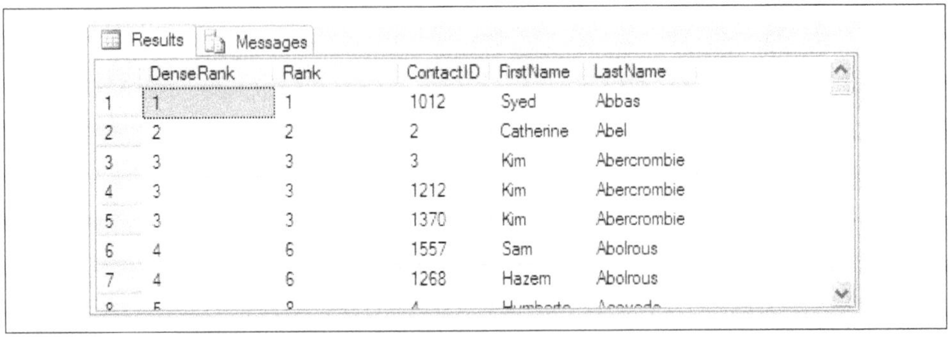

	DenseRank	Rank	ContactID	FirstName	LastName
1	1	1	1012	Syed	Abbas
2	2	2	2	Catherine	Abel
3	3	3	3	Kim	Abercrombie
4	3	3	1212	Kim	Abercrombie
5	3	3	1370	Kim	Abercrombie
6	4	6	1557	Sam	Abolrous
7	4	6	1268	Hazem	Abolrous

Figure 3-16. Results from DENSE_RANK() function example

NTILE( )

The `NTILE( )` function returns the group in which a row belongs within an ordered distribution of groups. Group numbering starts with `1`.

The NTILE( ) function syntax is:

```
NTILE(n) OVER ([<partition_by_clause>] <order_by_clause>)
```

where:

n   Specifies the number of groups that each partition should be divided into.

<partition_by_clause>
    Divides the result set into groups to which the NTILE( ) function is applied. The function is applied to each partition separately; computation restarts for each partition.

<order_by_clause>
    Specifies the column used to define the groups to which the NTILE( ) function is applied.

The following query distributes product list prices from AdventureWorks into four groups:

```
USE AdventureWorks

SELECT NTILE(4) OVER (ORDER BY ListPrice) GroupID,
    ProductID, Name, ListPrice
FROM Production.Product
WHERE ListPrice > 0
ORDER BY Name
```

Partial results are shown in Figure 3-17.

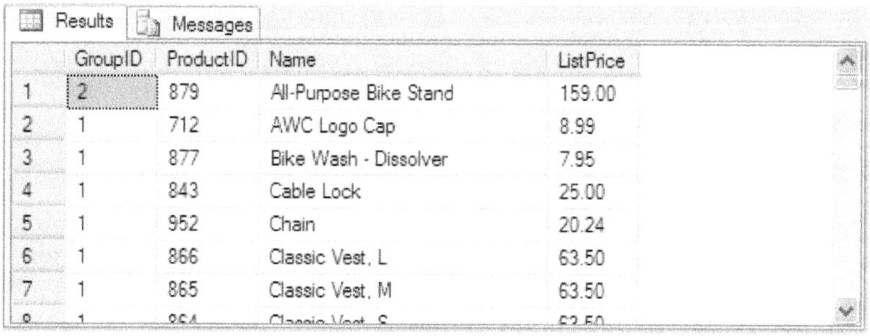

	GroupID	ProductID	Name	ListPrice
1	2	879	All-Purpose Bike Stand	159.00
2	1	712	AWC Logo Cap	8.99
3	1	877	Bike Wash - Dissolver	7.95
4	1	843	Cable Lock	25.00
5	1	952	Chain	20.24
6	1	866	Classic Vest, L	63.50
7	1	865	Classic Vest, M	63.50
8	1	864	Classic Vest, S	63.50

Figure 3-17. Results from NTILE() function example

If the number of rows is not evenly divisible by the number of groups, the size of the groups will differ by one.

Error Handling

SQL Server 2005 introduces structured exception handling similar to that found in C#. A group of T-SQL statements can be enclosed in a TRY block. If an error occurs within the TRY block, control is passed to a CATCH block containing T-SQL statements that handle the exception. Otherwise execution continues with the first statement following the CATCH block. If a CATCH block executes, control transfers to the first statement following the CATCH block once the CATCH block code completes.

A TRY...CATCH block does not trap warnings—messages with severity of 10 or lower—or errors with a severity level greater than 20—errors that typically terminate the Database Engine task.

TRY...CATCH blocks are subject to the following rules:

- A TRY block must be followed immediately by its associated CATCH block.
- Each TRY...CATCH block must be contained in a single batch, stored procedure, trigger, or function. A TRY block cannot span multiple batches—for example, more than one BEGIN...ELSE block or IF...ELSE block.
- TRY...CATCH blocks can be nested.
- You can use a GOTO statement to transfer control within a TRY or CATCH block or to exit a TRY or CATCH block. You cannot use a GOTO statement to enter a TRY or CATCH block.

The TRY...CATCH syntax is:

```
BEGIN TRY
{ sql_statement | sql_statement_block }
END TRY
BEGIN CATCH
{ sql_statement | sql_statement_block }
END CATCH
```

where:

sql_statement
    A T-SQL statement

sql_statement_block
    A group of T-SQL statements enclosed in a BEGIN...END block

For example, the Employee table in AdventureWorks has a check constraint that the Gender column can contain only M or F. The following statement updates the Gender for the employee with EmployeeID = 1 with the invalid value X:

```
USE AdventureWorks

BEGIN TRY
  UPDATE HumanResources.Employee
  SET Gender = 'X'
  WHERE EmployeeID = 1;
END TRY
BEGIN CATCH
  SELECT ERROR_NUMBER() ErrorNumber,
  ERROR_STATE() ErrorState,
  ERROR_SEVERITY() ErrorSeverity,
  ERROR_MESSAGE() ErrorMessage;
END CATCH
```

Executing this code returns a result set containing error information:

Column	Value
ErrorNumber	547
ErrorState	0
ErrorSeverity	16
ErrorMessage	UPDATE statement conflicted with CHECK constraint 'CK_Employee_Gender'. The conflict occurred in database 'AdventureWorks', table 'Employee', column 'Gender'.

As shown in the example, you can use the following functions to return information about the error caught by a CATCH block:

ERROR_MESSAGE( )
> Diagnostic information about the error. These messages often contain substitution variables that allow specific information, such as the database object that caused the error, to be included in the message.

ERROR_NUMBER( )
> The unique error number of the error. The ERROR_NUMBER( ) function returns the last error number every time it is called. This is different from @@ERROR, which works only if it immediately follows the error or is the first statement in the CATCH block.

ERROR_SEVERITY( )
> The severity level of the error. Error severities range from 0 to 24. Error levels 0 to 9 are warnings or informational.

ERROR_STATE( )
> The state of the error. A state code uniquely identifies specific conditions that cause errors with the same error number.

Data Definition Language (DDL) Triggers

Data Manipulation Language (DML) triggers are fired on actions that cause a change to the data in a table or a view—INSERT, UPDATE, or DELETE. SQL Server 2005 introduces Data Definition Language (DDL) triggers that fire in response to DDL statements that change the database schema or database server. These statements include CREATE, ALTER, DROP, GRANT, DENY, and REVOKE. DDL triggers are typically used for auditing and logging.

The syntax for a DDL trigger is:

```
CREATE TRIGGER trigger_name
ON { ALL SERVER | DATABASE }
[ WITH <ddl_trigger_option> [ ...,n ] ]
{ FOR | AFTER } { event_type | event_group } [ ,...n ]
```

```
AS { sql_statement [ ...n ] | EXTERNAL NAME < method specifier > }
[ ; ]

<ddl_trigger_option> ::=
    [ ENCRYPTION ]
    [ EXECUTE AS Clause ]

<method_specifier> ::=
    assembly_name.class_name.method_name
```

where:

trigger_name

The name of the trigger.

ON { ALL SERVER | DATABASE }

Defines the scope of the DDL trigger.

Triggers scoped as ALL SERVER fire whenever *event_type* or *event_group* happens anywhere in the current server. You must have at least CONTROL SERVER permission on the server to create a DDL trigger with server scope.

Triggers scoped as DATABASE fire whenever *event_type* or *event_group* occurs in the current database.

<ddl_trigger_option>

The WITH ENCRYPTION clause encrypts the CREATE TRIGGER statement body and prevents it from being accessed through catalog views or from being published as part of SQL Server replication.

The EXECUTE AS clause specifies the security context under which the trigger is executed.

{ FOR | AFTER }

FOR specifies that the trigger fires for each row affected by the triggering statement.

AFTER specifies that the trigger fires only when all operations in the triggering SQL statement have executed successfully. All referential cascade actions and constraint checks must also succeed. AFTER is the default.

event_type

A T-SQL event that causes the DDL trigger to fire once the event has finished executing. For a complete list of event types that are valid for use in DDL triggers, see Microsoft SQL Server 2005 Books Online.

event_group

The name of a predefined grouping of T-SQL events. The DDL trigger fires after any one of the events in *event_group* finishes executing. For a complete list of event groups that are valid for use in DDL triggers, see Microsoft SQL Server 2005 Books Online.

sql_statement

T-SQL that specifies both the conditions under which the DDL trigger is fired and the T-SQL that specifies the action or actions to be taken when the trigger fires.

<method_specifier>

Specifies the method of a registered assembly to bind with the trigger for CLR triggers. Creating CLR triggers is discussed in detail in Chapter 5.

As an example, look at the process for creating a DDL trigger to log CREATE TABLE and DROP TABLE operations to a log table:

1. Execute the following query to create a table named DdlLog in the ProgrammingSqlServer2005 database—create the database if you haven't previously. The DdlLog table will store the CREATE_TABLE and DROP_TABLE event information.

   ```
   USE ProgrammingSqlServer2005

   CREATE TABLE DdlLog
   (
       LogID int IDENTITY(1,1) NOT NULL,
       LogEntry xml NOT NULL,
           CONSTRAINT PK_Log PRIMARY KEY CLUSTERED
           (
               LogID ASC
           )
   )
   ```

2. Create a DDL trigger that will log created and dropped tables:

   ```
   USE ProgrammingSqlServer2005
   GO

   CREATE TRIGGER LogTableActivity
   ON DATABASE
   FOR CREATE_TABLE, DROP_TABLE
   AS
   INSERT INTO DdlLog (LogEntry)
   VALUES
   (
       EVENTDATA( )
   )
   ```

The EVENTDATA function returns information about database or server events. The function is called when the event notification fires. For events that fire a DDL trigger, the EVENTDATA function returns a value of xml type that contains:

- The time of the event.
- The System Process ID (SPID) of the connection during which the trigger executed.

- The type of event that fired the trigger.

- Additional information depending on the event type. For details about the schemas for specific event types, see the EVENTDATA (Transact-SQL) entry in Microsoft SQL Server 2005 Books Online.

3. Execute the following T-SQL statement to create and then drop a table named TestTable:

```
USE ProgrammingSqlServer2005

CREATE TABLE TestTable
(
    TestID int NOT NULL
)

DROP TABLE TestTable
```

4. Examine the table DdlLog. It contains two rows with details about the DDL CREATE_TABLE and DROP_TABLE events:

```
<EVENT_INSTANCE>
  <EventType>CREATE_TABLE</EventType>
  <PostTime>2005-09-15T22:23:06.030</PostTime>
  <SPID>51</SPID>
  <ServerName>WHAMILTONXP</ServerName>
  <LoginName>DANTECONSULTING\WHamilton</LoginName>
  <UserName>dbo</UserName>
  <DatabaseName>ProgrammingSqlServer2005</DatabaseName>
  <SchemaName>dbo</SchemaName>
  <ObjectName>TestTable</ObjectName>
  <ObjectType>TABLE</ObjectType>
  <TSQLCommand>
    <SetOptions ANSI_NULLS="ON" ANSI_NULL_DEFAULT="ON" ANSI_PADDING="ON"
      QUOTED_IDENTIFIER="ON" ENCRYPTED="FALSE" />
    <CommandText>CREATE TABLE TestTable
      (
          TestID int NOT NULL
      )

    </CommandText>
  </TSQLCommand>
</EVENT_INSTANCE>

<EVENT_INSTANCE>
  <EventType>DROP_TABLE</EventType>
  <PostTime>2005-09-15T22:23:06.063</PostTime>
  <SPID>51</SPID>
  <ServerName>WHAMILTONXP</ServerName>
  <LoginName>DANTECONSULTING\WHamilton</LoginName>
  <UserName>dbo</UserName>
  <DatabaseName>ProgrammingSqlServer2005</DatabaseName>
  <SchemaName>dbo</SchemaName>
  <ObjectName>TestTable</ObjectName>
  <ObjectType>TABLE</ObjectType>
```

```
<TSQLCommand>
  <SetOptions ANSI_NULLS="ON" ANSI_NULL_DEFAULT="ON" ANSI_PADDING="ON"
    QUOTED_IDENTIFIER="ON" ENCRYPTED="FALSE" />
  <CommandText>DROP TABLE TestTable
  </CommandText>
</TSQLCommand>
</EVENT_INSTANCE>
```

Metadata

SQL Server 2005 introduces *catalog views*—an interface to server metadata—which
expose information about database objects including tables, views, columns,
indexes, and stored procedures. Catalog views expose user-available catalog metadata and are the most efficient way to get, transform, and present catalog metadata.
Catalog views can be queried using a SELECT statement in the same way as any other
database view and return data as standard result sets. Catalog views are often joined
in queries to retrieve complex metadata.

Like *information schema views*—another way to retrieve metadata—catalog views
expose metadata independently of the underlying implementation of catalog tables.
If the underlying catalog tables change, applications that rely on catalog views will
not be affected. Unlike information schema views, catalog views expose metadata
specific to SQL Server.

Catalog views do not contain data about replication, backup, database maintenance
plans, or SQL Server Agent data.

The following query uses a catalog view to retrieve information about all the tables in
the AdventureWorks database. One record is returned in the result set for each table.

```
SELECT * FROM sys.tables
```

More information about specific catalog views appears throughout the book. For a
complete list of catalog views and their organization, see Microsoft SQL Server 2005
Books Online.

CHAPTER 4

Introduction to Common Language Runtime (CLR) Integration

The .NET Framework Common Language Runtime (CLR) is an environment that executes compiled code written in programming languages such as C# and VB.NET. The code is compiled to a file called an *assembly* that contains the compiled code together with an *assembly manifest*. The manifest contains metadata about the assembly, including types, methods, and inheritance relationships. Code running within the CLR is called *managed code*.

The CLR provides services such as automatic garbage collection, security support, and runtime type checking. Because the compiled code is executed by the CLR rather than directly by the operating system, managed code applications are platform- and language-independent.

SQL Server 2005 hosts the CLR in the Database Engine. This is called *CLR integration*. CLR integration lets you create database objects such as functions, stored procedures, triggers, user-defined types (UDTs), and user-defined aggregate (UDA) functions in programming languages supported by the CLR. Managed code running in SQL Server–hosted CLR is referred to as a *CLR routine*.

Prior to SQL Server 2005, the main way that SQL Server was extended was using extended stored procedures which let you create external routines using programming languages such as C. Extended stored procedures are used like regular stored procedures, however can have performance problems such as memory leaks and can cause the server to become unreliable. CLR integration lets you extend SQL Server with the safety and reliability of T-SQL and with the flexibility of extended stored procedures.

Managed code uses *code access security* (CAS) to control what operations assemblies can perform. CAS secures the code running within SQL Server and prevents the code from adversely affecting the operating system or the database server.

Generally, you should use T-SQL when the code in the routines primarily performs data access. CLR routines are best for CPU-intensive calculations and for supporting complex logic that would otherwise be difficult to implement using T-SQL.

The components needed to develop CLR routines are installed with SQL Server 2005. Although SQL Server 2005 ships with the .NET Framework and command-line compilers for C# and VB.NET, as well as a Visual Studio .NET IDE that lets you build Analysis Services and Reporting Services projects, you need to install Visual Studio 2005 to create CLR routines in Visual Studio 2005.

CLR Integration Design Objectives

Microsoft identifies the design objectives of SQL Server 2005 CLR integration as follows:

Reliability
> CLR routines cannot perform operations that compromise the integrity of the Database Engine process, nor are they allowed to overwrite Database Engine memory buffers and internal data structures.

Scalability
> SQL Server and the CLR have different models for threading, scheduling, and memory management. The design goal is to ensure scalability when user code calls APIs for threading, synchronization primitives, and memory.

Security
> User code running in the database must follow SQL Server authentication and authorization rules for accessing database objects. Additionally, administrators must be able to control access to operating system resources from code running within the database.

Performance
> User code running in the database must perform at least as well as equivalent implementations through native Database Engine functionality or T-SQL.

The CLR provides the following services to achieve these design objectives:

Type-safe verification
> After assemblies are loaded into the CLR but before they are compiled, the code is verified to ensure access to memory structures only in well-defined ways—code that passes this verification is *type-safe*.

Application domains
> Application domains are execution spaces within a host process where assemblies are loaded, unloaded, and executed. They provide isolation between executing assemblies.

Code access security
> CAS applies permissions to code to control the operations that the code can perform and the system resources it can access based on the identity of the code.

Host Protection Attributes (HPA)

HPA is a mechanism to annotate .NET-managed APIs with attributes of interest to host CLRs such as SQL Server. The host CLR can deny user code calls to APIs that are on a prohibited list.

SQL Server 2005 hosts the CLR in the Database Engine, effectively acting as the operating system for the CLR. The design goals for SQL Server 2005 CLR integration for reliability, scalability, and security are accomplished as follows:

Reliability

You cannot always recover from critical exceptions in .NET-managed code when a thread abort exception is raised. If there is any shared state in the application domain in which the thread abort exception occurs, the SQL Server–hosted CLR unloads that application domain, thereby stopping database transactions running in it.

Scalability

The CLR calls SQL Server APIs to create threads and calls SQL Server synchronization objects to synchronize threads. All threads and synchronization objects are known to SQL Server, so it can effectively schedule non-CLR threads, detect and remove deadlocks involving CLR synchronization objects, and detect and handle CLR threads that have not yielded in a reasonable amount of time.

The CLR calls SQL Server primitives to allocate and deallocate memory. This lets SQL Server stay within its configured memory limits—SQL Server can reject CLR memory requests when memory is constrained or ask the CLR to reduce its memory use as necessary.

Security

When a SQL Server registered assembly is created or altered, you can specify one of three permissions sets for the assembly: SAFE, EXTERNAL-ACCESS, or UNSAFE. SQL Server uses permission sets to set CAS permissions when the assembly executes. The three permission sets are described in Table 4-1.

Table 4-1. SQL Server CLR routine permission sets

Permission set	Description
SAFE	SAFE assemblies can access data from local SQL Server databases and can execute computations and business logic not involving resources outside the local databases.
	SAFE assemblies cannot access external system resources such as files, networks, environment variables, or the registry.
	The SAFE permission set can only be applied to code that is verifiably type-safe. It is the default permission set and the most restrictive.
EXTERNAL-ACCESS	EXTERNAL-ACCESS allows assemblies to access certain external system resources such as files, networks, environment variables, and the registry in addition to the access provided by the SAFE permission set.
	The EXTERNAL-ACCESS permission set can only be applied to code that is verifiably type-safe.

Table 4-1. SQL Server CLR routine permission sets (continued)

Permission set	Description
UNSAFE	UNSAFE assemblies have unrestricted access to resources both inside of and outside of SQL Server. An UNSAFE assembly can call unmanaged code.
	Only a database administrator can register an UNSAFE assembly.

The SQL Server–hosted CLR imposes the following security-related programming restrictions:

- Code marked SAFE or EXTERNAL-ACCESS cannot use static data members and variables.

- Calls cannot be made to .NET Framework API types or members annotated with the ExternalProcessMgmt, MayLeakOnAbort, SharedState, or Synchronization host protection attributes (HostProtectionAttribute)—this prevents code in assemblies marked as SAFE or EXTERNAL-ACCESS from calling APIs that might cause resource leaks on termination, that enable sharing state, or that perform synchronization.

Enabling CLR Integration

CLR integration is turned off by default in SQL Server 2005. Use the sp_configure system stored procedure to enable CLR integration, as shown here:

```
sp_configure 'clr enabled', 1
GO
RECONFIGURE
GO
```

The clr enabled server configuration option specifies whether .NET assemblies can be run by SQL Server (0 = do not allow; 1 = allow). The change takes effect immediately after sp_configure and reconfigure are executed—the server does not need to be restarted.

You need ALTER SETTINGS permissions at the server level to enable CLR integration.

Required .NET Namespaces

The components needed to create simple CLR routines are installed with SQL Server 2005 in the .NET Framework assembly named System.Data.dll—part of the base class library of the .NET Framework and located in both the Global Assembly Cache (GAC) and in the *<windir>\Microsoft.NET\Framework\<version>* directory. The key namespaces in this assembly are described in Table 4-2.

Table 4-2. .NET namespaces for CLR routines

System.Data.dll namespaces	Description
System.Data	Classes that comprise the ADO.NET architecture
System.Data.Sql	Classes that support SQL Server 2005–specific functionality
Microsoft.SqlServer.Server	Classes that support .NET CLR functionality inside SQL Server CLR routines—user-defined functions (UDFs), stored procedures, UDA functions, UDTs, and triggers
System.Data.SqlTypes	Classes that support native SQL Server data types
System.Data.SqlClient	.NET Frameworks data provider for SQL Server

Types of CLR Routines

SQL Server 2005 CLR integration lets you build database objects using .NET languages. Once a .NET Framework assembly is registered with SQL Server, you can create CLR routines that can be used anywhere a T-SQL equivalent routine can be used. Table 4-3 describes the available CLR routines.

Table 4-3. Types of CLR routines

Database object	.NET Framework assembly type	Description
Scalar-valued function	Public static method	A UDF that returns a single value.
Table-valued function	Public static method	A UDF that returns a table as the result set.
Stored procedure	Public static method	A routine that returns tabular result sets and messages to the client, invokes DDL and DML statements, and returns output parameters.
User-defined aggregate function	Class or structure	A UDA function that operates on values in a set of rows and returns a scalar.
User-defined type	Class or structure	Complex data types complete with methods that extend the scalar type system in SQL Server.
Trigger (DML and DDL)	Public static method	A type of stored procedure that automatically runs when a DML or DDL event occurs.

Hello World Example

This section shows how to create, configure, and use a SQL Server CLR routine by way of a sample CLR stored procedure that returns the text message "Hello world." This example is followed by an example that shows how to create the same .NET Framework assembly using a command-line compiler.

Follow these steps in Visual Studio 2005 to create the .NET Framework assembly containing the CLR stored procedure:

1. Select File → New → Project.

2. Select SQL Server Project in the New Project dialog box, shown in Figure 4-1, name it HelloWorld, specify the location, and click OK.

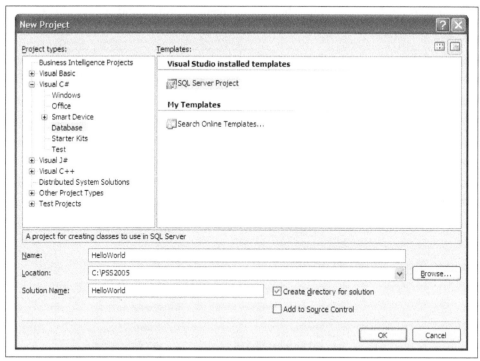

Figure 4-1. New Project dialog box

3. Because the stored procedure will not be accessing any data, click Cancel in the Add Database Reference dialog box, shown in Figure 4-2.

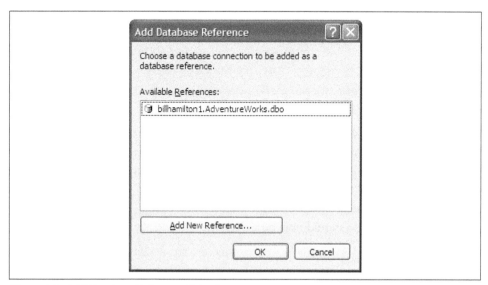

Figure 4-2. Add Database Reference dialog box

4. In Solution Explorer, right-click the HelloWorld project and select Add → Stored Procedure from the context menu, as shown in Figure 4-3.

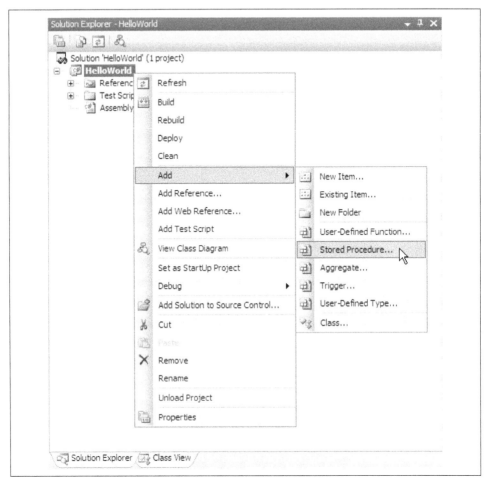

Figure 4-3. Add Stored Procedure menu item

5. In the Add New Item dialog box, shown in Figure 4-4, select the Stored Procedure template. Enter the name HelloWorldStoredProcedure.cs and click Add.

6. Add the following line of code to the HelloWorldStoredProcedure() method in HelloWorldStoredProcedure.cs:

```
SqlContext.Pipe.Send("Hello world.\n");
```

The complete code should now be as follows:

```
using System;
using System.Data;
using System.Data.Sql;
using System.Data.SqlTypes;
```

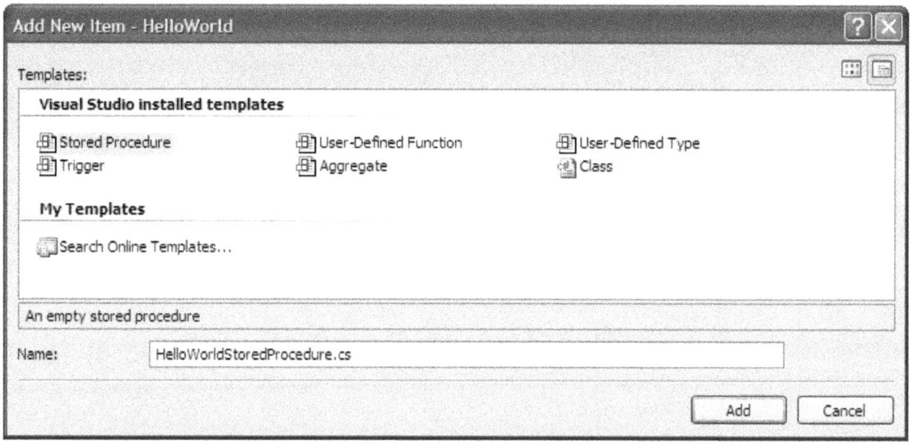

Figure 4-4. Add New Item dialog box

```
using Microsoft.SqlServer.Server;

    public partial class StoredProcedures
    {
        [SqlProcedure]
        public static void HelloWorldStoredProcedure()
        {
            SqlContext.Pipe.Send("Hello world.\n");
        }
    };
```

7. Build the solution by selecting Build → Build Solution from the Visual Studio 2005 main menu, by clicking the Build Solution button on the Build toolbar, or by right-clicking the HelloWorld project in Solution Explorer and selecting Build from the context menu. The stored procedure is compiled into an assembly called HelloWorld.dll in the *bin\Debug* subdirectory.

Once the stored procedure is compiled, you need to register the assembly with SQL Server before you can access the CLR stored procedure. This walkthrough and many of the examples in this book use a database called ProgrammingSqlServer2005. Follow these steps to register the assembly with SQL Server:

1. Right-click the ProgrammingSqlServer2005 database in Object Explorer and select New Query from the context menu, as shown in Figure 4-5.

2. Register the assembly HelloWorld.dll with the SQL Server assembly name HelloWorld by executing the following T-SQL statement:

```
USE ProgrammingSqlServer2005
GO

CREATE ASSEMBLY HelloWorld
FROM 'C:\PSS2005\HelloWorld\HelloWorld\bin\Debug\HelloWorld.dll'
```

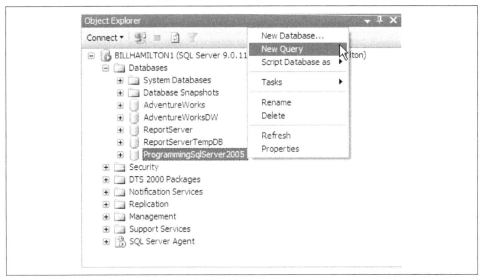

Figure 4-5. New Query menu item

The SQL Server assembly name and the .NET Framework assembly DLL name do not have to be the same. The SQL Server assembly name must be unique in the database.

You can confirm that the assembly is registered by expanding the Databases → ProgrammingSqlServer2005 → Programmability → Assemblies node in the Object Explorer tree view, as shown in Figure 4-6.

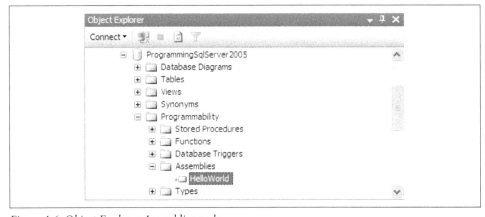

Figure 4-6. Object Explorer Assemblies node

3. Create a CLR stored procedure called HelloWorldSP based on the HelloWorld StoredProcedure() static method in the HelloWorld.dll assembly registered in Step 2. Execute the following query:

```
CREATE PROCEDURE HelloWorldSP
AS
EXTERNAL NAME HelloWorld.StoredProcedures.HelloWorldStoredProcedure
```

The EXTERNAL NAME clause has three parts, separated by periods:

- The SQL Server registered assembly name (from Step 2)—HelloWorld
- The class name in the .NET Framework assembly—StoredProcedures
- The name of the public static method implementing the stored procedure—HelloWorldStoredProcedure( )

You can confirm that the stored procedure was created by expanding the Databases → ProgrammingSqlServer2005 → Stored Procedure node in the Object Explorer tree view, as shown in Figure 4-7.

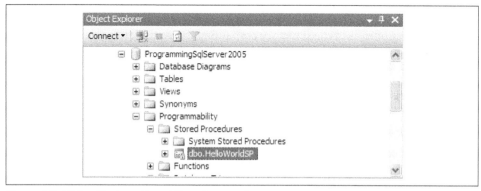

Figure 4-7. Object Explorer Stored Procedures node

You can now use the stored procedure just as you would use any other stored procedure.

Execute the HelloWorldSP stored procedure with the following T-SQL statement:

```
EXEC HelloWorldSP
```

The results follow:

```
Hello world.
```

The results are exactly the same as they would be if you had created and executed the following T-SQL stored procedure:

```
CREATE PROCEDURE HelloWorldSP2
AS
    PRINT 'Hello world.'
```

Once you have finished with the sample, you can remove the CLR stored procedure and registered .NET Framework assembly by executing the following statements:

```
DROP PROCEDURE HelloWorldSP
```

```
DROP ASSEMBLY HelloWorld
```

Command-Line Compiler

While the examples in this book use Visual Studio 2005, you can create the program files using any text editor and compile them using a .NET command-line compiler. SQL Server 2005 installs .NET Framework redistribution files, including command-line language compilers—for example *csc.exe* for C# and *vbc.exe* for VB.NET. The command-line compilers are installed in the directory *C:\<windir>\Microsoft.NET\Framework\<version>*, where:

<windir>
> The directory in which your version of Windows is installed—often *WINDOWS* or *WINNT*

<version>
> The .NET Framework version

To use the compiler, add the directory containing the compiler to your `Path` environment system variable defined in the `System variables` list box accessed through Control Panel → System → Advanced → Environment Variables.

To use the command-line C# compiler to compile the *HelloWorldStoredProcedure.cs* file created in the previous section, execute the following command:

```
csc /target:library /out:HelloWorld.dll HelloWorldStoredProcedure.cs
```

The `/target` compiler flag instructs the compiler to build a DLL. The `/out` flag instructs the compiler to override the default DLL name `HelloWorldStoredProcedure.dll` with the name `HelloWorld.dll`. For more information about Visual Studio .NET compilers and compiler flags, consult the Microsoft Developer Network (MSDN).

Once you have compiled the .NET Framework assembly, you register it and CLR routines in the same way as if you had used the Visual Studio 2005 compiler.

DDL Support for CLR Integration

SQL Server introduces new T-SQL statements to create and manage .NET assemblies and UDTs, and enhances other T-SQL statements to create and manage functions, stored procedures, triggers, and UDA functions created from CLR assemblies. These statements are described in Table 4-4.

Table 4-4. New and changed T-SQL statements to support CLR integration

Scope	DDL statement	New T-SQL statement	Description
.NET Framework assembly	CREATE ASSEMBLY	Yes	Loads assembly into SQL Server.
	ALTER ASSEMBLY	Yes	Changes a loaded assembly.
	DROP ASSEMBLY	Yes	Unloads an assembly from SQL Server.

Scope	DDL statement	New T-SQL statement	Description
User-defined aggregate function	CREATE AGGREGATE	Yes	Creates a UDA function in a SQL Server database from a UDA function implemented as a class in a .NET Framework assembly.
			The assembly containing the class must first be registered in SQL Server with the CREATE ASSEMBLY T-SQL statement.
	DROP AGGREGATE	Yes	Removes a UDA function from a SQL Server database.
User-defined type	CREATE TYPE	No	Creates a UDT in a SQL Server database from a type implemented as a class or structure in a .NET Framework assembly.
			The assembly containing the class or structure must first be registered in SQL Server with the CREATE ASSEMBLY T-SQL statement.
	DROP TYPE	No	Removes a UDT from a SQL Server database.
Stored procedure	CREATE PROCEDURE	No	Creates a stored procedure in a SQL Server database from a CLR stored procedure implemented as a method in a .NET Framework assembly.
			The assembly containing the method must first be registered in SQL Server with the CREATE ASSEMBLY T-SQL statement.
	ALTER PROCEDURE	No	Changes a stored procedure previously created with the CREATE PROCEDURE T-SQL statement.
	DROP PROCEDURE	No	Removes a stored procedure from a SQL Server database.
User-defined function (scalar-valued or table-valued)	CREATE FUNCTION	No	Creates a UDF in a SQL Server database from a CLR UDF implemented as a method in a .NET Framework assembly.
			The assembly containing the method must first be registered in SQL Server with the CREATE ASSEMBLY T-SQL statement.
	ALTER FUNCTION	No	Changes a UDF previously created with the CREATE FUNCTION T-SQL statement.
	DROP FUNCTION	No	Removes a UDF from a SQL Server database.
Trigger	CREATE TRIGGER	No	Creates a DML or DDL trigger in a SQL Server database from a CLR trigger implemented as a method in a .NET Framework assembly.
			The assembly containing the method must first be registered in SQL Server with the CREATE ASSEMBLY T-SQL statement.
	ALTER TRIGGER	No	Changes a trigger previously created with the CREATE TRIGGER T-SQL statement.
	DROP TRIGGER	No	Removes a trigger from a SQL Server database.

The statements are described in detail in the following subsections. Chapter 5 presents in-depth discussions and examples of creating these objects in C#.

CLR Routine Metadata

Catalog views return metadata used by the SQL Server 2005 Database Engine. The sys.all_objects catalog view returns a row for each user-defined object and system object in the current database. The type column specifies the object type—the CLR routine type values are shown in Table 4-5.

Table 4-5. CLR object type values

sys.all_objects type column value	CLR object type
AF	Aggregate function
FS	Scalar-valued function
FT	Table-valued function
PC	Stored procedure
TA	Trigger

For example, the following T-SQL statement returns information about all CLR stored procedures in the AdventureWorks database:

```
USE AdventureWorks
GO

SELECT * FROM sys.all_objects
WHERE type='PC'
```

The sys.all_objects catalog view does not return information for DDL triggers. Use the sys.triggers catalog view instead to return information for all DML and DDL triggers in the current database.

The sys.all_objects catalog view does not return information for UDTs. The sys.types catalog view returns information for all system and user-defined types in the current database. The sys.assembly_types catalog view returns information for all CLR UDTs.

SQL Server 2005 provides catalog views that contain information about registered assemblies and CLR functions, stored procedures, triggers, UDTs, and UDA functions defined from registered assemblies. These catalog views are described in Table 4-6 and detailed in the following subsections.

Table 4-6. Catalog views returning metadata about registered .NET Framework assemblies and CLR routines

Catalog view	Description
sys.assemblies	A row for each assembly registered in the current database
sys.assembly_files	A row for each file that makes up an assembly

Catalog view	Description
sys.assembly_modules	A row for each function, CLR stored procedure, or trigger
sys.assembly_references	A row for each pair of assemblies directly referencing each other
sys.assembly_types	A row for each CLR UDT

sys.assemblies

The sys.assemblies catalog view contains a row for each assembly registered in the current database. Table 4-7 describes the columns in this view.

Table 4-7. sys.assemblies catalog view columns

Column name	Description
name	The name of the assembly, unique within the schema.
principal_id	The ID of the principal that owns the schema.
assembly_id	The assembly ID number, unique within a database.
permission_set	The code access permissions for the assembly; one of the following numeric values: • 1 = Safe Access • 2 = External Access • 3 = Unsafe Access
permission_set_desc	A description of code access permissions specified by the value of the permission_set column; one of the following string values: SAFE_ACCESS, EXTERNAL_ACCESS, or UNSAFE_ACCESS.
is_visible	A numeric value indicating the visibility of the assembly: 0 = The assembly can be called only by other assemblies. 1 = The assembly can be used to create CLR UDFs, stored procedures, triggers, UDTs, and UDA functions.
clr_name	Canonical string that uniquely identifies the assembly. The string encodes the simple name, version number (version), culture (culture), public key (publickeytoken), and architecture (processorarchitecture) of the assembly.
create_date	The date that the assembly was created or registered.

The following T-SQL statement returns a result set of all the CLR assemblies registered in the current database:

```
SELECT * FROM sys.assemblies;
```

sys.assembly_files

The sys.assembly_files catalog view contains a row for each file in each registered assembly in the current database. Table 4-8 describes the columns in this view.

Table 4-8. sys.assembly_files catalog view columns

Column name	Description
assembly_id	The ID of the assembly to which the file belongs.
name	The name of the assembly file.
file_id	The ID of the file, unique within an assembly. The root assembly has a file ID of 1. Files added to the assembly have a file ID of 2 or greater.
content	The binary contents of the file.

sys.assembly_modules

The sys.assembly_modules catalog view contains a row for each CLR function (scalar-valued, table-valued, and aggregate), stored procedure, or trigger defined in a .NET Framework assembly in the current database. Table 4-9 describes the columns in this view.

Table 4-9. sys.assembly_modules catalog view columns

Column name	Description
object_id	The ID of the module (CLR routine), unique within the database.
assembly_id	The ID of the assembly from which the module was created.
assembly_class	The name of the class within the assembly that defines the module.
assembly_method	The name of the method within the assembly_class that defines this module. This value is NULL for aggregate functions.
null_on_null_input	Indicates whether the module returns NULL if any arguments are NULL.
execute_as_principal_id	The database principal ID for the execution context. If this value is NULL, the execution context is CALLER.

sys.assembly_references

The sys.assembly_references catalog view contains a row for each pair of assemblies registered in the current database where one assembly directly references another. Table 4-10 describes the columns in this view.

Table 4-10. sys.assembly_references catalog view columns

Column name	Description
assembly_id	The ID of the assembly that has a reference to another assembly
referenced_assembly_id	The ID of the assembly being referenced

sys.assembly_types

The sys.assembly_types catalog view contains a row for each UDT in the current database that is defined in a CLR assembly. Table 4-11 describes the columns in this view.

Table 4-11. sys.assembly_types catalog view columns

Column name	Description
`<inherited_columns>`	Columns inherited from `sys.types` catalog view
`assembly_id`	The ID of the assembly from which the UDT was created
`assembly_class`	The name of the class within the assembly that defines the UDT
`is_binary_ordered`	Indicates whether sorting the bytes of the type is equivalent to sorting the type using comparison operators
`is_fixed_length`	Indicates whether the length of the type is the same as the maximum length (`max_length` in `sys.types`)
`prog_id`	The `ProgID` of the type exposed to COM
`assembly_qualified_name`	The assembly qualified type name

Assembly Management

A .NET Framework assembly contains classes and methods that can implement CLR routines in SQL Server 2005. You first have to register the assembly with SQL Server by using the CREATE ASSEMBLY T-SQL statement as you did earlier in the "Hello World Example" section. A registered assembly can be modified using the ALTER ASSEMBLY statement, or removed from the server using the DROP ASSEMBLY statement. These three new T-SQL statements are described in the following subsections.

CREATE ASSEMBLY

The CREATE ASSEMBLY T-SQL statement registers a .NET Framework assembly as an object within SQL Server from which CLR stored procedures, UDFs, triggers, UDA functions, and UDTs can be created.

The CREATE ASSEMBLY syntax is:

```
CREATE ASSEMBLY assembly_name
  [ AUTHORIZATION owner_name ]
  FROM { client_assembly_specifier | assembly_bits [,...n] }
  [ WITH PERMISSION_SET = { SAFE | EXTERNAL_ACCESS | UNSAFE } ]

client_assembly_specifier :: =
  '[\\computer_name\]share_name\[path\]manifest_file_name'
  | '[local_path\]manifest_file_name'

assembly_bits :: =
  { varbinary_literal | varbinary_expression }
```

where:

assembly_name

Specifies the name of the assembly, which must be unique within the database.

AUTHORIZATION *owner_name*

Specifies the name of the user or role that is the owner of the assembly. If not specified, ownership is assigned to the current user.

FROM
   Specifies the .NET Framework assembly to load.

client_assembly_specifier
   Specifies the local path or Universal Naming Convention (UNC) network location where the assembly is located and the manifest filename for the assembly. Multi-module assemblies are not supported. Dependent assemblies are either automatically uploaded from the same location or loaded from the current database if owned by the same principal—CREATE ASSEMBLY fails if either is not possible.

assembly_bits
   Specifies a list of binary values that make up the assembly and its dependent assemblies. The root-level assembly must be specified first followed by the dependent assemblies in any order.

PERMISSION_SET = { SAFE | EXTERNAL_ACCESS | UNSAFE }
   Specifies the code-access security when SQL Server accesses the assembly. If not specified, the default is SAFE.

Multiple versions of the same assembly can be uploaded to the server. These assemblies must have different version numbers or cultures and must be registered using unique assembly names within SQL Server.

ALTER ASSEMBLY

The ALTER ASSEMBLY T-SQL statement modifies the properties of an assembly previously registered using the CREATE ASSEMBLY statement and refreshes the assembly with the latest version.

The ALTER ASSEMBLY syntax is:

```
ALTER ASSEMBLY assembly_name
  [ FROM { client_assembly_specifier | assembly_bits [ ,...n ] } ]
  [ WITH assembly_option [ ,...n ] ]
  [ DROP FILE { file_name [ ,...n ] | ALL } ]
  [ ADD FILE FROM
  {
    client_file_specifier [ AS file_name ]
    | file_bits AS file_name
  } [,...n ] ]

client_assembly_specifier :: =
  '\\computer_name\share-name\[path\]manifest_file_name'
  | '[local_path\]manifest_file_name'

assembly_bits :: =
  { varbinary_literal | varbinary_expression }

assembly_option :: =
  PERMISSION_SET { SAFE | EXTERNAL_ACCESS | UNSAFE }
  | VISIBILITY { ON | OFF } ]
  | UNCHECKED DATA
```

where:

assembly_name
>   Specifies the name of the registered assembly to alter.

FROM
>   Specifies the .NET Framework assembly to refresh with the latest copy.

DROP FILE { *file*_name [,...n] | ALL }
>   Removes the file associated with the assembly or all files associated with the assembly. DROP FILE executes before ADD FILE if both are specified.

ADD FILE FROM { *client_file_specifier* [AS *file_name*] | *file_bits* AS *file_name* }
>   Uploads a file that is to be associated with the assembly from the location specified by the *client_file_specifier* argument or from the binary values that make up the file specified by the *file_bits* argument. The *file_name* argument specifies the name to use to store the file in SQL Server. If the *file_name* argument is not specified with a *client_file_specified* argument, the filename part of the *client_file_specifier* is used as the name in SQL Server.

VISIBILITY { ON | OFF }
>   Specifies whether the assembly can be used to create CLR stored procedures, functions, triggers, UDTs, and UDA functions. Assemblies with VISIBILITY = OFF can be called only by other assemblies. The default VISIBILITY is ON.

UNCHECKED DATA
>   Alters the assembly even if there are tables with columns or check constraints that reference methods in the assembly or if there are CLR UDTs that are dependent on the assembly and use User-Defined serialization format. Only members of db_owner and db_ddlowner can specify this option.

Other arguments are the same as defined for the CREATE ASSEMBLY statement.

Executing ALTER ASSEMBLY does not affect currently executing sessions running the assembly being altered—they complete using the unaltered assembly. A new application domain is created running the latest bits for new users of the assembly.

If the FROM clause is not specified, the assembly is refreshed with the latest copy of the assembly rebinding CLR routines to the latest implementation in the assembly.

DROP ASSEMBLY

The DROP ASSEMBLY statement removes an assembly previously registered with the CREATE ASSEMBLY statement. The assembly and all of its associated files are removed from the database.

The DROP ASSEMBLY syntax is:

```
DROP ASSEMBLY assembly_name
[ WITH NO DEPENDENTS ]
```

where:

assembly_name
> Specifies the name of the registered assembly to drop

WITH NO DEPENDENTS
> Specifies that dependent assemblies are not to be dropped

Executing DROP ASSEMBLY does not affect currently executing sessions running the assembly being dropped—they run to completion. New attempts to invoke code in the assembly fail.

You cannot drop an assembly that is referenced by another assembly or that is used by a CLR function, stored procedure, trigger, UDT, or UDA function.

User-Defined Functions

A user-defined function (UDF) is a routine written by the user that returns either a scalar value (scalar-valued function) or a table (table-valued function). SQL Server 2005 functions can be created directly from T-SQL statements or from methods in a registered .NET Framework assembly.

UDFs are created, changed, and removed in SQL Server using the CREATE FUNCTION, ALTER FUNCTION, and DROP FUNCTION T-SQL statements. These statements have been enhanced in SQL Server 2005 to support CLR UDF management. The following subsections describe the enhancements.

CREATE FUNCTION

The CREATE FUNCTION T-SQL statement has been enhanced in SQL Server 2005 to let you create a CLR scalar-valued or table-valued UDF from a UDF implemented as a method in a .NET Framework assembly. You must first register the assembly using the CREATE ASSEMBLY statement. The CREATE FUNCTION syntax for creating CLR UDFs follows:

```
CREATE FUNCTION [ schema_name. ] function_name (
  [ { @parameter_name [AS] [ type_schema_name. ] scalar_parameter_data_type }
  [ ,...n ] ] )
RETURNS { scalar_return_data_type | TABLE clr_table_type_definition }
  [ WITH clr_function_option [ [,] ...n ] ]
  [ AS ] EXTERNAL NAME method_specifier [ ; ]

method_specifier ::=
  assembly_name.class_name.method_name

clr_table_type_definition ::=
  ( { column_name data_type }[ ,...n ] )
```

```
clr_function_option ::=
    [ RETURNS NULL ON NULL INPUT | CALLED ON NULL INPUT ]
    | [ EXECUTE_AS_Clause ]
```

where:

[*schema_name.*] *function_name*
> Specifies the name of the CLR UDF to create.

@parameter_name [AS] [*type_schema_name.*] *scalar_parameter_data_type*
> Defines zero or more parameters for the UDF:

> *@parameter_name*
>> Specifies the name of a parameter for the function. Specify a parameter using an ampersand (@) as the first character. DEFAULT parameters cannot be specified for CLR UDFs.

> [*type_schema_name.*] *scalar_parameter_data_type*
>> Specifies the parameter data type and optionally its schema. This can be any scalar data type supported by SQL Server except timestamp. The return value data type can also be a CLR UDT. char, varchar, and ntext data types cannot be specified for CLR scalar-valued UDFs—use nchar and nvarchar instead.

scalar_return_data_type
> Specifies the data type of the return value of a scalar-valued UDF. This can be any scalar data type supported by SQL Server except text, ntext, image, and timestamp. The return value data type can also be a CLR UDT. char and varchar data types cannot be specified for CLR scalar-valued UDFs—use nchar and nvarchar instead.

clr_table_type_definition
> Defines the CLR table returned from a table-valued UDF:

> *column_name*
>> Specifies the name of the column in the table.

> *data_type*
>> Specifies the data type of the column—timestamp and UDTs are not supported.

clr_function_option
> Specifies the OnNullCall attribute of a scalar-valued function:

> RETURNS NULL ON NULL INPUT
>> Specifies that SQL Server does not execute the function and returns NULL as the result of the function if any of the input arguments are NULL.

> CALLED ON NULL INPUT
>> Specifies that SQL Server executes the function even if one or more input arguments are NULL.

> If not specified, the default is CALLED ON NULL INPUT.

The CREATE FUNCTION value of the OnNullCall attribute takes precedence over the method's OnNullCall attribute if specified in the .NET code.

EXECUTE_AS_Clause
> Specifies the security execution context for the UDF.

method_specifier
> Specifies the method in the .NET Framework assembly that implements the UDF:

assembly_name
> Specifies the name of the registered assembly that contains the method implementing the CLR UDF.

class_name
> Specifies the name of the class in the assembly that implements the CLR UDF. The class name can be namespace-qualified, in which case it must be enclosed in brackets ([]).

method_name
> Specifies a public static method of the class that implements the CLR UDF functionality.

ALTER FUNCTION

The ALTER FUNCTION T-SQL statement has been enhanced in SQL Server 2005 to let you modify a CLR UDF previously created using the CREATE FUNCTION statement. The ALTER FUNCTION syntax for creating CLR UDFs follows:

```
ALTER FUNCTION [ schema_name. ] function_name
   ( { @parameter_name [AS] [ type_schema_name. ] scalar_parameter_data_type }
   [ ,...n ] )
RETURNS { scalar_return_data_type | TABLE <clr_table_type_definition> }
   [ WITH clr_function_option [ ,...n ] ]
   [ AS ] EXTERNAL NAME method_specifier

method_specifier ::=
   [ assembly_schema. ] assembly_name.class_name.method_name

clr_table_type_definition :: =
( { column_name data_type } [ ,...n ] )

clr_function_option ::=
[ RETURNS NULL ON NULL INPUT | CALLED ON NULL INPUT ]
| [ EXECUTE_AS_Clause ]
```

The arguments are the same as for the CREATE FUNCTION statement discussed in the preceding section.

DROP FUNCTION

The DROP FUNCTION T-SQL statement removes one or more UDFs previously created using the CREATE FUNCTION statement. The SQL Server 2005 DROP FUNCTION statement is the same as in SQL Server 2000. It now supports removing CLR UDFs.

The DROP FUNCTION syntax is:

```
DROP FUNCTION { [ schema_name. ] function_name } [ ,...n ]
```

DROP FUNCTION will fail if T-SQL functions or views in the database created with SCHEMABINDING or indexed computed columns reference this function.

Stored Procedures

A stored procedure is a saved collection of T-SQL statements or a reference to a CLR method that optionally takes and returns arguments and returns one or more result sets of data. SQL Server 2005 stored procedures can be created directly from T-SQL statements or from methods in registered .NET Framework assemblies.

Stored procedures are created, updated, and removed using the CREATE PROCEDURE, ALTER PROCEDURE, and DROP PROCEDURE T-SQL statements. These statements have been enhanced in SQL Server 2005 to support CLR stored procedure management. The following subsections describe these enhancements.

CREATE PROCEDURE

The CREATE PROCEDURE T-SQL statement has been enhanced in SQL Server 2005 to let you create a CLR stored procedure from a stored procedure implemented as a method in a .NET Framework assembly. You must first register the assembly using the CREATE ASSEMBLY statement as you did earlier in the "Hello World Example" section. The enhancements supporting CLR stored procedures are highlighted in the CREATE PROCEDURE syntax that follows:

```
CREATE PROC [ EDURE ] [schema_name.] procedure_name
  [ { @parameter [ type_schema_name. ] data_type }
  [ VARYING ] [ = default ] [ [ OUT [ PUT ] ] [ ,...n ]
  [ WITH <procedure_option> [ ,...n ]
  [ FOR REPLICATION ]
AS { sql_statement [ ...n ] | method_specifier }

procedure_option ::=
  [ ENCRYPTION ]
  [ RECOMPILE ]
  [ EXECUTE_AS_Clause ]

sql_statement ::=
  { [ BEGIN ] statements [ END ] }

method_specifier ::=
  EXTERNAL NAME assembly_name.class_name.method_name
```

where the new arguments are as follows:

method_specifier
> Specifies the method in the .NET Framework assembly that implements the stored procedure:
>
> *assembly_name*
>> Specifies the name of the registered assembly that contains the method implementing the stored procedure.
>
> *class_name*
>> Specifies the name of the class in the assembly that implements the stored procedure. The class name can be namespace-qualified, in which case it must be enclosed in brackets ([ ]).
>
> *method_name*
>> Specifies the name of the public static method implementing the CLR stored procedure.

ALTER PROCEDURE

The ALTER PROCEDURE T-SQL statement has been enhanced in SQL Server 2005 to let you modify a CLR stored procedure previously created using the CREATE PROCEDURE statement. The enhancements supporting CLR stored procedures are highlighted in the ALTER PROCEDURE syntax that follows:

```
ALTER PROC [ EDURE ] [schema_name.] procedure_name
    [ { @parameter [ type_schema_name. ] data_type }
    [ VARYING ] [ = default ] [ [ OUT [ PUT ] ] [ ,...n ]
    [ WITH procedure_option [ ,...n ] ]
    [ FOR REPLICATION ]
AS
    { sql_statement [ ...n ] | method_specifier }

procedure_option ::=
    [ ENCRYPTION ]
    [ RECOMPILE ]
    [ EXECUTE_AS_Clause ]

sql_statement ::=
    { [ BEGIN ] statements [ END ] }

method_specifier ::=
    EXTERNAL NAME [ assembly_schema. ] assembly_name.class_name.method_name
```

where the new arguments are as follows:

method_specifier
> Specifies the method in the .NET Framework assembly that implements the stored procedure:

assembly_schema

> Specifies the schema name for the assembly. If not specified, *assembly_name* must match an assembly in either the current user's schema or in the dbo schema.

assembly_name

> Specifies the name of the registered assembly that contains the method that implements the stored procedure.

class_name

> Specifies the name of the class in the assembly that implements the stored procedure. The class name can be namespace-qualified, in which case it must be enclosed in brackets ([ ]).

method_name

> Specifies the name of the public static method implementing the CLR stored procedure.

DROP PROCEDURE

The DROP PROCEDURE T-SQL statement removes one or more stored procedures previously created using the CREATE PROCEDURE statement. The SQL Server 2005 DROP PROCEDURE statement is the same as in SQL Server 2000. It now supports removing CLR stored procedures.

The DROP PROCEDURE syntax is:

```
DROP PROCEDURE { [ schema_name. ] procedure } [ ,...n ]
```

Metadata

The sys.procedures catalog view contains a row for each stored procedure in the current database. The view inherits columns from the sys.objects and sys.all_objects catalog views, so you can limit the rows returned to CLR stored procedures by filtering on the type column, as shown in the following statement:

```
SELECT * FROM sys.procedures
WHERE type='PC'
```

The WHERE clause specifying the type PC returns CLR stored procedures. Specifying type P returns SQL stored procedures.

User-Defined Aggregate Functions

User-defined aggregate (UDA functions compute a value over a group in a result set. SQL Server 2005 UDA functions can be created directly from T-SQL statements or from a class in a registered .NET Framework assembly.

UDA functions are created and removed in SQL Server using the CREATE AGGREGATE and DROP AGGREGATE T-SQL statements. These statements have been enhanced in SQL Server 2005 to support CLR UDA function management. The following subsections describe the enhancements.

CREATE AGGREGATE

The CREATE AGGREGATE T-SQL statement creates a UDA function from an implementation by a class in a registered assembly. The assembly must first be registered using the CREATE ASSEMBLY statement.

The CREATE AGGREGATE syntax is:

```
CREATE AGGREGATE [ schema_name. ] aggregate_name
..(@parameter input_sqltype )
RETURNS return_sqltype
EXTERNAL NAME assembly_name [ .class_name ]

input_sqltype ::=
..system_scalar_type | { [ udt_schema_name. ] udt_type_name }

return_sqltype ::=
..system_scalar_type | { [ udt_schema_name. ] udt_type_name }
```

where:

[schema_name.] aggregate_name
 Specifies the name of the CLR aggregate function to create.

@parameter input_sqltype
 Specifies the name of a parameter in the CLR aggregate function. The name must be prefixed with an ampersand (@). A parameter can specify a constant only, and not the names of database objects such as table names and columns names.

EXTERNAL NAME *assembly_name* [.*class_name*]
 Specifies the registered .NET Framework assembly and optionally the name of the class in the assembly that implements the CLR aggregate function. If *class_name* is not specified, it defaults to *aggregate_name*.

system_scalar_type
 Specifies a SQL Server scalar data type for the input or return value.

[udt_schema_name.] udt_type_name
 The name of a CLR UDT in SQL Server. If the schema name is not specified, it defaults to the schema of the current user.

DROP AGGREGATE

The DROP AGGREGATE T-SQL statement removes a UDA function previously created using the CREATE AGGREGATE statement.

The DROP AGGREGATE syntax follows:

```
DROP AGGREGATE [ schema_name. ] aggregate_name
```

where:

[*schema_name.*] *aggregate_name*
    Specifies the name of the UDA function to remove.

The DROP AGGREGATE statement does not execute if there are views, functions, or stored procedures created with schema binding that reference the UDA function.

User-Defined Types

SQL Server 2000 supports user-defined types (UDTs), also known as alias types. You create these by using the sp_addtypes system stored procedure. They are derived from SQL Server built-in data types and optionally have integrity constraints called rules.

SQL Server 2005 extends UDT functionality by letting you define CLR UDTs from a class in a registered .NET Framework assembly. A CLR UDT can store multiple items and expose methods, properties, and attributes. You can use a UDT as the data type for a column in a table, as a T-SQL variable, or as a parameter for stored procedures or functions.

UDTs are created and removed in SQL Server using the CREATE TYPE and DROP TYPE T-SQL statements. These statements have been enhanced in SQL Server 2005 to support CLR UDT management. The following subsections describe the enhancements.

CREATE TYPE

The CREATE TYPE statement has been enhanced in SQL Server 2005 to let you create a CLR UDT from a type implemented as a class or structure in a .NET Framework assembly. You must first register the assembly using the CREATE ASSEMBLY statement. The enhancements supporting CLR UDTs are highlighted in the CREATE TYPE syntax that follows:

```
CREATE TYPE [ schema_name. ] type_name
  { FROM base_type
  [ ( precision [ , scale ] ) ]
  [ NULL | NOT NULL ]
  | EXTERNAL NAME assembly_name [ .class_name ] }
```

where:

[*schema_name.*] *type_name*
    Specifies the name of the CLR UDT to create.

assembly_name
    Specifies the name of the registered assembly that implements the CLR UDT.

class_name
  Specifies the name of the class that implements the CLR UDT. The class name can be namespace-qualified, in which case it must be enclosed in brackets ([ ]).

DROP TYPE

The DROP TYPE T-SQL statement removes a UDT previously created using the CREATE TYPE statement. The SQL Server 2005 DROP TYPE statement is the same as in SQL Server 2000. It now supports removing CLR UDTs.

The DROP TYPE syntax is:

```
DROP TYPE [ schema_name. ] type_name
```

where:

[*schema_name.*] *type_name*
  Specifies the name of the UDT to remove

DROP TYPE will not execute if there are tables in the database with columns of the UDT, if there are columns of the sql_variant data type that contain the UDT, or if there are functions, stored procedures, or triggers in the database created with the WITH SCHEMABINDING clause that use variables or parameters of the UDT.

Metadata

The sys.assembly_types catalog view contains a row for all CLR UDTs in the current database. The view inherits all columns from the sys.types catalog view.

Triggers

A trigger is a type of stored procedure that executes in response to one or more specific database events. DML triggers execute when data is modified using T-SQL DML statements such as INSERT, UPDATE, or DELETE. DDL triggers execute when database objects are modified using T-SQL DDL statements such as CREATE, ALTER, and DROP. SQL Server 2005 DML and DDL triggers can be created directly from T-SQL statements or from methods in a registered .NET Framework assembly.

Triggers are created, changed, and removed using the CREATE TRIGGER, ALTER TRIGGER, and DROP TRIGGER T-SQL statements. These statements have been enhanced in SQL Server 2005 to support CLR trigger management. The following subsections describe the enhancements.

CREATE TRIGGER

The CREATE TRIGGER T-SQL statement has been enhanced in SQL Server 2005 to let you create a CLR DML or DDL trigger from a trigger implemented as a method in a .NET

Framework assembly. You must first register the assembly using the `CREATE ASSEMBLY` statement. The enhancements supporting CLR triggers are highlighted in this section.

The `CREATE TRIGGER` syntax for DML triggers is:

```
CREATE TRIGGER [ schema_name. ]trigger_name
  ON { TABLE | VIEW }
  [ WITH dml_trigger_option [ ,...n ] ]
  { FOR | AFTER | INSTEAD OF }
  { [ INSERT ] [ , ] [ UPDATE ] [ , ] [ DELETE ] }
  [ WITH APPEND ]
  [ NOT FOR REPLICATION ]
AS { sql_statement [ ...n ] | EXTERNAL NAME method specifier }

dml_trigger_option ::=
    [ ENCRYPTION ]
    [ EXECUTE AS Clause ]

method_specifier ::=
    assembly_name.class_name.method_name
```

The `CREATE TRIGGER` syntax for DDL triggers is:

```
CREATE TRIGGER trigger_name
  ON { ALL SERVER | DATABASE }
  [ WITH <ddl_trigger_option> [,...n ] ]
  { FOR | AFTER } { event_type | event_group } [ ,...n ]
AS { sql_statement [ ...n ] | EXTERNAL NAME <method specifier> }

ddl_trigger_option ::=
    [ ENCRYPTION ]
    [ EXECUTE AS Clause ]

method_specifier ::=
    assembly_name.class_name.method_name
```

where the new arguments for both DML and DDL triggers are:

method_specifier

Specifies the method in the .NET Framework assembly that implements the trigger:

assembly_name

Specifies the name of the registered assembly that contains the method that implements the trigger.

class_name

Specifies the name of the class in the assembly that implements the CLR trigger. The class name can be namespace-qualified, in which case it must be enclosed in brackets ([]).

method_name

Specifies the public static method of the class that implements the CLR trigger functionality.

ALTER TRIGGER

The ALTER TRIGGER T-SQL statement has been enhanced in SQL Server 2005 to let you modify a CLR DML or DDL trigger previously created using the CREATE TRIGGER statement. The enhancements supporting CLR triggers are highlighted in this section.

The ALTER TRIGGER syntax for DML triggers follows:

```
ALTER TRIGGER schema_name.trigger_name
  ON ( TABLE | VIEW )
  [ WITH dml_trigger_option [ ...,n ] ]
  ( FOR | AFTER | INSTEAD OF )
  { [ DELETE ] [ , ] [ INSERT ] [ , ] [ UPDATE ] }
  [ NOT FOR REPLICATION ]
AS { sql_statement [ ...n ] | EXTERNAL NAME method specifier }

dml_trigger_option ::=
  [ ENCRYPTION ]
  [ EXECUTE AS Clause ]

method_specifier ::=
   [ assembly_schema. ] assembly_name.class_name.method_name
```

The ALTER TRIGGER syntax for DDL triggers follows:

```
ALTER TRIGGER trigger_name
  ON { DATABASE | ALL SERVER }
  [ WITH ddl_trigger_option [ ...,n ] ]
  { FOR | AFTER } { event_type [ ,...n ] | event_group }
AS { sql_statement | EXTERNAL NAME method specifier }

ddl_trigger_option ::=
  [ ENCRYPTION ]
  [ EXECUTE AS Clause ]

method_specifier ::=
  [ assembly_schema. ] assembly_name.class_name.method_name
```

The new arguments for both DML and DDL triggers are the same as for the CREATE TRIGGER statement discussed in the preceding section.

DROP TRIGGER

The DROP TRIGGER T-SQL statement removes one or more DML or DDL triggers previously created using the CREATE TRIGGER statement. The SQL Server 2005 DROP TRIGGER statement is the same as in SQL Server 2000. It now supports removing CLR triggers.

The DROP TRIGGER syntax for DML triggers is:

```
DROP TRIGGER schema_name.trigger_name [ ,...n ]
```

The DROP TRIGGER syntax for DDL triggers is:

```
DROP TRIGGER trigger_name [ ,...n ]
ON { DATABASE | ALL SERVER }
```

Metadata

The sys.triggers catalog view contains a row for each trigger in the current database. You can limit the rows returned to CLR triggers by filtering on the type column, as shown in the following statement:

```
SELECT * FROM sys.triggers
WHERE type='TA'
```

ADO.NET In-Process Extensions Supporting CLR Programming

ADO.NET has four main in-process functional extensions that are used when programming .NET Framework routines. The SqlContext object provides access to context information, to a SqlPipe object for sending results to the client, and to a SqlTriggerContext object that provides information about the operation that caused a trigger to fire. The fourth—the SqlDataRecord object—returns to the caller a custom result set from a stored procedure. These four extensions are discussed in the following subsections.

SqlContext Object

Managed code is invoked in the server whenever a CLR routine is executed. Code running on the server executes in the context of the caller connection, so the CLR code needs access to the caller context. The SqlContext class in the Microsoft. SqlServer.Server namespace abstracts the context of the caller and provides access to the context components through its public static properties, described in Table 4-12.

Table 4-12. SqlContext public properties

Property	Return type	Description
IsAvailable	bool	Indicates whether the code that is executing is running inside SQL Server. If true, other members of SqlContext can be accessed. If false, all other properties will throw InvalidOperationException when accessed, and any attempts to open a connection using the context connection = true attribute in the connection string will fail.
Pipe	SqlPipe	A path for messages and result sets to flow to the client.
TriggerContext	SqlTriggerContext	Provides access to information about the operation that caused a DML or DDL trigger to fire. Also provides a map of the updated columns.
		You can retrieve TriggerContext only within a CLR trigger.

Table 4-12. SqlContext public properties (continued)

Property	Return type	Description
WindowsIdentity	System.Security. Principal. WindowsIdentity	Provides access to an impersonation token representing the Windows identity of the caller if the client that initiated execution of the stored procedure or function connected to SQL Server using integrated authentication. null is returned if the caller was authenticated using SQL Server authentication and the code cannot impersonate the caller.
		The SQL Server process account is the context for all CLR code invoked inside of SQL Server. The impersonation token is used to let the code perform actions using the identity of the caller instead of the identity of the process account.
		Only assemblies marked with EXTERNAL_ACCESS or UNSAFE permission can access the WindowsIdentity property.

You obtain an in-process connection using the new connection context connection string keyword. For example:

```
SqlConnection conn = new SqlConnection("context connection=true")
```

SqlPipe Object

Use the SqlPipe object to send messages and result sets from a CLR stored procedure to the calling client. The SqlPipe object cannot be directly instantiated. You obtain the SqlPipe object using the Pipe property of the SqlContext object within the body of a CLR routine, as shown in the "Hello World Example" section earlier in this chapter. The SqlPipe class has the public properties and methods described in Table 4-13.

Table 4-13. SqlPipe public properties and methods

Property	Description
IsSendingResults	Indicates whether the pipe is in the process of sending a result set, blocking it from use.
Method	
ExecuteAndSend( )	Executes a command specified as a SqlCommand object argument. The results are sent directly back to the client.
Send( )	Three overloads send one of the following to the client:
	• string (informational message—equivalent to T-SQL PRINT statement)
	• SqlDataRecord object (single-row result set)
	• SqlDataReader object (multiple-row result set)
SendResultsEnd( )	Marks the end of a custom result set from a stored procedure initiated by the SendResultsStart( ) method. Sets the SqlPipe object back to a state where other methods can be called on it. This method can be called only after SendResultsStart( ) is called.

Table 4-13. SqlPipe public properties and methods (continued)

Property	Description
SendResultsRow( )	Sends a row of data contained in a SqlDataRecord object to the client. This method can be called only after SendResultsStart( ) is called. Each row must conform to the SqlDataRecord argument describing the row that is supplied to the SendResultsStart( ) method.
SendResultsStart( )	Marks the start of a custom result set from a stored procedure. This method takes a SqlDataRecord argument to construct the metadata that describes the result set. All rows in the result set subsequently sent to the client using the SendResultsRow( ) method must conform to this metadata.

SqlTriggerContext Object

The SqlTriggerContext class provides context information about the CLR DML or DDL trigger. The SqlTriggerContext object cannot be directly instantiated. You obtain the SqlTrigger object using the TriggerContext property of the SqlContext object within the body of a CLR trigger. The SqlTriggerContext class has the public properties and methods described in Table 4-14.

Table 4-14. SqlTriggerContext public properties and methods

Property	Description
ColumnCount	The number of columns potentially affected by the UPDATE operation that caused the DML trigger to fire.
EventData	A SqlXml object containing XML describing the triggering operation for a DDL trigger.
TriggerAction	The type of action that caused the trigger to fire. This is one of the TriggerAction enumeration values.
IsUpdatedColumn( )	Indicates whether a column specified by its ordinal was modified by the UPDATE operation that caused the DML trigger to fire.

SqlDataRecord Object

The SqlDataRecord class represents a single row of data together with its metadata. The class allows stored procedures to return custom result sets to the client using the Send( ) or SendResultsRow( ) methods of the SqlPipe object.

You instantiate a SqlDataRecord object by passing to the constructor a SqlMetaData object array that contains an element of metadata for each column in the row. Each SqlMetaData object defines a column name, column type, and possibly other column attributes. For example, the following code defines a SqlDataRecord containing two columns:

```
SqlMetaData[] md = new SqlMetaData[2];
md[0] = new SqlMetaData("intCol", SqlDbType.Int);
md[1] = new SqlMetaData("stringCol", SqlDbType.NVarChar, 50);
SqlDataRecord row = new SqlDataRecord(md);
```

The `SqlDataRecord` class has accessor methods that let you get and set column values. This is similar to a `DataReader` except that you can write column values in addition to reading them. For example, the following code fills the two columns in the `SqlDataRecord` object defined in the preceding example:

```
row.SetSqlInt32(0, 1);
row.SetSqlString(1, "Record 1");
```

Custom Attributes for CLR Routines

The .NET CLR is extended using *attributes*—descriptive keywords saved in the assembly metadata that provide additional information for programming constructs. The custom attributes used with SQL Server 2005 CLR routines are defined in the `Microsoft.SqlServer.Server` namespace. Table 4-15 describes custom attributes used with SQL Server CLR routines.

Table 4-15. Custom attributes for CLR routines

Attribute	CLR routine	Description
SqlFacet	UDT	Specifies details about the return type of a UDT.
SqlFunction	UDF	Indicates that the method should be registered as a UDF.
SqlMethod	UDT	Specifies the determinism and data access properties of methods in a UDT.
SqlProcedure	Stored procedure	Indicates that the method should be registered as a stored procedure.
SqlTrigger	Trigger	Indicates that the method should be registered as a trigger.
SqlUserDefinedAggregate	UDA	Indicates that the method should be registered as a UDA.
SqlUserDefinedType	UDT	Indicates that the class or structure should be registered as a UDT.

These attributes are discussed in detail in Chapter 5 in the specific sections about the .NET Framework routines that use them.

SQL Server Data Types in the .NET Framework

The `System.Data.SqlTypes` namespace is part of the base class library of the .NET Framework. The namespace provides data types that map closely to native SQL Server data types. There are differences between `SqlTypes` data types and .NET Framework data types:

- `SqlTypes` data types support `NULL` values while .NET Framework data types do not. All arithmetic and bitwise operators and most functions return `NULL` if any `SqlTypes` operands or arguments are `NULL`.

- `SqlTypes` provides a `SqlBoolean` data type that represents a tristate logical value—`true`, `false`, and `null` (unknown value).

- The .NET Framework Decimal data type and the corresponding SQL Server Decimal data type have different maximum values. The Decimal data type assumes maximum precision, whereas the SqlDecimal data type and the SQL Server Decimal data type have the same maximum precision, scale, and semantics.

- Exceptions are thrown for all overflow and underflow errors and divide-by-zero errors when using SqlTypes data types. This behavior is not guaranteed with .NET Framework data types.

Table 4-16 lists SQL Server data types and their equivalents in the System.Data.SqlTypes namespace and in the .NET Framework.

Table 4-16. SQL Server, System.Data.SqlTypes, and .NET Framework data type equivalents

SQL Server data type	System.Data.SqlTypes data type	.NET Framework data type
varbinary	SqlBytes, SqlBinary	Byte[]
binary	SqlBytes, SqlBinary	Byte[]
image	None	None
varchar	None	None
char	None	None
nvarchar	SqlChars, SqlString	String, Char[]
nchar	SqlChars, SqlString	String, Char[]
text	None	None
ntext	None	None
uniqueidentifier	SqlGuid	Guid
rowversion	None	Byte[]
bit	SqlBoolean	Boolean
tinyint	SqlByte	Byte
smallint	SqlInt16	Int16
int	SqlInt32	Int32
bigint	SqlInt64	Int64
smallmoney	SqlMoney	Decimal
money	SqlMoney	Decimal
numeric	SqlDecimal	Decimal
decimal	SqlDecimal	Decimal
real	SqlSingle	Single
float	SqlDouble	Double
smalldatetime	SqlDateTime	DateTime
datetime	SqlDateTime	DateTime
sql_variant	None	Object
User-defined type (UDT)	None	Same class bound to the type in the registered assembly or dependent assembly

Table 4-16. SQL Server, System.Data.SqlTypes, and .NET Framework data type equivalents (continued)

SQL Server data type	System.Data.SqlTypes data type	.NET Framework data type
table	None	None
cursor	None	None
timestamp	None	None
xml	SqlXml	None

Testing and Debugging CLR Routines

SQL Server 2005 lets you debug both T-SQL database objects and CLR routines. SQL Server 2005 does not ship with a debugger, so you must use Visual Studio 2005.

Follow these steps to use the Visual Studio 2005 debugger to step through source code for registered CLR assemblies when executing T-SQL statements using .NET Framework routines:

1. Add the PDB file—a file containing debugging and project state information—to the registered assembly. For example, to add the PDB file to the HelloWorld stored procedure project in the "Hello World Example" section earlier in this chapter, execute the following T-SQL statement:

   ```
   ALTER ASSEMBLY HelloWorld
   ADD FILE FROM 'C:\PSS2005\HelloWorld\HelloWorld\bin\Debug\HelloWorld.pdb'
   ```

2. In the Visual Studio 2005 IDE, select Debug → Attach to Process.

3. Check the "Show processes from all users" checkbox in the Attach to Process dialog box.

4. Select *sqlservr.exe* from the Available Processes list box. Click the Attach button and close the dialog box.

5. Set a breakpoint in the source code at the following line:

   ```
   SqlContext.Pipe.Send("Hello world.\n");
   ```

6. Execute the stored procedure from SQL Server Management Studio:

   ```
   exec HelloWorldSP
   ```

   Execution will stop at the breakpoint you set in the Visual Studio IDE.

CHAPTER 5

Programming SQL Server CLR Routines

This chapter demonstrates how to create each type of SQL Server 2005 CLR routine: user-defined functions (scalar-valued functions and table-valued functions), stored procedures, user-defined aggregate (UDA) functions, user-defined types (UDTs), and both DML and DDL triggers. All examples in this section use Visual Studio 2005 to create and compile the CLR routines. If you don't have Visual Studio 2005, you can use the C# command-line compiler (*csc.exe*) discussed in Chapter 4.

Scalar-Valued Functions

A scalar-valued function (SVF) is a user-defined function (UDF) that returns a single value. Scalar-valued functions can take arguments and return values of any scalar data type supported by SQL Server except rowversion, text, ntext, image, timestamp, table, or cursor.

An SVF is implemented as a method of a class in a .NET Framework assembly. The return value of the method must be compatible with the SQL Server data type that the method returns. Table 4-16 lists SQL Server data types and their equivalent CLR data types.

You identify a .NET SVF or TVF by annotating the method where you implement the function with the SqlFunction attribute. In addition to indicating that the method should be registered as a function, the SqlFunction attribute can be used to define characteristics of the function. The SqlFunction attribute has the following syntax:

```
SqlFunction [ ( function-attribute [,...] ) ]

function-attribute::=
    IsDeterministic = {true | false}
  | DataAccess = { DataAccessKind.None | DataAccessKind.Read }
  | SystemDataAccess = { SystemDataAccessKind.None | SystemDataAccessKind.Read }
  | IsPrecise = { true | false }
  | FillRowMethodName = string
  | Name = string
  | TableDefinition = string
```

where:

IsDeterministic

Specifies whether the function always returns the same output values for the same set of input values and the same database state. This allows the server to do performance optimizations. The default value is false.

DataAccess = { DataAccessKind.None | DataAccessKind.Read }

Specifies the type of data access the function requires if it accesses data on the local SQL Server or on a remote server if transaction integration is required. The DataAccess argument takes one of two values of the DataAccessKind enumeration:

DataAccessKind.None

The function does not access data

DataAccessKind.Read

The function only reads data

The DataAccess property should be set to DataAccessKind.Read if a T-SQL statement is executed inside a CLR SVF or TVF routine.

User-defined functions cannot insert, update, or delete data.

SystemDataAccess = { SystemDataAccessKind.None | SystemDataAccessKind.Read }

Specifies the type of data access the function requires if it accesses data stored in the system catalogs or virtual system tables. The SystemDataAccess argument takes one of the two values of the SystemDataAccessKind enumeration:

SystemDataAccessKind.None

The function does not access data. This is the default value.

SystemDataAccessKind.Read

The function only reads data.

IsPrecise

Specifies whether the return value of the function depends on imprecise calculations involving single or double data types (float or real in SQL Server). This property is used to determine whether the computed columns using the function can be indexed. The default value is false.

FillRowMethodName

Specifies the name of the method used by a table-valued function to fill a row of data in the table returned by the function. Fill row methods are discussed in the next section, "Table-Valued Functions."

Name

Specifies the name with which the function should be registered in SQL Server.

TableDefinition

Specifies the layout of the table returned by a table-valued function.

The following example creates, registers, and executes a scalar-valued function. This function returns the total for a specific sales order by summing the LineTotal values in the Sales.SalesOrderDetail table in AdventureWorks for a specified sales order ID. Follow these steps:

1. Using the Visual Studio 2005 IDE, create a new SQL Server project named ScalarUdf.

2. Create a user-defined function item in the project by right-clicking on the project in Solution Explorer and selecting Add → User-Defined function from the context menu. Name the function SumLineTotal and click the Add button.

3. Add the following using directive to access the ADO.NET namespace:

   ```
   using System.Data.SqlClient;
   ```

4. Modify the SqlFunction attribute to indicate that the function will be reading data:

   ```
   [SqlFunction(DataAccess = DataAccessKind.Read)]
   ```

5. Change the return type of the SumLineTotal( ) method from SqlString to SqlMoney to match the data type of the LineTotal column being summed. Add an int argument named salesOrderID to the SumLineTotal( ) method.

6. Add code to the SumLineTotal( ) method to perform the calculation. The complete code follows:

   ```
   using System;
   using System.Data;
   using System.Data.Sql;
   using System.Data.SqlTypes;
   using Microsoft.SqlServer.Server;
   using System.Data.SqlClient;

   public partial class UserDefinedFunctions
   {
       [SqlFunction(DataAccess = DataAccessKind.Read)]
       public static SqlMoney SumLineTotal(int salesOrderID)
       {
           using (SqlConnection conn =
               new SqlConnection("context connection=true"))
           {
               conn.Open( );
               SqlCommand cmd = new SqlCommand(
                   "SELECT SUM(LineTotal) " +
                   "FROM Sales.SalesOrderDetail " +
                   "WHERE SalesOrderID=" + salesOrderID, conn);

               return (decimal)cmd.ExecuteScalar( );
           }
       }
   }
   ```

The function reads data from SQL Server, so the DataAccess property of the SqlFunction attribute is set to DataAccessKind.Read.

Notice that the return value is decimal, which is compatible with the SQL Server Money type. Table 4-16 lists SQL Server data types and their equivalent CLR data types.

7. Build the solution.

8. In SQL Server Management Studio, register the assembly and create the scalar-valued function by executing this query:

```
USE AdventureWorks
GO

CREATE ASSEMBLY ScalarUdf
FROM 'C:\PSS2005\ScalarUdf\ScalarUdf\bin\Debug\ScalarUdf.dll'
GO

CREATE FUNCTION SumLineTotal(@salesOrderID int)
RETURNS MONEY
AS EXTERNAL NAME ScalarUdf.UserDefinedFunctions.SumLineTotal
```

9. Execute the scalar-valued function with the following T-SQL statement:

```
SELECT dbo.SumLineTotal(43660)
```

The results are shown in Figure 5-1.

Figure 5-1. Results for scalar-valued function example

Table-Valued Functions

A table-valued function (TVF) is a UDF that returns a table. A TVF is implemented as a method of a class in a .NET Framework assembly that returns data as an IEnumerable or IEnumerator object. The columns of the return table cannot include timestamp columns or non-Unicode string data columns such as char, varchar, and text.

CLR TVFs are similar to their T-SQL counterparts—the main difference is that a T-SQL TVF temporarily stores results in an intermediate table, whereas a CLR TVF streams results back to the consumer. As a result, a T-SQL TVF supports constraints and unique indexes on the result set, whereas a CLR TVF can be consumed incrementally once the first row is available—the result set does not have to be fully materialized before returning values.

The following example creates, registers, and executes a table-valued function that returns a table containing the Name, Length, and ModifiedDate for each file in a specified directory. Follow these steps:

Enumerators

The IEnumerator interface supports simple iteration over a nongeneric collection. It is the base interface for all nongeneric enumerators. An enumerator can read the data in the underlying collection but cannot be used to modify the data. IEnumerator has one public property, Current, and two public methods, MoveNext( ) and Reset( ). Initially the enumerator is positioned before the first element in the collection.

- The Current property returns an object containing the current element in the collection. You must advance the enumerator from its initial position to the first element in the collection by calling MoveNext( ) before reading the value of the Current property. Reading the Current property when the enumerator is not positioned on an element in the collection (before the first element or after the last element) returns an InvalidOperationException.

- The MoveNext( ) method advances the enumerator to the next element in the collection. MoveNext( ) returns true if the enumerator was successfully advanced and false if the enumerator has passed the end of the collection.

- The Reset( ) method sets the enumerator to the initial position before the first element in the collection.

The IEnumerable interface has a single method, GetEnumerator( ), which returns an IEnumerator object.

1. Using the Visual Studio 2005 IDE, create a new SQL Server project named TableUdf.

2. Create a user-defined function item in the project. Name the function ReadDirectoryFileInfo.

3. Replace the code in the class with the following code:

```
using System;
using System.Collections;
using System.Data;
using System.Data.Sql;
using System.Data.SqlTypes;
using Microsoft.SqlServer.Server;
using System.IO;

public partial class UserDefinedFunctions
{
    [SqlFunction(FillRowMethodName = "FillRow", TableDefinition =
        "FileName nvarchar(256), Size int, DateModified datetime")]
    public static IEnumerator ReadDirectoryEntries(string path)
    {
        return new DirectoryLoader(path);
    }

    private static void FillRow(object obj, out SqlString fileName,
        out SqlInt64 fileLength, out SqlDateTime dateModified)
```

```
        {
            if (obj != null)
            {
                DirectoryEntry de = (DirectoryEntry)obj;
                fileName = de._fileName;
                fileLength = de._fileLength;
                dateModified = de._fileDateModified;
            }
            else
            {
                fileName = SqlString.Null;
                fileLength = SqlInt64.Null;
                dateModified = SqlDateTime.Null;
            }
        }
    }
}

public partial class DirectoryLoader : IEnumerator
{
    // array that stores the directory entries
    private FileInfo[] fia;
    private int index = -1;

    public DirectoryLoader(string path)
    {
        string[] files = Directory.GetFiles(path);
        fia = new FileInfo[files.Length];
        for (int i = 0; i < files.Length; i++)
            fia[i] = new FileInfo(files[i]);
    }

    public object Current
    {
        get
        {
            if (index != -1)
                return new DirectoryEntry(fia[index].Name,
                    fia[index].Length, fia[index].LastWriteTime);
            else
                return null;
        }
    }

    public bool MoveNext()
    {
        if (index == fia.Length - 1)
            return false;

        index++;
        return true;
    }

    public void Reset()
    {
```

```
        index = -1;
    }
}
public partial class DirectoryEntry
{
    internal string _fileName;
    internal long _fileLength;
    internal DateTime _fileDateModified;

    public DirectoryEntry(string fileName, long fileLength,
        DateTime fileDateModified)
    {
        _fileName = fileName;
        _fileLength = fileLength;
        _fileDateModified = fileDateModified;
    }
}
```

The code contains three classes—UserDefinedFunctions, which implements the TVF, and two helper classes:

UserDefinedFunctions

> The method ReadDirectoryEntries( ) implements the TVF. It is annotated with the SqlFunction attribute described in the preceding section, "Scalar-Valued Functions." The SqlFunction attribute identifies the public method FillRow( ) as the method that SQL Server uses to map the current enumerator element to a row in the table that is returned from the TVF. The SqlFunction attribute also specifies the TableDefinition property, which defines the record in the table returned from the TVF.

DirectoryLoader

> The enumerator that creates a collection of directory entries for a path specified as an argument to its constructor. The contents of the directory are stored in a FileInfo array named fia. The Current property of the enumerator returns a DirectoryEntry instance containing the filename, file length, and date modified.

DirectoryEntry

> Defines a class used to store the current element in the directory enumerator.

4. Build the solution.

5. In SQL Server Management Studio, register the assembly and create the table-valued function by executing this query:

```
USE ProgrammingSqlServer2005
GO

ALTER DATABASE ProgrammingSqlServer2005
SET TRUSTWORTHY ON
GO

CREATE ASSEMBLY TableUdf
FROM 'C:\PSS2005\TableUdf\TableUdf\bin\Debug\TableUdf.dll'
WITH PERMISSION_SET = EXTERNAL_ACCESS
```

```
GO

CREATE FUNCTION ReadDirectoryEntries(@path nvarchar(256))
RETURNS TABLE
  (FileName nvarchar(256), Length bigint, DateModified datetime)
AS
EXTERNAL NAME TableUdf.UserDefinedFunctions.ReadDirectoryEntries
```

Notice that the assembly is registered with EXTERNAL_ACCESS permission set to allow it to access the file system.

6. Execute the table-valued function with the following T-SQL statement:

```
SELECT * FROM ReadDirectoryEntries('c:\')
```

The results are shown in Figure 5-2.

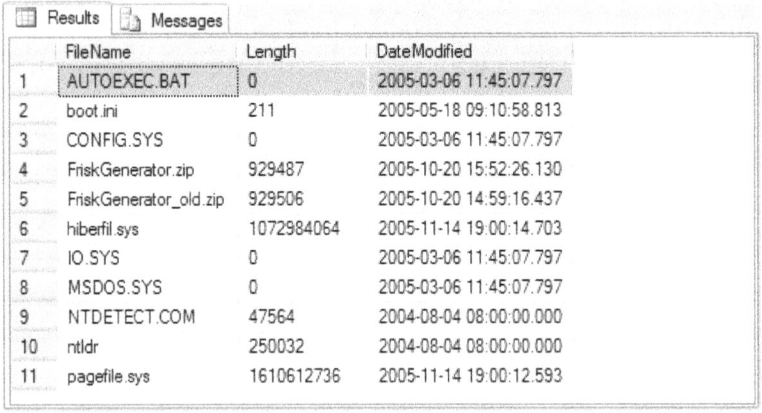

	FileName	Length	DateModified
1	AUTOEXEC.BAT	0	2005-03-06 11:45:07.797
2	boot.ini	211	2005-05-18 09:10:58.813
3	CONFIG.SYS	0	2005-03-06 11:45:07.797
4	FriskGenerator.zip	929487	2005-10-20 15:52:26.130
5	FriskGenerator_old.zip	929506	2005-10-20 14:59:16.437
6	hiberfil.sys	1072984064	2005-11-14 19:00:14.703
7	IO.SYS	0	2005-03-06 11:45:07.797
8	MSDOS.SYS	0	2005-03-06 11:45:07.797
9	NTDETECT.COM	47564	2004-08-04 08:00:00.000
10	ntldr	250032	2004-08-04 08:00:00.000
11	pagefile.sys	1610612736	2005-11-14 19:00:12.593

Figure 5-2. Results for TVF example

Stored Procedures

Stored procedures are routines that return tabular result sets, messages, and output parameters to the client and invoke DML and DDL statements. A CLR stored procedure is implemented as a public static method of a class in a .NET Framework assembly. The method is either void or returns an integer that is the return code from the stored procedure. A method declared void implicitly returns a stored procedure return code of 0.

You identify a stored procedure by annotating the method that implements the stored procedure with the SqlProcedure attribute. The SqlProcedure attribute indicates that the method should be registered as a stored procedure. The SqlProcedure attribute has the following syntax:

```
SqlProcedure [ ( procedure-attribute [ ,... ] ) ]

procedure-attribute::=
  Name = "procedure name"
```

where:

Name

 Specifies the name of the stored procedure.

Arguments to the stored procedure method can be any native SQL Server data type that has an equivalent in managed code.

CLR stored procedures can return information to the client as messages, tabular result sets, and output parameters. Send messages and tabular result sets using one of the Send( ) methods of the SqlPipe object or using the ExecuteAndSend( ) method of the SqlPipe object. The SqlPipe object is described in Chapter 4. Output parameters are arguments that are passed in the same way as other output arguments (i.e., using the out keyword in C#).

The following example creates, registers, and executes a stored procedure that returns a tabular result set of all employees that work a specified shift from the HumanResources.Shift table in AdventureWorks. The stored procedure takes the shift ID as its only argument. Follow these steps:

1. Using the Visual Studio 2005 IDE, create a new SQL Server project named StoredProcedure.

2. Create a stored procedure item in the project. Name the item EmployeesInShift.cs.

3. Replace the EmployeesInShiftCode.cs code with the following:

```
using System;
using System.Data;
using System.Data.Sql;
using Microsoft.SqlServer.Server;
using System.Data.SqlTypes;
using System.Data.SqlClient;

public partial class StoredProcedures
{
    [SqlProcedure]
    public static void EmployeesInShift(int shiftID)
    {
        using (SqlConnection conn = new SqlConnection("context connection=true"))
        {
            conn.Open( );
            SqlCommand cmd = new SqlCommand(
                "SELECT e.* FROM HumanResources.Employee e " +
                "JOIN HumanResources.EmployeeDepartmentHistory h " +
                "ON e.EmployeeID = h.EmployeeID " +
                "WHERE h.ShiftID = " + shiftID, conn);
            SqlContext.Pipe.ExecuteAndSend(cmd);
        }
    }
};
```

The `EmployeesInShift()` method implements the stored procedure and is annotated with the `StoredProcedure` attribute.

The tabular result set is returned to the client using the `ExecuteAndSend()` method of the `SqlPipe` object that executes a command and sends the tabular result set directly to the client. The method takes a single parameter that is a `SqlCommand` object associated with the context connection. Alternatively, you can send a tabular result set to the client using either the `Send(SqlDataReader)` or `Send(SqlDataRecord)` method of the `SqlPipe` object. The following line of code replaces the `ExecuteAndSend()` method used in this example with the `Send(SqlDataReader)` method:

```
SqlContext.Pipe.Send(cmd.ExecuteReader());
```

The `Send()` methods lets you manipulate the data before you send it to the client but is slightly slower because of additional overhead.

4. Build the solution.

5. Register the assembly and create the stored procedure by executing the following T-SQL statement in SQL Server Management Studio:

```
USE AdventureWorks
GO

CREATE ASSEMBLY EmployeeInShift
FROM 'C:\PSS2005\StoredProcedure\StoredProcedure\bin\Debug\StoredProcedure.dll'
GO

CREATE PROCEDURE EmployeeByShiftSP
  @shiftID int
AS EXTERNAL NAME EmployeeInShift.StoredProcedures.EmployeesInShift
```

6. Execute the stored procedure:

```
EXEC EmployeeByShiftSP @shiftID=1
```

The resulting set is all of the employees for the specified shift ID. Partial results are shown in Figure 5-3.

	EmployeeID	NationalIDNumber	ContactID	LoginID	ManagerID	Title	BirthDate	Ma
1	1	14417807	1209	adventure-works\guy1	16	Production Technician - WC60	1972-05-15 00:00:00.000	M
2	2	253022876	1030	adventure-works\kevin0	6	Marketing Assistant	1977-06-03 00:00:00.000	S
3	3	509647174	1002	adventure-works\roberto0	12	Engineering Manager	1964-12-13 00:00:00.000	M
4	4	112457891	1290	adventure-works\rob0	3	Senior Tool Designer	1965-01-23 00:00:00.000	S
5	4	112457891	1290	adventure-works\rob0	3	Senior Tool Designer	1965-01-23 00:00:00.000	S
6	5	480168528	1009	adventure-works\thierry0	263	Tool Designer	1949-08-29 00:00:00.000	M
7	6	24756624	1028	adventure-works\david0	109	Marketing Manager	1965-04-19 00:00:00.000	S
8	6	24756624	1028	adventure-works\david0	109	Marketing Manager	1965-04-19 00:00:00.000	S
9	8	690627818	1071	adventure-works\ruth0	185	Production Technician - WC10	1946-07-06 00:00:00.000	M
10	9	695256808	1005	adventure-works\gail0	2	Design Engineer	1942-10-29 00:00:00.000	M

Figure 5-3. Results for stored procedure example that returns a tabular result set

The following CLR stored procedure example returns an output parameter, a message, and a return code:

1. Add the following method to the StoredProcedure class created in the preceding example:

```
[SqlProcedure]
public static int EmployeeByShift2SP(out int outputVal)
{
    outputVal = 10;
    SqlContext.Pipe.Send("Test message.");
    return 5;
}
```

The limit for the return string is 8000 characters. Extra characters are truncated.

2. Build the solution.

3. Update the assembly registration in SQL Server and create the new stored procedure by executing this T-SQL statement:

```
ALTER ASSEMBLY EmployeeInShift
FROM 'C:\PSS2005\StoredProcedure\StoredProcedure\bin\Debug\StoredProcedure.dll'
GO

CREATE PROCEDURE EmployeeByShift2SP
    @outputVal int OUT
AS EXTERNAL NAME EmployeeInShift.StoredProcedures.EmployeeByShift2SP
```

4. Execute the stored procedure:

```
DECLARE @returnCode int
DECLARE @outputVal int

EXEC @returnCode = EmployeeByShift2SP @outputVal OUTPUT

PRINT 'Return code = ' + CAST(@returnCode AS CHAR(5))
PRINT 'Output value @outputVal = ' + CAST(@outputVal AS CHAR(5))
```

Results are shown in Figure 5-4.

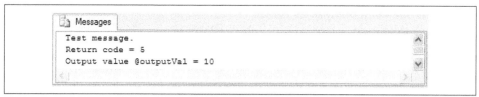

Figure 5-4. Results for stored procedure example that returns an output parameter, a message, and a return code

The following CLR stored procedure example returns a result set containing a single row of data created dynamically by the stored procedure, as shown next.

1. Add the following method to the `StoredProcedure` class created in the preceding example:

```
[SqlProcedure]
public static void DynamicSingleRow()
{
    SqlMetaData[] md = new SqlMetaData[2];
    md[0] = new SqlMetaData("intCol", SqlDbType.Int);
    md[1] = new SqlMetaData("stringCol", SqlDbType.NVarChar, 50);

    SqlDataRecord row = new SqlDataRecord(md);
    row.SetSqlInt32(0, 1);
    row.SetSqlString(1, "Record 1");

    SqlContext.Pipe.Send(row);
}
```

The method uses the `SqlMetaData` class to define the schema of the result set row. The row is created as an instance of the `SqlDataRecord` class. The row values are filled using the `Set()` methods of `SqlDataRecord`. The `Set()` methods take two arguments—an ordinal specifying the column number and the value. Finally, an overload of the `SqlPipe.Send()` method is used to return the instance of the `SqlDataRecord` class as the result set row.

You cannot extend this example to return a result set containing multiple rows since a new result set is returned each time the `Send()` method is called. The next example shows how to return a dynamically created result set containing multiple rows.

2. Build the solution.

3. Update the assembly registration in SQL Server and create the new stored procedure by executing this T-SQL statement:

```
ALTER ASSEMBLY EmployeeInShift
FROM 'C:\PSS2005\StoredProcedure\StoredProcedure\bin\Debug\StoredProcedure.dll'
GO

CREATE PROCEDURE DynamicSingleRow
AS EXTERNAL NAME EmployeeInShift.StoredProcedures.DynamicSingleRow
```

4. Execute the stored procedure:

```
EXEC DynamicSingleRow
```

Results are shown in Figure 5-5.

The following CLR stored procedure example returns a result set containing two rows of data created dynamically by the stored procedure:

1. Add the following method to the `StoredProcedure` class created in the preceding example:

```
[SqlProcedure]
public static void DynamicMultiRow()
{
```

Figure 5-5. Results for stored procedure example that returns a dynamically created single-row result set

```
SqlMetaData[] md = new SqlMetaData[2];
md[0] = new SqlMetaData("intCol", SqlDbType.Int);
md[1] = new SqlMetaData("stringCol", SqlDbType.NVarChar, 50);

SqlDataRecord row = new SqlDataRecord(md);
SqlContext.Pipe.SendResultsStart(row);

// create and send the first record
row.SetSqlInt32(0, 1);
row.SetSqlString(1, "Record 1");
SqlContext.Pipe.SendResultsRow(row);

// create and send the second record
row.SetSqlInt32(0, 2);
row.SetSqlString(1, "Record 2");
SqlContext.Pipe.SendResultsRow(row);

SqlContext.Pipe.SendResultsEnd( );
}
```

The `SqlResultsStart( )`, `SqlResultsSend( )`, and `SqlResultsEnd( )` methods of the `SqlPipe` class are used to send dynamically created result sets containing multiple rows. The `SqlResultsStart( )` method takes a `SqlMetaData` array argument from which the schema of the result set is inferred. The `SqlResultsRow( )` method is called for each row to return in the result set. It can be called any time after `SqlResultsStart( )` is called and before `SqlResultsEnd( )` is called marking the end of the result set.

2. Build the solution.

3. Update the assembly registration in SQL Server and create the new stored procedure by executing this T-SQL statement:

```
ALTER ASSEMBLY EmployeeInShift
FROM 'C:\PSS2005\StoredProcedure\StoredProcedure\bin\Debug\StoredProcedure.dll'
GO

CREATE PROCEDURE DynamicMultiRow
AS EXTERNAL NAME EmployeeInShift.StoredProcedures.DynamicMultiRow
```

4. Execute the stored procedure:

```
EXEC DynamicMultiRow
```

Results are shown in Figure 5-6.

Figure 5-6. Results for stored procedure example that returns a dynamically created multi-row result set

User-Defined Aggregate Functions

A user-defined aggregate (UDA) function returns a scalar result that is the result of a calculation on values in a set of rows. Examples of such functions include built-in SQL Server aggregate functions such as SUM, AVG, MIN, and MAX. A CLR UDA function is implemented as a structure or class in a .NET Framework assembly. A CLR UDA function can be invoked in T-SQL statements with the same rules that apply to system aggregate functions.

To implement a CLR UDA function, you have to write only the code that implements the accumulation logic—iteration over the result set and computing accumulated values are managed by the query processor. Specifically, you must implement an aggregation contract that defines mechanisms to save the intermediate state of the aggregation and to accumulate new values. This aggregation contract consists of four methods:

public void Init( )
> Invoked once for each group that the query processor is aggregating to initialize the aggregate computation. This method should clean up previous uses of the instance, because the query processor can choose to reuse an instance of an aggregate class to compute aggregates for multiple groups.

public void Accumulate(input_type value)
> The query processor invokes this method to accumulate aggregate values. The method is invoked for each value in the group being accumulated. The input_ type argument is the managed SQL Server data type equivalent to the native SQL Server data type specified by the argument.

public void Merge(udagg_class value)
> Used to merge a second instance of this aggregate class with the current instance. The query processor can invoke this method to merge partial computations of an aggregate on group partitions.

public return_type Terminate( )
> Completes the aggregation and returns the result. The return_type is a managed SQL Server data type equivalent to the return_sqltype specified in the CREATE AGGREGATE T-SQL statement used to create the CLR aggregate function.

You identify a UDA function by annotating the implementing class with the SqlUserDefinedAggregate attribute, which indicates that a class should be registered as a UDA function. The SqlUserDefinedAggregate attribute has the following syntax:

```
SqlUserDefinedAggregate [ (aggregate-attribute [,...] ) ]

aggregate-attribute::=
  Format = {Native | UserDefined}
  IsInvariantToDuplicates = {true | false}
  IsInvariantToNulls = {true | false}
  IsInvariantToOrder = {true | false}
  IsNullIfEmpty = {true | false}
  | MaxByteSize = n
```

where:

Format = {Native | UserDefined}
  Specifies the serialization format for the type—either Native or UserDefined.

  Native serialization uses a simple algorithm to efficiently serialize the type. Native serialization is recommended for simple types containing only fields of the following types: bool, byte, sbyte, short, ushort, int, uint, long, ulong, float, double, SqlByte, SqlInt16, SqlInt32, SqlInt64, SqlDateTime, SqlSingle, SqlDouble, SqlMoney, and SqlBoolean. Native serialization can also contain UDTs that use Native serialization.

  Native serialization has the following requirements:

  - All the fields of the type must be *blittable*—data types that have a common representation in both managed and unmanaged memory and therefore do not need to be converted when passed between managed and unmanaged code. The following types from the System namespace are blittable: Byte, SByte, UInt16, Int32, UInt32, Int64, IntPtr, and UIntPtr. One-dimensional arrays of blittable types and formatted value types containing only blittable types are also blittable.

  - The type must not specify the MaxByteSize property.

  - The type must not have any fields that are not serialized.

  UserDefined serialization controls the serialization through code and has the following requirements:

  - You must specify the MaxByteSize property of the SqlUserDefinedAggregate attribute.

  - The class or structure implementing the type must implement the Read( ) and Write( ) methods of the IBinarySerializable interface to read and write the byte stream.

IsInvariantToDuplicates
  Specifies whether the aggregate is invariant to duplicates. For example, MAX and MIN are invariant to duplicates, and AVG and SUM are not.

IsInvariantToNulls

Specifies whether the aggregate is invariant to nulls. For example, MAX and MIN are invariant to nulls, and COUNT is not (since nulls are included in the count).

IsInvariantToOrder

Specifies whether the aggregate is invariant to the order of the values. Specifying true gives the query optimizer more flexibility in choosing an execution plan and can result in improved performance.

IsNullIfEmpty

Specifies whether the aggregate returns a null reference if no values are accumulated. Otherwise the value that the initialized value of the variable returned by the Terminate( ) method is returned.

MaxByteSize

The maximum size of the UDT instance. MaxByteSize must be specified if the Format property is set to UserDefined.

The following example creates, registers, and executes a UDA function that returns the sum of a SqlMoney column in a table. Follow these steps:

1. Using the Visual Studio 2005 IDE, create a new SQL Server project named Uda.

2. Create an aggregate item in the project. Name the item SumMoney.cs. Empty code blocks are created for the four required methods.

3. Replace the code in SumMoney.cs with the following code:

```
using System;
using System.Data;
using System.Data.Sql;
using System.Data.SqlTypes;
using Microsoft.SqlServer.Server;

[Serializable]
[SqlUserDefinedAggregate(Format.Native)]
public struct SumMoney
{
    private SqlMoney sum;

    public void Init( )
    {
        sum = 0;
    }

    public void Accumulate(SqlMoney Value)
    {
        sum += Value;
    }

    public void Merge(SumMoney Group)
    {
```

```
        sum += Group.sum;
    }

    public SqlMoney Terminate( )
    {
        return sum;
    }
}
```

4. Build the solution.

5. In SQL Server Management Studio, register the assembly and create the UDA
   function by executing the following statement:

```
USE AdventureWorks
GO

CREATE ASSEMBLY SumMoney
FROM 'C:\PSS2005\Uda\Uda\bin\Debug\Uda.dll'
GO

CREATE AGGREGATE SumMoneyUda
( @Value money )
RETURNS money
EXTERNAL NAME SumMoney.SumMoney
```

6. Execute the aggregate function on the Sales.SalesOrderHeader table in Aventure-
   Works:

```
SELECT dbo.SumMoneyUda(SubTotal), dbo.SumMoneyUda(TaxAmt),
    dbo.SumMoneyUda(Freight), dbo.SumMoneyUda(TotalDue)
FROM Sales.SalesOrderHeader
```

The results shown in Figure 5-7 are returned (which are the same as the totals
returned by the built-in SUM function).

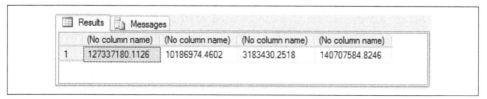

Figure 5-7. Results for UDA function example

User-Defined Types

In addition to supporting native and simple types as in previous versions of SQL
Server, SQL Server 2005 lets you define CLR user-defined types (UDTs). This lets
you extend the built-in data types and define complex data types. A CLR UDT can
be used in all contexts where a SQL Server system type can be used.

A CLR UDT is implemented as a class in a .NET Framework assembly. Identify a CLR
UDT by annotating the class that implements the UDT with the SqlUserDefinedType

attribute, which indicates that a class should be registered as a UDT. The SqlUserDefinedType attribute has the following syntax:

```
SqlUserDefinedType [ ( udt-property [,...] ) ]

udt-property::=
    Format = { Native | UserDefined }
  | MaxByteSize= n
  | IsByteOrdered= { true | false }
  | ValidationMethod = string
  | IsFixedLength = { true | false }
  | Name = string
```

where:

Format = { Native | UserDefined }

The serialization format of the UDT. For more information about these two values, see the Format property for the SqlUserDefinedAggregate attribute in the "User-Defined Aggregate Functions" section earlier in this chapter.

If the UDT is defined in a class rather than a structure, and if the Format property is Native, a StructLayout attribute must be specified and set to LayoutKind.Sequential. This forces the members in the class to be serialized in the same order in which they appear in the class.

MaxByteSize

Specifies the maximum size of an instance of the UDT between 1 and 8000 bytes. You must specify MaxByteSize if the Format property is set to UserDefined. Do not specify MaxByteSize if the Format property is set to Native.

IsByteOrdered

Specifies how binary comparisons are performed on the UDT by SQL Server. When IsByteOrdered is true, the UDT is ordered in the same way as its serialized binary representation and can be used to order the data. The following features are supported on the UDT column in a table when IsByteOrdered is true:

- Creating an index on the column
- Creating primary and foreign key constraints, and CHECK and UNIQUE constraints on the column
- Using the column in T-SQL ORDER BY, GROUP BY, and PARTITION BY clauses
- Using comparison operators in T-SQL statements on the column

ValidationMethod

Specifies the method used to validate instances of the UDT when the data is deserialized from a binary value. The converted method returns a Boolean indicating whether the UDT instance is valid.

The database engine automatically converts binary values to UDT values. The database engine prevents invalid values in the database by checking whether values are appropriate for the serialization format of the type and that the value can be deserialized. Default checking might be inadequate when, for example, UDT values are constrained by a value set or a range.

IsFixedLength

> Specifies whether all instances of the UDT are the same length. If the IsFixedLength property is true, all instances of the UDT must have the length, in bytes, specified by the MaxByteSize property. The property is used only when the Format property is set to UserDefined.

Name

> Specifies the name of the type.

When a field, method, or property is referenced as part of a query, the T-SQL type of the return value is inferred from the return type. The SqlFacet attribute can be used to return additional information about the return type of a non-void UDT expression—the SqlFacet attribute does not constrain the specific values that can be stored in the type. The syntax of the SqlFacet attribute is as follows:

```
SqlFacet[(facet-attribute [,...])]

facet-attribute::=
    IsFixedLength = { true | false }
  | MaxSize= { n }
  | Precision = { n }
  | Scale = { n }
  | IsNullable = { true | false }
```

where:

IsFixedLength

> Specifies whether the return type is a fixed length. IsFixedLength must be set to false if the MaxSize property is set to -1. The default value is false.

MaxSize

> Specifies the maximum size of the return type in bytes for binary types and characters for character field types. The default is 4000 for Unicode character types and 8000 for binary types. The value -1 indicates a large character or binary type.

Precision

> Specifies the precision (number of digits in the number) of the return type as a value from 1 to 38. This property is used only with numeric types. Scale must be specified if Precision is specified. The default value is 38.

Scale

> Specifies the scale (number of digits to the right of the decimal point) of the return type as a value from 0 to 38. This property is used only with numeric types. Precision must be specified if Scale is specified. The default value is 0.

IsNullable

> Indicates whether the value of the return type can be null. The default is true.

The properties specified for the SqlFacet attribute must be compatible with the return type. Table 5-1 shows SqlFacet properties that can be specified for each return type.

Table 5-1. Allowable SqlFacet properties by return type

Type	IsFixedLength	MaxSize	Precision	Scale	IsNullable
SqlBoolean	N	N	N	N	Y
SqlByte	N	N	N	N	Y
SqlInt16	N	N	N	N	Y
SqlInt32	N	N	N	N	Y
SqlInt64	N	N	N	N	Y
SqlSingle	N	N	N	N	Y
SqlDouble	N	N	N	N	Y
SqlDateTime	N	N	N	N	Y
SqlMoney	N	N	N	N	Y
SqlGuid	N	N	N	N	Y
SqlDecimal	N	N	Y	Y	Y
SqlString	Y	Y	N	N	Y
SqlBinary	Y	Y	N	N	Y
SqlXml	N	N	N	N	Y
SqlBytes	Y	Y	N	N	Y
SqlChars	Y	Y	N	N	Y
SqlUtcDateTime	N	N	N	N	Y
SqlDate	N	N	N	N	Y
SqlTime	N	N	N	N	Y
Embedded UDTs	N	N	N	N	Y
string	Y	Y	N	N	Y
Byte[]	Y	Y	N	N	Y
Char[]	Y	Y	N	N	Y
decimal	N	N	Y	Y	N

You must do the following when you define a CLR UDT:

- Annotate the class with the SqlUserDefinedType attribute.
- Specify the Serializable attribute, indicating that the UDT can be serialized.
- Implement the System.Data.SqlTypes.INullable interface so that the UDT can recognize a null value. This means that the UDT must implement a static IsNull property that returns a Boolean indicating whether the instance of the UDT is null.

- Implement a `public static` property named `Null` that returns a null instance of the UDT.

- Implement `public static ToString()` and `Parse()` methods to convert to and parse from a `string` representation of the type. The `Parse()` method takes a single argument of type `SqlString`.

- Implement the `IXmlSerializable` interface if all public fields and properties are XML serializable or marked with the `XmlIgnore` attribute. The `IXmlSerializable` interface provides custom XML serialization and deserialization by explicitly defining how an object is serialized and deserialized by the `XmlSerializer` class. The `IXmlSerializable` interface has three methods: `GetSchema()`, `ReadXml()`, and `WriteXml()`.

- Implement `Read()` and `Write()` methods if user-defined serialization is specified by implementing the `IBinarySerialize` interface.

A CLR UDT has the following restrictions:

- Public names cannot exceed 128 characters in length and must conform to SQL Server naming rules for identifiers.

- Only fields, properties, and methods defined in the type are callable from T-SQL. SQL Server is not aware of the inheritance hierarchy among UDTs.

- Members other than the class constructor cannot be overloaded.

- Static members must be declared either as constants or as read-only when the assembly permission is specified as `SAFE` or `EXTERNAL_ACCESS`.

The `SqlMethod` attribute is used to define characteristics of a UDT method or property. The syntax of the `SqlMethod` attribute is as follows:

```
SqlMethod [ ( method-attribute [ ,... ] ) ]

method-attribute::=
    function_attribute
  | IsMutator = { true | false }
  | OnNullCall = { true | false }
  | InvokeIfReceiverIsNull= { true | false }
```

where:

function_attribute
> The `SqlMethod` attribute inherits all properties of the `SqlFunction` attribute discussed in the "Scalar-Valued Functions" section earlier in this chapter.

`IsMutator`
> Specifies whether the method can modify the UDT instance. SQL Server looks for the `IsMutator` property of the `SqlMethod` attribute on `void` public methods in the UDT. If the `IsMutator` property is true on a `void` method, SQL Server marks the method as a mutator—a method that causes state change in the instance.

Mutator methods are not allowed in queries—their use is restricted to assignment statements or data modification statements. The default value of the IsMutator property is false.

OnNullCall

Specifies whether the method is evaluated if one or more null arguments are supplied. If false, the method returns null without evaluating the method if one or more of the arguments are null. If true, the method is evaluated regardless of whether arguments are null. The default value is true.

InvokeIfReceiverIsNull

Specifies whether SQL Server should invoke the method on a null reference. A value of true invokes the method on a null reference. The default value is false.

The following example creates, registers, and uses a UDT that defines a polygon and implements a single method that returns the area of the polygon as a double. Follow these steps:

1. Using the Visual Studio 2005 IDE, create a new SQL Server project named PolygonUdt.

2. Create an aggregate item in the project. Name the item Polygon.cs. Empty code blocks are created for the four required methods.

3. Replace the code in Polygon.cs with the following code:

```
using System;
using System.Data;
using System.Data.Sql;
using System.Data.SqlTypes;
using Microsoft.SqlServer.Server;

[Serializable]
[SqlUserDefinedType(Format.Native)]
public struct Polygon : INullable
{
    private bool isNull;

    private int numberSides;
    private double sideLength;

    public override string ToString()
    {
        if (this.isNull)
            return "null";
        else
            return string.Format("{0} sides each {1} units long",
                numberSides, sideLength);
    }

    public bool IsNull
    {
        get
```

```
    {
        return isNull;
    }
}

public static Polygon Null
{
    get
    {
        Polygon p = new Polygon( );
        p.isNull = true;

        return p;
    }
}

public static Polygon Parse(SqlString s)
{
    if (s.IsNull || s.Value.ToLower( ).Equals("null"))
        return Null;

    string[] sa = s.ToString( ).Split(',');
    if (sa.Length != 2)
        return Null;

    Polygon p = new Polygon( );

    try
    {
        p.numberSides = int.Parse(sa[0]);
        p.sideLength = double.Parse(sa[1]);

        if (p.numberSides > 2 && p.sideLength > 0)
            return p;
        else
            return Null;
    }
    catch (Exception)
    {
        return Null;
    }
}

public int NumberSides
{
    get { return numberSides; }
    set
    {
        if (value > 2)
        {
            numberSides = value;
            isNull = false;
        }
        else
```

```
                isNull = true;
        }
    }

    public double SideLength
    {
        get { return sideLength; }
        set
        {
            if (value > 0)
            {
                sideLength = value;
                isNull = false;
            }
            else
                isNull = true;
        }
    }

    [SqlMethod]
    public double Area( )
    {
        if (!isNull)
            return .25 * numberSides * Math.Pow(sideLength, 2) *
                (1 / Math.Tan(Math.PI / numberSides));
        else
            return 0;
    }

    [SqlMethod(IsMutator = true, OnNullCall = false)]
    public void SetValue(int numberSides, double sideLength)
    {
        if (numberSides > 2 && sideLength > 0)
        {
            this.numberSides = numberSides;
            this.sideLength = sideLength;
            this.isNull = false;
        }
        else
            isNull = true;
    }
}
```

The UDT is implemented as a struct marked with both a Serializable attribute and a SqlUserDefinedType attribute specifying Native serialization. A UDT must support both XML and binary serialization.

The UDT contains two private fields—numberSides and sideLength. The NumberSides and SideLength properties are used to get and set the value of these fields.

The UDT implements the INullable interface with the method IsNull( ), which simply returns the value of a private field, isNull, that keeps track of whether the polygon UDT is null. The UDT also implements the Null( ) method, which instantiates and returns a null instance of the Polygon UDT.

The UDT implements the required ToString( ) and Parse( ) methods. The ToString( ) method displays the value of the polygon as a string. The Parse( ) method converts a string to the polygon UDT and is used by the SQL Server CONVERT and CAST functions.

The UDT implements two methods. The Area( ) method returns the area of the polygon. The SetValue( ) method changes the number of sides and the length of the sides in the polygon UDT.

4. Build the solution.

5. Register the assembly and create the polygon UDT by executing the following T-SQL statement in SQL Server Management Studio:

```
USE ProgrammingSqlServer2005
GO

CREATE ASSEMBLY Polygon
FROM 'C:\PSS2005\PolygonUdt\PolygonUdt\bin\Debug\PolygonUdt.dll'
GO

CREATE TYPE Polygon
EXTERNAL NAME Polygon
```

6. Execute the following T-SQL statements:

```
DECLARE @p Polygon

SET @p = CONVERT(Polygon, '5, 4.2')

PRINT @p.IsNull
PRINT @p.ToString( )
PRINT @p.NumberSides
PRINT @p.SideLength
PRINT @p.Area( )

SET @p.SetValue(7, 3)
PRINT @p.ToString( )
PRINT @p.Area( )
```

The results are shown in Figure 5-8.

Triggers

A trigger is a type of stored procedure that executes automatically when an event occurs. SQL Server has two types of triggers:

Data Manipulation Language (DML) trigger
Executes when INSERT, UPDATE, and DELETE commands modify data in a table or view.

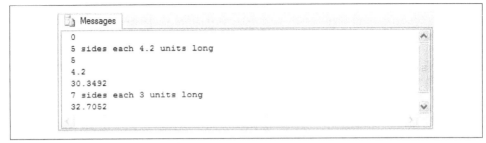

Figure 5-8. Results for UDT example

Data Definition Language (DDL) trigger
Executes in response to a DDL statement that is often used to make database schema changes. Examples include the CREATE, ALTER, and DROP statements.

A CLR trigger is implemented as a method of a class in a .NET Framework assembly.

The following two sections discuss creating CLR DML and DDL triggers.

DML Triggers

A CLR trigger is implemented as a public static void method in a .NET Framework assembly. You identify a CLR DML trigger by marking the method that implements the trigger with the SqlTrigger attribute, which indicates that a method should be registered as a DML trigger. The SqlTrigger attribute has the following syntax:

```
SqlTrigger [ ( trigger-attribute [ ,... ] ) ]

trigger-attribute::=
    Target = "table-name"
  | Event = "trigger-type update-action [, ...]"


trigger-type::=
  FOR | AFTER | INSTEAD OF

update-action::=
  UPDATE | DELETE | INSERT
```

where:

Target = "table-name"
Specifies the table to which the trigger applies

trigger-type
Specifies the type of trigger

update-action
Specifies the DML action that activates the trigger—UPDATE, DELETE, or INSERT

You can use the `TriggerAction` property of the `SqlTriggerContext` class instead of the `SqlTrigger` attribute. This is discussed later in this section in the example about creating a DDL trigger.

The following example creates update, insert, and delete DML triggers that log updates, inserts, and deletes to a table named `Volume`. These events are logged to a table named `VolumeAudit`. The example then registers the triggers and shows the results of executing DML statements against the `Volume` table. Follow these steps:

1. Execute the following T-SQL statements to create the `Volume` and `VolumeAudit` tables that are the target and logging destination of the triggers:

   ```
   USE ProgrammingSqlServer2005
   GO

   CREATE TABLE Volume
   (
       ID int NOT NULL,
       Length float NOT NULL,
       Width float NOT NULL,
       Height float NOT NULL,
       Volume float NOT NULL CONSTRAINT DF_Area_Area DEFAULT ((0)),
           CONSTRAINT PK_Volume PRIMARY KEY CLUSTERED
           (
               ID ASC
           )
   )
   GO

   CREATE TABLE VolumeAudit
   (
       Action varchar(50) NOT NULL,
       Description varchar(max) NOT NULL
   )
   ```

2. Using the Visual Studio 2005 IDE, create a new SQL Server project named `DmlTrigger`.

3. Create a trigger item in the project. Name the item `VolumeTriggers.cs`.

4. Replace the code in `VolumeTriggers.cs` with the following code:

   ```csharp
   using System;
   using System.Data;
   using System.Data.Sql;
   using Microsoft.SqlServer.Server;
   using System.Data.SqlClient;
   using System.Collections;

   public partial class Triggers
   {
       [SqlTrigger (Target="Volume", Event="FOR INSERT")]
       public static void InsertTrigger( )
       {
           using (SqlConnection conn = new SqlConnection("context connection=true"))
   ```

```
    {
        SqlDataAdapter da = new SqlDataAdapter("SELECT * FROM INSERTED",
            conn);
        DataTable dt = new DataTable( );
        da.Fill(dt);

        SqlCommand cmd = new SqlCommand( );
        cmd.Connection = conn;
        conn.Open( );
        foreach (DataRow row in dt.Rows)
        {
            int id = (int)row[0];
            double length = (double)row[1];
            double width = (double)row[2];
            double height = (double)row[3];
            double volume = length * width * height;

            string audit = string.Format("ID = {0}, Length = {1}, " +
                "Width = {2}, Height = {3}",
                id, length, width, height);

            cmd.CommandText = "INSERT INTO VolumeAudit VALUES ('INSERTED', '" +
                audit + "')";
            cmd.ExecuteNonQuery( );

            cmd.CommandText = "UPDATE Volume SET Volume = " + volume +
                " WHERE ID = " + id;
            cmd.ExecuteNonQuery( );

            SqlPipe pipe = SqlContext.Pipe;
            pipe.Send("Row inserted: " + audit);
        }
    }
}

[SqlTrigger(Target = "Volume", Event = "FOR UPDATE")]
public static void UpdateTrigger( )
{
    using (SqlConnection conn = new SqlConnection("context connection=true"))
    {
        SqlDataAdapter da = new SqlDataAdapter("SELECT * FROM DELETED",
            conn);
        DataTable dtDel = new DataTable( );
        da.Fill(dtDel);
        da = new SqlDataAdapter("SELECT * FROM INSERTED", conn);
        DataTable dtIns = new DataTable( );
        da.Fill(dtIns);

        SqlCommand cmd = new SqlCommand( );
        cmd.Connection = conn;
        conn.Open( );
        for (int i = 0; i < dtDel.Rows.Count; i++)
        {
            DataRow rowDel = dtDel.Rows[i];
```

```
            int delId = (int)rowDel[0];
            double delLength = (double)rowDel[1];
            double delWidth = (double)rowDel[2];
            double delHeight = (double)rowDel[3];
            double delVolume = (double)rowDel[4];

            string delAudit = string.Format("ID = {0}, Length = {1}, " +
                "Width = {2}, Height = {3}, Volume = {4}",
                delId, delLength, delWidth, delHeight, delVolume);

            DataRow rowIns = dtIns.Rows[i];
            int insId = (int)rowIns[0];
            double insLength = (double)rowIns[1];
            double insWidth = (double)rowIns[2];
            double insHeight = (double)rowIns[3];
            double insVolume = insLength * insWidth * insHeight;

            string insAudit = string.Format("ID = {0}, Length = {1}, " +
                "Width = {2}, Height = {3}, Volume = {4}",
                insId, insLength, insWidth, insHeight, insVolume);

            cmd.CommandText = "UPDATE Volume SET Volume = " + insVolume +
                " WHERE ID = " + insId;
            cmd.ExecuteNonQuery();

            cmd.CommandText = "INSERT INTO VolumeAudit VALUES " +
                "('UPDATED', 'Original: " + delAudit + "; " + "New: " +
                insAudit + "')";
            cmd.ExecuteNonQuery();

            SqlPipe pipe = SqlContext.Pipe;
            pipe.Send("Row updated: Original: " + delAudit + "; " + "New: " +
                insAudit);
        }
    }
}

[SqlTrigger(Target = "Volume", Event = "FOR DELETE")]
public static void DeleteTrigger()
{
    using (SqlConnection conn = new SqlConnection("context connection=true"))
    {
        SqlDataAdapter da = new SqlDataAdapter("SELECT * FROM DELETED",
            conn);
        DataTable dt = new DataTable();
        da.Fill(dt);

        SqlCommand cmd = new SqlCommand();
        cmd.Connection = conn;
        conn.Open();
        foreach(DataRow row in dt.Rows)
        {
            int id = (int)row[0];
            double length = (double)row[1];
```

```
                        double width = (double)row[2];
                        double height = (double)row[3];
                        double volume = (double)row[4];

                        string audit = string.Format("ID = {0}, Length = {1}, " +
                            "Width = {2}, Height = {3}, Volume = {4}",
                            id, length, width, height, volume);

                        cmd.CommandText = "INSERT INTO VolumeAudit VALUES ('DELETED', '"
                            + audit + "');";
                        cmd.ExecuteNonQuery();

                        SqlPipe pipe = SqlContext.Pipe;
                        pipe.Send("Row deleted: " + audit);
                    }
                }
            }
        }
```

5. Build the solution.

   Each of the three triggers is marked with the SqlTrigger attribute that specifies
   the Volume table as the target of the trigger together with the event that causes
   each trigger to execute.

6. In SQL Server Management Studio, register the assembly and create the DML
   insert, update, and delete triggers by executing the following query:

```
USE ProgrammingSqlServer2005
GO

CREATE ASSEMBLY VolumeTriggers
FROM 'C:\PSS2005\DmlTrigger\DmlTrigger\bin\Debug\DmlTrigger.dll'
GO

CREATE TRIGGER VolumeInsertTrigger
ON Volume
FOR INSERT
AS
EXTERNAL NAME VolumeTriggers.Triggers.InsertTrigger
GO

CREATE TRIGGER VolumeUpdateTrigger
ON Volume
FOR UPDATE
AS
EXTERNAL NAME VolumeTriggers.Triggers.UpdateTrigger
GO

CREATE TRIGGER VolumeDeleteTrigger
ON Volume
FOR DELETE
AS
EXTERNAL NAME VolumeTriggers.Triggers.DeleteTrigger
GO
```

7. Execute the following T-SQL statements to insert two rows into the Volume table:

```
INSERT INTO Volume (ID, Length, Width, Height) VALUES (1, 2.2, 3.4, 5.7)
INSERT INTO Volume (ID, Length, Width, Height) VALUES (2, 6, 2, 5.4)
```

The results are shown in Figure 5-9.

```
Messages

Row inserted: ID = 1, Length = 2.2, Width = 3.4, Height = 5.7

(1 row(s) affected)
Row inserted: ID = 2, Length = 6, Width = 2, Height = 5.4

(1 row(s) affected)
```

Figure 5-9. Results for DML trigger example

The output is generated by the following code in the insert DML trigger:

```
pipe.Send("Row inserted: " + audit);
```

The VolumeAudit table now contains the following records:

Action	Description
INSERTED	ID = 1, Length = 2.2, Width = 3.4, Height = 5.7
UPDATED	Original: ID = 1, Length = 2.2, Width = 3.4, Height = 5.7, Volume = 0; New: ID = 1, Length = 2.2, Width = 3.4, Height = 5.7, Volume = 42.636
INSERTED	ID = 2, Length = 6, Width = 2, Height = 5.4
UPDATED	Original: ID = 2, Length = 6, Width = 2, Height = 5.4, Volume = 0; New: ID = 2, Length = 6, Width = 2, Height = 5.4, Volume = 64.8

Although the update trigger on the Volume table updates the Volume table, the query is not recursive as long as the RECURSIVE_TRIGGERS database option is set to OFF—this is the default. You can check the status of all database options by executing the following T-SQL statement:

```
SELECT * FROM sys.databases
```

The is_recursive_triggers_on column contains the setting of the RECURSIVE_TRIGGERS option for each database.

You can change the value of a database option using the ALTER DATABASE statement. For example, execute the following T-SQL statement to change the recursive trigger behavior for the ProgrammingSqlServer2005 database to ON:

```
ALTER DATABASE ProgrammingSqlServer2005
SET RECURSIVE_TRIGGERS ON
```

There are four records—two inserted by the insert DML trigger and two inserted by the update DML trigger when the insert DML trigger updates the Volume field.

Execute the following T-SQL statement to update the first of the two rows previously inserted into the Volume table:

```
UPDATE Volume
SET Length = 1, Width = 4, Height = 7.2
WHERE ID = 1
```

The output follows:

```
Row updated:
Original: ID = 1, Length = 2.2, Width = 3.4, Height = 5.7, Volume = 42.636;
New: ID = 1, Length = 1, Width = 4, Height = 7.2, Volume = 28.8

(1 row(s) affected)
```

The VolumeAudit table now contains a new record inserted by the update DML trigger:

Action	Description
UPDATED	Original: ID = 1, Length = 2.2, Width = 3.4, Height = 5.7, Volume = 42.636; New: ID = 1, Length = 1, Width = 4, Height = 7.2, Volume = 28.8

Execute the following T-SQL statement to delete the two rows from the Volume table:

```
DELETE FROM Volume
```

The output follows:

```
Row deleted: ID = 2, Length = 6, Width = 2, Height = 5.4, Volume = 64.8
Row deleted: ID = 1, Length = 1, Width = 4, Height = 7.2, Volume = 28.8

(2 row(s) affected)
```

The VolumeAudit table now contains two new records inserted by the delete DML trigger:

Action	Description
DELETED	ID = 2, Length = 6, Width = 2, Height = 5.4, Volume = 64.8
DELETED	ID = 1, Length = 1, Width = 4, Height = 7.2, Volume = 28.8

DDL Triggers

A CLR trigger is implemented as a public static void method in a .NET Framework assembly. Instead of using the SqlTrigger attribute to define events for which a DDL trigger executes, the SqlTriggerContext is used to get context information about the trigger. This SqlTriggerContext class cannot be instantiated directly—call the TriggerContext property of the SqlContext class to get an instance.

The SqlTriggerContext class has a TriggerAction property that indicates the action that caused a trigger to fire. For DML triggers, the value can be TriggerAction. Update, TriggerAction.Insert, or TriggerAction.Delete. There are many DDL trigger actions—see Microsoft SQL Server 2005 Books Online for a complete list.

The following example creates, registers, and demonstrates a CLR DDL trigger that logs CREATE_TABLE and DROP_TABLE events to a table named Log. Follow these steps:

1. Create a table named Log to store the DDL event information in:

```
USE ProgrammingSqlServer2005
GO

CREATE TABLE Log
(
  LogID int IDENTITY(1,1) NOT NULL,
  LogEntry varchar(max) NOT NULL,
    CONSTRAINT PK_Log PRIMARY KEY CLUSTERED
    (
      LogID ASC
    )
)
```

2. Using the Visual Studio 2005 IDE, create a new SQL Server project named DdlTrigger.

3. Create a trigger item in the project. Name the item LogTableActivityTrigger.cs.

4. Replace the code in LogTableActivityTrigger.cs with the following code:

```
using System;
using System.Data;
using System.Data.Sql;
using Microsoft.SqlServer.Server;
using System.Data.SqlClient;

public partial class Triggers
{
    public static void LogTableActivityTrigger( )
    {
        SqlTriggerContext tc = SqlContext.TriggerContext;
        using (SqlConnection conn = new SqlConnection("context connection=true"))
        {
            conn.Open( );
            SqlCommand cmd = new SqlCommand( );
            cmd.Connection = conn;

            if (tc.TriggerAction == TriggerAction.CreateTable ||
                tc.TriggerAction == TriggerAction.DropTable)
            {
                cmd.CommandText = "INSERT INTO Log VALUES " +
                    "('" + tc.EventData.Value + "')";
                cmd.ExecuteNonQuery( );
            }
        }
    }
}
```

A single DDL trigger is defined in the Triggers class. The trigger checks the TriggerAction property of the SqlTriggerContext and then logs the EventData for the event that caused this trigger to fire. In this example, it is not necessary to check the trigger context, as all events for which the trigger is registered in Step 6 execute the same code to log the event. You could use the `TriggerAction` property to perform different actions for each of the different events that a DDL trigger is registered to handle.

5. Build the solution.

6. Register the assembly and create the DDL trigger by executing this statement in SQL Server Management Studio:

```
USE ProgrammingSqlServer2005
GO

CREATE ASSEMBLY DdlTrigger
FROM 'C:\PSS2005\DdlTrigger\DdlTrigger\bin\Debug\DdlTrigger.dll'
GO

CREATE TRIGGER LogTableActivity
ON DATABASE
FOR CREATE_TABLE, DROP_TABLE
AS
EXTERNAL NAME DdlTrigger.Triggers.LogTableActivityTrigger
```
The CREATE TRIGGER statement creates a DDL trigger that executes when CREATE TABLE and DROP TABLE DDL statements are executed.

7. Execute the following T-SQL statement to create and then drop a table named TestTable:

```
USE ProgrammingSqlServer2005
GO

CREATE TABLE TestTable
(
  TestID int NOT NULL,
    CONSTRAINT PK_TestTable PRIMARY KEY CLUSTERED
    (
      TestID ASC
    )
)
GO

DROP TABLE TestTable
GO
```

The Log table contains two rows, shown here, containing details about the DDL CREATE_TABLE and DROP_TABLE events:

```
<EVENT_INSTANCE>
  <EventType>CREATE_TABLE</EventType>
  <PostTime>2005-06-15T13:57:10.733</PostTime>
  <SPID>54</SPID>
  <ServerName>BILLHAMILTON1</ServerName>
  <LoginName>BILLHAMILTON1\whamilton</LoginName>
  <UserName>dbo</UserName>
  <DatabaseName>ProgrammingSqlServer2005</DatabaseName>
  <SchemaName>dbo</SchemaName>
```

```xml
    <ObjectName>TestTable</ObjectName>
    <ObjectType>TABLE</ObjectType>
    <TSQLCommand>
      <SetOptions ANSI_NULLS="ON" ANSI_NULL_DEFAULT="ON" ANSI_PADDING="ON"
        QUOTED_IDENTIFIER="ON" ENCRYPTED="FALSE" />
      <CommandText>
        CREATE TABLE TestTable
        (
          TestID int NOT NULL,
          CONSTRAINT PK_TestTable PRIMARY KEY CLUSTERED
          (
            TestID ASC
          )
        )
      </CommandText>
    </TSQLCommand>
  </EVENT_INSTANCE>

  <EVENT_INSTANCE>
    <EventType>DROP_TABLE</EventType>
    <PostTime>2005-06-15T13:57:10.937</PostTime>
    <SPID>54</SPID>
    <ServerName>BILLHAMILTON1</ServerName>
    <LoginName>BILLHAMILTON1\whamilton</LoginName>
    <UserName>dbo</UserName>
    <DatabaseName>ProgrammingSqlServer2005</DatabaseName>
    <SchemaName>dbo</SchemaName>
    <ObjectName>TestTable</ObjectName>
    <ObjectType>TABLE</ObjectType>
    <TSQLCommand>
      <SetOptions ANSI_NULLS="ON" ANSI_NULL_DEFAULT="ON" ANSI_PADDING="ON"
        QUOTED_IDENTIFIER="ON" ENCRYPTED="FALSE" />
      <CommandText>
        DROP TABLE TestTable
      </CommandText>
    </TSQLCommand>
  </EVENT_INSTANCE>
```

CHAPTER 6

.NET Client-Side Programming

This chapter describes SQL Server 2005 client-side programming technologies. These include:

SQL Native Client programming
Replaces the SQL OLE DB and SQL ODBC drivers; uses Microsoft Data Access Components (MDAC) and implements functionality supporting new features in SQL Server 2005.

SQLXML 4.0
Updates SQLXML 3.0 to accommodate new features in SQL Server 2005.

Exception Message Box programming
Extends the functionality of the regular message box in the System.Windows. Forms.MessageBox class to make it easier for you to control and to provide detailed information to users.

SQL Native Client Programming

Microsoft SQL Server 2005 introduces SQL Native Client, which is designed to simplify native access to data in SQL Server 7.0 or later using either OLE DB or ODBC. SQL Native Client replaces the SQL OLE DB provider and the SQL ODBC driver with a standalone API that combines both the SQL OLE DB provider and SQL ODBC driver functionality into a single DLL. The individual data access technologies are now referred to as *SQL Native Client (OLE DB)* and *SQL Native Client (ODBC)*. Additionally, SQL Native Client supports new SQL Server 2005 enhancements, as described in Table 6-1.

Table 6-1. SQL Native Client support for new functionality in SQL Server 2005

Function	Description
xml data type	Supports the SQL Server 2005 xml data type for columns, variable, parameters, and return types
Large value types	Supports SQL Server large-object data types—varchar(max), nvarchar(max), and varbinary(max)

Function	Description
User-defined types (UDTs)	Supports using UDTs in the SQL Server database
Multiple Active Result Sets (MARS)	Supports multiple result sets using a single SQL Server connection
Snapshot isolation	Supports snapshot isolation level in SQL Server 2005
Asynchronous operations	Allows methods to return immediately without blocking the calling thread
Database mirroring	Supports mirrored SQL Server 2005 databases
Query notifications	Supports client notifications when result sets are modified
Bulk copy	Supports transferring large amounts of data into or out of SQL Server
Password expiration	Supports handling expired passwords in SQL Server 2005 without administrator involvement

> If you are developing a new application or modifying an existing application written in a managed programming language such as C# or VB.NET, you should use a .NET Framework data provider for the database. Use SQL Native Client to access new features of SQL Server 2005 and also to access data sources using OLE DB or ODBC from other applications such as COM-based applications.

SQL Native Client is a separate product from MDAC, but it lets you evolve new data access functionality in applications without changing existing MDAC components. Although SQL Native Client uses MDAC, it is not dependent on a specific version of MDAC and can be used with any version installed with Windows 2000 SP3 or later. SQL Native Client does not include user-accessible functionality that already exists in the base MDAC components, such as connection pooling, ADO support, memory management, or client-side cursor support—it uses MDAC to provide that functionality. MDAC does not support enhancements in SQL Server 2005.

SQL Native Client components are installed by default with SQL Server 2005. These components are described in Table 6-2.

Table 6-2. SQL Native Client components

Component	Description	Directory
SQLNCLI.dll	Contains all SQL Native Client functionality, including both the OLE DB provider and ODBC provider.	<windows>\system32
SQLNCLIR.rll	The resource file for SQLNCLI.dll.	<windows>\system32
SQLNCLI.h	Contains all definitions needed to use SQL Native Client. Replaces both the ODBCSS.h and SQLOLEDB.h header files.	Program Files\Microsoft SQL Server\90\SDK\Include
SQLNCLI.lib	The library file needed to call the ODBC Bulk Copy Program (BCP) functions in SQL Native Client.	Program Files\Microsoft SQL Server\90\SDK\Lib

You need to redistribute SQL Native Client with your application so that it installs on client computers. An installation package named *SQLNCLI.msi* is included on the SQL Server 2005 installation CD, in the *Tools\Setup* directory. The *ReadmeSQL2005.htm* file in the *Tools* directory of the installation CD discusses client- and server-side prerequisites and provides installation instructions.

> See Microsoft SQL Server 2005 Books Online for information about SQL Native Client (OLE DB) and SQL Native Client (ODBC) programming.

SQLXML 4.0

SQL Server 2005 introduces SQLXML 4.0, which provides functionality found in previous releases and adds support for new SQL Server 2005 XML and web service functionality. SQLXML 4.0 is installed automatically with SQL Server 2005. You can also install SQLXML on clients' computers from the installation program *sqlxml4.msi*—you will also need to install MSXML 6.0 from the installation program *msxml6.msi*. These installation programs are on the SQL Server 2005 installation disk in the *Tools\Setup* subdirectory.

SQLXML 4.0 provides client-side XML functionality for writing applications that access XML data from SQL Server, process it, and send updated data back to the server. SQLXML bridges relational data to XML data in SQL Server. SQLXML is used to query relational data using T-SQL and return XML results, query relational data with XPath, and update relational data using XML. In addition to facilitating working with relational data as XML, SQLXML lets you execute XML template queries—queries embedded in a dynamic XML document—and server-side XPath queries in SQL Server 2005. The SQL Server .NET data provider, without SQLXML, does not provide this capability.

SQLXML 4.0 supports both the SQL Native Client and SQLOLEDB providers. The SQL Native Client provider is recommended, because it supports new SQL Server 2005 features such as the xml data type.

SQLXML Managed Classes

SQLXML managed classes expose SQLXML 4.0 functionality within .NET applications. The SQLXML managed classes provide methods to execute commands (SqlXmlCommand), create parameters for commands (SqlXmlParameter), and interact with the DataSet class (SqlXmlAdapter). These classes are described in the following subsections.

SqlXmlCommand

The SqlXmlCommand class executes a T-SQL command, stored procedure, XPath command, XML template file, UpdateGram, or DiffGram against a database. (Update-Grams and DiffGrams are discussed later in this chapter.)

The constructor for the SqlXmlCommand object is:

```
SqlXmlCommand(string connectionString)
```

where *connectionString* is an OLE DB connection string identifying the provider, server, database, and login information. For example:

```
Provider=SQLNCLI;Server=(local);database=AdventureWorks;Integrated Security=SSPI
```

You should normally set the Provider property of the connection to SQLNCLI, because the SQL Native Client data provider supports new SQL Server 2005 features such as the xml data type.

The SqlXmlCommand class has the public methods described in Table 6-3.

Table 6-3. SqlXmlCommand class public methods

Method	Description
ClearParameters( )	Removes SqlXmlParameter objects created for the command object
CreateParameter( )	Creates and returns a SqlXmlParameter object for the command object
ExecuteNonQuery( )	Executes the command and returns nothing
ExecuteStream( )	Returns a new Stream object containing the results of a query
ExecuteToStream(Stream)	Returns results to an existing Stream object
ExecuteXmlReader( )	Returns an XmlReader object containing the results of a query

The SqlXmlCommand class has the public properties described in Table 6-4.

Table 6-4. SqlXmlCommand class public properties

Property	Description
BasePath	A directory path used to resolve a relative mapping schema path (specified by the SchemaPath property), a relative XSL file path (specified by the XslPath property), or an external schema reference in an XML template (specified using the mapping-schema attribute).
ClientSideXml	Specifies whether the result set is converted to XML on the client side (middle tier).
CommandStream	A file containing the text of the command to execute. If a CommandStream file is used, only DiffGram, Template, and UpdateGram update CommandType values are allowed.
CommandText	The command text to execute. You can execute stored procedures with the SqlXmlCommand object by specifying the command text as follows: `EXEC storedProcedureName [ ? [ , ... n] ]` where the question mark (?) represents one or more parameters: instances of the SqlXmlParameter class, discussed in the next section.

Table 6-4. SqlXmlCommand class public properties (continued)

Property	Description
CommandType	The type of command to execute. One of the following values from the SqlXmlCommandType enumeration:
	Sql A T-SQL command (text or stored procedure)
	XPath An XPath command
	Template An XML template
	TemplateFile An XML template at the specified path
	UpdateGram An UpdateGram
	Diffgram A DiffGram
Namespaces	The namespaces for an XPath query.
OutputEncoding	The encoding for the returned stream. UTF-8 is the default.
RootTag	The root-level tag for returned XML results. If the command results in an XML fragment, this property can be used to make it a valid XML document.
SchemaPath	The name of the mapping schema for an XPath query, including the directory path. The path can be absolute or relative. If it is relative, the BasePath property is used to resolve the relative path.
XslPath	The name of the XSL transformation file, including the directory path to apply to the XML result set. The path can be absolute or relative. If it is relative, the BasePath property is used to resolve the relative path.

SqlXmlParameter

SqlXmlCommand objects support parameterized command text and stored procedure queries. Call the CreateParameter( ) method of the SqlXmlCommand class to create a parameter. The SqlXmlParameter class has the public properties described in Table 6-5.

Table 6-5. SqlXmlParameter class public properties

Property	Description
Name	Gets or sets the name of the parameter
Value	Gets or sets the value of the parameter

SqlXmlAdapter

The SqlXmlAdapter class is similar to the DataAdapter class. It provides a mechanism to load XML data into a DataSet and subsequently update the database with changes made offline to the data in the DataSet.

The SqlXmlAdapter has the following public constructors:

```
SqlXmlAdapter(SqlXmlCommand command)
SqlXmlAdapter(string commandText, SqlXmlCommandType commandType,
  string connectionString)
SqlXmlAdapter(Stream commandStream, SqlXmlCommandType commandType,
  string connectionString)
```

The SqlXmlAdapter has the public methods described in Table 6-6.

Table 6-6. SqlXmlAdapter public properties

Method	Description
Fill()	Executes a SqlXmlCommand object and loads the result set returned by that command into a DataSet object.
Update()	Propagates disconnected changes made to the DataSet object back to the database server

Using SQLXML Managed Classes

This section contains examples showing how to use the SQLXML managed classes to retrieve, process, output, and update data.

 Your Visual Studio 2005 projects require a reference to the Microsoft. Data.SqlXml namespace to use SQLXML managed classes.

Executing a query

The following example reads the top two employees from the HumanResources. Employee table in AdventureWorks into a Stream object:

```
using System;
using System.IO;
using Microsoft.Data.SqlXml;

class Program
{
    static void Main(string[] args)
    {
        SqlXmlCommand cmd = new SqlXmlCommand("Provider=SQLNCLI;Server=(local);" +
            "database=AdventureWorks;Integrated Security=SSPI");
        cmd.CommandText = "SELECT TOP 2 * FROM HumanResources.Employee " +
            "FOR XML AUTO";
        Stream stream = cmd.ExecuteStream();

        StreamReader sr = new StreamReader(stream);
        string s = sr.ReadToEnd();

        Console.WriteLine(s);
        Console.WriteLine(Environment.NewLine + "Press any key to continue.");
        Console.ReadKey();
    }
}
```

The example uses the StreamReader class to read the Stream into a string that is then output to the console. Results follow:

```
<HumanResources.Employee EmployeeID="1" NationalIDNumber="14417807"
  ContactID="1209" LoginID="adventure-works\guy1" ManagerID="16"
  Title="Production Technician- WC60" BirthDate="1972-05-15T00:00:00"
  MaritalStatus="M" Gender="M" HireDate="1996-07-31T00:00:00"
  SalariedFlag="0" VacationHours="21" SickLeaveHours="30"
  CurrentFlag="1" rowguid="AAE1D04A-C237-4974-B4D5-935247737718"
  ModifiedDate="2004-07-31T00:00:00"/>
<HumanResources.Employee EmployeeID="2" NationalIDNumber="253022876"
  ContactID="1030" LoginID="adventure-works\kevin0" ManagerID="6"
  Title="Marketing Assistant" BirthDate="1977-06-03T00:00:00"
  MaritalStatus="S" Gender="M" HireDate="1997-02-26T00:00:00"
  SalariedFlag="0" VacationHours="42" SickLeaveHours="41"
  CurrentFlag="1" rowguid="1B480240-95C0-410F-A717-EB29943C8886"
  ModifiedDate="2004-07-31T00:00:00"/>
```

Using parameters in a query

The following example uses a parameterized query to read the data for an employee:

```csharp
using System;
using System.IO;
using Microsoft.Data.SqlXml;

class Program
{
    static void Main(string[] args)
    {
        SqlXmlCommand cmd = new SqlXmlCommand("Provider=SQLNCLI;Server=(local);" +
            "database=AdventureWorks;Integrated Security=SSPI");
        cmd.CommandText = "SELECT * FROM HumanResources.Employee " +
            "WHERE EmployeeID=? FOR XML AUTO";
        // create the parameter to read data for EmployeeID = 5
        SqlXmlParameter parm = cmd.CreateParameter();
        parm.Value = "5";
        Stream stream = cmd.ExecuteStream();

        StreamReader sr = new StreamReader(stream);
        string s = sr.ReadToEnd();

        Console.WriteLine(s);
        Console.WriteLine(Environment.NewLine + "Press any key to continue.");
        Console.ReadKey();
    }
}
```

 OLE DB queries use a question mark (?) placeholder to identify parameters in the query. The parameters in the query string are replaced in the same order in which they are created from the SqlXmlCommand object using the CreateParameter() method.

Formatting with the FOR XML Clause

SQL Server 2005 lets you format the results of a T-SQL query into an XML document on either the server side or client side. You do this by using the SELECT statement's FOR XML clause. You can specify one of three FOR XML modes for server-side XML formatting:

RAW

> A single <row> element is returned in the XML document for each row in the result set.

AUTO

> An XML document is returned with a hierarchy automatically created based on the way the SELECT statement is specified. Nested FOR XML queries can overcome the limitations for the hierarchy that is automatically generated.

EXPLICIT

> An XML document is returned based on *shape information* in the query. Shape information lets you manipulate result set rows into hierarchies. EXPLICIT mode lets you create complex, custom XML structures for the result set.

> Client-side XML formatting formats a SQL query's result set into XML at the client rather than at the SQL Server. There are three client-side FOR XML modes:

RAW

> Identical to server-side RAW mode.

NESTED

> Similar to server-side AUTO mode with the following exceptions:

> A query against a view returns the base table name as the element name when using client-side formatting. When using server-side formatting, the view name is returned as the element name.

> A query against an aliased table returns the base table name as the element name when using client-side formatting. When using server-side formatting, the table alias is returned as the element name.

EXPLICIT

> Similar to server-side EXPLICIT mode.

You cannot use client-side formatting with queries that return multiple result sets. However, in an XML template, you can specify more than one <sql:query> block, each containing a query that returns a single result set.

If you specify FOR XML AUTO mode in a query, XML formatting occurs on the server even if client-side formatting is otherwise specified.

The results follow:

```
<HumanResources.Employee EmployeeID="5" NationalIDNumber="480168528"
  ContactID="1009" LoginID="adventure-works\thierry0" ManagerID="263"
  Title="Tool Designer" BirthDate="1949-08-29T00:00:00" MaritalStatus="M"
  Gender="M" HireDate="1998-01-11T00:00:00" SalariedFlag="0"
```

```
VacationHours="9" SickLeaveHours="24" CurrentFlag="1"
rowguid="1D955171-E773-4FAD-8382-40FD898D5D4D"
ModifiedDate="2004-07-31T00:00:00"/>
```

Handling an exception

The following example shows how to handle a SqlXmlException exception. This
example modifies the example in the preceding section—the parameter expected in
the query string is no longer created and, as a result, the code raises an exception
when executed.

```
using System;
using System.IO;
using Microsoft.Data.SqlXml;

class Program
{
    static void Main(string[] args)
    {
        SqlXmlCommand cmd = new SqlXmlCommand("Provider=SQLNCLI;Server=(local);" +
            "database=AdventureWorks;Integrated Security=SSPI");
        cmd.CommandText = "SELECT * FROM HumanResources.Employee " +
            "WHERE EmployeeID=? FOR XML AUTO";

        try
        {
            stream = cmd.ExecuteStream();

            StreamReader sr = new StreamReader(stream);
            string s = sr.ReadToEnd();

            Console.WriteLine(s);
        }
        catch (SqlXmlException ex)
        {
            Console.WriteLine(ex.Message);
        }

        Console.WriteLine(Environment.NewLine + "Press any key to continue.");
        Console.ReadKey();
    }
}
```

Results are shown in Figure 6-1.

Figure 6-1. Results for exception handling example

Retrieving an XmlReader object

The following example reads the data for the first two employees from the HumanResources.Employee table in AdventureWorks into an XmlTextReader object:

```
using System;
using Microsoft.Data.SqlXml;
using System.Xml;

class Program
{
    static void Main(string[] args)
    {
        SqlXmlCommand cmd = new SqlXmlCommand("Provider=SQLNCLI;Server=(local);" +
            "database=AdventureWorks;Integrated Security=SSPI");
        cmd.CommandText = "SELECT TOP 2 * FROM HumanResources.Employee " +
            "FOR XML AUTO";
        XmlReader xr = cmd.ExecuteXmlReader();

        using (XmlTextWriter xtw = new XmlTextWriter(Console.Out))
        {
            xtw.WriteNode(xr, false);
            xtw.Flush();
        }

        Console.WriteLine(Environment.NewLine + "Press any key to continue.");
        Console.ReadKey();
    }
}
```

The example uses an XmlTextWriter object to output the results in the XmlReader object to the console. Results follow:

```
<HumanResources.Employee EmployeeID="1" NationalIDNumber="14417807"
  ContactID="1209" LoginID="adventure-works\guy1" ManagerID="16"
  Title="Production Technician- WC60" BirthDate="1972-05-15T00:00:00"
  MaritalStatus="M" Gender="M" HireDate="1996-07-31T00:00:00" SalariedFlag="0"
  VacationHours="21" SickLeaveHours="30" CurrentFlag="1"
  rowguid="AAE1D04A-C237-4974-B4D5-935247737718"
  ModifiedDate="2004-07-31T00:00:00" />
<HumanResources.Employee EmployeeID="2" NationalIDNumber="253022876"
  ContactID="1030" LoginID="adventure-works\kevin0" ManagerID="6"
  Title="Marketing Assistant" BirthDate="1977-06-03T00:00:00"
  MaritalStatus="S" Gender="M" HireDate="1997-02-26T00:00:00" SalariedFlag="0"
  VacationHours="42" SickLeaveHours="41" CurrentFlag="1"
  rowguid="1B480240-95C0-410F-A717-EB29943C8886"
  ModifiedDate="2004-07-31T00:00:00" />
```

Processing an XML result set on the client

The following example returns a result set and uses the ClientSideXml property of the SqlXmlCommand object to process the results at the client side. It produces an XML document formatted using the FOR XML NESTED mode.

```
using System;
using System.IO;
using Microsoft.Data.SqlXml;

class Program
{
    static void Main(string[] args)
    {
        Stream stream;
        SqlXmlCommand cmd = new SqlXmlCommand("Provider=SQLNCLI;Server=(local);" +
            "database=AdventureWorks;Integrated Security=SSPI");
        cmd.CommandText = "SELECT TOP 2 * FROM HumanResources.Employee " +
            "FOR XML NESTED";
        cmd.ClientSideXml = true;
        stream = cmd.ExecuteStream();

        StreamReader sr = new StreamReader(stream);
        string s = sr.ReadToEnd();

        Console.WriteLine(s);
        Console.WriteLine(Environment.NewLine + "Press any key to continue.");
        Console.ReadKey();
    }
}
```

You can also specify a stored procedure that returns a regular non-XML result set.
Results follow:

```
<Employee EmployeeID="1" NationalIDNumber="14417807" ContactID="1209"
  LoginID="adventure-works\guy1" ManagerID="16"
  Title="Production Technician - WC60" BirthDate="1972-05-15T00:00:00"
  MaritalStatus="M" Gender="M" HireDate="1996-07-31T00:00:00"
  SalariedFlag="0" VacationHours="21" SickLeaveHours="30" CurrentFlag="1"
  rowguid="AAE1D04A-C237-4974-B4D5-935247737718"
  ModifiedDate="2004-07-31T00:00:00"/>
<Employee EmployeeID="2" NationalIDNumber="253022876" ContactID="1030"
  LoginID="adventure-works\kevin0" ManagerID="6"
  Title="Marketing Assistant" BirthDate="1977-06-03T00:00:00"
  MaritalStatus="S" Gender="M" HireDate="1997-02-26T00:00:00"
  SalariedFlag="0" VacationHours="42" SickLeaveHours="41" CurrentFlag="1"
  rowguid="1B480240-95C0-410F-A717-EB29943C8886"
  ModifiedDate="2004-07-31T00:00:00"/>
```

Filling a DataSet

The following example uses an XmlDataAdapter object to fill a DataSet object:

```
using System;
using Microsoft.Data.SqlXml;
using System.Data;

class Program
{
    static void Main(string[] args)
```

```
        {
            SqlXmlCommand cmd = new SqlXmlCommand("Provider=SQLNCLI;Server=(local);" +
                "database=AdventureWorks;Integrated Security=SSPI");
            cmd.CommandText = "SELECT TOP 2 * FROM HumanResources.Employee " +
                "FOR XML AUTO";

            DataSet ds = new DataSet();
            SqlXmlAdapter da = new SqlXmlAdapter(cmd);
            da.Fill(ds);

            foreach (DataRow row in ds.Tables[0].Rows)
                Console.WriteLine("{0} {1}", row["EmployeeID"], row["Title"]);

            Console.WriteLine(Environment.NewLine + "Press any key to continue.");
            Console.ReadKey();
        }
    }
```

Results are shown in Figure 6-2.

Figure 6-2. Results for filling a DataSet example

Applying an XSLT transformation to the XML result set

The following example applies an XSLT transformation to the XML result set containing the top 10 employees from the HumanResources.Employee table in AdventureWorks. The XSL file named *C:\PSS2005\Employee.xsl* follows:

```
<?xml version='1.0' encoding='UTF-8'?>
<xsl:stylesheet xmlns:xsl="http://www.w3.org/1999/XSL/Transform" version="1.0">
  <xsl:output method="html"/>
  <xsl:template match='*'>
    <xsl:apply-templates />
  </xsl:template>
  <xsl:template match='HumanResources.Employee'>
    <TR>
      <TD><xsl:value-of select='@EmployeeID'/></TD>
      <TD><xsl:value-of select='@Title'/></TD>
    </TR>
  </xsl:template>
  <xsl:template match='/'>
    <HTML>
      <HEAD/>
      <BODY>
       <TABLE>
         <TR>
           <TH>Employee ID</TH>
```

```
        <TH>Title</TH>
      </TR>
      <xsl:apply-templates select='ROOT'/>
    </TABLE>
    </BODY>
  </HTML>
  </xsl:template>
</xsl:stylesheet>
```

The code that generates the HTML file by applying the XSLT file *Employee.xsl* (stored in the *C:\PSS2005* directory) follows:

```
using System;
using System.IO;
using Microsoft.Data.SqlXml;

class Program
{
    static void Main(string[] args)
    {
        SqlXmlCommand cmd = new SqlXmlCommand("Provider=SQLNCLI;Server=(local);" +
            "database=AdventureWorks;Integrated Security=SSPI");
        cmd.CommandText = "SELECT TOP 10 * FROM HumanResources.Employee " +
            "FOR XML AUTO";
        cmd.CommandType = SqlXmlCommandType.Sql;
        cmd.RootTag = "ROOT";
        cmd.XslPath = @"C:\PSS2005\Employee.xsl";

        Stream s = cmd.ExecuteStream();
        byte[] b = new byte[s.Length];
        s.Read(b, 0, b.Length);
        FileStream fs = new FileStream(@"C:\PSS2005\Employee.html",
            FileMode.OpenOrCreate);
        fs.Write(b, 0, b.Length);
        fs.Flush();
    }
}
```

The CommandType property of the SqmXmlCommand object is set to SqlXmlCommandType.Sql from the values described in Table 6-4. This specifies that the SQL command in the CommandText property is processed. The ExecuteStream() method of the SqlXmlCommand object returns the results of executing the command—in this case a SQL query—as a Stream object.

The RootTag property of the SqlXmlCommand object specifies the root element for the XML generated by the query—in this case ROOT, which matches the xsl:apply-templates select element in the XSLT transformation file. The XslPath property specifies the full name of the XSLT transformation file to apply—the path to the file can be absolute or relative.

An excerpt from the resulting HTML file, named *C:\PSS2005\Employee.html*, follows:

```
<HTML>
<HEAD>
<META http-equiv="Content-Type" content="text/html; charset=utf-8">
</HEAD>
<BODY>
<TABLE>
<TR>
<TH>Employee ID</TH>
<TH>Title</TH>
</TR>
<TR>
<TD>1</TD>
<TD>Production Technician - WC60</TD>
</TR>
<TR>
<TD>2</TD>
<TD>Marketing Assistant</TD>
</TR>
<TR>

...

<TR>
<TD>10</TD>
<TD>Production Technician - WC10</TD>
</TR>
</TABLE>
</BODY>
</HTML>
```

Figure 6-3 shows the file displayed in Internet Explorer.

Annotated Mapping Schemas

An XML schema defines the structure of an XML document and any constraints on the data in the document. In an XML schema, the `<xs:schema>` element encloses the schema. The `<xs:schema>` element also contains attributes that define the namespace that the schema is in, as well as namespaces used in the schema. A valid XSD schema is derived from the XML schema namespace at *http://www.w3.org/2001/XMLSchema* and must have the `<xs:schema>` element defined as follows:

```
<xs:schema xmlns:xsd="http://www.w3.org/2001/XMLSchema">
```

Annotations are attributes used to map XML data to database tables and columns in a relational database, and to specify relationships between and constraints on multiple tables within an XSD schema. These mapping schemas let you do the following:

- Use XML template queries against XML views returned by the XSD schema and return the results as an XML document. Template queries are discussed later in this chapter in the section "XML Template Queries."

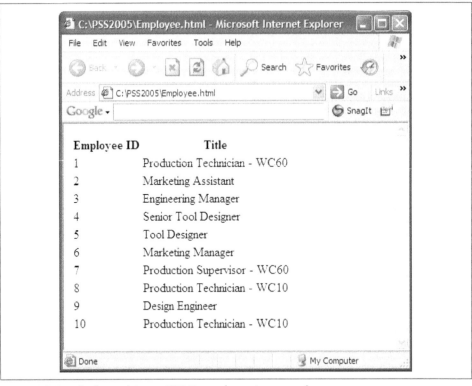

Figure 6-3. Results for applying an XSLT transformation example

- Use UpdateGrams to modify data in a SQL Server database. UpdateGrams are discussed later in this chapter in the section "UpdateGrams."

- Bulk load XML data into a SQL Server database. Bulk loading data is discussed in Chapter 7.

Annotations are defined in the `urn:schemas-microsoft-com:mapping-schema` namespace. Adding this namespace to the `<xs:schema>` element is the easiest way to specify the namespace:

```
<xs:schema xmlns:xs="http://www.w3.org/2001/XMLSchema"
           xmlns:sql="urn:schemas-microsoft-com:mapping-schema">
```

You can specify any prefix (instead of `sql`) for the namespace.

You can easily create an XSD schema using XML Schema Designer in Visual Studio 2005. For example, to create a schema for the `HumanResources.Employee` table in `AdventureWorks`, follow these steps:

1. Create a new a project in Visual Studio 2005.

2. Right-click the project in Solution Explorer and select Add → New Item from the context menu to open the Add New Item dialog box.

3. Select the XML schema template, give it the name Vendor.xsd, and click the Add button. The XML Schema designer surface is opened empty.

4. Open the Server Explorer window by selecting View → Server Explorer from the main menu.

5. Add a data connection to the AdventureWorks database, if it does not exist, by right-clicking the Data Connections node and selecting Add Connection in Server Explorer. Complete the Add Connection dialog box and click the OK button.

6. Drag the Employee (HumanResources) table in Server Explorer onto the XML Schema Designer surface Employee.xsd.

7. Right-click the XML Schema Designer surface and select View Code from the context menu to view the XSD schema that follows:

```xml
<?xml version="1.0" encoding="utf-8"?>
<xs:schema id="Employee"
  targetNamespace="http://tempuri.org/Employee.xsd"
elementFormDefault="qualified"
  xmlns="http://tempuri.org/Employee.xsd"
  xmlns:mstns="http://tempuri.org/Employee.xsd"
  xmlns:xs="http://www.w3.org/2001/XMLSchema"
  xmlns:msdata="urn:schemas-microsoft-com:xml-msdata">
  <xs:element name="Document">
    <xs:complexType>
      <xs:choice minOccurs="0" maxOccurs="unbounded">
        <xs:element name="Employee">
          <xs:complexType>
            <xs:sequence>
              <xs:element name="EmployeeID" type="xs:int" />
              <xs:element name="NationalIDNumber" type="xs:string" />
              <xs:element name="ContactID" type="xs:int" />
              <xs:element name="LoginID" type="xs:string" />
              <xs:element name="ManagerID" type="xs:int" minOccurs="0" />
              <xs:element name="Title" type="xs:string" />
              <xs:element name="BirthDate" type="xs:dateTime" />
              <xs:element name="MaritalStatus" type="xs:string" />
              <xs:element name="Gender" type="xs:string" />
              <xs:element name="HireDate" type="xs:dateTime" />
              <xs:element name="SalariedFlag" type="xs:boolean" />
              <xs:element name="VacationHours" type="xs:short" />
              <xs:element name="SickLeaveHours" type="xs:short" />
              <xs:element name="CurrentFlag" type="xs:boolean" />
              <xs:element name="rowguid" type="xs:string" />
              <xs:element name="ModifiedDate" type="xs:dateTime" />
            </xs:sequence>
          </xs:complexType>
        </xs:element>
      </xs:choice>
    </xs:complexType>
    <xs:unique name="DocumentKey1">
      <xs:selector xpath=".//mstns:Employee" />
```

```
            <xs:field xpath="mstns:EmployeeID" />
          </xs:unique>
        </xs:element>
      </xs:schema>
```

You can add annotations to this XSD schema and remove schema information that you do not need. The following example shows the same schema with `sql:relation` and `sql:field` mappings added and unnecessary information removed. Note the addition of the highlighted mapping-schema namespace in the `xs:schema` element.

```
<xs:schema xmlns:xsd="http://www.w3.org/2001/XMLSchema"
  xmlns:sql="urn:schemas-microsoft-com:mapping-schema">
  <xs:element name="Employee" sql:relation="HumanResources.Employee">
    <xs:complexType>
      <xs:sequence>
        <xs:element name="EmployeeID" type="xs:int" sql:field="EmployeeID" />
        <xs:element name="NationalIDNumber" type="xs:string"
          sql:field="NationalIDNumber" />
        <xs:element name="ContactID" type="xs:int" sql:field="ContactID" />
        <xs:element name="LoginID" type="xs:string" sql:field="LoginID" />
        <xs:element name="ManagerID" type="xs:int" sql:field="ManagerID" />
        <xs:element name="Title" type="xs:string" sql:field="Title" />
        <xs:element name="BirthDate" type="xs:date" sql:field="BirthDate" />
        <xs:element name="MaritalStatus" type="xs:string"
          sql:field="MaritalStatus" />
        <xs:element name="Gender" type="xs:string" sql:field="Gender" />
        <xs:element name="HireDate" type="xs:date" sql:field="HireDate" />
        <xs:element name="SalariedFlag" type="xs:boolean"
          sql:field="SalariedFlag" />
        <xs:element name="VacationHours" type="xs:int"
          sql:field="VacationHours" />
        <xs:element name="SickLeaveHours" type="xs:int"
          sql:field="SickLeaveHours" />
        <xs:element name="CurrentFlag" type="xs:boolean"
          sql:field="CurrentFlag" />
        <xs:element name="rowguid" type="xs:string" sql:field="rowguid" />
        <xs:element name="ModifiedDate" type="xs:date"
          sql:field="ModifiedDate" />
      </xs:sequence>
    </xs:complexType>
  </xs:element>
</xs:schema>
```

If the `sql:field` attribute is not specified for a field element or attribute, that element is automatically mapped to a column that has the same name, if one exists. The annotations in the example are actually unnecessary, because field elements and columns all have the same name.

The case-sensitivity of the table and field names defined by the `sql:relation` and `sql:field` attributes is determined by whether SQL Server is using case-sensitive collation.

Table 6-7 describes the most common mapping schema annotations.

Table 6-7. SQL Server 2005 mapping schema annotations

Annotation	Description
sql:encode	Specifies that an element or attribute mapped to a BLOB-type column is returned as a URL to the field rather than as Base64-encoded data within the XML document.
sql:field	Maps an element to a field in the table specified by the sql:relation attribute for the parent element.
sql:guid	Specifies that a GUID-type column value is used in the UpdateGram for that column rather than the value provided in the UpdateGram.
sql:hide	Hides an element or attribute specified in the schema in the resulting XML document.
sql:identity	Specifies for an identity-type column how the column is updated using an UpdateGram.
sql:inverse	Specifies that the UpdateGram should invert the update order of the parent-child relationship specified in a sql:relationship element. This overcomes primary key/foreign key violations when used with an UpdateGram or bulk load operation.
sql:is-constant	Specifies an element that does not map to a column in a table but is included in the XML document output.
sql:key-fields	Specifies columns that uniquely identify rows within a table.
sql:limit-field	Specifies that an attribute or element contains a limiting value specified using the sql:limit-value annotation.
sql:limit-value	Specifies the limit value in the column specified by the sql:limit-field annotation.
sql:mapped	Specifies whether elements are mapped to a table or column and whether they appear in the XML document output. The annotation takes the value 0 for false or 1 for true.
sql:max-depth	Specifies maximum depth in recursive relationships specified in the schema.
sql:overflow-field	Specifies the column that contains overflow data—unconsumed data from the source XML column.
sql:prefix	Prepends ID, IDREF, and IDREFS with a string prefix to ensure uniqueness within an XML document.
sql:relation	Maps an XML item to the specified table in the database.
sql:relationship	Specifies a relationship for a table (sql:relation) element using parent, child, parent-key, and child-key attributes to define the relationship.

Annotations are used to define the relational hierarchy of the data based on the relationships of the underlying tables. Specify a <sql:relationship> element for each relationship in the <xs:appinfo> element within the <xs:annotation> element in the XSD schema. The following code snippet defines a parent-child relationship between the Sales.Customer and Sales.SalesOrderHeader tables in AdventureWorks:

```
<xsd:annotation>
  <xsd:appinfo>
    <sql:relationship name="Customer-SalesOrderHeader"
      parent="Sales.Customer"
      parent-key="CustomerID"
      child="Sales.SalesOrderHeader"
      child-key="CustomerID" />
  </xsd:appinfo>
</xsd:annotation>
```

Add the <xsd:annotation> element immediately following the <xs:schema> element. Table 6-8 describes annotation attributes used to define an XSD relationship.

Table 6-8. sql:relationship annotation attributes

sql:relationship annotation attribute	Description
name	Unique name within the XSD schema for the relationship.
parent	Specifies the parent table. This element is optional—the parent will be inferred from the hierarchy if the parent attribute is missing.
parent-key	Specifies the parent key. Separate field names with a space if the key has more than one field.
child	Specifies the child table.
child-key	Specifies the child key that maps to the parent key. Separate field names with a space if the key has more than one field.

 For more information about XSD schemas, see Microsoft SQL Server 2005 Books Online.

XML Template Queries

An XML template query is an XML document with one or more T-SQL or XPath queries inside. An XML template query lets you query an XML document using T-SQL or XPath. The syntax is:

```
<rootName xmlns:sql="urn:schemas-microsoft-com:xml-sql" [ sql:xsl="stylesheet" ] >
    [ <sql:header>
        [ <sql:param name="paramName">paramValue</sql:param> [ ... n ] ]
    </sql:header> ]

    <sql:query client-side-xml="n">>
        tsqlQuery [ ... n ]
    </sql:query> [ ... n ]

    <sql:xpath-query mapping-schema="annotatedSchemaFile">
        xpathQuery
    </sql:xpath-query>
</rootname>
```

where:

rootName
    Specifies the name of the top-level element.

stylesheet
    Specifies the name of the XSLT stylesheet to apply to the result set before returning the formatted results to the client. If an XSLT stylesheet is specified, the

results are transformed before they are returned to the client as formatted results.

`<sql:param name="`*paramName*`">`*paramValue*`</sql:param>`

Specifies optional parameter values for parameterized T-SQL queries and stored procedures.

tsqlQuery

Specifies one or more T-SQL statements making up a batch. You can also specify one or more `<sql:query>` elements (i.e., one or more T-SQL statement batches).

annotatedSchemaFile

Specifies a reference to an annotated XSD schema. Annotated XML-Data Reduced (XDR) schemas are also supported for backward compatibility.

xpathQuery

Specifies an XPath query. A discussion about XPath queries is beyond the scope of this book. For information about XPath queries, see *XPath and XPointer* (O'Reilly, 2002) or the W3C XPath Specification at *http://www.w3.org/TR/1999/PR-xpath-19991008.html*.

The following example uses an XML template file containing a T-SQL query to return an XML document containing data about the top two employees in the `HumanResources.Employee` table in `AdventureWorks`. The XML template containing the T-SQL query follows:

```
<ROOT xmlns:sql="urn:schemas-microsoft-com:xml-sql">
  <sql:query>
    SELECT TOP 2 * FROM HumanResources.Employee FOR XML AUTO
  </sql:query>
</ROOT>
```

The code that executes the query in the XML template file (stored in the *C:\PSS2005* directory) follows:

```
using System;
using System.IO;
using Microsoft.Data.SqlXml;

class Program
{
    static void Main(string[] args)
    {
        SqlXmlCommand cmd = new SqlXmlCommand("Provider=SQLNCLI;Server=(local);" +
            "database=AdventureWorks;Integrated Security=SSPI");
        cmd.CommandType = SqlXmlCommandType.TemplateFile;
        cmd.CommandText = @"C:\PSS2005\TopTwoEmployeesTemplate.xml";

        Stream stream = cmd.ExecuteStream();

        StreamReader sr = new StreamReader(stream);
        string s = sr.ReadToEnd();
```

```
            Console.WriteLine(s);
            Console.WriteLine(Environment.NewLine + "Press any key to continue.");
            Console.ReadKey();
        }
    }
}
```

The results follow:

```
<ROOT xmlns:sql="urn:schemas-microsoft-com:xml-sql">
  <HumanResources.Employee EmployeeID="1" NationalIDNumber="14417807"
    ContactID="1209" LoginID="adventure-works\guy1" ManagerID="16"
    Title="Production Technician - WC60" BirthDate="1972-05-15T00:00:00"
    MaritalStatus="M" Gender="M" HireDate="1996-07-31T00:00:00" SalariedFlag="0"
    VacationHours="21" SickLeaveHours="30" CurrentFlag="1"
    rowguid="AAE1D04A-C237-4974-B4D5-935247737718"
    ModifiedDate="2004-07-31T00:00:00"/>
  <HumanResources.Employee EmployeeID="2" NationalIDNumber="253022876"
    ContactID="1030" LoginID="adventure-works\kevin0" ManagerID="6"
    Title="Marketing Assistant" BirthDate="1977-06-03T00:00:00"
    MaritalStatus="S" Gender="M" HireDate="1997-02-26T00:00:00" SalariedFlag="0"
    VacationHours="42" SickLeaveHours="41" CurrentFlag="1"
    rowguid="1B480240-95C0-410F-A717-EB29943C8886"
    ModifiedDate="2004-07-31T00:00:00"/>
</ROOT>
```

The CommandType property of the SqmXmlCommand object is set to SqlXmlCommandType.
TemplateFile from the values described in Table 6-4. This specifies that the template
file at the location specified by the CommandText property is executed. The
ExecuteStream() method of the SqlXmlCommand object returns the results of executing
the command—in this case a query in an XML template file—as a Stream object.

The next example shows how to execute an XPath query against a mapping schema
for the HumanResources.Employee table in the AdventureWorks database. The mapping
schema follows:

```
<xsd:schema xmlns:xsd="http://www.w3.org/2001/XMLSchema"
  xmlns:sql="urn:schemas-microsoft-com:mapping-schema">
  <xsd:element name="Employee" sql:relation="HumanResources.Employee">
    <xsd:complexType>
      <xsd:sequence>
        <xsd:element name="EmployeeID" type="xsd:int" sql:field="EmployeeID" />
        <xsd:element name="NationalIDNumber" type="xsd:string"
          sql:field="NationalIDNumber" />
        <xsd:element name="ContactID" type="xsd:int" sql:field="ContactID" />
        <xsd:element name="LoginID" type="xsd:string" sql:field="LoginID" />
        <xsd:element name="ManagerID" type="xsd:int" sql:field="ManagerID" />
        <xsd:element name="Title" type="xsd:string" sql:field="Title" />
        <xsd:element name="BirthDate" type="xsd:date" sql:field="BirthDate" />
        <xsd:element name="MaritalStatus" type="xsd:string"
          sql:field="MaritalStatus" />
        <xsd:element name="Gender" type="xsd:string" sql:field="Gender" />
        <xsd:element name="HireDate" type="xsd:date" sql:field="HireDate" />
        <xsd:element name="SalariedFlag" type="xsd:boolean"
          sql:field="SalariedFlag" />
```

```
          <xsd:element name="VacationHours" type="xsd:int"
            sql:field="VacationHours" />
          <xsd:element name="SickLeaveHours" type="xsd:int"
            sql:field="SickLeaveHours" />
          <xsd:element name="CurrentFlag" type="xsd:boolean"
            sql:field="CurrentFlag" />
          <xsd:element name="rowguid" type="xsd:string" sql:field="rowguid" />
          <xsd:element name="ModifiedDate" type="xsd:date"
            sql:field="ModifiedDate" />
        </xsd:sequence>
      </xsd:complexType>
    </xsd:element>
  </xsd:schema>
```

The code that returns an XML document containing data for the employee with
EmployeeID = 2 uses an XPath query and the preceding mapping file (stored in the *C:\ PSS2005* directory):

```
using System;
using System.IO;
using Microsoft.Data.SqlXml;

class Program
{
    static void Main(string[] args)
    {
        SqlXmlCommand cmd = new SqlXmlCommand("Provider=SQLNCLI;Server=(local);" +
            "database=AdventureWorks;Integrated Security=SSPI");
        cmd.CommandText = @"Employee[EmployeeID=2]";
        cmd.CommandType = SqlXmlCommandType.XPath;
        cmd.RootTag = "ROOT";
        cmd.SchemaPath = @"C:\PSS2005\Employee.xsd";

        Stream stream = cmd.ExecuteStream();

        StreamReader sr = new StreamReader(stream);
        string s = sr.ReadToEnd();

        Console.WriteLine(s);
        Console.WriteLine(Environment.NewLine + "Press any key to continue.");
        Console.ReadKey();
    }
}
```

The results follow:

```
<?xml version="1.0" encoding="utf-8" ?>
<ROOT>
  <Employee>
    <EmployeeID>2</EmployeeID>
    <NationalIDNumber>253022876</NationalIDNumber>
    <ContactID>1030</ContactID>
    <LoginID>adventure-works\kevin0</LoginID>
    <ManagerID>6</ManagerID>
    <Title>Marketing Assistant</Title>
```

```
      <BirthDate>1977-06-03</BirthDate>
      <MaritalStatus>S</MaritalStatus>
      <Gender>M</Gender>
      <HireDate>1997-02-26</HireDate>
      <SalariedFlag>0</SalariedFlag>
      <VacationHours>42</VacationHours>
      <SickLeaveHours>41</SickLeaveHours>
      <CurrentFlag>1</CurrentFlag>
      <rowguid>1B480240-95C0-410F-A717-EB29943C8886</rowguid>
      <ModifiedDate>2004-07-31</ModifiedDate>
    </Employee>
  </ROOT>
```

The CommandType property of the SqmXmlCommand object is set to SqlXmlCommandType.
Xpath from the values described in Table 6-4. This specifies that the XPath com-
mand in the CommandText property is executed. The ExecuteStream( ) method of the
SqlXmlCommand object returns the results of executing the command—in this case an
XPath query—as a Stream object.

UpdateGrams

An *UpdateGram* is an XML template used to insert, update, or delete data in the
database. An UpdateGram uses mapping information provided in the annotated
XML (XSD or XDR) schema. The UpdateGram format is:

```
<ROOT xmlns:updg="urn:schemas-microsoft-com:xml-updategram">
  <updg:sync [ mapping-schema= "AnnotatedSchemaFile.xml" ] >
    <updg:before>
      ...
    </updg:before>
    <updg:after>
      ...
    </updg:after>
  </updg:sync>
</ROOT>
```

where the following elements are defined in the urn:schemas-microsoft-com:xml-
updategram namespace:

<sync>
Contains one or more pairs of <before> and <after> blocks. These blocks must
be specified as pairs, even if they are empty. An UpdateGram can contain multiple <sync> blocks, each of which is treated as a transactional unit.

mapping-schema= "AnnotatedSchemaFile.xml"
Optionally specifies an annotated XSD or XDR mapping schema file used to
map elements and attributes in the <before> and <after> blocks to tables and
columns in the database.

<before>
Contains the original version (before state) of the record instance.

`<after>`

Contains the updated version (after state) of the record instance.

An UpdateGram uses the operations described in Table 6-9.

Table 6-9. *UpdateGram operations*

Operation	Description
insert	The record is inserted if it appears only in the `<after>` block.
update	The record is updated if it appears in the `<before>` block with a corresponding record in the `<after>` block. The record is updated to the values specified in the `<after>` block.
delete	The record is deleted if it appears only in the `<before>` block.

The UpdateGram mapping to the database can be implicit or explicitly specified using an XSD or XDR schema. Implicit mapping maps each element in the `<before>` and `<after>` elements to a table, and each attribute of the `<before>` and `<after>` elements to a column in the table.

Explicit mapping uses the annotated schema file specified by the mapping-schema attribute of the `<sync>` element to map elements and attributes in the `<before>` and `<after>` elements to tables and columns in the database. The path of the mapping schema file is specified relative to the location of the UpdateGram.

The examples in this section use a table named UpdateGramTable. Create the table using the following T-SQL statement:

```
USE ProgrammingSqlServer2005

CREATE TABLE UpdateGramTable
(
  ID int,
  Name varchar(50)
)
```

The following code executes an UpdateGram. To process the three UpdateGrams that follow the code, replace the full filename of the UpdateGram file passed into the StreamReader constructor with the name of each of the three UpdateGram files in the order in which they appear.

```
using System;
using System.IO;
using Microsoft.Data.SqlXml;

class Program
{
    static void Main(string[] args)
    {
        StreamReader sr = new StreamReader(@"C:\PSS2005\UpdateGram.xml");
        string s = sr.ReadToEnd( );
        sr.Close( );
```

```
            SqlXmlCommand cmd = new SqlXmlCommand("Provider=SQLNCLI;Server=(local);" +
                "database=ProgrammingSqlServer2005;Integrated Security=SSPI");
            cmd.CommandType = SqlXmlCommandType.UpdateGram;
            cmd.CommandText = s;

            cmd.ExecuteNonQuery();

            Console.WriteLine("Press any key to continue.");
            Console.ReadKey();
        }
    }
```

The CommandType property of the SqmXmlCommand object is set to SqlXmlCommandType. UpdateGram from the values described in Table 6-4. This specifies that the Update-Gram in the CommandText property is processed. The ExecuteNonQuery() method of the SqlXmlCommand object executes the command—in this case, processes the Update-Gram—and returns nothing.

The following UpdateGram inserts three records into the table UpdateGramTable:

```
<ROOT xmlns:updg="urn:schemas-microsoft-com:xml-updategram">
  <updg:sync >
    <updg:before>
    </updg:before>
    <updg:after>
      <UpdateGramTable ID="1" Name="Record 1"/>
      <UpdateGramTable ID="2" Name="Record 2"/>
      <UpdateGramTable ID="3" Name="Record 3"/>
    </updg:after>
  </updg:sync>
</ROOT>
```

The following UpdateGram deletes the record with ID = 2 from the table UpdateGramTable:

```
<ROOT xmlns:updg="urn:schemas-microsoft-com:xml-updategram">
  <updg:sync >
    <updg:before>
      <UpdateGramTable ID="2" Name="Record 2"/>
    </updg:before>
    <updg:after>
    </updg:after>
  </updg:sync>
</ROOT>
```

The following UpdateGram updates the record with ID = 3 in the table UpdateGramTable:

```
<ROOT xmlns:updg="urn:schemas-microsoft-com:xml-updategram">
  <updg:sync >
    <updg:before>
      <UpdateGramTable ID="3" Name="Record 3"/>
    </updg:before>
    <updg:after>
```

```
    <UpdateGramTable ID="3" Name="Updated Record 3"/>
      </updg:after>
    </updg:sync>
  </ROOT>
```

DiffGrams

A *DiffGram* is an XML document format introduced with the DataSet in Visual Studio .NET 1.0 and used to synchronize offline changes made to data with a database server or other persistent store using a DataAdapter. The DiffGram format is:

```
<?xml version="1.0"?>
<diffgr:diffgram
  xmlns:msdata="urn:schemas-microsoft-com:xml-msdata"
  xmlns:diffgr="urn:schemas-microsoft-com:xml-diffgram-v1"
  xmlns:xsd="http://www.w3.org/2001/XMLSchema">
    <DataInstance>
      ...
    </DataInstance>
    [<diffgr:before>
      ...
    </diffgr:before>]
</diffgr:diffgram>
```

where:

<DataInstance>

> Contains the most recent version of all data, including unchanged data and any changes made offline by the client

<before>

> Contains the original data instances (records) for data that has been updated or deleted

The DiffGram uses the following XML annotations that are defined in the urn: schemas-microsoft-com:xml-diffgram-v1 namespace:

id

> Associates data instance elements in the <DataInstance> and <before> blocks

hasChanges

> Specified as inserted or modified on elements in the <DataInstance> block for inserted or updated records

parentID

> Specifies parent-child relationships within the <before> block, and is used to determine the order in which updates are processed

A DiffGram identifies whether records are unchanged, deleted, updated, or inserted according to the rules described in Table 6-10.

Table 6-10. DiffGram record status rules

Record Status	Description
unchanged	Element exists in the `<DataInstance>` block but not in the `<before>` block.
inserted	Element exists in the `<DataInstance>` block but not in the `<before>` block. The element in the `<DataInstance>` block has the hasChanges attribute set to inserted.
updated	Element exists both in the `<DataInstance>` block and the `<before>` block. The records are associated using the id annotation, and the hasChanges attribute is set to modified on the element in the `<DataInstance>` block.
deleted	Element exists only in the `<before>` block.

Examples of using a DiffGram from SQLXML 4.0 managed classes to modify data in the database follow. The examples use a table named `DiffGramTable`. Create the table using the following T-SQL statement:

```
USE ProgrammingSqlServer2005

CREATE TABLE DiffGramTable
(
  ID int,
  Name varchar(50)
)
```

The examples in this section also use an XSD annotated mapping schema named `DiffGramTable.xsd` for the table `DiffGramTable`:

```
<xsd:schema xmlns:xsd="http://www.w3.org/2001/XMLSchema"
  xmlns:sql="urn:schemas-microsoft-com:mapping-schema">
  <xsd:element name="DiffGramTable" sql:relation="DiffGramTable">
    <xsd:complexType>
      <xsd:sequence>
        <xsd:element name="ID" type="xsd:int" sql:field="ID" />
        <xsd:element name="Name" type="xsd:string" sql:field="Name" />
      </xsd:sequence>
    </xsd:complexType>
  </xsd:element>
</xsd:schema>
```

The following code executes a DiffGram. To process the three DiffGrams that follow the code, replace the full filename of the DiffGram file passed into the highlighted StreamReader constructor with the name of each of the three DiffGram files in the order in which they appear.

```
using System;
using System.IO;
using Microsoft.Data.SqlXml;

class Program
{
    static void Main(string[] args)
    {
        StreamReader sr = new StreamReader(@"C:\PSS2005\DiffGram.xml");
```

```
        string s = sr.ReadToEnd();
        sr.Close();

        SqlXmlCommand cmd = new SqlXmlCommand("Provider=SQLNCLI;Server=(local);" +
            "database=ProgrammingSqlServer2005;Integrated Security=SSPI");
        cmd.CommandType = SqlXmlCommandType.DiffGram;
        cmd.CommandText = s;

        cmd.ExecuteNonQuery();

        Console.WriteLine("Press any key to continue.");
        Console.ReadKey();
    }
}
```

The CommandType property of the SqmXmlCommand object is set to SqlXmlCommandType.
DiffGram from the values described in Table 6-4. This specifies that the DiffGram in
the CommandText property is processed. The ExecuteNonQuery() method of the
SqlXmlCommand object executes the command—in this case processes the DiffGram—
and returns nothing.

The following DiffGram inserts three records into the table DiffGramTable. Note that
the hasChanges attribute is set to "inserted".

```
<ROOT xmlns:sql="urn:schemas-microsoft-com:xml-sql"
  sql:mapping-schema="c:\PSS2005\DiffGramTable.xsd">
  <diffgr:diffgram xmlns:msdata="urn:schemas-microsoft-com:xml-msdata"
    xmlns:diffgr="urn:schemas-microsoft-com:xml-diffgram-v1">
    <DocumentElement>
      <DiffGramTable diffgr:id="DiffGramTable1" msdata:rowOrder="0"
        diffgr:hasChanges="inserted">
        <ID>1</ID>
        <Name>Record 1</Name>
      </DiffGramTable>
      <DiffGramTable diffgr:id="DiffGramTable2" msdata:rowOrder="1"
        diffgr:hasChanges="inserted">
        <ID>2</ID>
        <Name>Record 2</Name>
      </DiffGramTable>
      <DiffGramTable diffgr:id="DiffGramTable3" msdata:rowOrder="2"
        diffgr:hasChanges="inserted">
        <ID>3</ID>
        <Name>Record 3</Name>
      </DiffGramTable>
    </DocumentElement>
  </diffgr:diffgram>
</ROOT>
```

The following DiffGram deletes the record with ID = 2 from the table DiffGramTable.
In this case, hasChanges is not used.

```
<ROOT xmlns:sql="urn:schemas-microsoft-com:xml-sql"
  sql:mapping-schema="c:\PSS2005\DiffGramTable.xsd">
  <diffgr:diffgram xmlns:msdata="urn:schemas-microsoft-com:xml-msdata"
```

```
    xmlns:diffgr="urn:schemas-microsoft-com:xml-diffgram-v1">
    <DocumentElement>
    </DocumentElement>
    <diffgr:before>
      <DiffGramTable diffgr:id="DiffGramTable2" msdata:rowOrder="1">
        <ID>2</ID>
        <Name>Record 2</Name>
      </DiffGramTable>
    </diffgr:before>
  </diffgr:diffgram>
</ROOT>
```

The following UpdateGram updates the record with ID = 3 in the table
UpdateGramTable. Here, hasChanges is set to ="modified".

```
<ROOT xmlns:sql="urn:schemas-microsoft-com:xml-sql"
  sql:mapping-schema="c:\PSS2005\DiffGramTable.xsd">
  <diffgr:diffgram xmlns:msdata="urn:schemas-microsoft-com:xml-msdata"
  xmlns:diffgr="urn:schemas-microsoft-com:xml-diffgram-v1">
    <DocumentElement>
      <DiffGramTable diffgr:id="DiffGramTable2" msdata:rowOrder="1"
        diffgr:hasChanges="modified">
        <ID>3</ID>
        <Name>Updated Record 3</Name>
      </DiffGramTable>
    </DocumentElement>
    <diffgr:before>
      <DiffGramTable diffgr:id="DiffGramTable2" msdata:rowOrder="1">
        <ID>3</ID>
        <Name>Record 3</Name>
      </DiffGramTable>
    </diffgr:before>
  </diffgr:diffgram>
</ROOT>
```

Exception Message Box

The exception message box API is installed with the SQL Server 2005 graphical components. It is implemented in the ExceptionMessageBox class in the Microsoft.
SqlServer.MessageBox namespace and enhances the standard message box implemented in the System.Windows.Forms.MessageBox class. The ExceptionMessageBox class
includes the following enhanced functionality:

- You can display up to five custom buttons.
- You can display custom text and symbols in the message box.
- The user can copy all information from the message box to the clipboard.
- You can display underlying error information in a hierarchical tree view, which
  the user can navigate.

- The user can decide whether the message should be displayed for subsequent occurrences of the same exception.

- The user can access online help for the exception by using a help link associated with the exception.

The following example shows how to use the exception message box within a .NET application. The example executes a RAISERROR T-SQL statement as the source of the error.

1. From Visual Studio 2005 main menu, select File → New → Project and create a new Windows Application project. Name the project ExceptionMessageBoxProject.

2. Add a reference to the Microsoft.ExceptionMessageBox.dll assembly. You might have to browse for it—the default installation directory is *C:\Program Files\ Microsoft SQL Server\90\SDK\Assemblies*.

3. Add a using directive for the exception message box namespace to Form1.cs:

   ```
   using Microsoft.SqlServer.MessageBox;
   ```

4. Add a button named raiseExceptionButton to Form1. In the click event handler for the button, add code to raise a SQL server error using the RAISERROR T-SQL statement in a try block and code to display the exception message box in the catch block. The complete code for this example follows:

   ```
   using System;
   using System.Collections.Generic;
   using System.ComponentModel;
   using System.Data;
   using System.Drawing;
   using System.Text;
   using System.Windows.Forms;

   using Microsoft.SqlServer.MessageBox;
   using System.Data.SqlClient;

   namespace ExceptionMesageBoxProject
   {
       public partial class Form1 : Form
       {
           public Form1()
           {
               InitializeComponent();
           }

           private void raiseExceptionButton_Click(object sender, EventArgs e)
           {
               SqlConnection conn = new SqlConnection("Data Source=(local);" +
                   "Integrated Security=SSPI;Initial Catalog=AdventureWorks");
               conn.Open();

               SqlCommand cmd = new SqlCommand(
                   "RAISEERROR('Test error', 15, 1)", conn);
   ```

```
                    try
                    {
                        cmd.ExecuteNonQuery( );
                    }
                    catch (Exception ex)
                    {
                        // create the exception message box and set some options
                        ExceptionMessageBox emb = new ExceptionMessageBox(ex);
                        emb.Buttons = ExceptionMessageBoxButtons.Custom;
                        emb.SetButtonText("Custom Button 1", "Custom Button 2",
                            "Custom Button 3");
                        emb.DefaultButton = ExceptionMessageBoxDefaultButton.Button2;
                        emb.Symbol = ExceptionMessageBoxSymbol.Question;
                        emb.ShowCheckBox = true;
                        emb.Show(this);

                        // display the button that was clicked
                        MessageBox.Show("You clicked " +
                            emb.CustomDialogResult.ToString( ));
                    }
                    finally
                    {
                        conn.Close( );
                    }
                }
            }
        }
```
5. Run the example. When you click the button, the exception message box is displayed, as shown in Figure 6-4.

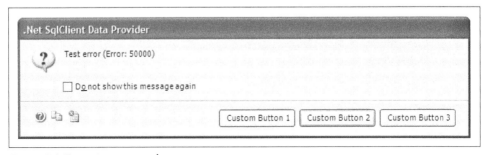

Figure 6-4. Exception message box

The Show( ) method of the ExceptionMessageBox class takes the parent window (type IWin32Window) as its only argument. Passing this as the parent makes the exception message box a child of the active window—this is usually the desired behavior.

You can specify up to five custom buttons using overloads of the ExceptionMessageBox constructor or using the overloaded SetButtonText() method—both take the button text for up to five custom buttons as arguments. The CustomDialogResult property indicates which custom button was clicked.

This example displays the optional checkbox on the exception message box. The checkbox lets the user control whether the message box is displayed for subsequent occurrences of the same exception.

Clicking the Show Technical Details icon (rightmost icon in the toolbar at the bottom left of the message box) brings up the Advanced Information dialog box, containing a hierarchy of error information that the user can drill down through, as shown in Figure 6-5.

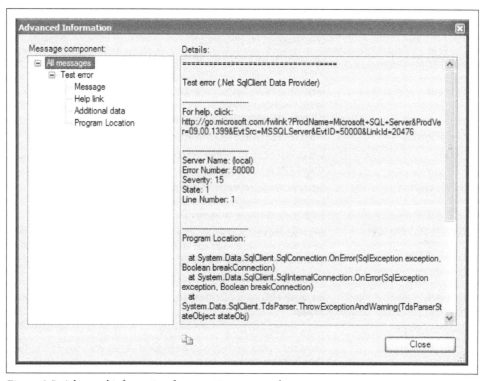

Figure 6-5. Advanced information for exception message box

An ExceptionMessageBox instance has public properties that let you control its appearance and functionality, as described in Table 6-11.

Table 6-11. ExceptionMessageBox instance properties

Property	Description
Beep	Gets or sets whether to play a sound when the message box is displayed.
Buttons	Gets or sets the buttons to display in the message box. A value from the ExceptionMessageBoxButtons enumeration.
Caption	Gets or sets the caption for the exception message box.
CheckBoxRegistryKey	Gets or sets the registry key that specifies the initial checkbox value if the ShowCheckBox property is true. This property is used together with the CheckBoxRegistryValue property.
CheckBoxRegistryMeansDo NotShowDialog	Gets or sets whether the registry value indicated by the CheckBoxRegistryKey and CheckBoxRegistryValue properties indicates that the user decided not to view the message.
CheckBoxRegistryValue	Gets or sets the registry value that specifies the initial checkbox value if the ShowCheckBox property is true. This property is used together with the CheckBoxRegistryKey property.
CheckBoxText	Gets or sets the text to display for the checkbox on the exception message box when the ShowCheckbox property is true.
CustomDialogResult	Gets the custom message box button that was clicked. This is a value from the ExceptionMessageBoxDialogResult enumeration. None is returned if the Buttons property is not set to ExceptionMessageBoxButtons.Custom.
CustomSymbol	Gets or sets a Bitmap to use as the symbol on the message box.
Data	Gets an IDictionary interface for help link and advanced information details associated with the top-level message.
DefaultButton	Gets or sets the default button in the message box when Buttons is ExceptionMessageBoxButtons.Custom. A value from the ExceptionMessageBoxDefaultButton enumeration.
DefaultDialogResult	Gets or sets the value as a member of the DialogResult enumeration returned by the Show( ) method when the user has specified not to show the dialog box for subsequent occurrences of the same message.
Font	Gets or sets the font used in the message box.
HelpLink	Gets or sets a link to a help file or web page as help as additional help to the top-level message.
InnerException	Gets or sets the inner exception of the message box as an Exception instance.
IsCheckBoxChecked	Gets or sets whether the checkbox on the exception message box is checked when the ShowCheckboxProperty is true.
Message	Gets or sets the exception (as an Exception instance) for the message box.
MessageLevelDefault	Gets or sets the number of message levels to display in the message box.
Options	Gets or sets display options for the message box using values in the ExceptionMessageBoxOptions enumeration.

Table 6-11. ExceptionMessageBox instance properties (continued)

Property	Description
ShowCheckBox	Gets or sets whether to show the checkbox on the exception message box—the check-box lets the user control whether the message box is displayed for subsequent occur-rences of the same exception.
ShowToolbar	Gets or sets whether to display the toolbar with the help, copy, and show advanced information buttons.
Symbol	Gets or sets the symbol to display in the message box using a value from the ExceptionMessageBoxSymbol enumeration.
Text	Gets or sets the text to display in the message box.
UseOwnerFont	Gets or sets whether to retrieve and use the font of the parent window as the font for the message box.

CHAPTER 7

XML Data

SQL Server 2005 provides extensive support for XML data storage and processing. You can store XML documents and fragments natively as columns and T-SQL variables of the new xml data type. xml data type columns can be indexed, typed according to an XML schema, and manipulated using XQuery and XML Data Manipulation Language (DML).

A relational model is particularly suited to data that is highly structured with a well-known, well-defined schema. XML data, on the other hand, is suitable to handling data with a flexible, evolving, or unknown structure. XML is also well suited to storing data that represents a containment hierarchy.

Some reasons to store data as XML include the following:

- Using the administrative capabilities of SQL Server to manage your XML data
- Efficiently sharing, querying, and making fine-grained modifications to your XML data
- Ensuring that data is validated against an existing XML schema

In addition to natively storing XML data, SQL Server 2005 lets you map relational data to XML data using XQuery extension functions and map XML data to relational data using the FOR XML clause.

SQL Server 2005 includes SQLXML 4.0. This extends and enhances the client-side XML functionality introduced in SQLXML 3.0, which shipped as a web release after the release of SQL Server 2000.

xml Data Type

The new xml data type supports storing both XML documents and fragments in the database. An XML fragment is an XML instance that does not have a single top-level (root) element. You can create columns, parameters, and variables of the new xml type and store XML instances in them. xml data type instances have a maximum size of 2GB.

An XML schema collection can be associated with a column, parameter, or variable of xml data type. An xml data type with an associated schema is referred to as being *typed*. The XML schema validates xml data type instances against constraints and provides data type information about the elements and attributes in the instance. The schema also helps SQL Server optimize data storage. The XML schema collection must be registered with SQL Server before it can be used to create typed xml instances. Registration is described in the "Managing XML Schema Collections" section later in this chapter.

If you want to use xml data type query methods against xml data type columns or variables, or want to create or rebuild indexes on XML data type columns, you must set the SQL Server 2005 database configuration options listed in Table 7-1. By default, the values are set as required. They may be changed using the SET statement. You can check the values for each database by executing the following T-SQL query:

```
SELECT * FROM sys.databases
```

Table 7-1. SQL Server 2005 database configuration option settings for using xml data type query methods

SET option	Required value
ANSI_NULLS	ON
ANSI_PADDING	ON
ANSI_WARNINGS	ON
ARITHABORT	ON
CONCAT_NULL_YIELDS_NULL	ON
NUMERIC_ROUNDABORT	OFF
QUOTED_IDENTIFIER	ON

Creating xml Data Type Columns and Variables

The following subsections describe how to create xml data type columns and T-SQL variables.

Columns

Use the CREATE TABLE statement to create a table that contains one or more xml data type columns. The syntax for creating a table with an xml data type column is:

```
CREATE TABLE table_name (
   ...

  xml_column_name xml
  [ [DOCUMENT | CONTENT] (schema_name.xml_schema_collection_name ) ],

   ...
)
```

where:

table_name
> The name of the table in the database.

xml_column_name
> The name of the xml data type column in the table.

[DOCUMENT | CONTENT]
> The DOCUMENT facet constrains the typed xml data type instance to allow only a single top-level element.
>
> The CONTENT facet explicitly allows the typed xml data type instance to have zero or more top-level elements and text nodes in top-level elements. The default is CONTENT.

schema_name
> The XML schema in the XML schema collection to associate with the xml data type column.

xml_schema_collection_name
> The name of an existing XML schema collection.

The following example creates a table named xmlTest that has an untyped xml data type column named xmlCol. The example also creates a clustered primary key on the ID column for use in later examples.

```
USE ProgrammingSqlServer2005

CREATE TABLE xmlTable
(
  ID int NOT NULL,
  xmlCol xml,
CONSTRAINT PK_xmlTable
  PRIMARY KEY CLUSTERED (ID)
)
```

You can query the sys.columns catalog view to get information about the xml data type columns in a database. The following query returns the xml data type columns in a database:

```
USE AdventureWorks

SELECT o.name, c.* FROM sys.columns c
JOIN sys.objects o ON c.object_id = o.object_id
WHERE EXISTS
    (SELECT * FROM sys.types t
    WHERE c.system_type_id = t.system_type_id AND
    name='xml')
```

Partial results for running the query against the AdventureWorks database are shown in Figure 7-1.

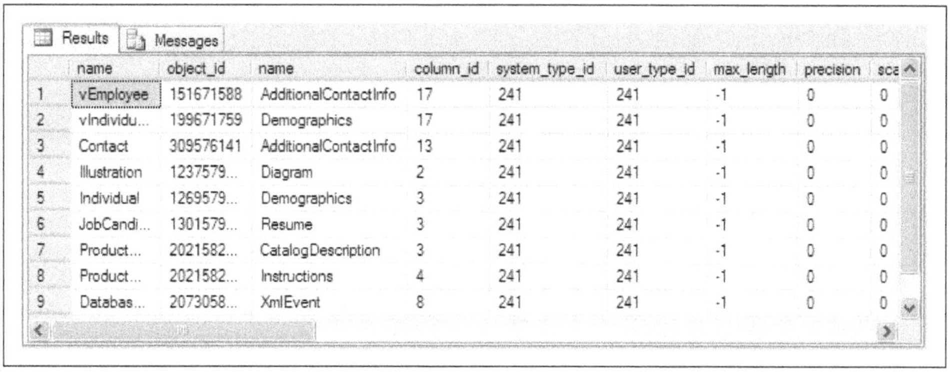

Results | Messages

name	object_id	name	column_id	system_type_id	user_type_id	max_length	precision	sca
1	vEmployee	151671588	AdditionalContactInfo	17	241	241	-1	0	0
2	vIndividu...	199671759	Demographics	17	241	241	-1	0	0
3	Contact	309576141	AdditionalContactInfo	13	241	241	-1	0	0
4	Illustration	1237579...	Diagram	2	241	241	-1	0	0
5	Individual	1269579...	Demographics	3	241	241	-1	0	0
6	JobCandi...	1301579...	Resume	3	241	241	-1	0	0
7	Product...	2021582...	CatalogDescription	3	241	241	-1	0	0
8	Product...	2021582...	Instructions	4	241	241	-1	0	0
9	Databas...	2073058...	XmlEvent	8	241	241	-1	0	0

Figure 7-1. Results for sys.columns catalog view example

This query joins the sys.columns catalog view to the sys.objects catalog view to return the table or view that the xml data type column belongs to as the first column in the result set. The EXISTS clause filters the results to include only xml data types.

Variables

The DECLARE statement is used to create T-SQL variables. The syntax for creating an xml data type variable is:

```
DECLARE variable_name [AS] xml
    [ ( [ DOCUMENT | CONTENT] schema_name.xml_schema_collection_name ) ]
```

where:

variable_name

> The name of the xml data type variable. The variable name must be prefixed with an ampersand (@).

The other parameters are the same as those discussed in the preceding "Columns" section.

The following example uses an xml data type variable to insert a row into the xmlTable created in the preceding "Columns" section:

```
USE ProgrammingSqlServer2005

DECLARE @xmlVar xml
SET @xmlVar = '<rootNode><childElement/></rootNode>'

INSERT INTO xmlTable (ID, xmlCol)
VALUES (1, @xmlVar)
```

The following example creates a stored procedure to modify a row in the xmlTable table:

```
USE ProgrammingSqlServer2005
GO
```

```
CREATE PROCEDURE updateXmlTable
    @ID int,
    @xmlCol xml
AS
BEGIN
    UPDATE xmlTable
    SET xmlCol = @xmlCol
    WHERE ID = @ID
END
```

Execute the stored procedure using the following code to update the xmlCol value for the row with ID = 1:

```
USE ProgrammingSqlServer2005

SELECT * FROM xmlTable

EXEC updateXmlTable 1, '<newRootNode><newChildElement/></newRootNode>'

SELECT * FROM xmlTable
```

The before and after result sets returned by the query are shown in Figure 7-2.

Figure 7-2. Result sets for stored procedure using xml data type example

Limitations

The xml data type has the following limitations:

- It cannot be stored in a sql_variant instance.
- It cannot be cast or converted to the text or ntext data types.
- It does not support PRIMARY KEY, FOREIGN KEY, UNIQUE, COLLATE, or RULE constraints.
- Only string data types can be cast to an xml data type.
- It cannot be compared or sorted and, as a result, cannot be used in a GROUP BY clause.
- It cannot be used in distributed partitioned views. Partitioned views join horizontally partitioned data from a set of member tables, making it appear as one table. In a distributed partitioned view, at least one of the tables resides on a remote server instance.

- It cannot be used as a parameter to any scalar built-in function other than ISNULL, COALESCE, or DATALENGTH.
- It cannot be used as a key column in an index.
- XML declaration processing instructions (PIs) (<?xml ... ?>) are not preserved when the XML instance is stored in the database. All other PIs in the XML instance are preserved.
- The order of attributes in XML instances stored in xml type columns is not preserved.
- By default, insignificant whitespace is not preserved. Whitespace can be preserved for an xml data type instance by specifying the optional style argument to the CONVERT function.
- Single quotation marks (') and double quotation marks (") around attribute values are not preserved because the data is stored as name/value pairs in the database.
- Namespace prefixes are not preserved and may change when xml data type instances are retrieved.

Creating xml Data Type Instances

You can create instances of XML data by casting or converting from strings. You can even take advantage of implicit casting by simply using a string in place of an xml type value. The next two subsections go into more detail on these topics, and the third shows you how to bulk load XML data. A fourth way to create a value of xml type is to issue a SELECT statement with a FOR XML clause. You'll find that method discussed in detail in "XML Results Using the FOR XML Clause" later in this chapter.

Casting and Converting Strings

You can cast or convert (CONVERT function) any string data type instance—[n][var]char, [n]text, varbinary, and image—to an xml data type instance. Untyped data is checked to ensure that it is well formed. Instances of typed XML data are validated against the associated schema.

The XML parser discards insignificant whitespace when converting string data types to xml data types when either of the following is true:

- The xml:space attribute is not defined on an element or its ancestors.
- The xml:space attribute defined on an element or one of its ancestors has the value of default.

You can override the default whitespace handling behavior by setting the optional style (third) parameter of the CONVERT function to 1. You cannot override the default whitespace handling when using the CAST function to cast a string data type instance to an xml data type instance.

The following example inserts a row into the xmlTable table created in the "Creating xml Data Type Columns and Variables" section earlier in this chapter. The example specifies the style attribute (third argument) of the CONVERT function to preserve whitespace when converting a string to an xml data type instance.

```
USE ProgrammingSqlServer2005

INSERT INTO xmlTable (ID, xmlCol)
VALUES (2, CONVERT(xml, '<rootNode2>  <childElement/>  </rootNode2>', 1))
```

If the style argument is not specified or set to 0, the xml data type instance will be stripped of whitespace and stored as follows:

```
<rootNode2><childElement/></rootNode2>
```

Constant Assignment

A string constant can be used where an xml data type instance is expected. An implicit cast to the xml data type is performed. If the xml data type is typed, the XML in the string is validated against the associated XML schema. The following example implicitly casts a string to an xml data type variable:

```
DECLARE @xmlVar xml
SET @xmlVar = '<rootNode><childElement/></rootNode>'

SELECT @xmlVar
```

The xml data type instance is returned as shown in Figure 7-3.

Figure 7-3. Results for xml constant assignment example

Bulk Loading Data with OPENROWSET

Enhanced OPENROWSET functionality in SQL Server 2005 lets you bulk load XML from files into xml data type columns. The syntax for the OPENROWSET statement for bulk loading data is as follows:

```
OPENROWSET
(BULK 'data_file',
      { FORMATFILE = 'format_file_path' [ <bulk_options> ]
      | SINGLE_BLOB | SINGLE_CLOB | SINGLE_NCLOB }
} )
```

```
<bulk_options> ::=
    [ , CODEPAGE = { 'ACP' | 'OEM' | 'RAW' | 'code_page' }]
    [ , ERRORFILE = 'file_name' ]
    [ , FIRSTROW = first_row ]
    [ , LASTROW = last_row ]
    [ , MAXERRORS = maximum_errors ]
    [ , ROWS_PER_BATCH = rows_per_batch ]
```

where:

BULK *'data_file'*

Uses a BULK rowset provider from the data file with the full path specified by *data_file*.

FORMATFILE

Specifies the full path of the format file—a file that defines column types in the result set. XML and non-XML format file types are supported. The non-XML format file is the same as that used with bcp.exe or the BULK INSERT statement. See Microsoft SQL Server 2005 Books Online for more information.

The format file is not needed when SINGLE_BLOB, SINGLE_CLOB, or SINGLE_NCLOB is specified.

<bulk_options>

Specifies one or more of the following options for the BULK option:

CODEPAGE = { 'ACP' | 'OEM' | 'RAW' | 'code_page' }

The codepage of the data in the data file. CODEPAGE is relevant only if the data contains char, varchar, or text columns with character values less than 32 or greater than 127.

ERRORFILE

The full path to the file used to log nonconforming rows—rows that are not loaded.

FIRSTROW

The number of the first row to load. The default value is 1, meaning the first row in the data file.

LASTROW

The number of the last row to load. The default value is 0, meaning the last row in the data file.

MAXERRORS

The maximum number of syntax errors or nonconforming rows before OPENROWSET returns an error. The default value is 10.

ROWS_PER_BATCH

OPENROWSET always bulk loads a data file as a single batch. ROWS_PER_BATCH specifies the approximate number of rows in the data file and is used by the query processor as a hint for allocating resources in the query plan. The default value is 0, meaning that ROWS_PER_BATCH is not known.

SINGLE_BLOB
> Returns the contents of the data file as a single-column, single-row result set of the varbinary(max) data type.

SINGLE_CLOB
> The data file is read as ASCII and returned as a single-column, single-row result set of the varchar(max) data type.

SINGLE_NCLOB
> The data file is read as UNICODE and returned as a single-column, single-row result set of the nvarchar(max) data type.

The following example bulk loads data from the following tab-delimited file *OpenRowSetData.txt*. Make sure that the ID and ValueCol values are separated with a tab.

```
1    Value 1
2    Value 2
3    Value 3
4    Value 4
```

First create the table, OpenRowSetTable, that will be the destination for the bulk-loaded data by executing the following statement:

```
USE ProgrammingSqlServer2005

CREATE TABLE OpenRowSetTable
(
  ID int,
  ValueCol varchar(50)
)
```

Create a non-XML format file named OpenRowSetData.fmt that describes the data being bulk loaded:

```
9.0
2
1    SQLCHAR    0    12    "\t"      1    ID           ""
2    SQLCHAR    0    50    "\r\n"    2    ValueCol     SQL_Latin1_General_CP1_CI_AS
```

Executing the following OPENROWSET statement loads the data using the non-XML format file into the OpenRowSetTable table:

```
INSERT INTO OpenRowSetTable(ID, ValueCol)
SELECT rs.ID, rs.ValueCol
FROM OPENROWSET( BULK N'C:\PSS2005\OpenRowSet\OpenRowSetData.txt',
    FORMATFILE = N'C:\PSS2005\OpenRowSet\OpenRowSetData.fmt') AS rs
```

Examining the OpenRowSetTable table reveals four rows, as shown in Figure 7-4.

Next, you will bulk load the data from the text file to the OpenRowSetTable table using an XML format file. Create the following XML format file and name it *OpenRowSetData.xml*:

```
<?xml version="1.0"?>
<BCPFORMAT xmlns="http://schemas.microsoft.com/sqlserver/2004/bulkload/
  format" xmlns:xsi="http://www.w3.org/2001/XMLSchema-instance">
 <RECORD>
  <FIELD ID="1" xsi:type="CharTerm" TERMINATOR="\t" MAX_LENGTH="12"/>
  <FIELD ID="2" xsi:type="CharTerm" TERMINATOR="\r\n" MAX_LENGTH="50"
    COLLATION="SQL_Latin1_General_CP1_CI_AS"/>
 </RECORD>
 <ROW>
  <COLUMN SOURCE="1" NAME="ID" xsi:type="SQLINT"/>
  <COLUMN SOURCE="2" NAME="ValueCol" xsi:type="SQLVARYCHAR"/>
 </ROW>
</BCPFORMAT>
```

Bulk load the data using the XML format file into the OpenRowSetTable table using the same statement as before but specifying the XML format file:

```
INSERT INTO OpenRowSetTable(ID, ValueCol)
SELECT rs.ID, rs.ValueCol
```

Figure 7-4. Results for bulk load example

```
FROM OPENROWSET( BULK N'C:\PSS2005\OpenRowSet\OpenRowSetData.txt',
    FORMATFILE = N'C:\PSS2005\OpenRowSet\OpenRowSetData.xml') AS rs
```

The OpenRowSetTable now contains eight rows.

XML Data Type Methods

The xml data type provides helper methods to query xml data type columns and variables. Internally, the xml data type methods are treated as subqueries. As a result, an xml data type method cannot be used in a PRINT statement or in a GROUP BY clause.

The examples in this section use a table called xmldtmTable. Create this table and add two rows to it by executing the following statement:

```
USE ProgrammingSqlServer2005

CREATE TABLE xmldtmTable
(
  ID int,
  xmlCol xml,
CONSTRAINT PK_xmldtmTable
  PRIMARY KEY CLUSTERED (ID)
)

INSERT INTO xmldtmTable (ID, xmlCol)
VALUES (1, '<root><childElement1 value="1"/><childElement2 value="2"/></root>')

INSERT INTO xmldtmTable (ID, xmlCol)
VALUES (2, '<root><childElement value="1"/><childElement value="2"/></root>')
```

The T-SQL statement creates a table with the two rows shown in Figure 7-5.

	ID	xmlCol
▶	1	<root><childElement1 value="1" /><childElement2 value="2" /></root>
	2	<root><childElement value="1" /><childElement value="2" /></root>
*	NULL	NULL

Figure 7-5. Results for XML data type methods example

The xml data type methods are described in the following subsections.

query( )

The xml data type query( ) method queries an xml data type instance and returns an untyped xml data type instance. The query( ) syntax is:

```
query(XQuery)
```

where:

XQuery

An XQuery expression that queries for XML nodes in an xml data type instance

The following example uses the query( ) method to extract the childElement2 element from the xml data type instance in the column xmlCol for ID = 1:

```
SELECT xmlCol.query('/root/childElement2')
FROM xmldtmTable
WHERE ID = 1
```

The result set is shown in Figure 7-6.

Figure 7-6. Result set for query() method example

value( )

The xml data type value( ) method performs a query against an xml data type instance and returns a scalar value of SQL data type. The value( ) method syntax is:

```
value(XQuery, SQLType)
```

where:

XQuery

An XQuery expression that retrieves data from the xml data type instance. An error is returned if the expression does not return at least one value.

SQLType

A string literal of the SQL data type to be returned. *SQLType* cannot be an xml, CLR UDT, image, text, ntext, or sql_variant data type.

The value( ) method uses the T-SQL CONVERT function implicitly to convert the result of the XQuery expression to the SQL data type.

The following example uses the value( ) method to extract the attribute value from the xml data type instance in the column xmlCol for ID = 1:

```
SELECT xmlCol.value('(/root/childElement2/@value)[1]', 'int') Value
FROM xmldtmTable
WHERE ID = 1
```

The result set is shown in Figure 7-7.

Figure 7-7. Result set for value() method example

The value( ) operator requires a single operand, so [1] is required to specify the first childElement2. The value attributes could be accessed for other childElement2 elements, if they existed, using the appropriate index.

exist( )

The xml data type exist( ) method returns a value indicating whether an XQuery expression against an xml data type instance returns a nonempty result set. The return value is one of the following:

1

> The XQuery expression returns at least one XML node.

0

> The XQuery expression returns an empty result set.

NULL

> The xml data type instance against which the query is executed is NULL.

The exist( ) method syntax is:

```
exist (XQuery)
```

where:

XQuery

> An XQuery expression

The following example uses the exist( ) method to determine whether the attribute value from the xml data type instance in the column xmlCol is a specified value for ID = 1:

```
SELECT xmlCol.exist('/root/childElement2[@value=1]')
FROM xmldtmTable
WHERE ID = 1
```

The result is shown in Figure 7-8.

Figure 7-8. Result for exist( ) method example

The value of 0 means that the attribute value does not have the value 1. If the exist( ) method is changed to exist('/root/childElement2[@value=2]'), the result is 1.

modify( )

The xml data type modify( ) method modifies the content of an xml data type instance. The modify( ) method syntax follows:

```
modify (XML_DML)
```

where:

XML_DML

An XML Data Manipulation Language statement. The XML DML statement inserts, updates, or deletes nodes from an xml data type instance.

The modify( ) method can only be used in the SET clause of an UPDATE statement.

XML DML and the modify( ) method are discussed in more detail in the "XML Data Manipulation Language" section later in this chapter.

nodes( )

The xml data type nodes( ) method shreds an xml data type instance into relational data by identifying nodes that will be mapped to a new row. The nodes( ) syntax is:

```
nodes (XQuery) as Table(Column)
```

where:

XQuery

An XQuery expression that constructs nodes that are subsequently exposed as a result set

Table

The table name for the result set

Column

The column name for the result set

The following example uses the nodes( ) method to return the value attributes for each child element childElement as an int:

```
SELECT T.C.value('@value', 'int') AS Value
FROM xmldtmTable
```

```
CROSS APPLY xmlCol.nodes('/root/childElement') AS T(C)
WHERE ID = 2
```

The result set is shown in Figure 7-9.

Figure 7-9. Result set for nodes( ) method example

The CROSS APPLY operator lets you invoke the nodes( ) method for each row returned by the query.

Viewing XML Data as Relational Data

OPENXML is a T-SQL function that provides access to in-memory XML documents through a mechanism similar to a relational result set. OPENXML can be used in SELECT and SELECT INTO statements wherever rowset providers such as a table or view, or the OPENROWSET function, can appear.

Before you can use OPENXML, you must call the system stored procedure sp_xml_preparedocument to parse the XML document and return the handle of the parsed internal representation of the document. The document handle is passed to OPENXML, which provides a relational rowset view of the document.

The syntax of the OPENXML keyword is:

```
OPENXML( idoc, rowpattern, [flags] )
  [ WITH ( <schemaDeclaration>  [ ,...n ] | tableName ) ]

<schemaDeclaration> ::=
  colName colType [colPattern | metaProperty]
```

where:

idoc
> The document handle of the internal representation of the XML document. The handle is obtained using the sp_xml_preparedocument system stored procedure.

rowpattern
> The XPath pattern that identifies the nodes in the XML document to be processed as rows.

flags
> Optionally specifies the mapping between the XML data and the rowset, and how the spillover column should be filled. The *flags* option is a byte created from the values described in Table 7-2.

Table 7-2. OPENXML flags option values

Value	Description
0	Defaults to attribute-centric mapping. 0 is the default if the *flags* option is not specified.
1	Attribute-centric mapping—XML attributes map to the columns defined in schemaDeclaration. When combined with XML_ELEMENTS, attribute-centric mapping is applied first followed by element-centric mapping for all unmapped columns.
2	Element-centric mapping—XML elements map to the columns specified in schemaDeclaration. When combined with XML_ATTRIBUTES, element-centric mapping is applied first followed by attribute-centric mapping for all unmapped columns.
8	In the context of retrieval, indicates that consumed data should not be copied to the overflow property @mp : xmltext. This flag can be combined with XML_ATTRIBUTES or XML_ELEMENTS.

schemaDeclaration

The schema definition, in the form where:

colName

The name of the column in the rowset.

colType

The SQL data type of the column in the rowset.

colPattern

An XPath pattern specifying how XML nodes are mapped to columns in the rowset. The *colPattern* mapping overrides the mapping specified by the flags option.

metaProperty

An OPENXML metaproperty that lets you extract information about XML nodes, including relative position and namespace information.

tableName

A table name can be specified instead of a schema definition if a table with the desired schema exists and column patterns are not needed.

If the WITH clause is not specified, the results are returned in *edge table format* instead of a rowset format. An edge table represents an XML document in a single table with the structure described in Table 7-3.

Table 7-3. Edge table schema

Column name	Data type	Description
id	bigint	Unique ID of the XML document node. The root node has an id value of 0. Negative values are reserved.
parentid	bigint	The ID of the parent node. The root node has a parentid value of NULL.
nodetype	int	The node type based on XML DOM node type numbering, where 1 = element node; 2 = attribute node; 3 = text node.
localname	nvarchar	The local name of the element or attribute. The localname value is NULL if the DOM object does not have a name.

Table 7-3. Edge table schema (continued)

Column name	Data type	Description
prefix	nvarchar	The namespace prefix of the node name.
namespaceuri	nvarchar	The namespace URI of the node. The namespaceuri value is NULL if a namespace is not present.
datatype	nvarchar	The actual data type of the element or attribute, and NULL otherwise. The data type is inferred from the inline DTD or schema.
prev	bigint	The node ID of the previous sibling element. The prev value is NULL if there is no direct previous sibling.
text	ntext	The element content or attribute value in text form. The text value is NULL if the edge table does not need a value for the entry.

The syntax of the sp_xml_preparedocument system stored procedure is:

```
sp_xml_preparedocument hDoc OUTPUT
    [ , xmlText ] [ , xpathNamespaces ]
```

where:

hDoc

   The handle to the parsed internal representation of the XML document

xmlText

   The original XML document

xPathNamespaces

   The namespaces used in row and column XPath expressions in OPENXML

Once you have finished using the internal representation of the document, call the sp_xml_removedocument system stored procedure to remove it and invalidate the document handle. The syntax of sp_xml_removedocument is:

```
sp_xml_removedocument hDoc
```

where:

hDoc

   The handle to the parsed internal representation of the XML document

The following example uses OPENXML to extract manufacturing location information for product model 7 from the Instructions xml data type column in the Production. ProductModel table in AdventureWorks. An excerpt of the data follows:

```
<root xmlns="http://schemas.microsoft.com/sqlserver/2004/07/
    adventure-works/ProductModelManuInstructions">
    Adventure Works CyclesFR-210B Instructions for Manufacturing HL Touring
    FrameSummaryThis document contains manufacturing instructions for
    manufacturing the HL Touring Frame, Product Model 7. Instructions are

    ...

    <Location LaborHours="2.5" LotSize="100" MachineHours="3" SetupHours="0.5"
```

```
LocationID="10">Work Center - 10 Frame FormingThe following instructions
pertain to Work Center 10. (Setup hours = .5, Labor Hours = 2.5,
Machine Hours = 3, Lot Sizing = 100)
<step>Insert
  <material>aluminum sheet MS-2341</material>
  into the
  <tool>T-85A framing tool</tool>
  .
</step>

...

</Location>
<Location LaborHours="1.75" LotSize="1" MachineHours="2" SetupHours="0.15"
  LocationID="20">Work Center 20 - Frame WeldingThe following instructions
  pertain to Work Center 20. (Setup hours = .15, Labor Hours = 1.75,
. </Location>

...

</root>
```

Execute the following statement to extract manufacturing location information for product model ID 7 as a tabular result set. Note that you must enter the emphasized line in the example on a single line rather than on two lines, done here only to fit the page width.

```
USE AdventureWorks

DECLARE @idoc int
DECLARE @instructions xml
SET @instructions = (SELECT Instructions FROM Production.ProductModel
  WHERE ProductModelID = 7)

EXEC sp_xml_preparedocument @idoc OUTPUT, @instructions,
  N'<root xmlns:ns="http://schemas.microsoft.com/sqlserver/2004/07/
    adventure-works/ProductModelManuInstructions" />'

SELECT * FROM OPENXML(@idoc, N'/ns:root/ns:Location')
WITH (
  LaborHours float N'@LaborHours',
  LotSize float '@LotSize',
  MachineHours float '@MachineHours',
  SetupHours float '@SetupHours',
  LocationID int '@LocationID'
)

EXEC sp_xml_removedocument @idoc
```

The result set is shown in Figure 7-10.

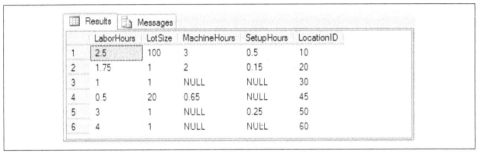

Figure 7-10. Result set for OPENXML example

Indexing XML Data

xml data type instances are stored as binary large objects (BLOB) in xml data type columns. If these columns are not indexed, they must be shredded at runtime for each row in the table to evaluate a query. This can be costly, especially with large xml data type instances or a large number of rows in the table. Building primary and secondary XML indexes on xml data type columns can significantly improve query performance.

 Shredding is the process of mapping and converting an XML document into tables in a relational database.

An xml data type column can have one primary XML index and multiple secondary XML indexes, where:

Primary XML index
> A relational index on the shredded and persisted representation of all tags, values, and paths of XML instances in the xml data type column. The index creates several rows of data for each instance in the column.
>
> A primary XML index requires a clustered index on the primary key of the table containing the xml data type being indexed.

Secondary XML index
> Further improves performance for specific types of queries. A primary XML index must exist on the xml data type column before a secondary XML index can be created.

There are three types of secondary XML indexes:

PATH index
> Optimizes queries based on path expressions

VALUE index
> Optimizes value-based queries for paths that include wildcards or are not fully specified

PROPERTY index

Optimizes queries based on properties in a specific XML instance stored in a column

An XML index can be created only on a single xml data type column. XML indexes cannot be created on the following:

- A non-xml data type column

- An xml data type column in a view

- A table-valued variable with xml data type columns

- An xml data type variable

- A computed xml data type column

A relational index cannot be created on an xml data type column.

You must set the SQL Server 2005 options listed in Table 7-4 when creating or rebuilding an XML index on an xml data type column. If these options are not set, you will not be able to create or rebuild the XML index, and you will not be able to insert values into or modify values in indexed xml data type columns.

Table 7-4. SQL Server 2005 option settings for creating and rebuilding an index on an XML column

SET option	Required value
ANSI_NULLS	ON
ANSI_PADDING	ON
ANSI_WARNINGS	ON
ARITHABORT	ON
CONCAT_NULL_YIELDS_NULL	ON
NUMERIC_ROUNDABORT	OFF
QUOTED_IDENTIFIER	ON

Primary and secondary indexes on xml data type columns are created, changed, and dropped similarly to indexes on non-xml data type columns. The following subsections describe managing indexes on xml data type columns.

Creating an XML Index

The CREATE INDEX statement is used to create a new primary or secondary XML index on an xml data type column. The syntax is:

```
CREATE [ PRIMARY ] XML INDEX index_name
    ON <object> ( xml_column_name )
    [ USING XML INDEX xml_index_name
        [ FOR { VALUE | PATH | PROPERTY } ]
    [ WITH ( <xml_index_option> [ ,...n ] ) ]
[ ; ]
```

```
<object> ::=
{ [ database_name . [ schema_name ] . | schema_name . ] table_name }

<xml_index_option> ::=
{
    PAD_INDEX = { ON | OFF }
  | FILLFACTOR = fillfactor
  | SORT_IN_TEMPDB = { ON | OFF }
  | STATISTICS_NORECOMPUTE = { ON | OFF }
  | DROP_EXISTING = { ON | OFF }
  | ALLOW_ROW_LOCKS = { ON | OFF }
  | ALLOW_PAGE_LOCKS = { ON | OFF }
  | MAXDOP = max_degree_of_parallelism
}
```

where:

[PRIMARY] XML INDEX

> The xml data type column on which to create the index. If PRIMARY is specified, a clustered index is created on the column. Each xml data type column can have one primary and multiple secondary indexes. A primary index must exist on an xml data type column before a secondary index can be created on the column.

index_name

> The name of the index, which must be unique within the table. A primary XML index name cannot begin with the following characters: #, ##, @, or @@.

<object> :: = { [*database_name*. [*schema_name*] . | *schema_name* .] *table_name* }

> The object to be indexed, fully qualified or not, where:

> *database_name*

>> The name of the database.

> *schema_name*

>> The name of the schema to which the table belongs.

> *table_name*

>> The name of the table to be indexed.

xml_column_name

> The xml data type column on which to create the index.

USING XML INDEX *xml_index_name*

> The primary XML index used to create the secondary XML index.

FOR { VALUE | PATH | PROPERTY }

> The type of secondary XML index to create, where:

> VALUE

>> Creates a VALUE secondary XML index on the VALUE, HID, PK, and XID columns of the primary XML index.

PATH

   Creates a PATH secondary XML index on the HID, VALUE, PK, and XID columns
   of the primary XML index.

PROPERTY

   Creates a PROPERTY secondary XML index on the PK, HID, VALUE, and XID columns of the primary XML index and includes the LVALUE and LVALUEBIN columns.

<xml_index_option> ::=

   Options used to create the XML index, where:

PAD_INDEX = { ON | OFF }

   Specifies index padding. If PAD_INDEX is ON, the FILLFACTOR is used to compute the padding (free space) applied to intermediate-level pages of the
   index. The default is OFF.

FILLFACTOR

   Specifies the percentage of free space, as an integer value from 1 to 100, that
   should be left in the leaf level of each index page during index creation or
   change.

SORT_IN_TEMPDB = { ON | OFF }

   Specifies whether to store sort results in tempdb. The default is OFF, meaning
   that intermediate sort results are stored in the same database as the index.

STATISTICS_NORECOMPUTE = { ON | OFF }

   Specifies whether out-of-date distribution statistics are automatically recom-
   puted. The default is OFF, enabling automatic statistics updating.

DROP_EXISTING = { ON | OFF }

   Specifies whether the existing XML index is automatically dropped and
   rebuilt. The default is OFF, meaning that an error is returned if the specified
   index name already exists.

ALLOW_ROW_LOCKS = { ON | OFF }

   Specifies whether row locks are allowed when accessing the index. The
   default is ON, meaning that row locks are allowed.

ALLOW_PAGE_LOCKS = { ON | OFF }

   Specifies whether page locks are allowed when accessing the index. The
   default is ON, meaning that page locks are allowed.

MAX_DOP

   Overrides the maximum degree of parallelism for the duration of the index
   operation by limiting the number of processors used in a parallel plan execution. Parallel indexing operations and parallel query processing are available
   only in SQL Server 2005 Enterprise Edition.

A table must have a clustered primary key with less than 16 columns in it before a
primary XML index can be created.

The following example creates a primary XML index on the `xmlCol` xml data type column in the `xmlTable` table created in the "Creating xml Data Type Columns and Variables" section earlier in this chapter:

```
CREATE PRIMARY XML INDEX xmlColIndex
ON xmlTable(xmlCol)
```

The following example creates a secondary `VALUE` index on the `xmlCol` column:

```
CREATE XML INDEX xmlColValueIndex
ON xmlTable(xmlCol)
USING XML INDEX xmlColIndex
FOR VALUE
```

Altering an XML Index

The `ALTER INDEX` statement is used to modify an existing XML index created using the `CREATE INDEX` statement. The syntax is:

```
ALTER INDEX { index_name | ALL }
    ON <object>
    { REBUILD
        [ WITH ( <rebuild_index_option> [ ,...n ] ) ]
    | DISABLE
    | SET ( <set_index_option> [ ,...n ] )
    }
[ ; ]

<object> ::=
{
    [ database_name. [ schema_name ] . | schema_name. ]
        table_or_view_name
}

<rebuild_index_option > ::=
{
    PAD_INDEX = { ON | OFF }
  | FILLFACTOR = fillfactor
  | SORT_IN_TEMPDB = { ON | OFF }
  | STATISTICS_NORECOMPUTE = { ON | OFF }
  | ALLOW_ROW_LOCKS = { ON | OFF }
  | ALLOW_PAGE_LOCKS = { ON | OFF }
  | MAXDOP = max_degree_of_parallelism
}

<set_index_option>::=
{
    ALLOW_ROW_LOCKS= { ON | OFF }
  | ALLOW_PAGE_LOCKS = { ON | OFF }
  | STATISTICS_NORECOMPUTE = { ON | OFF }
}
```

The arguments are described in the "Creating an XML Index" subsection earlier in this section. You need supply arguments only for index characteristics that you are changing.

Dropping an XML Index

The DROP INDEX statement is used to remove one or more XML indexes from the database. The syntax is:

```
DROP INDEX
{ index_name ON <object> [ ,...n ] }

<object> ::=
{
    [ database_name. [ schema_name ] . | schema_name. ]
        table_or_view_name
}
```

The arguments are described in the "Creating an XML Index" subsection earlier in this section.

The following example drops the secondary value index created on the xmlTable table in the "Creating an XML Index" subsection earlier in this section:

```
DROP INDEX xmlColValueIndex ON xmlTable
```

Viewing XML Indexes

The xml_indexes catalog view returns information about primary and secondary XML indexes in a database. The following query returns the XML indexes on the Individual table in AdventureWorks:

```
USE AdventureWorks

SELECT o.name TableName, xi.*
FROM sys.xml_indexes xi
    JOIN sys.objects o ON xi.object_id = o.object_id
WHERE o.name = 'Individual'
```

Partial results are shown in Figure 7-11.

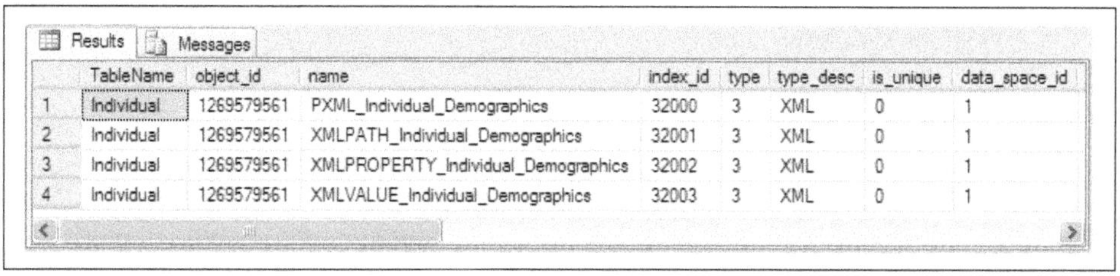

	TableName	object_id	name	index_id	type	type_desc	is_unique	data_space_id
1	Individual	1269579561	PXML_Individual_Demographics	32000	3	XML	0	1
2	Individual	1269579561	XMLPATH_Individual_Demographics	32001	3	XML	0	1
3	Individual	1269579561	XMLPROPERTY_Individual_Demographics	32002	3	XML	0	1
4	Individual	1269579561	XMLVALUE_Individual_Demographics	32003	3	XML	0	1

Figure 7-11. Results for viewing XML indexes example

In the example, the sys.xml_indexes catalog view is joined to the sys.objects catalog view to return as the first column in the result set the table that the index belongs to.

Managing XML Schema Collections

An XML schema collection is a metadata object in the database that contains one or more XML Schema Definition (XSD) language schemas. It is used to validate xml data type instances. You can associate XML schema collections with xml data type instances in columns or variables. An XML schema collection associated with an xml data type column validates the column instance data against the schema—the data is stored in the database if it conforms. XML schema collections are managed similarly to other database objects, using CREATE, ALTER and DROP T-SQL statements. The following subsections describe commands to create, modify, delete, and interrogate XML schema collections.

Creating XML Schema Collections

The CREATE XML SCHEMA COLLECTION statement is used to import XML schemas into the database. The syntax is:

```
CREATE XML SCHEMA COLLECTION [<relational_schema>.]sql_identifier AS expression
```

where:

relational_schema
>   The name of the relational schema. If not specified, the default relational schema—dbo by default—is used.

sql_identifier
>   The name of the XML schema collection.

expression
>   The XML schema specified as a string constant or scalar variable of [n]varchar, [n]varbinary, or xml type.

The following example creates an XML schema collection for a Contact xml data type. The schema specifies that a contact has an element named Contact with three attributes: FirstName, LastName, and PhoneNumber.

```
USE ProgrammingSqlServer2005

CREATE XML SCHEMA COLLECTION ContactSchemaCollection AS
N'<?xml version="1.0" encoding="utf-16"?>
<xs:schema targetNamespace="http://tempuri.org/ContactSchema"
  elementFormDefault="qualified"
  attributeFormDefault="unqualified"
  xmlns="http://tempuri.org/ContactSchema"
  xmlns:mstns="http://tempuri.org/ContactSchema"
```

```
    xmlns:xs="http://www.w3.org/2001/XMLSchema">
      <xs:element name="Contact">
          <xs:complexType>
              <xs:sequence>
              </xs:sequence>
              <xs:attribute name="FirstName" type="xs:string" />
              <xs:attribute name="LastName" type="xs:string" />
              <xs:attribute name="PhoneNumber" type="xs:string" />
          </xs:complexType>
      </xs:element>
    </xs:schema>'
```

You can view the new XML schema collection in Object Explorer in SQL Server Management Studio by selecting Databases → ProgrammingSqlServer2005 → Programmability → Types → XML Schema Collections.

The following example creates a table with a single xml data type column named Contact. The Contact column is typed using the ContactSchemaCollection XML schema collection.

```
USE ProgrammingSqlServer2005

CREATE TABLE Contacts
(
    Contact xml (ContactSchemaCollection)
)
```

You insert data into a typed xml data type column in the same way as for an untyped xml data type column. The following statement adds a contact:

```
INSERT INTO Contacts (Contact)
VALUES ('<Contact xmlns="http://tempuri.org/ContactSchema"
  FirstName="John" LastName="Doe" PhoneNumber="555-555-5555" />')
```

An error results if the data you try to insert or update in a column does not conform to the XML schema. For example, the following statement incorrectly specifies an attribute named Phone instead of PhoneNumber:

```
INSERT INTO Contacts (Contact)
VALUES ('<Contact xmlns="http://tempuri.org/ContactSchema"
  FirstName="John" LastName="Doe" Phone="555-555-5555" />')
```

Executing the statement returns the message shown in Figure 7-12.

Figure 7-12. Message for XML schema violation example

Modifying XML Schema Collections

The `ALTER XML SCHEMA COLLECTION` statement lets you add new schemas to an existing XML schema collection created previously with the `CREATE XML SCHEMA COLLECTION` statement. The syntax is:

```
ALTER XML SCHEMA COLLECTION [relational_schema.]sql_identifier
    ADD 'Schema Component'
```

where:

relational_schema
> The name of the relational schema. If not specified, the default relational schema—dbo by default—is used.

sql_identifier
> The name of the XML schema collection to add the XML schema to.

Schema Component
> The XML schema to insert into the schema collection, specified as a `string` constant or scalar variable of `[n]varchar`, `[n]varbinary`, or `xml` type.

Removing XML Schema Collections

The `DROP XML SCHEMA COLLECTION` statement deletes an entire XML schema collection previously created using the `CREATE XML SCHEMA COLLECTION` statement. All components of the XML schema collection are dropped. The syntax is:

```
DROP XML SCHEMA COLLECTION [relational_schema.]sql_identifier
```

where:

relational_schema
> The name of the relational schema. If not specified, the default relational schema—dbo by default—is used.

sql_identifier
> The name of the XML schema collection to drop.

The `DROP XML SCHEMA COLLECTION` statement is a transactional operation that can be rolled back if performed inside of a transaction.

You cannot drop an XML schema collection that is in use—that is, if any of the following are true:

- It is associated with an `xml` data type column or parameter.
- It is specified in a table constraint.
- It is referenced in a schema-bound function or stored procedure.

The `ContactSchemaCollection` XML schema collection is used by the `Contacts` table, so you must make the `Contact` column untyped by executing an `ALTER TABLE` T-SQL statement before you can remove the XML schema collection. The following code example uses the `ALTER TABLE` statement to untype the `Contact` column in the `Contacts` table:

```
ALTER TABLE Contacts ALTER COLUMN Contact xml
```

You can also drop either the `Contact` column or the `Contacts` table to remove the association with the XML schema collection. Once the XML schema collection is no longer associated with the `Contact` column, you can remove the XML schema collection by executing the `DROP XML SCHEMA COLLECTION` T-SQL statement, as shown in the following example:

```
DROP XML SCHEMA COLLECTION ContactSchemaCollection
```

Viewing XML Schema Collections

The catalog view `xml_schema_collections` enumerates the XML schema collections in a database, as shown in the following example:

```
USE AdventureWorks

SELECT s.name SchemaName, xsc.name XmlSchemaCollectionName
FROM sys.xml_schema_collections xsc
  JOIN sys.schemas s ON xsc.schema_id = s.schema_id
```

The result set is shown in Figure 7-13.

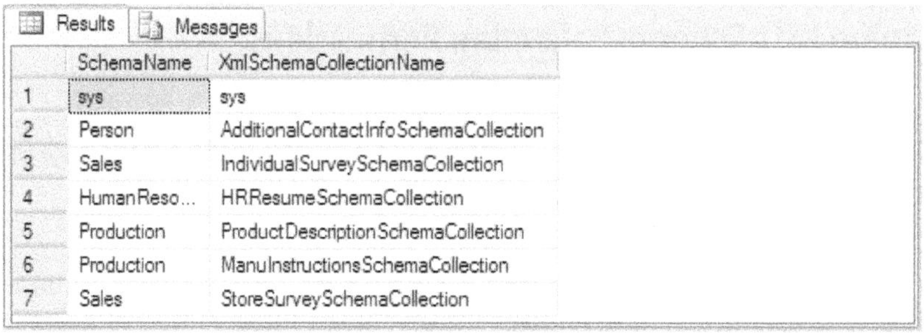

	SchemaName	XmlSchemaCollectionName
1	sys	sys
2	Person	AdditionalContactInfoSchemaCollection
3	Sales	IndividualSurveySchemaCollection
4	HumanReso...	HRResumeSchemaCollection
5	Production	ProductDescriptionSchemaCollection
6	Production	ManuInstructionsSchemaCollection
7	Sales	StoreSurveySchemaCollection

Figure 7-13. Result set for XML schema collections example

The `xml_schema_namespace` intrinsic function reconstructs the XML schema collection from the schema components stored in the database and returns an `xml` data type instance. The syntax of the `xml_schema_namespace` function is:

```
xml_schema_namespace ( schemaName, xmlSchemaCollectionName, [ targetNamespace ] )
```

where:

`schemaName`
: The name of the XML schema in the `xmlSchemaCollection`

`xmlSchemaCollectionName`
: The name of the XML schema collection

targetNamespace
> The namespace URI within the XML schema collection

You can run this function against any of the rows returned by the previous query except the row representing the sys.sys schema collection. For example:

```
SELECT xml_schema_namespace('Person', 'AdditionalContactInfoSchemaCollection')
```

The result set is an `xml` data type instance that contains the `Person` schema in the `AdditionalContactInfoSchemaCollection` XML schema collection. A fragment of the result set is shown in Figure 7-14.

```
<xsd:schema xmlns:xsd="http://www.w3.org/2001/XMLSchema"
  xmlns:t="http://schemas.microsoft.com/sqlserver/2004/07/adventure-works/ContactInfo"
  targetNamespace="http://schemas.microsoft.com/sqlserver/2004/07/adventure-works/ContactInfo">
  <xsd:element name="AdditionalContactInfo">
    <xsd:complexType mixed="true">
      <xsd:complexContent mixed="true">
        <xsd:restriction base="xsd:anyType">
          <xsd:sequence>
            <xsd:any namespace="http://schemas.microsoft.com/sqlserver/2004/07/adventure-works/ContactRecord
              http://schemas.microsoft.com/sqlserver/2004/07/adventure-works/ContactTypes"
              minOccurs="0" maxOccurs="unbounded" />
          </xsd:sequence>
        </xsd:restriction>
      </xsd:complexContent>
    </xsd:complexType>
  </xsd:element>
</xsd:schema>
```

Figure 7-14. Fragment of results for view XML schema collection example

Managing XML Schema Collection Permissions

The XML schema collection permission model lets you do the following:

- Grant, revoke, and deny a user (principal) permission to create and use XML schema collections
- Transfer ownership of XML schema collections
- Use the XML schema collection objects to type `xml` data type columns, variables, and parameters or to constrain tables or columns

Granting permissions

You can grant a user permission to create an XML schema collection by granting the user `CREATE XML SCHEMA COLLECTION` permission on the database together with `ALTER` permission either on the schema or on the database.

For existing XML schema collection objects, you can grant `CONTROL`, `TAKE OWNERSHIP`, `ALTER`, `EXECUTE`, `REFERENCES`, or `VIEW DEFINITION` permissions using the `GRANT` T-SQL statement.

For more information about the GRANT T-SQL statement, see Microsoft SQL Server 2005 Books Online.

Revoking permissions

You can revoke permission to create an XML schema collection in one of the following ways:

- Revoke a user's ALTER permission on the schema. The user will no longer be able to create an XML schema collection in the relational schema.

- Revoke a user's ALTER permission on the database. The user will no longer be able to create an XML schema collection anywhere in the database.

- Revoke either CREATE XML SCHEMA COLLECTION or ALTER ANY XML SCHEMA COLLECTION from the user. This prevents the user from importing an XML schema collection in the database.

For existing XML schema collection objects, you can revoke CONTROL, TAKE OWNERSHIP, ALTER, EXECUTE, REFERENCES, or VIEW DEFINITION permissions by using the REVOKE T-SQL statement.

For more information about the REVOKE T-SQL statement, see Microsoft SQL Server 2005 Books Online.

Denying permissions

You can deny permission to create an XML schema collection in one of the following ways:

- Deny the user's ALTER permission on the schema. The user will no longer be able to create an XML schema collection anywhere in the relational schema.

- Deny the user's CONTROL permission on the schema.

- Deny the user's ALTER ANY SCHEMA permission on the database. The user will no longer be able to create an XML schema collection anywhere in the database.

For existing XML schema collection objects, you can revoke CONTROL, TAKE OWNERSHIP, ALTER, EXECUTE, REFERENCES, or VIEW DEFINITION XML schema collection permissions by using the DENY T-SQL statement.

For more information about the DENY T-SQL statement, see Microsoft SQL Server 2005 Books Online.

Limitations of XML Schema Collections

XML schema validation of xml data type columns is subject to some limitations:

- xsi:schemaLocation and xsi:noNamespaceSchemaLocation attribute values are ignored.
- The <xsd:include> element is not allowed.
- The <xsd:unique>, <xsd:key>, and <xsd:keyref> constraints are not supported.
- Canonical representations of values in the XML document must not violate a pattern restriction for its type.
- The processContents attribute of wildcard elements (<xsd:any> and <xsd:anyAttribute>) does not support lax—it must be set to skip or strict.
- The <xsd:redefine> element is not supported.
- Types derived from xs:QName using an XML schema restriction element are not supported.
- Schemas containing list types with union type items are not supported.
- <xsd:simple> types are restricted as described in Table 7-5.

Table 7-5. <xsd:simple> types

Simple type	Restriction
duration	The year part must be in the range -2^{31} to $2^{31} - 1$.
	The month, day, hour, minute, and second parts must all be in the range 0 to 9999.
	The second part has an additional three digits of precision after the decimal point.
dateTime	The year part must be in the range −9999 to 9999.
	The month part must be in the range 1 to 12.
	The day part must be in the range 1 to 31 and must be a valid calendar date.
	The hour part must be in the range −14 to 14.
date	The year part must be in the range −9999 to 9999.
	The month part must be in the range 1 to 12.
	The day part must be in the range 1 to 31 and must be a valid calendar date.
gYearMonth	The year part must be in the range −9999 to 9999.
gYear	The year part must be in the range −9999 to 9999.
gMonthDay	The month part must be in the range 1 to 12.
	The day part must be in the range 1 to 31.
gDay	The day part must be in the range 1 to 31.
gMonth	The month part must be in the range 1 to 12.
decimal	Must conform to the format of the SQL Server numeric data type—up to 38 digits of precision are allowed with up to 10 of those being fractional.
	Variable precision decimal values are not supported.

Table 7-5. <xsd:simple> types (continued)

Simple type	Restriction
float	Must conform to the format of the SQL Server real data type.
double	Must conform to the format of the SQL Server float data type.
string	Must conform to the format of the SQL Server nvarchar(max) data type.
anyURI	Cannot be more than 4000 Unicode characters in length.

- xs:decimal instanced values are represented internally by SQL server as data type numeric (38, 10). Variable precision decimals are not supported.
- Time zone information for date, time, and dateTime simple types is normalized to Greenwich Mean Time (GMT). The GMT zone is added to data that does not have a time zone.
- The length, minLength, and maxLength facets are stored as a long data type.
- The minOccurs and maxOccurs attributes must fit in 4-byte integers.
- Schema component identifiers are limited to a length of 1000 Unicode characters. Supplementary character pairs used in some languages are not supported within identifiers.
- The NaN simple type value is not supported.
- XML schemas having types that have pattern facets or enumerations that violate those facets are rejected.
- A schema containing an <xsd:choice> particle must either have children or explicitly define its minOccurs attribute with a value of 0.
- block and final attributes cannot have repeated values.
- The namespace attribute for <xsd:any> cannot be an empty string. Explicitly specify the namespace as ##local to indicate an unqualified element or attribute.
- The uniqueness of the ID attribute is enforced only for the <xsd:attribute> component and not for the <xsd:element> component. The ID attribute for <xsd:attribute> must be unique within the schema collection.
- The NOTATION type is not supported.

XQuery Support

XQuery is a language for querying XML data. SQL Server 2005 supports a subset of XQuery for querying the xml data type. The implementation is aligned with the July 2004 draft of XQuery. For more information about using the XQuery language, see the World Wide Web Consortium (W3C) web site at *http://www.w3.org/TR/2004/ WD-xquery-20040723/* and Microsoft SQL Server 2005 Books Online.

xml Data Type Functions

The XQuery functions described in Table 7-6 can be used with XQuery against the xml data type. These functions are part of the *http://www.w3.org/2004/07/xpath-functions* namespace. The W3C specification uses a namespace prefix of fn: for these functions. However, use of fn: is not required in the SQL Server 2005 implementation.

Table 7-6. XQuery functions

Category	XQuery function	Description
Numeric	ceiling	Returns the smallest integer that is not smaller than the argument
	floor	Returns the largest integer that is not larger than the argument
	round	Returns the integer closest to the argument
String	concat	Returns a string concatenation of zero or more string arguments
	contains	Returns an xs:boolean value indicating whether a string argument contains a string specified by a second argument
	substring	Returns the specified part of a string argument
	string-length	Returns the length of a string argument
Booleans	not	Returns a Boolean value for the logical NOT of a Boolean argument
Nodes	number	Returns the numeric value of a specified node
Context	last	Returns an unsigned integer indicating the number of items in the sequence currently being processed
	position	Returns an unsigned integer indicating the number position of the context item in the sequence currently being processed
Sequences	empty	Returns a Boolean value indicating whether the specified sequence is an empty sequence
	distinct-values	Returns a sequence containing the distinct values in a specified sequence
Aggregate	count	Returns the number of items in a specified sequence
	avg	Returns the average of the values in a specified sequence
	min	Returns the smallest value in a specified sequence
	max	Returns the largest value in a specified sequence
	sum	Returns the sum of the values in a specified sequence
Constructor	Constructor Functions	Creates an instance of any XSD built-in or user-defined atomic type
Data accessor	string	Returns the string representation of a node or atomic value argument
	data	Returns the typed value of the specified node

The following query uses XQuery to retrieve the work center having the most labor hours for each product from the Instructions xml data type column in the Production.ProductModel table in AdventureWorks. Note that you must enter the emphasized line in the example on a single line.

```
USE AdventureWorks

SELECT ProductModelID, Name,
    Instructions.query('
    declare namespace AWMI=
      "http://schemas.microsoft.com/sqlserver/2004/07/
        adventure-works/ProductModelManuInstructions";
    for $Location in /AWMI:root/AWMI:Location
    where $Location/@LaborHours = max(/AWMI:root/AWMI:Location/@LaborHours)
    return <Location WCID="{ $Location/@LocationID }"
      LaborHrs="{ $Location/@LaborHours }" />') Result
FROM  Production.ProductModel
WHERE Instructions IS NOT NULL
```

Partial results are shown in Figure 7-15.

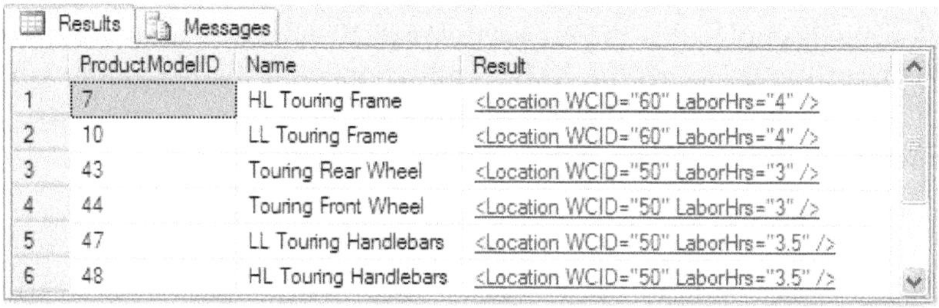

Figure 7-15. Results for XQuery example

xml Data Type Operators

The XQuery operators described in Table 7-7 can be used in queries that run against xml data type instances.

Table 7-7. XQuery operators

Category	Operators
Numeric	+, -, *, div, mod
Value comparison	eq, ne, lt, gt, le, ge
General comparison	=, !=, <, >, <=, >=

Using XQuery Extension Functions to Bind Relational Data Inside XML Data

In addition to xml data type methods, SQL Server provides two XQuery extension functions—sql:column( ) and sql:variable( )—to bind relational data inside XML data. These functions bring in data from a non-xml data type column or from a T-SQL variable so that you can investigate or manipulate the relational data as you would an xml data type instance. Bound relational data is read-only.

The XQuery extension functions cannot be used to reference data in columns or variables of xml, CLR UDT, timestamp, text, ntext, sql_variant, or image data types.

sql:column( ) function

The sql:column( ) function exposes relational data from a non-xml data type column, letting you return relational data as part of an XML result set. The syntax is:

```
sql:column(columnName)
```

where:

columnName

    The name of a column in the row being processed

The following example adds the ProductionModelID and Name columns and the SQL variable @laborHourTarget to the XML result containing the maximum labor hours for each product model from the Instructions xml data type column. Note that you must enter the emphasized line in the example on a single line.

```
USE AdventureWorks

DECLARE @laborHourTarget int;
SET @laborHourTarget = 2.5;

SELECT Instructions.query('
  declare namespace pmmi="http://schemas.microsoft.com/sqlserver/
    2004/07/adventure-works/ProductModelManuInstructions";
  <ProductModel
    ProductModelID=   "{ sql:column("pm.ProductModelID") }"
    Name=             "{ sql:column("pm.Name") }"
    LaborHourTarget=  "{ sql:variable("@laborHourTarget") }" >
    { attribute MaxLaborHours {max(/pmmi:root/pmmi:Location/@LaborHours)} }
  </ProductModel>
') AS Result
FROM Production.ProductModel pm
WHERE Instructions IS NOT NULL
```

Partial results are shown in Figure 7-16.

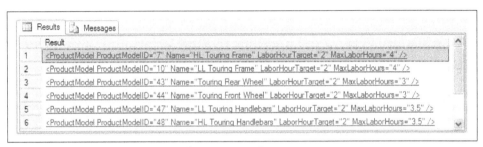

Figure 7-16. Results for sql:column() function example

sql:variable( ) function

The sql:variable( ) function used in the preceding example exposes data in a non-xml data type T-SQL variable inside XML. The syntax is:

```
sql:variable(variableName)
```

where:

variableName
    The name a T-SQL variable

XML Data Manipulation Language

XML DML extends the XQuery language to support data modification in xml data type instances. XML DML adds the insert, delete, and replace value of keywords to the XQuery language.

The examples in the subsections that follow use a table named xmldmlTable. Create this table by executing the following statement:

```
USE ProgrammingSqlServer2005

CREATE TABLE xmldmlTable
(
  ID int,
  xmlCol xml,
CONSTRAINT PK_xmldmlTable
  PRIMARY KEY CLUSTERED (ID)
)
```

The added XML DML keywords are used to modify xml data type instances as detailed in the following three subsections.

insert

The XML DML insert statement inserts one or more nodes as child nodes or siblings of a specified node in an xml data type instance. The syntax for the insert keyword follows:

```
insert Expression1 ( {as first | as last} into | after | before
  Expression2 )
```

where:

Expression1
    A constant XML instance or an XQuery expression identifying one or more nodes to insert. It cannot resolve to the root (/) node. If multiple nodes are specified by the constant XML instance, they must be enclosed in parentheses and separated by commas.

into

Nodes identified by *Expression1* are inserted as child nodes of the node identified by *Expression2*.

{ as first | as last }

If the node identified by *Expression2* already has one or more child nodes, you must use either the as first or as last keywords to specify the location in which to insert the new child nodes—either at the beginning or at the end of the child list.

The as first and as last keywords are ignored when inserting attributes.

after

Nodes identified by *Expression1* are inserted as siblings immediately after the node identified by *Expression2*. The after keyword cannot be used to insert attributes.

before

Nodes identified by *Expression1* are inserted immediately before the node identified by *Expression2*. The before keyword cannot be used to insert attributes.

Expression2

A constant XML instance or an XQuery expression identifying a single existing node. Nodes identified by *Expression1* are inserted relative to this node. The insert fails if *Expression2* identifies more than one node.

The following example creates a record in the xmldmlTable with ID = 1 and the xmlCol xml data type column set to a simple XML document. The example then adds a child element named childElement0 as the first child of the root node using an insert XML DML statement.

```
INSERT INTO xmldmlTable (ID, xmlCol)
VALUES (1, '<root><childElement1 value="1"/></root>')

SELECT xmlCol FROM xmldmlTable WHERE ID = 1

UPDATE xmldmlTable
SET xmlCol.modify('insert <childElement0 value="0"/> as first into (/root)[1]')
WHERE ID = 1

SELECT xmlCol FROM xmldmlTable WHERE ID = 1
```

Two result sets are returned, as shown in Figure 7-17.

The first result set shows the xmlCol value before the XML DML insert. The second result set after the insert XML DML command shows the new childelement0 element as the first child of the root element.

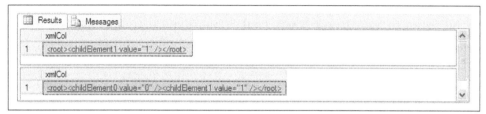

Figure 7-17. Results for XML DML insert example

delete

The XML DML delete statement deletes one or more nodes from an xml data type instance. The syntax of the delete keyword is:

    delete *Expression*

where:

Expression

An XQuery expression specifying one or more nodes to delete. All nodes specified by the XQuery expression and all contained (child) nodes are deleted. The expression cannot be the root (/) node.

The following example creates a record in the xlmdmlTable with ID = 2. It assigns the elements childElement1 and childElement2 to the xlmCol column, then deletes childElement1.

```
INSERT INTO xmldmlTable (ID, xmlCol)
VALUES (2, '<root><childElement1 value="1"/>
  <childElement2 value="2"/></root>')

SELECT xmlCol FROM xmldmlTable WHERE ID = 2

UPDATE xmldmlTable
SET xmlCol.modify('delete (/root/childElement1)')
WHERE ID = 2

SELECT xmlCol FROM xmldmlTable WHERE ID = 2
```

Two result sets are returned, as shown in Figure 7-18.

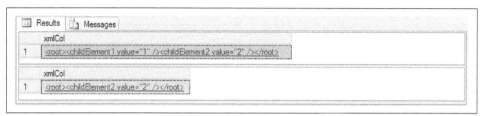

Figure 7-18. Results for XML DML delete example

The first result set shows the xmlCol value before the XML DML delete. The second result set after the delete XML DML command shows the removal of the childelement1 element from the root element.

replace value of

The XML DML replace value of statement updates the value of a node in an xml data type instance. The syntax of replace value of is:

```
replace value of Expression1 with Expression2
```

where:

Expression1
    A constant XML instance or an XQuery expression identifying a single node to update. An error will result if multiple nodes are specified. *Expression1* must identify an element with simply typed content, a text node, or an attribute node—specifying a union type, complex type, processing instruction, document node, or comment node will return an error.

Expression2
    The new value of the node. When updating a type xml data type instance, *Expression2* must have the same subtype as *Expression1*.

The following example updates the value attribute for element childElement1:

```
INSERT INTO xmldmlTable (ID, xmlCol)
VALUES (3, '<root><childElement1 value="1"/></root>')

SELECT xmlCol FROM xmldmlTable WHERE ID = 3

UPDATE xmldmlTable
SET xmlCol.modify('replace value of (/root/childElement1/@value)[1] with "100"')
WHERE ID = 3

SELECT xmlCol FROM xmldmlTable WHERE ID = 3
```

Two result sets are returned, as shown in Figure 7-19. The first result set shows the xmlCol value before the XML DML replace value of. The second result set after the replace value of XML DML command shows the value attribute of the childElement1 element changed from 1 to 100.

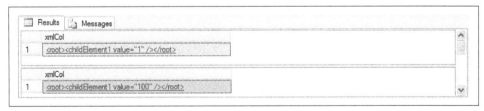

Figure 7-19. Results for XML DML replace value of example

XML DML Limitations and Restrictions

XML DML cannot be used to insert, delete, or modify the following:

- xmlns, xmlns.*, or xml:base attributes in either typed or untyped xml data type instances.
- xsi:nil or xsi:type attributes in typed xml data type instances.

Additionally, XML DML has the following restriction:

- The xml:base attribute cannot be inserted into either typed or untyped xml data type instances.

XML Results Using the FOR XML Clause

You can return the result set of a SELECT statement as XML by specifying the FOR XML clause in the query. The FOR XML clause was introduced in SQL Server 2000. SQL Server 2005 enhances the functionality, as discussed in the "FOR XML Updates and Enhancements" section later in this chapter. The FOR XML clause syntax is:

```
[ FOR { BROWSE | <XML> } ]

<XML> ::=
  XML
  {
    { RAW [ ('ElementName') ] | AUTO }
    [
      <CommonDirectives>
      [ , { XMLDATA | XMLSCHEMA [ ( TargetNameSpaceURI ) ]} ]
      [ , ELEMENTS [ XSINIL | ABSENT ]
    ]
    | EXPLICIT
    [
      <CommonDirectives>
      [ , XMLDATA ]
    ]
    | PATH [ ('ElementName') ]
    [
      <CommonDirectives>
      [ , ELEMENTS [ XSINIL | ABSENT ] ]
    ]
  }

<CommonDirectives> ::=
  [ , BINARY BASE64 ]
  [ , TYPE ]
  [ , ROOT [ ('RootName') ] ]
```

where:

RAW[('*ElementName*')]

Transforms each row in the result set into an XML element with the name specified in the *ElementName* parameter. The identifier defaults to <row> if the *ElementName* parameter is not specified.

AUTO

Returns the query results as a simple, nested XML hierarchy. Each table in the FROM clause with at least one column selected is returned as an XML element.

XMLDATA

Returns an inline XML-Data Reduced (XDR) schema in the returned XML.

XMLSCHEMA [(*TargetNameSpaceURI*)]

Returns an inline XSD Schema prepended to the resulting XML document. If the *TargetNameSpaceURI* argument is specified, the specified namespace is returned in the schema. You cannot use the XMLSCHEMA directive with the ROOT directive or when a row tag name is specified.

ELEMENTS [XSINIL | ABSENT]

Specifies that columns are returned as subelements rather than mapped to attributes. The ELEMENTS option is supported only for RAW, AUTO, and PATH modes.

The XSINIL option specifies that an element with the xsi:nil attribute set to true is created for a column with a NULL value. If not specified, or the ABSENT option is specified, no element is created for a column with a NULL value.

EXPLICIT

Explicitly specifies the XML hierarchy for the query result.

PATH

A simpler way than EXPLICIT mode to specify the XML hierarchy for the result set. PATH uses nested FOR XML queries to mix elements and attributes and to specify the nesting used to represent complex properties. Attributes must appear before other node types in the same level.

BINARY BASE64

Specifies that any binary data returned by the query is represented in Base64-encoded format. This option must be specified when returning binary data using RAW or EXPLICIT mode. By default, binary data is returned as a reference in AUTO mode.

TYPE

Specifies that the results of the query are returned as an xml data type instance.

ROOT[('*RootName*')]

Adds a single top-level (root) element to the returned XML result with the name specified by the *RootName* argument. If the *RootName* argument is not specified, the name of the top-level element defaults to root.

Some FOR XML Examples

The examples in this subsection show the effect of the FOR XML clause on the result set returned by the following SELECT statement:

```
USE AdventureWorks

SELECT TOP 2 DepartmentID, Name
FROM HumanResources.Department
```

The SELECT statement without the FOR XML clause returns the ID and name of the top two departments, as shown in Figure 7-20.

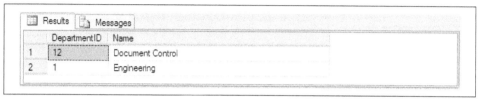

Figure 7-20. Results for SELECT example

Now add the FOR XML RAW clause to the statement:

```
SELECT TOP 2 DepartmentID, Name
FROM HumanResources.Department
FOR XML RAW
```

The result set is a single row with one xml data type column containing the XML fragment shown in Figure 7-21.

Figure 7-21. Results for FOR XML example

Add the ROOT directive to the FOR XML clause to add a root node Departments and turn the XML fragment into an XML document:

```
SELECT TOP 2 DepartmentID, Name
FROM HumanResources.Department
FOR XML RAW, ROOT ('Departments')
```

The results are shown in Figure 7-22.

Specifying the XMLSCHEMA directive returns an inline XSD schema in the result set:

```
SELECT TOP 2 DepartmentID, Name
FROM HumanResources.Department
FOR XML RAW, XMLSCHEMA
```

```
<Departments>
    <row DepartmentID="12" Name="Document Control" />
    <row DepartmentID="1" Name="Engineering" />
</Departments>
```

Figure 7-22. Results for FOR XML with ROOT directive example

The results are shown in Figure 7-23.

```
<xsd:schema targetNamespace="urn:schemas-microsoft-com:sql:SqlRowSet1"
            xmlns:xsd="http://www.w3.org/2001/XMLSchema"
            xmlns:sqltypes="http://schemas.microsoft.com/sqlserver/2004/sqltypes"
            elementFormDefault="qualified">
    <xsd:import namespace="http://schemas.microsoft.com/sqlserver/2004/sqltypes"
            schemaLocation="http://schemas.microsoft.com/sqlserver/2004/sqltypes/sqltypes.xsd" />
    <xsd:element name="row">
        <xsd:complexType>
            <xsd:attribute name="DepartmentID" type="sqltypes:smallint" use="required" />
            <xsd:attribute name="Name" use="required">
                <xsd:simpleType sqltypes:sqlTypeAlias="[AdventureWorks].[dbo].[Name]">
                    <xsd:restriction base="sqltypes:nvarchar" sqltypes:localeId="1033"
                                sqltypes:sqlCompareOptions="IgnoreCase IgnoreKanaType IgnoreWidth"
                                sqltypes:sqlSortId="52">
                        <xsd:maxLength value="50" />
                    </xsd:restriction>
                </xsd:simpleType>
            </xsd:attribute>
        </xsd:complexType>
    </xsd:element>
</xsd:schema>
<row xmlns="urn:schemas-microsoft-com:sql:SqlRowSet1" DepartmentID="12" Name="Document Control" />
<row xmlns="urn:schemas-microsoft-com:sql:SqlRowSet1" DepartmentID="1" Name="Engineering" />
```

Figure 7-23. Results for FOR XML with XMLSCHEMA directive

The following example uses AUTO mode to return sales order information:

```
SELECT soh.SalesOrderID, soh.OrderDate, soh.CustomerID,
    sod.ProductID, sod.OrderQty
FROM Sales.SalesOrderHeader soh, Sales.SalesOrderDetail sod
WHERE soh.SalesOrderID = sod.SalesOrderID
FOR XML AUTO
```

Partial results are shown in Figure 7-24.

One element is created for each table specified in the FROM clause, with the table aliases specified in the FROM clause used as element names. AUTO mode uses the column order in the SELECT statement to nest elements in the XML document hierarchy. Values of selected columns are added to the elements as attributes. The ORDER BY clause is needed to ensure that all child elements are nested under a single parent element.

The following example uses PATH mode to return contact information for vendors:

```
SELECT
    v.VendorID "@ID",
    v.Name "@Name",
    c.FirstName "Contact/First",
    c.LastName "Contact/Last"
```

```
⊟ <soh SalesOrderID="43659" OrderDate="2001-07-01T00:00:00" CustomerID="676">
    <sod ProductID="776" OrderQty="1" />
    <sod ProductID="777" OrderQty="3" />
    <sod ProductID="778" OrderQty="1" />
    <sod ProductID="771" OrderQty="1" />
    <sod ProductID="772" OrderQty="1" />
    <sod ProductID="773" OrderQty="2" />
    <sod ProductID="774" OrderQty="1" />
    <sod ProductID="714" OrderQty="3" />
    <sod ProductID="716" OrderQty="1" />
    <sod ProductID="709" OrderQty="6" />
    <sod ProductID="712" OrderQty="2" />
    <sod ProductID="711" OrderQty="4" />
  </soh>
⊟ <soh SalesOrderID="43660" OrderDate="2001-07-01T00:00:00" CustomerID="117">
    <sod ProductID="762" OrderQty="1" />
    <sod ProductID="758" OrderQty="1" />
  </soh>
⊟ <soh SalesOrderID="43661" OrderDate="2001-07-01T00:00:00" CustomerID="442">
```

Figure 7-24. Results for FOR XML with AUTO mode example

```
FROM Purchasing.Vendor v, Purchasing.VendorContact vc, Person.Contact c
WHERE v.VendorID = vc.VendorID AND vc.ContactID = c.ContactID
ORDER BY v.Name
FOR XML PATH ('Vendor')
```

Partial results are shown in Figure 7-25.

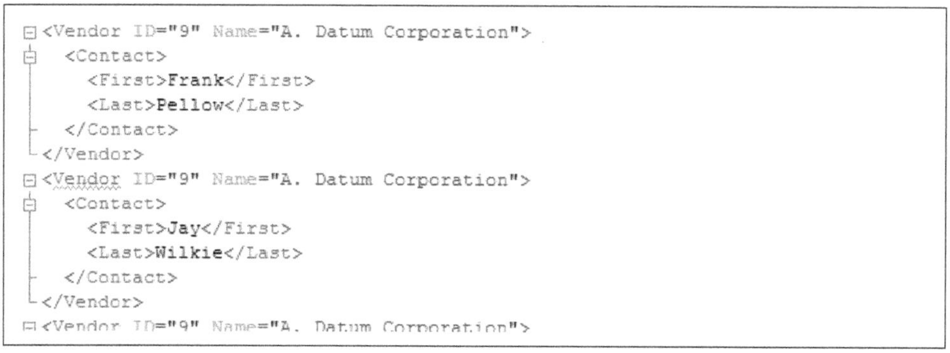

```
⊟ <Vendor ID="9" Name="A. Datum Corporation">
⊟   <Contact>
      <First>Frank</First>
      <Last>Pellow</Last>
    </Contact>
  </Vendor>
⊟ <Vendor ID="9" Name="A. Datum Corporation">
⊟   <Contact>
      <First>Jay</First>
      <Last>Wilkie</Last>
    </Contact>
  </Vendor>
⊟ <Vendor ID="9" Name="A. Datum Corporation">
```

Figure 7-25. Results for FOR XML with PATH mode example

The ampersand (@) preceding the VendorID and Name column names results in the output of attributes in the XML document. The slash (/) in the FirstName and LastName column names results in the output of XML subelements in the XML document.

The following example uses EXPLICIT mode to return contact information for vendors:

```
SELECT DISTINCT
    1          AS Tag,
    NULL       AS Parent,
```

```
    v.VendorID   AS [Vendor!1!ID],
    v.Name       AS [Vendor!1!Name],
    NULL         AS [Contact!2!FirstName],
    NULL         AS [Contact!2!LastName]
FROM Purchasing.Vendor v, Purchasing.VendorContact vc, Person.Contact c
WHERE v.VendorID = vc.VendorID AND vc.ContactID = c.ContactID

UNION ALL

SELECT
    2            AS Tag,
    1            AS Parent,
    v.VendorID,
    v.Name,
    c.FirstName,
    c.LastName
FROM Purchasing.Vendor v, Purchasing.VendorContact vc, Person.Contact c
WHERE v.VendorID = vc.VendorID AND vc.ContactID = c.ContactID

ORDER BY [Vendor!1!ID], [Contact!2!LastName]
FOR XML EXPLICIT
```

Partial results are shown in Figure 7-26.

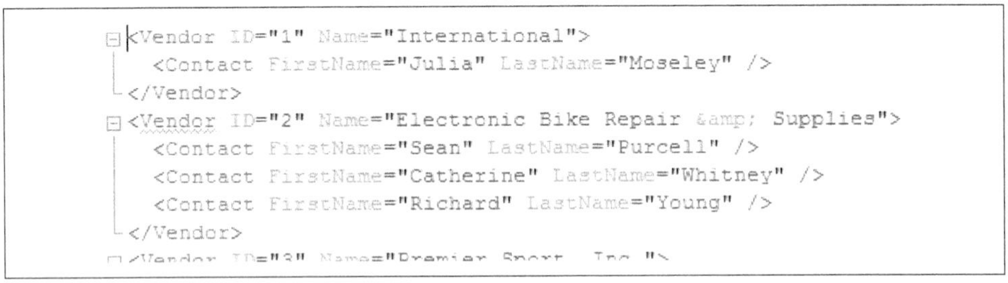

Figure 7-26. Results for FOR XML with EXPLICIT mode example

The Tag and Parent metacolumns determine the XML document hierarchy. Columns are selected at each level of the hierarchy and combined into a nested XML document using the UNION ALL operator. The column name syntax is *elementName! elementLevel!attributeName*.

FOR XML Support for SQL Server Data Types

The following SQL Server data types have limitations or special handling as described when used with the FOR XML clause:

xml

> If an xml data type is specified in the SELECT clause, column values are mapped to and serialized as elements in the returned XML regardless of whether the ELEMENTS directive is specified. XML declarations in the xml data type column are not serialized.

User-Defined Types (UDT)
CLR UDTs are not supported.

String
Whitespace characters in the data are entitized. For example, carriage returns, tabs, and line feeds are converted to , 	, and
, respectively.

timestamp
timestamp data type instances are treated as varbinary(8) data and are always Base 64 encoded. If an XSD or XSR schema is requested, it reflects this.

FOR XML Updates and Enhancements

SQL Server 2005 updates and enhances FOR XML functionality in SQL Server 2000 as described in the following list:

TYPE directive
In SQL Server 2000, a FOR XML query returns results either as a text or image type. In SQL Server 2005, the TYPE directive lets you return a result set from a FOR XML query as an xml data type.

RAW mode enhancements
RAW mode now lets you specify the row element name, retrieve element-centric XML, and specify the root element for the XML result.

AUTO mode enhancements
AUTO mode shapes the returned XML hierarchy by comparing columns in adjacent rows in the query. In SQL Server 2000, ntext, text, and image data types are not compared. In SQL Server 2005, xml data type columns are also not compared. The new varchar(max), nvarchar(max), and varbinary(max) data types are compared.

Derived table support has been improved, allowing it to be used to group columns from different tables under the same element while hiding the join from the AUTO mode shaping mechanism.

EXPLICIT mode enhancements
EXPLICIT mode now supports the CDATA directive with an element name and the xsi:nil column mode.

Nested queries
Using the xml data type and the TYPE directive in FOR XML queries lets you further process the XML result set on the server. This lets you build nested FOR XML queries.

Generating elements for NULL values
The XSINIL parameter of the ELEMENTS directive lets you create elements for NULL column values. These elements have an xsi:nil attribute set to true.

Inline XSD and XDR schema generation
A query with a FOR XML clause can return an inline schema in the XML returned.

Specify the XMLSCHEMA keyword to return an XSD schema. XMLSCHEMA can be specified only in RAW or AUTO mode, not in EXPLICIT mode. A nested FOR XML query that specifies the TYPE directive returns an untyped xml data type instance.

Specify the XMLDATA keyword in the FOR XML clause to return an XDR schema. The XDR schema does not support all new data types and enhancements in SQL Server 2005. Specifically:

- XDR does not support FOR XML query result sets that include xml data type columns.
- The varchar(max), nvarchar(max), and varbinary(max) data types are mapped to varchar(n), nvarchar(n), and varbinary(n).
- When compatibility mode is set to 90, timestamp values are treated as varbinary(8) data and Base64-encoded when binary base64 is specified, and URL-encoded in AUTO mode when binary base64 is not specified.

XML Catalog Views

The catalog views described in Table 7-8 return information about the xml entities in a database.

Table 7-8. Catalog views for XML entities

Catalog view	Description
sys.xml_attributes	A row per xml component that is an attribute (symbol_space = A).
	This view inherits from sys.xml_components.
sys.xml_component_placements	A row per placement for xml components.
sys.xml_components	A row per component of an XML schema.
sys.xml_elements	A row per xml component that is an element (symbol_space = E).
	This view inherits from sys.xml_components.
sys.xml_facets	A row per facet of an xml-type definition.
	This view inherits from sys.xml_components.
sys.xml_indexes	A row per xml index.
	This view inherits from sys.indexes.
sys.xml_model_groups	A row per xml component that is a Model-Group (symbol_space = M).
	This view inherits from sys.xml_components.
sys.xml_schema_collections	A row per XML schema collection.
sys.xml_schema_components	A row per XML schema component.
sys.xml_schema_namespaces	A row per XSD-defined XML namespace.

Table 7-8. Catalog views for XML entities (continued)

Catalog view	Description
sys.xml_types	A row per xml component that is a Type (symbol_space = T).
	This view inherits from sys.xml_components.
sys.xml_wildcard_namespaces	A row per enumerated namespace for an xml wildcard.
sys.xml_wildcards	A row per xml component that is an Attribute-Wildcard (kind V) or Element-Wildcard (kind W) both with symbol_space = N.
	This view inherits from sys.xml_components.

CHAPTER 8

Native XML Web Services

SQL Server 2005 supports native XML web services for both SOAP 1.1 and SOAP 1.2 clients. The SQL Server Database Engine can be configured as an HTTP listener, allowing heterogeneous clients to access its data. You can send SOAP message requests to SQL Server over HTTP to execute T-SQL batch statements (with or without parameters), stored procedures, extended stored procedures, and scalar-valued user-defined functions (UDFs).

In SQL Server 2000, web service support is provided by SQLXML 3.0 and Internet Information Services (IIS), as well as the Microsoft Data Access Components (MDAC) stack installed on the client to access SQL Server. The inclusion of native web services in SQL Server 2005 allows a much wider group of clients to access the database, consistent with the platform and operating system interoperability goals for web services.

A client needs only HTTP and XML to access web services exposed by SQL Server 2005. This broadens access to SQL Server data across the extended enterprise from heterogeneous environments, including Unix and Linux systems and mobile devices. SQL Server 2005 includes built-in security measures to control client access.

Open Standards

SQL Server 2005 native XML web services are based on the following open standards:

Hypertext Transfer Protocol (HTTP)
   A platform-independent protocol for exchanging data. HTTP is the underlying protocol for the Web. HTTP defines the format for messages, how they are transmitted, and the actions that web servers and browsers should take in response to the message commands.

   Native HTTP support in SQL Server 2005 requires the kernel-mode HTTP listener (http.sys), which is available only in Windows Server 2003 or Windows

XP SP2 or later. The HTTP Configuration Utility (`httpcfg.exe`) is used to configure `http.sys`.

Simple Object Access Protocol (SOAP)
> A lightweight XML-based messaging protocol used to encode web service request and response information and transmit that information over a network. SOAP is platform- and operating system–independent and can be transported over a variety of Internet protocols, including HTTP, TCP, and SMTP.

Web Service Description Language (WSDL)
> An XML document format that describes the capabilities of a web service.

Creating a Web Service

Follow these steps to create an XML web service in SQL Server 2005:

1. Establish an HTTP endpoint on the SQL Server instance. An endpoint is an interface through which HTTP-based clients can query the server. You establish an endpoint by using the `CREATE ENDPOINT` T-SQL DDL statement.

2. Expose stored procedures or UDFs as *web methods.* You do this by defining existing stored procedures or UDFs for web access by using either the `CREATE ENDPOINT` or `ALTER ENDPOINT` T-SQL DDL statement.

3. Create the WSDL that describes the web service and make it available to clients, allowing them to access the web service. The WSDL can be generated by SQL Server or you can custom-build it.

The next section in this chapter gives an example of how to create a web service in SQL Server 2005.

Creating the HTTP Endpoint and Exposing a Web Method Example

The example in this section creates a stored procedure and defines an HTTP SOAP endpoint with a single web method that accesses the stored procedure. A .NET client is created to call the stored procedure via a web service call and to display the results.

Follow these steps to create the endpoint and expose a web method:

1. Create a stored procedure to return purchase orders for a specific employee, or all purchase orders if an employee is not specified. Execute the following query in the `AdventureWorks` database to create the stored procedure:

```
USE AdventureWorks

CREATE PROCEDURE GetPurchaseOrder
    @EmployeeID [int] = NULL
WITH EXECUTE AS CALLER
```

```
AS
IF @EmployeeID IS NOT NULL
    BEGIN
        SELECT * FROM Purchasing.PurchaseOrderHeader
        WHERE EmployeeID = @EmployeeID
    END
ELSE
    SELECT * FROM Purchasing.PurchaseOrderHeader
```

2. Create an HTTP SOAP endpoint named GetPurchaseOrderEndpoint to expose this stored procedure as a web method named GetPurchaseOrder. The following T-SQL statement creates the HTTP endpoint with a single web method:

```
USE AdventureWorks

CREATE ENDPOINT GetPurchaseOrderEndpoint
    STATE = STARTED
    AS HTTP (
        path = '/sql/GetPurchaseOrder',
        AUTHENTICATION = (INTEGRATED),
        PORTS = (CLEAR)
    )
    FOR SOAP(
        WEBMETHOD 'GetPurchaseOrder'
            (NAME = 'AdventureWorks.dbo.GetPurchaseOrder',
            SCHEMA = STANDARD),
        BATCHES = ENABLED,
        WSDL = DEFAULT,
        SCHEMA = STANDARD,
        DATABASE = 'AdventureWorks',
        NAMESPACE = 'http://tempUri.org/'
    )
```

 Under Windows XP, you cannot create endpoints using port 80 if IIS is running, because IIS listens on port 80. You can either stop the World Wide Web Publishing service or create the endpoint on a port other than 80 by specifying the CLEAR_PORT clause in the CREATE ENDPOINT or ALTER ENDPOINT statement.

Stop the World Wide Web Publishing service by selecting Start → Administrative Tools → Services. In the Services dialog box, right-click World Wide Web Publishing and choose Stop from the context menu.

Creating and managing HTTP endpoints is described in detail in the "Creating an HTTP Endpoint" section later in this chapter.

You can confirm that the endpoint has been created by querying the catalog view sys.http_endpoints:

```
SELECT * FROM sys.http_endpoints
```

You can confirm the existence of the web method by querying the catalog view sys. endpoint_webmethods:

```
SELECT * FROM sys.endpoint_webmethods
```

Catalog views that contain information about the HTTP endpoints defined in the SQL Server instance are described in the "Endpoint Metadata" section later in this chapter.

This permission controls whether a principal can see metadata for a specific endpoint:

```
{ GRANT | DENY | REVOKE | }  ON ENDPOINT::endPointName
    TO server_principal
```

This permission does not give the principal access to the endpoint.

The next step is to consume this web method. The following example uses a C# .NET client. Follow these steps in Visual Studio 2005:

1. From the Visual Studio 2005 menu, select File → New → Project.

2. In the New Project dialog box, select Visual C# in the tree view and Windows Application from the installed templates.

3. Specify where you want to save the project. Name the project GetPurchase-OrderSoapApp. Click OK.

4. In the Solution Explorer window, right-click References and select Add Web Reference from the context menu.

5. In the Add Web Reference dialog box, enter *http://localhost/sql/GetPurchase Order?wsdl*. You can specify a server name instead of localhost if your SQL Server is not local. Figure 8-1 shows that the GetPurchaseOrder() method is available, together with sqlbatch(), which permits ad hoc queries to be executed.

6. Change the Web reference name listbox to GetPurchaseOrderWS. Click the Add Reference button.

7. Double-click Form1 in Solution Explorer to open the Form Designer.

8. Add a DataGridView control to the form. Uncheck the Enable Adding, Enable Editing, and Enable Deleting checkboxes. Set the Name property to PODataGridView.

9. Add a Label control to the form. Set the Text property to Employee ID:.

10. Add a TextBox control to the form. Set the Name property to employeeIDTextBox.

11. Add a Button control to the form. Set the Text property to Go and the Name property to goButton.

    Figure 8-2 shows the completed form.

12. Double-click the goButton to add a click event handler named goButton_Click for the button.

13. Add the following code to the goButton_Click event handler:

```
GetPurchaseOrderWS.GetPurchaseOrderEndpoint proxy =
    new GetPurchaseOrderWS.GetPurchaseOrderEndpoint();
proxy.Credentials = System.Net.CredentialCache.DefaultCredentials;
```

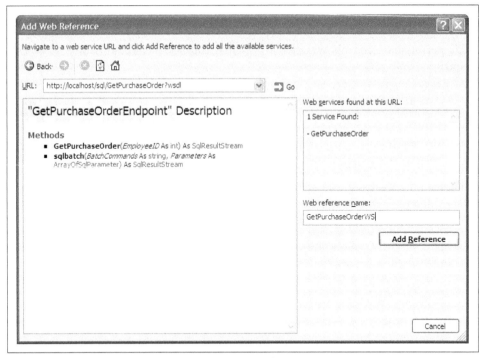

Figure 8-1. Adding a web reference for GetPurchaseOrder( )

Figure 8-2. Web client application user interface

```
object[] results;

int employeeID = -1;
try
{
    employeeID = int.Parse(employeeIDTextBox.Text);
```

```
        }
        catch (Exception) { }

        // execute the GetPurchaseOrder( ) method passing in either null or
        // an Employee ID
        if (employeeID != -1)
            results = proxy.GetPurchaseOrder(employeeID);
        else
            results = proxy.GetPurchaseOrder(System.Data.SqlTypes.SqlInt32.Null);

        // iterate over the array of objects returned from the web service and
        // handle each of them
        foreach (object o in results)
        {
            if (o.GetType( ).IsPrimitive)
                MessageBox.Show("SP Return Code = " + o);
            else
                switch (o.GetType().ToString( ))
                {
                    case "System.Data.DataSet":
                        // cast the object to a DataSet and fill the DataGridView
                        PODataGridView.DataSource = ((DataSet)o).Tables[0];
                        break;
                    case "GetPurchaseOrderSoapApp.GetPurchaseOrderWS.SqlRowCount":
                        MessageBox.Show("RowCount = " +
                        ((GetPurchaseOrderSoapApp.GetPurchaseOrderWS.SqlRowCount)o).Count);
                        break;
                }
        }
```

14. Execute the application. Enter a value for the Employee ID (for example, 244), or leave it blank to retrieve all employees. Click the Go button, and the DataGridView is filled with the DataSet returned by the web method. Results for Employee ID = 244 are shown in Figure 8-3.

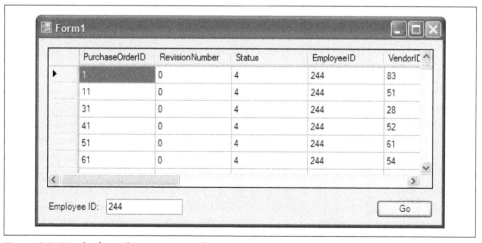

Figure 8-3. Results for web service example

SQL Batches

Web-service endpoints can be configured to support ad hoc queries. The BATCHES language-specific argument for SOAP in the CREATE ENDPOINT and ALTER ENDPOINT configures this. You execute an ad hoc query by calling the sqlbatch( ) method of the HTTP endpoint, passing in the queries (multiple queries must be separated with semicolons) and any parameters.

In a SOAP SQL batch request, the SOAP <body> element contains a single, <sqlbatch>. This element has two child elements:

<BatchCommands>
Specifies the query, or multiple queries separated by semicolons (;).

<Parameters>
Specifies an optional list of parameters. Each parameter is specified as a <SqlParameter> child element of the <Parameters> element. For each parameter, you must pass the parameter name as the name attribute of the <Parameter> element and the parameter value as a <Value> child element of the <Parameter> element.

The following example demonstrates ad hoc query support by altering the preceding client. This new version returns the purchase orders for an employee using an ad hoc query instead of the GetPurchaseOrder( ) web method. Replace the code for the goButton_Click event handler with the following code:

```
int employeeID = -1;
try
{
    employeeID = int.Parse(employeeIDTextBox.Text);
}
catch (Exception) { }

// execute the query only if a valid employee ID is entered
if (employeeID != -1)
{
    GetPurchaseOrderWS.GetPurchaseOrderEndpoint proxy =
        new GetPurchaseOrderWS.GetPurchaseOrderEndpoint( );
    proxy.Credentials = System.Net.CredentialCache.DefaultCredentials;

    // SQL parameterized command that returns purchase orders for an employee
    string commandText = "SELECT * FROM Purchasing.PurchaseOrderHeader " +
        "WHERE EmployeeID = @employeeID FOR XML AUTO";

    // create the employee ID parameter
    GetPurchaseOrderWS.SqlParameter[] parm =
        new GetPurchaseOrderWS.SqlParameter[1];
    parm[0] = new GetPurchaseOrderWS.SqlParameter( );
    parm[0].name = "employeeID";
    parm[0].Value = employeeID;
    parm[0].sqlDbType = GetPurchaseOrderWS.sqlDbTypeEnum.Int;
    parm[0].direction = GetPurchaseOrderWS.ParameterDirection.Input;
```

```
// call the web service sqlbatch method to execute the ad hoc query
object[] results = proxy.sqlbatch(commandText, ref parm);

// iterate over the array of objects returned from the web service and
// handle each of them
foreach (object o in results)
{
    if (o.GetType( ).IsPrimitive)
        MessageBox.Show("Return Code = " + o);
    else
        switch (o.GetType().ToString( ))
        {
            case "System.Xml.XmlElement":
                // retrieve the XmlElement and convert to a DataSet
                System.Xml.XmlElement xmlResult = (System.Xml.XmlElement)o;
                System.Xml.XmlNodeReader xnr =
                    new System.Xml.XmlNodeReader(xmlResult);
                DataSet ds = new DataSet( );
                ds.ReadXml(xnr);
                PODataGridView.DataSource = ds.Tables[0];

                break;
            case "GetPurchaseOrderSoapApp.GetPurchaseOrderWS.SqlRowCount":
                MessageBox.Show("RowCount = " +
                    ((GetPurchaseOrderSoapApp.GetPurchaseOrderWS.SqlRowCount)
                    o).Count);
                break;
        }
    }
}
```

The results are the same as in the previous example, except that you must specify an employee ID.

SOAP Request and Response Messages

When you are building a Visual Studio .NET application, Visual Studio .NET creates the necessary proxy class so that you can call a web service method almost exactly like you call any other method. The Visual Studio .NET application automatically builds the SOAP envelope for the request, and SQL Server processes the request, returning results in an object array or a single DataSet object.

If you are building an application that builds its own SOAP requests and processes its own SOAP responses, you need to understand the SOAP request and response message structures and the SOAP fault message structure. For more information, see Microsoft SQL Server 2005 Books Online.

Managing HTTP Endpoints

An HTTP endpoint is an interface through which HTTP-based clients send queries to the server. You must use the CREATE ENDPOINT T-SQL statement to configure the SQL Server instance to listen natively for HTTP requests before you can send a native HTTP/SOAP request to the server.

SQL Server HTTP endpoints can listen and receive requests on any valid port including TCP port 80—the same port used by the IIS World Wide Web Publishing service. Each URL—whether used for an HTTP endpoint or by IIS—is registered with the Windows operating system through the system HTTP listener process (http.sys).

This section discusses how to create, change, and remove endpoints, and how to grant and change permissions on endpoint objects.

Creating an HTTP Endpoint

An endpoint is an interface on which the server listens for HTTP requests from clients. The CREATE ENDPOINT T-SQL statement creates and configures an endpoint and web methods exposed by the endpoint.

The syntax for the CREATE ENDPOINT statement is:

```
CREATE ENDPOINT endPointName [ AUTHORIZATION login ]
STATE = { STARTED | STOPPED | DISABLED }
AS { HTTP | TCP } (
   <protocol_specific_arguments>
      )
FOR { SOAP | TSQL | SERVICE_BROKER | DATABASE_MIRRORING } (
   <language_specific_arguments>
        )
```

where:

endPointName
>   The name of the endpoint being created.

AUTHORIZATION *login*
>   The SQL Server or Windows account that is assigned ownership of the new endpoint. The caller must have IMPERSONATE permissions on the specified *login* to specify AUTHORIZATION. If this clause is omitted, the caller becomes the owner.
>
>   You can reassign ownership of an endpoint with the ALTER ENDPOINT statement.

STATE = { STARTED | STOPPED | DISABLED }
>   The state of the endpoint when created.
>
>   STARTED
>   >   The endpoint is started and listening for requests.
>
>   DISABLED
>   >   The endpoint is disabled and does not respond to requests.

STOPPED

The endpoint is stopped and returns an error in response to requests.

STOPPED is the default state.

Use the ALTER ENDPOINT statement to change the state of an endpoint.

AS { HTTP | TCP } (<protocol_specific_arguments>)

Specifies the transport protocol to use—HTTP or TCP. The AS clause specifies transport protocol–specific information for the endpoint, including the listening port, the authentication method, and a list of IP addresses that are restricted from accessing the endpoint.

The AS clause is described in the following subsection, "Protocol-specific arguments."

FOR { SOAP | TSQL | SERVICE_BROKER | DATABASE_MIRRORING }
(<language_specific_arguments>)

Specifies the payload type—SOAP, TSQL, SERVICE_BROKER, or DATABASE_MIRRORING. The FOR clause defines the payload and specifies additional SOAP configuration information, such as whether ad hoc queries are allowed, whether to return the XSD schema for the result set, and how to handle invalid characters in the XML.

The FOR clause is described in the upcoming subsection "Language-specific items."

Protocol-specific arguments

The syntax for HTTP protocol-specific items in the AS clause is:

```
<AS HTTP_protocol_specific_arguments> ::=
AS HTTP (
  PATH = 'url',
  AUTHENTICATION =( { BASIC | DIGEST | INTEGRATED | NTLM | KERBEROS } [ ,...n ] ),
  PORTS = ( { CLEAR | SSL} [ ,... n ] )
  [ SITE = {'*' | '+' | 'webSite' },]
  [, CLEAR_PORT = clearPort ]
  [, SSL_PORT = SSLPort ]
  [, AUTH_REALM = { 'realm' | NONE } ]
  [, DEFAULT_LOGON_DOMAIN = { 'domain' | NONE } ]
  [, RESTRICT_IP = { NONE | ALL } ]
  [, COMPRESSION = { ENABLED | DISABLED } ]
  [, EXCEPT_IP = ( { <4-part-ip> | <4-part-ip>:<mask> } [ ,...n ] ) ]
)
```

where:

PATH

The URL path for the endpoint on the host computer specified by the SITE argument. The PATH together with the SITE argument specifies the URL that the client uses to send HTTP SOAP requests to the server.

For example, in the URL http://<site>/<path>, site is the computer specified by the SITE argument and path is the URL specified by the PATH argument.

AUTHENTICATION

The authentication method for the endpoint—one or more of BASIC, DIGEST, INTEGRATED, NTLM, or KERBEROS. (If you specify more than one authentication method, separate the methods with commas).

Authentication is discussed in detail in the "Endpoint Authentication" section later in this chapter.

PORTS = ({ CLEAR | SSL} [,…n])

One or more listening ports for the endpoint. The listening ports can be CLEAR, SSL, or both. If CLEAR is specified, incoming requests must use standard HTTP requests (*http://*). If SSL is specified, incoming requests must use Secure HTTP requests (*https://*).

SITE = {'*' | '+' | 'webSite' }

The name of the host computer. Either a specific hostname webSite or one of two wildcards can be specified:

Plus sign (+)

Specifies listening on all possible hostnames for the computer

Asterisk (*)

Specifies listening on all possible hostnames for the computer that are not otherwise explicitly reserved

If the SITE argument is not specified, the default value is asterisk (*).

CLEAR_PORT

The listening clear port number, if the PORTS argument specifies clear port listening (PORTS = CLEAR). The default value is 80 if CLEAR_PORT is not explicitly specified.

SSL_PORT

The listening SSL port number, if the PORTS argument specifies SSL port listening (PORTS = SSL). The default value is 443 if SSL_PORT is not explicitly specified.

AUTH_REALM = { 'realm' | NONE }

The hint returned to the client as part of the HTTP challenge for digest authentication (AUTHENTICATION = DIGEST). The default value is NONE.

DEFAULT_LOGIN_DOMAIN{ 'domain' | NONE }

The default login domain for basic authentication (AUTHENTICATION = BASIC). The default value is NONE.

RESTRICT_IP = { NONE | ALL }

This parameter together with EXCEPT_IP specifies which IP addresses can send requests to an endpoint:

NONE

Indicates that all IP addresses except the list specified by the EXCEPT_IP parameter can send requests to the endpoint.

ALL

Indicates that only IP addresses specified in the EXCEPT_IP parameter can send requests to the endpoint (i.e., all IP addresses are restricted except for the list defined by the EXCEPT_IP parameter).

The default is NONE, allowing all IP addresses to send requests to the endpoint.

COMPRESSION = { ENABLED | DISABLED }

Specifies whether the endpoint honors *gzip*-encoded requests and returns compressed responses. The default value is DISABLED, indicating that gzip requests are not honored.

EXCEPT_IP = ({ <4-part-ip> | <4-part-ip>:<mask> } [,...n])

A list of IP addresses that together with the RESTRICT_IP argument specifies which IP addresses are either allowed to send or not allowed to send requests to the endpoint.

The syntax for TCP protocol-specific items in the AS clause is:

```
<AS TCP_protocol_specific_arguments> ::=
AS TCP (
  LISTENER_PORT = listenerPort
  [ , LISTENER_IP = ALL | (<4-part-ip> | <ip_address_v6> ) ]
  [ , RESTRICT_IP = ALL | NONE ]
  [ , EXCEPT_IP = ( { <4-part-ip> | <4-part-ip>:<mask> } [ ,...n ] ) ]
```

where:

LISTENER_PORT

The listening port number for the TCP/IP protocol. The default value is 4022.

LISTENER_IP = ALL | (<4-part-ip> | <ip_address_v6>)

The IP address that the endpoint listens on. The default value is ALL, meaning the endpoint will accept a connection on any valid IP address.

RESTRICT_IP

The RESTRICT_IP clause is described in the preceding discussion about HTTP protocol-specific items.

EXCEPT_IP

The EXCEPT_IP clause is described in the preceding discussion about HTTP protocol-specific items.

Language-specific arguments

The syntax for SOAP language-specific arguments is:

```
<FOR SOAP_language_specific_arguments> ::=
FOR SOAP(
  [ { WEBMETHOD [ 'namespace' .] 'method_alias'
  (   NAME = 'database.owner.name'
      [ , SCHEMA = { NONE | STANDARD | DEFAULT } ]
      [ , FORMAT = { ALL_RESULTS | ROWSETS_ONLY | NONE} ]
  )
```

```
      } [ ,...n ] ]
    [   BATCHES = { ENABLED | DISABLED } ]
    [ , WSDL = { NONE | DEFAULT | 'sp_name' } ]
    [ , SESSIONS = { ENABLED | DISABLED } ]
    [ , LOGIN_TYPE = { MIXED | WINDOWS } ]
    [ , SESSION_TIMEOUT = timeoutInterval | NEVER ]
    [ , DATABASE = { 'database_name' | DEFAULT }
    [ , NAMESPACE = { 'namespace' | DEFAULT } ]
    [ , SCHEMA = { NONE | STANDARD } ]
    [ , CHARACTER_SET = { SQL | XML }]
    [ , MAX_SOAP_HEADERS_SIZE = { int | DEFAULT }]
 )
```

where:

WEBMETHOD ['namespace' .] 'method_alias'

A method for which you can send SOAP requests to the endpoint. Each WEBMETHOD clause describes a single method. However, an endpoint can expose multiple methods. The ALTER ENDPOINT statement can be used to add or remove web methods from an existing endpoint.

If the namespace is not specified, the namespace of the endpoint is used.

NAME = 'database.owner.name'

The name of the stored procedure or UDF corresponding to the web method. The NAME must be specified as a three-part name in the format database.owner. name.

SCHEMA = {NONE | STANDARD | DEFAULT}

Specifies whether an inline XSD schema is returned in the SOAP response from the web method.

NONE

The web method is omitted from the schema if one is sent in the SOAP response.

STANDARD

An XSD schema is not returned with the SOAP response.

DEFAULT

The value specified for the endpoint SCHEMA option determines whether an XSD schema is returned.

FORMAT= { ALL_RESULTS | ROWSETS_ONLY | NONE }

Specifies whether the row count, error messages, and warnings are returned with the result set.

ALL_RESULTS

The row count, error messages, and warnings are returned with the result set in the SOAP response.

ROWSETS_ONLY

Only the result set is returned in the SOAP response.

NONE

SOAP-specific markup is suppressed from the SOAP response.

The default value is ALL_RESULTS.

BATCHES = { ENABLED | DISABLED }

Specifies whether ad hoc SQL requests are supported on the endpoint through the sqlbatch( ) method. The default value is DISABLED.

Ad hoc SQL requests are detailed earlier in this chapter in the section "SQL Batches."

WSDL = { NONE | DEFAULT | 'sp_name' }

Specifies whether a WSDL document is generated and returned for WSDL queries submitted to the endpoint.

NONE

No WSDL file is generated or returned for WSDL queries to the endpoint.

DEFAULT

The default WSDL file is generated and returned for WSDL queries to the endpoint.

'sp_name'

A custom WSDL file generated by the stored procedure sp_name is returned for WSDL queries on the endpoint.

SESSIONS = { ENABLED | DISABLED }

Specifies whether SQL Server allows sessions—multiple SOAP request/response pairs identified as part of a single SOAP session. The default value is DISABLED.

LOGIN_TYPE = { MIXED | WINDOWS }

The SQL Server authentication mode for the endpoint. LOGIN_TYPE is used only to further restrict the authentication mode for endpoints based on the authentication mode selected when the SQL Server instance was installed.

WINDOWS

Only Windows authentication is used.

MIXED

Either SQL or Windows authentication is used. Mixed authentication cannot be used if it was not selected as the global authentication mode when SQL Server was installed. An endpoint using SQL Server–based authentication must be configured to use an SSL port.

The default value is WINDOWS.

SESSION_TIMEOUT = int | NEVER

The time, in seconds, after which a SOAP session expires at the server if no requests (identified by a session ID in the SOAP header) are made. After the session times out, subsequent requests with the expired session ID return a SOAP fault. The SOAP session never expires if a value of NEVER is specified for SESSION_TIMEOUT.

DATABASE = { 'database_name' | DEFAULT }
> The database in which the operation is executed. If not specified or if DEFAULT is specified, the default database for the login is used.

NAMESPACE = { 'namespace' | DEFAULT }
> The namespace for the endpoint. If not specified or if specified as DEFAULT, *http://tempuri.org* is used.

SCHEMA = { NONE | STANDARD }
> Specifies whether an XSD schema is returned by the endpoint with the SOAP result sent to the client.

> STANDARD
>> An inline schema is included in the SOAP response.

> NONE
>> The inline schema is not included in the SOAP response.

> An inline schema is required to load SOAP results into a .NET DataSet object.

> The default is STANDARD.

CHARACTER_SET = { SQL | XML }
> Specifies the behavior if the results of an operation include characters that are not valid in XML.

> XML
>> An error is returned if the result includes invalid XML characters.

> SQL
>> Invalid characters are encoded as character references and returned in the results—this might result in invalid XML.

> The default value is XML.

MAX_SOAP_HEADERS_SIZE = { int | DEFAULT }
> Specifies the maximum size, in bytes, of the SOAP header within the SOAP envelope. The server throws a parsing error if the SOAP header is larger than the specified value. The maximum header size is 8KB if DEFAULT is specified or if a value is not specified.

The syntax for Service Broker–specific items is:

```
<FOR SERVICE_BROKER_language_specific_arguments> ::=
FOR SERVICE_BROKER (
  [ AUTHENTICATION = { WINDOWS [ { NTLM | KERBEROS | NEGOTIATE } ] |
      CERTIFICATE certificateName |
      WINDOWS [ { NTLM | KERBEROS | NEGOTIATE } ] CERTIFICATE certificateName |
      CERTIFICATE certificateName WINDOWS [ { NTLM | KERBEROS | NEGOTIATE } ] } ]
  [ , ENCRYPTION = {DISABLED | SUPPORTED | REQUIRED }
      [ALGORITHM {RC4 | AES | AES RC4 | RC4 AES } ] ] }
  [ , MESSAGE_FORWARDING = { ENABLED | DISABLED } ]
  [ , MESSAGE_FORWARD_SIZE = forwardSize ]
)
```

where:

AUTHENTICATION

> The TCP/IP authentication requirements for connections for the endpoint—either WINDOWS or CERTIFICATE. The default is WINDOWS. If both authentication methods are specified, they are attempted in the order specified until one succeeds or both fail.

> WINDOWS

>> Windows Authentication is used to authenticate the endpoints users. You can optionally specify an authorization method—NTLM, KERBEROS, or NEGOTIATE—to force Windows Authentication to use that authorization method. If you specify NEGOTIATE, the endpoint uses Windows negotiating protocol to select either NTLM or Kerberos. NEGOTIATE is the default authorization method.

> CERTIFICATE

>> Endpoint connects using the specified certificate to establish identity for authorization. The endpoint needs a certificate with the public key for the specified certificate.

ENCRYPTION = {DISABLED | SUPPORTED | REQUIRED }

> Specifies whether encryption is used in the process.

> DISABLED

>> Data sent over the connection is not encrypted.

> SUPPORTED

>> Data is encrypted if the opposite endpoint connection specifies SUPPORTED or REQUIRED.

> REQUIRED

>> Data must be encrypted. The opposite endpoint must specify SUPPORTED or REQUIRED for the ENCRYPTION option.

> The default is REQUIRED.

ALGORITHM

> Specifies the encryption algorithm. If both endpoints specify different encryption algorithms, the accepting endpoint prevails.

MESSAGE_FORWARDING = { ENABLED | DISABLED }

> Specifies whether messages received by the endpoint for services located elsewhere are forwarded.

> ENABLED

>> Messages are forwarded if a forwarding address is available.

> DISABLED

>> Messages for services located elsewhere are discarded.

> The default value is DISABLED.

MESSAGE_FORWARD_SIZE

Specifies the maximum amount of storage, in megabytes, allocated for use by the endpoint for storing messages that will be forwarded.

The syntax for database mirroring–specific items is:

```
<FOR DATABASE_MIRRORING_language_specific_arguments> ::=
FOR DATABASE_MIRRORING (
    [ AUTHENTICATION = { WINDOWS [ { NTLM | KERBEROS | NEGOTIATE } ] |
        CERTIFICATE certificateName } ]
    [ [ , ] ENCRYPTION = { DISABLED |SUPPORTED | REQUIRED }
        [ ALGORITHM { RC4 | AES | AES RC4 | RC4 AES } ] ] }
    [ , ] ROLE = { WITNESS | PARTNER | ALL }
)
```

where:

AUTHENTICATION

The AUTHENTICATION clause is described in the preceding discussion about Service Broker–specific items.

ENCRYPTION = { DISABLED |SUPPORTED | REQUIRED }

The ENCRYPTION clause is described in the preceding discussion about Service Broker–specific items.

ROLE = { WITNESS | PARTNER | ALL }

Specifies the database mirroring role or roles that the endpoint supports in the SQL Server mirroring process.

WITNESS

The endpoint performs the role of witness in the mirroring process.

PARTNER

The endpoint performs the role of partner in the mirroring process.

ALL

The endpoint performs the role of both witness and partner in the mirroring process.

Altering an ENDPOINT

The ALTER ENDPOINT statement lets you change an existing endpoint—you can add methods to the endpoint, change or drop existing endpoint methods, and change properties of the endpoint.

In the ALTER ENDPOINT statement, specify only properties that you want to update— unspecified properties will remain unchanged.

Endpoints can be altered by members of the sysadmin role, the owner of the endpoint, or by users granted ALTER ANY ENDPOINT permission or ALTER ON ENDPOINT permission for the specific endpoint. The ALTER AUTHORIZATION statement changes the owner of an existing endpoint—this command is discussed in the "Endpoint Authentication" section later in this chapter.

Most of the clauses and arguments for the ALTER ENDPOINT statement are the same as those for the CREATE ENDPOINT statement, discussed in the previous section. Only different arguments and clauses are discussed in this section.

The syntax for the ALTER ENDPOINT statement is:

```
ALTER ENDPOINT endPointName
[ AFFINITY = { NONE | <64bit_integer> | ADMIN } ]
[ STATE = { STARTED | STOPPED | DISABLED } ]
AS { TCP | HTTP } (
    <protocol_specific_items> )
FOR { SOAP | TSQL | SERVICE_BROKER | DATABASE_MIRRORING } (
    <language_specific_items> )
```

where:

AFFINITY

Specifies the endpoint affinity.

STATE

The STATE argument is the same as described in the discussion for the CREATE ENDPOINT statement earlier in this chapter.

If the state is changed to DISABLED, the server needs to be restarted for the change to take effect.

Protocol-specific items

The syntax for HTTP protocol-specific items is:

```
<AS HTTP_protocol_specific_arguments> ::=
AS HTTP (
  PATH = 'url',
  AUTHENTICATION = ( { BASIC | DIGEST | NTLM | KERBEROS | INTEGRATED } [ ,...n ] ),
  PORTS = ( { CLEAR | SSL } [ ,...n ] )
  [ SITE = { '*' | '+' | 'webSite' } , ]
  [ , CLEAR_PORT = clearPort ]
  [ , SSL_PORT = SSLPort ]
  [ , AUTH_REALM = { 'realm' | NONE } ]
  [ , DEFAULT_LOGON_DOMAIN = { 'domain' | NONE } ]
  [ , RESTRICT_IP = { NONE | ALL } ]
  [ , COMPRESSION = { ENABLED | DISABLED } ]
  [ , ADD EXCEPT_IP = ( { <4-part-ip> | <4-part-ip>:<mask> } [ ,...n ] )
  [ , DROP EXCEPT_IP = ( { <4-part-ip> | <4-part-ip>:<mask> } [ ,...n ] )
)
```

where:

ADD EXCEPT_IP

Adds IP addresses to the IP addresses in the EXCEPT_IP parameter for the endpoint.

The `RESTRICT_IP` parameter specified in the `CREATE ENDPOINT` statement controls whether requests from these IP addresses are allowed or denied access to the endpoint.

`DROP EXCEPT_IP`

Removes IP addresses from the IP addresses in the `EXCEPT_IP` parameter for the endpoint.

The `RESTRICT_IP` parameter specified in the `CREATE ENDPOINT` statement controls whether requests from these IP addresses are allowed or denied access to the endpoint.

The syntax for TCP protocol-specific items is:

```
<AS TCP_protocol_specific_arguments> ::=
AS TCP (
  LISTENER_PORT = listenerPort
  [ , LISTENER_IP = ALL | (<4-part-ip> | <ip_address_v6> ) ]
  [ , RESTRICT_IP = ALL | NONE ]
  [ , EXCEPT_IP = ( { <4-part-ip> | <4-part-ip>:<mask> } [ ,...n ] ) ]
)
```

Language-specific items

The syntax for SOAP language-specific items is:

```
<FOR SOAP_language_specific_arguments> ::=
(
  [ { ADD WEBMETHOD [ 'namespace' .] 'method_alias'
  (   NAME = 'database.owner.name'
      [ , SCHEMA = {NONE | STANDARD | DEFAULT } ]
      [ , FORMAT = { ALL_RESULTS | ROWSETS_ONLY } ]
  )
  } [ ,...n ] ]

  [ { ALTER WEBMETHOD [ 'namespace' .] 'method_alias'
  (   NAME = 'database.owner.name'
      [ , SCHEMA = {NONE | STANDARD | DEFAULT} ]
      [ , FORMAT = { ALL_RESULTS | ROWSETS_ONLY } ]
  )
  } [ ,...n] ]

  [ { DROP WEBMETHOD [ 'namespace' .] 'method_alias' } [ ,...n ] ]

  [   BATCHES = { ENABLED | DISABLED } ]
  [ , WSDL = { NONE | DEFAULT | 'sp_name' } ]
  [ , SESSIONS = { ENABLED | DISABLED } ]
  [ , SESSION_TIMEOUT = int ]
  [ , DATABASE = { 'database_name' | DEFAULT }
  [ , NAMESPACE = { 'namespace' | DEFAULT } ]
  [ , SCHEMA = { NONE | STANDARD } ]
  [ , CHARACTER_SET = { SQL | XML } ]
)
```

where:

ADD WEBMETHOD
> Adds a method to the endpoint.

ALTER WEBMETHOD
> Changes the definition of an existing method on the endpoint.

DROP WEBMETHOD
> Removes an existing method from the endpoint.

The syntax for Service Broker–specific items is:

```
<FOR SERVICE_BROKER_language_specific_arguments> ::=
FOR SERVICE_BROKER (
  [ AUTHENTICATION = ENABLED | REQUIRED* | NONE ]
  [ , MESSAGE_FORWARDING = ENABLED | DISABLED* ]
  [ , MESSAGE_FORWARD_SIZE = forwardSize
)
```

The syntax for database mirroring–specific items is:

```
<FOR DATABASE_MIRRORING_language_specific_arguments> ::=
FOR DATABASE_MIRRORING (
  [ ENCRYPTION = ENABLED | DISABLED ] |
  ROLE = WITNESS | PARTNER | ALL
)
```

Dropping an ENDPOINT

The DROP ENDPOINT statement removes an existing endpoint. Endpoints can be dropped by members of the sysadmin role, the owner of the endpoint, or users granted CONTROL permission on the endpoint.

The DROP ENDPOINT statement syntax is:

```
DROP ENDPOINT endPointName
```

where:

endPointName
> The name of the endpoint to remove.

Endpoint Authentication

Each endpoint is configured for an authentication type and access permissions that allow users to connect to the endpoint.

A user must be an authenticated Windows user—either a trusted Windows user or a member account on the local computer—to access an endpoint. Anonymous authentication on an endpoint is not supported.

The AUTHENTICATION clause in the CREATE ENDPOINT and ALTER ENDPOINT statements specifies how endpoint authentication is performed. The following authentication types are supported:

BASIC

An HTTP 1.1 authentication mechanism that uses an authentication header containing a Base64-encoded username and password separated by a colon (:). The credentials must map to a valid Windows account. Because Base64 encoding can easily be decoded, SQL Server requires that a Secure Sockets Layer (SSL) port be used for the HTTP connection—BASIC authentication is not allowed for endpoints where the PORTS value is CLEAR.

DIGEST

An HTTP 1.1 authentication mechanism consisting of a username and password hashed with the MD5 algorithm. The server has access to either the actual password or an MD5 hash of the password, allowing the client to prove the password without actually sending it to the server. The credentials must map to a valid Windows domain account—local users are not supported for digest authentication.

NTLM

The authentication mechanism supported by Windows 9x and Windows NT 4.0. NTLM is an encrypted challenge/response protocol that uses a domain name, username, and one-way password hash.

Although Microsoft Kerberos is the protocol of choice, NTLM is provided for backward compatibility.

KERBEROS

An Internet standard mutual-authentication mechanism between client and server designed for use over an open or unsecured network. Clients obtain an authentication ticket from a Kerberos Key Distribution Center (KDC) and present that ticket to servers when connections are established. Kerberos is supported in Windows 2000 or later by the Security Support Provider Interface (SSPI).

To use Kerberos authentication, you must register a service principal name (SPN) with the SQL Server account that it is running on by using the SetSPN.exe tool. For more information, see Microsoft SQL Server 2005 Books Online.

INTEGRATED

The endpoint can respond to either Kerberos or NTLM authentication-type challenges. The server tries to authenticate the client using the authentication type that the client uses in the authentication request.

Native HTTP SOAP can user either Windows user and group accounts or SQL Server logins as security principals. You control this via the LOGIN_TYPE value in the SOAP language-specific arguments for the CREATE ENDPOINT or ALTER ENDPOINT statement.

If SQL logins are used, your application must use *WS-Security* headers to submit the SQL username and password login credentials to the server for SQL Server authentication.

 WS-Security is an open-standard set of SOAP extensions used to build secure web services and to implement message content integrity and confidentiality.

For more information about WS-Security, get the latest draft from the Organization for the Advancement of Structured Information Standards (OASIS) web site at *http://www.oasis-open.org*.

To use SQL Server authentication, the following conditions must be met:

- The SQL Server installation is mixed mode, supporting both Windows and SQL logins.
- The endpoint is configured with `LOGIN_TYPE = MIXED` and `PORTS = (SSL)`.
- Endpoint permissions have been granted to the appropriate SQL Server logins.

A generic WS-Security header that can be used in a SOAP request header to transport SQL Server authentication credentials is:

```
<SOAP-ENV:Header>
  <wsse:Security
    xmlns:wsse="http://docs.oasis-open.org/wss/2004/01/
      oasis-200401-wss-wssecurity-secext-1.0.xsd">
    <wsse:UsernameToken>
      <wsse:Username>sqlLoginUserName</wsse:Username>
      <wsse:Password Type="http://docs.oasis-open.org/wss/2004/01/
        oasis-200401-wss-username-token-profile-1.0#PasswordText">
        sqlLoginPassword
      </wsse:Password>
    </wsse:UsernameToken>
  </wsse:Security>
</SOAP-ENV:Header>
```

The `<wsse:UserName>` element contains the SQL Server user login name, and the `<wsse:Password>` element contains the password for the login.

Managing Permissions on Endpoints

Endpoint permissions specify whether a login can create, alter, connect, or transfer ownership of an endpoint. Requests against endpoints can be executed by members of the sysadmin role, the owner of the endpoint, or users granted `CONNECT` permission on the endpoint.

All T-SQL statements governing permissions must be executed on the master database. This section discusses the statements used for managing endpoint permissions.

The prototypes in the subsections use the following arguments:

server_principal
> The principal to which the permission is granted, denied, or revoked. *server_principal* is one of the following:
>
> * A SQL Server login
> * A SQL Server login created from a Windows login
> * A SQL Server login mapped to a certificate
> * A SQL Server login mapped to an asymmetric key

endPointName
> The name of the endpoint for which the permission is granted.

Create permission

A server-scoped permission controls whether a login can create an endpoint object. The syntax is:

```
{ GRANT | DENY | REVOKE } CREATE ENDPOINT TO server_principal
```

Alter permission

You can assign permissions to a user to alter an endpoint in three different ways:

* At the server scope. Granting this permission lets the login alter or drop any endpoint on the server:

  ```
  { GRANT | DENY | REVOKE } ALTER ANY ENDPOINT TO server_principal
  ```

* For a specific endpoint. Granting this permission lets the login alter or drop a specific endpoint on the server:

  ```
  { GRANT | DENY | REVOKE } ALTER ON ENDPOINT::endPointName TO server_principal
  ```

Control permission

This permission lets the principal alter or drop a specific endpoint on the server and transfer its ownership:

```
{ GRANT | DENY | REVOKE } CONTROL ON ENDPOINT::endPointName TO server_principal
```

Connect permission

This permission controls whether a login can execute requests against a specific endpoint:

```
{ GRANT | DENY | REVOKE } CONNECT ON ENDPOINT::endPointName TO server_principal
```

Take Ownership permission

This permission controls whether a user specified in the AUTHORIZATION clause of a CREATE ENDPOINT or ALTER ENDPOINT statement can take ownership of an endpoint:

```
{ GRANT | DENY | REVOKE } TAKE OWNERSHIP ON ENDPOINT::endPointName TO
    server_principal>
```

Endpoint Metadata

You can query the catalog views described in Table 8-1 for information about all endpoints defined in the system.

Table 8-1. Catalog views for endpoint information

Catalog view	Description
sys.database_mirroring_endpoints	General endpoint information and detailed database mirroring–specific information for each database mirroring endpoint in the system
sys.endpoints	General information about each HTTP endpoint in the system, including the name, ID, principal ID, protocol, type, and state information
sys.endpoint_webmethods	Detailed information for each SOAP method defined on a SOAP-enabled HTTP endpoint
sys.http_endpoints	General endpoint information and HTTP-specific information, including site information and authentication type for endpoints in the system that use HTTP
sys.tcp_endpoints	General endpoint information and TCP-specific information for endpoints in the system that use TCP
sys.service_broker_endpoints	General endpoint information and Service Broker–specific information for each Service Broker endpoint in the system
sys.soap_endpoints	General endpoint information and SOAP-specific information for each endpoint in the system that carries a SOAP payload
sys.via_endpoints	General endpoint information and Virtual Interface Adapter (VIA)–specific information for each VIA endpoint in the system

CHAPTER 9

SQL Server Management Objects (SMO)

SQL Server Management Objects (SMO) is a collection of namespaces introduced in SQL Server 2005 for programming all aspects of SQL Server 2005 management. SMO supersedes SQL Server Distributed Management Objects (SQL-DMO). Besides extending SQL-DMO functionality, SMO is easier to use. SMO adds functionality to support new SQL Server 2005 features, in addition to providing all SQL-DMO functionality.

SMO uses SQL-DMO terminology where possible to facilitate the migration. However, some DMO properties have been moved or renamed in the transition. For more information, see the Microsoft SQL Server 2005 Books Online section "SMO Mapping to DMO."

There is no way to upgrade a SQL-DMO application to SMO—the application must be rewritten. SMO applications can interface with both SMO and SQL-DMO within the same process.

SMO is compatible with SQL Server 2000 and SQL Server 7.0. This allows you to use SMO to manage environments with a mix of different SQL Server versions. You cannot use SMO to manage a database with compatibility level 60 (SQL Server version 6.0) or 65 (SQL Server version 6.5).

SMO uses the SQL Server data provider (System.Data.SqlClient) to communicate with SQL Server instances. SMO clients must have SQL Server Native Client installed. SQL Server Native Client ships with both SQL Server 2005 and .NET Framework 2.0 and is described in more detail in Chapter 6.

SMO clients require one of the following operating systems: Windows NT 4.0 SP5 or later, Windows 2000, Windows XP, or Windows Server 2003. SMO clients also require MDAC 9.0, which ships with SQL Server 2005.

SMO assemblies are installed automatically as part of the Client Tools option when installing SQL Server 2005. The default installation directory is *C:\Program Files\ Microsoft SQL Server\90\SDK\Assemblies*.

This chapter introduces SMO, provides an overview of the SMO object model, and demonstrates a simple SMO programming example. The next four chapters explore SMO programming in detail:

Chapter 10, *SQL Server Management Objects (SMO) Instance Classes, Part 1*
SMO contains a class hierarchy that matches the SQL Server database hierarchy. This chapter describes the SMO classes used to administer database objects that store and access data, such as tables, indexes, triggers, and stored procedures. It also shows how to use the SMO classes programmatically to administer these objects. In addition, it shows how to subscribe to SMO events and handle exceptions.

Chapter 11, *SQL Server Management Objects (SMO) Instance Classes, Part 2*
SMO contains classes for administering database objects that do not store or access data, such as data and log files, logins, users, roles, and .NET Framework assemblies. This chapter describes how to use these classes programmatically.

Chapter 12, *SQL Server Management Objects (SMO) Utility Classes*
SMO utility classes are used to perform tasks that are independent of a SQL Server instance. These classes include scripting, backup and restore, transfer, mail, and tracing classes. This chapter shows how to use these classes programmatically.

Chapter 13, *Programming Windows Management Instrumentation (WMI)*
WMI can be used to manage SQL Server services, network settings, and server alias settings. This chapter describes the SMO classes that you use to access WMI and shows you how to program these classes.

SMO Object Model

The SMO object model contains two types of classes:

Instance classes
Form a hierarchy that matches the database server object hierarchy. The top object is a SQL Server instance represented by the Server object. Under this object is a hierarchy of instance objects, including databases, tables, columns, indexes, and stored procedures. Instance classes are discussed in detail in Chapters 10 and 11.

Utility classes
Perform specific tasks and are independent of the server instance. Utility classes are discussed in detail in Chapters 12 and 13.

SMO has a collection of namespaces that represent different areas of functionality. These are described in Table 9-1.

Table 9-1. SMO namespaces

Namespace	Description
Microsoft.SqlServer.Management.Common	Classes common to SMO and Replication Management Objects (RMO)—primarily classes used to establish a connection to a SQL Server instance
Microsoft.SqlServer.Management.Nmo	Classes used to develop and administer Notification Services instances and applications
Microsoft.SqlServer.Management.Smo	Instance classes, utility classes, event handlers, exceptions, and enumerations used to programmatically control SQL Server
Microsoft.SqlServer.Management.Smo.Agent	Classes that represent SQL Server Agent
Microsoft.SqlServer.Management.Smo.Broker	Classes that represent Service Broker
Microsoft.SqlServer.Management.Smo.Mail	Classes that represent Database Mail
Microsoft.SqlServer.Management.Smo.RegisteredServers	Classes that represent registered servers and schemas
Microsoft.SqlServer.Management.Smo.Wmi	Classes that provides programmatic access to the WMI provider for Configuration Management
Microsoft.SqlServer.Management.Trace	Classes that provide programmatic access for tracing and recording events, manipulating and analyzing trace logs, and replaying trace events

Creating an SMO Project in Visual Studio .NET

This example shows you how to build a simple C# SMO Console application using Visual Studio 2005. Follow these steps:

1. Select File → New → Project from the Visual Studio 2005 main menu.

2. In the New Project dialog box, select Visual C# as the project type and select Console Application from the installed templates.

3. Enter a name for the project and specify the location in which to save the project. Click OK.

4. Right-click References in the Solution Explorer window. Select Add Reference from the context menu.

5. In the Add Reference dialog box, add a reference to the Microsoft.SqlServer. ConnectionInfo.dll and Microsoft.SqlServer.Smo.dll assemblies.

6. Click OK to close the dialog box and add the references.

7. In the Solution Explorer window, right-click the file Program.cs. Select View → Code from the context menu.

8. Expose SMO types by adding the following using directives to the code:

```
using Microsoft.SqlServer.Management.Smo;
using Microsoft.SqlServer.Management.Common;
```

Add using directives for any other types that you need access to.

A Simple SMO Application

This example displays the product title for the local SQL Server instance and the hardware platform for the computer running the SQL Server instance. You need a reference to the Microsoft.SqlServer.ConnectionInfo.dll and Microsoft.SqlServer.Smo.dll assemblies to compile and execute this example.

```
using System;

using Microsoft.SqlServer.Management.Smo;

class Program
{
    static void Main(string[] args)
    {
        Server server = new Server("localhost");
        Console.WriteLine("Product:    " + server.Information.Product);
        Console.WriteLine("Platform:   " + server.Information.Platform);

        Console.WriteLine(Environment.NewLine +
            "Press any key to continue.");
        Console.ReadKey();
    }
}
```

The console output looks something like the output shown in Figure 9-1.

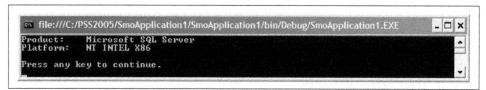

Figure 9-1. Console output for a simple SMO application

The Information property of the Server class returns an Information object that exposes information about the SQL Server instance through its properties.

CHAPTER 10

SQL Server Management Objects (SMO) Instance Classes, Part 1

SMO instance classes form a hierarchy matching the database server hierarchy. The top SMO objects are SQL Server instances represented by the Server object, under which is a hierarchy of instance objects that includes databases, tables, columns, indexes, and stored procedures.

This chapter provides an overview of the SMO instance classes for administering database objects that are used to store data. Following this overview, the chapter shows how to use these classes programmatically, how to subscribe to SMO events, and how to handle SMO exceptions. The chapter concludes with a reference to all SMO classes used to programmatically administer data storage objects. Chapter 11 covers SMO classes for administering database objects that are not used to store data.

Programming SMO Instance Classes for Administering Data Storage Objects

The following SQL Server objects are considered to store data. They are used to identify the SMO instance classes that administer SQL Server data storage objects.

- SQL Server instances
- Databases
- Schemas
- Tables
- Views
- Columns
- Indexes
- Foreign keys
- Check constraints
- Rules

- Stored procedures, extended stored procedures, and numbered stored procedures
- DML and DDL triggers
- User-defined aggregates, user-defined functions, and user-defined types
- Data types
- System data types

Figure 10-1 shows the relationship between SMO instance classes used to administer the preceding list of SQL Server objects. A reference to these classes is included in the "SMO Instance Classes for Administering Data Storage Objects Reference" section, later in this chapter.

The following subsections show how to programmatically use SMO instance classes for data storage. The examples in this section are all built using Visual Studio 2005. You need a reference to the following assemblies to compile and run the examples:

- Microsoft.SqlServer.ConnectionInfo
- Microsoft.SqlServer.Smo

Additional assembly references for examples will be indicated where required.

Connecting to and Disconnecting from SQL Server

This example demonstrates how to instantiate an SMO instance class and iterate through a collection. The example connects to the local SQL Server instance, lists the databases on the instance, and disconnects from the instance:

```
using System;

using Microsoft.SqlServer.Management.Common;
using Microsoft.SqlServer.Management.Smo;

class Program
{
    static void Main(string[] args)
    {
        Server server = new Server();

        DatabaseCollection dbs = server.Databases;

        foreach (Database db in dbs)
            Console.WriteLine(db.Name);

        server.ConnectionContext.Disconnect();

        Console.WriteLine("Press any key to continue.");
        Console.ReadKey();
    }
}
```

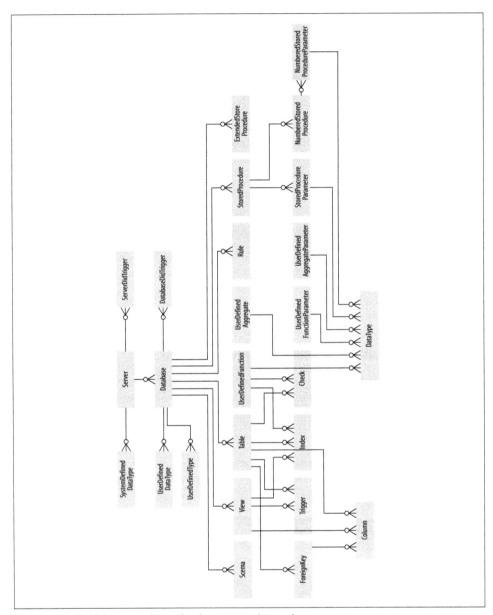

Figure 10-1. SMO instance classes for data storage hierarchy

Results are shown in Figure 10-2.

The Server class is the top-level class in the SMO hierarchy, and represents a SQL Server instance. The Server instance is used to access the collection of Database objects in the DatabaseCollection object and enumerate the names of the databases on the server. The SMO classes used to manage SQL Server databases are described

Figure 10-2. Results for listing server databases example

later in the chapter, in the section "SMO Instance Classes for Administering Data Storage Objects Reference."

The ServerConnection object (represented by the Server.ConnectionContext property) contains the information needed to connect to and disconnect from a SQL Server instance. You can reuse a ServerConnection object, which is helpful if the connection information that it contains is extensive. You do not need to call the Connect() method on the ServerConnection object. SMO will automatically open and close a connection to the server as required. The Disconnect() method of the ServerConnection class explicitly disconnects the connection instead of simply allowing it to disconnect automatically when the connection goes out of scope.

The Server object constructor has three overloads. The default constructor (used in the preceding example) automatically tries to connect to the default SQL Server instance with default connection settings.

The second overload specifies the SQL Server instance name as a constructor argument, as shown in the following example:

```
Server server = new Server("localhost");
```

The third overload creates the Server object by using a ServerConnection object, as shown in the following example:

```
ServerConnection sc = new ServerConnection();
sc.ServerInstance = "localhost";
Server server = new Server(sc);
```

Navigating the Server Hierarchy

This example iterates over all databases on the local SQL Server instance, listing the tables and columns in each:

```
using System;
using System.Data;

using Microsoft.SqlServer.Management.Common;
using Microsoft.SqlServer.Management.Smo;
```

```
class Program
{
    static void Main(string[] args)
    {
        Server server = new Server("localhost");

        foreach (Database db in server.Databases)
        {
            Console.WriteLine("DATABASE: " + db.Name);
            foreach (Table t in db.Tables)
            {
                Console.WriteLine("  TABLE: " + t.Name);
                Console.WriteLine("    COLUMNS:");
                foreach (Column c in t.Columns)
                    Console.WriteLine("      " + c.Name);
            }
            Console.WriteLine();
        }

        Console.WriteLine("Press any key to continue.");
        Console.ReadKey();
    }
}
```

Partial results are shown in Figure 10-3.

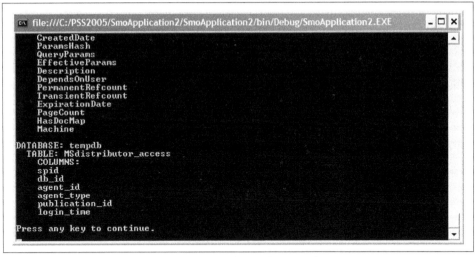

Figure 10-3. Partial results for navigating server hierarchy example

The Database object exposes a collection of Table objects representing the tables in the database. Each Table object in turn exposes a collection of Column objects representing the columns in the table. Accessing the other collections of data storage objects is similar to accessing the Table and Column collections. Figure 10-1, earlier in the chapter, shows the class hierarchy, which will help you understand the relationships among the classes, and the "SMO Instance Classes for Administering Data Storage Objects Reference" section, later in this chapter, provides more detailed information.

Enumerating Database Properties

This example enumerates the properties of the AdventureWorks database on the local SQL Server instance, using the Database.Properties collection:

```
using System;

using Microsoft.SqlServer.Management.Common;
using Microsoft.SqlServer.Management.Smo;

class Program
{
    static void Main(string[] args)
    {
        Server server = new Server("localhost");

        DatabaseCollection dbs = server.Databases;
        Database db = dbs["AdventureWorks"];
        foreach (Property p in db.Properties)
            Console.WriteLine(p.Name + ": " + p.Value);

        Console.WriteLine(Environment.NewLine + "Press any key to continue.");
        Console.ReadKey();
    }
}
```

Results are shown in Figure 10-4.

Enumerating Database Objects

This example enumerates all objects in the AdventureWorks database:

```
using System;
using System.Data;

using Microsoft.SqlServer.Management.Common;
using Microsoft.SqlServer.Management.Smo;

class Program
{
    static void Main(string[] args)
    {
        Server server = new Server("localhost");

        Database db = server.Databases["AdventureWorks"];

        using (DataTable dt = db.EnumObjects())
        {
```

```
file:///C:/PSS2005/SmoApplication2/SmoApplication2/bin/Debug/SmoApplication2.EXE
ActiveConnections: 0
CompatibilityLevel: Version90
CreateDate: 6/8/2005 2:25:14 PM
DataSpaceUsage: 101472
DboLogin: True
DefaultFileGroup: PRIMARY
DefaultSchema:
ID: 8
IndexSpaceUsage:
IsAccessible: True
IsDbAccessAdmin:
IsDbBackupOperator:
IsDbDatareader:
IsDbDatawriter:
IsDbDdlAdmin:
IsDbDenyDatareader:
IsDbDenyDatawriter:
IsDbOwner:
IsDbSecurityAdmin:
IsFullTextEnabled: True
IsSystemObject: False
LastBackupDate:
LastLogBackupDate:
Owner: BILLHAMILTON1\whamilton
PrimaryFilePath:
ReplicationOptions: 0
Size:
SpaceAvailable:
Status: Normal
UserName:
CaseSensitive: False
Collation: SQL_Latin1_General_CP1_CI_AS
IsUpdateable: True
Version:
AutoCreateStatisticsEnabled: True
AutoUpdateStatisticsEnabled: True
DatabaseGuid: 8b5d5479-b68a-48e3-8b21-ee6d564ef124
DatabaseSnapshotBaseName:
DefaultFullTextCatalog:
IsDatabaseSnapshot: False
IsDatabaseSnapshotBase:
IsMailHost:
IsMirroringEnabled: False
LogReuseWaitStatus: Nothing
MirroringFailoverLogSequenceNumber:
MirroringID:
MirroringPartner:
MirroringRole:
MirroringRoleSequence:
MirroringSafetyLevel: None
MirroringSafetySequence:
MirroringStatus: None
MirroringWitness:
MirroringWitnessStatus: None
RecoveryForkGuid: c3c9a0be-fe80-4cdd-972c-72a46d3d996c

Press any key to continue.
```

Figure 10-4. Results for enumerating database properties example

```
            foreach (DataRow row in dt.Rows)
            {
                for (int i = 0; i < dt.Columns.Count; i++)
                    Console.WriteLine(dt.Columns[i].ColumnName +
                        ": " + row[i]);
                Console.WriteLine();
            }
        }

        Console.WriteLine("Press any key to continue.");
        Console.ReadKey();
    }
}
```

Partial results are shown in Figure 10-5.

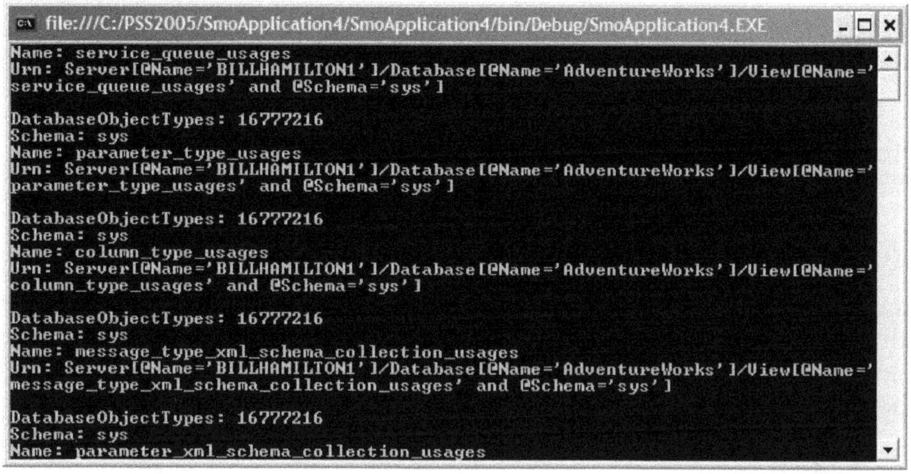

Figure 10-5. Results for enumerating database example

The EnumObjects() method of the Database class returns a DataTable with the columns described in Table 10-1.

Table 10-1. DataTable columns returned by Database.EnumObjects()

Column	Description
DatabaseObjectTypes	A value from the DatabaseObjectTypes enumeration identifying the object type
Schema	The schema to which the database object belongs
Name	The name of the database object
Urn	The Uniform Resource Name (URN) for the database object

The EnumObjects() method has three overloads. Besides the no-argument version that you've just seen, there are two that let you specify the type of object to enumerate as a value from the DatabaseObjectTypes enumeration. The following are the prototypes for the EnumObjects() methods:

```
Database.EnumObjects()
Database.EnumObjects(DatabaseObjectTypes)
Database.EnumObjects(DatabaseObjectTypes, SortOrder)
```

where:

DatabaseObjectTypes

Enumeration of database object types—for example, All, DatabaseRole, Schema, Table, and View. If not specified, the default is All. For a complete list, see Microsoft SQL Server 2005 Books Online.

SortOrder
Enumeration of sort orders—Name, Schema, Type, and Urn.

For example, the following line of code returns information about tables in the database:

```
db.EnumObjects(DatabaseObjectTypes.Table)
```

DatabaseObjectTypes enumeration values can be logically ORed to return a table containing multiple object types.

Creating a Database Object

This example demonstrates how to create new SMO instance objects. It creates a table named SmoTestTable in the ProgrammingSqlServer2005 database. The table contains two columns, with a primary key index on the first. You need to add a reference to Microsoft.SqlServer.SqlEnum to compile and execute this example.

```
using System;
using System.Data;

using Microsoft.SqlServer.Management.Common;
using Microsoft.SqlServer.Management.Smo;

class Program
{
    static void Main(string[] args)
    {
        Server server = new Server("localhost");
        Database db = server.Databases["ProgrammingSqlServer2005"];

        // create a table
        Table t = new Table(db, "SmoTestTable");

        DataType dt = new DataType(SqlDataType.Int);
        Column c = new Column(t, "ID", dt);
        c.Nullable = false;
        t.Columns.Add(c);

        dt = new DataType(SqlDataType.VarChar, 100);
        c = new Column(t, "Name", dt);
        t.Columns.Add(c);

        t.Create();

        // create a primary key index on the table
        Index i = new Index(t, "PK");
        IndexedColumn ic = new IndexedColumn(i, "ID");
        i.IndexedColumns.Add(ic);
        i.IndexKeyType = IndexKeyType.DriPrimaryKey;
        i.Create();
```

```
            Console.WriteLine("Press any key to continue.");
            Console.ReadKey();
        }
    }
```

The process for creating SMO instance objects typically follows the pattern in this example:

1. Instantiate the SMO instance object.
2. Set the mandatory properties of the object.
3. Call the Create( ) method of the object.

In this example, a new table is created by instantiating a Table object, passing in arguments for the database in which the table is created and the name of the table. Columns are added to the table by instantiating a Column object, passing in arguments for the table to which you are adding them, the name of the column, and the data type as a DataType instance. Finally, the table is created in the database by calling the Create( ) method of the Table object.

The primary key index is created by instantiating an Index, passing in arguments for the table in which the index is created and the name of the index. A column is added as part of the index by instantiating an IndexedColumn object, passing in arguments for the index to which it is added, and the name of the column. Next, you specify the type of index you want by setting the IndexKeyType property to a value from the IndexKeyType enumeration—DriPrimaryKey, DriUniqueKey, or None. Finally, you create the index by calling the Create( ) method of the Index object.

The Alter( ) method of SMO instance objects is used to update the object properties with new values. The Drop( ) method of SMO instance objects is used to drop the object.

Checking Database Table Integrity

This example checks the integrity of all tables and their indexes in AdventureWorks and writes the errors (if any) to the console:

```
using System;
using System.Collections.Specialized;

using Microsoft.SqlServer.Management.Common;
using Microsoft.SqlServer.Management.Smo;

class Program
{
    static void Main(string[] args)
    {
        Server server = new Server("localhost");

        DatabaseCollection dbs = server.Databases;
        Database db = dbs["AdventureWorks"];
```

```
        StringCollection sc = db.CheckTables(RepairType.None);

        foreach (object o in sc)
            Console.WriteLine("{0}", o);

        Console.WriteLine("Press any key to continue.");
        Console.ReadKey();
    }
}
```

There is no output from this example unless you run it against a corrupted database, in which case the errors are output to the console.

The CheckTables() method of the Database class tests the database pages implementing storage for all tables and indexes defined on tables. The CheckTables() method takes a single argument—a value from the RepairType enumeration described in Table 10-2.

Table 10-2. RepairType enumeration

Value	Description
AllowDataLoss	Attempt to repair all data pages even if data is lost.
Fast	Repair data pages in fast mode. This option is for backward compatibility.
None	Do not repair data pages.
Rebuild	Repair data pages by rebuilding them.

The CheckTables() method is implemented using the T-SQL DBCC CHECKDB statement. The StringCollection returned from the method is a collection of error messages returned by DBCC CHECKDB. The database must be in single-user mode to use any of the three repair options (other than None).

Transacting SMO Operations

SMO commands can be wrapped in transactions so that multiple commands either succeed or fail as a group. This example transacts a set of SMO commands that creates a table named SmoTestTable in the ProgrammingSqlServer2005 database. If the user enters a Y at the prompt, the transaction commits and the table is created. Otherwise, the transaction rolls back.

```
using System;
using System.Data;

using Microsoft.SqlServer.Management.Common;
using Microsoft.SqlServer.Management.Smo;

class Program
{
    static void Main(string[] args)
    {
        Server server = new Server("localhost");
```

```
    server.ConnectionContext.BeginTransaction( );

    Database db = server.Databases["ProgrammingSqlServer2005"];

    // create a table
    Table t = new Table(db, "SmoTestTable2");

    DataType dt = new DataType(SqlDataType.Int);
    Column c = new Column(t, "ID", dt);
    c.Nullable = false;
    t.Columns.Add(c);

    dt = new DataType(SqlDataType.VarChar, 100);
    c = new Column(t, "Name", dt);
    t.Columns.Add(c);

    t.Create( );

    Console.WriteLine("Commit new table (Y/N)?");
    ConsoleKeyInfo cki = Console.ReadKey( );

    if ((char)cki.Key == 'Y')
    {
        server.ConnectionContext.CommitTransaction( );
        Console.WriteLine(Environment.NewLine + "Table created.");
    }
    else
    {
        server.ConnectionContext.RollBackTransaction( );
        Console.WriteLine(Environment.NewLine + "Table not created.");
    }

    Console.WriteLine("Press any key to continue.");
    Console.ReadKey( );
    }
}
```

The Server class exposes a ServerConnection object through its ConnectionContext
property. The ServerConnection object lets you programmatically interrogate and
manage the connection with the SQL Server instance. ServerConnection also provides support for transactions through its BeginTransaction( ), CommitTransaction( ),
and RollbackTransaction( ) methods.

Capture Mode

SMO applications can capture and record T-SQL statements that are equivalent to
the operations performed by the SMO statements. This example captures the T-SQL
commands generated by SMO programming and outputs them to the console
window:

```
using System;
using System.Data;
```

```
using Microsoft.SqlServer.Management.Common;
using Microsoft.SqlServer.Management.Smo;

class Program
{
    static void Main(string[] args)
    {
        Server server = new Server("localhost");
        server.ConnectionContext.SqlExecutionModes = SqlExecutionModes.CaptureSql;
        server.ConnectionContext.Connect();

        Database db = server.Databases["ProgrammingSqlServer2005"];

        // create a table
        Table t = new Table(db, "SmoTestTable");

        DataType dt = new DataType(SqlDataType.Int);
        Column c = new Column(t, "ID", dt);
        c.Nullable = false;
        t.Columns.Add(c);

        dt = new DataType(SqlDataType.VarChar, 100);
        c = new Column(t, "Name", dt);
        t.Columns.Add(c);

        t.Create();

        // create a primary key index on the table
        Index i = new Index(t, "PK");
        IndexedColumn ic = new IndexedColumn(i, "ID");
        i.IndexedColumns.Add(ic);
        i.IndexKeyType = IndexKeyType.DriPrimaryKey;
        i.Create();

        // output the captured T-SQL
        foreach (string s in server.ConnectionContext.CapturedSql.Text)
            Console.WriteLine(s);

        Console.WriteLine(Environment.NewLine + "Press any key to continue.");
        Console.ReadKey();
    }
}
```

Results are shown in Figure 10-6.

This example uses the same table creation code as the example in the "Creating a Database Object" section. The generated T-SQL code is captured and output. It is *not* sent to the server and it is *not* executed.

The mode is controlled by the SqlExecutionModes property of the Server object ConnectionContext. It takes a value from the SqlExecutionModes enumeration that specifies whether the code is executed (ExecuteSql), captured (CaptureSql), or both (ExecuteAndCaptureSql).

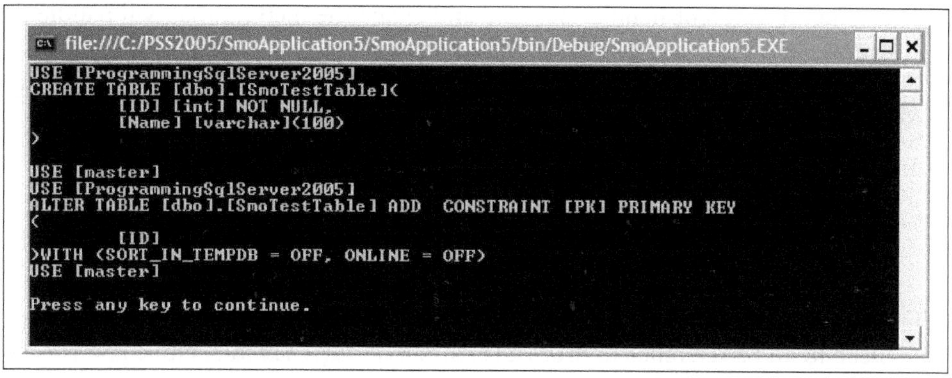

```
ca  file:///C:/PSS2005/SmoApplication5/SmoApplication5/bin/Debug/SmoApplication5.EXE      _ □ ×
USE [ProgrammingSqlServer2005]
CREATE TABLE [dbo].[SmoTestTable](
        [ID] [int] NOT NULL,
        [Name] [varchar](100)
)

USE [master]
USE [ProgrammingSqlServer2005]
ALTER TABLE [dbo].[SmoTestTable] ADD  CONSTRAINT [PK] PRIMARY KEY
(
        [ID]
)WITH (SORT_IN_TEMPDB = OFF, ONLINE = OFF)
USE [master]

Press any key to continue.
```

Figure 10-6. Results for capturing T-SQL example

Captured SQL is written to the CapturedSql object (exposed as a property of the Server object's ConnectionContext) and accessed through the CapturedSql.Text property, which exposes it as a StringCollection object.

Event Notification

Events let you monitor the SQL Server Database Engine. Event monitoring can be set up for the following SMO instance classes, some of which are not described until Chapter 11:

> Server
> Database
> Schema
> Table
> View
> Index
> Stored procedure
> DML and DDL triggers
> User-defined functions
> User-defined types
> Synonyms
> Logins
> Users
> SQL assemblies
> Application roles
> Certificates
> Partition functions and schemes

Subscribing to events for the different SMO instance classes follows a similar pattern:

1. Instantiate an event set object.
2. Add events for which you want notification to this event set.

3. Instantiate an event-handler delegate and create the method that will handle the events.

4. Call the SubscribeToEvents( ) method to specify the events to receive with the event set from Step 1.

5. Call the StartEvents( ) method to start receiving events.

6. Call the StopEvents( ) method to stop receiving events. Call the Unsubscribe-FromEvents( ) method or the UnsubscribeAllEvents( ) method to clear some or all event settings and remove some or all event handlers.

This example shows how to configure a database-event handler and subscribe to it. You need to add a reference to Microsoft.SqlServer.SqlEnum to compile and execute this example.

```
using System;
using System.Data;

using Microsoft.SqlServer.Management.Common;
using Microsoft.SqlServer.Management.Smo;

class Program
{
    static void Main(string[] args)
    {
        Server server = new Server( );
        Database db = server.Databases["ProgrammingSqlServer2005"];

        DatabaseEventSet des = new DatabaseEventSet( );
        des.CreateTable = true;
        des.DropTable = true;
        ServerEventHandler seh = new ServerEventHandler(OnDatabaseEvent);
        db.Events.SubscribeToEvents(des, seh);

        db.Events.StartEvents( );

        // create a table with a single column
        Table t = new Table(db, "SmoTestTable3");

        DataType dt = new DataType(SqlDataType.Int);
        Column c = new Column(t, "ID", dt);
        c.Nullable = false;
        t.Columns.Add(c);

        t.Create( );

        // drop the table
        t.Drop( );

        db.Events.StopEvents( );

        Console.WriteLine(Environment.NewLine + "Press any key to continue.");
        Console.ReadKey( );
```

```
        }

        protected static void OnDatabaseEvent(object sender, ServerEventArgs e)
        {
            if (e.EventType.ToString() == "CreateTable")
                Console.WriteLine("A table named " +
                    e.Properties["ObjectName"].Value + " was created.");
            else if (e.EventType.ToString() == "DropTable")
                Console.WriteLine("A table named " +
                    e.Properties["ObjectName"].Value + " was dropped.");
        }
    }
```

Results are shown in Figure 10-7.

Figure 10-7. Results for database event example

The SubscribeToEvents( ) method of the DatabaseEvents object (exposed through the Events property of the Database class) takes two arguments—a DatabaseEventSet object that specifies the events to monitor, and a ServerEventHandler delegate that handles the database events with the OnDatabaseEvent( ) method.

Alternatively, the DatabaseEventSet object can be created from the sum of the corresponding properties in the DatabaseEvent class, as shown in the following code:

```
DatabaseEventSet des = DatabaseEvent.CreateTable + DatabaseEvent.DropTable;
```

Handling Exceptions

This example shows how to catch and handle an SMO exception. An exception is raised when an attempt is made to create the database AdventureWorks, which already exists.

```
using System;
using System.Data;

using Microsoft.SqlServer.Management.Common;
using Microsoft.SqlServer.Management.Smo;

class Program
{
    static void Main(string[] args)
    {
        Server server = new Server("localhost");
```

```
        Database db = new Database(server, "AdventureWorks");
        try
        {
            db.Create();
            Console.WriteLine(Environment.NewLine +
                "Database created. Press any key to continue.");
        }
        catch (SmoException ex)
        {
            Console.WriteLine(ex.SmoExceptionType.ToString());
            Console.WriteLine(ex.Message);
            if (ex.InnerException != null)
                Console.WriteLine(ex.InnerException.Message);
            Console.WriteLine(Environment.NewLine + "Press any key to continue.");
        }

        Console.ReadKey();
    }
}
```

Results are shown in Figure 10-8.

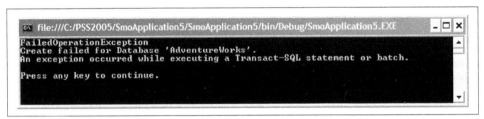

Figure 10-8. Results for handling a database exception example

The SmoException class in the Microsoft.SqlServer.Management.Smo namespace represents an exception raised during a SMO operation. The SmoException class inherits from the Exception class and has additional public properties, listed in Table 10-3.

Table 10-3. SmoException class additional public properties

Property	Description
HelpLink	The help link for more information from Microsoft about the SMO exception.
ProductName	The name of the product that caused the SMO exception.
SmoExceptionType	The type of SMO exception. This is a value from the SmoExceptionType enumeration.

The SmoExceptionType enumeration values are described in Table 10-4.

Table 10-4. SmoExceptionType enumeration

Value	Description
CollectionNotAvailableException	Attempting to retrieve a collection that is not available.
FailedOperationException	An operation fails.

Table 10-4. SmoExceptionType enumeration (continued)

Value	Description
InternalEnumeratorException	An error occurs during an enumeration operation.
InternalSmoErrorException	An internal SMO exception occurs.
InvalidConfigurationFileEnumeratorException	An invalid configuration file is encountered.
InvalidPropertyUsageEnumeratorException	An object property is accessed incorrectly.
InvalidQueryExpressionEnumeratorException	An invalid query expression is encountered.
InvalidSmoOperationException	An invalid SMO operation is called.
InvalidVersionEnumeratorException	The version is not valid.
InvalidVersionSmoOperationException	An invalid version of an SMO operation is called.
MissingObjectException	An object is missing.
PropertyCannotBeRetrievedException	A property cannot be retrieved.
PropertyNotSetException	A property value has not been set and is required to be set.
PropertyReadOnlyException	Attempt to set a read-only property.
PropertyTypeMismatchException	Attempt to set a property with a value having an incorrect data type.
PropertyWriteException	An error occurs updating the value of a property.
ServiceRequestException	An error occurs during a service request.
SmoException	An SMO exception occurs.
UnknownPropertyEnumeratorException	An unknown property enumerator is encountered.
UnknownPropertyException	An unknown property is requested.
UnknownTypeEnumeratorException	An unknown type enumerator is encountered.
UnsupportedFeatureException	An unsupported feature is requested.
UnsupportedObjectNameException	An object name is not supported.
UnsupportedVersionException	An unsupported version of SQL Server is encountered.
WrongPropertyValueException	A property is assigned an incorrect value.

The exception classes derived from the SmoException class have the same names as the SMO exception types listed in Table 10-4. For example, there is a class named CollectionNotAvailableException that is derived from the SmoException class.

SMO Instance Classes for Administering Data Storage Objects Reference

This section describes the SMO classes used to administer SQL Server objects that store data. The classes are arranged into functional groups. A hierarchical diagram of these classes is shown in Figure 10-1, earlier in this chapter.

SQL Server Instances

The SMO classes used to manage SQL Server instances are described in Table 10-5.

Table 10-5. SMO classes for managing a SQL Server instance

Class	Description
Information	Represents nonconfigurable information about the SQL Server instance. The `Information` property of the `Server` class returns an `Information` object for the SQL Server instance.
Server	Represents a SQL Server instance.
ServerActiveDirectory	Represents Active Directory settings for a SQL Server instance. The `ActiveDirectory` property of the `Server` class returns a `ServerActiveDirectory` object for the SQL Server instance.
ServerEvent	Represents a SQL Server event that can be included in a `ServerEventSet` object.
ServerEventArgs	Represents the arguments used to report a server event.
ServerEvents	Represents the settings required for SQL Server event notification. The `ServerEvents` object is obtained using the `Events` property of the `Server` object and cannot be created as a standalone object. The `SubscribeToEvents( )` method of the `ServerEvents` class specifies the events to receive as either a `ServerEventSet` or `ServerTraceEventSet` object.
ServerEventSet	Represents a set of SQL Server events as `ServerEvent` objects.
ServiceMasterKey	Represents the service master key for the SQL Server instance. The `ServiceMasterKey` property of the `Server` class returns a `ServiceMasterKey` object for the SQL server instance.
ServerProxyAccount	Represents a SQL Server proxy account permitting impersonation of job-step execution. The `ProxyAccount` property of the `Server` class returns a `ServerProxyAccount` object for the SQL server instance.
ServerTraceEvent	Represents a SQL Server trace event. The `ServerTraceEvent` class contains a property for each trace event that the server can respond to.
ServerTraceEventSet	Represents a set of SQL Server trace events.
Settings	Represents configurable settings about the SQL Server instance. The `Settings` property of the `Server` class returns a `Settings` object for the SQL Server instance.

Databases

The SMO classes used to manage SQL Server databases are described in Table 10-6.

Table 10-6. SMO classes for managing databases

Class	Description
Database	Represents a SQL Server database.
DatabaseActiveDirectory	Represents Active Directory settings for a database. The `ActiveDirectory` property of the `Database` class returns a `DatabaseActiveDirectory` object for the database.

Table 10-6. SMO classes for managing databases (continued)

Class	Description
DatabaseCollection	Represents a collection of databases as Database objects. The Databases property of the Server class returns the databases defined on the SQL Server instance.
DatabaseEvent	Represents a SQL Server database event that can be included in a DatabaseEventSet object.
DatabaseEventArgs	Represents the arguments used to report a database event.
DatabaseEvents	Represents the settings required for SQL Server database-event notification. The DatabaseEvents object is obtained using the Events property of the Database object and cannot be created as a standalone object.
	The SubscribeToEvents() method of the DatabaseEvents class specifies the events to receive as a DatabaseEventSet object.
DatabaseEventSet	Represents a set of SQL Server database events as a DatabaseEvent object
DatabaseOptions	Represents SQL Server database options. The DatabaseOptions property of the Database class returns a DatabaseOptions object for the database.
MasterKey	Represents the database master key used to symmetrically encrypt and decrypt the private key of certificates. The MasterKey property of the Database class returns a MasterKey object for the database.

Tables

The SMO classes used to manage SQL Server tables are described in Table 10-7.

Table 10-7. SMO classes for managing tables

Class	Description
Table	Represents a table.
TableCollection	Represents a collection of tables as Table objects. The Tables property of the Database class returns the tables defined in the database.
TableEvent	Represents a SQL Server table event that can be included in a TableEventSet object.
TableEvents	Represents the settings required for SQL Server table-event notification. The TableEvents object is obtained using the Events property of the Table object and cannot be created as a standalone object.
	The SubscribeToEvents() method of the TableEvents class specifies the events to receive as a TableEventSet object.
TableEventSet	Represents a set of SQL Server table events as TableEvent objects.

Columns

The SMO classes used to manage SQL Server columns are described in Table 10-8.

Table 10-8. SMO classes for managing columns

Class	Description
Column	Represents a column.
ColumnCollection	Represents a collection of columns as Column objects.
	The Columns property of the Table class returns the collection of columns in the table.
	The Columns property of the View class returns the collection of columns in the view.
DefaultConstraint	Represents a default constraint on a column. A default constraint specifies the value to use for a column if a value is not specified when a row is inserted. The DefaultConstraint object is accessed through the DefaultConstraint property of the Column class.

Views

The SMO classes used to manage SQL Server views are described in Table 10-9.

Table 10-9. SMO classes for managing views

Class	Description
View	Represents a view.
ViewCollection	Represents a collection of views defined on a table as View objects. The Views property of the Database class returns the views defined in the database.
ViewEvent	Represents a SQL Server view event that can be included in a ViewEventSet object.
ViewEvents	Represents the settings required for SQL Server view-event notification. The ViewEvents object is obtained using the Events property of the View object and cannot be created as a standalone object.
	The SubscribeToEvents( ) method of the ViewEvents class specifies the events to receive as a ViewEventSet object.
ViewEventSet	Represents a set of SQL Server view events as ViewEvent objects.

Indexes

The SMO classes used to manage SQL Server indexes are described in Table 10-10.

Table 10-10. SMO classes for managing indexes

Class	Description
Index	Represents an index.
IndexCollection	Represents a collection of indexes as Index objects.
	The Indexes property of the Table class returns the collection of indexes defined on a table.
	The Indexes property of the View class returns the collection of indexes defined on a view.
	The Indexes property of the UserDefinedFunction class returns the collection of indexes defined on a user-defined function.

Table 10-10. SMO classes for managing indexes (continued)

Class	Description
IndexedColumn	Represents a column in an index.
IndexedColumnCollection	Represents a collection of index columns as IndexColumn objects. The IndexColumns property of the Index class returns the collection of columns in the index.
IndexEvents	Represents the setting required for SQL Server index-event notification. The IndexEvents object is obtained using the Events property of the Index object and cannot be created as a standalone object.
	The SubscribeToEvents( ) method of the IndexEvents class specifies the events to receive as an ObjectEventSet object.

Foreign Keys

A foreign-key constraint is a column or combination of columns used to enforce a link between two tables. The column or columns that make up the primary key in one table are referenced by a column or columns in a second table. The column or columns in the second table constitute a foreign key. The SMO classes used to manage SQL Server foreign-key constraints are described in Table 10-11.

Table 10-11. SMO classes for managing foreign keys

Class	Description
ForeignKey	Represents a foreign key.
ForeignKeyCollection	Represents a collection of foreign keys as ForeignKey objects. The ForeignKeys property of the Table class returns the collection of foreign keys defined on the table.
ForeignKeyColumn	Represents a column in a foreign key.
ForeignKeyColumnCollection	Represents a collection of foreign-key columns as ForeignKeyColumn objects. The Columns property of the ForeignKey class returns the collection of columns in the foreign key.

Check Constraints

Check constraints limit the values that can be stored in a column based on a logical expression that returns either true or false. A column can have multiple check constraints, and a check constraint can be applied to multiple columns. The SMO classes used to manage SQL Server check constraints are described in Table 10-12.

Table 10-12. SMO classes for managing check constraints

Class	Description
Check	Represents a check constraint.
CheckCollection	Represents a collection of check constraints as Check objects.
	The Checks property of the Table class returns the collection of check constraints defined on a table.
	The Checks property of the UserDefinedFunction class returns the collection of check constraints defined on a user-defined function.

Rules

A rule is used to restrict the values in a column. The SMO classes used to manage SQL Server rules are described in Table 10-13.

Table 10-13. SMO classes for managing rules

Class	Description
Rule	Represents the attributes of a rule.
RuleCollection	Represents a collection of rules as Rule objects. The Rules property of the Database class returns the collection of rules defined on the database.

 Rules are included for backward compatibility and will be removed in a future version of SQL Server. Use a check constraint instead of a rule in new development.

Stored Procedures

The SMO classes used to manage SQL Server stored procedures are described in Table 10-14.

Table 10-14. SMO classes for managing stored procedures

Class	Description
StoredProcedure	Represents a stored procedure.
StoredProcedureCollection	Represents a collection of stored procedures as StoredProcedure objects. The StoredProcedures property of the Database class returns the collection of stored procedures in the database.
StoredProcedureEvent	Represents a stored-procedure event that can be included in a StoredProcedure EventSet object.
StoredProcedureEvents	Represents the settings required for SQL Server stored-procedure event notification. The StoredProcedureEvents object is obtained using the Events property of the StoredProcedure object and cannot be created as a standalone object.
	The SubscribeToEvents( ) method of the StoredProcedureEvents class specifies the events to receive as a StoredProcedureEventSet object.

Table 10-14. SMO classes for managing stored procedures (continued)

Class	Description
StoredProcedureEventSet	Represents a set of stored-procedure events as StoredProcedureEvent objects.
StoredProcedureParameter	Represents a parameter for a stored procedure.
StoredProcedureParameter Collection	Represents a collection of stored-procedure parameters as StoredProcedureParameter objects. The Parameters property of the StoredProcedure class returns the collection of parameters for the stored procedure.

Numbered Stored Procedures

The SMO classes used to manage SQL Server numbered stored procedures are described in Table 10-15.

Table 10-15. SMO classes for managing numbered stored procedures

Class	Description
NumberedStoredProcedure	Represents a numbered stored procedure.
NumberedStoredProcedureCollection	Represents a collection of numbered stored procedures as NumberedStoredProcedure objects. The NumberedStoredProcedures property of the StoredProcedure class returns the collection of numbered stored procedures.
NumberedStoredProcedureParameter	Represents a parameter for a numbered stored procedure.
NumberedStoredProcedureParameterCollection	Represents a collection of numbered stored-procedure parameters as NumberedStoredProcedureParameter objects. The Parameters property of the NumberedStoredProcedure class returns the collection of parameters for the numbered stored procedure.

 Numbered stored procedures are included for backward compatibility and will be removed in a future version of SQL Server. Do not use them in new development.

Extended Stored Procedures

The SMO classes used to manage SQL Server extended stored procedures are described in Table 10-16.

Table 10-16. SMO classes for managing extended stored procedures

Class	Description
ExtendedStoredProcedure	Represents an extended stored procedure.
ExtendedStoredProcedureCollection	Represents a collection of extended stored procedures as Extended-StoredProcedure objects. The ExtendedStoredProcedures property of the Database class returns the collection of extended stored procedures in a database.

 Extended stored procedures are included for backward compatibility and will be removed in a future version of SQL Server. Do not use them in new development.

DML Triggers

The SMO classes used to manage SQL Server DML triggers are described in Table 10-17.

Table 10-17. SMO classes for managing DML triggers

Class	Description
Trigger	Represents a DML trigger.
TriggerCollection	Represents a collection of triggers as Trigger objects.
	The Triggers property of the Table class returns the collection of triggers defined on a table.
	The Triggers property of the View class returns the collection of triggers defined on a view.
TriggerEvents	Represents the settings required for SQL Server trigger-event notification. The TriggerEvents object is obtained using the Events property of the Trigger object and cannot be created as a standalone object.
	The SubscribeToEvents( ) method of the TriggerEvents class specifies the events to receive as an ObjectEventSet object.

DDL Triggers

The SMO classes used to manage server- and database-scoped DDL triggers are described in Table 10-18.

Table 10-18. SMO classes for managing DDL triggers

Class	Description
DatabaseDdlTrigger	Represents a DDL trigger scoped to the database.
DatabaseDdlTriggerCollection	Represents a collection of DDL triggers scoped to the database as DatabaseDdlTrigger objects. The Triggers property of the Database class returns the collection of triggers scoped to a database.
DatabaseDdlTriggerEvent	Represents a database DDL trigger event that can be included in a DatabaseDdlEventSet object.

Table 10-18. SMO classes for managing DDL triggers (continued)

Class	Description
DatabaseDdlTriggerEventSet	Represents a set of database DDL trigger events as DatabaseDdlTriggerEvent objects.
ServerDdlTrigger	Represents a DDL trigger scoped to the SQL Server instance.
ServerDdlTriggerCollection	Represents a collection of DDL triggers scoped to the SQL Server instance as ServerDdlTrigger objects. The Triggers property of the Server class returns the collection of triggers scoped to the SQL Server instance.
ServerDdlTriggerEvent	Represents a server DDL trigger event that can be included in a ServerDdlEventSet object.
ServerDdlTriggerEventSet	Represents a set of server DDL trigger events as ServerTriggerEvent objects.

User-Defined Objects

The SMO classes used to manage user-defined aggregates, user-defined functions, and user-defined types are described in Table 10-19.

Table 10-19. SMO classes for managing user-defined objects

Class	Description
UserDefinedAggregate	Represents a user-defined aggregate.
UserDefinedAggregateCollection	Represents a collection of user-defined aggregates as UserDefinedAggregate objects. The UserDefinedAggregates property of the Database class returns the collection of user-defined aggregates in a database.
UserDefinedAggregateParameter	Represents a parameter used with a user-defined aggregate.
UserDefinedAggregateParameter Collection	Represents a collection of user-defined aggregate parameters as UserDefinedAggregateParameter objects. The UserDefinedAggregateParameters property of the UserDefinedAggregate class returns the collection of parameters for the user-defined aggregate.
UserDefinedDataType	Represents a user-defined type based on a SQL Server data type.
UserDefinedDataTypeCollection	Represents a collection of user-defined types as UserDefinedDataType objects. The UserDefinedDataTypes property of the Database class returns the collection of user-defined types in a database.
UserDefinedFunction	Represents a user-defined function.
UserDefinedFunctionCollection	Represents a collection of user-defined functions as UserDefinedFunction objects. The UserDefinedFunctions property of the Database class returns the collection of user-defined functions in a database.
UserDefinedFunctionEvent	Represents a SQL Server user-defined function event that can be included in a UserDefinedFunctionEventSet object.

Table 10-19. SMO classes for managing user-defined objects (continued)

Class	Description
UserDefinedFunctionEvents	Represents the settings required for SQL Server user-defined function event notification. The UserDefinedFunctionEvents object is obtained using the Events property of the UserDefinedFunction object and cannot be created as a standalone object.
	The SubscribeToEvents( ) method of the UserDefinedFunctionEvents class specifies the events to receive as an UserDefinedFunctionEventSet object.
UserDefinedFunctionEventSet	Represents a set of user-defined function events as UserDefinedFunctionEvent objects.
UserDefinedFunctionParameter	Represents a parameter for a user-defined function.
UserDefinedFunctionParameter Collection	Represents a collection of user-defined function parameters as UserDefinedFunctionParameter objects. The Parameters property of the UserDefinedFunction class returns the collection of parameters for the user-defined function.
UserDefinedType	Represents a user-defined type based on a .NET data type.
UserDefinedTypeCollection	Represents a collection of user-defined types as UserDefinedType objects. The UserDefinedTypes property of the Database class returns the collection of user-defined types in a database.
UserDefinedTypeEvents	Represents the settings required for SQL Server user-defined type event notification. The UserDefinedTypeEvents object is obtained using the Events property of the UserDefinedType object and cannot be created as a standalone object.
	The SubscribeToEvents( ) method of the UserDefinedTypeEvents class specifies the events to receive as an ObjectEventSet object.

Data Types

The SMO class used to manage SQL Server data types are described in Table 10-20.

Table 10-20. SMO classes for managing data types

Class	Description
DataType	Represents a SQL Server data type.
	The DataType property of the following classes returns a DataType object representing its data type:
	• Column
	• NumberedStoredProcedureParameter
	• StoredProcedureParameter
	• UserDefinedAggregate
	• UserDefinedAggregateParameter
	• UserDefinedFunction
	• UserDefinedFunctionParameter

System Data Types

The SMO classes used to manage SQL Server system data types are described in Table 10-21.

Table 10-21. SMO classes for managing system data types

Class	Description
SystemDataType	Represents a system data type.
SystemDataTypeCollection	Represents a collection of system data types as SystemDataType objects. The SystemDataTypes property of the Server class returns the collection of system data types defined on a SQL Server instance.

Schemas

A schema is an ownership context for SQL Server objects such as tables, views, and stored procedures. The SMO classes used to manage SQL Server schemas are described in Table 10-22.

Table 10-22. SMO classes for managing schemas

Class	Description
Schema	Represents a SQL Server schema.
SchemaCollection	Represents a collection of schemas as Schema objects. The Schemas property of the Database class returns the schemas defined for a database.
SchemaEvents	Represents the setting required for SQL Server schema-event notification. The SchemaEvents object is obtained using the Events property of the Schema object and cannot be created as a standalone object. The SubscribeToEvents( ) method of the SchemaEvents class specifies the events to receive as an ObjectEventSet object.

SQL Server Objects

The SMO classes used to manage SQL Server objects are described in Table 10-23.

Table 10-23. SMO classes for managing SQL Server objects

Class	Description
ObjectAlteredEventArgs	Represents the arguments passed by the event that is raised when an object is altered.
ObjectCreatedEventArgs	Represents the arguments passed by the event that is raised when an object is created.
ObjectDroppedEventArgs	Represents the arguments passed by the event that is raised when an object is dropped.
ObjectEvent	Represents a SQL Server object event that can be included in an ObjectEventSet object.

Table 10-23. SMO classes for managing SQL Server objects (continued)

Class	Description
ObjectEventSet	Represents a set of object events as `ObjectEvent` objects.
ObjectPermission	Represents a SQL Server object permission.
ObjectPermissionInfo	Represents information about a SQL Server object permission.
ObjectPermissionSet	Represents a set of SQL Server object permissions as `ObjectPermission` objects.
ObjectProperty	Represents a set of attributes for a SQL Server object property.
ObjectRenamedEventArgs	Represents the arguments passed by the event that is raised when an object is renamed.

SQL Server Management Objects (SMO) Instance Classes, Part 2

This chapter provides an overview of the SMO instance classes for administering database objects that do not store data. Following this overview, the chapter shows how to use these classes programmatically. Chapter 10 covers SMO classes for administering database objects that do store data.

Programming SMO Instance Classes for Administering Database Objects Not Used for Data Storage

The following SQL Server objects are considered not to store data. They identify the SMO instance classes that administer them.

    Server configuration
    Registered servers
    Linked servers
    Database defaults
    Data files, log files, and filegroups
    Partition functions and schemes
    Logins
    Users
    Server, database, and application roles
    Server and database permissions
    .NET Framework assemblies
    Endpoints
    XML schemas
    Languages
    Statistics
    Certificates
    Credentials
    Symmetric and asymmetric keys
    Synonyms

System- and user-defined messages
Full-Text Search
OLE DB provider

A reference to the SMO classes that implement this functionality is included in the "SMO Instance Classes for Administering Objects Not Used for Data Storage Reference" section at the end of this chapter.

This section shows how to programmatically use SMO instance classes that are not used for data storage. The examples in this section are all built using Visual Studio 2005. You need a reference to the following assemblies to compile and run the examples:

- Microsoft.SqlServer.ConnectionInfo
- Microsoft.SqlServer.Smo

Additional assembly references for examples will be indicated where required.

Registered Server and Server Groups

Registered servers let you save connection information for SQL Servers. Server groups create a hierarchy similar to an operating system directory to facilitate organization of registered servers. You can view registered servers and server groups in the Registered Servers pane in SQL Server Management Studio.

The SMO RegisteredServer class represents a registered server. Similarly, the ServerGroup class represents a group of registered servers. These classes reside in the Microsoft.SqlServer.Management.Smo.RegisteredServers namespace. The static SqlServerRegistrations property of the SmoApplication class representing the SMO application contains collections of both registered servers and server groups called RegisteredServers and ServerGroups. The following example enumerates registered servers and server groups using these collections.

The SMO classes used to manage registered servers and server groups are described in Table 11-2 in the section "SMO Instance Classes for Administering Objects Not Used for Data Storage Reference" later in the chapter.

```
using System;
using System.Data;
using System.Collections;

using Microsoft.SqlServer.Management.Common;
using Microsoft.SqlServer.Management.Smo;
using Microsoft.SqlServer.Management.Smo.RegisteredServers;

class Program
{
    static void Main(string[] args)
    {
        Console.WriteLine("---SERVER GROUPS---");
        foreach (ServerGroup sg in
```

```
    SmoApplication.SqlServerRegistrations.ServerGroups)
{
    Console.WriteLine(sg);
    foreach (RegisteredServer rs in sg.RegisteredServers)
        Console.WriteLine("  " + rs.Name);
}

Console.WriteLine(Environment.NewLine + "---REGISTERED SERVERS---");
foreach (RegisteredServer rs in
    SmoApplication.SqlServerRegistrations.RegisteredServers)
    Console.WriteLine(rs.Name);

Console.WriteLine(Environment.NewLine + "Press any key to continue.");
Console.ReadKey();
    }
}
```

Sample results are shown in Figure 11-1, indicating that one server group and one server are defined.

Figure 11-1. Results for enumerating server groups and servers example

Managing Logins

This example reads the Logins property of the Server object. Logins is a collection of Login objects, representing all the logins defined on the target server. A Login object represents a SQL Server login account granted access to SQL Server through either Windows or SQL Server standard authentication.

For each Login object found in the Logins collection, the example displays the login name (Login.Name), the default database (Login.DefaultDatabase), and the login mode (Login.WindowsLoginAccessType).

The SMO classes used to manage logins are described in Table 11-8 in the section "SMO Instance Classes for Administering Objects Not Used for Data Storage Reference," later in this chapter.

You need to add a reference to the Microsoft.SqlServer.SqlEnum assembly to compile and execute this example.

```
using System;
using System.Data;
using System.Collections;
```

```
using Microsoft.SqlServer.Management.Common;
using Microsoft.SqlServer.Management.Smo;

class Program
{
    static void Main(string[] args)
    {
        Server server = new Server("localhost");

        foreach (Login l in server.Logins)
        {
            Console.WriteLine("Name: " + l.Name);
            Console.WriteLine("DefaultDatabase: " + l.DefaultDatabase);
            Console.WriteLine("WindowsLoginAccessType:" +
                l.WindowsLoginAccessType);
            Console.WriteLine();
        }

        Console.WriteLine("Press any key to continue.");
        Console.ReadKey();
    }
}
```

Partial results are shown in Figure 11-2.

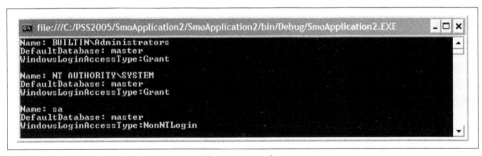

Figure 11-2. Partial results for enumerate logins example

The results are the same as opening the Security → Logins node in the Object Explorer window of SQL Server Management Studio.

This example creates a new login called TestLogin. It does so by instantiating a Login object, setting its LoginType to LoginType.SqlLogin, and then invoking its Create() method.

```
using System;
using System.Data;
using System.Collections;

using Microsoft.SqlServer.Management.Common;
using Microsoft.SqlServer.Management.Smo;

class Program
{
```

```
static void Main(string[] args)
{
    Server server = new Server("localhost");

    Login l = new Login(server, "TestLogin");
    l.LoginType = LoginType.SqlLogin;
    l.Create("tempPassword");

    Console.WriteLine("Press any key to continue.");
    Console.ReadKey();
}
}
```

If you specify a LoginType of SqlLogin, you must set the Password property using one of the overloads of the Create( ) method. If you specify a LoginType of WindowsUser, you must specify the server name and the Windows account name as the login account name argument to the Login class constructor. The following lines of code create a Windows user login:

```
Login l = new Login(server, @"serverName\windowsAccountName");
l.LoginType = LoginType.WindowsUser;
l.Create();
```

Managing Users

This example enumerates the Users property of a Database object representing the AdventureWorks database. Users is a collection of User objects, which represent SQL Server users—security principals used for controlling access permission within a database. While you create logins at the server level, users map to a single SQL Server login in the database where the user is defined. The DatabaseMapping class describes how logins map to database users.

For each user in the Database.Users collection, the example displays the username (User.Name), creation date (User.CreateDate), associated login (User.Login), and user type (User.UserType).

The SMO classes used to manage users are described in Table 11-9 in the section "SMO Instance Classes for Administering Objects Not Used for Data Storage Reference," later in this chapter.

You need to add a reference to the Microsoft.SqlServer.SqlEnum assembly to compile and execute this example.

```
using System;
using System.Data;
using System.Collections;

using Microsoft.SqlServer.Management.Common;
using Microsoft.SqlServer.Management.Smo;

class Program
```

```
{
    static void Main(string[] args)
    {
        Server server = new Server("localhost");
        Database db = server.Databases["AdventureWorks"];

        foreach (User u in db.Users)
        {
            Console.WriteLine("Name: " + u.Name);
            Console.WriteLine("CreateDate: " + u.CreateDate);
            Console.WriteLine("Login: " + u.Login);
            Console.WriteLine("UserType: " + u.UserType);
            Console.WriteLine();
        }

        Console.WriteLine("Press any key to continue.");
        Console.ReadKey();
    }
}
```

Results are shown in Figure 11-3.

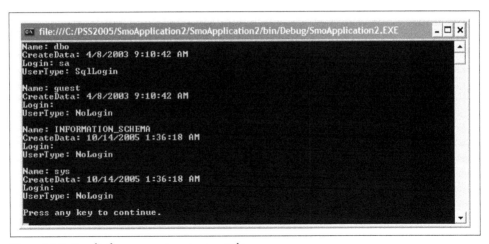

Figure 11-3. Results for enumerate users example

The results are the same as opening the Security → Users node for a database in the Object Explorer window of SQL Server Management Studio.

This example creates a new user, TestUser, in the AdventureWorks database and associates it with the TestLogin SQL Server login account created in the example earlier in this section. It does so by instantiating a new User object, setting its Login property to the string "TestLogin", and then calling its Create() method.

```
using System;
using System.Data;
using System.Collections;
```

```
using Microsoft.SqlServer.Management.Common;
using Microsoft.SqlServer.Management.Smo;

class Program
{
    static void Main(string[] args)
    {
        Server server = new Server("localhost");
        Database db = server.Databases["ProgrammingSqlServer2005"];

        User u = new User(db, "TestUser");
        u.Login = "TestLogin";
        u.Create();

        Console.WriteLine("Press any key to continue.");
        Console.ReadKey();
    }
}
```

Managing Roles

This example enumerates the roles in the AdventureWorks database. It does so by reading the Roles property of the Database object. Each element in the Roles collection is a DatabaseRole object. The example displays the name (DatabaseRole.Name), creation date (DatabaseRole.CreateDate), and owner (DatabaseRole.Owner) for each DatabaseRole object, and also prints the role members by calling the DatabaseRole.EnumMembers() method.

The SMO classes used to manage server roles are described in Table 11-10. The SMO classes used to manage database roles are described in Table 11-11. Both tables are located in the section "SMO Instance Classes for Administering Objects Not Used for Data Storage Reference," later in this chapter

You need to add a reference to the Microsoft.SqlServer.SqlEnum assembly to compile and execute this example.

```
using System;
using System.Data;
using System.Collections;

using Microsoft.SqlServer.Management.Common;
using Microsoft.SqlServer.Management.Smo;

class Program
{
    static void Main(string[] args)
    {
        Server server = new Server("localhost");
        Database db = server.Databases["AdventureWorks"];

        foreach (DatabaseRole dr in db.Roles)
        {
```

```
            Console.WriteLine("Name: " + dr.Name);
            Console.WriteLine("CreateDate: " + dr.CreateDate);
            Console.WriteLine("Owner: " + dr.Owner);
            Console.WriteLine("Members:");
            foreach(string s in dr.EnumMembers())
                Console.WriteLine("  " + s);
            Console.WriteLine();
        }

        Console.WriteLine("Press any key to continue.");
        Console.ReadKey();
    }
}
```

Partial results are shown in Figure 11-4.

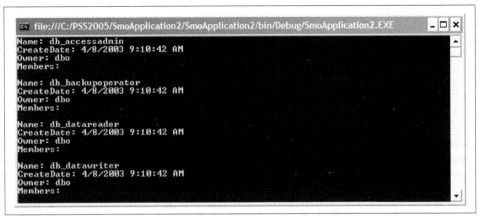

Figure 11-4. Results for enumerate roles example

The results are the same as opening the Security → Roles → Database Roles node for a database in the Object Explorer window of SQL Server Management Studio.

This example adds the user TestUser created in an example earlier in this section to the db_backupoperator role. It does so by calling the AddToRole() method of the User class.

```
using System;
using System.Data;
using System.Collections;

using Microsoft.SqlServer.Management.Common;
using Microsoft.SqlServer.Management.Smo;

class Program
{
    static void Main(string[] args)
    {
        Server server = new Server("localhost");
        Database db = server.Databases["ProgrammingSqlServer2005"];
```

```
        User u = db.Users["TestUser"];
        u.AddToRole("db_backupoperator");

        Console.WriteLine("Press any key to continue.");
        Console.ReadKey( );
    }
}
```

Alternatively, you can instantiate a specific DatabaseRole object and add the user to the role by using the AddMember( ) method:

```
DatabaseRole r = db.Roles["db_backupoperator"];
r.AddMember("TestUser");
```

Managing Server Permissions

This example grants, denies, and revokes server permissions to and from the SQL server login account TestLogin created in the "Managing Logins" section earlier in this chapter. It uses several SMO classes to accomplish this:

Server
 Exposes methods Grant( ), Deny( ), Revoke( ), and EnumServerPermissions( ) used to retrieve and specify server permissions.

ServerPermissionInfo
 Captures the set of server permissions returned by EnumServerPermissions( ).

ServerPermissionSet
 Passes a set of server permissions to the Server methods Grant( ), Deny( ), and Revoke( ).

ServerPermission
 Represents a single permission in a set of server permissions.

The SMO classes used to manage server permissions are described in Table 11-12 in the section "SMO Instance Classes for Administering Objects Not Used for Data Storage Reference," later in this chapter.

```
using System;
using System.Data;

using Microsoft.SqlServer.Management.Common;
using Microsoft.SqlServer.Management.Smo;

class Program
{
    static void Main(string[] args)
    {
        Server server = new Server("localhost");

        ServerPermissionInfo[] spi;
        ServerPermissionSet sps;
```

```
        spi = server.EnumServerPermissions("TestLogin");
        for (int i = 0; i < spi.Length; i++)
            Console.WriteLine(spi[i].ToString());
        Console.WriteLine();

        // grant "create any database"
        sps = new ServerPermissionSet(ServerPermission.CreateAnyDatabase);
        server.Grant(sps, "TestLogin");

        // deny "view any database"
        sps = new ServerPermissionSet(ServerPermission.ViewAnyDatabase);
        server.Deny(sps, "TestLogin");

        spi = server.EnumServerPermissions("TestLogin");
        for (int i = 0; i < spi.Length; i++)
            Console.WriteLine(spi[i].ToString());
        Console.WriteLine();

        // revoke previous grant and deny
        sps = new ServerPermissionSet(new ServerPermission[] {
            ServerPermission.CreateAnyDatabase, ServerPermission.ViewAnyDatabase});
        server.Revoke(sps, "TestLogin");

        spi = server.EnumServerPermissions("TestLogin");
        for (int i = 0; i < spi.Length; i++)
            Console.WriteLine(spi[i].ToString());
        Console.WriteLine();

        Console.WriteLine("Press any key to continue.");
        Console.ReadKey();
    }
}
```

Results are shown in Figure 11-5.

Figure 11-5. Results for managing server permissions example

Enumerating .NET Framework Assemblies

SQL Server 2005 through CLR integration lets you create database objects such as functions, stored procedures, triggers, user-defined data types, and user-defined aggregate functions from .NET Framework assemblies.

The following example outputs a list of all .NET Framework assemblies defined in the AdventureWorks database and lists the files associated with each. It does so by enumerating the Assemblies property of the Database object, which is a collection of SqlAssembly objects. SqlAssembly in turn contains a collection called SqlAssemblyFiles, whose elements are SqlAssemblyFile objects.

The SMO classes used to manage .NET Framework assemblies are described in Table 11-15 in the section "SMO Instance Classes for Administering Objects Not Used for Data Storage Reference," later in this chapter.

```
using System;
using System.Data;

using Microsoft.SqlServer.Management.Common;
using Microsoft.SqlServer.Management.Smo;

class Program
{
    static void Main(string[] args)
    {
        Server server = new Server("localhost");
        Database db = server.Databases["AdventureWorks"];

        foreach (SqlAssembly sa in db.Assemblies)
        {
            Console.WriteLine(sa.Name + " " + sa.CreateDate);
            foreach (SqlAssemblyFile saf in sa.SqlAssemblyFiles)
                Console.WriteLine("   " + saf.Name);
        }

        Console.WriteLine(Environment.NewLine + "Press any key to continue.");
        Console.ReadKey();
    }
}
```

Results are shown in Figure 11-6.

Figure 11-6. Results for enumerate assemblies example

The SqlAssembly class has methods that let you create, alter, and drop .NET Framework assemblies from the database.

Statistics

Statistics contain information about the distribution of values in a column. The query optimizer uses statistics to calculate the optimal query plan. Specifically, statistics help it estimate the cost of using an index or column to evaluate the query.

When the AUTO_CREATE_STATISTICS database option is set to ON (the default), SQL Server automatically stores statistical information about indexed columns and columns without indexes that are used in a predicate. You might need to manually define statistics, especially if you have disabled automatic statistics on SQL Server. When the AUTO_UPDATE_STATISTICS database option is set to ON (the default), SQL Server periodically updates the statistics as data in the underlying tables changes. Out-of-date statistics can cause the query optimizer to make suboptimal decisions about how to process a query. SQL Server 2005 introduces the AUTO_UPDATE_STATISTICS_ASYNC database option, which, when set to ON (the default is OFF), allows for asynchronous automatic updating of statistics. This lets queries continue to use out-of-date statistical information while it is being updated, rather than blocking the query until the update is complete.

You can view the status of the statistics database options by querying the sys.databases catalog view:

```
SELECT  name,
        is_auto_create_stats_on,
        is_auto_update_stats_on,
        is_auto_update_stats_async_on
FROM sys.databases
```

This example uses SMO to display the columns in each statistics counter on the HumanResources.Employee table in AdventureWorks. It instantiates a Table object representing HumanResources.Employee. The Table object exposes the statistic counters defined for the table as a collection of Statistic objects. The example scans this collection, enumerating the StatisticColumns object containing the collection of columns defined in the statistics counter.

The SMO classes used to manage statistics are described in Table 11-19 in the section "SMO Instance Classes for Administering Objects Not Used for Data Storage Reference," later in this chapter.

```
using System;
using System.Data;
using System.Collections;

using Microsoft.SqlServer.Management.Common;
using Microsoft.SqlServer.Management.Smo;

class Program
{
    static void Main(string[] args)
    {
```

```
            Server server = new Server("localhost");
            Database db = server.Databases["AdventureWorks"];
            Table t = db.Tables["Employee", "HumanResources"];

            StatisticCollection sc = t.Statistics;
            for (int i = 0; i < sc.Count; i++)
            {
                Console.WriteLine(sc[i].Name);
                foreach (StatisticColumn scol in sc[i].StatisticColumns)
                    Console.WriteLine("   " + scol.Name);

                Console.WriteLine();
            }

            Console.WriteLine(Environment.NewLine + "Press any key to continue.");
            Console.ReadKey();
        }
    }
```

Results are shown in Figure 11-7.

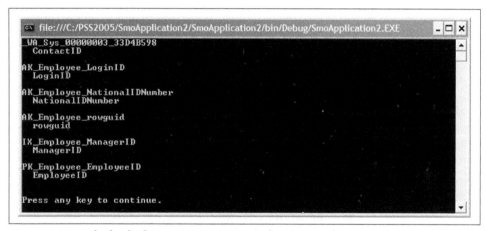

Figure 11-7. Results for displaying statistics counter columns example

This example creates a new statistics counter named IX_Employee_ContactID on the ContactID column of the HumanResources.Employee table in AdventureWorks. It first creates a Table object representing this table. Next it instantiates a new Statistic object, and then associates it with ContactID in a new StatisticColumn object. It adds this StatisticColumn object to the StatisticColumns collection of the Statistic object. Finally, it calls Statistic.Create().

```
using System;
using System.Data;
using System.Collections;

using Microsoft.SqlServer.Management.Common;
using Microsoft.SqlServer.Management.Smo;
```

```
class Program
{
    static void Main(string[] args)
    {
        Server server = new Server("localhost");
        Database db = server.Databases["AdventureWorks"];
        Table t = db.Tables["Employee", "HumanResources"];

        Statistic s = new Statistic(t, "IX_Employee_ContactID");
        StatisticColumn sc = new StatisticColumn(s, "ContactID");
        s.StatisticColumns.Add(sc);
        s.Create();

        Console.WriteLine("Press any key to continue.");
        Console.ReadKey();
    }
}
```

You can see the new statistics counter by opening the Databases → AdventureWorks → Tables → HumanResources.Employee → Statistics node in the Object Explorer window of SQL Server Management Studio.

This following code drops the statistics counter IX_Employee_ContactID created in the preceding example:

```
using System;
using System.Data;
using System.Collections;

using Microsoft.SqlServer.Management.Common;
using Microsoft.SqlServer.Management.Smo;

class Program
{
    static void Main(string[] args)
    {
        Server server = new Server("localhost");
        Database db = server.Databases["AdventureWorks"];
        Table t = db.Tables["Employee", "HumanResources"];

        t.Statistics["IX_Employee_ContactID"].Drop();

        Console.WriteLine("Press any key to continue.");
        Console.ReadKey();
    }
}
```

Synonyms

A *synonym* is a database object that provides an alternate name for another database object either on the local server or on a remote server. From a design point of view, a synonym provides a layer of abstraction that allows changes to be made to underlying objects without affecting client applications. A synonym can be created for the following database objects:

- Tables, including global and local temporary tables
- Views
- SQL scalar functions, inline table-valued functions, table-valued functions, and stored procedures
- CLR stored procedures, scalar functions, table-valued functions, and aggregate functions
- Replication-filter procedures
- Extended stored procedures

A synonym cannot reference a user-defined aggregate function. A synonym object cannot be the base object for another synonym.

This example creates a synonym for the HumanResources.Employees table and uses the synonym to query the table. It instantiates a new Synonym object, associating it with the AdventureWorks database. It then sets several relevant properties:

- Schema and BaseSchema are both set to "HumanResources".
- BaseDatabase is set to the AdventureWorks database.
- BaseObject is set to the name of the underlying object, in this case the Employee table.

Finally, it calls the Synonym.Create( ) method.

The SMO classes used to manage synonyms are described in Table 11-23 in the section "SMO Instance Classes for Administering Objects Not Used for Data Storage Reference," later in this chapter.

```
using System;
using System.Data;
using System.Data.SqlClient;

using Microsoft.SqlServer.Management.Common;
using Microsoft.SqlServer.Management.Smo;

class Program
{
    static void Main(string[] args)
    {
        Server server = new Server("localhost");
        Database db = server.Databases["AdventureWorks"];
        Synonym s = new Synonym(db, "EmployeeSynonym");
        s.Schema = "HumanResources";
        s.BaseDatabase = "AdventureWorks";
        s.BaseSchema = "HumanResources";
        s.BaseObject = "Employee";
        s.Create( );
```

```
SqlConnection conn = new SqlConnection(
    "Data Source=localhost;Integrated Security=SSPI;" +
    "Initial Catalog=AdventureWorks");
SqlDataAdapter da = new SqlDataAdapter(
    "SELECT TOP 5 EmployeeID, LoginID, Title " +
    "FROM HumanResources.EmployeeSynonym", conn);
DataTable dt = new DataTable();
da.Fill(dt);

foreach (DataRow row in dt.Rows)
    Console.WriteLine(row["EmployeeID"] + ", " +
        row["LoginID"] + ", " + row["Title"]);

Console.WriteLine(Environment.NewLine + "Press any key to continue.");
Console.ReadKey();
    }
}
```

Results are shown in Figure 11-8.

Figure 11-8. Results for synonym example

You can see the new synonym by opening the Databases → AdventureWorks → Synonyms node in the Object Explorer window of SQL Server Management Studio.

The following code drops the synonym named EmployeeSynonym created in the preceding example:

```
using System;

using Microsoft.SqlServer.Management.Common;
using Microsoft.SqlServer.Management.Smo;

class Program
{
    static void Main(string[] args)
    {
        Server server = new Server("localhost");
        Database db = server.Databases["AdventureWorks"];

        db.Synonyms["EmployeeSynonym", "HumanResources"].Drop();

        Console.WriteLine("Press any key to continue.");
        Console.ReadKey();
    }
}
```

Messages

The sys.messages catalog view contains a row for each system-defined and user-defined message in the SQL Server instance. Messages with IDs less than 50001 are reserved for system messages. Catalog views are the recommended mechanism for accessing information in system tables. The sys.sysmessages view contains similar information as the sys.messages catalog view and is provided for backward compatibility.

The SMO class representing a system message is SystemMessage. The Server object exposes the collection of SystemMessage objects through its SystemMessages property. The following example enumerates the collection of system messages for the local machine, and lists the ID, language ID, and text for each of them.

The SMO classes used to manage messages are described in Tables 11-24 and 11-25. Both tables are located in the section "SMO Instance Classes for Administering Objects Not Used for Data Storage Reference," later in this chapter.

```
using System;
using System.Data;
using System.Collections;

using Microsoft.SqlServer.Management.Common;
using Microsoft.SqlServer.Management.Smo;

class Program
{
    static void Main(string[] args)
    {
        Server server = new Server("localhost");
        foreach (SystemMessage sm in server.SystemMessages)
        Console.WriteLine(sm.ID + "[" + sm.Language + "]: " + sm.Text);
        Console.WriteLine(Environment.NewLine + "Press any key to continue.");
        Console.ReadKey();
    }
}
```

Partial results are shown in Figure 11-9.

The following code directly accesses the message with an ID of 105:

```
Server server = new Server("localhost");
SystemMessage sm = server.SystemMessages[105, "us_english"];
```

In addition to an indexer, the SystemMessageCollection class also has two methods for getting a specific SystemMessage object. The methods are ItemByIdAndLanguage( ) and ItemByIdAndLanguageID( ), both of which take two arguments, like the indexer. The first argument is the message ID for both methods. The second argument specifies the language as a string for the first method and as a language ID for the second method.

The sys.syslanguages catalog view contains a row for each language installed on the SQL Server instance. The SystemMessage indexer and the accessor methods require

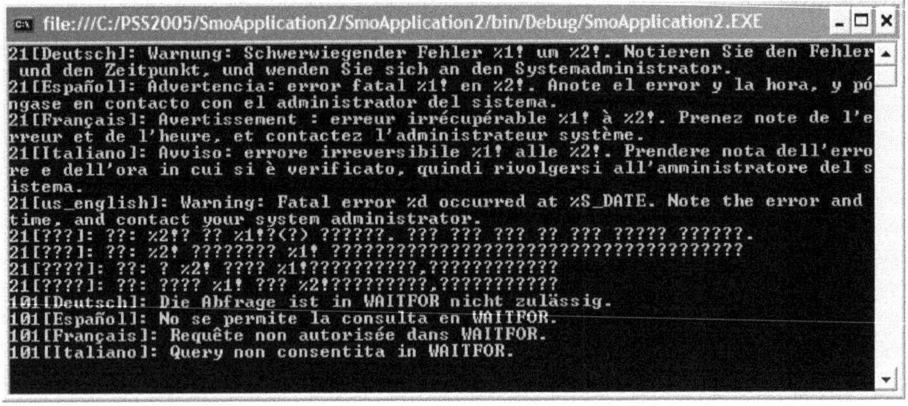

Figure 11-9. Partial results for enumerating messages example

either the language ID (langid column) or name (name column) from this table as the language argument.

Working with user-defined messages is similar to working with system-defined messages with the exception that you can create, alter, and drop them using the UserDefinedMessage class. The following example shows how:

```
Server server = new Server("localhost");
UserDefinedMessage udm = new UserDefinedMessage(server, 50001,
    "us_english", 1, "test user-defined message", false);
udm.Create();
```

The following code drops the user-defined message:

```
Server server = new Server("localhost");
UserDefinedMessage udm = server.UserDefinedMessages[50001, "us_english"];
udm.Drop();
```

Full-Text Search

Full-Text Search lets you index text data in SQL Server and perform linguistic searches against the words and phrases in the data by using rules of the language that the data is in. You can create full-text indexes on char, varchar, and nvarchar data type columns, as well as columns that contain formatted binary data stored in varbinary(max) or image columns. You can build a full-text index on a table that has a single unique column that does not allow NULL values.

A *full-text index* stores information about significant words in a column.

A *full-text index catalog* contains zero or more full-text indexes. Each catalog contains indexing information for one or more tables in the database.

This example creates a full-text index on the Description column of the Production. ProductDescription table in AdventureWorks. These are the steps:

1. It instantiates a FullTextCatalog object, sets its IsDefault property to true, and then calls its Create( ) method.

2. It associates a Table object with Production.ProductDescription.

3. It instantiates a FullTextIndex object, linking it to the Table created in Step 2.

4. It creates a FullTextIndexColumn object tied to the Description column.

5. It adds the FullTextIndexColumn object created in Step 4 to the IndexedColumns collection of the FullTextIndex object created in Step 3.

6. It sets the CatalogName property of the FullTextIndex object to point to the FullTextCatalog object created in Step 1.

7. It calls the Create( ) method of the FullTextIndex object.

The SMO classes used to manage Full-Text Search catalogs and indexes are described in Table 11-26 in the section "SMO Instance Classes for Administering Objects Not Used for Data Storage Reference," later in this chapter.

```
using System;
using System.Data;
using System.Collections;

using Microsoft.SqlServer.Management.Common;
using Microsoft.SqlServer.Management.Smo;

class Program
{
    static void Main(string[] args)
    {
        Server server = new Server("localhost");
        Database db = server.Databases["AdventureWorks"];

        FullTextCatalog ftc = new FullTextCatalog(db, "PSS2005_AW_Catalog");
        ftc.IsDefault = true;
        ftc.Create();

        Table t = db.Tables["ProductDescription", "Production"];
        FullTextIndex fti = new FullTextIndex(t);
        fti.IndexedColumns.Add(new FullTextIndexColumn(fti, "Description"));
        fti.UniqueIndexName = "PK_ProductDescription_ProductDescriptionID";
        fti.CatalogName = "PSS2005_AW_Catalog";
        fti.Create();

        Console.WriteLine("Press any key to continue.");
        Console.ReadKey();
    }
}
```

You can see the new full-text index by opening the Databases → AdventureWorks → Storage → Full Text Catalogs node in the Object Explorer window of SQL Server Management Studio.

SMO Instance Classes for Administering Objects Not Used for Data Storage Reference

This section describes the classes used to administer SQL Server SMO instance classes that are not used to store data. The classes are arranged into functional groups.

Server Configuration

The SMO classes used to manage configuration information for a SQL Server instance are described in Table 11-1.

Table 11-1. SMO classes for managing SQL Server configuration

Class	Description
ConfigProperty	Represents configuration option information.
ConfigPropertyCollection	Represents a collection of ConfigProperty objects. The Properties property of the Configuration class returns the collection of configuration.
Configuration	Represents configuration information for a SQL Server instance. The configuration information object for a configuration option setting is exposed through the properties of the Configuration object that returns a ConfigProperty object.
	The Configuration object is accessed through the Configuration property of the Server class.

Registered Servers

Registered servers let you save connection information for SQL Server instances. Server groups create a hierarchy similar to an operating system directory to facilitate organization of registered servers. Registered servers and server groups can be viewed in the Registered Servers view in SQL Server Management Studio.

The SMO classes used to manage registered SQL servers and server groups are described in Table 11-2. These classes are located in the Microsoft.SqlServer. Management.Smo.RegisteredServers namespace.

Table 11-2. SMO classes for managing registered servers and server groups

Class	Description
RegisteredServer	Represents a registered SQL Server.
RegisteredServerCollection	Represents a collection of registered SQL Servers as RegisteredServer objects.
	The RegisteredServers property of the ServerGroup class returns a RegisteredServerCollection object containing SQL servers included in the parent server group.
	The RegisteredServers property of the SmoApplication.SqlServer-Registrations class returns a RegisteredServerCollection object containing SQL servers defined on the SmoApplication object.

Table 11-2. SMO classes for managing registered servers and server groups (continued)

Class	Description
ServerGroup	Represents a group of registered SQL Server instances.
ServerGroupCollection	Represents a collection of registered SQL Server groups as ServerGroup objects. The ServerGroups property of the SmoApplication.SqlServer-Registrations class returns a ServerGroupCollection object containing SQL server groups defined on the SmoApplication object.

Linked Servers

A linked server is a database system other than SQL Server that is linked to a SQL Server instance through an OLE DB driver. The SMO classes used to manage linked servers are described in Table 11-3.

Table 11-3. SMO classes for managing linked servers

Class	Description
LinkedServer	Represents a database system other than SQL Server.
LinkedServerCollection	Represents a collection of linked servers as LinkedServer objects. The LinkedServers property of the Server class returns the collection of linked servers registered with the SQL Server instance.
LinkedServerLogin	Represents a SQL Server logon account that has permission to connect to a linked server.
LinkedServerLoginCollection	Represents a collection of linked server logins as LinkedServerLogin objects. The LinkedServerLogins property of the LinkServer class returns the collection of linked server logins defined on the linked server.

Database Defaults

The SMO classes used to manage database defaults are described in Table 11-4.

Table 11-4. SMO classes for managing database defaults

Class	Description
Default	Represents a SQL Server database default.
DefaultCollection	Represents a collection of database defaults as Default objects. The Defaults property of the Database class returns the collection of defaults defined on the database.

Files and Filegroups

A SQL Server database is mapped over a series of operating system files with data files and log files always stored in separate files. Data can be mapped to both a single primary data file (*.mdf* file), which is the starting point for all database operations, and optional secondary data files (*.ndf* files). Log files contain information used to recover the database and are mapped to one or more operating system files (*.ldf* files).

Filegroups are used to group together database objects and files for allocation and administrative purposes. Log files are not part of a filegroup and are managed separately from the data space.

The SMO classes used to manage data files, log files, and filegroups are described in Table 11-5.

Table 11-5. SMO classes for managing files and filegroups

Class	Description
DataFile	Represents a SQL Server data file.
DataFileCollection	Represents a collection of data files as DataFile objects. The Files property of the FileGroup class returns the collection of data files defined in the filegroup.
FileGroup	Represents a SQL Server filegroup.
FileGroupCollection	Represents a collection of filegroups as FileGroup objects. The FileGroups property of the Database class returns the collection of filegroups defined on the database.
LogFile	Represents a SQL Server log file.
LogFileCollection	Represents a collection of log files as LogFile objects. The LogFiles property of the Database class returns the collection of log files defined on the database.

Partition Functions

Partitioning a database splits large tables into smaller tables to improve performance and simplify maintenance. A partition function maps each row of a table or index into a partition based on the values of a specified column. A partition is scoped at the database level.

The SMO classes used to manage partition functions are described in Table 11-6.

Table 11-6. SMO classes for managing partition functions

Class	Description
PartitionFunction	Represents a partition function.
PartitionFunctionCollection	Represents a collection of partition functions as Partition-Function objects. The PartitionFunctions property of the Database class returns the collection of partition functions defined on the database.
PartitionFunctionEvents	Represents the settings required for SQL Server partition function event notification. The PartitionFunctionEvents object is obtained using the Events property of the Partition-Function object and cannot be created as a standalone object.
PartitionFunctionParameter	Represents a partition function parameter.
PartitionFunctionParameterCollection	Represents a collection of partition function parameters as PartitionFunctionParameter objects. The Partition-FunctionParameters property of the PartitionFunction class returns the collection of partition function parameters defined on the partition function.

Partition Schemes

A partition scheme maps partitions of a partitioned table or index to filegroups. The SMO classes used to manage partition schemes are described in Table 11-7.

Table 11-7. SMO classes for managing partition schemes

Class	Description
PartitionScheme	Represents a partition scheme.
PartitionSchemeCollection	Represents a collection of partition schemes as PartitionScheme objects. The PartitionSchemes property of the Database class returns the collection of partition schemes defined on the database.
PartitionSchemeEvents	Represents the settings required for SQL Server partition scheme event notification. The PartitionSchemeEvents object is obtained using the Events property of the PartitionScheme object and cannot be created as a standalone object.
	The SubscribeToEvents( ) method of the PartitionScheme-Events class specifies the events to receive as an ObjectEventSet object.
PartitionSchemeParameter	Represents a partition scheme parameter.
PartitionSchemeParameterCollection	Represents a collection of partition scheme parameters as Partition-SchemeParameter objects. The PartitionSchemeParameters property of both the Table and Index classes returns the collection of partition scheme parameters defined on the table or index.

Logins

The SMO classes used to manage logins are described in Table 11-8.

Table 11-8. SMO classes for managing logins

Class	Description
DatabaseMapping	Represents a SQL Server database mapping of logins to database users for each database.
	The EnumDatabaseMappings( ) method of the Login class returns an array of DatabaseMapping objects for the login account.
Login	Represents a SQL Server login account granted access to SQL Server through either Windows or SQL Server standard authentication.
LoginCollection	Represents a collection of Login objects. The Logins property of the Server class returns a LoginsCollection object containing all login accounts defined on the SQL Server instance.
LoginEvents	Represents the settings required for SQL Server login event notification. The LoginEvents object is obtained using the Events property of the Login object and cannot be created as a standalone object.
	The SubscribeToEvents( ) method of the LoginEvents class specifies the events to receive as an ObjectEventSet object.

Users

The SMO classes used to manage users are described in Table 11-9.

Table 11-9. SMO classes for managing users

Class	Description
User	Represents a SQL Server user—a security principal used for controlling access permission within a database. While a login is created at the server level, a user maps to a single SQL Server login in the database in which the user is defined.
UserCollection	Represents a collection of User objects. The Users property of the Database class returns a UserCollection object containing all users defined for the database.
UserEvents	Represents the settings required for SQL Server user event notification. The UserEvents object is obtained using the Events property of the User object and cannot be created as a standalone object.
	The SubscribeToEvents( ) method of the UserEvents class specifies the events to receive as an ObjectEventSet object.
UserOptions	Represents a set of configurable server options relating to users. The UserOptions object is obtained using the UserOptions property of the Server object and cannot be created as a standalone object.

Server Roles

The SMO classes used to manage server roles are described in Table 11-10.

Table 11-10. SMO classes for managing server roles

Class	Description
ServerRole	Represents a server security role.
ServerRoleCollection	Represents a collection of server roles as ServerRole objects. The Roles property of the Server class returns the collection of roles defined on the SQL Server instance.

Database Roles

The SMO classes used to manage database roles are described in Table 11-11.

Table 11-11. SMO classes for managing database roles

Class	Description
DatabaseRole	Represents a SQL Server database security role.
DatabaseRoleCollection	Represents a collection of DatabaseRole objects. The Roles property of the Database class returns a DatabaseRoleCollection object containing all roles defined for the database.

Server Permissions

The SMO classes used to manage server permissions are described in Table 11-12.

Table 11-12. SMO classes for managing server permissions

Class	Description
ServerPermission	Represents a server permission. A ServerPermissionSet object containing a set of ServerPermission objects is used to specify permissions for the Grant( ), Deny( ), and Revoke( ) methods of the Server object.
ServerPermissionInfo	Represents information about a server-level permission for a database server. The EnumServerPermissions( ) method of the Server class returns permission information as an array of ServerPermissionInfo objects.
ServerPermissionSet	Represents a set of server permissions. The ServerPermissionSet class is used to specify multiple permissions for the Grant( ), Deny( ), and Revoke( ) methods of the Server object.

Database Permissions

The SMO classes used to manage database permissions are described in Table 11-13.

Table 11-13. SMO classes for managing database permissions

Class	Description
DatabasePermission	Represents a SQL Server database permission. A DatabasePermissionSet object containing a set of DatabasePermission objects is used to specify permissions for the Grant( ), Deny( ), and Revoke( ) methods of the Database object.
DatabasePermissionInfo	Represents information about a server-level permission for a database server. The EnumDatabasePermissions( ) method of the Database class returns permission information as an array of DatabasePermissionInfo objects.
DatabasePermissionSet	Represents a set of database permissions. The DatabasePermissionSet class is used to specify multiple permissions for the Grant( ), Deny( ), and Revoke( ) methods of the Database object.

Application Roles

The SMO classes used to manage application roles are described in Table 11-14.

Table 11-14. SMO classes for managing application roles

Class	Description
ApplicationRole	Represents an application security role used to set privileges from an application.
ApplicationRoleCollection	Represents a collection of application roles as ApplicationRole objects. The ApplicationRoles property of the Database class returns the collection of roles defined on the database.
ApplicationRoleEvents	Represents the settings required for SQL Server application role event notification. The ApplicationRoleEvents object is obtained using the Events property of the ApplicationRole object and cannot be created as a standalone object. The SubscribeToEvents( ) method of the ApplicationRoleEvents class specifies the events to receive as an ObjectEventSet object.

.NET Framework Assemblies

SQL Server 2005, through CLR integration, lets you create database objects such as functions, stored procedures, triggers, user-defined data types, and user-defined aggregate functions from .NET Framework assemblies. The SMO classes used to manage .NET Framework assemblies are described in Table 11-15.

Table 11-15. SMO classes for managing .NET Framework assemblies

Class	Description
SqlAssembly	Represents a .NET Framework assembly.
SqlAssemblyCollection	Represents a collection of .NET Framework assemblies as SqlAssembly objects. The Assemblies property of the Database class returns a SqlAssembly-Collection object containing all .NET Framework assemblies defined on the database.
SqlAssemblyEvent	Represents an assembly event. The SqlAssemblyEvent class contains a property for each event that the database can respond to.
SqlAssemblyEvents	Represents the settings required for SQL Server assembly event notification. The SqlAssemblyEvents object is obtained using the Events property of the SqlAssembly object and cannot be created as a standalone object.
	The SubscribeToEvents( ) method of the SqlAssemblyEvents class specifies the events to receive as an SqlAssemblyEventSet object.
SqlAssemblyEventSet	Represents a set of SQL Server database events and is used to specify the set of events for the DatabaseEvent class.
SqlAssemblyFile	Represents the binary file that stores a .NET Framework assembly.
SqlAssemblyFileCollection	Represents a collection of .NET Framework assembly files as SqlAssemblyFile objects. The SqlAssemblyFiles property of the SqlAssembly class returns a SqlAssemblyFileCollection object containing all files associated with the .NET Framework assemblies.

Endpoints

An endpoint is a service that can listen natively for requests. An endpoint can expose methods to calling clients. Endpoints can use either an HTTP or TCP protocol, and handle SOAP, Service Broker, T-SQL, or database mirroring payloads. The SMO classes used to manage endpoints are described in Table 11-16.

Table 11-16. SMO classes for managing endpoints

Class	Description
DatabaseMirroringPayload	Represents a SQL Server database mirroring payload. The Database-Mirroring property of the Payload class returns a DatabaseMirroring-Payload object representing the database mirroring payload for the endpoint.
Endpoint	Represents a SQL Server endpoint service.

Table 11-16. SMO classes for managing endpoints (continued)

Class	Description
EndpointCollection	Represents a collection of endpoints as Endpoint objects. The Endpoints property of the Server class returns the collection of endpoints defined on the SQL Server instance.
EndpointProtocol	Represents an endpoint protocol. The Protocol property of the Endpoint class returns a Protocol object representing the protocol for the endpoint.
HttpProtocol	Represents an HTTP protocol. The Http property of the Protocol class returns an HttpProtocol object representing the HTTP protocol.
Payload	Represents an HTTP endpoint payload. The Payload property of the Endpoint class returns a Payload object representing the payload for the endpoint.
Protocol	Represents a protocol used by an endpoint.
ServiceBrokerPayload	Represents a SQL Server Service Broker payload. The ServiceBroker property of the Payload class returns a ServiceBrokerPayload object representing the Service Broker payload for the endpoint.
SoapPayload	Represents a SQL Server SOAP payload. The Soap property of the Payload class returns a SoapPayload object representing the SOAP payload for the endpoint.
SoapPayloadMethod	Represents a SOAP payload method.
SoapPayloadMethodCollection	Represents a collection of SOAP payload methods as SoapPayloadMethod objects. The SoapPayloadMethods property of the SoapPayload class returns the collection of SOAP payload methods defined for the SOAP payload.
TcpProtocol	Represents a TCP protocol. The Tcp property of the Protocol class returns a TcpProtocol object representing the TCP protocol.

XML Schemas

XML schemas are used to validate XML documents and data type instances and to define complex XML data types. The SMO classes used to manage XML schemas are described in Table 11-17.

Table 11-17. SMO classes for managing XML schemas

Class	Description
XmlSchemaCollection	Represents a collection of XML namespaces.
XmlSchemaCollectionCollection	Represents a collection of XML namespaces as XmlSchemaCollection objects. The XmlSchemaCollections property of the Database class returns the collection of XML namespaces defined on the database.

Languages

The SMO classes used to manage supported languages are described in Table 11-18.

Table 11-18. SMO classes for managing supported languages

Class	Description
Language	Represents a SQL Server language.
LanguageCollection	Represents a collection of SQL Server languages as Language objects. The Languages property of the Server class returns the collection of languages supported by the SQL Server instance.

Statistics

Statistics contain information about the distribution of values in a column. This information is used to calculate optimal query plans. The SMO classes used to manage SQL Server statistics are described in Table 11-19.

Table 11-19. SMO classes for managing statistics

Class	Description
Statistic	Represents a SQL Server statistics counter.
StatisticCollection	Represents a collection of SQL Server statistic counters as Statistic objects. The Statistics property of the Table class returns a StatisticCollection object containing all statistics counters defined for the table.
StatisticColumn	Represents a column defined in a SQL Server statistics counter.
StatisticColumnCollection	Represents a collection of columns defined in a SQL Server statistics counter as StatisticColumn objects. The StatisticColumns property of the Statistic class returns a StatisticColumnCollection object containing all statistic columns defined in the statistics counter.
StatisticEvents	Represents the setting required for SQL Server statistic-event notification. The StatisticEvents object is obtained using the Events property of the Statistic object and cannot be created as a standalone object.
	The SubscribeToEvents( ) method of the StatisticEvents class specifies the events to receive as an ObjectEventSet object.

Certificates

A certificate is a digitally signed statement that binds the value of a public key to a person, service, or device that holds the corresponding private key. The SMO classes used to manage certificates are described in Table 11-20.

Table 11-20. SMO classes for managing certificates

Class	Description
Certificate	Represents a SQL Server certificate.
CertificateCollection	Represents a collection of SQL Server certificates as Certificate objects. The Certificates property of the Database class returns the collection of certificates defined on a database.

Table 11-20. SMO classes for managing certificates (continued)

Class	Description
CertificateEvents	Represents the settings required for SQL Server certificate event notification. The CertificateEvents object is obtained using the Events property of the Certificate object and cannot be created as a standalone object.
	The SubscribeToEvents( ) method of the CertificateEvents class specifies the events to receive as an ObjectEventSet object.

Credentials

A credential contains authentication information needed to connect to a secured resource outside of SQL Server. A credential can be associated with multiple SQL Server logins, but a login can only be mapped to one credential. The SMO classes used to manage credentials are described in Table 11-21.

Table 11-21. SMO classes for managing credentials

Class	Description
Credential	Represents a SQL Server credential.
CredentialCollection	Represents a collection of SQL Server credentials as Credential objects. The Credentials property of the Server class returns the collection of credentials defined on the SQL Server instance.

Keys

The SMO classes used to manage asymmetric and symmetric keys are described in Table 11-22.

Table 11-22. SMO classes for managing keys

Class	Description
AsymmetricKey	Represents a SQL Server asymmetric key.
AsymmetricKeyCollection	Represents a collection of asymmetric keys as AsymmetricKey objects. The AsymmetricKeys property of the Database class returns the collection of asymmetric keys defined on the database.
SymmetricKey	Represents a SQL Server symmetric key.
SymmetricKeyCollection	Represents a collection of symmetric keys as SymmetricKey objects. The SymmetricKeys property of the Database class returns the collection of symmetric keys defined on the database.
SymmetricKeyEncryption	Represents the type of encryption (asymmetric, certificate, password, or symmetric) used when encrypting a symmetric key object.
	The AddKeyEncryption( ) method of the SymmetricKey Class adds a type of encryption to the symmetric key.

Synonyms

A synonym is a database object that provides an alternate name for a database object either on the local server or on a remote server. The SMO classes used to manage SQL Server synonyms are described in Table 11-23.

Table 11-23. SMO classes for managing synonyms

Class	Description
Synonym	Represents a SQL Server synonym.
SynonymCollection	Represents a collection of SQL Server synonyms as Synonym objects. The Synonyms property of the Database class returns a SynonymCollection object containing synonyms defined on the database.
SynonymEvents	Represents settings required for SQL Server synonym event notification.

System Messages

The SMO classes used to manage system messages are described in Table 11-24.

Table 11-24. SMO classes for managing system messages

Class	Description
SystemMessage	Represents a system message defined on a SQL Server instance.
SystemMessageCollection	Represents a collection of SQL Server system messages as SystemMessage objects. The SystemMessages property of the Server class returns a SystemMessageCollection object containing all system messages defined on the SQL server instance.

User-Defined Messages

The SMO classes used to manage user-defined error and warning messages are described in Table 11-25.

Table 11-25. SMO classes for managing user-defined messages

Class	Description
UserDefinedMessage	Represents a user-defined message on a SQL Server instance.
UserDefinedMessageCollection	Represents a collection of SQL Server user-defined messages as UserDefinedMessage objects. The UserDefinedMessages property of the Server class returns a UserDefinedMessageCollection object containing all user-defined messages defined on the SQL server instance.

Full-Text Search

Full-Text Search lets you perform linguistic searches against the words and phrases in your data. The SMO classes used to manage Full-Text Search catalogs and indexes are described in Table 11-26.

Table 11-26. SMO classes for managing Full-Text Search

Class	Description
FullTextCatalog	Represents a full-text catalog letting you programmatically create, manage, and configure the catalog.
FullTextCatalogCollection	Represents a collection of full-text catalogs as FullTextCatalog objects. The FullTextCatalogs property of the Database class returns a FullTextCatalogCollection object containing all full-text catalogs defined on the database.
FullTextIndex	Represents a full-text index letting you programmatically create, manage, and configure the index.
	The FullTextIndex property of the Table or View class returns the full-text index on the table or view.
FullTextIndexColumn	Represents a column in a full-text index letting you programmatically create, manage, and configure the column.
FullTextIndexColumnCollection	Represents a collection of full-text index columns as FullTextIndex-Column objects. The IndexedColumns property of the FullTextIndex class returns a FullTextIndexColumnCollection object containing all columns defined on the full-text index.
FullTextService	Provides programmatic access to the Full-Text Search settings. The FullText property of the Server class returns the full-text service implementation for the SQL Service instance.

OLE DB Providers

The SMO classes used to manage SQL Server OLE DB providers are described in Table 11-27.

Table 11-27. SMO classes for managing OLE DB Providers

Class	Description
OleDbProviderSettings	Represents the settings for a SQL Server OLE DB provider.
OleDbProviderSettingsCollection	Represents a collection of OleDbProviderSettings objects. The OleDbProviderSettings property of the Settings class returns the collection of OLE provider settings defined on the SQL Server instance. The Settings property of the Server class returns a Settings object representing a set of configurable settings on the SQL Server instance.

CHAPTER 12

SQL Server Management Objects (SMO) Utility Classes

SMO utility classes perform specific tasks and are work independently of the SQL Server instance. SMO utility classes can be grouped according to their function:

- Database scripting operations
- Backup and restore databases
- Transfer schema and data between database instances
- Trace and trace replay operations
- Administering the Database Mail subsystem

The sections in this chapter describe these SMO utility classes and shows how to use them through programming examples.

There are three more SMO utility classes that are discussed in later chapters:

- SMO classes used to administer SQL Server Agent are covered in Chapter 16.
- SMO classes used to administer Service Broker are covered in Chapter 17.
- SMO classes used to administer Notification Services are covered in Chapter 18.

The examples in this section are all built using Visual Studio 2005. The examples need a reference to the following assemblies:

- Microsoft.SqlServer.ConnectionInfo
- Microsoft.SqlServer.Smo

Additional assembly references will be given for examples in which the assemblies are required.

Scripting

You can document a database schema by generating T-SQL scripts for the different objects. Possible uses for these scripts include the following:

- As a backup, allowing objects to be recreated if necessary
- To create development, testing, staging, and production environments

SQL Server Management Studio lets you script selected database objects. You can choose to use either a manual process or the Generate SQL Server Scripts Wizard.

The SMO classes used for scripting operations are described in Table 12-1. These classes are located in the `Microsoft.SqlServer.Management.Smo` namespace.

Table 12-1. SMO classes for scripting operations

Class	Description
Scripter	Provides programmatic access to scripting settings and functionality, including finding dependencies, outputting scripts, and managing the context of a scripting operation.
ScriptingErrorEventArgs	Represents the arguments used to report an error during a scripting operation. ScriptingErrorEventArgs is derived from EventArgs.
ScriptingOptions	Represents options for scripting operations. These options identify the SQL Server items to script and control the scripting operation.
ScriptOption	Represents a SQL Server scripting option. The ScriptOption class contains a property for each type of SQL Server item that can be scripted.

This section shows how to programmatically use SMO scripting classes. You need to add a reference to the `Microsoft.SqlServer.SmoEnum` assembly to compile and execute the examples in this section.

A Uniform Resource Name (URN) address uniquely identifies each SQL Server object. The first example and the next one use URNs to specify which objects to script.

The first example shows how to use the `Scripter` class to script the objects in the AdventureWorks database:

```
using System;
using System.Data;
using System.Collections.Specialized;

using Microsoft.SqlServer.Management.Common;
using Microsoft.SqlServer.Management.Smo;

class Program
{
    static void Main(string[] args)
    {
        Server server = new Server("localhost");
        Database db = server.Databases["AdventureWorks"];

        Scripter scripter = new Scripter(server);
        StringCollection sc = scripter.Script(new Urn[] { db.Urn });

        foreach (string s in sc)
```

```
            Console.WriteLine(s);

            Console.WriteLine(Environment.NewLine + "Press any key to continue.");
            Console.ReadKey();
        }
    }
```

Results are shown in Figure 12-1.

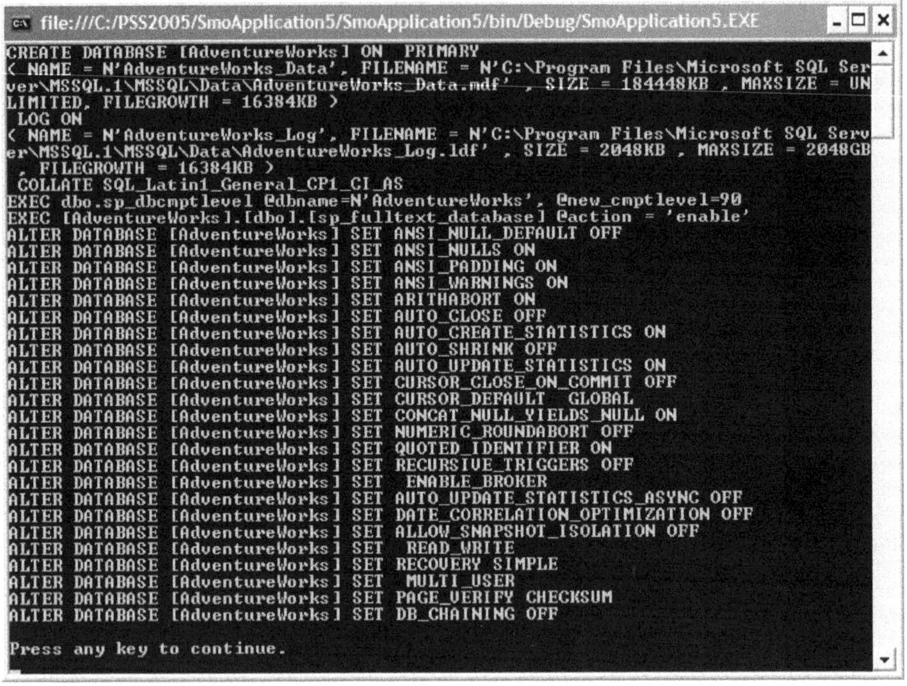

Figure 12-1. Results for scripting AdventureWorks database objects

The Script( ) method of the Scripter class generates T-SQL that can be used to create SQL Server objects identified by either a SqlSmoObject array, Urn array, or
UrnCollection object passed as an argument to the constructor. The Script( )
method returns the T-SQL as a StringCollection object. The Options property
exposes a ScriptingOptions object that lets you control scripting operations.

The following example scripts all tables in AdventureWorks:

```
using System;
using System.Data;
using System.Collections.Specialized;

using Microsoft.SqlServer.Management.Common;
using Microsoft.SqlServer.Management.Smo;
```

```
class Program
{
    static void Main(string[] args)
    {
        Server server = new Server("localhost");
        Database db = server.Databases["AdventureWorks"];

        UrnCollection urnc = new UrnCollection();
        foreach (Table t in db.Tables)
            urnc.Add(t.Urn);

        Scripter scripter = new Scripter(server);
        StringCollection sc = scripter.Script(urnc);

        foreach (string s in sc)
            Console.WriteLine(s);

        Console.WriteLine(Environment.NewLine + "Press any key to continue." );
        Console.ReadKey();
    }
}
```

Partial results are shown in Figure 12-2.

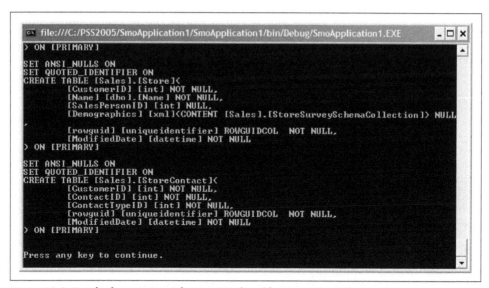

Figure 12-2. Results for scripting AdventureWorks tables using UrnCollection class example

The Script( ) method of the Scripter class is overloaded. In addition to accepting a UrnCollection object as shown in the preceding example, it can also take a list of objects as a Urn array or a SqlSmoObject array.

The SMO classes used to manage URN addresses are described in Table 12-2.

Table 12-2. SMO classes for managing URN addresses

Class	Description
Urn	Represents a URN address
UrnCollection	Represents a collection of Urn objects

The SqlSmoObject class is a generic class that represents all SQL Server objects. The following example uses the SqlSmoObject class to produce the same result as the preceding example:

```
using System;
using System.Data;
using System.Collections.Specialized;

using Microsoft.SqlServer.Management.Common;
using Microsoft.SqlServer.Management.Smo;

class Program
{
    static void Main(string[] args)
    {
        Server server = new Server("localhost");
        Database db = server.Databases["AdventureWorks"];

        Table[] ta = new Table[db.Tables.Count];
        db.Tables.CopyTo(ta, 0);
        SqlSmoObject[] ssoa = new SqlSmoObject[db.Tables.Count];
        Array.Copy(ta, ssoa, ta.Length);

        Scripter scripter = new Scripter(server);
        StringCollection sc = scripter.Script(ssoa);

        foreach (string s in sc)
            Console.WriteLine(s);

        Console.WriteLine(Environment.NewLine + "Press any key to continue.");
        Console.ReadKey();
    }
}
```

Partial results are shown in Figure 12-3.

The static EnumDependencies() method of the Scripter class returns a UrnCollection object that contains the specified object and either its parents or children, depending on the value of the second argument from the DependencyType enumeration.

The following example uses the EnumDependencies() method to script the first table in AdventureWorks and its child objects:

```
using System;
using System.Data;
using System.Collections.Specialized;
```

Figure 12-3. Results for scripting AdventureWorks tables using SqlSmoObject class example

```
using Microsoft.SqlServer.Management.Common;
using Microsoft.SqlServer.Management.Smo;

class Program
{
    static void Main(string[] args)
    {
        Server server = new Server("localhost");
        Database db = server.Databases["AdventureWorks"];

        Scripter scripter = new Scripter(server);
        UrnCollection urnc = Scripter.EnumDependencies(
            db.Tables[0], DependencyType.Children);
        StringCollection sc = scripter.Script(urnc);

        foreach (string s in sc)
            Console.WriteLine(s);

        Console.WriteLine(Environment.NewLine + "Press any key to continue.");
        Console.ReadKey();
    }
}
```

Results are shown in Figure 12-4.

The output contains the T-SQL script to generate both the table named AWBuildVersion and its children—a single update trigger on the table.

The Scripter object raises three types of events, described in Table 12-3.

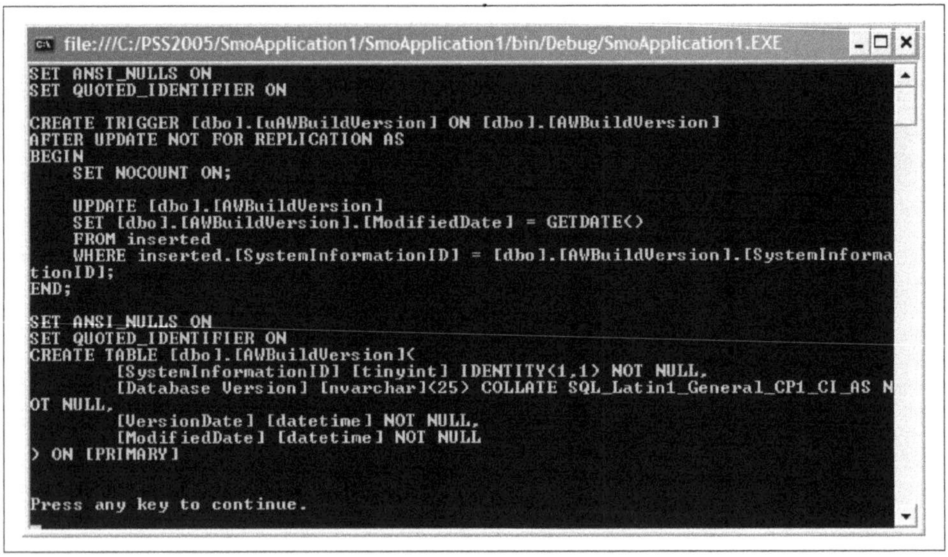

Figure 12-4. Results for scripting single AdventureWorks table and its children example

Table 12-3. Scripter events

Event	Description
DiscoveryProgress	Reports progress at intervals during the DiscoverDependencies() method
ScriptingError	Reports an error during a scripting operation
ScriptingProgress	Reports progress at intervals during the Script() method

This example receives and handles the ScriptingProgress event:

```
using System;
using System.Data;
using System.Collections.Specialized;

using Microsoft.SqlServer.Management.Common;
using Microsoft.SqlServer.Management.Smo;

class Program
{
    static void Main(string[] args)
    {
        Server server = new Server("localhost");
        Database db = server.Databases["AdventureWorks"];

        UrnCollection urnc = new UrnCollection();
        foreach (Table t in db.Tables)
            urnc.Add(t.Urn);

        Scripter scripter = new Scripter(server);
        scripter.ScriptingProgress +=
```

```
                new ProgressReportEventHandler(ScriptingProgressEventHandler);
            StringCollection sc = scripter.Script(urnc);

            Console.WriteLine(Environment.NewLine + "Press any key to continue.");
            Console.ReadKey();
        }

        protected static void ScriptingProgressEventHandler(
            object sender, ProgressReportEventArgs e)
        {
            Console.WriteLine("(" + e.TotalCount + "/" + e.Total + ") " + e.Current);
        }
    }
```

Partial results are shown in Figure 12-5.

Figure 12-5. Results for monitoring scripting progress example

Backing Up and Restoring Data

The SMO backup and restore classes serve several purposes:

- To back up and restore data and logs
- To perform integrity checks
- To examine database consistency

The SMO backup and restore classes are described in Table 12-4. These classes are located in the Microsoft.SqlServer.Management.Smo namespace.

Table 12-4. SMO classes for managing backup and restore operations

Class	Description
Backup	Provides programmatic access to SQL Server backup operations.
BackupDevice	Represents a SQL Server backup device—a tape drive or disk drive used in a backup operation.
BackupDeviceCollection	Represents a collection of backup devices as BackupDevice objects. The BackupDevices property of the Server class returns the collection of all backup devices on an instance of SQL Server.
BackupDeviceItem	Provides programmatic access to SQL Server backup devices by name.
PercentCompleteEventArgs	Represents the details of the event that occurs when a backup or restore process reaches a percent-complete marker.
RelocateFile	Provides a mechanism to relocate files during a restore operation. The Relocate-File class is used with the RelocateFiles property of the Restore class.
Restore	Provides programmatic access to SQL Server restore operations. The Restore class lets you restore all or part of a database and transaction log records, verify the integrity of a backup medium, identify the contents of a backup medium, and monitor the status of a restore operation.
VerifyCompleteEventArgs	Represents the details of the event that occurs when a backup verification completes.

This section shows how to use SMO backup and restore classes programmatically.

This example backs up the AdventureWorks database to a file:

```
using System;
using System.Data;
using System.Collections;

using Microsoft.SqlServer.Management.Common;
using Microsoft.SqlServer.Management.Smo;

class Program
{
    static void Main(string[] args)
    {
        BackupDeviceItem bdi =
            new BackupDeviceItem("AdventureWorks.bak", DeviceType.File);

        Backup bu = new Backup( );
        bu.Database = "AdventureWorks";
        bu.Devices.Add(bdi);
        bu.Initialize = true;

        // add percent complete and complete event handlers
        bu.PercentComplete +=
            new PercentCompleteEventHandler(Backup_PercentComplete);
        bu.Complete +=new ServerMessageEventHandler(Backup_Complete);

        Server server = new Server("localhost");
        bu.SqlBackup(server);
```

```
            Console.WriteLine(Environment.NewLine + "Press any key to continue.");
            Console.ReadKey();
        }

        protected static void Backup_PercentComplete(
            object sender, PercentCompleteEventArgs e)
        {
            Console.WriteLine(e.Percent + "% processed.");
        }

        protected static void Backup_Complete(object sender, ServerMessageEventArgs e)
        {
            Console.WriteLine(Environment.NewLine + e.ToString());
        }
    }
```

Once complete, the backup file *AdventureWorks.bak* is located (by default) in the *C:\ Program Files\Microsoft SQL Server\MSSQL.1\MSSQL\Backup* directory. Results are shown in Figure 12-6.

Figure 12-6. Results for backup example

The Backup class provides programmatic access to SQL Server backup operations. Three properties are set to configure the Backup object in this example:

Database
    Specifies the database to backup

Devices
    Sets the backup device as a BackupDeviceItem instance

Initialize
    Specifies whether the backup device is initialized as part of the backup operation

There are other optional properties that further control the backup operation.

A PercentCompleteEventHandler is added so that the progress of the backup operation can be displayed to the console. A ServerMessageEventHandler is added to display the status of the BACKUP DATABASE operation.

Finally, the SqlBackup( ) method is called to perform the database backup operation.

The following example restores the backup created in the preceding example:

```
using System;
using System.Data;
using System.Collections;

using Microsoft.SqlServer.Management.Common;
using Microsoft.SqlServer.Management.Smo;

class Program
{
    static void Main(string[] args)
    {
        Server server = new Server("localhost");

        BackupDeviceItem bdi = new BackupDeviceItem(
            "AdventureWorks.bak", DeviceType.File);

        Restore r = new Restore( );
        r.Database = "AdventureWorks";
        r.ReplaceDatabase = true;
        r.Devices.Add(bdi);

        //add percent complete and complete event handlers
        r.PercentComplete +=
            new PercentCompleteEventHandler(Restore_PercentComplete);
        r.Complete += new ServerMessageEventHandler(Restore_Complete);

        r.SqlRestore(server);

        Console.WriteLine(Environment.NewLine + "Press any key to continue.");
        Console.ReadKey( );
    }

    protected static void Restore_PercentComplete(
        object sender, PercentCompleteEventArgs e)
    {
        Console.WriteLine(e.Percent + "% processed.");
    }

    protected static void Restore_Complete(object sender, ServerMessageEventArgs e)
    {
        Console.WriteLine(Environment.NewLine + e.ToString( ));
    }
}
```

Results are shown in Figure 12-7.

The Restore class provides programmatic access to SQL Server restore operations. Three properties are set to configure the Restore object in this example:

```
file:///C:/PSS2005/SmoApplication1/SmoApplication1/bin/Debug/SmoApplication1.EXE
10% processed.
20% processed.
30% processed.
40% processed.
50% processed.
60% processed.
70% processed.
80% processed.
90% processed.
100% processed.

System.Data.SqlClient.SqlError: RESTORE DATABASE successfully processed 21106 pa
ges in 24.878 seconds (6.949 MB/sec).

Press any key to continue.
```

Figure 12-7. Results for restore example

- The Database property, which specifies the database on which the restore operation runs.

- The ReplaceDatabase property, which specifies whether the backup operation creates a new image of the restored database.

- The Devices property, which sets the backup device for the restore operation as a BackupDeviceItem instance.

There are other optional properties not used in this example that further control the backup operation.

A PercentCompleteEventHandler event handler is added so that the progress of the restore operation can be displayed to the console. A ServerMessageEventHandler event handler is added to display the details of the RESTORE DATABASE event.

Finally, the SqlRestore( ) method is called to perform the database restore operation.

 The restore operation requires exclusive access to the database being restored.

Transferring Data

The SMO Transfer class is used to programmatically transfer (copy) data and schemas within and between SQL Server instances. This class is in the Microsoft. SqlServer.Management.Smo namespace.

This example shows how to transfer the AdventureWorks database to a new database called AdventureWorksCopy:

```
using System;
using System.Data;

using Microsoft.SqlServer.Management.Common;
using Microsoft.SqlServer.Management.Smo;
```

```
class Program
{
    static void Main(string[] args)
    {
        Server server = new Server("localhost");
        Database db = server.Databases["AdventureWorks"];

        // create the destination database
        Database dbCopy = new Database(server, "AdventureWorksCopy");
        dbCopy.Create();

        // transfer the data
        Transfer t = new Transfer(db);
        t.CopyAllTables = true;
        t.Options.WithDependencies = true;
        t.DestinationServer = server.Name;
        t.DestinationDatabase = "AdventureWorksCopy";
        t.CopySchema = true;
        t.CopyData = true;

        // wire up event handler to monitor progress
        t.DataTransferEvent +=
            new DataTransferEventHandler(DataTransferEvent_Handler);

        t.TransferData();

        Console.WriteLine("Press any key to continue.");
        Console.ReadKey();
    }

    protected static void DataTransferEvent_Handler(
        object sender, DataTransferEventArgs e)
    {
        Console.WriteLine("[" + e.DataTransferEventType + "] " + e.Message);
    }
}
```

Partial results are shown in Figure 12-8.

Six properties are set to configure the Transfer object in this example:

- The CopyAllTables property is set to true.
- The Options.WithDependencies property is set to true.
- The DestinationServer property is set to the name of the destination server for the object copy. In this case, the destination server is the local server, which is the same as the source server.
- The DestinationDatabase property is set to the name of the database on the destination server.
- The CopySchema property is set to true.
- The CopyData property is set to true.

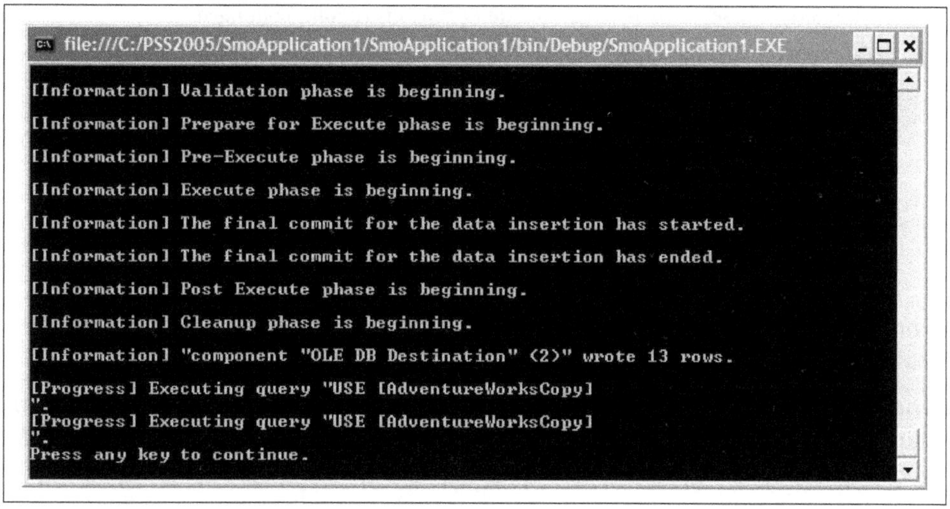

Figure 12-8. Results for transfer data example

There are other optional properties not used in this example that further control the transfer operation.

A DataTransfer event handler is added so that the progress as each database is copied is output to the console window.

Finally, the TransferData( ) method is called to perform the data transfer operation.

Tracing

The SMO trace and replay classes provide an interface with which to trace and record events, manipulate and analyze trace data, and replay recorded trace events. SQL Profiler and the SQL Trace system stored procedures can also perform these tasks.

The SMO classes used to manage trace and replay operations are described in Table 12-5. These classes are located in the Microsoft.SqlServer.Management.Trace namespace.

Table 12-5. SMO classes for managing trace and replay operations

Class	Description
ReplayEventArgs	Represents arguments used to report events that occur during replay operations.
TraceEventArgs	Represents arguments used to report events that occur during trace operations.
TraceFile	Represents a trace logfile.
TraceReplay	Represents a replay operation for trace logfiles and tables.

Table 12-5. SMO classes for managing trace and replay operations (continued)

Class	Description
TraceReplayOptions	Represents configuration settings for replaying a trace. The Options property of the TraceReplay class returns a TraceReplayOptions object for the replay operation.
TraceServer	Represents a new trace on a SQL Server instance.
TraceTable	Represents a table of trace information. The OutputTable property of the TraceReplay class returns a TraceTable object for the replay operation.

The examples in this section show how to programmatically use the SMO trace classes to capture and replay trace events.

The first example logs the name of the first 20 trace log events to the console using the standard trace definition file *Standard.tdf*, installed by default in the *C:\Program Files\ Microsoft SQL Server\90\Tools\Profiler\Templates\Microsoft SQL Server\90* directory:

```
using System;

using Microsoft.SqlServer.Management.Common;
using Microsoft.SqlServer.Management.Smo;
using Microsoft.SqlServer.Management.Trace;

class Program
{
    static void Main(string[] args)
    {
        TraceServer ts = new TraceServer( );

        ConnectionInfoBase ci = new SqlConnectionInfo("localhost");
        ((SqlConnectionInfo)ci).UseIntegratedSecurity = true;
        ts.InitializeAsReader(ci,
          @"C:\Program Files\Microsoft SQL Server\90\Tools\Profiler\" +
          @"Templates\Microsoft SQL Server\90\Standard.tdf");

        int eventNumber = 0;
        while (ts.Read( ))
        {
            Console.Write(ts.GetValue(0) + Environment.NewLine);
            eventNumber++;
            if (eventNumber == 20)
                break;
        }
        ts.Close( );

        Console.WriteLine(Environment.NewLine + "Press any key to continue.");
        Console.ReadKey( );
    }
}
```

Results are shown in Figure 12-9.

Figure 12-9. Results for tracing example

The trace definition file determines the information contained in the trace—which events and what columns of trace data are captured for each event. This example displays only the first column—the name of the trace event. You can get a complete list of columns by viewing the standard definition file using SQL Server Profiler.

The next example replays an existing trace logfile. Use an existing trace file or create a trace file to use with SQL Server Profiler by following these steps:

1. Open SQL Server Profiler by selecting Start → Microsoft SQL Server 2005 → Performance Tools → SQL Server Profiler.

2. From the main menu, select File → New Trace.

3. Complete the Connect to Server dialog box and click the Connect button.

4. Accept the defaults for the Trace Properties dialog box and click the Run button.

5. Let the trace run for about 20 events and then stop it by selecting File → Stop Trace.

6. Save the trace by selecting File → Save. Save the trace file as *C:\PSS2005\Trace\ TestTrace.trc* and click the Save button.

The source code for the example follows:

```
using System;
using System.Data;
using System.Collections;

using Microsoft.SqlServer.Management.Common;
using Microsoft.SqlServer.Management.Smo;
using Microsoft.SqlServer.Management.Trace;

class Program
{
```

```
static void Main(string[] args)
{
    TraceReplay tr = new TraceReplay();
    TraceFile tf = new TraceFile();
    tf.InitializeAsReader(@"C:\PSS2005\Trace\TestTrace.trc");
    tr.Source = tf;
    tr.Connection = new SqlConnectionInfo("localhost");
    tr.ReplayEvent += new ReplayEventHandler(tr_ReplayEvent);
    tr.Start();

    Console.WriteLine(Environment.NewLine + "Press any key to continue.");
    Console.ReadKey();
}

static void tr_ReplayEvent(object sender, ReplayEventArgs args)
{
    Console.WriteLine("--- Record number: " + args.RecordNumber + " ---");
    for (int i = 0; i < args.CurrentRecord.FieldCount; i++)
        Console.WriteLine(args.CurrentRecord[i].ToString());

    Console.WriteLine();
}
}
```

Partial results are shown in Figure 12-10. Of course, your results will be slightly different.

The example displays all of the data in the trace file. In this example, there are 17 records, the last 2 of which are shown.

Database Mail

The SMO SqlMail class gives you programmatic access to configure and monitor the SQL Server Database Mail subsystem. The SqlMail class does not give you access to mailboxes or the ability to send or receive mail messages.

 For security reasons, Database Mail is inactive by default. You must use either the SQL Server Surface Area Configuration tool or the Database Mail Configuration Wizard to enable Database Mail.

A Database Mail *profile* is a collection of accounts. A Database Mail *account* contains information for email servers. An account can be part of one or more profiles.

Applications send email by using profiles rather than accounts. This improves both flexibility and reliability because accounts can be added to and removed from profiles without changing the application or its configuration. Profiles can be configured to automatically failover. Users and applications can have access to one or more profiles.

Profiles are either public or private. Public profiles are defined at the server level and are available to users in all host databases for sending and receiving email. Private

```
file:///C:/PSS2005/SmoApplication5/SmoApplication5/bin/Debug/SmoApplication5.EXE

---- Record number: 16 ----
NT AUTHORITY\SYSTEM
11/21/2005 1:53:06 AM
51
0
exec sp_executesql N'
                                declare @BatchID uniqueidentifier

                                set @BatchID = newid()

                                UPDATE [Notifications] WITH (TABLOCKX)
                                  SET [BatchID] = @BatchID,
                                      [ProcessStart] = GETUTCDATE(),
                                      [ProcessHeartbeat] = GETUTCDATE()
                                FROM (
                                      SELECT TOP 2 [NotificationID] FROM [Not
ifications] WITH (TABLOCKX) WHERE ProcessStart is NULL and
                                      (ProcessAfter is NULL or ProcessAfte
r < GETUTCDATE()) ORDER BY [NotificationEntered]
                                    ) AS t1
                                WHERE [Notifications].[NotificationID] = t1.
[NotificationID]

                                select top 2
                                            -- Notification data
                                            N.[NotificationID],
                                            N.[SubscriptionID],
                                            N.[ActivationID],
                                            N.[ReportID],
                                            N.[SnapShotDate],
                                            N.[DeliveryExtension],
                                            N.[ExtensionSettings],
                                      N.[Locale],
                                            N.[Parameters],
                                            N.[SubscriptionLastRunTime],

                                            N.[ProcessStart],
                                            N.[NotificationEntered],
                                            N.[Attempt],
                                            N.[IsDataDriven],
                                            SUSER_SNAME(Owner.[Sid]),
                                            Owner.[UserName],
                                            -- Report Data
                                            O.[Path],
                                            O.[Type],
                                            SD.NtSecDescPrimary,
                                      N.[Version]
                                      from
                                            [Notifications] N with (TABL
OCKX) inner join [Catalog] O on O.[ItemID] = N.[ReportID]
                                            inner join [Users] Owner on
N.SubscriptionOwnerID = Owner.UserID
                                            left outer join [SecData] SD
 on O.[PolicyID] = SD.[PolicyID] AND SD.AuthType = @AuthType
                                      where
                                            N.[BatchID] = @BatchID
                                ORDER BY [NotificationEntered]
                                ',N'@AuthType tinyint',@AuthType=1
1844
304
0
System.Byte[]
SYSTEM
Report Server
11/21/2005 1:53:06 AM
0

---- Record number: 17 ----
11/21/2005 1:53:09 AM

Press any key to continue.
```

Figure 12-10. Partial results for trace replay example

profiles are defined in a specific database, and access is generally restricted to specific users and roles for sending email using the profile. Profiles are private by default.

Figure 12-11 shows the relationship between SMO Database Mail classes.

The SMO Database Mail classes are described in Table 12-6. These classes are in the Microsoft.SqlServer.Management.Smo.Mail namespace.

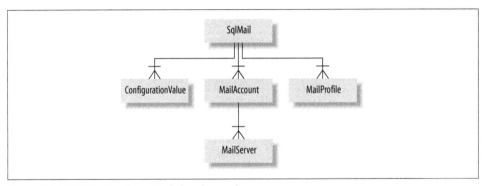

Figure 12-11. SMO Database Mail class hierarchy

Table 12-6. SMO classes for Database Mail

Class	Description
ConfigurationValue	Represents a SQL Server Database Mail configuration option.
ConfigurationValueCollection	Represents a collection of SQL Server Database Mail configuration options as ConfigurationValue objects. The ConfigurationValues property of the SqlMail class returns the collection of options defined on the SQL Server Database Mail subsystem.
MailAccount	Represents a SQL Server Database Mail account.
MailAccountCollection	Represents a collection of SQL Server Database Mail accounts as MailAccount objects. The Accounts property of the SqlMail class returns the collection of mail accounts defined on the SQL Server Database Mail subsystem.
MailProfile	Represents a SQL Server Database Mail profile.
MailProfileCollection	Represents a collection of SQL Server Database Mail profiles as MailProfile objects. The Profiles property of the SqlMail class returns the collection of mail profiles defined on the SQL Server Database Mail subsystem.
MailServer	Represents a SQL Server Database Mail server.
MailServerCollection	Represents a collection of SQL Server Database Mail servers as MailServer objects. The MailServers property of the MailAccount class returns the collection of mail servers associated with a mail account.
SqlMail	Represents the SQL Server Database Mail subsystem.

The following example enumerates the SQL Server Database Mail profiles and the accounts within each profile:

```
using System;
using System.Data;

using Microsoft.SqlServer.Management.Common;
using Microsoft.SqlServer.Management.Smo;
using Microsoft.SqlServer.Management.Smo.Mail;

class Program
{
    static void Main(string[] args)
```

```
        {
            Server server = new Server("localhost");
            SqlMail mail = server.Mail;

            foreach (MailProfile mp in mail.Profiles)
            {
                Console.WriteLine(mp.Name);
                DataTable dt = mp.EnumAccounts();
                foreach (DataRow row in dt.Rows)
                    for (int i = 0; i < dt.Columns.Count; i++)
                        Console.WriteLine("  " + dt.Columns[i].ColumnName +
                            ": " + row[i]);
                Console.WriteLine();
            }

            Console.WriteLine("Press any key to continue.");
            Console.ReadKey();
        }
    }
```

Results are shown in Figure 12-12.

Figure 12-12. Results for enumerating SQL Server Database Mail example

The results show that the example SQL Server instance has one profile, named Test profile, that has one account, named Test account.

The Mail property of the Server class returns a SqlMail object that represents the SQL Server Database Mail subsystem for the server. The Profiles property of the SqlMail class returns a collection of MailProfile objects representing the mail profiles defined on the mail subsystem. The EnumAccounts() method of the MailProfile class returns a DataTable object containing information about the email accounts associated with the profile.

CHAPTER 13

Programming Windows Management Instrumentation (WMI)

You view and manage SQL Server services, network settings, and server-alias settings using the Windows Management Instrumentation (WMI) Provider for Configuration Management. The `ManagedComputer` class in the `Microsoft.SqlServer.Management.Smo.Wmi` namespace represents a WMI installation on a SQL Server instance. It provides access to the WMI Provider for Configuration Management.

The `ManagedComputer` class is the top class in the SMO WMI hierarchy, just as the `Server` class is the top class in the SMO instance classes. `ManagedComputer` objects operate independently of `Server` objects.

You can use the WMI Provider for Configuration Management in one of three ways:

- Use a Windows Management Instrumentation Query Language (WQL) editor or query tool such as `WBEMTest.exe` to execute queries.

- Use a scripting language such as VBScript, JScript, or Perl in which you can embed and execute WQL queries.

- Use the `ManagedComputer` class in the `Microsoft.SqlServer.Management.Smo.Wmi` namespace from a .NET SMO application.

This book deals only with using the `ManagedComputer` class in a .NET SMO application. For more information about the other alternatives, see Microsoft SQL Server 2005 Books Online.

Programming SMO WMI Classes

Figure 13-1 shows the relationship between SMO classes used with the WMI Provider for Configuration Management.

This section shows how to programmatically use SMO WMI classes. The examples in this section are all built using Visual Studio 2005. You need a reference to the following assemblies to compile and run the examples:

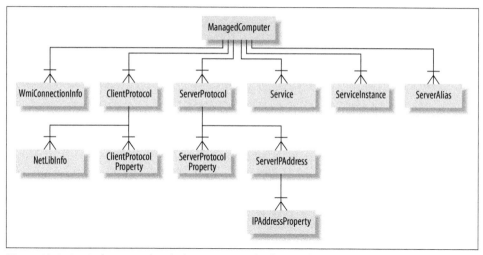

Figure 13-1. SMO classes used with the WMI Provider for Configuration Management

- Microsoft.SqlServer.ConnectionInfo
- Microsoft.SqlServer.Smo
- Microsoft.SqlServer.WmiEnum

Additional assembly references will be indicated for examples in which they are required.

Enumerating the WMI Installation

This example demonstrates how to instantiate a ManagedComputer object and iterate through its hierarchy of collections to enumerate information about the WMI installation. The example lists client protocols, connection settings, server aliases, service instances, and services on the local machine.

```
using System;
using System.Data;

using Microsoft.SqlServer.Management.Common;
using Microsoft.SqlServer.Management.Smo;
using Microsoft.SqlServer.Management.Smo.Wmi;

class Program
{
    static void Main(string[] args)
    {
        ManagedComputer mc = new ManagedComputer();

        Console.WriteLine("-Client Protocols-");
        foreach (ClientProtocol cp in mc.ClientProtocols)
            Console.WriteLine(cp.DisplayName + ": " +
                (cp.IsEnabled ? "Enabled" : "Disabled"));
```

```
            Console.WriteLine(Environment.NewLine + "-Connection Settings-");
            WmiConnectionInfo wci = mc.ConnectionSettings;
            Console.WriteLine("MachineName = " + wci.MachineName);
            Console.WriteLine("Timeout = " + wci.Timeout);
            Console.WriteLine("Username = " + wci.Username);

            Console.WriteLine(Environment.NewLine + "-Server Aliases-");
            foreach (ServerAlias sa in mc.ServerAliases)
                Console.WriteLine(sa.Name + ": " + sa.State);

            Console.WriteLine(Environment.NewLine + "-Server Instances-");
            foreach (ServerInstance si in mc.ServerInstances)
                Console.WriteLine(si.Name + ": " + si.State);

            Console.WriteLine(Environment.NewLine + "-Services-");
            foreach (Service s in mc.Services)
                Console.WriteLine(s.Name + ": " + s.ServiceState);

            Console.WriteLine(Environment.NewLine + "Press any key to continue.");
            Console.ReadKey();
        }
    }
```

Results are shown in Figure 13-2.

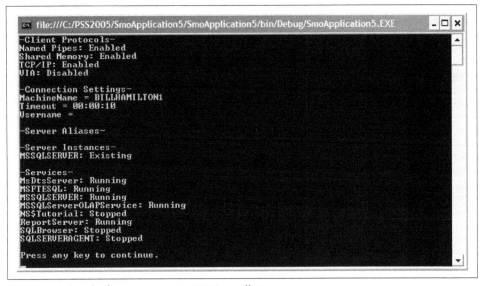

Figure 13-2. Results from enumerating WMI installation

The ManagedComputer class, which represents a WMI installation on a SQL Server instance, has an overloaded constructor. The overload used in the preceding example takes no arguments and initializes a new instance for the default SQL Server instance. The other two overloads let you specify the name of the computer to connect to, and optionally a login name and password. The ManagedComputer class exposes WMI functionality through the set of properties described in Table 13-1.

Table 13-1. ManagedComputer class public properties

Property	Return value	Description
ClientProtocols	ClientProtocolCollection	Gets a collection of ClientProtocol objects, each representing a client protocol defined on the WMI installation
ConnectionSettings	WmiConnectionInfo	Gets the connection settings for the WMI installation
Name	string	Gets the name of the WMI object
Properties	PropertyCollection	Gets a collection of Property objects, each representing a property defined on the WMI object
ServerAliases	ServerAliasCollection	Gets a collection of ServerAlias objects, each representing a server alias on the WMI installation
ServerInstances	ServerInstanceCollection	Gets a collection of ServerInstance objects, each representing an instance of SQL Server on the WMI installation
Services	ServiceCollection	Gets a collection of Service objects, each representing a SQL Server service on the WMI installation
State	SqlSmoState	Gets the state of the WMI object
Urn	Urn	Gets the URN address for the WMI object
UserData	object	Gets or sets user-defined data associated with the WMI object

Four collections accessed through properties of the ManagedComputer class allow access to most WMI functionality. These collections expose the objects described further in Table 13-2.

Table 13-2. ManagedComputer class collections

Class	Function
ClientProtocol	The ClientProtocol class represents a network protocol installed on a client that allows communication with a SQL Server instance over a network. The ClientProtocol class lets you: • Get or set the display name of the protocol • Enable or disable the protocol • Get the network library information file for the protocol as a NetLibInfo object • Get the network library filename for the protocol • Get or set the order in which the protocol is listed and applied relative to the supported protocols in the ClientProtocolCollection object • Access and modify the collection of attributes (as ProtocolProperty objects) defined on the protocol The collection of ClientProtocol objects is accessed through the ClientProtocols property.

Table 13-2. ManagedComputer class collections (continued)

Class	Function
ServerAlias	A server alias is an alternate name that you can use to connect to an instance of SQL Server. The ServiceAlias class lets you: • Get or set the connection string used by the alias to connect to the SQL Server instance • Get or set the name of the alias • Get or set the parent (as a ManagedComputer object) of the alias • Get or set the name of the protocol used by the alias • Get or set the SQL Server instance that the alias connects to • Create, refresh, and drop server aliases The collection of ServerAlias objects is accessed though the ServerAliases property.
ServerInstance	The ServerInstance class represents an instance of SQL Server and lets you: • Get or set the name of the server instance • Get or set the parent (as a ManagedComputer object) of the server instance • Access and modify the collection of protocols (as a collection of ServerProtocol objects) defined on the server in the WMI installation The collection of ServerInstance objects is accessed though the ServerInstances property.
Service	The Service class represents an instance of a SQL Server service and lets you: • Find out whether the service can be paused or stopped • Get a list of services that are dependent on the service • Get the name and display name of the service • Get the parent of the service (as a ManagedComputer object) • Get the path of the binary file that implements the service • Get the process ID that uniquely identifies the service • Get the account under which the service is running • Get the state of the service (e.g., stopped, paused, running) • Get the method by which the service is started (as a ServiceStartMode enumeration value) • Get startup parameters for the service • Change the password for the account under which the service is running • Stop, pause, start, and resume the service • Refresh the service • Set the account under which the service runs The collection of Service objects is accessed though the Services property.

The SMO classes for WMI are described in Table 13-3.

Table 13-3. SMO classes used with the WMI Provider for Configuration Management

Class	Description
ClientProtocol	Represents a client network protocol that allows the client to communicate with a SQL Server instance over a network.
ClientProtocolCollection	Represents a collection of client protocols as ClientProtocol objects. The ClientProtocols property of the ManagedComputer class returns the client protocols defined on the WMI installation.

Class	Description
ClientProtocolProperty	Represents an attribute of a WMI client network protocol.
ClientProtocolPropertyCollection	Represents a collection of client protocol properties as ClientProtocolProperty objects. The ProtocolProperties property of the ClientProtocol class returns the attributes of the client protocol.
IPAddressProperty	Represents an attribute of an IP address.
IPAddressPropertyCollection	Represents a collection of IP address properties as IPAddressProperty objects. The IPAddressProperties property of the ServerIPAddress class returns the attributes of the IP address.
ManagedComputer	Represents a WMI installation on a SQL Server instance.
NetLibInfo	Represents information about a network library file. The NetLibInfo property of the ClientProtocol class returns the NetLibInfo object for the protocol.
ServerAlias	Represents an alias for a server connection.
ServerAliasCollection	Represents a collection of server aliases as ServerAlias objects. The ServerAliases property of the ManagedComputer class returns the server aliases defined on the WMI installation.
ServerInstance	Represents a SQL Server instance.
ServerInstanceCollection	Represents a collection of SQL Server instances as ServerInstance objects. The ServerInstances property of the ManagedComputer class returns the server instances defined on the WMI installation.
ServerIPAddress	Represents an IP address of a server protocol defined on the WMI installation.
ServerIPAddressCollection	Represents a collection of IP addresses as ServerIPAddress objects. The IPAddresses property of the ServerProtocol class returns the IP addresses defined on the WMI installation.
ServerProtocol	Represents a server network protocol that allows the server to communicate with SQL Server clients over a network.
ServerProtocolCollection	Represents a collection of server protocols as ServerProtocol objects. The ServerProtocols property of the ManagedComputer class returns the server protocols defined on the WMI installation.
ServerProtocolProperty	Represents an attribute of a WMI server network protocol.
ServerProtocolPropertyCollection	Represents a collection of server protocol properties as ServerProtocolProperty objects. The ProtocolProperties property of the ServerProtocol class returns the attributes of the server protocol.
Service	Represents an instance of a SQL Server service.
ServiceCollection	Represents a collection of SQL Server services as Service objects. The Services property of the ManagedComputer class returns the services defined on the WMI installation.
WmiConnectionInfo	Represents connection information used by a WMI installation. The ConnectionSettings property of the ManagedComputer class returns the WmiConnectionInfo object for the WMI installation.

Creating a Server Alias

This example demonstrates how to create new SMO WMI objects. The example creates a new server alias on the local SQL Server instance. It does so by instantiating a new ServerAlias object, associating it with the ManagedComputer object that represents WMI, and then invoking the Create( ) method of ServerAlias.

```
using System;
using System.Data;

using Microsoft.SqlServer.Management.Common;
using Microsoft.SqlServer.Management.Smo;
using Microsoft.SqlServer.Management.Smo.Wmi;

class Program
{
    static void Main(string[] args)
    {
        ManagedComputer mc = new ManagedComputer( );

        ServerAlias sa = new ServerAlias( );
        sa.ConnectionString = "1433";
        sa.Name = "PSS2005 Alias";
        sa.Parent = mc;
        sa.ProtocolName = "tcp";
        sa.ServerName = "localhost";
        sa.Create( );

        Console.WriteLine(Environment.NewLine + "Press any key to continue.");
        Console.ReadKey( );
    }
}
```

Figure 13-3 shows the new alias using the SQL Server Configuration Manager tool (Start → Microsoft SQL Server 2005 → Configuration Tools → SQL Server Configuration Manager).

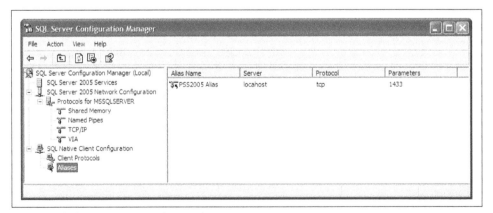

Figure 13-3. Creating a server alias results

Starting and Stopping a Service

This example shows how to stop and start a service by stopping and restarting SQL Server Reporting Services:

```
using System;
using System.Data;

using Microsoft.SqlServer.Management.Common;
using Microsoft.SqlServer.Management.Smo;
using Microsoft.SqlServer.Management.Smo.Wmi;
using System.Threading;

class Program
{
    static void Main(string[] args)
    {
        ManagedComputer mc = new ManagedComputer();

        Service s = mc.Services["ReportServer"];
        Console.WriteLine("ReportServer status: " + s.ServiceState);

        s.Stop();
        Thread.Sleep(10000);
        s.Refresh();
        Console.WriteLine("ReportServer status: " + s.ServiceState);
        s.Start();
        Thread.Sleep(10000);
        s.Refresh();
        Console.WriteLine("ReportServer status: " + s.ServiceState);

        Console.WriteLine(Environment.NewLine + "Press any key to continue.");
        Console.ReadKey();
    }
}
```

Results are shown in Figure 13-4.

Figure 13-4. Results from stopping and starting service example

The Service class has methods to control the state of a service—Start(), Pause(), Resume(), and Stop(). The AcceptsPause and AcceptsStop properties should be checked before calling Pause() or Stop() to ensure that the service can be paused or stopped.

The example uses the static Sleep( ) method of the Thread class to pause for 10 seconds to allow the service state change operations to complete. The Refresh( ) method of the Service class refreshes the SQL Server service to ensure the status is current.

CHAPTER 14

SQL Server Reporting Services (SSRS)

SQL Server 2005 Reporting Services (SSRS) is a middle-tier server that provides a reporting environment running on top of Internet Information Services (IIS). You can build reports from any data source that has a .NET Framework–managed data provider, an OLE DB provider, or an ODBC provider. This lets you build reports based on relational, multidimensional, and XML data sources from a wide range of database servers. You can access a report by using a URL, the report viewer control in either a web or Windows application, or Report Server web services.

SSRS supports tabular, matrix, chart, and free-form report layouts—the layouts, together with graphical elements, can be combined in a single report if required. You can include links to additional information or to related reports and drill-down functionality. Reports can contain both mandatory and optional parameters. Ad hoc reporting is supported through use of Report Builder—a ClickOnce Windows application that is accessed through the URL *http://<servername>/reportserver/reportbuilder/reportbuilder.application* from the report server or from Report Manager.

SSRS supports a variety of output formats, including HTML 3.2, HTML 4.0, MHTML, PDF, XML, Excel, CSV, and Image (TIFF). SSRS automatically provides a navigation toolbar for those formats that support toolbars. Additionally, you can add document maps and bookmarks to facilitate navigation in large reports.

Three tools are provided for designing reports. Report Designer is a report-authoring application hosted within Business Intelligence Development Studio. Report Designer lets you define, preview, and publish reports. Report Designer provides query builders, an expression editor, and wizards to help you work with images and to create simple reports. Ad hoc reporting is supported by two tools: Model Designer, which you use to define, edit, and publish report models—business-oriented abstractions of underlying data used to help build ad hoc reports—and Report Builder, which you use to create ad hoc reports based on published report models and manage them as you would any other reports.

SSRS includes configuration, monitoring, and management tools. Role-based security controls access to folders, reports, and resources. Report-delivery options include on-demand, through included SharePoint Web parts that let you view a report from a SharePoint site, automated by subscription, or automated based on data.

SSRS is an open and extensible reporting platform. You can use the API to develop, install, and manage SSRS component extensions to support custom-data, delivery, and rendering requirements. Report Definition Language (RDL) is used to describe the layout and content of a report. RDL is an XML-based grammar that you can extend to implement custom functionality. RDL can be generated manually or programmatically using Report Designer.

This chapter discusses how to programmatically access SSRS reports, and how to incorporate them into your applications. For more information about designing, defining, deploying, delivering, and securing reports, see Microsoft SQL Server 2005 Books Online.

Getting Started

The examples in this chapter use the AdventureWorks database and sample reports. Follow these instructions to install and deploy the sample reports:

1. From the Start menu, select Microsoft SQL Server 2005 → Documentation and Tutorials → Samples → Microsoft SQL Server 2005 Samples to install the sample reports.

2. Open SQL Server Business Intelligence Development Studio.

3. Open the solution *C:\Program Files\Microsoft SQL Server\90\Samples\Reporting Services\Report Samples\AdventureWorks Sample Reports\AdventureWorks Sample Reports.sln.*

4. Select the Production solution configuration (instead of the default, Debug) on the standard toolbar.

5. From the main menu, select Build → Deploy AdventureWorks Sample Reports to publish the reports.

6. Open a web browser and navigate to the reports virtual directory of your report server, *http://<servername>/reports.* If your report server is on the local machine, enter the URL *http://localhost/reports.* The AdventureWorks Sample Reports folder is listed in the Report Manager contents, as shown in Figure 14-1.

7. Click the AdventureWorks Sample Reports folder to view the reports it contains. Click one of the reports to render it.

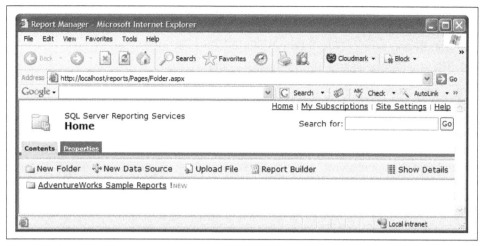

Figure 14-1. Report Manager

Integrating Reports into Applications

SSRS lets you integrate reports into applications in three different ways:

- Issue URL-based requests to navigate, access, and view reports. This is the most efficient way to render reports, because URL-based requests directly access the server. URL-based reports are also easy and efficient to implement. You can use URL-based requests in both web and Windows applications. In a Windows application, launch a web browser in a separate window or display the report in the web browser control on the form.

- Use the freely distributable report viewer control for Visual Studio 2005 to embed Reporting Services functionality into either a Windows or web application.

- Access the report server through Report Server web service using SOAP over HTTP as the communication interface between the client and the report server. In addition to providing the capabilities of URL-based requests, the web service exposes report management functionality that is not available through URL access. This includes content, subscription, and data-source management. You can use the SOAP API in both Windows and web applications.

A typical enterprise application uses more than one of these methods to meet reporting needs. The three methods are discussed in more detail in the following subsections.

URL Access

The URL request contains information identifying the report server to use, as well as parameters that are processed by the report server and that control the formatting and rendering of the report. The parameters, parameter prefixes, and combination of supplied parameters in the URL determine how the report server handles a specific request. Report server URLs follow W3C/IETF formatting guidelines:

- Parameters are separated by an ampersand (&).
- Name-value pairs are separated by an equals sign (=).
- The order of parameters is not significant.

For example, enter the URL *http://localhost/ReportServer?/AdventureWorks Sample Reports/Sales Order Detail&rs:Command=Render*. The report shown in Figure 14-2 is rendered in the browser.

Figure 14-2. Sales order detail report

The information in the URL specifies that you want to do the following:

- Use the local report server.
- Access a report in the report server virtual root named ReportServer.
- Access the report named AdventureWorks Sample Reports/Sales Order Detail.
- Render the report in the default rendering format for the browser.

The report server URL syntax is:

```
protocol://server/virtualroot?[/pathinfo]&[prefix:]param=
    value[&prefix:param=value]...n]
```

where:

protocol
> The URL protocol, usually http or https.

server
> The name of the computer running the report server.

virtualroot
> The name of the virtual root of the report server.

pathinfo
> The full pathname of the item being accessed from the report server database. The item can be one of four types, described in Table 14-1.

Table 14-1. URL item types

Item type	Description
Data Source	Displays the data source if the user is authenticated with Read Contents permission for the data source
Folder	Returns a generic folder-navigation page containing links to subfolders, reports, data sources, and resources in the folder
Report	Renders and returns the specified report
Resource	Returns the specified resource for a report

prefix
> Accesses a specific process running in the report server. If not specified, the parameter is processed as a report (rs) parameter. Table 14-2 describes the available prefixes.

Table 14-2. URL parameter prefixes

Parameter prefix	Description
rc	Specifies device-information settings, including those for reports targeted for the HTML Viewer. HTML device-information settings are described in Table 14-5.
	The device is specified using the report server rs:Format parameter. Valid values depend on the rendering extensions installed on the report server. Common devices include HTML 3.2, HTML 4.0, CSV, Excel, Image (TIFF), MHTML, PDF, and XML.
rs	Specifies configuration settings to the report server.
dsu	Specifies a username to access a data source.
dsp	Specifies a password to access a data source.

param

The name of the parameter. Parameters control how reports are processed and rendered.

value

The value of the parameter.

Report server parameters are prefixed with rs and are used to control report processing. Table 14-3 describes report server parameters.

Table 14-3. Report server parameters

Parameter	Description
Command	Specifies the type of request made to the report server. Table 14-4 describes possible values.
	If the rs:Command parameter is not specified, the report server evaluates the URL and selects the appropriate command value. Specifying the rs:Command value will improve performance.
	Only one rs:Command parameter can be specified in a URL.
Format	Specifies the format for rendering the report. The ListExtensions( ) method of the ReportingService class (in the ReportService web service) returns the rendering extensions installed on a report server instance. The following code snippet shows how:

	``
	ReportingService rs = new ReportingService( );
	rs.Credentials =
	    System.Net.CredentialCache.DefaultCredentials;
	Extension[] re =
	    rs.ListExtensions(ExtensionTypeEnum.Render);
	``

ParameterLanguage	Specifies the language for URL parameters that is independent of the browser language. The value is a culture value, such as en-US. The default is the browser language.
Snapshot	Renders the report based on a report-history snapshot. The value of this parameter must be a valid snapshot ID in the ISO 8601 standard format YYYY-MM-DDTHH:MM:SS.

Table 14-4 describes the rs:Command parameter values.

Table 14-4. rs:Command parameter values

Value	Description
GetDataSourceContents	Displays the value of a specified data source as XML. This parameter value corresponds to calling the GetDataSourceContents( ) web-service method.
GetResourceContents	Renders a resource and displays it as HTML. This parameter value corresponds to calling the GetResourceContents( ) web-service method.
ListChildren	Displays children for the item passed in the URL. This parameter value corresponds to calling the ListChildren( ) web-service method.
Render	Renders the specified report. This parameter value corresponds to calling the Render( ) web-service method.

For example, entering this URL in your browser will display all child items of the AdventureWorks Sample Reports folder: *http://localhost/reportserver?/AdventureWorks SampleReports&rs:Command=ListChildren*.

HTML device-information settings control how the report is rendered in HTML format. HTML device-information settings, and other device-information settings, are prefixed with rc. Table 14-5 describes HTML device-information settings. See Microsoft SQL Server 2005 Books Online for details about settings for other devices.

Table 14-5. HTML device-information settings

Parameter	Description
BookmarkID	The bookmark ID to jump to in the report.
DocMap	Specifies whether the report document map is visible. The value true displays the document map and the value false hides it. The default value is true.
DocMapID	The document map ID to scroll to in the report.
EndFind	The last page in the report to search. The default value is the current page. Use this parameter together with the StartFind parameter.
FallbackPage	The number of the page to display if a search or document map selection fails. The default is the current page.
FindString	The text to search for in the report. The default value is an empty string.
GetImage	The icon for the HTML Viewer user interface.
HTMLFragment	Specifies whether an HTML fragment is created instead of a full HTML document. The HTML fragment omits the <HTML> and <BODY> HTML tags. The default value is false.
Icon	The icon for the specified rendering extension.
JavaScript	Specifies whether JavaScript is supported in the rendered report.
LinkTarget	The target for hyperlinks in the report. This value can be a specific window or frame, a new window by setting the parameter value to _blank, or the values _self, _parent, and _top.
Parameters	Specifies whether the parameters area of the toolbar is visible. The value true displays the parameters area and the value false hides it. The default value is true.
ReplacementRoot	The path used for prefixing the value of the href attribute of A elements in the HTML report returned by the server. By default, the server provides this value.
Section	The page in the report to display. The default value is 1. The last page is displayed if the parameter value is greater than the number of pages in the report.
StartFind	The first page in the report to search. The default value is the current page. Use this parameter together with the EndFind parameter.
StreamRoot	The path used for prefixing the value of the src attribute of the IMG element in the HTML report returned by the server. By default, the server provides this value.
StyleSheet	The stylesheet to apply to the HTML Viewer.
StyleStream	Specifies whether styles and scripts are created as a separate stream instead of in the document. The value true creates a separate stream and the value of false puts styles and scripts in the document. The default value is false.
Toolbar	Specifies whether the toolbar is visible. The value true displays the toolbar for rendering formats that support a toolbar. The value false hides the toolbar. The default value is true.
Type	The short name of the browser as defined in browscap.ini.
Zoom	The report zoom value. The value can be a percent integer or the string constant Page Width or Whole Page. The default value is the percent integer 100.

You can use a report server parameter to control the rendering format for the report. The URL *http://localhost/reportserver?/AdventureWorks Sample Reports/Company Sales&rs:Command=Render&rs:Format=IMAGE* renders the report as a TIFF image. The URL *http://localhost/reportserver?/AdventureWorks Sample Reports/Company Sales&rs:Command=Render&rs:Format=XML* renders the report as an XML file.

HTML device-information settings control how the report is displayed in a browser. The URL *http://localhost/reportserver?/AdventureWorks Sample Reports/Company Sales&rs:Command=Render&rc:Toolbar=false&rc:Zoom=200* renders the report at twice the default size without a toolbar.

Report parameters are passed in the URL as name-value pairs separated by an equals sign (=). Pass a null parameter using the syntax `parameterName:isNull=true`. Note that report parameters are not prefixed. For example, the report `Employee Sales Summary` takes three parameters: `ReportMonth` (integer), `ReportYear` (integer), and `EmpID` (string). When you run the report normally, the RDL populates the employee drop-down list using the `DataSet` named `SalesEmps`. This corresponds to the following query:

```
SELECT E.EmployeeID, C.FirstName + N' ' + C.LastName AS Employee
FROM HumanResources.Employee E
INNER JOIN Sales.SalesPerson SP ON E.EmployeeID = SP.SalesPersonID
INNER JOIN Person.Contact C ON E.ContactID = C.ContactID
ORDER BY C.LastName, C.FirstName
```

We need to run this query to determine the employee ID for each employee. Jillian Carson has employee ID 277. The URL:

http://localhost/reportserver?/AdventureWorks Sample Reports/Employee SalesSummary&rsCommand=Render&EmpID=277&ReportMonth=7& ReportYear=2002

sets the report parameters to return the sales summary report for Jillian Carson for July 2002.

The preceding examples show how to request a report using a URL. This is equivalent to an HTTP GET method. You can also request a report using an HTTP POST method, which transfers the parameter name/value pairs in the HTTP header instead of the URL. Using an HTTP POST method overcomes the maximum allowable URL length limit in cases where a parameter list is long, and is also more secure because the user cannot directly modify the parameter names and values. The following HTML returns the same sales summary report for Jillian Carson for July 2002 as in the preceding example but uses an HTTP POST method:

```
<form id="postRenderForm"
  action="http://localhost/reportserver?/AdventureWorks Sample Reports/
  Employee Sales Summary" method="post" target="_self">
    <input type="hidden" name="rs:Command" value="Render"/>
    <input type="hidden" name="EmpID" value="277"/>
```

```
<input type="hidden" name="ReportMonth" value="7"/>
<input type="hidden" name="ReportYear" value="2002"/>
<input type="submit" value="Render"/>
</form>
```

Report Viewer Control

The report viewer control is a freely distributable control that ships with Visual Studio 2005. The control is called ReportViewer and is in the Data section of the Toolbox in the Visual Studio 2005 IDE.

Use the control by dragging it onto either a Windows form or a web form surface. The ReportViewer control menu prompts you to either "Choose Report" from a dropdown list or "Design a new report." Click "Design a new report" to bring up Report Designer. Select <Server Report>, and you are prompted for the Report Server Url and the Report Path. Fill in these values and run the application—the report appears in the control.

For example, set the value of Report Server Url to *http://localhost/reportserver* and the Report Path to /AdventureWorks Sample Reports/Company Sales. Run the application—if you created a Windows Forms application, the resulting output will look like Figure 14-3.

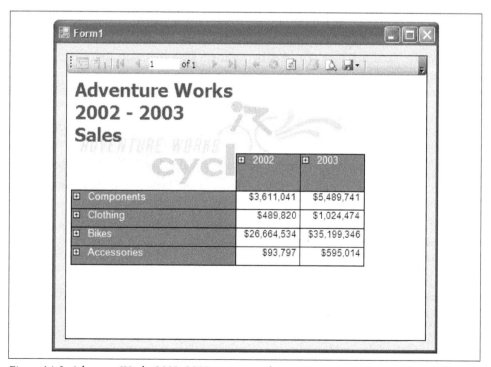

Figure 14-3. AdventureWorks 2002–2003 company sales report

The report server and report path can be specified at runtime through the properties of the `ServerReport` object exposed by the `ServerReport` property of the control, as shown in the following code snippet:

```
reportViewer1.ServerReport.ReportServerUrl =
    new Uri(@"http://localhost/reportserver");
reportViewer1.ServerReport.ReportPath =
    @"/AdventureWorks Sample Reports/Company Sales";
```

Report Server Web Service

SSRS provides full access to report server functionality through Report Server web services. The web service provides methods and properties for both report execution—controlling the processing and rendering of reports—and report management.

You can develop Reporting Services applications that use Report Server web services with the .NET Framework, by using the Reporting Services script environment and the rs utility (rs.exe), or by using any development tools capable of invoking SOAP methods. This section discusses only the first approach. For information on the other two approaches, see Microsoft SQL Server 2005 Books Online.

These are the steps you follow to create an application that uses Report Server web services (you'll build a real example shortly):

1. Create a new Windows application in Visual Studio 2005.

2. Using Solution Explorer, add a web reference to the `ReportService` web service from the local machine. Do this by right-clicking the Web References node in Solution Explorer and selecting Add Web Reference from the context menu. This displays the Add Web Reference dialog box, Start Browsing for Web Services page, shown in Figure 14-4.

3. Click the "Web services on the local machine" link to display the dialog box shown in Figure 14-5.

4. Click the `ReportService` service to display the dialog box shown in Figure 14-6.

   Specify `ReportService` in the Web reference name listbox and click the Add Reference button.

5. Add a using directive to the top of the class for the `ReportService` web service. For example, if you named the application `MyApp`, the using directive would be as follows:

   ```
   using MyApp.ReportService;
   ```

6. Create an instance of the proxy class, as shown in the following snippet:

   ```
   ReportingService rs = new ReportingService();
   ```

7. Pass authentication credentials to the web service. The following code passes default Windows credentials:

   ```
   rs.Credentials = System.Net.CredentialCache.DefaultCredentials;
   ```

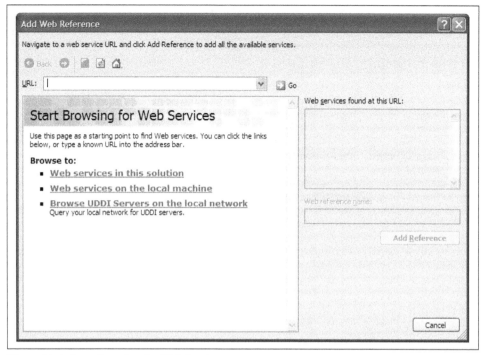

Figure 14-4. Start Browsing for Web Services page

8. Call report server web service methods from your application. Once the proxy is instantiated and the caller is authenticated, this is done in the same way as with any .NET Framework method.

As an example, let's build a Windows Forms application that presents a drop-down list of the reports available in the *AdventureWorks Sample Reports* folder, as shown in Figure 14-7.

When you select a report from the list and click the Render button, the report is saved to a web page (HTML) file. Note that if you select a report that requires parameters, such as Employee Sales Summary, a ReportParameterValueNotSetException is raised. The ParameterValue array argument is always passed as null to keep this example simple.

To build the example, create a Windows application named ReportServerWebService. Add a listbox to the form and name it reportListBox. Add a button to the form and name it renderButton. Add a web reference to the ReportService web service and give it the name ReportService. Copy the following code into the form:

```
using System;
using System.Collections.Generic;
using System.ComponentModel;
using System.Data;
using System.Drawing;
```

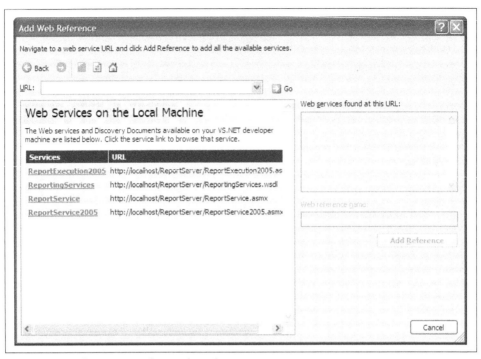

Figure 14-5. Web Services on the Local Machine page

```csharp
using System.Text;
using System.Windows.Forms;
using System.IO;

using ReportServerWebService.ReportService;

namespace ReportServerWebService
{
    public partial class MainForm : Form
    {
        private string reportPath = @"/AdventureWorks Sample Reports";

        public MainForm()
        {
            InitializeComponent();
        }

        private void MainForm_Load(object sender, EventArgs e)
        {
            ReportingService rs = new ReportingService();
            rs.Credentials = System.Net.CredentialCache.DefaultCredentials;

            CatalogItem[] cis = rs.ListChildren(reportPath, false);
            foreach (CatalogItem ci in cis)
            {
```

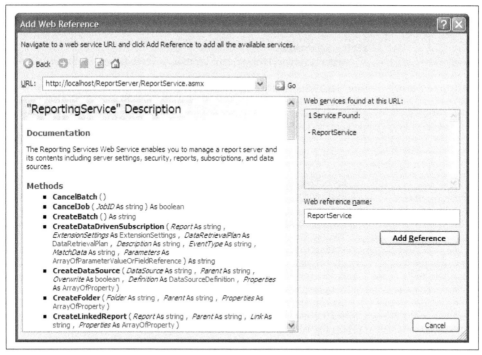

Figure 14-6. "ReportingService" Description page

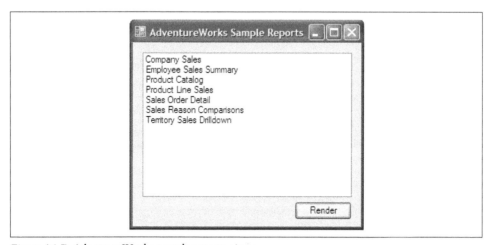

Figure 14-7. AdventureWorks sample reports viewer

```
            if(ci.Type == ItemTypeEnum.Report)
                reportListBox.Items.Add(ci.Name);
        }
    }

    private void renderButton_Click(object sender, EventArgs e)
```

```
        {
            if (reportListBox.SelectedIndex >= 0)
            {
                string reportName =
                    reportListBox.Items[reportListBox.SelectedIndex].ToString( );

                SaveFileDialog sfd = new SaveFileDialog( );
                sfd.Filter = "Web page format (*.html)|*.html";
                sfd.FileName = reportName;
                if (sfd.ShowDialog( ) == DialogResult.OK)
                {
                    string renderFileName = sfd.FileName;

                    ReportingService rs = new ReportingService( );
                    rs.Credentials = System.Net.CredentialCache.DefaultCredentials;

                    string reportFullName = reportPath + "/" + reportName;
                    string format = "HTML4.0";
                    string historyID = null;
                    string deviceInfo = null;
                    ParameterValue[] pv = null;
                    DataSourceCredentials[] dsc = null;
                    string showHideToggle = null;
                    string encoding;
                    string mimeType;
                    ParameterValue[] parameterUsed = null;
                    Warning[] warning = null;
                    string[] streamIds = null;
                    byte[] report;

                    try
                    {
                        report = rs.Render(reportFullName, format, historyID,
                            deviceInfo, pv, dsc, showHideToggle, out encoding,
                            out mimeType, out parameterUsed, out warning,
                            out streamIds);

                        using (FileStream fs = File.OpenWrite(renderFileName))
                            fs.Write(report, 0, report.Length);
                    }
                    catch (Exception ex)
                    {
                        MessageBox.Show(ex.Message, "Error",
                            MessageBoxButtons.OK, MessageBoxIcon.Error);
                    }
                }
            }
        }
    }
}
```

Running the example launches the application window with a listbox containing the available reports. Select the Company Sales report and click the Render button. The report is saved as *Company Sales.html* in the location you specify. An excerpt from this file follows:

```
<!DOCTYPE HTML PUBLIC "-//W3C//DTD HTML 4.01 Transitional//EN">
<html>
<head>
<title>
Company Sales
</title>
<META http-equiv="Content-Type" content="text/html; charset=utf-8">
<META http-equiv="Content-Style-Type" content="text/css">
<META http-equiv="Content-Script-Type" content="text/javascript">

...

<IMG BORDER="0" SRC="http://localhost/ReportServer?%2f
AdventureWorks+Sample+Reports%2fCompany+Sales&amp;
rs:Command=Get&amp;rc:GetImage=9.00.1399.00TogglePlus.gif"/></a>
 Bikes</DIV></TD>
<TD class="a17"><DIV class="a16">$26,664,534</DIV></TD>
<TD class="a17"><DIV class="a16">$35,199,346</DIV></TD></TR>
<TR VALIGN="top"><TD WIDTH="0" style="HEIGHT:6.35mm"></TD>
<TD class="a8" COLSPAN="2"><DIV class="a10">
<a href="http://localhost/ReportServer?%2f
AdventureWorks+Sample+Reports%2fCompany+Sales&amp;
rc%3aZoom=200&amp;rc%3aSection=0&amp;rs%3aFormat=HTML4.0&amp;
rs%3aShowHideToggle=368&amp;rs%3aSnapshot%3aisnull=True">
<IMG BORDER="0" SRC="http://localhost/ReportServer?%2f
AdventureWorks+Sample+Reports%2fCompany+Sales&amp;rs:Command=Get&amp;
rc:GetImage=9.00.1399.00TogglePlus.gif"/></a>
 Accessories</DIV></TD>
<TD class="a17"><DIV class="a16">$93,797</DIV></TD>
<TD class="a17"><DIV class="a16">$595,014</DIV></TD></TR></TABLE></TD></TR>
<TR><TD style="HEIGHT:1.59mm"></TD></TR></TABLE></DIV></TD>
<TD WIDTH="100%" HEIGHT="0"></TD></TR><TR>
<TD WIDTH="0" HEIGHT="100%"></TD></TR></TABLE></DIV>
</body>
</html>
```

Figure 14-8 shows the report when opened in Internet Explorer.

The Render( ) method takes arguments that identify the report and specify how to render the results to a byte stream that can be saved to a file or displayed.

Device-information settings are passed to the Render( ) method as a <DeviceInfo> XML element. HTML device-information settings are described in Table 14-5, earlier in the chapter. For example, to zoom the report 200%, set the *deviceInfo* argument of the Render( ) method to the following:

```
<DeviceInfo>
    <Zoom>200</Zoom>
</DeviceInfo>
```

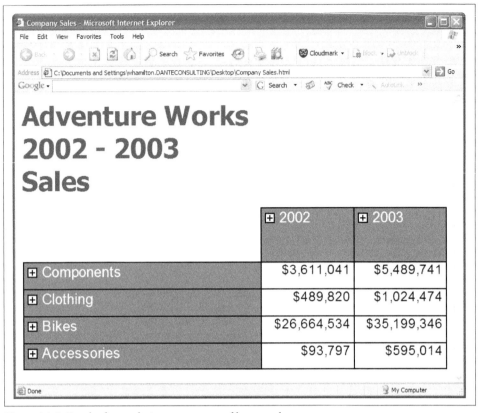

Figure 14-8. Results for rendering a report to a file example

Reporting Services Extensions

SQL Server Reporting Services is designed to be extensible. The Microsoft. ReportingServices.DataProcessing namespace contains interfaces that let you extend Reporting Services to integrate custom data into your reports. The Microsoft. ReportingServices.Interfaces namespace contains interfaces that let you extend Reporting Services delivery mechanisms and build custom security extensions for Reporting Services. The Microsoft.Reporting.ReportRendering namespace contains classes and interfaces that let you extend the report-rendering capabilities of Reporting Services. For more information about developing Reporting Services extensions, see Microsoft SQL Server 2005 Books Online.

CHAPTER 15

SQL Server Integration Services (SSIS)

SQL Server Integration Services (SSIS) is a platform for building data integration and workflow solutions and extract, transform, and load (ETL) solutions for data warehousing. Common integration scenarios include merging data from heterogeneous data sources, populating data warehouses and data marts, standardizing data, and performing administrative functions such as backing up, copying, and loading data.

SQL Server 2005 provides graphical tools for constructing data integration solutions. You can also construct, maintain, manage, and run data integration programmatically using either native or managed code. This chapter provides an overview of SSIS and demonstrates SSIS managed-code programming.

Architecture

SSIS consists of four key parts:

Integration Services service
> Manages storage of packages and monitors running Integration Services packages.

Integration Services object model
> Comprises native and managed APIs for accessing Integration Services tools, command-line utilities, and custom applications.

Integration Services runtime
> Saves the layout of packages, runs packages, and supports logging, breakpoints, configuration, connections, and transactions. SSIS runtime executables are the packages, containers, tasks, and event handlers that perform workflow functionality.

Data flows
> Move data from source to destination with optional transformation. There are three types of data-flow components—source, transformation, and destination (load).

SSIS Objects

The SSIS object model is built on eight primary objects:

Package
> A collection of connections, control-flow elements, data-flow elements, event handlers, variables, and configurations either created using SSIS graphical-design tools or built programmatically.

Control flow
> Tasks, containers, and constraints that connect executables into an ordered flow.

Data flow
> Sources and destinations that extract and load the data, data transformations, and paths linking sources, transformations, and destinations. The data flow is created within a data-flow task—an executable that creates, orders, and runs the data flow.

Connection manager
> Defines the connection string for accessing data that tasks, transformations, and event handlers in the package use.

Event handler
> A workflow that runs in response to events raised by a package, task, or container.

Configuration
> A set of name-value pairs that defines the properties of the package and its tasks, containers, variables, connections, and event handlers when the package runs. Separating configuration from the package lets you change the properties of the package without changing the package. These objects also facilitate deploying packages from development servers to production servers and moving packages between servers/environments.

Log provider
> Defines the destination type and format used to log runtime information for packages, containers, and tasks.

System and user-defined variables
> Stores values that SSIS packages, tasks, and event handlers use at runtime and exposes information about packages at runtime.

Figure 15-1 shows the relationship between the SSIS objects.

The following subsections describe each of these objects in more detail.

Control-Flow Elements

SSIS provides three different types of control-flow elements that can be nested:

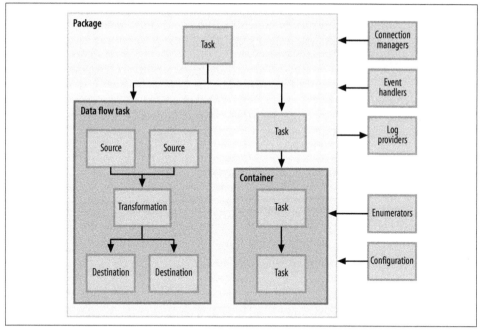

Figure 15-1. SSIS object relationship

Containers

> Provide structures for grouping tasks and implementing repeating control flow in packages. SSIS provides three types of containers:

Foreach Loop container

> Repeats control flow for each element in a collection.

For Loop container

> Repeats control flow while a test expression evaluates as true.

Sequence container

> Defines a subset of the control flow in a package. This lets you manage and execute a group of executables (tasks and containers) as a single unit.

Tasks

> Provide functionality within the package. SSIS provides seven types of tasks:

Workflow tasks

> Communicate with other processes to run packages or programs, send and receive messages between packages, send email messages, read Windows Management Instrumentation (WMI) data, and monitor WMI events.

Data-flow tasks

> Define and run data flows that extract, transform, and load data.

Data-preparation tasks
> Copy files and directories, download files and data, save data returned by web methods, and manipulate XML documents.

SQL Server tasks
> Access, copy, create, modify, and delete SQL Server data and objects.

Analysis Services tasks
> Create, modify, delete, and process Analysis Services objects. Analysis Services is discussed in Chapter 20.

Scripting tasks
> Extend package functionality with custom scripts.

Maintenance tasks
> Perform numerous administrative functions—back up the database, check database integrity, execute SQL Service Agent jobs, execute T-SQL statements, clean up history, notify operators, rebuild and reorganize indexes, shrink databases, and update statistics.

Precedent constraints
> Connect containers and tasks within packages in an ordered flow. You can control the sequence of execution and specify conditions that determine whether containers and tasks run.

Data-Flow Components

Data-flow components are connected within a data-flow task using integration service paths. These paths map the outputs of one data-flow component to the inputs of the next data-flow component in the data-flow task. SSIS provides three types of data-flow components:

Source
> Retrieve data from an external data source available to components in the data flow. A source has one or more outputs that make source columns available to the next component in the data flow, and can have one or more error outputs. SSIS provides the sources described in Table 15-1. You can develop custom sources if these do not meet your needs.

Table 15-1. SSIS data-flow sources

Source	Description
DataReader	Data from a .NET Framework data provider
Excel	Data from an Excel file
Flat File	Data from a flat file
OLE DB	Data from an OLE DB provider
Raw File	Raw data from a file

Table 15-1. SSIS data-flow sources (continued)

Source	Description
Script Component	Data from the results of executing a script
XML	Data from an XML file

Transformation

Performs tasks such as updating, aggregating, cleaning, distributing, and merging data. A transformation can have single or multiple inputs and outputs depending on the task it performs, and can also have one or more error outputs. SSIS provides business intelligence, row, rowset, split and join transformations, as well as other miscellaneous transformations. You can develop custom transformations if these do not meet your needs. See Microsoft SQL Server 2005 Books Online for more information about the built-in transformations.

Destination

Loads data from a data flow into external data sources or creates an in-memory DataSet. Destinations have one or more inputs and optionally one or more error outputs. SSIS provides the destinations described in Table 15-2. You can develop custom destinations if these do not meet your needs.

Table 15-2. SSIS data-flow destinations

Destination	Description
Data Mining Model Training	Trains a data-mining model
DataReader	Exposes data through an ADO.NET DataReader interface
Dimension Processing	Loads and processes an Analysis Services dimension
Excel	Loads an Excel file
Flat File	Loads a flat file
OLE DB	Loads an OLE DB data destination
Partition Processing	Loads and processes an Analysis Services partition
Raw File	Loads a raw file
Recordset	Exposes data through an ADO.NET Recordset
Script Component	Loads data using a script
SQL Server Mobile	Loads a SQL Server Mobile database
SQL Server Destination	Bulk loads data to a SQL Server 2005 table or view

Connection Managers

A connection manager describes the connection to a data source for accessing data that tasks, transformations, and event handlers in the package use. SSIS creates the connections when a package runs. You can define multiple connections for a package. SSIS provides the connection manager types described in Table 15-3.

Table 15-3. SSIS connection manager types

Type	Description
ADO	Connects to a data source using ADO
ADO.NET	Connects to a data source using the ADO.NET data provider
EXCEL	Connects to an Excel file
FILE	Connects to a single file or folder
FLATFILE	Connects to data in a single flat file
FTP	Connects to an FTP server
HTTP	Connects to a web service or web site
MSMQ	Connects to a Microsoft Message Queue (MSMQ) queue
MSOLAP90	Connects to an instance of Analysis Services or to an Analysis Services project
MULTIFILE	Connects to multiple files and folders
MULTIFLATFILE	Connects to data in multiple flat files
ODBC	Connects to a data source using ODBC
OLEDB	Connects to a data source using OLE DB
SMOServer	Connects to SQL Server Management Objects (SMO)
SMTP	Connects to an SMTP server
SQLMOBILE	Connects to a SQL Server Mobile database
WMI	Connects to a WMI server

Events

SSIS executables—packages, Foreach Loop containers, For Loop containers, Sequence containers, and task host containers—raise events at runtime. You can write custom event handlers to extend package functionality and simplify administration. If an event does not have a handler, the event bubbles up to the next container in the package hierarchy until it is finally raised to the package. Table 15-4 describes the SSIS runtime events.

Table 15-4. SSIS runtime events

Event	Description
OnError	Raised by an executable when an error occurs
OnExecStatusChanged	Raised by an executable when its execution status changes
OnInformation	Raised by an executable during validation and execution to report information
OnPostExecute	Raised by an executable immediately after it finishes running
OnPostValidate	Raised by an executable immediately after it finishes validating
OnPreExecute	Raised by an executable immediately before it starts running
OnPreValidate	Raised by an executable immediately before it starts validating
OnProgress	Raised by an executable when progress has been made during execution

Table 15-4. SSIS runtime events (continued)

Event	Description
OnQueryCancel	Raised by an executable to determine whether it should stop running
OnTaskFailed	Raised by a task when it fails
OnVariableValueChanged	Raised by an executable when the value of a variable changes
OnWarning	Raised by an executable when a warning occurs

Package Configurations

SSIS provides package configurations for updating property values at runtime. Each package configuration is a property-value pair. Configurations simplify deploying packages to multiple servers, simplify moving packages between servers, and add flexibility to packages by allowing configuration properties to be easily changed. SSIS supports the package-configuration types described in Table 15-5.

Table 15-5. SSIS package-configuration types

Type	Description
XML configuration file	Configuration information is stored in an XML file, which can contain multiple configurations.
Environment variable	Configuration information is stored in an environment variable.
Registry entry	Configuration information is stored in the registry.
Parent package variable	Configuration information is stored in a variable in the package.
SQL Server table	Configuration information is stored in a SQL Server table, which can contain multiple configurations.

Log Providers

SSIS includes log providers that implement logging in packages, containers, and tasks to help you audit and troubleshoot. SSIS offers five log providers, as described in Table 15-6. You can develop custom log providers if these do not meet your needs.

Table 15-6. Log providers

Provider	ProgID	Description
Text file	DTS.LogProviderTextFile.1	Writes log entries to a text file in comma-separated value (CSV) format
SQL Server Profiler	DTS.LogProviderSQLProfiler.1	Writes log entries to SQL Server traces that can be viewed using SQL Server Profiler
SQL Server	DTS.LogProviderSQLServer.1	Writes log entries to the sysdtslog90 table in a SQL Server 2005 database
Windows Event log	DTS.LogProviderEventLog.1	Writes log entries to the Application log in the Windows Event log on the local computer
XML file	DTS.LogProviderXMLFile.1	Writes log entries to an XML file

Variables

Variables store values that SSIS packages, tasks, and event handlers use at runtime. SSIS supports two types of variables: user-defined variables and system variables. User-defined variables are defined by package developers, and system variables are defined by SSIS. You can create user-defined variables for all SSIS container types—packages, Foreach Loop containers, For Loop containers, Sequence containers, tasks, and event handlers. Variables are scoped within the scope of a container and are accessible to the children of the container. A variable can raise an event when its value changes.

Tools

SQL Server 2005 provides the following tools for designing and managing Integration Services:

Business Intelligence Development Studio
    Helps to develop, test, debug, and deploy integration packages.

SQL Server 2005 Management Studio
    Manages packages in production.

SSIS Designer
    A graphical tool in Business Intelligence Development Studio that is used to construct control flows and data flows in packages, add event handlers to the packages and package objects, view package contents, and view execution progress of packages.

Integration Services Wizards
    Wizards for copying data between data sources, constructing simple packages, creating package configurations, deploying Integration Services projects, and migrating SQL Server 2000 DTS packages.

Command-line utilities
    Tools to manage packages, specify package runtime configuration, and run packages from the command line, as described in Table 15-7.

Table 15-7. SSIS command-line utilities

Command-line utility	Description
dtexecui	Specifies runtime configuration and runs an existing package on the local computer
dtexec	Configures and runs an existing package stored in a SQL Server database, the SSIS package store, and the filesystem
dtutil	Manages, copies, deletes, moves, and verifies the existence of existing packages stored in a SQL Server database, the SSIS package store, and the filesystem

Programming SSIS

SSIS lets you programmatically create, load, modify, and execute packages, as well as other objects, including connection managers, log providers, and enumerators. In this section, you'll see how to program SSIS in managed code.

There are two engines that you program against when developing SSIS solutions:

Runtime engine
    Manages packages and the execution infrastructure

Data-flow engine
    Supports the data-flow task used to extract, transform, and load data

The following two sections contain examples that show how to programmatically perform common tasks when programming against these two engines.

All examples in this section are built using Visual Studio 2005. Each example needs a reference to the `Microsoft.SqlServer.ManagedDTS` assembly. Additional assembly references are indicated for examples in which they are required.

Control-Flow Programming

Control-flow programming uses the SSIS object model to build packages, add stock and custom tasks, connect tasks, and run packages. Control-flow programming also lets you build objects such as connection managers, variables, log providers, enumerators, event handlers, and configuration files. The following subsections show how.

Creating a package

This example creates an empty package—the top-level container for all other SSIS objects:

```
using System;

using Microsoft.SqlServer.Dts.Runtime;

class Program
{
    static void Main(string[] args)
    {
        // create an empty package
        Package p = new Package();

        Console.WriteLine("Press any key to continue.");
        Console.ReadKey();
    }
}
```

The Package class represents the package container and exposes collections of other containers, connections, tasks, log providers, variables, configurations, precedence constraints, and event handlers.

Saving a package

This example creates an empty package and saves it to disk using the Application class:

```
using System;

using Microsoft.SqlServer.Dts.Runtime;

class Program
{
    static void Main(string[] args)
    {
        // create an empty package
        Package p = new Package();

        // save the package to the File System folder
        Application a = new Application();
        a.SaveToDtsServer(p, null, @"File System\TestPackage", "localhost");

        Console.WriteLine("Press any key to continue.");
        Console.ReadKey();
    }
}
```

Results are shown in Figure 15-2.

Figure 15-2. Results for saving package example

After running this example, you can view the package in the Object Explorer window in SQL Server Management Studio. Select View → Registered Server Types → Integration Services from the main menu. In the Registered Servers window, right-click the SSIS server and select Connect → Object Explorer from the context menu.

In the Object Explorer window, expand the Stored Packages → File System node for the Integration Services instance, as shown in Figure 15-3.

Figure 15-3. Viewing packages using Object Explorer

By default, package (*.dtsx*) files in the File System node are saved in *C:\Program Files\ Microsoft SQL Server\90\DTS\Packages*. You can open the file using Business Intelligence Studio or you can reload the file programmatically, as described in the next section.

The Application class discovers, accesses, and manages Package objects and provides access to information about the system and available components through its properties.

Loading a package

This example loads the package named TestPackage (created in the preceding example) from disk:

```
using System;

using Microsoft.SqlServer.Dts.Runtime;

class Program
{
    static void Main(string[] args)
    {
        // load the package to the File System folder
        Application a = new Application();
        Package p = a.LoadFromDtsServer(@"File System\TestPackage",
            "localhost", null);

        Console.WriteLine("Package: " + p.CreationName + " " +
            p.Name + " loaded.");

        Console.WriteLine(Environment.NewLine + "Press any key to continue.");
        Console.ReadKey();
    }
}
```

Results follow in Figure 15-4.

Figure 15-4. Results for loading a package example

Adding a task to the package

This example creates a package and adds a `ForLoop` container and a `SendMail` task to it. A `SQLTask` task is added to the `ForLoop` container.

```
using System;

using Microsoft.SqlServer.Dts.Runtime;

class Program
{
    static void Main(string[] args)
    {
        // create an empty package
        Package p = new Package( );

        // add a foreach loop
        ForLoop fl = (ForLoop)p.Executables.Add("STOCK:ForLoop");
        // add a SQL task to the ForLoop
        fl.Executables.Add("STOCK:SQLTask");

        // add a send mail task
        p.Executables.Add("STOCK:SendMailTask");

        // enumerate the tasks in the package
        foreach (Executable e in p.Executables)
        {
            if (e.ToString( ) == "Microsoft.SqlServer.Dts.Runtime.TaskHost")
            {
                Console.WriteLine(((TaskHost)e).InnerObject.GetType().ToString( ));
            }
            else if (e.ToString( ) == "Microsoft.SqlServer.Dts.Runtime.ForLoop")
            {
                // enumerate the tasks in the ForLoop container
                Console.WriteLine(e.ToString( ));
                foreach (Executable e2 in ((ForLoop)e).Executables)
                    Console.WriteLine("  " +
                        ((TaskHost)e2).InnerObject.GetType().ToString( ));
            }
        }

        Console.WriteLine(Environment.NewLine + "Press any key to continue.");
```

```
            Console.ReadKey();
        }
    }
}
```

The output is shown in Figure 15-5.

Figure 15-5. Output for adding tasks example

The output from the example enumerates the tasks once after they have been created. Enumerating tasks is discussed in the section "Enumerating task properties," later in this chapter.

You can add tasks to Package, Sequence, ForLoop, ForEachLoop, and DtsEventHandler objects—these objects are all containers. Each container has an Executables collection containing Executable objects.

You add an object to a container by calling the Add( ) method of the container object. The Remove( ) method removes objects from the container. The Add( ) method takes a single string parameter that contains the CLSID, PROGID, or STOCK moniker, or a CreationName that identifies the task or container. Table 15-8 describes the SSIS tasks.

Table 15-8. SSIS tasks

STOCK name	Description
ActiveXScriptTask	Creates and uses ActiveX scripts created in SQL Server 2000.
	This feature is intended only for backward compatibility and will be removed in the next version of SQL Server.
BulkInsertTask	Runs bulk inserts.
DMQueryTask	Runs prediction queries based on data-mining models built in Analysis Services.
Exec80PackageTask	Runs packages created in SQL Server 2000 as part of a workflow.
ExecutePackageTask	Runs other SSIS packages as part of a workflow.
ExecuteProcessTask	Runs an application or batch file as part of a workflow.
FileSystemTask	Runs a command against the filesystem.
FtpTask	Uses FTP to download and upload files and manage directories.
MessageQueueTask	Sends or receives messages to and from an MSMQ queue.
PipelineTask	Moves data between source and destination with optional transformation.
ScriptTask	Runs custom code to perform functions not available using the built-in SSIS tasks.

Table 15-8. SSIS tasks (continued)

STOCK name	Description
SendMailTask	Sends an email message.
SQLTask	Executes T-SQL commands.
TransferDatabaseTask	Transfers databases from one SQL Server instance to another.
TransferErrorMessagesTask	Copies user-defined error messages from one SQL Server instance to another.
TransferJobsTask	Transfers SQL Server Agent jobs from one SQL Server instance to another.
TransferLoginsTask	Transfers logins from one SQL Server instance to another.
TransferSqlServerObjectsTask	Copies SQL Server objects from one SQL Server instance to another.
TransferStoredProceduresTask	Copies stored procedures from the master database of one SQL Server instance to another.
WebServiceTask	Runs a web method and stores the results in a specified location.
WmiDataReaderTask	Configures and runs a WMI query.
WmiEventWatcherTask	Runs a WMI query and waits for events associated with the query.
XMLTask	Retrieves, manipulates, and saves XML documents stored in files.

The container classes described in Table 15-9 have the same collections as the Package class, letting you nest tasks within the package to an arbitrary depth. You have already encountered the Executables collection; more of the collections will appear throughout the remainder of this chapter.

Table 15-9. SSIS containers

STOCK name	Description
ForEachLoop	Defines an iterative workflow using the for each iteration element.
ForLoop	Defines an iterative workflow using the for iteration element.
Sequence	Defines a control flow that is a subset of the workflow of the parent container.

Adding a connection manager

This example creates a package and adds a SQL Server ADO.NET connection manager to it:

```
using System;

using Microsoft.SqlServer.Dts.Runtime;

class Program
{
    static void Main(string[] args)
    {
        // create an empty package
        Package p = new Package();

        Console.WriteLine("Beginning number of connections: " +
```

```
            p.Connections.Count);

        // add a connection to AdventureWorks
        ConnectionManager cm;
        cm = p.Connections.Add("ADO.NET");
        Console.WriteLine("Connection added.");
        // configure connection
        cm.ConnectionString = "Data Source=localhost;" +
            "Integrated Security=SSPI;Initial Catalog=AdventureWorks";

        Console.WriteLine("Ending number of connections: " + p.Connections.Count);

        Console.WriteLine(Environment.NewLine + "Press any key to continue.");
        Console.ReadKey();
    }
}
```

Results are shown in Figure 15-6.

Figure 15-6. Results for adding connection manager example

The ConnectionManager class represents a connection to a data source. The connection type is specified as an argument to the constructor from the connection types described in Table 15-3. It provides a layer of abstraction so that you can interact with a variety of data sources in a consistent manner. The Connections property of the Package class exposes the collection of connection managers associated with the Package class. The ConnectionInfos property of the Application class returns a collection of information about connections installed on the computer as ConnectionInfo objects.

The runtime engine manages connections for the package as it runs so that you do not need to perform tasks such as opening and closing connections.

Running a package

This example creates a package with a SQLTask task and runs the package. You need to add a reference to the Microsoft.SqlServer.SQLTask assembly to build and execute this example.

```
using System;

using Microsoft.SqlServer.Dts.Runtime;
using Microsoft.SqlServer.Dts.Tasks.ExecuteSQLTask;
```

```
class Program
{
    static void Main(string[] args)
    {
        // create an empty package
        Package p = new Package();

        // add a connection manager
        ConnectionManager cm = p.Connections.Add("ADO.NET");
        cm.Name = "CM_ProgrammingSqlServer2005";
        cm.ConnectionString = "Data Source=localhost;" +
            "Integrated Security=SSPI;Initial Catalog=ProgrammingSqlServer2005";

        // add a SQL task to the package
        Executable e = p.Executables.Add("STOCK:SQLTask");
        TaskHost th = (TaskHost)e;
        ExecuteSQLTask est = (ExecuteSQLTask)th.InnerObject;
        est.Connection = cm.Name;
        est.SqlStatementSourceType = SqlStatementSourceType.DirectInput;
        est.SqlStatementSource = "CREATE TABLE TestTable " +
            "( ID int NOT NULL, Description nchar(100))";

        // run the package
        DTSExecResult r = p.Execute();

        // check the status and result of the package run
        Console.WriteLine("Status: " + p.ExecutionStatus.ToString());

        if (r == DTSExecResult.Success)
            Console.WriteLine("Package executed successfully.");

        Console.WriteLine(Environment.NewLine + "Press any key to continue.");
        Console.ReadKey();
    }
}
```

Results are shown in Figure 15-7.

Figure 15-7. Results for running a package example

Running the package creates the table TestTable in the ProgrammingSqlServer2005 database when the package runs.

The example creates a Package object and a ConnectionManager object containing connection information to the ProgrammingSqlServer2005 database. A SQL task executable is added to the package by passing the string STOCK:SQLTask to the Add() method of the Executables collection for the package. The Executable object is cast to a TaskHost object, which is then cast to a ExecuteSQLTask object. The SQL task is configured by setting properties of the ExecuteSQLTask object.

The TaskHost class is a wrapper for a task. It is used to retrieve additional properties of and methods on the task. The InnerObject property of the TaskHost class accesses the task object, and can be cast to the specific type of task.

SSIS executable objects implement an Execute() method that runs the executable. The ExecutionStatus property of a container returns a value from the DTSExecStatus enumeration, described in Table 15-10, indicating the status of the task execution.

Table 15-10. DTSExecStatus enumeration

Name	Description
Abend	The task terminated abnormally because of an internal error.
Completed	The task completed and returned either a Failure or Success result for the execution result (DTSExecResult).
Executing	The task is running.
None	The task is idle.
Suspended	The task is suspended.
Validating	The task is validating.

The Execute() method of a container returns a value from the DTSExecResult enumeration, described in Table 15-11, indicating the result of executing the package.

Table 15-11. DTSExecResult enumeration

Name	Description
Canceled	The task was cancelled.
Completion	The task ran to completion.
Failure	The task failed.
Success	The task succeeded.

Validating a package

This example creates and validates a package. You need to add a reference to the Microsoft.SqlServer.SQLTask assembly to build and execute this example.

```
using System;

using Microsoft.SqlServer.Dts.Runtime;
using Microsoft.SqlServer.Dts.Tasks.ExecuteSQLTask;

class Program
{
    static void Main(string[] args)
```

```
{
    // create an empty package
    Package p = new Package( );

    // add a connection manager
    ConnectionManager cm = p.Connections.Add("ADO.NET");
    cm.Name = "CM_ProgrammingSqlServer2005";
    cm.ConnectionString = "Data Source=localhost;" +
        "Integrated Security=SSPI;Initial Catalog=ProgrammingSqlServer2005";

    // add a SQL task to the package
    Executable e = p.Executables.Add("STOCK:SQLTask");
    TaskHost th = (TaskHost)e;
    ExecuteSQLTask est = (ExecuteSQLTask)th.InnerObject;
    est.Connection = cm.Name;
    est.SqlStatementSourceType = SqlStatementSourceType.DirectInput;
    est.SqlStatementSource = "CREATE TABLE TestTable " +
        "( ID int NOT NULL, Description nchar(100))";

    // validate the package
    DTSExecResult r = p.Validate(p.Connections, p.Variables, null, null);
    Console.WriteLine("Validation result: " + r);

    Console.WriteLine(Environment.NewLine + "Press any key to continue.");
    Console.ReadKey( );
    }
}
```

The output is shown in Figure 15-8.

Figure 15-8. Output for validate package example

The Package class and other containers have a Validate( ) method that validates dependencies and settings for the object to verify that it will successfully execute. The method ensures that required values are set and contain appropriate values. When connections are validated, a connection to the data is not actually made and data at the data source is not checked. The Validate( ) method can raise and log events.

Enumerating task properties

This example creates a package, adds a TransferDatabaseTask task to it, and enumerates the task properties. You need to add a reference to the Microsoft.SqlServer. TransferDatabase assembly to compile and run this example.

```
using System;

using Microsoft.SqlServer.Dts.Runtime;
using Microsoft.SqlServer.Dts.Tasks.TransferDatabaseTask;

class Program
{
    static void Main(string[] args)
    {
        // create an empty package
        Package p = new Package();

        Executable e = p.Executables.Add("STOCK:TransferDatabaseTask");

        TaskHost th = (TaskHost)e;
        TransferDatabaseTask tdt = (TransferDatabaseTask)th.InnerObject;
        Console.WriteLine("Type = " + tdt.GetType().ToString());
        Console.WriteLine("Version = " + tdt.Version);
        Console.WriteLine();

        foreach (DtsProperty dp in th.Properties)
            Console.WriteLine(dp.Name + " = " + dp.GetValue(th));

        Console.WriteLine(Environment.NewLine + "Press any key to continue.");
        Console.ReadKey();
    }
}
```

Results are shown in Figure 15-9.

The Properties collection of DtsProperty objects for the TaskHost class exposes a container-specific collection of properties. The property values are accessed by calling the GetValue() method of the DtsProperty class.

Connecting tasks

This example creates a package, adds two tasks, and sets a constraint that does not allow the second task to execute until the first completes:

```
using System;

using Microsoft.SqlServer.Dts.Runtime;

class Program
{
    static void Main(string[] args)
    {
        // create an empty package
        Package p = new Package();

        // create the tasks
        Executable e1 = p.Executables.Add("STOCK:TransferDatabaseTask");
        Executable e2 = p.Executables.Add("STOCK:SendMailTask");
```

Figure 15-9. Results for enumerating task properties example

```
// create the precedence constraint
PrecedenceConstraint pc = p.PrecedenceConstraints.Add(e1, e2);
pc.Name = "e1 before e2 precedence constraint";
pc.Value = DTSExecResult.Completion;

foreach (PrecedenceConstraint pc1 in p.PrecedenceConstraints)
{
    Console.WriteLine(pc1.Name);
    Console.WriteLine("  From: " +
        ((TaskHost)pc1.PrecedenceExecutable).InnerObject);
    Console.WriteLine("  To:   " +
        ((TaskHost)pc1.ConstrainedExecutable).InnerObject);
}

Console.WriteLine(Environment.NewLine + "Press any key to continue.");
```

```
                Console.ReadKey( );
            }
    }
```

Results are shown in Figure 15-10.

Figure 15-10. Results for connecting tasks example

The `PrecedenceConstraint` class configures precedence between two containers. The `Add( )` method for the `PrecedenceConstraints` collection for a container takes two arguments—the executable before the constraint and the executable after the constraint. The `Value` property of the `PrecedenceConstraints` collection specifies the constraint type—a value from the `DTSExecResult` enumeration described in Table 15-11.

Using variables

You can use variables to dynamically set values in packages, containers, tasks, and event handlers. This example adds a user variable to an empty package and iterates over all variables in the package:

```
using System;

using Microsoft.SqlServer.Dts.Runtime;

class Program
{
    static void Main(string[] args)
    {
        // create an empty package
        Package p = new Package( );

        // create a variable
        p.Variables.Add("Variable1", false, "", 1);

        foreach (Variable v in p.Variables)
            Console.WriteLine(v.Name + " = " + v.Value +
                " [" + v.DataType + "]");

        Console.WriteLine(Environment.NewLine + "Press any key to continue.");
        Console.ReadKey( );
    }
}
```

The output is shown in Figure 15-11.

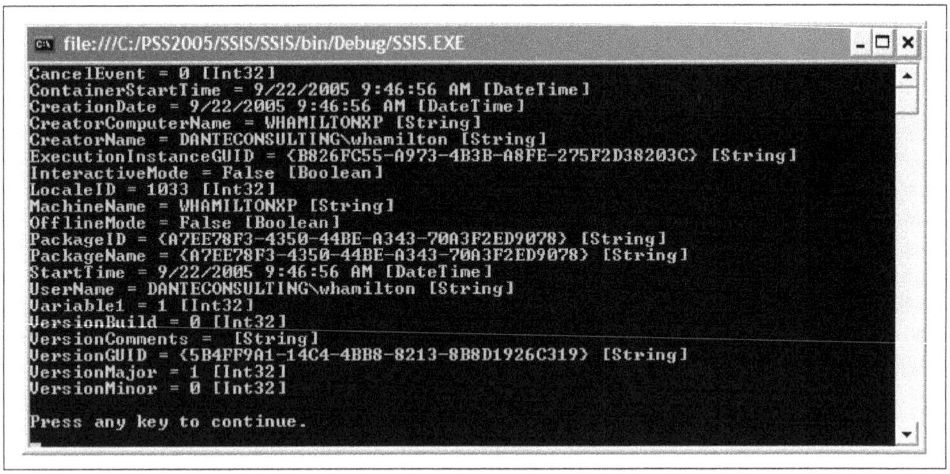

Figure 15-11. Output for add variable example

The Variables property of container objects accesses the collection of Variable objects for the container. You can see the variable named Variable1 that was added programmatically in the output.

SSIS provides two default namespaces for variables. The User namespace is the default location for variables created programmatically. The System namespace contains variables that store information about the running package and its objects.

Configuring a package

This example creates a configuration file for a new package. You need to create the directory *C:\PSS2005\Packages* or specify a different location to run the examples in this section.

```
using System;

using Microsoft.SqlServer.Dts.Runtime;

class Program
{
    static void Main(string[] args)
    {
        string packagePath = @"C:\PSS2005\Packages\";

        // create an empty package
        Package p = new Package();
        // enable configurations
        p.EnableConfigurations = true;
        p.ExportConfigurationFile(packagePath + "SamplePackageConfig.xml");

        // create a variable
        Variable v = p.Variables.Add("Variable1", false, "", 1);
```

```
            // create the configuration file
            Configuration c = p.Configurations.Add( );
            c.ConfigurationString = "SamplePackageConfig.xml";
            c.ConfigurationType = DTSConfigurationType.ConfigFile;
            c.Description = "Sample configuration file";
            c.PackagePath = v.GetPackagePath( );

            // save the package with the configuration file to an XML file
            Application a = new Application( );
            a.SaveToXml(packagePath + "SamplePackage.xml", p, null);

            Console.WriteLine("Press any key to continue.");
            Console.ReadKey( );
        }
    }
```

Running the example creates the configuration file shown in Figure 15-12.

The Configuration class represents information about how a package is configured. The Configurations class represents a collection of Configuration objects. The Package class exposes its collection of configurations through the Configurations property.

The EnableConfigurations property of the Package class indicates whether a package supports loading configuration files when the package is loaded. If the value of EnableConfigurations is false, the package uses configuration values persisted within the package. The ExportConfigurationFile( ) method of the Package class creates an XML file containing all deployable variables in the package. You can see this in the <DTS:Configuration> element in the XML in Figure 15-12.

The ConfigurationType property of the Configuration class specifies the way in which configuration information is stored. The property takes a value from the DTSConfigurationType enumeration, described in Table 15-12. The ConfigurationString property specifies the location of the configuration.

Table 15-12. DTSConfigurationType enumeration

Value	Description
ConfigFile	Configuration file
EnvVariable	Environment variable
IConfigFile	Environment variable that contains information about the configuration flat file
IParentVariable	Environment variable that contains information about the package variable
IRegEntry	Environment variable that contains information about the registry entry
ISqlServer	Environment variable that contains information about the SQL Server instance
ParentVariable	Package variable
RegEntry	Registry entry
SqlServer	SQL Server msdb database

```
<?xml version="1.0" ?>
<DTS:Executable xmlns:DTS="www.microsoft.com/SqlServer/Dts" DTS:ExecutableType="MSDTS.Package.1">
  <DTS:Property DTS:Name="PackageFormatVersion">2</DTS:Property>
  <DTS:Property DTS:Name="VersionComments" />
  <DTS:Property DTS:Name="CreatorName">DANTECONSULTING\whamilton</DTS:Property>
  <DTS:Property DTS:Name="CreatorComputerName">WHAMILTONXP</DTS:Property>
  <DTS:Property DTS:Name="CreationDate" DTS:DataType="7">11/20/2005 2:43:47 PM</DTS:Property>
  <DTS:Property DTS:Name="PackageType">0</DTS:Property>
  <DTS:Property DTS:Name="ProtectionLevel">1</DTS:Property>
  <DTS:Property DTS:Name="MaxConcurrentExecutables">-1</DTS:Property>
  <DTS:Property DTS:Name="PackagePriorityClass">0</DTS:Property>
  <DTS:Property DTS:Name="VersionMajor">1</DTS:Property>
  <DTS:Property DTS:Name="VersionMinor">0</DTS:Property>
  <DTS:Property DTS:Name="VersionBuild">0</DTS:Property>
  <DTS:Property DTS:Name="VersionGUID">{AC4411AB-4D58-4233-90BC-016888943EF9}</DTS:Property>
  <DTS:Property DTS:Name="EnableConfig">-1</DTS:Property>
  <DTS:Property DTS:Name="CheckpointFileName" />
  <DTS:Property DTS:Name="SaveCheckpoints">0</DTS:Property>
  <DTS:Property DTS:Name="CheckpointUsage">0</DTS:Property>
  <DTS:Property DTS:Name="SuppressConfigurationWarnings">0</DTS:Property>
  <DTS:Configuration>
    <DTS:Property DTS:Name="ConfigurationType">1</DTS:Property>
    <DTS:Property DTS:Name="ConfigurationString">SamplePackageConfig.xml</DTS:Property>
    <DTS:Property DTS:Name="ConfigurationVariable">\Package.Variables[::Variable1]</DTS:Property>
    <DTS:Property DTS:Name="ObjectName">{A6EEAF45-D885-43AD-9B40-18FC90760C48}</DTS:Property>
    <DTS:Property DTS:Name="DTSID">{A6EEAF45-D885-43AD-9B40-18FC90760C48}</DTS:Property>
    <DTS:Property DTS:Name="Description">Sample configuration file</DTS:Property>
    <DTS:Property DTS:Name="CreationName" />
  </DTS:Configuration>
  <DTS:Property DTS:Name="ForceExecValue">0</DTS:Property>
  <DTS:Property DTS:Name="ExecValue" DTS:DataType="3">0</DTS:Property>
  <DTS:Property DTS:Name="ForceExecutionResult">-1</DTS:Property>
  <DTS:Property DTS:Name="Disabled">0</DTS:Property>
  <DTS:Property DTS:Name="FailPackageOnFailure">0</DTS:Property>
  <DTS:Property DTS:Name="FailParentOnFailure">0</DTS:Property>
  <DTS:Property DTS:Name="MaxErrorCount">1</DTS:Property>
  <DTS:Property DTS:Name="ISOLevel">1048576</DTS:Property>
  <DTS:Property DTS:Name="LocaleID">1033</DTS:Property>
  <DTS:Property DTS:Name="TransactionOption">1</DTS:Property>
  <DTS:Property DTS:Name="DelayValidation">0</DTS:Property>
  <DTS:Variable>
    <DTS:Property DTS:Name="Expression" />
    <DTS:Property DTS:Name="EvaluateAsExpression">0</DTS:Property>
    <DTS:Property DTS:Name="Namespace" />
    <DTS:Property DTS:Name="ReadOnly">0</DTS:Property>
    <DTS:Property DTS:Name="RaiseChangedEvent">0</DTS:Property>
    <DTS:VariableValue DTS:DataType="3">1</DTS:VariableValue>
    <DTS:Property DTS:Name="ObjectName">Variable1</DTS:Property>
    <DTS:Property DTS:Name="DTSID">{5EF6D450-FE5F-4BCB-B89F-292AAC907861}</DTS:Property>
    <DTS:Property DTS:Name="Description" />
    <DTS:Property DTS:Name="CreationName" />
  </DTS:Variable>
  <DTS:LoggingOptions>
    <DTS:Property DTS:Name="LoggingMode">0</DTS:Property>
    <DTS:Property DTS:Name="FilterKind">1</DTS:Property>
    <DTS:Property DTS:Name="EventFilter" DTS:DataType="8" />
  </DTS:LoggingOptions>
  <DTS:Property DTS:Name="ObjectName">{AD8ED863-8F2B-4EDF-8208-F9CCF490959E}</DTS:Property>
  <DTS:Property DTS:Name="DTSID">{AD8ED863-8F2B-4EDF-8208-F9CCF490959E}</DTS:Property>
  <DTS:Property DTS:Name="Description" />
  <DTS:Property DTS:Name="CreationName">MSDTS.Package.1</DTS:Property>
  <DTS:Property DTS:Name="DisableEventHandlers">0</DTS:Property>
</DTS:Executable>
```

Figure 15-12. Package configuration file example

Finally, the SaveToXml() method of the Application class saves the package and configuration information to the *SamplePackage.xml* file.

This example loads the package created in the preceding example and displays the configuration information:

```csharp
using System;

using Microsoft.SqlServer.Dts.Runtime;

class Program
{
    static void Main(string[] args)
    {
        string packagePath = @"C:\PSS2005\Packages\";

        Application a = new Application();
        Package p = a.LoadPackage(packagePath + "SamplePackage.xml", null);

        // output the user variables
        foreach (Variable v in p.Variables)
        {
            if (!v.SystemVariable)
                Console.WriteLine(v.Name + " = " + v.Value);
        }

        // output the configurations
        Console.WriteLine();
        foreach (Configuration c in p.Configurations)
        {
            Console.WriteLine("ConfigurationString = " + c.ConfigurationString);
            Console.WriteLine("ConfigurationType = " + c.ConfigurationType);
            Console.WriteLine("CreationName = " + c.CreationName);
            Console.WriteLine("Description = " + c.Description);
            Console.WriteLine("ID = " + c.ID);
            Console.WriteLine("Name = " + c.Name);
            Console.WriteLine("PackagePath = " + c.PackagePath);
        }

        Console.WriteLine(Environment.NewLine + "Press any key to continue.");
        Console.ReadKey();
    }
}
```

Results are shown in Figure 15-13.

Figure 15-13. Results for loading package configuration file example

Handling events

The SSIS runtime provides a set of events that occur before, during, and after the validation and execution of a package, as described in Table 15-4. You can create event handlers that execute a workflow when an event is raised. The events can be captured either by implementing the IDTSEvents interface in a class or by creating a DtsEventHandler object in the workflow.

The first example shows how to use the IDTSEvents interface:

```
using System;

using Microsoft.SqlServer.Dts.Runtime;

class Program : DefaultEvents
{
    static void Main(string[] args)
    {
        // create an empty package
        Package p = new Package();

        // ... build the package

        // execute the package providing an instance of the Program class
        // as an argument
        Program program = new Program();
        DTSExecResult r = p.Execute(null, null, program, null, null);

        Console.WriteLine(Environment.NewLine + "Press any key to continue.");
        Console.ReadKey();
    }

    public override void OnPreExecute(Executable exec, ref bool fireAgain)
    {
        Console.WriteLine("Event: OnPreExecute");
    }
}
```

The output is shown in Figure 15-14.

Figure 15-14. Output from IDTSEvents example

You can receive event notifications during execution or validation of a container by building a class that implements the IDTSEvents interface. You can also derive a class from the DefaultEvents class and override the events you are interested in handling—this is the approach used in this example. You need to create an instance of the Program class and provide it as the third argument to the Execute( ) method of the package to receive event notifications.

The second example creates a DtsEventHandler object and uses it to handle the OnTaskFailed event. You need to add a reference to the Microsoft.SqlServer.SQLTask assembly to compile and run this example.

```
using System;

using Microsoft.SqlServer.Dts.Runtime;
using Microsoft.SqlServer.Dts.Tasks.ExecuteSQLTask;

class Program
{
    static void Main(string[] args)
    {
        // create an empty package
        Package p = new Package( );

        // add a connection manager
        ConnectionManager cm = p.Connections.Add("ADO.NET");
        cm.Name = "CM_ProgrammingSqlServer2005";
        cm.ConnectionString = "Data Source=localhost;" +
            "Integrated Security=SSPI;Initial Catalog=ProgrammingSqlServer2005";

        // add a SQL task to the package
        Executable e = p.Executables.Add("STOCK:SQLTask");
        TaskHost th = (TaskHost)e;
        ExecuteSQLTask est = (ExecuteSQLTask)th.InnerObject;
        est.Connection = cm.Name;
        est.SqlStatementSourceType = SqlStatementSourceType.DirectInput;
        est.SqlStatementSource = "CREATE TABLE TestTable2 " +
            "( ID int NOT NULL, Description nchar(100))";

        // add the event handler
        DtsEventHandler deh = (DtsEventHandler)p.EventHandlers.Add("OnTaskFailed");

        // Add task to fire when the event handler executes
        Executable e2 = deh.Executables.Add("STOCK:SQLTask");
        TaskHost th2 = (TaskHost)e2;
        ExecuteSQLTask est2 = (ExecuteSQLTask)th2.InnerObject;
        est2.Connection = cm.Name;
        est2.SqlStatementSourceType = SqlStatementSourceType.DirectInput;
        est2.SqlStatementSource = "CREATE TABLE TestTable3 " +
            "( ID int NOT NULL, Description nchar(100))";

        DTSExecResult r = p.Execute( );
        Console.WriteLine("Status: " + r.ToString( ));

        Console.WriteLine(Environment.NewLine + "Press any key to continue.");
        Console.ReadKey( );
    }
}
```

You need to run this example twice:

1. The first run successfully creates a table named TestTable2 in the ProgrammingSqlServer2005 database. The OnTaskFailed event handler never executes, because no task in the package failed when the package was run—the table TestTable3 is not created. Confirm that table TestTable2 exists and table TestTable3 does not exist by using Object Explorer in SQL Server Management Studio.

2. The second run tries but fails to create the table TestTable2, because it already exists from the previous package run. The failure causes the OnTaskFailed event handler to run, creating TestTable3. Confirm that both TestTable2 and TestTable3 exist.

The DtsEventHandler class represents a container that runs when specific events occur. You create and add workflow for the event handler in the same way as for any other container.

Logging

This example enables logging for a package and writes log information to an XML file. You need to create the directory *C:\PSS2005\Logs* to compile and execute this example.

```
using System;
using System.IO;

using Microsoft.SqlServer.Dts.Runtime;

class Program
{
    static void Main(string[] args)
    {
        // create an empty package
        Package p = new Package();

        // add a file connection manager
        ConnectionManager cm = p.Connections.Add("FILE");
        cm.Name = "Logging";
        cm.ConnectionString = @"C:\PSS2005\Logs\TestLog.xml";

        // enable logging
        p.LoggingMode = DTSLoggingMode.Enabled;

        // create a log provider in the package and select it for logging
        LogProvider lp = p.LogProviders.Add("DTS.LogProviderXmlFile.1");
        lp.ConfigString = cm.Name;
        p.LoggingOptions.SelectedLogProviders.Add(lp);
        // set the events to include in the logging
        p.LoggingOptions.EventFilterKind = DTSEventFilterKind.Inclusion;
        p.LoggingOptions.EventFilter =
            new string[] { "OnPreExecute", "OnPostExecute", "OnTaskFailed" };
```

```
        // run the package
        DTSExecResult r = p.Execute( );
        Console.WriteLine("Status: " + r);

        Console.WriteLine(Environment.NewLine + "Press any key to continue.");
        Console.ReadKey( );
    }
}
```

The log file *C:\PSS2005\Logs\TestLog.xml* is shown in Figure 15-15.

The LogProvider class contains information about a log provider for a container. The
LogProviders property of the Package class exposes the collection of all log providers
associated with the package. The Add( ) method of the LogProviders class adds the
specified log provider to the collection of log providers. The log provider is specified
by passing either the ProgID or ClassID of one of the five included log providers or of
a custom log provider as the argument to the Add( ) method. Table 15-6 lists
included log providers and corresponding ProgIDs. The ConfigString property sup-
plies configuration information specific to the log provider. The XML log provider
used in this example and most log providers use the ConfigString property to specify a ConnectionManager object used to connect to the log destination.

> The LogProviderInfos property of the Application class returns a col-
> lection of information about log providers installed on the computer.

The LoggingMode property of each container specifies whether event information for
the container is logged. It takes a value from the DTSLoggingMode enumeration—
Disabled, Enabled, or UseParentSetting. If LoggingMode is not specified, it defaults to
the logging mode of the parent container. The package is the top-level container, and
its LoggingMode property defaults to Disabled. Each provider has different configuration options set through the ConfigString property.

The LoggingOptions.EventFilter property of the container takes a string array of
events that you want to log. The LoggingOptions.EventFilterKind property takes a
value from DTSEventFilterKind indicating whether the array of events is included or
excluded from logging. Logging can be further filtered by setting columns in the
DTSEventColumnFilter structure to true or false to select whether the columns are
logged, and assigning the structure to LoggingOptions using the SetColumnFilter( )
method.

Data-Flow Programming

A data flow lets you load, transform, and save data. You build a data flow by adding
pipeline components—data-flow sources, transformations, and destinations—to the
data flow, and then configuring and connecting the components.

```xml
<?xml version="1.0" ?>
<dtslogs>
  <dtslog />
  <dtslog>
    <record>
      <event>PackageStart</event>
      <message>Beginning of package execution.</message>
      <computer>WHAMILTONXP</computer>
      <operator>DANTECONSULTING\whamilton</operator>
      <source>{942DBD49-F935-4AF2-83F4-49527D306E18}</source>
      <sourceid>{942DBD49-F935-4AF2-83F4-49527D306E18}</sourceid>
      <executionid>{2CA8F591-5318-4A1E-BA4A-F6B3808D7136}</executionid>
      <starttime>11/20/2005 5:58:26 PM</starttime>
      <endtime>11/20/2005 5:58:26 PM</endtime>
      <datacode>0</datacode>
      <databytes>0x</databytes>
    </record>
    <record>
      <event>OnPreExecute</event>
      <message>(null)</message>
      <computer>WHAMILTONXP</computer>
      <operator>DANTECONSULTING\whamilton</operator>
      <source>{942DBD49-F935-4AF2-83F4-49527D306E18}</source>
      <sourceid>{942DBD49-F935-4AF2-83F4-49527D306E18}</sourceid>
      <executionid>{2CA8F591-5318-4A1E-BA4A-F6B3808D7136}</executionid>
      <starttime>11/20/2005 5:58:26 PM</starttime>
      <endtime>11/20/2005 5:58:26 PM</endtime>
      <datacode>0</datacode>
      <databytes>0x</databytes>
    </record>
    <record>
      <event>OnPostExecute</event>
      <message>(null)</message>
      <computer>WHAMILTONXP</computer>
      <operator>DANTECONSULTING\whamilton</operator>
      <source>{942DBD49-F935-4AF2-83F4-49527D306E18}</source>
      <sourceid>{942DBD49-F935-4AF2-83F4-49527D306E18}</sourceid>
      <executionid>{2CA8F591-5318-4A1E-BA4A-F6B3808D7136}</executionid>
      <starttime>11/20/2005 5:58:26 PM</starttime>
      <endtime>11/20/2005 5:58:26 PM</endtime>
      <datacode>0</datacode>
      <databytes>0x</databytes>
    </record>
    <record>
      <event>PackageEnd</event>
      <message>End of package execution.</message>
      <computer>WHAMILTONXP</computer>
      <operator>DANTECONSULTING\whamilton</operator>
      <source>{942DBD49-F935-4AF2-83F4-49527D306E18}</source>
      <sourceid>{942DBD49-F935-4AF2-83F4-49527D306E18}</sourceid>
      <executionid>{2CA8F591-5318-4A1E-BA4A-F6B3808D7136}</executionid>
      <starttime>11/20/2005 5:58:26 PM</starttime>
      <endtime>11/20/2005 5:58:26 PM</endtime>
      <datacode>0</datacode>
      <databytes>0x</databytes>
    </record>
  </dtslog>
</dtslogs>
```

Figure 15-15. Results for logging to XML file example

This example enumerates the available pipeline components—data-flow sources, transformations, and destinations:

```
using System;

using Microsoft.SqlServer.Dts.Runtime;

class Program
{
    static void Main(string[] args)
    {
        Application a = new Application();

        foreach (PipelineComponentInfo pci in a.PipelineComponentInfos)
        {
            Console.WriteLine(pci.Name);
            Console.WriteLine("   " + pci.ComponentType);
            Console.WriteLine("   " + pci.CreationName);
            Console.WriteLine("   " + pci.Description);
            Console.WriteLine();
        }

        Console.WriteLine("Press any key to continue.");
        Console.ReadKey();
    }
}
```

Partial results are shown in Figure 15-16.

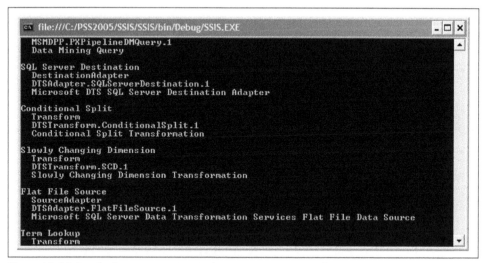

Figure 15-16. Results for enumerating pipeline components example

The Application class exposes a PipelineComponentInfos collection. It contains a PipelineComponentInfo object for each installed pipeline component. The ComponentType property of the PipelineComponentInfo class identifies the type of component as a value from the DTSPipelineComponent enumeration—DestinationAdapter, SourceAdapter, Transform, or View.

Data-flow programming—programmatically constructing and configuring a data flow, developing custom source, transformation, and load components that participate in the data flow, and programming custom data-flow components—is beyond the scope of this chapter. See Microsoft SQL Server 2005 Books Online for more information about these topics.

CHAPTER 16

SQL Server Agent

SQL Server Agent automates administrative tasks by running jobs, monitoring SQL Server, and processing alerts.

You can define jobs and their schedules, alerts, and operators by using Object Explorer in SQL Server Management Studio, by using T-SQL scripts, or by using SQL Server Management Objects (SMO). Using SMO is the focus of this chapter.

SQL Server Agent is disabled by default. Start SQL Server Agent by connecting to a server instance in Object Explorer. Right-click the SQL Server Agent node and click Start on the context menu to start SQL Server Agent.

Set SQL Server Agent to start automatically by launching SQL Server Configuration Manager from Microsoft SQL Server 2005 → Configuration Tools. Select SQL Server 2005 Services in the left panel, right-click SQL Server Agent from the list of services in the right panel, and select Properties from the context menu to launch the SQL Server Agent Properties dialog box. Select the Service tab and change the Start Mode to Automatic.

Programming SQL Server Agent

Figure 16-1 shows the key SMO SQL Server Agent classes and defines the relationships between them.

These classes are in the `Microsoft.SqlServer.Management.Smo.Agent` namespace.

The rest of this chapter presents programming examples that show how to use SMO SQL Server Agent classes and provides descriptions of the classes. You need a reference to the following assemblies to compile and run the examples:

- Microsoft.SqlServer.ConnectionInfo
- Microsoft.SqlServer.Smo
- Microsoft.SqlServer.SmoEnum
- Microsoft.SqlServer.SqlEnum

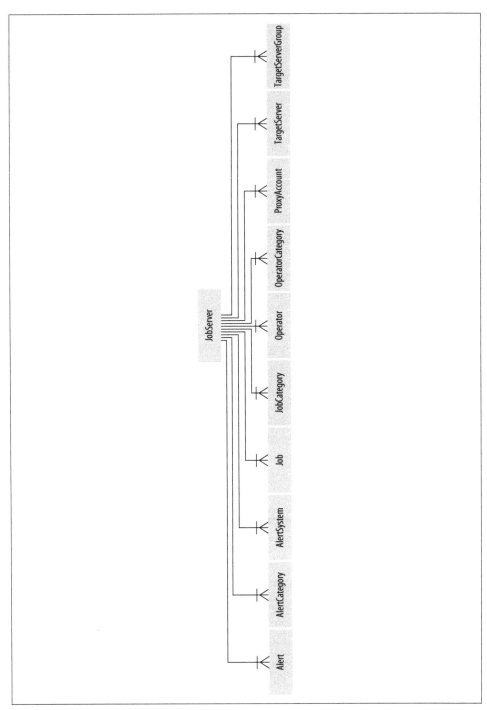

Figure 16-1. SQL Server Agent class hierarchy

Creating a Job

A SQL Server Agent *job* specifies a series of *job steps* (actions) that SQL Server Agent performs according to a schedule, in response to an alert, or by executing the sp_start_job stored procedure. This example creates a SQL Server Agent job named TestJob. The job has a single job step named TestJob that runs a database consistency check on the AdventureWorks database.

```
using System;

using Microsoft.SqlServer.Management.Common;
using Microsoft.SqlServer.Management.Smo;
using Microsoft.SqlServer.Management.Smo.Agent;

class Program
{
    static void Main(string[] args)
    {
        Server server = new Server("(local)");
        JobServer jobServer = server.JobServer;

        // create the job
        Job j = new Job(jobServer, "TestJob");
        j.Create();

        // set the execution target server (same as sp_add_jobserver)
        j.ApplyToTargetServer("(local)");

        // create the job step
        JobStep js = new JobStep(j, "Step 1");
        js.SubSystem = AgentSubSystem.TransactSql;
        js.Command = "DBCC CHECKDB('AdventureWorks') WITH NO_INFOMSGS";
        js.OnFailAction = StepCompletionAction.QuitWithFailure;
        js.Create();

        Console.WriteLine("Press any key to continue.");
        Console.ReadKey();
    }
}
```

 You must specify the server by using the string (local) if the job is to run on the local server. The string localhost will not work.

In this example, a job step is added to the job by creating a JobStep object and adding it to the job by passing a reference to the job in the JobStep constructor.

After you run the example, expand and refresh the SQL Server Agent → Jobs node in Object Explorer to show the new job TestJob. Right-click the TestJob node and select Properties from the context menu to show the Job Properties dialog box. Select the Steps page to display the single step you added to the job, as shown in Figure 16-2.

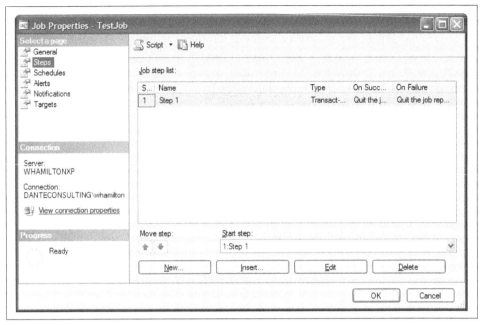

Figure 16-2. Job Properties dialog box

The SubSystem property of the JobStep class specifies the SQL Server subsystem that is used by the job step. It is a value from the AgentSubSystem enumeration described in Table 16-1. In this example, the single step added uses the Transact SQL subsystem.

Table 16-1. AgentSubSystem enumeration

Value	SQL Server subsystem
ActiveScripting	Active Scripting
AnalysisCommand	Analysis Command
AnalysisQuery	Analysis Query
CmdExec	Operating System Command executive
Distribution	Distribution Agent
LogReader	Log Reader Agent
Merge	Merge Agent
QueueReader	Queue Reader Agent
Snapshot	Snapshot Agent
Ssis	SQL Server Integration Services (SSIS)
TransactSql	Transact-SQL

SMO has classes used to manage SQL Server Agent jobs, job steps, job categories, filters, and schedules. These classes are described in Table 16-2.

Table 16-2. SMO classes for administering SQL Server Agent jobs

Class	Description
Job	Represents a SQL Server Agent job.
JobCategory	Represents attributes that allow jobs to be categorized.
JobCategoryCollection	Represents a collection of job categories as JobCategory objects. The JobCategories property of the JobServer class returns the job categories defined on SQL Server Agent.
JobCollection	Represents a collection of jobs as Job objects. The Jobs property of the JobServer class returns the jobs defined on SQL Server Agent.
JobFilter	Represents constraints used to restrict output of the EnumJobs( ) method of the JobServer class.
JobHistoryFilter	Represents constraints used to restrict output of the EnumJobHistory( ) method of the JobServer class.
JobSchedule	Represents a SQL Server Agent job schedule.
JobScheduleCollection	Represents a collection of job schedules as JobSchedule objects.
	The SharedSchedule property of the JobServer class returns the shared schedules defined on SQL Server Agent.
	The JobSchedules property of the Job class returns the job schedules assigned to the job.
JobServer	Represents the SQL Server Agent subsystem.
JobStep	Represents a SQL Server Agent job step.
JobStepCollection	Represents a collection of job steps as JobStep objects. The JobSteps property of the Job class returns the job steps defined for the job.

Running a Job

This example runs the job created in the preceding example:

```
using System;

using Microsoft.SqlServer.Management.Common;
using Microsoft.SqlServer.Management.Smo;
using Microsoft.SqlServer.Management.Smo.Agent;

class Program
{
    static void Main(string[] args)
    {
        Server server = new Server("(local)");
        JobServer jobServer = server.JobServer;

        Job j = jobServer.Jobs["TestJob"];
        j.Start( );

        Console.WriteLine("Press any key to continue.");
        Console.ReadKey( );
    }
}
```

The Start( ) method of the Job class runs the job. If you open SQL Server Agent Job Activity Monitor by selecting SQL Server Agent → Job Activity Monitor in Object Explorer, you will see that the job TestJob is executing, as shown in Figure 16-3. You have to click the Refresh button on the toolbar to update the status.

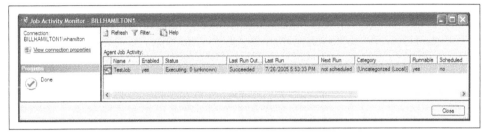

Figure 16-3. SQL Server Agent Job Activity Monitor

You can view the history for the job TestJob by right-clicking the SQL Server Agent → Jobs → TestJob node in Object Explorer and then selecting View History from the context menu.

Creating a Schedule

A SQL Server Agent *schedule* specifies when a job runs—either whenever SQL Server Agent starts, whenever CPU utilization is at a level defined as idle, at a specified date and time, or on a recurring basis. This example creates a job schedule that runs once daily at 4:00 A.M. A later example associates this schedule with the job named TestJob created in the first example in this section.

```
using System;

using Microsoft.SqlServer.Management.Common;
using Microsoft.SqlServer.Management.Smo;
using Microsoft.SqlServer.Management.Smo.Agent;

class Program
{
    static void Main(string[] args)
    {
        Server server = new Server("(local)");
        JobServer jobServer = server.JobServer;

        JobSchedule js = new JobSchedule(jobServer, "TestSchedule");
        js.FrequencyTypes = FrequencyTypes.Daily;
        js.FrequencyInterval = 1;
        js.ActiveStartTimeOfDay = TimeSpan.FromHours(4);
        js.IsEnabled = true;
        js.Create( );

        Console.WriteLine("Press any key to continue.");
        Console.ReadKey( );
    }
}
```

After you run this program, you can view and manage the new schedule by right-clicking the SQL Server Agent → Jobs node in Object Explorer and selecting Manage Schedules from the context menu.

The schedule is defined using the properties of the JobSchedule class described in Table 16-3.

Table 16-3. Properties of the JobSchedule class used to define schedule

Property	Description
ActiveEndDate	The date and time when the schedule ends.
ActiveEndTimeOfDay	The time when the schedule stops for the day.
ActiveStartDay	The date and time when the schedule starts.
ActiveStartTimeOfDay	The time when the schedule starts for the day.
FrequencyInterval	The frequency interval that specifies how often the job is scheduled to run. The FrequencyInterval property is relative to the value of the FrequencyTypes property.
FrequencyRecurrenceFactor	The number of weeks or months between scheduled jobs having weekly or monthly frequency
FrequencyRelativeIntervals	The value of a day relative to the first day of the month.
FrequencySubDayIntervals	The time (hours or minutes) between scheduled jobs having daily frequency, with a frequency subday type of hour or minute.
FrequencySubDayTypes	The unit of time used to specify the interval between scheduled jobs having daily frequency. The value is from the FrequencySubDayTypes enumeration—Hour, Minute, Once, or Unknown.
FrequencyTypes	The frequency specifying how often the schedule executes. The value is from the FrequencyTypes enumeration—AutoStart, Daily, Monthly, MonthlyRelative, OneTime, OnIdle, Unknown, or Weekly.

Scheduling a Job

This example associates the job named TestJob, created in the first example in this section, with the schedule named TestSchedule, created in the preceding section:

```
using System;

using Microsoft.SqlServer.Management.Common;
using Microsoft.SqlServer.Management.Smo;
using Microsoft.SqlServer.Management.Smo.Agent;

class Program
{
    static void Main(string[] args)
    {
        Server server = new Server("(local)");
        JobServer jobServer = server.JobServer;

        JobSchedule js = jobServer.SharedSchedules["TestSchedule"];
```

```
            Job j = jobServer.Jobs["TestJob"];
            j.AddSharedSchedule(js.ID);

            Console.WriteLine("Press any key to continue.");
            Console.ReadKey();
        }
    }
```

The AddSharedSchedule() method of the Job class associates the schedule with the job. The method uses the schedule ID number to identify the schedule.

After you run this program, you can see that job TestJob is associated with the schedule TestSchedule by right-clicking the SQL Server Agent → Jobs → TestJob node in Object Explorer and selecting Properties from the context menu. This opens the Job Properties dialog box. Select the Schedules page to view the list of schedules for the job. You can also right-click the SQL Server Agent → Jobs node and select Manage Schedules from the context menu. This opens the Manage Schedules dialog box. Click the value in the Jobs in schedule column to display the Jobs Referencing a Schedule dialog box, which lists the jobs associated with the schedule.

Creating an Operator

A SQL Server Agent *operator* defines contact information for a SQL Server administrator. An alert can notify using email, a pager through email, or net send. This example creates an operator named Test Operator and assigns an email address to the operator:

```
using System;

using Microsoft.SqlServer.Management.Common;
using Microsoft.SqlServer.Management.Smo;
using Microsoft.SqlServer.Management.Smo.Agent;

class Program
{
    static void Main(string[] args)
    {
        Server server = new Server("(local)");
        JobServer jobServer = server.JobServer;

        Operator o = new Operator(jobServer, "Test Operator");
        o.EmailAddress = "test@operator.org";
        o.Enabled = true;
        o.Create();

        Console.WriteLine("Press any key to continue.");
        Console.ReadKey();
    }
}
```

The `EmailAddress`, `NetSendAddress`, and `PagerAddress` properties of the `Operator` class specify the address for the operator for the different communication options.

After you run this program, you can view the new operator by refreshing and expanding the SQL Server Agent → Operators node.

The SMO classes used to manage SQL Server Agent operators are described in Table 16-4.

Table 16-4. SMO classes for administering SQL Server Agent operators

Class	Description
Operator	Represents a SQL Server Agent operator.
OperatorCategory	Represents attributes that allow operators to be categorized.
OperatorCategoryCollection	Represents a collection of operator categories as `OperatorCategory` objects. The `OperatorCategories` property of the `JobServer` class returns the operator categories defined on SQL Server Agent.
OperatorCollection	Represents a collection of operators as `Operator` objects. The `Operators` property of the `JobServer` class returns the operators defined on SQL Server Agent.

Creating an Alert

A SQL Server Agent *alert* specifies an automatic response to a specific condition—either a SQL Server event, a SQL Server performance condition, or a Windows Management Instrumentation (WMI) event. The alert either notifies one or more operators or runs a job.

This example creates an alert that emails the operator named `Test Operator`, created in the preceding example, when an error with a severity of 20 is encountered:

```
using System;

using Microsoft.SqlServer.Management.Common;
using Microsoft.SqlServer.Management.Smo;
using Microsoft.SqlServer.Management.Smo.Agent;

class Program
{
    static void Main(string[] args)
    {
        Server server = new Server("(local)");
        JobServer jobServer = server.JobServer;

        Alert a = new Alert(jobServer, "Test Alert");
        a.Severity = 20;     // Fatal error in current process
        a.Create();

        a.AddNotification("Test Operator", NotifyMethods.NotifyEmail);
```

```
            Console.WriteLine("Press any key to continue.");
            Console.ReadKey();
        }
    }
}
```

After you run this program, you can view the new alert by refreshing and expanding the SQL Server Agent → Alerts node.

Execute the following T-SQL statement to trigger the alert:

```
RAISERROR ('test error', 20, 1) WITH LOG
```

The following message is displayed as a result of the error:

```
Msg 2745, Level 16, State 2, Line 1
Process ID 59 has raised user error 50000, severity 20. SQL Server is
  terminating this process.
Msg 50000, Level 20, State 1, Line 1
test error
Msg 0, Level 20, State 0, Line 0
A severe error occurred on the current command.  The results, if any,
  should be discarded.
```

You can check that the alert Test Alert occurred by right-clicking the SQL Server Agent → Alerts → Test Alert node in Object Explorer and selecting Properties from the context menu. Select the History page in the Alert Properties dialog box to see the date of the last alert, the date of the last response, and the total number of occurrences.

When creating an alert, you must specify one of the following:

- A non-zero message ID
- A non-zero severity
- A non-null performance condition
- A non-null WMI namespace and query

SQL Server Agent Mail is turned off by default. To enable it, right-click the SQL Server Agent node in Object Explorer and select Properties from the context menu. Next, select the Alert System page in the SQL Server Agent Properties dialog box, check the Enable mail profile checkbox, and complete the rest of the Mail Session section of the dialog page.

The SMO classes used to manage SQL Server Agent alerts are described in Table 16-5.

Table 16-5. SMO classes for administering SQL Server Agent alerts

Class	Description
Alert	Represents a SQL Server alert.
AlertCategory	Represents attributes that allow alerts to be categorized.

Table 16-5. SMO classes for administering SQL Server Agent alerts (continued)

Class	Description
AlertCategoryCollection	Represents a collection of alert categories as AlertCategory objects. The AlertCategories property of the JobServer class returns the alert categories defined on SQL Server Agent.
AlertCollection	Represents a collection of alerts as Alert objects. The Alerts property of the JobServer class returns the alerts defined on SQL Server Agent.
AlertSystem	Represents defaults for all alerts defined on a SQL Server instance. The AlertSystem property of the JobServer class returns the alert system information defined on SQL Server Agent.

Creating a Proxy Account

A SQL Server Agent *proxy account* defines a security context in which a job step can run. This example creates a proxy account named Test Proxy, gives the public database role access to the proxy, and lets job steps use the Active Scripting and Operating System (CmdExec) subsystems:

```
using System;

using Microsoft.SqlServer.Management.Common;
using Microsoft.SqlServer.Management.Smo;
using Microsoft.SqlServer.Management.Smo.Agent;

class Program
{
    static void Main(string[] args)
    {
        Server server = new Server("(local)");
        JobServer jobServer = server.JobServer;

        ProxyAccount p = new ProxyAccount(jobServer, "Test Proxy");
        // see note below about credentials
        p.CredentialName = "Test Credential";
        p.IsEnabled = true;
        p.Create();

        // give the public database role access to the proxy account
        p.AddMsdbRole("public");

        // allow Active Scripting and Operating System
        p.AddSubSystem(AgentSubSystem.ActiveScripting);
        p.AddSubSystem(AgentSubSystem.CmdExec);

        Console.WriteLine("Press any key to continue.");
        Console.ReadKey();
    }
}
```

You must create a *credential* before creating a proxy. Credentials contain authentication information that authenticated SQL Server users require to access resources outside of SQL Server—on the local machine or on the network domain. The credential used to create the proxy must be for a valid Windows user. Add credentials from Object Explorer in SQL Server Management Studio by selecting Security → Credentials → New Credential in Object Explorer. Alternatively, you can add and manage credentials by using the SMO Credential class, discussed in Chapter 11.

After you run the code, you can view the proxies by refreshing and opening either the SQL Server Agent → Proxies → ActiveXScript node or the SQL Server Agent → Proxies → Operating System (CmdExec) node in Object Explorer.

Assign a proxy to a job step by using the ProxyName property of the JobStep class. The AgentSubSystem property of the ProxyAccount class specifies the SQL Server subsystems that can be used by the proxy. You can give SQL login, database role, or server role principals access to the proxy account by using the AddLogin( ), AddMsdbRole( ), or AddServerRole( ) methods, respectively, of the ProxyAccount class.

The SMO classes used to manage SQL Server Agent proxies are described in Table 16-6.

Table 16-6. SMO classes for administering SQL Server Agent proxy accounts

Class	Description
ProxyAccount	Represents a SQL Server Agent proxy account.
ProxyAccountCollection	Represents a collection of proxy accounts as ProxyAccount objects. The ProxyAccounts property of the JobServer class returns the proxy accounts defined on SQL Server Agent.

Multiserver Environments

A *master server* defines SQL Server Agent jobs that are run on remote (target) servers. A *target server* downloads and executes jobs defined on a master server. Target servers are defined only on a master SQL Server Agent. For information about setting up a multiserver administration group, see Microsoft SQL Server 2005 Books Online.

Target server instances are automatically populated when you connect to a SQL Server instance defined as a master in a multiserver administration group. The SMO target server objects let you retrieve information about a target server and set the location for a target server. The SMO classes used to manage SQL Server Agent target servers are described in Table 16-7.

Table 16-7. SMO classes for administering SQL Server Agent target servers

Class	Description
TargetServer	Represents a target server for multiserver administration on SQL Server Agent. The TargetServer object is obtained using an item from the TargetServer-Collection object returned by the TargetServers property of the JobServer object and cannot be created as a standalone object.
TargetServerCollection	Represents a collection of target servers as TargetServer objects. The TargetServers property of the JobServer class returns the target servers defined on SQL Server Agent.
TargetServerGroup	Represents a target server group for multiserver administration on SQL Server Agent.
TargetServerGroupCollection	Represents a collection of target server groups as TargetServerGroup objects. The TargetServerGroups property of the JobServer class returns the target server groups defined on SQL Server Agent.

CHAPTER 17

Service Broker

SQL Server 2005 introduces Service Broker—a technology that is part of the Database Engine that helps you to build scalable, loosely coupled database applications. Service Broker provides a message-based communications platform that integrates independent application components. Service Broker makes it easier to build distributed applications by providing an asynchronous programming framework that includes queuing and reliable messaging. Service Broker can be used both for applications that use a single SQL Server instance and for applications that are distributed across multiple instances. The Service Broker Framework provides a T-SQL Data Manipulation Language (DML) interface for sending and receiving streams of asynchronous messages.

Architecture

Before you look at the message flow within a Service Broker solution, there are some key Service Broker terms with which you should be familiar.

A *message* is a unit of information exchanged between applications that use Service Broker. Internally, a message is stored in SQL Server as a varbinary(max) data type. Each message has a *message type* that defines the name and type of data that a message contains. Each message has a unique identity. Each message also has a unique *sequence number* within its conversation, which is used to enforce message ordering.

A *conversation* is a reliable, persistent communications channel made up of a series of messages. Messages are guaranteed to arrive in the order in which they were sent and are guaranteed to arrive exactly once.

A *conversation group* is a set of related conversations for completing a specific task. A conversation group is defined by a participant and is not shared between participants in a conversation—each participant can group conversations as needed. Service Broker automatically adds a conversation group identifier to messages in related conversations. A conversation group facilitates the coordination of the messages within related conversations. A conversation group is associated with a specific service, and all conversations within the conversation group are messages to and from that service.

A *contract* specifies the message types used to perform a specific task and the message types that each participant in a conversation can use.

An application sends a message to a *service*—a collection of related tasks—and receives messages from a *queue*, which holds messages in a database. Generally, one queue is used per service, although it is possible to share a queue across multiple services. A service specifies the contracts for which it is the target. A *target service* is an address that accepts requests for tasks identified by the contract specified by the service. An *initiating service* is the return address for a conversation with a target service.

A *dialog* is a conversation between two services. Dialogs use the message conversation identifier and sequence number to identify related messages and put them in the correct order. In this way, dialogs provide exactly-once-in-order message delivery. The *initiator* begins a dialog, and the *target* accepts the conversation started by the initiator.

Message delivery between applications is asynchronous and transactional. If a transaction rolls back, all Service Broker operations within the transaction are rolled back, including send and receive operations.

A *route* specifies where to deliver messages and specifies a service name, a broker instance identifier that uniquely identifies a Service Broker database, and a network address. SQL Server uses the service name and broker instance specified when a conversation is started to determine the route for a conversation.

A *remote service binding* relates a local database user, the certificate for the user, and the name of a remote service and is used to provide dialog security for conversations that target a remote service.

Figure 17-1 shows the flow of messages from an initiating client to a target, which processes the message and responds to the client.

Programming Service Broker

SMO Service Broker classes are used to manage Service Broker objects programmatically. SMO Service Broker classes do not support creating conversations or sending and receiving messages. You send and receive streams of asynchronous messages using T-SQL DML statements, which are discussed in the "Implementing a Service Broker Service" section later in this chapter. Figure 17-2 shows the relationship between SMO classes for Service Broker programming.

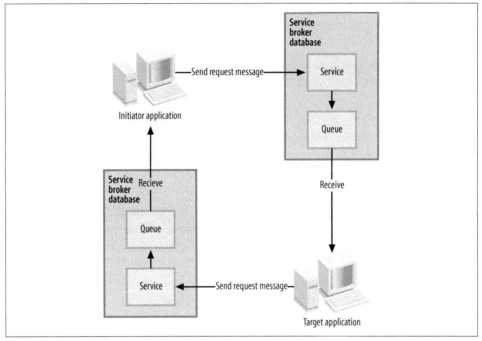

Figure 17-1. Service Broker message flow

The remainder of this chapter contains examples that show how to use the SMO Service Broker classes and provides descriptions of the classes. You need a reference to the following assemblies to compile and run the examples:

- Microsoft.SqlServer.ConnectionInfo
- Microsoft.SqlServer.ServiceBrokerEnum
- Microsoft.SqlServer.Smo

The ServiceBroker object described in is the top-level class in the SMO Service Broker class hierarchy and represents the implementation of Service Broker on a SQL Server database. The ServiceBroker property of the Database class returns the Service Broker implementation on a database.

Enumerating Service Broker Objects

This example enumerates all Service Broker objects—message types, contracts, queues, services, routes, and remote service bindings:

```
using System;

using Microsoft.SqlServer.Management.Smo;
using Microsoft.SqlServer.Management.Common;
using Microsoft.SqlServer.Management.Smo.Broker;
```

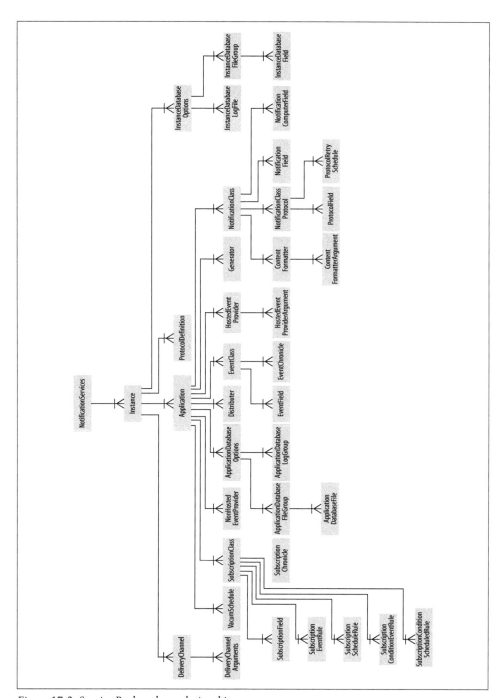

Figure 17-2. Service Broker class relationships

```
class Program
{
    static void Main(string[] args)
    {
        Server server = new Server("localhost");
        Database db = server.Databases["AdventureWorks"];
        ServiceBroker sb = db.ServiceBroker;

        Console.WriteLine("MESSAGE TYPES:");
        foreach (MessageType mt in sb.MessageTypes)
            Console.WriteLine("    " + mt.Name);

        Console.WriteLine(Environment.NewLine + "CONTRACTS:");
        foreach (ServiceContract sc in sb.ServiceContracts)
            Console.WriteLine(sc.Name);

        Console.WriteLine(Environment.NewLine + "QUEUES:");
        foreach (ServiceQueue sq in sb.Queues)
            Console.WriteLine("    " + sq.Name);

        Console.WriteLine(Environment.NewLine + "SERVICES:");
        foreach (BrokerService bs in sb.Services)
            Console.WriteLine("    " + bs.Name);

        Console.WriteLine(Environment.NewLine + "ROUTES:");
        foreach (ServiceRoute sr in sb.Routes)
            Console.WriteLine("    " + sr.Name);

        Console.WriteLine(Environment.NewLine + "REMOTE SERVICE BINDINGS:");
        foreach (RemoteServiceBinding rsb in sb.RemoteServiceBindings)
            Console.WriteLine("    " + rsb.Name);

        Console.WriteLine(Environment.NewLine + "Press any key to continue.");
        Console.ReadKey();
    }
}
```

Results are shown in Figure 17-3.

The ServiceBroker class exposes a set of collections of the following Service Broker objects: message types, contracts, queues, services, routes, and remote service bindings. A discussion of the classes used to programmatically manage these objects follows.

The classes used to manage Server Broker message types are described in Table 17-1.

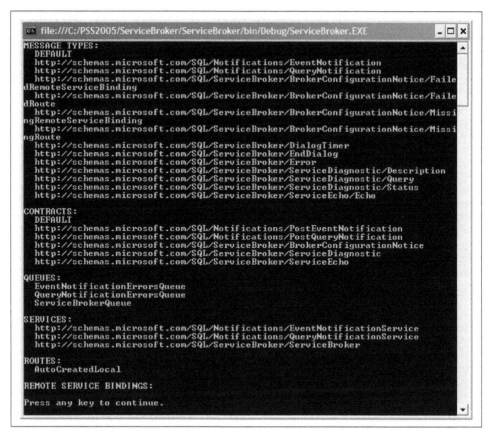

Figure 17-3. Results for enumerating Service Broker objects example

Table 17-1. SMO classes for administering Service Broker message types

Class	Description
MessageType	Represents a message type.
MessageTypeCollection	Represents a collection of message types as MessageType objects. The MessageTypes property of the ServiceBroker class returns the message types defined on a Service Broker instance.
MessageTypeEvents	Represents the settings required for message type event notification. The BrokerServiceEvents object is obtained using the Events property of the MessageType object and cannot be created as a standalone object.
	The SubscribeToEvents( ) method of the BrokerServiceEvents class specifies the events to receive as an ObjectEventSet object.
MessageTypeMapping	Represents a relationship between a message type and a service contract.
MessageTypeMappingCollection	Represents a collection of message type mappings as MessageTypeMapping objects. The MessageTypeMappings property of the ServiceContract class returns the message types defined on a service contract.

The classes used to manage Server Broker service contracts programmatically are described in Table 17-2.

Table 17-2. SMO classes for administering Service Broker service contracts

Class	Description
ServiceContract	Represents a contract.
ServiceContractCollection	Represents a collection of contracts as ServiceContract objects. The ServiceContracts property of the ServiceBroker class returns the contracts defined on a Service Broker instance.
ServiceContractEvents	Represents the settings required for service contract event notification. The ServiceContractEvents object is obtained using the Events property of the ServiceContract object and cannot be created as a standalone object. The SubscribeToEvents( ) method of the ServiceContractEvents class specifies the events to receive as an ObjectEventSet object.
ServiceContractMapping	Represents a collection of contracts mapped to the Service Broker service.
ServiceContractMappingCollection	Represents a collection of service contract mappings as ServiceContractMapping objects. The ServiceContractMappings property of the BrokerService class returns the contracts mapped to the Service Broker instance.

The classes used to manage Server Broker message queues programmatically are described in Table 17-3.

Table 17-3. SMO classes for administering Service Broker message queues

Class	Description
ServiceQueue	Represents a message queue.
ServiceQueueCollection	Represents a collection of queues as ServiceQueue objects. The Queues property of the ServiceBroker class returns the queues defined on a Service Broker instance.
ServiceQueueEvents	Represents the settings required for service queue event notification. The ServiceQueueEvents object is obtained using the Events property of the ServiceQueue object and cannot be created as a standalone object. The SubscribeToEvents( ) method of the ServiceQueueEvents class specifies the events to receive as a ServiceEventSet object.
ServiceQueueEvent	Represents a service queue event that can be included in a ServiceQueueEventSet object.
ServiceQueueEventSet	Represents a set of service queue events as ServiceQueueEvent objects.

The classes used to programmatically manage Server Broker services are described in Table 17-4.

Table 17-4. SMO classes for managing Service Broker services

Class	Description
BrokerService	Represents a Service Broker service.
BrokerServiceCollection	Represents a collection of Service Broker services as BrokerService objects. The Services property of the ServiceBroker class returns the Service Broker services defined on a Service Broker implementation.
BrokerServiceEvents	Represents the settings required for Service Broker service event notification. The BrokerServiceEvents object is obtained using the Events property of the BrokerService object and cannot be created as a standalone object. The SubscribeToEvents( ) method of the BrokerServiceEvents class specifies the events to receive as an ObjectEventSet object.

The SMO classes used to manage Server Broker routes programmatically are described in Table 17-5.

Table 17-5. SMO classes for administering Service Broker routes

Class	Description
ServiceRoute	Represents a Service Broker route.
ServiceRouteCollection	Represents a collection of routes as ServiceRoute objects. The Routes property of the ServiceBroker class returns the routes defined on a Service Broker instance.
ServiceRouteEvents	Represents the settings required for service route event notification. The ServiceRouteEvents object is obtained using the Events property of the ServiceRoute object and cannot be created as a standalone object. The SubscribeToEvents( ) method of the ServiceRouteEvents class specifies the events to receive as an ObjectEventSet object.

The SMO classes used to manage Server Broker remote service bindings programmatically are described in Table 17-6.

Table 17-6. SMO classes for administering Service Broker remote service bindings

Class	Description
RemoteServiceBinding	Represents the settings that Service Broker uses for security and authentication when communicating with a remote service.
RemoteServiceBindingCollection	Represents a collection of remote service bindings as RemoteServiceBinding objects. The RemoteServiceBindings property of the ServiceBroker class returns the remote service bindings defined on a Service Broker instance.
RemoteServiceBindingEvents	Represents the settings required for remote service binding event notification. The RemoteServiceBindingEvents object is obtained using the Events property of the RemoteServiceBinding object and cannot be created as a standalone object. The SubscribeToEvents( ) method of the RemoteService-BindingEvents class specifies the events to receive as an ObjectEventSet object.

Implementing a Service Broker Service

This example sets up Service Broker objects used in the examples later in this chapter. The following objects are created:

- Request and response message types, using the MessageType class.
- A contract that maps the request and response message types to initiator and target roles, using the ServiceContract and MessageTypeMapping classes.
- Initiator and target queues, using the ServiceQueue class.
- Request and response services, using the BrokerService class. These services are associated with the appropriate contract by using the ServiceContractMapping class.

The source code follows:

```
using System;

using Microsoft.SqlServer.Management.Smo;
using Microsoft.SqlServer.Management.Common;
using Microsoft.SqlServer.Management.Smo.Broker;

class Program
{
    static void Main(string[] args)
    {
        Server server = new Server("localhost");
        Database db = server.Databases["ProgrammingSqlServer2005"];
        ServiceBroker sb = db.ServiceBroker;

        // create the request and response message types
        MessageType requestMessage = new MessageType(sb, "HelloWorldRequest");
        requestMessage.MessageTypeValidation = MessageTypeValidation.Xml;
        requestMessage.Create();
        MessageType responseMessage = new MessageType(sb, "HelloWorldResponse");
        responseMessage.MessageTypeValidation = MessageTypeValidation.Xml;
        responseMessage.Create();

        // create the service contract
        ServiceContract contract = new ServiceContract(sb, "HelloWorldContract");
        contract.MessageTypeMappings.Add(new MessageTypeMapping(
            contract, "HelloWorldRequest", MessageSource.Initiator));
        contract.MessageTypeMappings.Add(new MessageTypeMapping(
            contract, "HelloWorldResponse", MessageSource.Target));
        contract.Create();

        // create the queues
        ServiceQueue initiatorQueue = new ServiceQueue(sb, "HelloWorldInitiator");
        initiatorQueue.Create();
        ServiceQueue targetQueue = new ServiceQueue(sb, "HelloWorldTarget");
        targetQueue.Create();
```

```
        // create the services
        BrokerService requestService =
            new BrokerService(sb, "HelloWorldRequestService");
        requestService.QueueName = "HelloWorldTarget";
        requestService.ServiceContractMappings.Add(
            new ServiceContractMapping(requestService, "HelloWorldContract"));
        requestService.Create();

        BrokerService responseService =
            new BrokerService(sb, "HelloWorldResponseService");
        responseService.QueueName = "HelloWorldInitiator";
        responseService.ServiceContractMappings.Add(
            new ServiceContractMapping(responseService, "HelloWorldContract"));
        responseService.Create();

        Console.WriteLine("Press any key to continue.");
        Console.ReadKey();
    }
}
```

You can view the newly created objects in Object Explorer in SQL Server Management Studio by opening the Databases → ProgrammingSqlServer2005 → Service Broker node.

This example does not specify all of the possible properties when creating the objects. For example, the message owner is not specified and defaults to the Windows account. The rest of the discussion for this example describes a generic approach for creating the different objects.

Creating a message type defines the name of the message, the owner of the message type as a database user or role, and how the message is validated as a value from the MessageTypeValidation enumeration, as described in Table 17-7.

Table 17-7. MessageTypeValidation enumeration

Value	Description
Empty	Message body must be null.
None	Validation is not performed.
Xml	Message body must contain well-formed XML.
XmlSchemaCollection	Message body must contain XML that validates against the XML schema collection specified for the message type by the ValidationXmlSchemaCollection property.

Creating a contract defines the name of the contract, the owner of the contract as a database user or role, message types included in the contract, and which endpoints (MessageSource.Initiator, MessageSource.InitiatorAndTarget, or MessageSource.Target) can send each message type.

Creating a queue defines the name of the queue, the status (indicating whether the queue is available for use), the retention (specifying whether messages are removed from the queue once retrieved), and, optionally, a stored procedure that runs when a message arrives on the queue, to process the message automatically.

Creating a service defines the name of the service, the owner of the service as a database user or role, the queue that receives messages for the service, and the name of one or more contracts for which the service is a target. The service can initiate conversations only if no contracts are specified.

Creating a route defines the name of the route, the owner of the route as a database user or role, the name of the remote service that the route points to, the database that hosts the target service, the length of time that SQL Server retains the route in the routing table, and network addresses for the route.

Additionally, the other object you can create is a remote service binding. Creating a remote service binding defines the name of the remote service binding, the owner of the binding as a database user or role, the database principal that owns the certificate associated with the remote service, and the remote service to bind to the user.

The preceding example corresponds to the following T-SQL DML batch:

```
USE [ProgrammingSqlServer2005]
GO

CREATE MESSAGE TYPE [HelloWorldRequest] VALIDATION = WELL_FORMED_XML
CREATE MESSAGE TYPE [HelloWorldResponse] VALIDATION = WELL_FORMED_XML

CREATE CONTRACT [HelloWorldContract]
(
    [HelloWorldRequest] SENT BY INITIATOR,
    [HelloWorldResponse] SENT BY TARGET
)

CREATE QUEUE [HelloWorldInitiator]
CREATE QUEUE [HelloWorldTarget]

CREATE SERVICE [HelloWorldRequestService] ON QUEUE [HelloWorldTarget]
(
    [HelloWorldContract]
)

CREATE SERVICE [HelloWorldResponseService] ON QUEUE [HelloWorldInitiator]
(
    [HelloWorldContract]
)
```

The following T-SQL batch starts a conversation from the HelloWorldRequestService service to the HelloWorldResponseService service by using the HelloWorldContract and sends a message of type HelloWorldRequest by using the conversation:

```
BEGIN TRANSACTION
DECLARE @conversationHandle uniqueidentifier
```

```
BEGIN DIALOG @conversationHandle
   FROM SERVICE [HelloWorldRequestService]
   TO SERVICE 'HelloWorldResponseService'
   ON CONTRACT [HelloWorldContract]
   WITH ENCRYPTION = OFF;

SEND ON CONVERSATION @conversationHandle
   MESSAGE TYPE [HelloWorldRequest]
   (
      CAST(N'<Request>Hello world request</Request>' AS XML)
   )
COMMIT
```

The BEGIN DIALOG T-SQL statement starts a conversation between two services. The new converstation is assigned a system-generated conversation handle with a data type of uniqueidentifier. All messages are part of a conversation. You can specify a conversation group when starting a conversation. If one is not specified, SQL Server automatically creates a new conversation group for the new conversation.

The SEND T-SQL statement sends a message to a service using an existing conversation—the conversation that the message belongs to is identified by a conversation handle such as the one returned by the BEGIN DIALOG statement in the preceding example. If the SEND statement is not the first statement in a batch, you must terminate the preceding T-SQL statement with a semicolon (;).

The following T-SQL batch retrieves the first message from the HelloWorldInitiator queue. If the message type name is HelloWorldRequest, a response is sent (again using a SEND T-SQL statement) as part of the conversation initiated in the preceding example and the conversation is ended.

```
DECLARE @conversationHandle uniqueidentifier
DECLARE @message_body nvarchar(MAX)
DECLARE @message_type_name sysname;

BEGIN TRANSACTION;

RECEIVE TOP(1)
    @message_type_name = message_type_name,
    @conversationHandle = conversation_handle,
    @message_body = message_body
FROM [HelloWorldInitiator]

IF @message_type_name = 'HelloWorldRequest'
BEGIN
    SEND ON CONVERSATION @conversationHandle
        MESSAGE TYPE [HelloWorldResponse]
        (
            CAST(N'<Response>Hello world response</Response>' AS XML)
        );
    END CONVERSATION @conversationHandle;
END
COMMIT
```

The RECEIVE T-SQL statement retrieves one or more messages from a message queue. A RECEIVE statement can specify a conversation handle or conversation group ID to retrieve specific messages. The RECEIVE statement has an optional WAITFOR clause that specifies the length of time to wait for a message. The RECEIVE statement removes the message from the queue unless the RETENTION property of the queue is set to on. If the RECEIVE statement is not the first statement in a batch, you must terminate the preceding statement with a semicolon.

The END CONVERSATION T-SQL statement ends one side of an existing conversation. A conversation ends when initiator and target both end the conversation or when the conversation expires, specified by the LIFETIME argument in the BEGIN DIALOG T-SQL statement. When a conversation ends, Service Broker removes all messages for the conversation from the service queue.

You can use the BEGIN CONVERSATION TIMER T-SQL statement to start a timer. When the timer expires, a message of the type http://schemas.Microsoft.com/SQL/ServiceBroker/Messages/DialogTimer is put on the local queue for the conversation. Each side of the conversation has its own conversation timer.

You can also use the GET TRANSMISSION STATUS T-SQL statement to return a description of the last transmission error for one side of a conversation. An empty string is returned if the last transmission succeeded.

You can see the message by querying the HelloWorldTarget queue, using a SELECT T-SQL statement:

```
SELECT * FROM HelloWorldTarget
```

Service Broker manages the contents of the queue. So, although you can issue SELECT statements to query the contents of the queue, the queue cannot be the target of an INSERT, UPDATE, or DELETE statement.

This T-SQL batch retrieves a response message from the HelloWorldTarget queue, outputs the response, and ends the conversation:

```
DECLARE @conversationHandle uniqueidentifier
DECLARE @message_body nvarchar(MAX)
DECLARE @message_type_name sysname;

BEGIN TRANSACTION;

RECEIVE TOP(1)
    @message_type_name = message_type_name,
    @conversationHandle = conversation_handle,
    @message_body = message_body
FROM [HelloWorldTarget]

IF @message_type_name = 'HelloWorldResponse'
BEGIN
    PRINT @message_type_name;
    PRINT @conversationHandle;
```

```
    PRINT @message_body;

    END CONVERSATION @conversationHandle;
END
COMMIT
```

Results are shown in Figure 17-4.

Figure 17-4. Results for retrieve response example

CHAPTER 18
Notification Services

Notification Services is a programming framework based on XML and T-SQL. It is used to create applications that generate and send messages to subscribers. Notifications can be sent according to a schedule, or in response to conditions or events. Notifications can be sent using built-in or custom delivery protocols. They can be delivered to messaging systems such as email or cell phones.

Notification Services applications have a variety of uses, including:

Customer applications
> Notify customers about statuses, service changes, or products that might meet a customer's criteria

Business applications
> Monitor line-of-business data, company operations, and business intelligence data

Employee applications
> Connect employees as part of workflow or keep them updated with timely information

Architecture

Notification Services applications are based on a subscriber/subscription model. Here are some key terms used to describe the entities participating in a Notification Services application:

Subscriber
> A user or application that requests and receives the notification

Subscription
> A request for information, delivery mechanism, and destination for requested notifications

Event

A piece of information or an occurrence in which the subscriber is interested

Notification

A message containing the information requested by the subscriber in the subscription

Figure 18-1 shows the relationship between these entities.

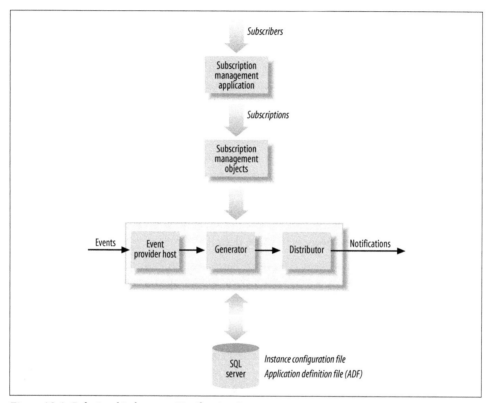

Figure 18-1. Relationship between Notification Services entities

The Notification Services platform stores system data, and it generates and distributes notifications. It comprises the following:

- Notification Services engine, which contains the provider host, generator, and distributor
- Notification Services database

A Notification Services application is hosted in a Notification Services instance. The application generates and sends messages to the application's subscribers—users or other applications. The subscriber creates subscriptions to the application. The application monitors and collects events. Notification Services matches subscriptions to events and generates, formats, and sends a notification to the subscriber when an event and subscription match. The *application database* stores event, subscription, and notification data and metadata about the Notification Services application. The applications in a Notification Services instance can share subscribers and delivery mechanisms, which allows them to be administered as a group.

A subscription management application manages subscriber and subscription information in Notification Services. Subscription management is the process of managing the subscribers, the information they are interested in (subscriptions), and where to send notifications (device information). Subscription management is handled by a Windows or web application that uses subscription management objects supplied in the Notification Services Management Objects (NMO) classes—a collection of classes used to create and administer Notification Services instances and applications programmatically. The subscription management classes are used to write and read subscriber, subscription, and subscriber device data from Notification Services.

To support both Notification Services applications and subscription management applications, Notification Services provides an API that stores and retrieves subscriber and subscription information, collects and stores event data, matches subscriptions and events to generate notifications, formats the event data into messages according to delivery protocol, and sends messages to subscribers. The remainder of this section describes this process in more detail.

An *event provider* collects event data from various sources and submits this data to a Notification Services application, which uses one or more event providers. Notification Services ships with three standard event providers:

File System Watcher event provider
> Triggered when an XML file is added to a watched directory. The `ClassName` for this event provider is `FileSystemWatcherProvider`.

SQL Server event provider
> Uses a T-SQL query to get information from a database and create Notification Services events based on the result. The `ClassName` for this event provider is `SQLProvider`.

Analysis Services event provider
> Uses a static or dynamic multidimensional expression (MDX) query to get information from an Analysis Services cube, and creates Notification Services events based on the results. SQL Services Analysis Services (SSAS) and MDX queries are discussed in Chapter 18. The `ClassName` for this provider is `AnalysisServicesProvider`.

You can develop a custom event provider if the standard event providers do not meet your needs.

An event provider is either *hosted* or *nonhosted*. A hosted event provider runs within Notification Services, either continuously or according to a schedule. Nonhosted event providers run as external applications and submit events on their own schedule.

An *event class* represents one type of event that can be submitted to a Notification Services application and used to generate notifications. An event class definition includes field names and data types for the event and supporting data. The event class is used to implement the underlying SQL Server database objects for storing the event data and supporting data.

An *event chronicle* is a supplemental storage tables for event data. An event chronicle is generally used to store most-recent event data to support scheduled subscriptions. This data is updated as it changes and used whenever a scheduled subscription is evaluated. An *event chronicle rule* contains the T-SQL queries that maintain the event chronicle data in the underlying SQL Server tables.

A *subscription class* represents one type of subscription to a Notification Services application. The subscription class definition includes both fields for storing subscription data and a *notification generation rule* that matches events to subscription data. The subscription class is used by SQL Server to implement the underlying database objects for storing the subscription data and supporting data.

Once events are collected by the event provider, the *generator* processes subscriptions against those events by applying notification generation rules. The generator settings include which computer runs the generator and how many threads the generator can use when it processes application rules.

A *notification class* represents one type of notification produced by a Notification Services application. The notification class definition includes fields and data types defining the data that is sent to subscribers, information about the content formatter, and information about how the delivery protocols are used to deliver notifications. The notification class is used to implement the underlying SQL Server database objects for storing the notification data and supporting data.

A *distributor* is run by the Notification Services engine and governs notification formatting and delivery. Every *distributor quantum*—a configurable interval—the distributor looks for a *work item*—a group of notifications—to process. If the distributor finds a work item, it calls the content formatter to transform the notification data and send the formatted notifications to the subscriber using the specified delivery protocol.

The *content formatter* transforms raw notification data into readable messages in each combination of subscriber locale and device. A content formatter is required for each combination of locale and device. The formatted message can contain raw notification data, dynamic formatted data that is calculated at formatting time, and static text specified by the content formatter.

A *delivery channel* represents a delivery endpoint. Formatted notifications are sent to one or more delivery channels. These in turn package the notifications into delivery protocol packets and send them to the services that deliver the notification messages to a subscriber. Notification Services includes the following standard *delivery protocols*:

Simple Mail Transfer Protocol (SMTP)
    Creates and routes notification messages for delivery by an SMTP service.

File protocol
    Creates and routes notifications to a text file; intended for application testing.

You can develop a custom delivery protocol if the standard ones do not meet your requirements.

In addition to standard message-by-message formatting and delivery, Notification Services offers two options: digest delivery, which groups multiple notification messages to a subscriber into a single message, and multicast delivery, which sends a single notification to multiple subscribers.

Creating a Notification Services Application

You can create and configure Notification Services instances and applications by using XML configuration files and SQL Server 2005 Management Studio, or programmatically by using NMO. An application created and configured using XML configuration files can be managed programmatically using NMO. The next section, "Programming Notification Services," discusses programming using NMO.

You need to perform the following tasks to create and configure a Notification Services application using XML configuration files:

1. Create and configure the Notification Services instance. You can do this in one of two ways:
    - Create an instance configuration file (ICF) for the Notification Services instance. An ICF is an XML file that describes a Notification Services instance. The ICF names the instance and contains metadata about the instance, the SQL Server instance that hosts the instance database, delivery protocols, delivery channels, and encryption. The configuration file also lists applications hosted in the instance.
    - Use NMO to programmatically configure the Notification Services instance.

2. Create and configure the Notification Services application. This includes the structure of events, subscriptions, and notifications; configuration information for the distributor and generator; and application execution settings. You can create and configure an application in one of two ways:

- Create an application definition file (ADF) for the Notification Services application. An ADF is an XML file that contains metadata defining a Notification Services application. An ADF is required for each application hosted in the Notification Services instance.

- Use NMO to configure the Notification Services instance programmatically.

3. Create a subscription management application that lets users sign up and manage their subscriptions and target devices.

4. Create a subscription management application using NMO subscription management classes.

5. Create custom event providers, content formatters, and delivery protocols as required.

6. Deploy the Notification Services application.

For more information about creating and using ICF and ADF files and the schemas for each file type, see Microsoft SQL Server 2005 Books Online.

Programming Notification Services

You can build a Notification Services solution by configuring the Notification Services instance in the IDF file and defining an ADF for the application, as described in the preceding section. Alternatively, you can use NMO classes to configure the instance and define the instance. Programming with NMO classes is the focus of this section.

NMO contains classes that are used to programmatically create and administer Notification Services instances and applications. Figure 18-2 shows the relationship between NMO classes.

The NMO namespace `Microsoft.SqlServer.Management.Nmo` contains classes used to develop Notification Services instances and applications. The `Microsoft.SqlServer.NotificationServices` namespace contains classes and interfaces for developing custom event providers, content formatters, and delivery protocols. It also contains the subscription management interfaces.

The remainder of this chapter describes the NMO classes and provides examples that show how to use them. You need a reference to the following assemblies to compile and run the examples:

- Microsoft.SqlServer.ConnectionInfo
- Microsoft.SqlServer.NotificationServices
- Microsoft.SqlServer.Smo

`NotificationServices` is the top-level class in the NMO class hierarchy and represents a Notification Services server.

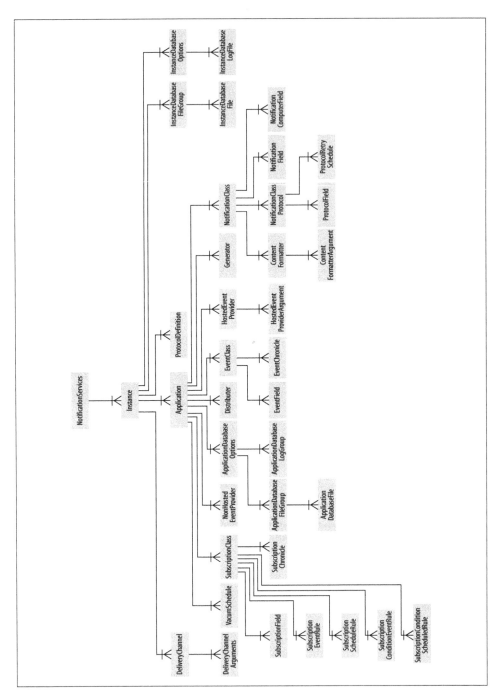

Figure 18-2. NMO class hierarchy

Creating a Notification Services Application and Service

This section creates a complete Notification Services application that creates file and email notifications based on changes in a stock price. For the purpose of this example, the stock price information is limited to a stock ticker symbol and price. Two subscribers are created—one that is notified by entries in a text file and one that is notified using email. Each of the two users monitors a single stock—ticker symbols ABC and DEF.

This section shows the application that creates the StockWatch Notification Services application and adds two subscribers and a subscription for each. Subsequent sections discuss the different parts of the application in detail.

Follow these steps to create the StockWatch Notification Services application with two subscribers and a subscription for each, start the service, and generate notifications:

1. Create a Visual Studio 2005 C# console application in the *C:\PSS2005* directory. Name the project NotificationServices.

2. Add the following references to the project:
   - Microsoft.SqlServer.ConnectionInfo
   - Microsoft.SqlServer.NotificationServices
   - Microsoft.SqlServer.Smo

3. Replace the code in *Program.cs* with the code in Example 18-1. This code is explained in detail throughout the rest of this chapter.

Example 18-1. Notification Services example

```
using System;

using Microsoft.SqlServer.Management.Smo;
using Microsoft.SqlServer.Management.Nmo;
using ns = Microsoft.SqlServer.NotificationServices;

class Program
{
    private static Instance nsi;
    private static Application a;

    private const string baseDirectoryPath = @"C:\PSS2005\NotificationServices";
    private const string nsServer = "NSServerName";
    private const string serviceUserName = "NSUSerName";
    private const string servicePassword = "NSPassword";

    static void Main(string[] args)
    {
        Server server = new Server("(local)");

        // create a new instance
```

Example 18-1. Notification Services example (continued)

```
        NotificationServices ns = server.NotificationServices;
        nsi = new Instance(ns, "StockWatch");

        CreateDeliveryChannel();

        // create a new application in the StockWatch instance
        a = new Application(nsi, "StockWatchApp");
        a.BaseDirectoryPath = baseDirectoryPath;

        CreateEventClass();
        CreateSubscriptionClass();
        CreateNotificationClass();
        CreateHostedEventProvider();
        CreateGenerator();
        CreateDistributor();
        CreateVacuumSchedule();

        a.QuantumDuration = new TimeSpan(0, 0, 15);
        a.PerformanceQueryInterval = new TimeSpan(0, 0, 5);
        a.SubscriptionQuantumLimit = 1;
        a.ChronicleQuantumLimit = 1;
        a.VacuumRetentionAge = new TimeSpan(0, 0, 1);

        nsi.Applications.Add(a);

        Console.WriteLine("Added application.");

        nsi.Create();
        nsi.RegisterLocal(serviceUserName, servicePassword);
        nsi.Enable();

        Console.WriteLine("Application enabled." + Environment.NewLine);

        CreateSubscriber();
        CreateSubscription();

        Console.WriteLine(Environment.NewLine + "Press any key to continue.");
        Console.ReadKey();
    }

    private static void CreateDeliveryChannel()
    {
        DeliveryChannelArgument dca;
        // add file delivery channel
        DeliveryChannel dcFile =
            new DeliveryChannel(nsi, "StockWatchFileDeliveryChannel");
        dcFile.ProtocolName = "File";
        dca = new DeliveryChannelArgument(dcFile, "FileName");
        dca.Value = baseDirectoryPath + @"\Notifications\FileNotifications.txt";
        dcFile.DeliveryChannelArguments.Add(dca);
        nsi.DeliveryChannels.Add(dcFile);
        Console.WriteLine("Added delivery channel: " + dcFile.Name);
```

Example 18-1. Notification Services example (continued)

```
        // add email delivery channel
        DeliveryChannel dcEmail =
            new DeliveryChannel(nsi, "StockWatchEmailDeliveryChannel");
        dcEmail.ProtocolName = "SMTP";
        nsi.DeliveryChannels.Add(dcEmail);
        Console.WriteLine("Added delivery channel: " + dcEmail.Name);
    }

    private static void CreateEventClass()
    {
        EventClass ec = new EventClass(a, "StockWatchEvents");

        EventField ef;
        ef = new EventField(ec, "Symbol");
        ef.Type = "nvarchar(6)";
        ec.EventFields.Add(ef);
        ef = new EventField(ec, "Price");
        ef.Type = "float";
        ec.EventFields.Add(ef);

        a.EventClasses.Add(ec);

        Console.WriteLine("Added event class: " + ec.Name);
    }

    private static void CreateSubscriptionClass()
    {
        SubscriptionClass sc = new SubscriptionClass(a, "StockWatchSubscriptions");

        SubscriptionField sf;
        sf = new SubscriptionField(sc, "DeviceName");
        sf.Type = "nvarchar(255)";
        sc.SubscriptionFields.Add(sf);
        sf = new SubscriptionField(sc, "SubscriberLocale");
        sf.Type = "nvarchar(10)";
        sc.SubscriptionFields.Add(sf);
        sf = new SubscriptionField(sc, "Symbol");
        sf.Type = "nvarchar(6)";
        sc.SubscriptionFields.Add(sf);
        sf = new SubscriptionField(sc, "Price");
        sf.Type = "float";
        sc.SubscriptionFields.Add(sf);

        SubscriptionEventRule ser =
            new SubscriptionEventRule(sc, "StockWatchSubscriptionsEventRule");
        ser.Action = @"INSERT INTO StockWatchNotifications (" +
            "SubscriberId, DeviceName, SubscriberLocale, Symbol, Price) " +
            "SELECT s.SubscriberId, s.DeviceName, s.SubscriberLocale, " +
            "e.Symbol, e.Price " +
            "FROM StockWatchEvents e, StockWatchSubscriptions s " +
            "WHERE e.Symbol = s.Symbol";
```

Example 18-1. Notification Services example (continued)

```
        ser.EventClassName = "StockWatchEvents";

        sc.SubscriptionEventRules.Add(ser);

        a.SubscriptionClasses.Add(sc);

        Console.WriteLine("Added subscription class: " + sc.Name);
    }

    private static void CreateNotificationClass()
    {
        NotificationClass nc = new NotificationClass(a, "StockWatchNotifications");

        NotificationField nf;
        nf = new NotificationField(nc, "Symbol");
        nf.Type = "nvarchar(6)";
        nc.NotificationFields.Add(nf);
        nf = new NotificationField(nc, "Price");
        nf.Type = "float";
        nc.NotificationFields.Add(nf);

        ContentFormatter cf = new ContentFormatter(nc, "XsltFormatter");

        ContentFormatterArgument cfa;
        cfa = new ContentFormatterArgument(cf, "XsltBaseDirectoryPath");
        cfa.Value = a.BaseDirectoryPath + @"\AppDefinition";
        cf.ContentFormatterArguments.Add(cfa);
        cfa = new ContentFormatterArgument(cf, "XsltFileName");
        cfa.Value = "StockWatch.xslt";
        cf.ContentFormatterArguments.Add(cfa);

        nc.ContentFormatter = cf;
        nc.DigestDelivery = true;

        ProtocolField pf;

        // add file notification class protocol
        NotificationClassProtocol ncpFile =
            new NotificationClassProtocol(nc, "File");

        pf = new ProtocolField(ncpFile, "Symbol");
        pf.FieldReference = "Symbol";
        ncpFile.ProtocolFields.Add(pf);
        pf = new ProtocolField(ncpFile, "Price");
        pf.FieldReference = "Price";
        ncpFile.ProtocolFields.Add(pf);

        nc.NotificationClassProtocols.Add(ncpFile);

        // add email notification class protocol
        NotificationClassProtocol ncpEmail =
            new NotificationClassProtocol(nc, "SMTP");
```

Example 18-1. Notification Services example (continued)

```
        pf = new ProtocolField(ncpEmail, "Subject");
        pf.SqlExpression = "'Stock watch: ' + CONVERT(nvarchar(30), GETDATE( ))";
        ncpEmail.ProtocolFields.Add(pf);
        pf = new ProtocolField(ncpEmail, "BodyFormat");
        pf.SqlExpression = "'html'";
        ncpEmail.ProtocolFields.Add(pf);
        pf = new ProtocolField(ncpEmail, "From");
        pf.SqlExpression = "'notification@StockWatchService.com'";
        ncpEmail.ProtocolFields.Add(pf);
        pf = new ProtocolField(ncpEmail, "Priority");
        pf.SqlExpression = "'Normal'";
        ncpEmail.ProtocolFields.Add(pf);
        pf = new ProtocolField(ncpEmail, "To");
        pf.SqlExpression = "DeviceAddress";
        ncpEmail.ProtocolFields.Add(pf);

        nc.NotificationClassProtocols.Add(ncpEmail);

        nc.ExpirationAge = new TimeSpan(1, 0, 0);

        a.NotificationClasses.Add(nc);

        Console.WriteLine("Added notification class: " + nc.Name);
    }

    private static void CreateHostedEventProvider( )
    {
        HostedEventProvider hep = new HostedEventProvider(a, "StockWatchHEP");
        hep.ClassName = "FileSystemWatcherProvider";
        hep.SystemName = nsServer;

        HostedEventProviderArgument hepa;
        hepa = new HostedEventProviderArgument(hep, "WatchDirectory");
        hepa.Value = baseDirectoryPath + @"\Events";
        hep.HostedEventProviderArguments.Add(hepa);
        hepa = new HostedEventProviderArgument(hep, "SchemaFile");
        hepa.Value = baseDirectoryPath + @"\AppDefinition\EventsSchema.xsd";
        hep.HostedEventProviderArguments.Add(hepa);
        hepa = new HostedEventProviderArgument(hep, "EventClassName");
        hepa.Value = "StockWatchEvents";
        hep.HostedEventProviderArguments.Add(hepa);

        a.HostedEventProviders.Add(hep);
    }

    private static void CreateGenerator( )
    {
        // create a new generator for the application
        Generator g = new Generator(a, "StockWatchGenerator");
        g.SystemName = nsServer;
        a.Generator = g;
```

Example 18-1. Notification Services example (continued)

```
        Console.WriteLine("Created generator: " + g.Name);
    }

    private static void CreateDistributor()
    {
        Distributor d = new Distributor(a, "StockWatchDistributor");
        d.SystemName = nsServer;
        d.QuantumDuration = new TimeSpan(0, 0, 15);
        a.Distributors.Add(d);

        Console.WriteLine("Added distributor: " + d.Name);
    }

    private static void CreateVacuumSchedule()
    {
        VacuumSchedule vs = new VacuumSchedule(a, "StockWatchVacuumSchedule");
        vs.StartTime = new TimeSpan(0, 0, 0);
        a.VacuumSchedules.Add(vs);

        Console.WriteLine("Added vacuum schedule: " + vs.Name);
    }

    private static void CreateSubscriber()
    {
        ns.NSInstance swnsi = new ns.NSInstance("StockWatch");

        ns.Subscriber s;
        ns.SubscriberDevice sd;

        // create a subscriber
        s = new ns.Subscriber(swnsi);
        s.SubscriberId = @"KristinHamilton";
        s.Add();
        Console.WriteLine("Added subscriber: " + s.SubscriberId);

        // create a file subscriber device
        sd = new ns.SubscriberDevice();
        sd.Initialize(swnsi);
        sd.DeviceName = "StockWatchSubscriberDevice";
        sd.SubscriberId = "KristinHamilton";
        sd.DeviceTypeName = "File";
        sd.DeviceAddress = "KristinH@StockWatch.ns";
        sd.DeliveryChannelName = "StockWatchFileDeliveryChannel";
        sd.Add();
        Console.WriteLine("Added subscriber file device.");

        // create a subscriber
        s = new ns.Subscriber(swnsi);
        s.SubscriberId = @"TonyHamilton";
        s.Add();
        Console.WriteLine("Added subscriber: " + s.SubscriberId);
```

Example 18-1. Notification Services example (continued)

```
        // create an email subscriber device
        sd = new ns.SubscriberDevice( );
        sd.Initialize(swnsi);
        sd.DeviceName = "StockWatchSubscriberDevice";
        sd.SubscriberId = "TonyHamilton";
        sd.DeviceTypeName = "Email";
        sd.DeviceAddress = "TonyH@StockWatchNS.ns";
        sd.DeliveryChannelName = "StockWatchEmailDeliveryChannel";
        sd.Add( );
        Console.WriteLine("Added subscriber email device.");
    }

    private static void CreateSubscription( )
    {
        ns.NSInstance swnsi = new ns.NSInstance("StockWatch");
        ns.NSApplication a = new ns.NSApplication(swnsi, "StockWatchApp");

        ns.Subscription s;

        // add subscriptions
        s = new ns.Subscription( );
        s.Initialize(a, "StockWatchSubscriptions");
        s.SetFieldValue("DeviceName", "StockWatchSubscriberDevice");
        s.SetFieldValue("SubscriberLocale", "en-us");
        s.SubscriberId = "KristinHamilton";
        s.SetFieldValue("Symbol", "ABC");
        s.SetFieldValue("Price", "0.00");
        s.Add( );
        Console.WriteLine("Added subscription: " + s.SubscriberId);

        s = new ns.Subscription( );
        s.Initialize(a, "StockWatchSubscriptions");
        s.SetFieldValue("DeviceName", "StockWatchSubscriberDevice");
        s.SetFieldValue("SubscriberLocale", "en-us");
        s.SubscriberId = "TonyHamilton";
        s.SetFieldValue("Symbol", "DEF");
        s.SetFieldValue("Price", "0.00");
        s.Add( );
        Console.WriteLine("Added subscription: " + s.SubscriberId);
    }
}
```

4. Replace the following string constant values in lines 13 to 15:

   NSServerName
   > The server that runs the Notification Services engine components. Use the
   > name of the local computer for this example.

   NSUserName
   > The account the NS$StockWatch service runs under.

   NSPassword
   > The password for the *NSUserName* account.

5. Compile and execute the code. The results are shown in Figure 18-3.

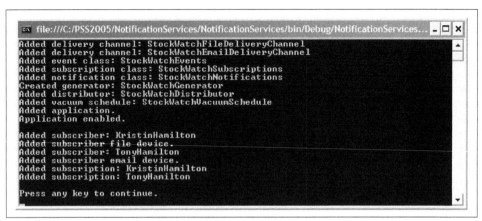

Figure 18-3. Results for Notification Services example

6. Two databases are created when the NMO application is run—StockWatchNSMain and StockWatchStockWatchApp. Ensure that the service login account specified in Step 4 has at least the NSRunService database role membership for both of these databases.

7. Refresh the Notification Services node in Object Explorer in SQL Server Management Studio to view the new Notification Services service, as shown in Figure 18-4.

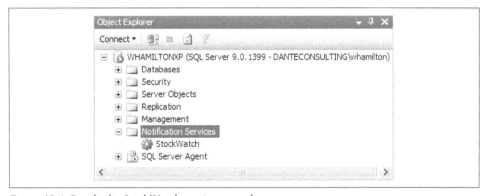

Figure 18-4. Results for StockWatch service example

8. Right-click the StockWatch service and select Start from the context menu to start the service.

9. Right-click the StockWatch service and select Properties from the context menu to display the Instance Properties dialog box, shown in Figure 18-5.

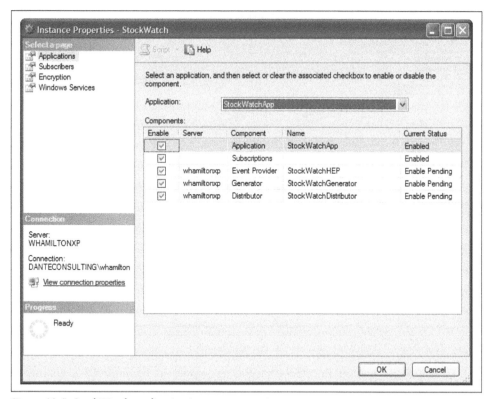

Figure 18-5. StockWatch application instance properties

10. Select the Windows Services page to display the service status, as shown in Figure 18-6. The service should be running.

11. Ensure that the SMTP service—a component of Internet Information Services (IIS)—is installed and started. For more information, see Microsoft SQL Server 2005 Books Online.

12. Create the following three folders in the *C:\PSS2005\NotificationServices* directory:

    AppDefinition
    The folder containing the XSLT transformation file used to format notifications (*StockWatch.xslt* in this example) and the schema for the event data (*EventSchema.xsd* in this example). These two files are discussed in Steps 13 and 14.

    Events
    The folder in which event data is placed as XML files (named *EventData.xml* in this example).

    Notifications
    The folder in which file notifications are created.

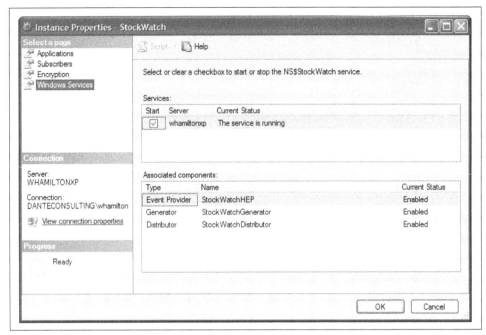

Figure 18-6. StockWatch Windows Services instance properties

13. Create a file named *EventSchema.xsd*, as shown in Example 18-2, in the *C:\ PSS2005\NotificationServices\AppDefinition* folder. This file describes the schema of the event data in the *EventData.xml* file described in Step 15.

Example 18-2. EventSchema.xsd

```
<xsd:schema xmlns:xsd="http://www.w3.org/2001/XMLSchema"
  xmlns:sql="urn:schemas-microsoft-com:mapping-schema">
  <xsd:element name="event" sql:relation="FlightEvents">
    <xsd:complexType>
      <xsd:sequence>
        <xsd:element name="Symbol" type="xsd:string" />
        <xsd:element name="Price" type="xsd:float" />
      </xsd:sequence>
    </xsd:complexType>
  </xsd:element>
</xsd:schema>
```

14. Create a file named *StockWatch.xslt*, as shown in Example 18-3, in the *C:\ PSS2005\NotificationServices\AppDefinition* folder. This file is used to format the notification data for both file and email notifications.

Example 18-3. StockWatch.xslt

```
<?xml version="1.0" encoding="UTF-8" ?>
<xsl:stylesheet version="1.0" xmlns:xsl="http://www.w3.org/1999/XSL/Transform">
```

Example 18-3. StockWatch.xslt (continued)

```
<xsl:template match="notifications">
<html>
    <body>
        StockWatch Price Update<br/><br/>
        <xsl:apply-templates/>
        <br/><br/>
        <i>SQL Server StockWatch Notification Services</i><br/><br/>
    </body>
    </html>
    </xsl:template>

    <xsl:template match="notification">
        The price of <b><xsl:value-of select="Symbol" /></b> is now <b>
        $<xsl:value-of select="Price" /></b>.<br/>
    </xsl:template>
</xsl:stylesheet>
```

15. Create a file named *EventData.xml*, as shown in Example 18-4, in the *C:\ PSS2005\NotificationServices* folder. This XML file contains the event data. In this example, the events for symbols ABC and DEF have subscriptions and generate notifications. The event for symbol GHI has no subscriptions and does not generate a notification.

Example 18-4. EventData.xml

```
<eventData>
    <event>
        <Symbol>ABC</Symbol>
        <Price>3.83</Price>
    </event>
    <event>
        <Symbol>DEF</Symbol>
        <Price>5.75</Price>
    </event>
    <event>
        <Symbol>GHI</Symbol>
        <Price>1.22</Price>
    </event>
</eventData>
```

16. Copy the *EventData.xml* file into the *C:\PSS2005\NotificationServices\Events* folder to submit events. The File System Watcher event provider reads data from the application, submits the data to the application StockWatchApp, and changes the extension of the event datafile to *.done* once the file is processed. If there is an error processing the file, the extension of the datafile is changed to *.err*.

17. After less than a minute, a notification file named *FileNotification.txt* is created in the *C:\PSS2005\NotificationServices\Notifications* folder, as shown in Figure 18-7.

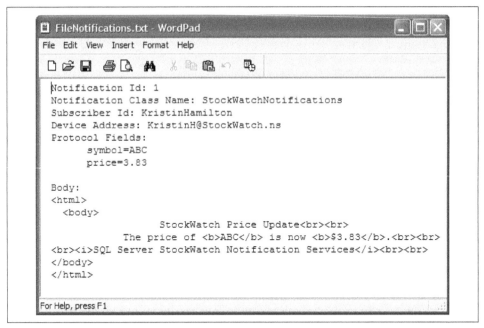

Figure 18-7. FileNotification.txt

The email message shown in Figure 18-8 is also generated. It appears in the *C:\Inetpub\mailroot\Queue* folder briefly as a file with an *.eml* extension and is then moved to the *C:\Inetpub\mailroot\Badmail* folder because the email address is not valid. To deliver the email, change the email address for the user `TonyHamilton` in the `CreateSubscriber( )` method of Example 18-1 to a valid email address by changing the `DeviceAddress` property of the `SubscriberDevice` object for that user.

Notice that both the file and email notifications are formatted using the XSLT transformation *StockWatch.xslt*, discussed in Step 14.

The remainder of this chapter discusses the code that creates the `StockWatch` service, subscribers, and subscriptions.

Creating a Notification Services Instance and Application

The Notification Services instance named `StockWatch` and a Notification Services application named `StockWatchApp` are created in the `Main( )` method of Example 18-1. The code follows—the code that creates the Notification Services instance and application is highlighted:

```
static void Main(string[] args)
{
    Server server = new Server("(local)");
```

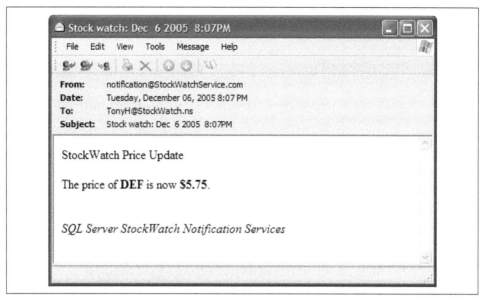

From: notification@StockWatchService.com
Date: Tuesday, December 06, 2005 8:07 PM
To: TonyH@StockWatch.ns
Subject: Stock watch: Dec 6 2005 8:07PM

StockWatch Price Update

The price of **DEF** is now $5.75.

SQL Server StockWatch Notification Services

Figure 18-8. StockWatch notification email

```
// create a new instance
NotificationServices ns = server.NotificationServices;
nsi = new Instance(ns, "StockWatch");

CreateDeliveryChannel();

// create a new application in the StockWatch instance
a = new Application(nsi, "StockWatchApp");
a.BaseDirectoryPath = baseDirectoryPath;

CreateEventClass();
CreateSubscriptionClass();
CreateNotificationClass();
CreateHostedEventProvider();
CreateGenerator();
CreateDistributor();
CreateVacuumSchedule();

a.QuantumDuration = new TimeSpan(0, 0, 15);
a.PerformanceQueryInterval = new TimeSpan(0, 0, 5);
a.SubscriptionQuantumLimit = 1;
a.ChronicleQuantumLimit = 1;
a.VacuumRetentionAge = new TimeSpan(0, 0, 1);

nsi.Applications.Add(a);

Console.WriteLine("Added application.");

nsi.Create();
nsi.RegisterLocal(serviceUserName, servicePassword);
```

```
    nsi.Enable();

    Console.WriteLine("Application enabled." + Environment.NewLine);

    CreateSubscriber();
    CreateSubscription();

    Console.WriteLine(Environment.NewLine + "Press any key to continue.");
    Console.ReadKey();
}
```

The NotificationServices object represents a Notification Services server. The Instances property of the NotificationServices class returns an InstanceCollection object containing a collection of Notification Services instances as Instance objects. At a minimum, you must define a DeliveryChannel object and an Application object to create an Instance object—in this example, this is done by the CreateDeliveryChannel() and Main() methods.

The RegisterLocal() method of the Instance class registers an instance of Notification Services on the local computer. This is the same as registering a Notification Services instance using SQL Server Management Studio by right-clicking the Notification Services instance and selecting Tasks → Register from the context menu. You can also register a Notification Services instance by using the nscontrol register command. Registering an instance creates or updates registry entries for the instance, creates performance counters, and optionally creates a Windows Service to run the instance.

The Enable() method of the Instance class enables all instance and application components, allowing event collection, notification generation, notification distribution, and subscription management. A NotificationServices instance is disabled when you create it.

The NMO classes used to manage Notification Services instances are described in Table 18-1.

Table 18-1. NMO classes for managing Notification Services instances

Class	Description
Instance	Represents a Notification Services instance.
InstanceCollection	Represents a collection of instances as Instance objects. The Instances property of the NotificationServices class returns the Notification Services instances on the server.

The Application object represents a Notification Services application. At a minimum, you must define a Generator object and a Distributor object for an Application object—in this example, this is done by the CreateGenerator() and CreateDistributor() methods.

This example configures the Application object by setting the following properties:

BaseDirectoryPath
> Specifies the base directory path for the ADF

QuantumDuration
> Specifies how frequently the generator tries to process work

PerformanceQueryInterval
> Specifies how frequently the application updates its performance counters

SubscriptionQuantumLimit
> Specifies how far the logical clock can fall behind the real-time clock before skipping subscription rule firings

ChronicleQuantumLimit
> Specifies how far the logical clock can fall behind the real-time clock before skipping event chronicle firings

VacuumRetentionAge
> Specifies the minimum age at which event and notification data is considered obsolete and can be removed

The NMO classes used to manage Notification Services applications are described in Table 18-2.

Table 18-2. NMO classes for managing applications

Class	Description
Application	Represents a Notification Services application.
ApplicationCollection	Represents a collection of Notification Services applications as `Application` objects. The `Applications` property of the `Instance` class returns the Notification Services applications hosted on the Notification Services instance.

Creating a Delivery Channel

A file delivery channel named StockWatchFileDeliveryChannel and an email delivery channel named StockWatchEmailDeliveryChannel are created in the CreateDeliveryChannel( ) method of Example 18-1. The code follows:

```
private static void CreateDeliveryChannel( )
{
    DeliveryChannelArgument dca;
    // add file delivery channel
    DeliveryChannel dcFile =
        new DeliveryChannel(nsi, "StockWatchFileDeliveryChannel");
    dcFile.ProtocolName = "File";
    dca = new DeliveryChannelArgument(dcFile, "FileName");
    dca.Value = baseDirectoryPath + @"\Notifications\FileNotifications.txt";
    dcFile.DeliveryChannelArguments.Add(dca);
    nsi.DeliveryChannels.Add(dcFile);
    Console.WriteLine("Added delivery channel: " + dcFile.Name);

    // add email delivery channel
```

```
DeliveryChannel dcEmail =
    new DeliveryChannel(nsi, "StockWatchEmailDeliveryChannel");
dcEmail.ProtocolName = "SMTP";
nsi.DeliveryChannels.Add(dcEmail);
Console.WriteLine("Added delivery channel: " + dcEmail.Name);
}
```

You have to add at least one delivery channel to a Notification Services instance before creating it. The ProtocolName property of the DeliveryChannel object must be set to SMTP, File, or the name of a custom delivery protocol.

The NMO classes used to manage delivery channels are described in Table 18-3.

Table 18-3. NMO classes for managing delivery channels

Delivery channel	Description
DeliveryChannel	Represents a delivery channel.
DeliveryChannelArgument	Represents a name-value pair specifying delivery channel configuration and authentication information for the delivery service.
DeliveryChannelArgumentCollection	Represents a collection of delivery channel arguments as Delivery-ChannelArgument objects. The DeliveryChannelArguments property of the DeliveryChannel class returns the delivery channel arguments for the delivery channel.
DeliveryChannelCollection	Represents a collection of delivery channels as DeliveryChannel objects. The DeliveryChannels property of the Instance class returns the delivery channels for the Notification Services instance.

Creating an Event Class

An event class named StockWatchEvents is created in the CreateEventClass( ) method of Example 18-1. The code follows:

```
private static void CreateEventClass( )
{
    EventClass ec = new EventClass(a, "StockWatchEvents");

    EventField ef;
    ef = new EventField(ec, "Symbol");
    ef.Type = "nvarchar(6)";
    ec.EventFields.Add(ef);
    ef = new EventField(ec, "Price");
    ef.Type = "float";
    ec.EventFields.Add(ef);

    a.EventClasses.Add(ec);

    Console.WriteLine("Added event class: " + ec.Name);
}
```

An event class represents a type of event used by a Notification Services application. The event class has two fields—Symbol of type nvarchar(6) and Price of type float.

The NMO classes for managing event classes, fields, and chronicles are described in Table 18-4.

Table 18-4. NMO classes for managing events

Class	Description
EventChronicle	Represents an event chronicle.
EventChronicleCollection	Represents a collection of event chronicles as EventChronicle objects. The EventChronicles property of the EventClass class returns the event chronicles for the event class.
EventChronicleRule	Represents an event chronicle maintenance query that the generator runs.
EventClass	Represents an event class.
EventClassCollection	Represents a collection of event classes as EventClass objects. The Event-Classes property of the Application class returns the event classes for the Notification Services application.
EventField	Represents a field in an event class schema.
EventFieldCollection	Represents a collection of event class schema fields as EventField objects. The EventFields property of the EventClass class returns the event fields for the event class.

Creating a Subscription Class and Subscription Event Rule

A subscription class with a single subscription event rule is created in the CreateSubscriptionClassMethod( ) method of Example 18-1. The code follows:

```
private static void CreateSubscriptionClass( )
{
    SubscriptionClass sc = new SubscriptionClass(a, "StockWatchSubscriptions");

    SubscriptionField sf;
    sf = new SubscriptionField(sc, "DeviceName");
    sf.Type = "nvarchar(255)";
    sc.SubscriptionFields.Add(sf);
    sf = new SubscriptionField(sc, "SubscriberLocale");
    sf.Type = "nvarchar(10)";
    sc.SubscriptionFields.Add(sf);
    sf = new SubscriptionField(sc, "Symbol");
    sf.Type = "nvarchar(6)";
    sc.SubscriptionFields.Add(sf);
    sf = new SubscriptionField(sc, "Price");
    sf.Type = "float";
    sc.SubscriptionFields.Add(sf);

    SubscriptionEventRule ser =
        new SubscriptionEventRule(sc, "StockWatchSubscriptionsEventRule");
    ser.Action = @"INSERT INTO StockWatchNotifications (" +
        "SubscriberId, DeviceName, SubscriberLocale, Symbol, Price) " +
        "SELECT s.SubscriberId, s.DeviceName, s.SubscriberLocale, " +
```

```
                    "e.Symbol, e.Price " +
                    "FROM StockWatchEvents e, StockWatchSubscriptions s " +
                    "WHERE e.Symbol = s.Symbol";

                ser.EventClassName = "StockWatchEvents";

                sc.SubscriptionEventRules.Add(ser);

                a.SubscriptionClasses.Add(sc);

                Console.WriteLine("Added subscription class: " + sc.Name);
            }
```

A SubscriptionClass object defines a type of subscription within a Notification Services application. The SubscriptionField objects added to the Subscription object represent fields in the subscription class schema. A SubscriptionChronicle object lets you store subscription information outside of tables used by the subscription class—this example does not use a subscription chronicle.

The NMO classes for managing subscription chronicles, subscription classes, and subscription fields are described in Table 18-5.

Table 18-5. NMO classes for managing subscription chronicles, classes, and fields

Class	Description
SubscriptionChronicle	Represents a subscription chronicle.
SubscriptionChronicleCollection	Represents a collection of subscription chronicles as SubscriptionChronicle objects. The SubscriptionChronicles property of the SubscriptionClass class returns the subscription chronicles for the subscription class.
SubscriptionClass	Represents a subscription class.
SubscriptionClassCollection	Represents a collection of subscription classes as SubscriptionClass objects. The SubscriptionClasses property of the Application class returns the subscription classes for the Notification Services application.
SubscriptionField	Represents a field in the subscription class schema.
SubscriptionFieldCollection	Represents a collection of fields as SubscriptionField objects. The SubscriptionFields property of the SubscriptionClass class returns the fields for the subscription class schema.

A SubscriptionEventRule object represents a rule that uses T-SQL queries to generate notifications when event batches arrive. The Action property represents the T-SQL query for the SubscriptionEventRule object. In this example, notifications are generated when the ticker symbol of an event matches the ticker symbol specified in a subscription.

The NMO classes for managing the different types of subscription rules are described in Table 18-6.

Table 18-6. NMO classes for managing subscription rules

Class	Description
SubscriptionConditionEventRule	Represents a subscription rule that the generator runs against subscriptions that use conditions to generate notifications.
SubscriptionConditionEventRuleCollection	Represents a collection of subscription condition event rules as SubscriptionConditionEventRule objects. The SubscriptionConditionEvent-Rules property of the SubscriptionClass class returns the subscription condition event rules for the subscription class.
SubscriptionConditionScheduledRule	Represents a subscription rule that the generator runs against scheduled subscriptions that use conditions to generate notifications.
SubscriptionConditionScheduledRuleCollection	Represents a collection of subscription condition scheduled rules as SubscriptionConditionScheduled-Rule objects. The SubscriptionCondition-ScheduledRules property of the SubscriptionClass class returns the subscription condition scheduled rules for the subscription class.
SubscriptionEventRule	Represents an event rule that contains simple (not conditional) actions.
SubscriptionEventRuleCollection	Represents a collection of subscription event rules as SubscriptionEventRule objects. The SubscriptionEventRules property of the SubscriptionClass class returns the subscription event rules for the subscription class.
SubscriptionScheduledRule	Represents a scheduled rule that contains actions that do not use conditions to generate notifications.
SubscriptionScheduledRuleCollection	Represents a collection of scheduled rules as SubscriptionScheduledRule objects. The SubscriptionScheduledRules property of the SubscriptionClass class returns the scheduled rules for the subscription class.

Creating a Notification Class, Content Formatter, and Notification Class Protocol

A notification class named StockWatchNotifications, a content formatter named XsltFormatter, and two notification class protocols named File and SMTP are created in the CreateNotificationClass( ) method of Example 18-1. The code follows:

```
private static void CreateNotificationClass( )
{
    NotificationClass nc = new NotificationClass(a, "StockWatchNotifications");

    NotificationField nf;
    nf = new NotificationField(nc, "Symbol");
```

```
nf.Type = "nvarchar(6)";
nc.NotificationFields.Add(nf);
nf = new NotificationField(nc, "Price");
nf.Type = "float";
nc.NotificationFields.Add(nf);

ContentFormatter cf = new ContentFormatter(nc, "XsltFormatter");

ContentFormatterArgument cfa;
cfa = new ContentFormatterArgument(cf, "XsltBaseDirectoryPath");
cfa.Value = a.BaseDirectoryPath + @"\AppDefinition";
cf.ContentFormatterArguments.Add(cfa);
cfa = new ContentFormatterArgument(cf, "XsltFileName");
cfa.Value = "StockWatch.xslt";
cf.ContentFormatterArguments.Add(cfa);

nc.ContentFormatter = cf;
nc.DigestDelivery = true;

ProtocolField pf;

// add file notification class protocol
NotificationClassProtocol ncpFile =
    new NotificationClassProtocol(nc, "File");

pf = new ProtocolField(ncpFile, "Symbol");
pf.FieldReference = "Symbol";
ncpFile.ProtocolFields.Add(pf);
pf = new ProtocolField(ncpFile, "Price");
pf.FieldReference = "Price";
ncpFile.ProtocolFields.Add(pf);

nc.NotificationClassProtocols.Add(ncpFile);

// add email notification class protocol
NotificationClassProtocol ncpEmail =
    new NotificationClassProtocol(nc, "SMTP");

pf = new ProtocolField(ncpEmail, "Subject");
pf.SqlExpression = "'Stock watch: ' + CONVERT(nvarchar(30), GETDATE())";
ncpEmail.ProtocolFields.Add(pf);
pf = new ProtocolField(ncpEmail, "BodyFormat");
pf.SqlExpression = "'html'";
ncpEmail.ProtocolFields.Add(pf);
pf = new ProtocolField(ncpEmail, "From");
pf.SqlExpression = "'notification@StockWatchService.com'";
ncpEmail.ProtocolFields.Add(pf);
pf = new ProtocolField(ncpEmail, "Priority");
pf.SqlExpression = "'Normal'";
ncpEmail.ProtocolFields.Add(pf);
pf = new ProtocolField(ncpEmail, "To");
pf.SqlExpression = "DeviceAddress";
ncpEmail.ProtocolFields.Add(pf);
```

```
    nc.NotificationClassProtocols.Add(ncpEmail);

    nc.ExpirationAge = new TimeSpan(1, 0, 0);

    a.NotificationClasses.Add(nc);

    Console.WriteLine("Added notification class: " + nc.Name);
}
```

The NotificationClass object represents a type of notification supported by a Notification Services application. A NotificationField object represents a field in a notification class schema. The notification class in this example has two fields—Symbol of type nvarchar(6) and Price of type float.

The NMO classes for managing notification classes and fields are described in Table 18-7.

Table 18-7. NMO classes for managing notification classes and fields

Class	Description
NotificationClass	Represents a notification class.
NotificationClassCollection	Represents a collection of notification classes as NotificationClass objects. The NotificationClasses property of the Application class returns the notification classes for the Notification Services application.
NotificationComputedField	Represents a computed field in a notification class schema.
NotificationComputedFieldCollection	Represents a collection of computed fields as NotificationComputedField objects. The NotificationComputedFields property of the NotificationClass class returns the computed fields for the notification class.
NotificationField	Represents a noncomputed field in a notification class schema.
NotificationFieldCollection	Represents a collection of fields as NotificationField objects. The NotificationFields property of the NotificationClass class returns the fields for the notification class.

A content formatter formats notifications for a notification class. Each notification class has one content formatter that can perform different formatting based on field values in the notification. The content formatter takes three arguments:

XsltBaseDirectoryPath
    The root directory for all XSLT files.

XsltFileName
    The name of the XSLT file used to transform raw notification data into formatted data for notification delivery.

DisableEscaping

An optional Boolean argument indicating that the event data contains either HTML or XML data preventing further transformation. The default value is false.

The NMO classes for managing content formatters are described in Table 18-8.

Table 18-8. NMO classes for managing content formatters

Class	Description
ContentFormatter	Represents a content formatter. The ContentFormatter property of the NotificationClass class returns the content formatter for the notification class.
ContentFormatterArgument	Represents a name-value pair for a content formatter initialization argument.
ContentFormatterArgumentCollection	Represents a collection of initialization arguments as ContentFormatterArgument objects. The ContentFormatterArguments property of the ContentFormatter class returns the initialization arguments for the content formatter.

A notification class protocol represents a delivery protocol for a notification class. A ProtocolField object represents a protocol header field used by some delivery protocols. Protocol field headers are different for file and email notification—examine the code and examine the file and email notifications shown in Figure 18-7 and Figure 18-8 to see the result of setting the protocol fields. The value of the ProtocolField object is set using either the SqlExpression or FieldReference property. This lets you use either a T-SQL expression or a notification field to define a protocol field value.

The NMO classes for managing protocols are described in Table 18-9.

Table 18-9. NMO classes for managing protocols

Class	Description
NotificationClassProtocol	Represents a delivery protocol for a notification class.
NotificationClassProtocolCollection	Represents a collection of notification class protocols as NotificationClassProtocol objects. The NotificationClassProtocols property of the NotificationClass class returns the delivery classes for the notification class.
ProtocolDefinition	Represents a custom delivery protocol.
ProtocolDefinitionCollection	Represents a collection of custom delivery protocols as ProtocolDefinition objects. The ProtocolDefinitions property of the Instance class returns the custom delivery protocols for the Notification Services instance.
ProtocolField	Represents a protocol header field.

Table 18-9. NMO classes for managing protocols (continued)

Class	Description
ProtocolFieldCollection	Represents a collection of protocol header fields as ProtocolField objects. The ProtocolFields property of the NotificationClassProtocol class returns the protocol header fields for the delivery protocol.
ProtocolRetrySchedule	Represents a retry schedule interval.
ProtocolRetryScheduleCollection	Represents a collection of retry schedule intervals as ProtocolRetrySchedule objects. The ProtocolRetrySchedules property of the NotificationClassProtocol class returns the retry schedules for notifications sent using the delivery protocol.

Creating an Event Provider

A hosted event provider is created in the CreateHostedEventProvider() method of Example 18-1. The code follows:

```
private static void CreateHostedEventProvider()
{
    HostedEventProvider hep = new HostedEventProvider(a, "StockWatchHEP");
    hep.ClassName = "FileSystemWatcherProvider";
    hep.SystemName = nsServer;

    HostedEventProviderArgument hepa;
    hepa = new HostedEventProviderArgument(hep, "WatchDirectory");
    hepa.Value = baseDirectoryPath + @"\Events";
    hep.HostedEventProviderArguments.Add(hepa);
    hepa = new HostedEventProviderArgument(hep, "SchemaFile");
    hepa.Value = baseDirectoryPath + @"\AppDefinition\EventsSchema.xsd";
    hep.HostedEventProviderArguments.Add(hepa);
    hepa = new HostedEventProviderArgument(hep, "EventClassName");
    hepa.Value = "StockWatchEvents";
    hep.HostedEventProviderArguments.Add(hepa);

    a.HostedEventProviders.Add(hep);
}
```

Event providers collect event data and submit it to an event class. Hosted event providers are run by the Notification Services engine. Nonhosted event providers, on the other hand, run outside of the engine, and have no interaction with Notification Services.

The ClassName property of the HostedEventProvider class specifies the class that implements the event provider. Notification Services has three built-in event providers, described in the "Architecture" section earlier in this chapter. You can also use a custom event provider. This example uses the File System Watcher event provider (with a ClassName of FileSystemWatcherProvider), which gathers events of the

StockWatchEvents event class from a file in the *C:\PSS2005\NotificationServices\ Events* directory. The event file must conform to the schema defined in the *C:\ PSS2005\NotificationServices\AppDefinition\EventsSchema.xsd* file.

The NMO classes for managing hosted and nonhosted event providers are described in Table 18-10.

Table 18-10. NMO classes for managing hosted and nonhosted event providers

Class	Description
HostedEventProvider	Represents a hosted event provider for a Notification Services application.
HostedEventProviderArgument	Represents a name-value pair specifying hosted event provider configuration.
HostedEventProviderArgumentCollection	Represents a collection of hosted event provider arguments as HostedEventProviderArgument objects. The HostedEventProviderArguments property of the HostedEventProvider class returns the hosted event provider arguments for the hosted event provider.
HostedEventProviderCollection	Represents a collection of hosted event providers as HostedEventProvider objects. The HostedEventProviders property of the Application class returns the hosted event providers for the Notification Services application.
NonHostedEventProvider	Represents a nonhosted event provider.
NonHostedEventProviderCollection	Represents a collection of nonhosted event providers as NonHostedEventProvider objects. The NonHostedEventProviders property of the Application class returns the nonhosted event providers for the Notification Services application.

Creating a Generator

A generator named StockWatchGenerator is created in the CreateGenerator( ) method of Example 18-1. The code follows:

```
private static void CreateGenerator( )
{
    // create a new generator for the application
    Generator g = new Generator(a, "StockWatchGenerator");
    g.SystemName = nsServer;
    a.Generator = g;

    Console.WriteLine("Created generator: " + g.Name);
}
```

The Generator object represents the generator for a Notification Services application. The Generator property of the Application class returns the generator for the application. You have to specify the Generator property of the Application object before adding the application to the Notification Services instance. An application has only one generator, which handles rule processing for the application.

The SystemName property of the Generator class must be specified, and cannot be any of the following: localhost, ., an IP address, or any string containing a backslash (\).

Creating a Distributor

A distributor named StockWatchDistributor is created in the CreateDistributor() method of Example 18-1. The code follows:

```
private static void CreateDistributor()
{
    Distributor d = new Distributor(a, "StockWatchDistributor");
    d.SystemName = nsServer;
    d.QuantumDuration = new TimeSpan(0, 0, 15);
    a.Distributors.Add(d);

    Console.WriteLine("Added distributor: " + d.Name);
}
```

The Distributor object represents a distributor for a Notification Services application. Each application must have one distributor that controls formatting and distribution of notifications. If an application has multiple distributors, each one must be installed on a different server. The QuantumDuration property specifies the distributor work item polling interval, which is 15 seconds in this example.

The NMO classes for managing distributors are described in Table 18-11.

Table 18-11. NMO classes for managing distributors

Class	Description
Distributor	Represents a distributor for a Notification Services application.
DistributorCollection	Represents a collection of distributors as Distributor objects. The Distributors property of the Application class returns the distributors used to distribute notifications to delivery channels for the Notification Services application.

Creating a Vacuum Schedule

A vacuum schedule named StockWatchVacuumSchedule is created in the CreateVacuumSchedule() method of Example 18-1. The code follows:

```
private static void CreateVacuumSchedule()
{
    VacuumSchedule vs = new VacuumSchedule(a, "StockWatchVacuumSchedule");
    vs.StartTime = new TimeSpan(0, 0, 0);
    a.VacuumSchedules.Add(vs);

    Console.WriteLine("Added vacuum schedule: " + vs.Name);
}
```

Vacuuming removes old event and notification data from the application database on a daily schedule. The StartTime property specifies the daily time in Universal Coordinated Time (UTC) for the data removal process to start. Although specifying a vacuum schedule is optional, old data is not removed from the database if a vacuum schedule is not specified.

The NMO classes for managing vacuum schedules are described in Table 18-12.

Table 18-12. NMO classes for managing vacuum schedules

Class	Description
VacuumSchedule	Represents a data removal schedule.
VacuumScheduleCollection	Represents a collection of data removal schedules as VacuumSchedule objects. The VacuumSchedules property of the Application class returns the data removal schedules for the application.

Creating a Subscriber and Subscriber Device

Two subscribers, each with a single subscriber device, are created in the CreateSubscriber( ) method of Example 18-1. The code follows:

```
private static void CreateSubscriber( )
{
    ns.NSInstance swnsi = new ns.NSInstance("StockWatch");

    ns.Subscriber s;
    ns.SubscriberDevice sd;

    // create a subscriber
    s = new ns.Subscriber(swnsi);
    s.SubscriberId = @"KristinHamilton";
    s.Add( );
    Console.WriteLine("Added subscriber: " + s.SubscriberId);

    // create a file subscriber device
    sd = new ns.SubscriberDevice( );
    sd.Initialize(swnsi);
    sd.DeviceName = "StockWatchSubscriberDevice";
    sd.SubscriberId = "KristinHamilton";
    sd.DeviceTypeName = "File";
    sd.DeviceAddress = "KristinH@StockWatch.ns";
    sd.DeliveryChannelName = "StockWatchFileDeliveryChannel";
    sd.Add( );
    Console.WriteLine("Added subscriber file device.");

    // create a subscriber
    s = new ns.Subscriber(swnsi);
    s.SubscriberId = @"TonyHamilton";
    s.Add( );
    Console.WriteLine("Added subscriber: " + s.SubscriberId);
```

```
      // create an email subscriber device
      sd = new ns.SubscriberDevice( );
      sd.Initialize(swnsi);
      sd.DeviceName = "StockWatchSubscriberDevice";
      sd.SubscriberId = "TonyHamilton";
      sd.DeviceTypeName = "Email";
      sd.DeviceAddress = "TonyH@StockWatchNS.ns";
      sd.DeliveryChannelName = "StockWatchEmailDeliveryChannel";
      sd.Add( );
      Console.WriteLine("Added subscriber email device.");
    }
```

The NSInstance class represents a Notification Services instance that is registered in the Windows registry.

The Subscriber class represents a subscriber in a Notification Services instance. The SubscriberEnumeration class represents a collection of subscribers as Subscriber objects in a Notification Services instance.

The SubscriberEnumeration class is used to retrieve a Subscriber object from the collection of subscribers to the Notification Services instance. The Delete( ) method removes a subscriber, the Add( ) method adds a subscriber, and the Update( ) method updates the information for an existing subscriber. The following code deletes the subscriber AnySubscriber from a Notification Service instance named HelloWorld:

```
NSInstance nins = new NSInstance("HelloWorld");
SubscriberEnumeration se = new SubscriberEnumeration(nins);
se["AnySubscriber"].Delete( );
```

The SubscriberDevice class represents a device that can receive notifications. A single subscriber device is added to each subscriber. Each subscriber device specifies the following properties:

DeviceName
> The name of the subscriber device.

SubscriberId
> The ID of the subscriber with which the subscriber device is associated.

DeviceTypeName
> The name of the device type for the subscriber device.

DeviceAddress
> The address used to contact the device.

DeliveryChannelName
> The name of the delivery channel that the device uses. This example assigns the StockWatchFileDeliveryChannel delivery channel to one subscriber and the StockWatchEmailDeliveryChannel delivery channel to the other—these delivery channels are created in the code described in the "Creating a Delivery Channel" section earlier in this chapter.

The SubscriberDeviceEnumeration class is used to retrieve a SubscriberDevice object from the collection of devices for a subscriber. The Delete( ) method removes a device, the Add( ) method adds a device, and the Update( ) method updates the information for an existing device.

Creating a Subscription

Two subscriptions are created in the CreateSubscription( ) method of Example 18-1. The code follows:

```
private static void CreateSubscription( )
{
    ns.NSInstance swnsi = new ns.NSInstance("StockWatch");
    ns.NSApplication a = new ns.NSApplication(swnsi, "StockWatchApp");

    ns.Subscription s;

    // add subscriptions
    s = new ns.Subscription( );
    s.Initialize(a, "StockWatchSubscriptions");
    s.SetFieldValue("DeviceName", "StockWatchSubscriberDevice");
    s.SetFieldValue("SubscriberLocale", "en-us");
    s.SubscriberId = "KristinHamilton";
    s.SetFieldValue("Symbol", "ABC");
    s.SetFieldValue("Price", "0.00");
    s.Add( );
    Console.WriteLine("Added subscription: " + s.SubscriberId);

    s = new ns.Subscription( );
    s.Initialize(a, "StockWatchSubscriptions");
    s.SetFieldValue("DeviceName", "StockWatchSubscriberDevice");
    s.SetFieldValue("SubscriberLocale", "en-us");
    s.SubscriberId = "TonyHamilton";
    s.SetFieldValue("Symbol", "DEF");
    s.SetFieldValue("Price", "0.00");
    s.Add( );
    Console.WriteLine("Added subscription: " + s.SubscriberId);
}
```

The NSApplication class represents a Notification Services application. The Subscription class represents a subscription in a Notification Services application. Both subscriptions use the subscriber device named StockWatchSubscriberDevice created in the "Creating a Subscriber and Subscriber Device" section earlier in this chapter. The subscription for KristinHamilton is for events for ticker symbol ABC, while the subscription for subscriber TonyHamilton is for events for ticker symbol DEF. The results can be seen in the notifications shown in Figures 18-7 and 18-8.

The SubscriptionEnumeration class represents a collection of subscriptions as Subscription objects in a Notification Services application. Use the SubscriptionEnumeration class to iterate over a collection of subscriptions for an application and manage the individual subscriptions in the collection. These two classes are implemented in the Microsoft.SqlServer.NotificationServices namespace.

Enumerating a Notification Services Instance Database

This example enumerates the filegroup, database files, and logfiles for the StockWatch Notification Services instance created in Example 18-1:

```
using System;

using Microsoft.SqlServer.Management.Smo;
using Microsoft.SqlServer.Management.Nmo;

class Program
{
    static void Main(string[] args)
    {
        Server server = new Server("(local)");
        NotificationServices ns = server.NotificationServices;
        Instance ins = ns.Instances["StockWatch"];

        InstanceDatabaseOptions ido = ins.InstanceDatabaseOptions;
        Console.WriteLine("INSTANCE DATABASE OPTIONS:");
        Console.WriteLine("  Name: " + ido.Name);
        Console.WriteLine("  DefaultFileGroup: " + ido.DefaultFileGroup);

        Console.WriteLine(Environment.NewLine + "FILE GROUPS:");
        foreach (InstanceDatabaseFileGroup idfg in ido.InstanceDatabaseFileGroups)
        {
            Console.WriteLine("  Name: " + idfg.Name);

            Console.WriteLine(Environment.NewLine + "DATABASE FILES");
            foreach (InstanceDatabaseFile idf in idfg.InstanceDatabaseFiles)
                Console.WriteLine("  Name: " + idf.Name);
        }

        Console.WriteLine(Environment.NewLine + "LOG FILES:");
        foreach (InstanceDatabaseLogFile idlf in ido.InstanceDatabaseLogFiles)
            Console.WriteLine("  Name: " + idlf.Name);

        Console.WriteLine(Environment.NewLine + "Press any key to continue.");
        Console.ReadKey();
    }
}
```

Results are shown in Figure 18-9.

Each Notification Services instance has one database that can optionally contain one or more filegroups. If you define filegroups, one must be called PRIMARY. Use SQL Server Management Studio if you need to alter the Notification Services instance database after creating the instance.

Figure 18-9. Results for enumerating a Notification Services instance database example

The NMO classes for managing the instance database, filegroups, files, and logfiles are described in Table 18-13.

Table 18-13. NMO classes for managing instance databases

Instance	Description
InstanceDatabaseFile	Represents an instance database file.
InstanceDatabaseFileCollection	Represents a collection of instance databases as InstanceDatabase objects. The InstanceDatabaseFiles property of the InstanceDatabaseFileGroup class returns the instance databases in the instance database filegroup.
InstanceDatabaseFileGroup	Represents an application database filegroup.
InstanceDatabaseFileGroupCollection	Represents a collection of instance database filegroups as InstanceDatabaseFileGroup objects. The Instance-DatabaseFileGroups property of the InstanceDatabase-Options class returns the instance database filegroups in the application.
InstanceDatabaseLogFile	Represents an instance database logfile.
InstanceDatabaseLogFileCollection	Represents a collection of instance database logfiles as Instance-DatabaseLogFile objects. The InstanceDatabase-LogFiles property of the InstanceDatabaseOptions class returns the instance database logfiles in the application.
InstanceDatabaseOptions	Represents database options for the instance database. The InstanceDatabaseOptions property of the Instance class returns the database properties for the instance.

Enumerating a Notification Services Application Database

This example enumerates the filegroup, database files, and logfiles for the HelloWorldApp Notification Services application created in Example 18-1:

```
using System;

using Microsoft.SqlServer.Management.Smo;
using Microsoft.SqlServer.Management.Nmo;

class Program
{
```

```
static void Main(string[] args)
{
    Server server = new Server("(local)");
    NotificationServices ns = server.NotificationServices;
    Instance ins = ns.Instances["StockWatch"];
    Application a = ins.Applications["StockWatchApp"];

    ApplicationDatabaseOptions ado = a.ApplicationDatabaseOptions;
    Console.WriteLine("APPLICATION DATABASE OPTIONS:");
    Console.WriteLine(" Name: " + ado.Name);
    Console.WriteLine(" DefaultFileGroup: " + ado.DefaultFileGroup);

    Console.WriteLine(Environment.NewLine + "FILE GROUPS:");
    foreach (ApplicationDatabaseFileGroup adfg in
        ado.ApplicationDatabaseFileGroups)
    {
        Console.WriteLine(" Name: " + adfg.Name);

        Console.WriteLine(Environment.NewLine + "DATABASE FILES");
        foreach (ApplicationDatabaseFile adf in adfg.ApplicationDatabaseFiles)
            Console.WriteLine(" Name: " + adf.Name);
    }

    Console.WriteLine(Environment.NewLine + "LOG FILES:");
    foreach (ApplicationDatabaseLogFile adlf in
        ado.ApplicationDatabaseLogFiles)
        Console.WriteLine(" Name: " + adlf.Name);

    Console.WriteLine(Environment.NewLine + "Press any key to continue.");
    Console.ReadKey();
}
}
```

Results are shown in Figure 18-10.

Figure 18-10. Results for enumerating a Notification Services application database example

Each Notification Services application has one database that can optionally contain one or more filegroups. If you define filegroups, one must be called PRIMARY. Use SQL Server Management Studio if you need to alter the application database after creating the instance.

The NMO classes for managing the application database, filegroups, files, and log-files are described in Table 18-14.

Table 18-14. NMO classes for managing application databases

Class	Database
ApplicationDatabaseFile	Represents an application database file.
ApplicationDatabaseFileCollection	Represents a collection of application databases as ApplicationDatabaseFile objects. The ApplicationDatabaseFiles property of the ApplicationDatabaseFileGroup class returns the application databases in the application database filegroup.
ApplicationDatabaseFileGroup	Represents an application database filegroup.
ApplicationDatabaseFileGroupCollection	Represents a collection of application database filegroups as ApplicationDatabaseFileGroup objects. The ApplicationDatabaseFileGroups property of the ApplicationDatabaseOptions class returns the application database filegroups in the application.
ApplicationDatabaseLogFile	Represents an application database logfile.
ApplicationDatabaseLogFileCollection	Represents a collection of application database logfiles as ApplicationDatabaseLogFile objects. The ApplicationDatabaseLogFiles property of the ApplicationDatabaseOptions class returns the application database logfiles in the application.
ApplicationDatabaseOptions	Represents database options for the application database. The ApplicationDatabaseOptions property of the Application class returns the database properties for the application.

CHAPTER 19

Replication

Replication copies and distributes data and database objects from one database to another and provides a mechanism to keep the data synchronized. Data can be replicated from server to server or from server to client.

Before you look at programming replication, there are some key terms with which you should be familiar:

Publisher

A SQL Server instance that makes its data available through replication, detects changes to the data, and maintains information about one or more publications and articles.

Distributor

A SQL Server instance that stores replication metadata for one or more publishers. Each distributor has a distribution database that stores history data, transactions, and metadata. When a single SQL Server instance acts as both publisher and distributor, the distributor is called a *local distributor*. When the publisher and distributor are on different SQL Server instances, the distributor is called a *remote distributor*.

Subscriber

A SQL Server instance that receives replicated data.

Publication

A collection of one or more articles. A publication can be either pushed to the subscriber or pulled by the subscriber.

Article

A database object included in a publication.

Subscription

A request for the publication that defines where and when the publication will be received.

SQL Server 2005 provides three types of replication:

Snapshot
> Distributes data as it appears at a moment in time. The entire snapshot is generated and sent to subscribers when synchronization occurs and is not monitored for updates to the published data.

Transactional
> Schema and data changes are sent to subscribers when they occur. Data changes are applied to the subscriber data in the same order and within the same transaction boundaries in which they occurred at the publisher, guaranteeing transactional consistency within each publication. Transactional replication usually starts with a snapshot of the schema and data, and is typically used in server-to-server replication scenarios.

Merge
> Schema and data changes are tracked with triggers. Data is synchronized when the subscriber connects to the publisher; all changes made since the last synchronization occurred are included. Merge replication typically starts with a snapshot of the schema and data, and is normally used in server-to-client replication scenarios.

You can implement and administer replication by using SQL Server Management Studio, by using Windows Synchronization Manager, or programmatically by using replication APIs. The rest of this chapter discusses the third option, programmatic implementation and administration of replication. For more information about the other two methods, consult Microsoft SQL Server 2005 Books Online.

Replication uses a set of programs called agents to perform tasks associated with replication. The agents are described in the "Agents Supporting Replication" sidebar.

Implementing replication involves five steps:

1. Configure the publisher and distributor.
2. Define the publication—database objects, type of replication, and filtering—and the type of replication.
3. Identify a location for storing snapshot files and define when initial synchronization will occur.
4. Create subscriptions.
5. Synchronize the data, including the initial synchronization to the snapshot.

Programming Replication

SQL Server Replication Management Objects (RMO) is a collection of namespaces introduced in SQL Server 2005 for programming all aspects of SQL Server 2005 replication. RMO supersedes replication functionality in SQL-DMO. RMO is compatible with SQL Server 2000 and SQL Server 7.0, which lets you manage replication in environments having a mix of different SQL Server versions.

The following subsections provide examples that show how to use the replication classes and include descriptions of the classes. The examples use merge replication, but transactional replication is similar. You need a reference to the following assemblies to compile and run the examples:

- Microsoft.SqlServer.ConnectionInfo
- Microsoft.SqlServer.Replication .NET Programming Interface

Additional assembly references are indicated for examples in which they are required.

The ReplicationServer object described in is the top-level class in the RMO class hierarchy. It represents a SQL Server instance involved in replication. The server can take the role of distributor, publisher, subscriber, or a combination of those roles.

Prerequisites

Most of the examples in this chapter build on each other. There are a few things you need to do before you start.

Disable replication if it is enabled. This will let you run the first two examples, which install a distributor and create a publisher. To disable replication, right-click the Replication node in Object Explorer in SQL Server Management Studio, select Disable Replication from the context menu, and follow the instructions in the wizard.

Create a database named ReplicationDestination by right-clicking the Databases node in Object Explorer and selecting New Database from the context menu. In the New Database dialog box, set the Database name listbox to ReplicationDestination, accept the defaults, and click OK to create the database.

Ensure that the setup is correct by following these steps:

1. Right-click the Databases node in Object Explorer and select Refresh from the context menu.
2. Expand the Databases node in Object Explorer by clicking the plus sign next to it.
3. Right-click the Replication node in Object Explorer and select Refresh from the context menu.
4. Expand the Replication node in Object Explorer by clicking the plus sign next to it.
5. Right-click the Replication node in Object Explorer.

The context menu should appear as shown in Figure 19-1. You should also see the new ReplicationDestination database.

Installing a Distributor

This example shows how to install a distributor onto the local SQL Server instance. It instantiates a ServerConnection object representing the local machine, and then creates a ReplicationServer object based on this ServerConnection object.

The next object created is a DistributionDatabase object, called distribution and linked to the ServerConnection object named sc. A distribution database stores replication information on the distributor.

Finally, the InstallDistributor( ) method of the ReplicationServer class installs a distributor onto the currently connected or remote SQL Server instance. The distribution database is created as a system database. The password for the InstallDistributor( ) method must conform to your password policy.

The source code for the example follows:

```
using System;

using Microsoft.SqlServer.Management.Common;
using Microsoft.SqlServer.Replication;
```

Figure 19-1. Prerequisite configuration

```
class Program
{
    static void Main(string[] args)
    {
        ServerConnection sc = new ServerConnection("localhost");
        // create the distributor
        ReplicationServer dist = new ReplicationServer(sc);

        // install the distributor
        DistributionDatabase dDb = new DistributionDatabase(
            "distribution", sc);
        dist.InstallDistributor("password1", dDb);

        sc.Disconnect();

        Console.WriteLine("Press any key to continue.");
        Console.ReadKey();
    }
}
```

Once you have executed the example, confirm that the distributor has been installed by right-clicking the Replication node in Object Explorer. The context menu should appear as shown in Figure 19-2. The Configure Distribution context menu item is replaced by two new menu items—Distributor Properties and Disable Publishing and Distribution.

Figure 19-2. Replication context menu after installing a distributor

You can see the new distribution database in Object Explorer in SQL Server Management Studio by right-clicking the Replication node and selecting Distributor Properties from the context menu. The distributor properties are displayed in the Distributor Properties dialog box, shown in Figure 19-3.

The RMO classes used to programmatically manage distribution and distributor objects are described in Table 19-1.

Table 19-1. RMO classes for managing distribution databases

Class	Description
DistributionDatabase	Represents a distribution database that stores replication information on the distributor.
DistributionDatabaseCollection	Represents a collection of DistributionDatabase objects. The DistributionDatabases property of the ReplicationServer class returns a DistributionDatabaseCollection object containing all distribution databases on the distributor.

Creating a Publisher

This example creates a publisher on the local SQL Server instance. The example instantiates a DistributionPublisher object and associates it with the target ServerConnection object. The DistributionPublisher class represents a computer that acts as both a publisher and a distributor.

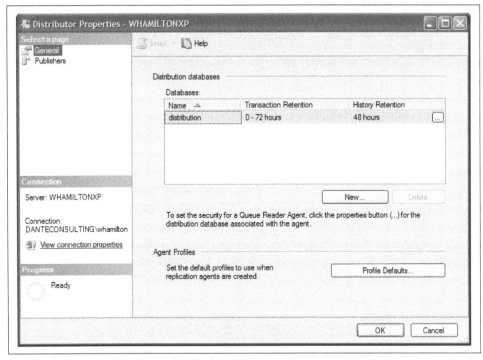

Figure 19-3. Distributor Properties dialog box

Next, several properties of the DistributionPublisher object are set, and then its Create() method is called. The DistributionDatabase property links this DistributionPublisher object with the DistributionDatabase object you created in the previous example. The PublisherSecurity property accesses the security context as a ConnectionSecurityContext object. It is used by the replicating agent to connect to the distribution publisher. The ConnectionSecurityContext object specifies an authentication mode and, if SQL Server authentication is used, the login and password. This example uses Windows authentication.

> Before you execute this example, replace the *ServerName* argument in the DistributionPublisher constructor with the name of your database server and create the directory *C:\PSS2005\Replication*.

The source code for the example follows:

```
using System;

using Microsoft.SqlServer.Management.Common;
using Microsoft.SqlServer.Replication;

class Program
{
```

```
static void Main(string[] args)
{
    ServerConnection sc = new ServerConnection("(local)");

    DistributionPublisher dp = new DistributionPublisher(
        "ServerName", sc);
    dp.DistributionDatabase = "distribution";
    dp.WorkingDirectory = @"C:\PSS2005\Replication";
    dp.PublisherSecurity.WindowsAuthentication = true;
    dp.Create();

    sc.Disconnect();

    Console.WriteLine("Press any key to continue.");
    Console.ReadKey();
}
}
```

Once you have executed the example, confirm that the publisher has been created by right-clicking the Replication node in Object Explorer. The context menu should appear as shown in Figure 19-4. A new context item, Publisher Properties, has been added.

Figure 19-4. Replication context menu after creating a publisher

The RMO classes used to manage publishers programmatically are described in Table 19-2.

Table 19-2. RMO classes for managing publishers

Class	Description
DistributionPublisher	Represents a computer that acts as both publisher and distributor.
DistributionPublisherCollection	Represents a collection of DistributionPublisher objects. The DistributionPublishers property of the ReplicationServer class returns a DistributionPublisherCollection object containing all publishers that use the SQL Server instance as a distributor.
PublisherConnectionSecurityContext	Represents login information when connecting to a publisher server instance. The PublisherSecurity property of the PullSubscription class returns the security context used by the synchronization agent when connecting to the publisher.

As mentioned earlier in the section, the PublisherSecurity property of the PublisherSubscriber class accesses the security context as a ConnectionSecurityContext object that is used by the replicating agent to connect to the distribution publisher. The RMO class used to programmatically manage security context information is described in Table 19-3.

Table 19-3. RMO class for managing connection security context information

Class	Description
ConnectionSecurityContext	Represents information for connecting to SQL Server replication publishers, distributors, and subscribers. The connection security context information specifies an authentication mode and, if SQL Server authentication is used, the login and password.

Enabling a Database for Publication

This example enables the AdventureWorks database for merge publication. It does so by creating a ReplicationDatabase object and associating it with the AdventureWorks database. ReplicationDatabase represents a replication database, either a publisher or a subscriber.

The EnableMergePublishing and EnableTransPublishing properties of the ReplicationDatabase class control whether a database is available for merge and transactional replication publication.

The source code for the example follows:

```
using System;

using Microsoft.SqlServer.Management.Common;
using Microsoft.SqlServer.Replication;
```

```
class Program
{
    static void Main(string[] args)
    {
        ServerConnection sc = new ServerConnection("localhost");

        ReplicationDatabase rDb = new ReplicationDatabase(
            "AdventureWorks", sc);
        rDb.EnabledMergePublishing = true;

        sc.Disconnect();

        Console.WriteLine("Press any key to continue.");
        Console.ReadKey();
    }
}
```

 The code in this example only enables the merge publishing of the AdventureWorks database. It does not actually publish anything. Subsequent examples will show you how to publish an article.

After you run the code, confirm that the AdventureWorks database is enabled for merge publication by selecting Replication → Publisher Properties in Object Explorer and then selecting the Publication Databases page. Figure 19-5 shows AdventureWorks enabled for merge publication.

Creating a Publication

This example creates a merge publication named AdventureWorks_MergePub for the AdventureWorks database. It does so by instantiating a MergePublication object and then setting its Name, DatabaseName, ConnectionContext, and Status properties. Finally, it invokes its Create() method.

The source code for the example follows:

```
using System;

using Microsoft.SqlServer.Management.Common;
using Microsoft.SqlServer.Replication;

class Program
{
    static void Main(string[] args)
    {
        ServerConnection sc = new ServerConnection("localhost");

        MergePublication mp = new MergePublication();
        mp.Name = "AdventureWorks_MergePub";
        mp.DatabaseName = "AdventureWorks";
        mp.ConnectionContext = sc;
```

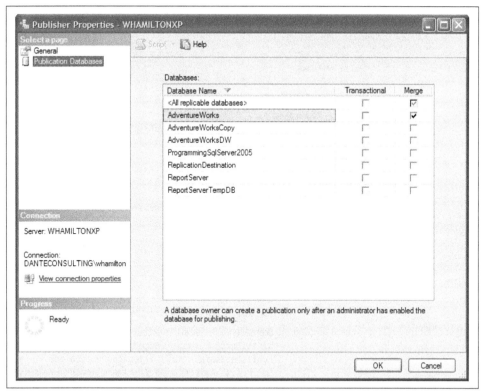

Figure 19-5. Publisher Properties dialog box showing AdventureWorks database

```
        mp.Status = State.Active;
        mp.Create( );

        sc.Disconnect( );

        Console.WriteLine("Press any key to continue.");
        Console.ReadKey( );
    }
}
```

After executing this example, you can view the new publication in Object Explorer by refreshing and expanding the Replication → Local Publications node in Object Explorer, as shown in Figure 19-6.

The publication will not publish anything, because no articles have been defined for it. The next section, "Creating an Article," defines an article to publish.

The RMO classes used to manage publications are described in Table 19-4.

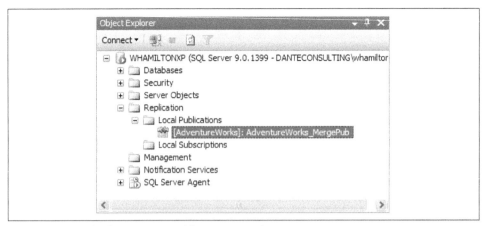

Figure 19-6. Results for creating a publication example

Table 19-4. RMO classes for managing publications

Class	Description
DistributionPublication	Represents read-only information about the distributor image of a snapshot, transactional, or merge publication.
DistributionPublicationCollection	Represents a collection of DistributionPublication objects. The DistributionDatabases property of the Distribution-Publisher class returns a DistributionPublication-Collection object containing all distribution publications defined on the distribution database.
MergeDynamicSnapshotJob	Represents information about the Snapshot Agent job that generates the snapshot data for a subscription to a merge publication with a parameterized row filter. The EnumDynamicSnapshotJobs( ) method of the MergePublication class returns an ArrayList object of dynamic snapshot jobs for the merge publication.
MergePartition	Represents information about a subscriber partition for a merge publication with a parameterized row filter. The EnumMergePartitions( ) method of the MergePublication class returns an ArrayList object of subscriber partitions for the merge publication.
MergePublication	Represents a merge publication. The EnumMergePublications( ) method of the ReplicationDatabase class returns an ArrayList object of merge publications that use the replication database.
MergePublicationCollection	Represents a collection of MergePublication objects. The MergePublications property of the ReplicationDatabase class returns a MergePublicationCollection object containing all merge publications defined on the replication database. The MergePublications property of the Distribution-Publisher class returns a MergePublicationCollection object containing all merge publications defined on the distribution publisher.
PublicationAccess	Represents login information in the publication access list (PAL) for a publication.
TransPublication	Represents a transactional or snapshot publication.

Table 19-4. RMO classes for managing publications (continued)

Class	Description
TransPublicationCollection	Represents a collection of TransPublication objects.
	The TransPublications property of the ReplicationDatabase class returns a TransPublicationCollection object containing all transactional and snapshot publications defined on the replication database.
	The TransPublications property of the Distribution-Publisher class returns a TransPublicationCollection object containing all transactional and snapshot publications defined on the distribution publisher.

Creating an Article

This example creates an article named Article_1 in the AdventureWorks_MergePub merge publication created in the preceding section, "Creating a Publication." The steps are the same as you've seen previously:

1. Instantiate the appropriate object, in this case a MergeArticle object (which represents an article in a merge publication).
2. Set the appropriate properties.
3. Call the object's Create( ) method.

The properties of interest for a MergeArticle object are as follows:

Name
    The name under which SQL Server stores the article

PublicationName
    The name of the merge publication through which the article is exposed for replication

DatabaseName
    The name of the underlying database

ConnectionContext
    The ServerConnection object representing the target machine

SourceObjectName
    The name of the object in the database

SourceObjectOwner
    The name of the owner (schema) of the database object being published

The source code for the example follows:

```
using System;

using Microsoft.SqlServer.Management.Common;
using Microsoft.SqlServer.Replication;

class Program
```

```
{
    static void Main(string[] args)
    {
        ServerConnection sc = new ServerConnection("localhost");

        MergeArticle ma = new MergeArticle();
        ma.Name = "Article_1";
        ma.PublicationName = "AdventureWorks_MergePub";
        ma.DatabaseName = "AdventureWorks";
        ma.ConnectionContext = sc;
        ma.SourceObjectName = "Vendor";
        ma.SourceObjectOwner = "Purchasing";
        ma.Create();

        sc.Disconnect();

        Console.WriteLine("Press any key to continue.");
        Console.ReadKey();
    }
}
```

After running the code, you can see the publication by right-clicking the Replication
→ Local Publications → [AdventureWorks]: AdventureWorks_MergePub node in
Object Explorer and selecting Properties from the context menu. Select the Articles
page in the Publication Properties dialog box to view the articles to publish, as
shown in Figure 19-7.

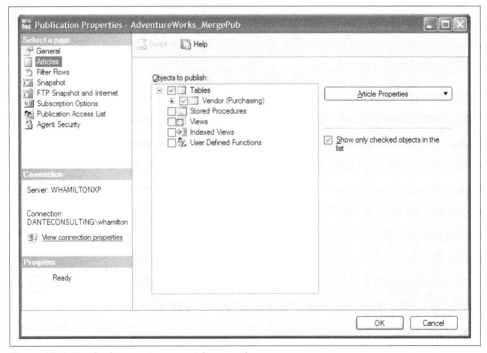

Figure 19-7. Results for creating an article example

The RMO classes used to manage publications are described in Table 19-5.

Table 19-5. RMO classes for managing articles

Class	Description
ArticleConflict	Represents information about the merge replication conflict table. The EnumConflictTables( ) method of the ReplicationDatabase object returns an ArrayList object of conflict information for all merge publications and subscriptions.
DistributionArticle	Represents read-only information about the distributor image of a snapshot, transactional, or merge article.
DistributionArticleCollection	Represents a collection of DistributionArticle objects. The DistributionArticles property of the Distribution-Publication class returns a DistributionArticleCollection object containing all distribution articles defined on the distribution publication.
MergeArticle	Represents an article in a merge publication. The EnumArticles( ) method of the MergePublication class returns an ArrayList object of articles in the publication.
MergeArticleCollection	Represents a collection of MergeArticle objects. The MergeArticles property of the MergePublication class returns a MergeArticleCollection object containing all articles in the merge publication.
MergeJoinFilter	Represents a join filter or logical record relationship between merge articles. The EnumMergeJoinFilters( ) method of the MergeArticle class returns an ArrayList object of join filters defined for the merge article.
TransArticle	Represents an article in either a transactional or snapshot publication. The EnumArticles( ) method of the TransPublication class returns an ArrayList object of articles in the publication.
TransArticleCollection	Represents a collection of TransArticle objects. The TransArticles property of the TransPublication class returns a TransArticleCollection object containing all articles in the transactional or snapshot publication.

Enumerating Items Available for Replication

This example enumerates the tables and columns available for replication in the AdventureWorks database. It does so using the EnumReplicationTables( ) method on the ReplicationDatabase class. This method returns an ArrayList object of ReplicationTable objects. The example then scans this ArrayList object and calls the EnumReplicationColumns( ) method for each ReplicationTable object. For each column reported, the example displays the column's name and data type.

The source code for the example follows:

```
using System;
using System.Collections;

using Microsoft.SqlServer.Management.Common;
using Microsoft.SqlServer.Replication;
```

```
class Program
{
    static void Main(string[] args)
    {
        ServerConnection sc = new ServerConnection("localhost");
        ReplicationDatabase rDb = new ReplicationDatabase(
            "AdventureWorks", sc);

        ArrayList ta = rDb.EnumReplicationTables();
        for (int i = 0; i < ta.Count; i++)
        {
            ReplicationTable t = (ReplicationTable)ta[i];
            Console.WriteLine(t.OwnerName + "." + t.Name);

            ArrayList ca = t.EnumReplicationColumns();
            for (int j = 0; j < ca.Count; j++)
            {
                ReplicationColumn c = (ReplicationColumn)ca[j];
                Console.WriteLine("   " + c.Name + " " + c.Datatype);
            }

            Console.WriteLine(Environment.NewLine);
        }

        sc.Disconnect();

        Console.WriteLine("Press any key to continue.");
        Console.ReadKey();
    }
}
```

Partial results are show in Figure 19-8.

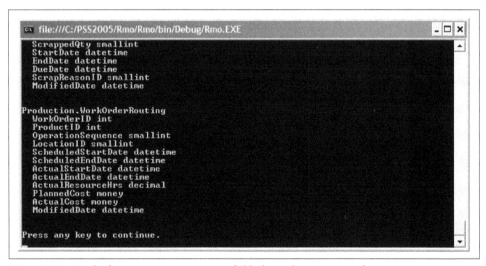

Figure 19-8. Results for enumerating items available for replication example

The RMO classes used to manage replication items are described in Table 19-6.

Table 19-6. RMO classes for managing objects being replicated

Class	Description
HeterogeneousColumn	Represents a column in a table on a non-SQL Server publisher. The EnumHeterogeneouscolumns( ) method of the Replication-Server class returns an ArrayList object of heterogeneous columns in a table that can be replicated.
HeterogeneousTable	Represents a table on a non-SQL Server publisher. The EnumHeterogeneousTables( ) method of the ReplicationServer class returns an ArrayList object of heterogeneous tables that can be replicated.
IdentityRangeInfo	Represents identity range management settings for a published article when the source table contains an identity column. The EnumIdentity-RangeInfo( ) method of the ReplicationTable class returns an ArrayList object of identity range information about articles based on the table.
ReplicationColumn	Represents information about a column (in a table) required for replication. The EnumReplicationColumns( ) method of the Replication-Table class returns an ArrayList object of columns that can be replicated.
ReplicationDatabase	Represents a replication database, either publication or subscription.
ReplicationDatabaseCollection	Represents a collection of replication databases. The EnumReplication-Databases( ) method of the ReplicationServer class returns an ArrayList object of all databases enabled for replication on the replication server.
ReplicationSchemaBoundView	Represents information about a schema-bound view required for replication. The EnumReplicationSchemaBoundViews( ) method of the ReplicationDatabase class returns an ArrayList object of schema-bound views that can be replicated.
ReplicationStoredProcedure	Represents information about a stored procedure required for replication. The EnumReplicationStoredProcedures( ) method of the ReplicationDatabase class returns an ArrayList object of stored procedures that can be replicated.
ReplicationTable	Represents information about a table required for replication. The Enum-ReplicationTables( ) method of the ReplicationDatabase class returns an ArrayList object of tables that can be replicated.
ReplicationUserDefinedAggregate	Represents information about a user-defined aggregate required for replication. The EnumReplicationUserDefinedAggregates( ) method of the ReplicationDatabase class returns an ArrayList object of user-defined aggregates that can be replicated.
ReplicationUserDefinedFunction	Represents information about a user-defined function required for replication. The EnumReplicationUserDefinedFunctions( ) method of the ReplicationDatabase class returns an ArrayList object of user-defined functions that can be replicated.
ReplicationView	Represents information about a user-defined view required for replication. The EnumReplicationViews( ) method of the Replication-Database class returns an ArrayList object of views that can be replicated.

Filtering an Article

This example partitions the article created in the "Creating an Article" section earlier in this chapter both horizontally (row-based) and vertically (column-based). It does so by using the MergeArticle class, which exposes one property and two methods of interest.

The FilterClause property of the MergeArticle class defines subsets of rows that are available for the article, similar to horizontally partitioning the data. The syntax of the filter clause follows that of a T-SQL WHERE clause without the word WHERE. In this example, the full WHERE clause is WHERE CreditRating = 1 AND PreferredVendorStatus = 'true'. Only records matching this criterion will be published.

The AddReplicatedColumns( ) and RemoveReplicatedColumns( ) methods add columns to and remove columns from the article, similar to vertically partitioning the data. Only columns that are nullable or defined with a default value can be removed from a vertical partition. This example removes the PurchasingWebServiceURL column from the article.

The source code for the example follows:

```
using System;

using Microsoft.SqlServer.Management.Common;
using Microsoft.SqlServer.Replication;

class Program
{
    static void Main(string[] args)
    {
        ServerConnection sc = new ServerConnection("localhost");
        ReplicationDatabase rDb = new ReplicationDatabase(
            "AdventureWorks", sc);

        MergeArticle ma = rDb.MergePublications["AdventureWorks_MergePub"].
            MergeArticles["Article_1"];
        ma.FilterClause = "CreditRating = 1 AND PreferredVendorStatus = 'true'";
        ma.RemoveReplicatedColumns(new string[] {"PurchasingWebServiceURL"});

        sc.Disconnect();

        Console.WriteLine("Press any key to continue.");
        Console.ReadKey();
    }
}
```

You can examine the article by right-clicking the Replication → Local Publications → [AdventureWorks]: AdventureWorks_MergePub node in Object Explorer and selecting Properties from the context menu. Then select the Articles page to see that the PurchasingWebServiceURL column has been removed from the article, as shown in Figure 19-9.

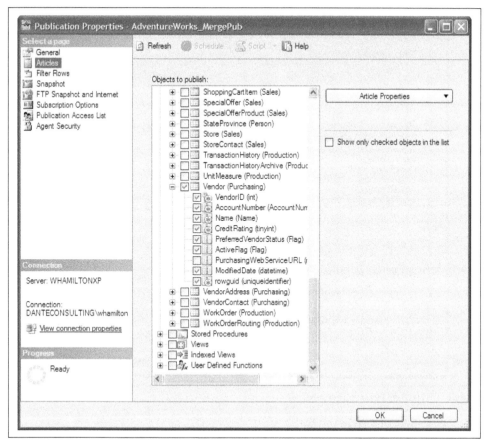

Figure 19-9. Publication Properties dialog box

You can examine the filter you added by selecting the Filter Rows page in the Publication Properties dialog box, selecting the Vendor (Purchasing) filtered tables, and clicking the Edit button to open the Edit Filter dialog box, as shown in Figure 19-10.

Registering a Subscriber

This example creates a subscriber named Subscriber_1. It does so by using the RegisteredSubscriber class in a very simple manner:

1. It instantiates the RegisteredSubscriber object, associating it with the ServerConnection object that represents the target SQL Server.

2. It calls its Create( ) method.

The source code for the example follows:

```
using System;

using Microsoft.SqlServer.Management.Common;
```

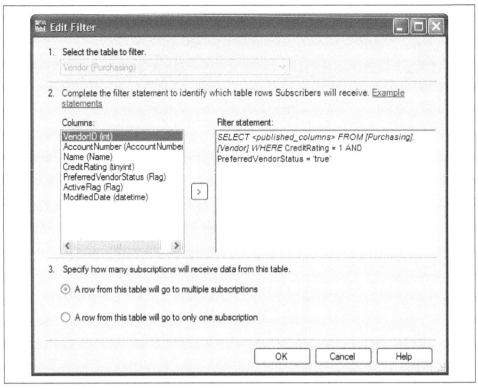

Figure 19-10. Edit Filter dialog box

```
using Microsoft.SqlServer.Replication;

class Program
{
    static void Main(string[] args)
    {
        ServerConnection sc = new ServerConnection("localhost");

        RegisteredSubscriber rs = new RegisteredSubscriber("Subscriber_1", sc);
        rs.Create();

        sc.Disconnect();

        Console.WriteLine("Press any key to continue.");
        Console.ReadKey();
    }
}
```

The sp_helpsubscriberinfo system stored procedure returns information about registered subscribers.

The RMO classes used to manage subscribers are provided for backward compatibility, as it is no longer necessary to explicitly register a subscriber at the publisher in SQL Server 2005. These classes are described in Table 19-7.

Table 19-7. RMO classes for managing subscribers

Class	Description
RegisteredSubscriber	Represents a subscriber registered at a publisher or distributor. The EnumRegisteredSubscribers( ) method of the DistributionPublisher and ReplicationServer classes returns an ArrayList object of registered subscribers.
RegisteredSubscriberCollection	The RegisteredSubscribers property of the DistributionPublisher and ReplicationServer classes returns a RegisteredSubscriberCollection object containing all registered subscribers.

Creating a Subscription

This example creates a pull merge subscription for the publication AdventureWorks_MergePub created in the section "Creating a Publication," earlier in this chapter. It does so in the usual manner, but with one additional method call:

1. It instantiates a MergePullSubscription object.
2. It sets properties as appropriate.
3. It calls the object's Create( ) method.
4. It calls its Refresh( ) method.

The properties that the example sets are as follows:

ConnectionContext
    The target SQL Server instance.

DatabaseName
    The name of the subscription database.

PublisherName
    The name associated with the DistributionPublisher object when it was created.

PublicationDBName
    The name the publisher has assigned to the database.

PublicationName
    The name assigned to the publication.

SubscriberType
    A value from the MergeSubscriberType enumeration.

CreateSyncAgentByDefault
    Setting this property of the MergePullSubscription class creates the agent job used to synchronize the subscription.

There are two additional steps you must perform:

1. Configure the MergePublication object so that it allows pull.
2. Register the merge pull subscription at the publisher.

These are the steps to configure the MergePublication object (AdventureWorks_MergePub) to allow pull, and to register the subscription:

1. Instantiate a MergePublication object and associate it with AdventureWorks_MergePub.
2. Load the publication's properties.
3. Make sure the Attributes property indicates that the publication supports pull.
4. If the publication does not support pull, change the Attributes, and then call CommitPropertyChanges() and Refresh() on the MergePublication object.
5. Call the MakePullSubscriptionWellKnown() method on the MergePublication object.

 Before you execute this example, replace the *ServerName* argument used to set the MergePullSubscription.PublisherName property and used in the MergePublication.MakePullSubscription() method with the name of your database server.

The source code for the example follows:

```
using System;

using Microsoft.SqlServer.Management.Common;
using Microsoft.SqlServer.Replication;

class Program
{
    static void Main(string[] args)
    {
        ServerConnection sc = new ServerConnection("localhost");

        // create the pull subscription
        MergePullSubscription mps = new MergePullSubscription();
        mps.ConnectionContext = sc;
        mps.PublisherName = "ServerName";
        mps.PublicationDBName = "AdventureWorks";
        mps.PublicationName = "AdventureWorks_MergePub";
        mps.DatabaseName = "ReplicationDestination";
        mps.SubscriberType = MergeSubscriberType.Local;
        mps.CreateSyncAgentByDefault = true;
        mps.Create();

        MergePublication mp = new MergePublication(
            "AdventureWorks_MergePub", "AdventureWorks", sc);
        mp.LoadProperties();

        // allow pull if not already allowed
```

```
        if ((mp.Attributes & PublicationAttributes.AllowPull) == 0)
        {
            mp.Attributes = mp.Attributes | PublicationAttributes.AllowPull;
            mp.CommitPropertyChanges( );
            mp.Refresh( );
        }

        // register the merge pull subscription at the publisher
        mp.MakePullSubscriptionWellKnown(
            "ServerName", "ReplicationDestination",
            mps.SyncType, mps.SubscriberType, mps.Priority);

        sc.Disconnect( );

        Console.WriteLine("Press any key to continue.");
        Console.ReadKey( );
    }
}
```

To examine the subscription, refresh and expand the Replication → Local Subscriptions node in Object Explorer, right-click the [ReplicationDestination] – [ServerName].[AdventureWorks]: AdventureWorks_MergePub local subscription, and select Properties from the context menu to display the Subscription Properties dialog box. Figure 19-11 shows the details of the new subscription.

Setting the CreateSyncAgentByDefault property of the MergePullSubscription class creates the agent job used to synchronize the subscription. Open the SQL Server Agent jobs by selecting SQL Server Agent → Jobs and you will see that a new merge replication job has been created.

The RMO classes used to manage subscriptions are described in Table 19-8.

Table 19-8. RMO classes for managing subscriptions

Class	Description
DistributionSubscription	Represents read-only information about the distributor image of a snapshot or transactional subscription. Use this class to create a subscription to a heterogeneous publication.
DistributionSubscriptionCollection	Represents a collection of DistributionSubscription objects. The DistributionSubscriptions property of the DistributionPublication class returns a DistributionPublicationCollection object containing all distribution subscriptions defined on the distribution publication.
LastValidationDateTime	Represents the date and time of the last merge subscription validation.
MergePullSubscription	Represents a pull subscription to a merge publication.
	The EnumMergePullSubscriptions property of the ReplicationDatabase class returns an ArrayList object of all merge pull subscriptions that use the database.

Table 19-8. RMO classes for managing subscriptions (continued)

Class	Description
MergePullSubscriptionCollection	Represents a collection of MergePullSubscription objects.
	The MergePullSubscriptions property of the Replication-Database class returns a MergePullSubscription-Collection object containing all merge pull subscriptions defined on the replication database.
MergeSubscription	Represents a subscription to merge publication.
MergeSubscriptionCollection	Represents a collection of MergeSubscription objects.
	The MergeSubscriptions property of the Replication-Database class returns a MergeSubscriptionCollection object containing all merge push subscriptions defined on the replication database.
SubscriptionBackupInformation	Represents information for backup devices used for setting an "initial from backup" subscription.
SubscriberSubscription	Represents a lightweight object of limited subscription information on the subscribing server.
TransPullSubscription	Represents a pull subscription to a transactional or snapshot publication. The EnumTransPullSubscriptions property of the ReplicationDatabase class returns an ArrayList object of all merge pull subscriptions that use the database.
TransPullSubscriptionCollection	Represents a collection of TransPullSubscription objects.
	The TransPullSubscriptions property of the ReplicationDatabase class returns a TransPullSubscriptionCollection object containing all transactional and snapshot pull subscriptions defined on the replication database.
TransSubscription	Represents a subscription to a transactional or snapshot publication.
TransSubscriptionCollection	Represents a collection of TransSubscription objects. The TransSubscriptions property of the ReplicationDatabase class returns a TransSubscriptionCollection object containing all transactional or snapshot subscriptions defined on the replication database.

Generating the Initial Snapshot

This example generates the initial snapshot used to initialize the subscriber for a new subscription. It uses the SnapshotGenerationAgent class, which represents the Snapshot Agent. It creates an instance of this class, and then sets the following properties:

Publisher
    The name given to the distribution publisher

PublisherDatabase
    The name of the database being published for replication

Publication
    The name of the publication

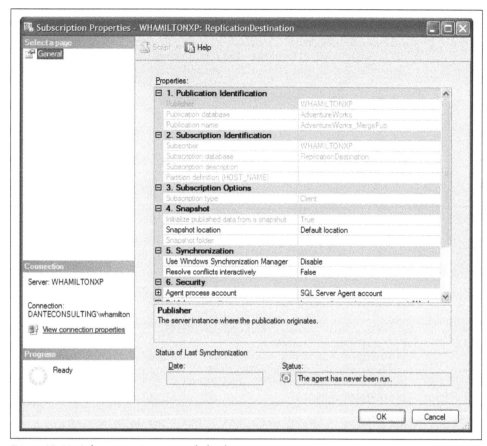

Figure 19-11. Subscription Properties dialog box

Distributor

The name of the distributor (in this case, the same as Publisher)

PublisherSecurityMode

A value from the SecurityMode enumeration (SecurityMode.Integrated in this case)

DistributorSecurityMode

A value from the SecurityMode enumeration (SecurityMode.Integrated in this case)

ReplicationType

A value from the ReplicationType enumeration (ReplicationType.Merge in this case)

The last step is to call the GenerateSnapshot() method of the SnapshotGenerationAgent. In this case, GenerateSnapshot() runs the Snapshot Agent synchronously to generate the initial snapshot for the merge publication named AdventureWorks_MergePub.

You need to add a reference to the `Microsoft.SqlServer.Replication.dll` assembly, installed by default in the *C:\Program Files\Microsoft SQL Server\90\SDK\Assemblies* directory, to compile and execute this example. Before you execute this example, replace the *ServerName* argument used to set the `SnapshotGenerationAgent.Publisher` and `SnapshotGenerationAgent.Distributor` properties with the name of your database server.

The source code for the example follows:

```
using System;

using Microsoft.SqlServer.Management.Common;
using Microsoft.SqlServer.Replication;

class Program
{
    static void Main(string[] args)
    {
        SnapshotGenerationAgent sga = new SnapshotGenerationAgent();
        sga.Publisher = "ServerName";
        sga.PublisherDatabase = "AdventureWorks";
        sga.Publication = "AdventureWorks_MergePub";
        sga.Distributor = "ServerName";
        sga.PublisherSecurityMode = SecurityMode.Integrated;
        sga.DistributorSecurityMode = SecurityMode.Integrated;
        sga.ReplicationType = ReplicationType.Merge;
        sga.GenerateSnapshot();

        Console.WriteLine(Environment.NewLine + "Press any key to continue.");
        Console.ReadKey();
    }
}
```

Partial results are shown in Figure 19-12.

The `StartSnapshotGenerationAgentJob()` method of the `MergePublication` and `TransPublication` classes generates a snapshot asynchronously.

Synchronizing a Subscription to an Initial Snapshot

This example uses the snapshot created in the preceding section, "Generating the Initial Snapshot," to initialize the subscriber when the data is first synchronized.

Before you execute this example, replace the *ServerName* argument used to set the `MergePullSubscription.PublisherName` property with the name of your database server.

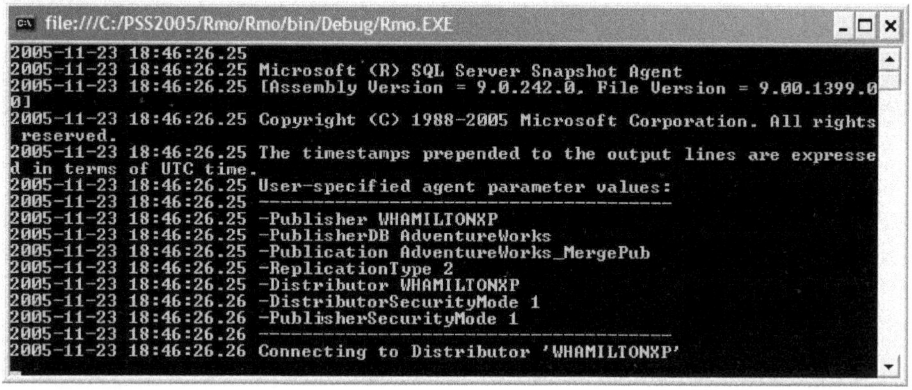

Figure 19-12. Partial results for generating initial snapshot example

The source code for the example follows:

```
using System;

using Microsoft.SqlServer.Management.Common;
using Microsoft.SqlServer.Replication;

class Program
{
    static void Main(string[] args)
    {
        ServerConnection sc = new ServerConnection("localhost");

        MergePullSubscription mps = new MergePullSubscription();
        mps.ConnectionContext = sc;
        mps.DatabaseName = "ReplicationDestination";
        mps.PublisherName = "ServerName";
        mps.PublicationDBName = "AdventureWorks";
        mps.PublicationName = "AdventureWorks_MergePub";
        mps.LoadProperties();
        mps.SynchronizeWithJob();

        sc.Disconnect();

        Console.WriteLine("Press any key to continue.");
        Console.ReadKey();
    }
}
```

After you run this code, the table named Vendor is created in the subscriber database
ReplicationDestination.

The SynchronizeWithJob() method of the MergeSubscription, MergePullSubscription,
TransSubscription, and TransPullSubscription classes starts the Merge Agent job to

synchronize the subscription. The snapshot is transferred to and applied to the subscriber when the subscription is first synchronized.

If you select View Synchronization Status from the context menu for the local subscription, the status of the last synchronization indicates something similar to the following:

```
Applied the snapshot and merged 0 data change(s) (0 insert(s), 0 update(s),
0 delete(s), 0 conflict(s)).
```

If you run the code a second time, the snapshot is not applied and the status of the last synchronization indicates something similar to this:

```
Merge completed with no data changes processed.
```

Replication allows multiple nodes to make data changes, so it is possible that changes made at one node may conflict with changes made at another.

The RMO classes used to manage merge and transactional replication conflict information are described in Table 19-9.

Table 19-9. RMO classes for managing replication conflicts

Class	Description
MergeConflictCount	Represents conflict count information for a table article in merge replication. The EnumMergeConflictCounts( ) method of the ReplicationDatabase class returns an ArrayList object of conflicts in a merge publication or subscription database.
TransConflictCount	Represents conflict count information for a table article in transactional replication. The EnumTransConflictCounts( ) method of the ReplicationDatabase class returns an ArrayList object of conflicts in a transactional publication or subscription database.

Retrieving Agent History

This example displays status information about the last synchronization job that was run. It uses the LastAgentJobHistoryInfo( ) method of the MergePullSubscription class, which returns this information as an AgentJobHistoryInfo object. This class represents the results from the last run of the replication agent. It then shows the LastRunDateTime and Status properties of this object.

 Before you execute this example, replace the *ServerName* argument used to set the MergePullSubscription.PublisherName property with the name of your database server.

The source code for the example follows:

```
using System;

using Microsoft.SqlServer.Management.Common;
using Microsoft.SqlServer.Replication;
```

```
class Program
{
    static void Main(string[] args)
    {
        ServerConnection sc = new ServerConnection("localhost");

        MergePullSubscription mps = new MergePullSubscription();
        mps.ConnectionContext = sc;
        mps.DatabaseName = "ReplicationDestination";
        mps.PublisherName = "ServerName";
        mps.PublicationDBName = "AdventureWorks";
        mps.PublicationName = "AdventureWorks_MergePub";
        mps.LoadProperties();

        AgentJobHistoryInfo ajhi = mps.LastAgentJobHistoryInfo();
        Console.WriteLine("Last Run Date/Time: " + ajhi.LastRunDateTime);
        Console.WriteLine("Status:           " + ajhi.Status);

        sc.Disconnect();

        Console.WriteLine(Environment.NewLine + "Press any key to continue.");
        Console.ReadKey();
    }
}
```

Results are shown in Figure 19-13.

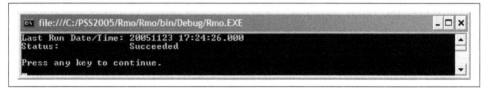

Figure 19-13. Results for retrieving agent history example

The RMO classes used to manage agents are described in Table 19-10.

Table 19-10. RMO classes for managing agents

Class	Description
AgentJobHistoryInfo	Represents the results from the last run of the replication agent. The LastAgentJobHistoryInfo property of the MergePullSubscription and TransPullSubscription classes returns an AgentJobHistoryInfo object with information about the last synchronization agent job that was run.
AgentProfile	Represents a replication agent profile. The EnumAgentProfiles() method of the ReplicationServer class returns an ArrayList object of all replication agent profiles supported on the server.
	Replication agent profiles define default values when agent jobs get created.

Table 19-10. RMO classes for managing agents (continued)

Class	Description
AgentProfileParameter	Represents a parameter in a replication agent profile. The EnumParameter( ) method of the AgentProfile class returns an ArrayList object of information about parameters for the replication agent profile.
AgentProfileParameterInfo	Represents information about a replication agent parameter. The EnumParameter( ) method of the AgentProfile class returns an ArrayList object of information about parameters for the replication agent profile.

Specifying a Replication Schedule

This example sets the subscription created in the "Creating a Subscription" section to pull replication data from the publication every five minutes. It does so by setting several properties of the MergePullSubscription object:

AgentSchedule.FrequencyType
> Takes a value from the ScheduleFrequencyType enumeration (ScheduleFrequency-Type.Daily in this case).

AgentSchedule.FrequencySubDay
> Takes a value from the ScheduleFrequencySubDay enumeration (Schedule-FrequencySubDay.Minute in this case).

AgentSchedule.FrequencySubDayInterval
> Specifies the number of units of the AgentSchedule.FrequencySubDay. This example sets replication to occur every one hour.

The last step is to call the CommitPropertyChanges( ) method on the MergePull-Subscription object.

 Before you execute this example, replace the *ServerName* argument used to set the MergePullSubscription.PublisherName property with the name of your database server.

The source code for the example follows:

```
using System;

using Microsoft.SqlServer.Management.Common;
using Microsoft.SqlServer.Replication;

class Program
{
    static void Main(string[] args)
    {
        ServerConnection sc = new ServerConnection("localhost");

        MergePullSubscription mps = new MergePullSubscription( );
        mps.ConnectionContext = sc;
```

```
                mps.DatabaseName = "ReplicationDestination";
                mps.PublisherName = "ServerName";
                mps.PublicationDBName = "AdventureWorks";
                mps.PublicationName = "AdventureWorks_MergePub";
                mps.LoadProperties();
                mps.AgentSchedule.FrequencyType = ScheduleFrequencyType.Daily;
                mps.AgentSchedule.FrequencySubDay = ScheduleFrequencySubDay.Hour;
                mps.AgentSchedule.FrequencySubDayInterval = 1;
                mps.CommitPropertyChanges();

                sc.Disconnect();

                Console.WriteLine("Press any key to continue.");
                Console.ReadKey();
        }
    }
```

After you execute the example, confirm the new job schedule in Object Explorer by refreshing SQL Server Agent → Jobs, right-clicking the *ServerName*-AdventureWorks-AdventureWorks_MergePub-*ServerName*-ReplicationDestination-0 job, and selecting Properties from the context menu to open the Job Properties dialog box, shown in Figure 19-14.

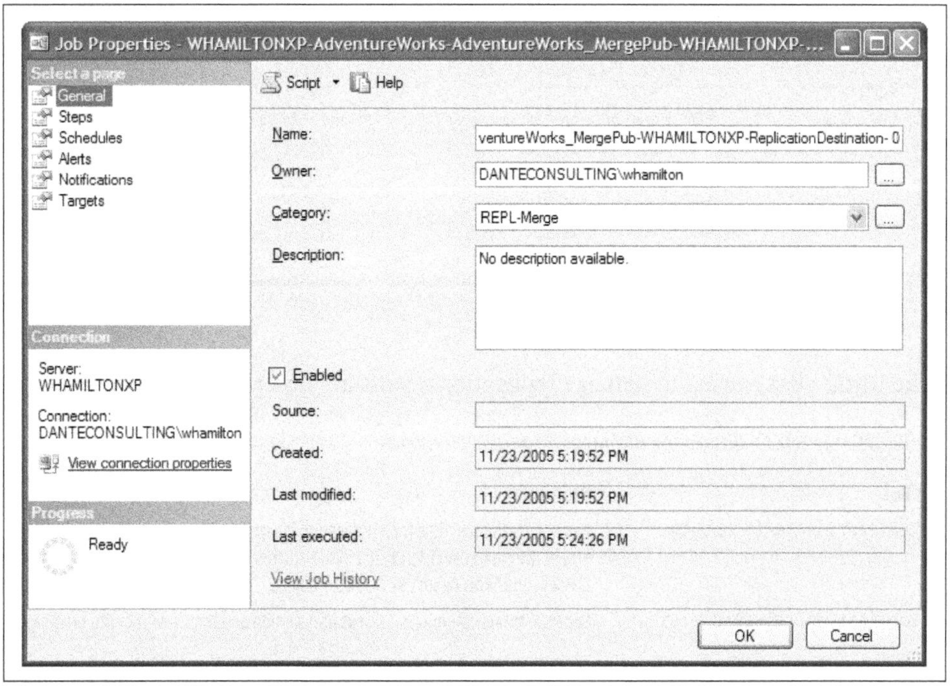

Figure 19-14. Job Properties dialog box

Select the Schedules page and then click the Edit button to display the Job Schedules Properties dialog box, shown in Figure 19-15.

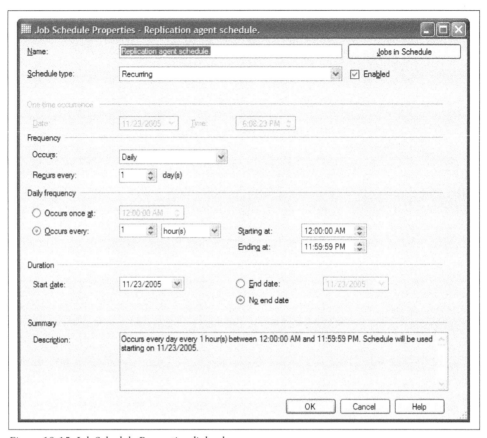

Figure 19-15. Job Schedule Properties dialog box

The RMO classes used to manage replication agents are described in Table 19-11.

Table 19-11. RMO classes for managing replication agents

Class	Description
ReplicationAgentSchedule	Represents the schedule for a replication agent job. The AgentSchedule property of the MergePullSubscription and TransPullSubscription classes returns an AgentSchedule object.
ReplicationStatusAndWarning	Represents replication agent status information and threshold monitor warnings.

Validating Subscriber Data

This example validates the subscription to the AdventureWorks_MergePub publication created in the earlier "Creating a Publication" section. It first calls the Validate-

Subscription() method of the MergePublication class, which marks the subscription for validation in the next synchronization. It then forces synchronization by calling MergePullSubscription.SynchronizeWithJob().

 Before you execute this example, replace the *ServerName* argument used in the MergePublication.ValidateSubscription() constructor and to set the MergePullSubscription.PublisherName property with the name of your database server.

The source code for the example follows:

```
using System;

using Microsoft.SqlServer.Management.Common;
using Microsoft.SqlServer.Replication;

class Program
{
    static void Main(string[] args)
    {
        ServerConnection sc = new ServerConnection("localhost");

        // mark the subscription for validation
        MergePublication mp = new MergePublication();
        mp.ConnectionContext = sc;
        mp.Name = "AdventureWorks_MergePub";
        mp.DatabaseName = "AdventureWorks";
        mp.LoadProperties();
        mp.ValidateSubscription("ServerName", "ReplicationDestination",
            ValidationOption.Checksum80);

        // synchronize the subscription.
        MergePullSubscription mps = new MergePullSubscription();
        mps.ConnectionContext = sc;
        mps.DatabaseName = "ReplicationDestination";
        mps.PublisherName = "ServerName";
        mps.PublicationDBName = "AdventureWorks";
        mps.PublicationName = "AdventureWorks_MergePub";
        mps.LoadProperties();
        mps.SynchronizeWithJob();

        sc.Disconnect();

        Console.WriteLine("Press any key to continue.");
        Console.ReadKey();
    }
}
```

The ValidateSubscription() method of the MergePublication class marks the subscription for validation in the next synchronization. To view the subscription, refresh and expand the Replication → Local Subscriptions node in Object Explorer, right-click

the [ReplicationDestination] – [*ServerName*].[AdventureWorks]: AdventureWorks_
MergePub local subscription, and select View Job History from the context menu to
display the Log File Viewer dialog box. The results of the validation appear in the
details for the job in the bottom pane, as shown in Figure 19-16.

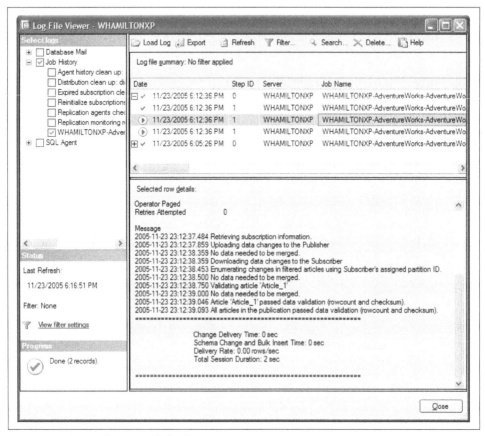

Figure 19-16. Log File Viewer dialog box

Monitoring Replication

This example displays summary and detailed merge session information using three
classes:

MergeSubscriberMonitor
    Represents server-side monitoring of merge publication subscriptions.

MergeSessionSummary
    Represents Merge Agent session information. An array of `MergeSessionSummary`
    objects is returned by a call to the `MergeSubscriberMonitor.GetSessionsSummary()`
    method.

MergeSessionDetail

Represents information about a step in a Merge Agent session. An array of MergeSessionDetail objects is returned by a call to the MergeSubscriberMonitor. GetSessionDetails() method.

The example shows the StartTime, Duration, and Status properties of each MergeSessionSummary object. It also obtains details about each step by calling MergeSubscriberMonitor.GetSessionDetails(), and displays the DetailType and Message properties.

> Before you execute this example, replace the *ServerName* argument used to set the MergeSubscriberMonitor.Publisher property with the name of your database server.

The source code for the example follows:

```
using System;

using Microsoft.SqlServer.Management.Common;
using Microsoft.SqlServer.Replication;

class Program
{
    static void Main(string[] args)
    {
        ServerConnection sc = new ServerConnection("localhost");
        MergeSubscriberMonitor msm = new MergeSubscriberMonitor(sc);
        msm.Publisher = "ServerName";
        msm.Publication = "AdventureWorks_MergePub";
        msm.PublisherDB = "AdventureWorks";
        msm.SubscriberDB = "ReplicationDestination";

        // display the merge session summary information
        MergeSessionSummary[] mssa = msm.GetSessionsSummary();
        foreach (MergeSessionSummary mss in mssa)
        {
            Console.WriteLine(mss.StartTime + ", " + mss.Duration + ", " +
                mss.Status);

            // display the merge session detail information for the session
            MergeSessionDetail[] msda = msm.GetSessionDetails(mssa[0].SessionId);
            foreach (MergeSessionDetail msd in msda)
                Console.WriteLine("   " + msd.DetailType + ": " + msd.Message);

            Console.WriteLine();
        }

        sc.Disconnect();

        Console.WriteLine(Environment.NewLine + "Press any key to continue.");
```

```
            Console.ReadKey();
        }
    }
}
```

Partial results are shown in Figure 19-17.

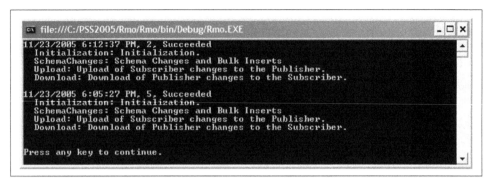

Figure 19-17. Results for monitoring replication example

The RMO classes used to manage monitors and access merge session information are described in Tables 19-12 and 19-13.

Table 19-12. RMO classes for managing monitors

Class	Description
MergeSubscriberMonitor	Represents server-side monitoring of subscriptions to merge publications.
MonitorThreshold	Represents a threshold metric used to monitor a publication. The EnumMonitorThresholds( ) method of the PublicationMonitor class returns an ArrayList object of monitor thresholds defined for the publication.
PendingCommandInfo	Represents information about pending commands for a subscription to a transactional publication. The TransPendingCommandInfo property of the PublicationMonitor class returns information about pending commands for a subscription.
PublicationMonitor	Represents publisher-side monitoring of a publication.
PublicationMonitorCollection	The PublicationMonitors property of the PublisherMonitor class returns a PublicationMonitorCollection object containing information about monitors defined for the publication.
PublisherMonitor	Represents distributor-side monitoring of a publisher.
PublisherMonitorCollection	The PublisherMonitors property of the ReplicationMonitor class returns a PublisherMonitorCollection object containing information about monitors used to monitor publishers.
ReplicationMonitor	Represents a monitor for a replication server.
TracerToken	Represents tracer token information. The EnumTracerTokens( ) method of the PublicationMonitor class returns an ArrayList object of tracer tokens that have been inserted into the monitored transactional publication.

Table 19-13. RMO classes for managing merge session information

Class	Description
MergeSessionDetail	Represents information about a step in a Merge Agent session. The GetSession-Details() method of the MergeSubscriberMonitor class returns an array of MergeSessionDetail objects containing detailed Merge Agent information.
MergeSessionError	Represents information about errors during a Merge Agent session. The Errors property of the MergeSessionSummary class returns a MergeSessionError object.
MergeSessionSummary	Represents Merge Agent session information.

Business Logic Handlers

You can execute business logic in managed code assemblies during the merge synchronization process to provide custom handling for conditions during synchronization, such as data changes, conflicts, and errors. These assemblies are called business logic handlers. You can use COM-based resolvers—either custom or those supplied with SQL Server 2005—for the same purpose.

The RMO classes used to manage business logic handlers and COM-based resolvers are described in Table 19-14.

Table 19-14. RMO classes for managing business logic handlers and COM-based resolvers

Class	Description
BusinessLogicHandler	Represents server registration for the managed code assembly implementing a business logic handler. The EnumBusinessLogicHandlers() method of the ReplicationServer class returns an ArrayList object of business logic handlers registered at the server.
CustomResolver	Represents a COM-based resolver registration at a server used for merge replication. The EnumCustomResolvers() method of the ReplicationServer class returns an ArrayList object of custom conflict resolvers registered on the SQL Server instance.

For more information about implementing custom business logic using business logic handlers or COM-based resolvers, see Microsoft SQL Server 2005 Books Online.

CHAPTER 20

SQL Server Analysis Services (SSAS)

SQL Server Analysis Services (SSAS) provides *online analytical processing* (OLAP) and *data mining* functionality using a combination of client- and server-side components.

A *data warehouse* is a data repository used to overcome issues arising from performing strategic analysis on data in an *online transaction processing* (OLTP) database. An OLTP database supports the day-to-day business activity of the organization and is configured to let applications write data for a single transaction as quickly as possible. A data warehouse provides users easy access to information used to make strategic business decisions.

Dimension tables store information used to categorize and hierarchically organize the information stored in fact tables. The columns of a dimension table are called *attributes*. Attributes are used to hierarchically organize the rows of dimension tables in a way that is meaningful for business users.

OLAP is a combination of products and processes used to aggregate large amounts of heterogeneous data and interactively examine the results in a dimensional model. OLAP evolved from the need to interactively examine large volumes of data warehouse information.

Like a data warehouse, OLAP uses dimensional modeling to represent data. Unlike a data warehouse, which typically uses a relational database to store and access data, OLAP uses cubes—multidimensional data structures organized hierarchically along a business attribute for each dimension of the cube, with each cell containing one or more measures.

This chapter provides an overview of SSAS, the languages used with SSAS, programmatically querying data and metadata, and programmatically administering an SSAS instance and its objects. Because SSAS is a very large topic, the goal of this chapter is simply to provide an introduction to key elements and concepts. See Microsoft SQL Server 2005 Books Online for in-depth information about SSAS.

Before You Begin

The examples in this chapter use the sample Adventure Works DW (Standard Edition or Enterprise Edition) SSAS database. If this is not installed, follow the instructions in the topic "Running Setup to Install AdventureWorks Sample Databases and Samples" in Microsoft SQL Server 2005 Books Online.

You have to process the database prior to using it. Right-click the database in Object Explorer and select Process from the context menu.

View the SSAS databases in Object Explorer to ensure that the Adventure Works DW database is available by following these steps:

1. Open SQL Server Management Studio.

2. Select View → Registered Server Types → Analysis Services.

3. Right-click the Analysis Services server in the Registered Servers window and click Connect → Object Explorer from the context menu.

4. Expand the Databases node under the registered Analysis Services server to display the newly deployed Analysis Services Tutorial database, as shown in Figure 20-1.

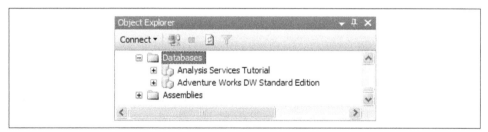

Figure 20-1. Object Explorer view of Analysis Services Tutorial database

SSAS Overview

A data warehouse combines data from multiple sources into a single homogenous repository that is organized for efficient analytical query processing rather than transaction processing. Data warehouses use dimensional modeling to represent business information. Data is stored in two types of tables—*fact tables* and *dimension tables*.

Fact tables contain numeric performance information from transactional data. The columns of a fact table are one of two types—*measures* or *attributes*. A measure is quantitative business data and is usually numeric. An attribute is used to associate the measures with a row in the dimension table.

Multidimensional data is represented by structures called *cubes*, each representing a set of data called a *measure*, hierarchically organized by one or more *dimensions*. Dimensions organize data within a cube by using *hierarchies* and *attributes* instead of tables. Cubes are typically built from data in relational data sources. A *member* is an item in a dimension that represents one or more data instances, similar to records in a relational database.

A hierarchy organizes the members of a dimension into one or more *levels*, and lets you navigate and aggregate data within the cube. Each attribute in a hierarchy definition corresponds to a level in the hierarchy from the most summarized down to the most detailed. For example, you can have a Geography dimension that organizes the hierarchy into levels based on Country, State, and City attributes. The member in the lowest level is called a *leaf member*, and other members are called *nonleaf* members.

Multiple data values called *measures* exist at each intersection of the dimensions. A measure is a special dimension that represents the data organized according to the other dimensions in the cube. Every cube must have a measure dimension. Calculated measures can be created that derive from existing measures.

SSAS Database

An SSAS *database* is a container for all objects required for an SSAS solution, as described in Table 20-1.

Table 20-1. SSAS database objects

Database object	Description
Data source	Encapsulates provider-specific connection information used to access source data.
Data-source view	A logical model based on one or more data sources creating a layer of abstraction to the source data.
Cube	Multidimensional data structure organized hierarchically along a business attribute and providing an easy and responsive mechanism for querying data.
Dimension	A combination of hierarchies and attributes used to categorize data according to areas of interest within a cube.
Data-mining structure	A data structure that defines the data domain from which data-mining models are built. The data-mining structure contains mining structure columns that describe the data in the data source.
Data-mining model	Data from the data-mining structure processed using an algorithm that identifies rules and patterns for populating the mining model.
Role	Used to manage security for databases, cubes, and mining models.
Assembly	CLR managed code that extends the business functionality of MDX and DMX.

SSAS Languages

SSAS provides the following languages used to query and manipulate data and schemas:

Multidimensional Expressions (MDX)
    Used to refine, work with, and retrieve data from multidimensional objects

Data Mining Extensions (DMX)
Used to create and work with data-mining models

XML for Analysis (XMLA)
Open-standard, SOAP-based protocol for accessing standard multidimensional data sources, including SSAS data sources, on the Web

Analysis Services Scripting Language (ASSL)
Used to create, manage, and deploy SSAS objects

The following subsections describe the SSAS languages.

Multidimensional Expressions (MDX)

A relational database represents two-dimensional data defined by columns and rows. The intersection of a column and row identifies a field containing a single data value. T-SQL statements query relational data by using SELECT queries, specifying columns to retrieve and limiting values retrieved by using a WHERE clause.

MDX is a statement-based scripting language used to define, retrieve, and manipulate multidimensional objects and data. Although MDX is similar to T-SQL, it is not an extension to T-SQL. The MDX language provides the following:

- A Data Manipulation Language (DML) used to retrieve and manipulate data from multidimensional objects
- A Data Definition Language (DDL) used to create, alter, and drop multidimensional objects
- A scripting language used to manage scope, context, and control flow within MDX scripts
- Operators and functions, both built-in and user-defined, for manipulating data retrieved from multidimensional objects

Each MDX expression has a SELECT clause to request data, a FROM clause to identify the data source, and a WHERE clause to filter data. These elements, together with other keywords, are used to extract multidimensional data from cubes and manipulate the data retrieved through a set of built-in or user-defined functions. MDX also provides a DDL to manage SSAS objects.

MDX returns the results of a query against a cube in a structure called a *cellset*, which is analogous to the result set returned by T-SQL statements issued against relational data sources. A cube contains a collection of cells, and the intersection point of a member from each dimension of the cube defines a *cell*. A cell contains one measure together with its properties, such as the data type and format. A *tuple* is an expression that contains an ordered collection of one member of each dimension uniquely identifying a cell. A set is an ordered collection of tuples.

A SELECT statement is used in MDX to retrieve data from cubes. A simple SELECT statement contains a SELECT clause and a FROM clause with an optional WHERE clause.

The following example executes an MDX SELECT query against the Adventure Works cube in the Adventure Works DW database. Right-click that database in Object Explorer and select New Query → MDX from the context menu. Execute the following query to retrieve a cellset from the Adventure Works cube:

```
SELECT {[Measures].[Sales Amount], [Measures].[Gross Profit Margin]} ON COLUMNS,
    {[Product].[Product Model Categories].[Category]} ON ROWS
FROM [Adventure Works]
WHERE ([Sales Territory Country].[United States])
```

Results are shown in Figure 20-2.

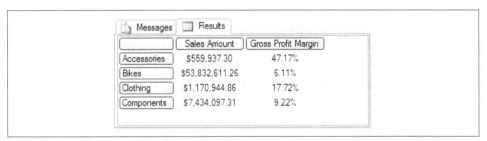

Figure 20-2. Results for MDX query example

The preceding example defines two query axes—Sales Amount and Gross Profit Margin as columns and [Product].[Product Model Categories].[Category] as a row—and restricts the data returned from the measure to the United States.

In T-SQL, the fields specified in a SELECT statement, together with a WHERE clause, are used to limit the data retrieved by a query. In MDX, the SELECT clause specifies the dimensions and members returned, which are referred to as the *query axis* dimensions. The WHERE clause restricts the data returned in the cellset to specific dimensions and member criteria, which are referred to as the *slicer axis* dimensions.

The SELECT clause determines the query axes—the edges—of the cellset returned by an MDX query. Each axis dimension is associated with a number, starting with 0 and incrementing sequentially with no breaks. The first five axes can be referred to by the aliases COLUMNS, ROWS, PAGES, SECTIONS, and CHAPTERS. If you specify more than two dimensions in the query, you will not be able to see those dimensions in the Results window in SQL Server Management Studio.

You can use a calculated measure in a query by specifying it using a WITH MEMBER clause, as shown in the following example:

```
WITH MEMBER [Measures].[Total Amount] AS
    '[Measures].[Sales Amount] + [Measures].[Tax Amount]'
SELECT {[Measures].[Total Amount]} ON COLUMNS,
    {[Product].[Product Model Categories].[Category]} ON ROWS
FROM [Adventure Works]
WHERE ([Sales Territory Country].[United States])
```

Results are shown in Figure 20-3.

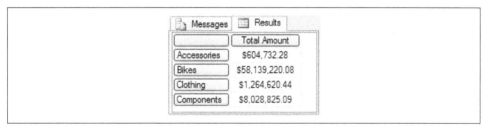

Figure 20-3. Results for MDX query using WITH MEMBER clause example

Data Mining Extensions (DMX)

DMX is a language used to create new data-mining model structures, train models, manage models, and browse and predict against models. DMX consists of DML statements, DDL statements, functions, and operators.

The OLE DB for Data Mining specification defines a structure in which to store the definition of a mining model and a language for creating, managing, and working with data-mining models. You can use DMX with this structure to create and work with models.

There are two types of DMX statements—data manipulation and data definition. Use DMX data-manipulation statements to browse and create predictions against existing models. Use DMX data-definition statements to create, import, export, and drop mining models and mining structures from a database.

You create a new DMX statement by right-clicking an SSAS database in Object Explorer and selecting New Query → DMX from the context menu. As an example, execute the following DMX data-manipulation statement to return information about the mining model schema rowset for the Forecasting mining model:

```
SELECT MODEL_CATALOG, MODEL_NAME, ATTRIBUTE_NAME, NODE_NAME,
  NODE_UNIQUE_NAME, NODE_DISTRIBUTION
FROM [Forecasting].CONTENT
```

Results are shown in Figure 20-4.

XML for Analysis (XMLA)

XMLA is a SOAP-based XML protocol used for universal data access to any standard multidimensional data source on the Web. XMLA lets you explore and query multidimensional data through web services.

The XMLA open specification has two methods—Discover and Execute—that handle incoming and outgoing information on an SSAS instance. The Discover method

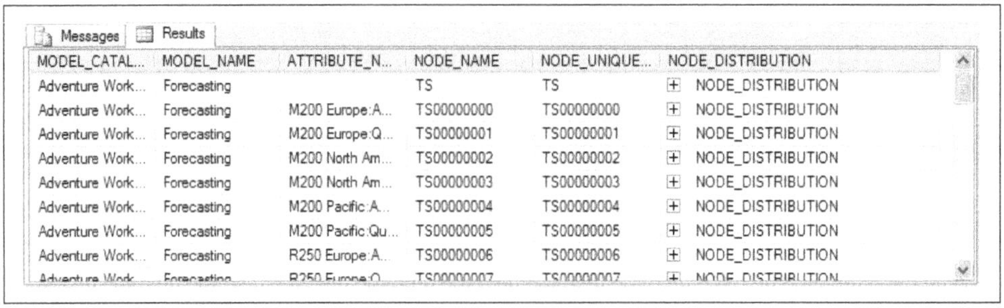

Messages | Results

MODEL_CATAL...	MODEL_NAME	ATTRIBUTE_N...	NODE_NAME	NODE_UNIQUE...	NODE_DISTRIBUTION
Adventure Work...	Forecasting		TS	TS	+ NODE_DISTRIBUTION
Adventure Work...	Forecasting	M200 Europe:A...	TS00000000	TS00000000	+ NODE_DISTRIBUTION
Adventure Work...	Forecasting	M200 Europe:Q...	TS00000001	TS00000001	+ NODE_DISTRIBUTION
Adventure Work...	Forecasting	M200 North Am...	TS00000002	TS00000002	+ NODE_DISTRIBUTION
Adventure Work...	Forecasting	M200 North Am...	TS00000003	TS00000003	+ NODE_DISTRIBUTION
Adventure Work...	Forecasting	M200 Pacific:A...	TS00000004	TS00000004	+ NODE_DISTRIBUTION
Adventure Work...	Forecasting	M200 Pacific:Qu...	TS00000005	TS00000005	+ NODE_DISTRIBUTION
Adventure Work...	Forecasting	R250 Europe:A...	TS00000006	TS00000006	+ NODE_DISTRIBUTION
Adventure Work...	Forecasting	R250 Europe:Q...	TS00000007	TS00000007	+ NODE_DISTRIBUTION

Figure 20-4. Results for DMX data-manipulation statement example

returns information and metadata from a web service. The Execute method lets you run commands against XMLA data sources.

XMLA is the native protocol for SQL Server 2005 and is used by client applications to communicate with SSAS instances. SSAS uses XMLA exclusively when communicating with client applications, and significantly extends the XMLA 1.1 specification for this purpose.

The following example shows an Execute XMLA query that is the same as the first query in the "Multidimensional Expressions (MDX)" section earlier in this chapter. Create a new XMLA query in SQL Server Management Studio by right-clicking the SSAS instance and selecting New Query → XMLA from the context menu.

```
<Execute xmlns="urn:schemas-microsoft-com:xml-analysis">
  <Command>
    <Statement>
      SELECT {[Measures].[Sales Amount], [Measures].[Gross Profit Margin]}
        ON COLUMNS,
      {[Product].[Product Model Categories].[Category]} ON ROWS
      FROM [Adventure Works]
      WHERE ([Sales Territory Country].[United States])
    </Statement>
  </Command>
  <Properties>
    <PropertyList>
      <Catalog>Adventure Works DW Standard Edition</Catalog>
      <Format>Multidimensional</Format>
      <AxisFormat>ClusterFormat</AxisFormat>
    </PropertyList>
  </Properties>
</Execute>
```

The results are returned in the <CellData> element of the XML document partially shown in Figure 20-5.

The next example uses a Discover XMLA query to return the available data sources for the SSAS server and information required to connect to them:

```
<Discover xmlns="urn:schemas-microsoft-com:xml-analysis">
  <RequestType>DISCOVER_DATASOURCES</RequestType>
```

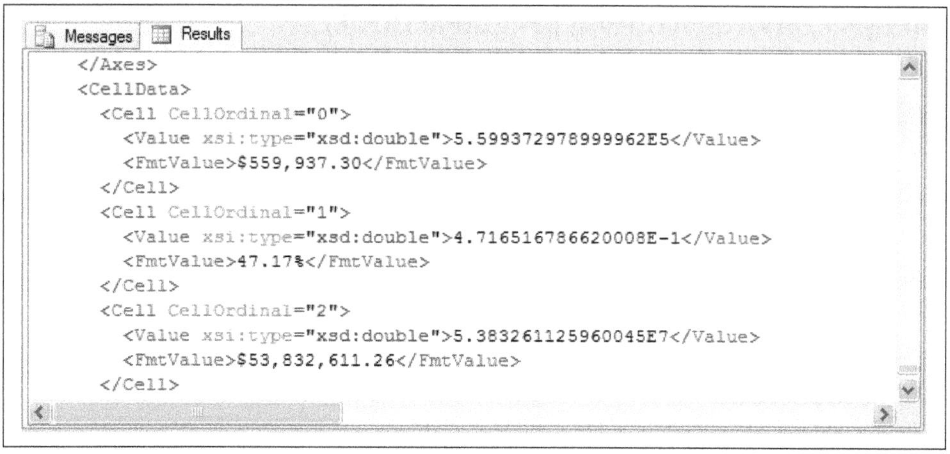

```
  </Axes>
  <CellData>
    <Cell CellOrdinal="0">
      <Value xsi:type="xsd:double">5.599372978999962E5</Value>
      <FmtValue>$559,937.30</FmtValue>
    </Cell>
    <Cell CellOrdinal="1">
      <Value xsi:type="xsd:double">4.716516786620008E-1</Value>
      <FmtValue>47.17%</FmtValue>
    </Cell>
    <Cell CellOrdinal="2">
      <Value xsi:type="xsd:double">5.383261125960045E7</Value>
      <FmtValue>$53,832,611.26</FmtValue>
    </Cell>
```

Figure 20-5. Partial results for XMLA Execute method example

```
    <Restrictions>
    </Restrictions>
    <Properties>
    </Properties>
  </Discover>
```

The results are returned in the <row> element of the XML document partially shown in Figure 20-6.

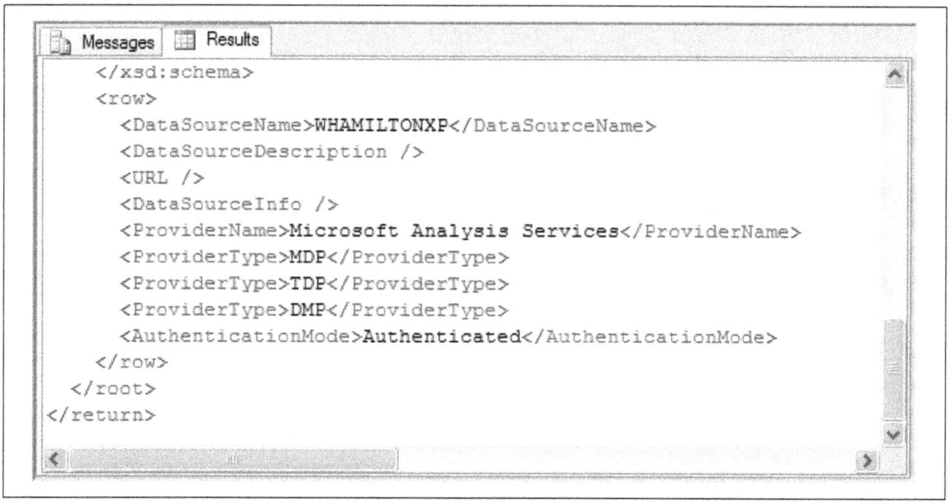

```
    </xsd:schema>
    <row>
      <DataSourceName>WHAMILTONXP</DataSourceName>
      <DataSourceDescription />
      <URL />
      <DataSourceInfo />
      <ProviderName>Microsoft Analysis Services</ProviderName>
      <ProviderType>MDP</ProviderType>
      <ProviderType>TDP</ProviderType>
      <ProviderType>DMP</ProviderType>
      <AuthenticationMode>Authenticated</AuthenticationMode>
    </row>
  </root>
</return>
```

Figure 20-6. Partial results for XMLA Discover method example

The RequestType parameter specifies the type of information the Discover method should return. The Restrictions parameter filters the returned result set based on column values. The Properties element specifies properties of the Discover method.

Analysis Services Scripting Language (ASSL)

ASSL is a dialect for SOAP messages used by client applications to communicate with SSAS instances. ASSL has two parts:

- A DDL that defines an SSAS instance, the database, and the database objects contained in the instance. Client applications use the DDL to describe, create, alter, and deploy SSAS objects.
- A command language that sends actions to an SSAS instance using XMLA.

For more information about ASSL, see Microsoft SQL Server 2005 Books Online.

Development

You create an Analysis Services database by using SQL Server Management Studio. Right-click the Database folder for the Analysis Server instance and select New Database from the context menu to open the New Database dialog box. Although you cannot create an Analysis Services database by using Business Intelligence Development Studio or Visual Studio 2005, you can define objects on an existing Analysis Services database by using either SQL Server Management Studio or Business Intelligence Development Studio.

You develop, deploy, and manage SSAS solutions by using Business Intelligence Development Studio and SQL Server Management Studio. You use Business Intelligence Development Studio to create business intelligence solutions—either SSAS or report projects. You use SQL Server Management Studio to administer Analysis Services instances and manage and create Analysis Services objects using SSAS Scripts Projects. These project types are described in the following subsections.

SSAS Project

An SSAS project contains object definitions such as data sources, data-source views, dimensions, and cubes for a single SSAS database stored in XML files. These projects are part of SSAS solutions that can contain projects from other SQL Server components. You can create an SSAS project that is independent of a specific SSAS instance by using Business Intelligence Development Studio.

SSAS Scripts Project

An SSAS Scripts Project contains scripts written in MDX, DMX, and XMLA. SSAS Scripts Projects let you group related scripts for development and administrative purposes. You can create an SSAS Scripts Project with SQL Server Management Studio.

Accessing Data by Using ADOMD.NET

ADOMD.NET is a .NET Framework data provider that lets client applications access multidimensional data sources such as SSAS. ADOMD.NET uses XMLA 1.1 to communicate with data sources. The ADOMD.NET namespace is `Microsoft.AnalysisServices.AdomdClient`, which is implemented in the `Microsoft.AnalysisServices.AdomdClient.dll` assembly. This is located by default in the *C:\Program Files\Microsoft.NET\ADOMD.NET\90* directory.

This section shows how to use ADOMD.NET to retrieve data and metadata from an SSAS instance. You need a reference to the `Microsoft.AnalysisServices.AdomdClient` assembly to compile and run the examples.

Querying an SSAS Database

This section shows how to use ADOMD.NET to retrieve multidimensional data from a managed client application.

The first example shows how to use the ADOMD.NET data provider to retrieve data from the Adventure Works cube by using an MDX query that populates a data reader:

```
using System;
using System.Data;

using Microsoft.AnalysisServices.AdomdClient;

class Program
{
    static void Main(string[] args)
    {
        AdomdConnection conn = new AdomdConnection(
            "Data Source=localhost;Catalog=Adventure Works DW Standard Edition");
        conn.Open( );

        string commandText = "SELECT {[Measures].[Sales Amount], " +
            "[Measures].[Gross Profit Margin]} ON COLUMNS, " +
            "{[Product].[Product Model Categories].[Category]} ON ROWS " +
            "FROM [Adventure Works] " +
            "WHERE ([Sales Territory Country].[United States])";

        AdomdCommand cmd = new AdomdCommand(commandText, conn);
        AdomdDataReader dr = cmd.ExecuteReader(CommandBehavior.CloseConnection);

        // output the rows in the DataReader
        while (dr.Read( ))
        {
            for (int i = 0; i < dr.FieldCount; i++)
                Console.Write(dr[i] + (i == dr.FieldCount - 1 ? "" : ", "));

            Console.WriteLine( );
        }
```

```
            dr.Close();
            Console.WriteLine(Environment.NewLine + "Press any key to continue.");
            Console.ReadKey();
        }
    }
```

The results shown in Figure 20-7 correspond to those from executing the same query in the "Multidimensional Expressions (MDX)" section earlier in this chapter.

Figure 20-7. Results for ADOMD.NET query example

The AdomdConnection class represents a connection to a multidimensional data source. The AdomdDataReader class retrieves a forward-only, read-only stream of data from a data source and is similar to other data reader classes in ADO.NET. The stream of results is returned as the query executes, letting you access data as soon as the first row is available, rather than waiting for the entire set of results to be returned. The AdomdDataReader object is created by calling the Execute() or ExecuteReader() method of the AdomdCommand object. The Read() method of the AdomdDataReader object retrieves the next row of results.

The CellSet class in ADOMD.NET is an in-memory cellset that can be manipulated while disconnected and later synchronized to the data source. The CellSet class is analogous to the DataSet class in ADO.NET. This example shows how to use the CellSet class to manipulate data extracted from the Adventure Works cube:

```
using System;
using System.Data;

using Microsoft.AnalysisServices.AdomdClient;

class Program
{
    static void Main(string[] args)
    {
        AdomdConnection conn = new AdomdConnection(
            "Data Source=localhost;Catalog=Adventure Works DW Standard Edition");
        conn.Open();

        string commandText = "SELECT {[Measures].[Sales Amount], " +
            "[Measures].[Gross Profit Margin]} ON COLUMNS, " +
            "{[Product].[Product Model Categories].[Category]} ON ROWS " +
            "FROM [Adventure Works] " +
            "WHERE ([Sales Territory Country].[United States])";
```

```
AdomdCommand cmd = new AdomdCommand(commandText, conn);
CellSet cs = cmd.ExecuteCellSet();

// iterate over the rows and column positions
foreach (Position pRow in cs.Axes[1].Positions)
{
    foreach (Position pCol in cs.Axes[0].Positions)
    {
        // get the formatted value based on the row and column positions
        Console.Write(
            cs[pCol.Ordinal, pRow.Ordinal].FormattedValue + ", ");
    }
    Console.WriteLine();
}

conn.Close();

Console.WriteLine(Environment.NewLine + "Press any key to continue.");
Console.ReadKey();
    }
}
```

Results are shown in Figure 20-8.

Figure 20-8. Results for ADOMD.NET CellSet example

The results correspond to those from the first query executed in the "Multidimensional Expressions (MDX)" section earlier in this chapter.

The CellSet class contains a collection of Cell objects hierarchically organized to the tuples and axes specified by the Axes and FilterAxis properties. The cells in the cellset are accessed by index, a pair of indexes corresponding to the column and row, or an array of indexes corresponding to the dimensions of the cellset containing more than two dimensions.

The following example retrieves a cellset as an XmlReader object and uses an XmlDocument object to output the contents of the XmlReader object to the console:

```
using System;
using System.Data;
using System.Xml;

using Microsoft.AnalysisServices.AdomdClient;

class Program
```

```
{
    static void Main(string[] args)
    {
        AdomdConnection conn = new AdomdConnection(
            "Data Source=localhost;Catalog=Adventure Works DW Standard Edition");
        conn.Open( );

        string commandText = "SELECT {[Measures].[Sales Amount], " +
            "[Measures].[Gross Profit Margin]} ON COLUMNS, " +
            "{[Product].[Product Model Categories].[Category]} ON ROWS " +
            "FROM [Adventure Works] " +
            "WHERE ([Sales Territory Country].[United States])";

        AdomdCommand cmd = new AdomdCommand(commandText, conn);
        XmlReader xr = cmd.ExecuteXmlReader( );
        XmlDocument xd = new XmlDocument( );
        xd.Load(xr);
        Console.WriteLine(xd.InnerXml);

        xr.Close( );
        conn.Close( );

        Console.WriteLine(Environment.NewLine + "Press any key to continue.");
        Console.ReadKey( );
    }
}
```

The data portion of the resulting XML document is shown in Figure 20-9.

Figure 20-9. Results for ADOMD.NET XmlDocument example

The ExecuteXmlReader( ) property of the AdomdCommand class returns the cellset as an XmlReader object. As with the example in the "XML for Analysis (XMLA)" section earlier in this chapter, the results are returned in the <CellData> element of the XML document.

Retrieving Schema Information

A schema rowset contains metadata, monitoring, and support information from an SSAS instance. This section shows how to use ADOMD.NET to retrieve schema information from a managed client application.

This example shows how to use the AdomdDataReader class to get schema information about a cellset:

```
using System;
using System.Data;

using Microsoft.AnalysisServices.AdomdClient;

class Program
{
    static void Main(string[] args)
    {
        AdomdConnection conn = new AdomdConnection(
            "Data Source=localhost;Catalog=Adventure Works DW Standard Edition");
        conn.Open();

        string commandText = "SELECT {[Measures].[Sales Amount], " +
            "[Measures].[Gross Profit Margin]} ON COLUMNS, " +
            "{[Product].[Product Model Categories].[Category]} ON ROWS " +
            "FROM [Adventure Works] " +
            "WHERE ([Sales Territory Country].[United States])";

        AdomdCommand cmd = new AdomdCommand(commandText, conn);
        AdomdDataReader dr = cmd.ExecuteReader(CommandBehavior.CloseConnection);

        // retrieve the schema information into a table
        DataTable dt = dr.GetSchemaTable();

        foreach (DataRow row in dt.Rows)
        {
            foreach (DataColumn col in dt.Columns)
                Console.WriteLine(col.ColumnName + " = " + row[col].ToString());

            Console.WriteLine();
        }

        dr.Close();

        Console.WriteLine(Environment.NewLine + "Press any key to continue.");
        Console.ReadKey();
    }
}
```

Partial results are shown in Figure 20-10.

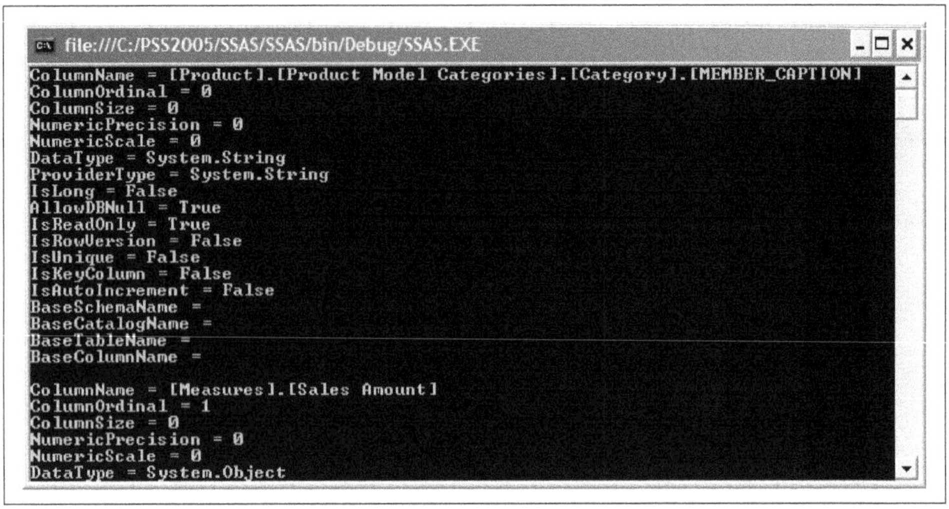

```
file:///C:/PSS2005/SSAS/SSAS/bin/Debug/SSAS.EXE

ColumnName = [Product].[Product Model Categories].[Category].[MEMBER_CAPTION]
ColumnOrdinal = 0
ColumnSize = 0
NumericPrecision = 0
NumericScale = 0
DataType = System.String
ProviderType = System.String
IsLong = False
AllowDBNull = True
IsReadOnly = True
IsRowVersion = False
IsUnique = False
IsKeyColumn = False
IsAutoIncrement = False
BaseSchemaName =
BaseCatalogName =
BaseTableName =
BaseColumnName =

ColumnName = [Measures].[Sales Amount]
ColumnOrdinal = 1
ColumnSize = 0
NumericPrecision = 0
NumericScale = 0
DataType = System.Object
```

Figure 20-10. Partial results for retrieving cellset schema example

The GetSchemaTable() method of the AdomdDataReader class returns a DataTable object containing schema information about the cellset. Each row of the DataTable corresponds to a column in the cellset. The columns of the DataTable contain properties for the cellset column.

The connection to the SSAS instance can also be used to retrieve schema information for the objects in an SSAS instance. This example shows how:

```csharp
using System;
using System.Data;

using Microsoft.AnalysisServices.AdomdClient;

class Program
{
    static void Main(string[] args)
    {
        AdomdConnection conn = new AdomdConnection(
            "Data Source=localhost;Catalog=Analysis Services Tutorial");
        conn.Open();
        DataSet ds = conn.GetSchemaDataSet(AdomdSchemaGuid.Dimensions, null);

        DataTable dt = ds.Tables[0];
        foreach(DataRow row in dt.Rows)
        {
            foreach (DataColumn col in dt.Columns)
                Console.WriteLine(col.ColumnName + " = " + row[col].ToString());

            Console.WriteLine();
        }

        conn.Close();
```

```
        Console.WriteLine("Press any key to continue.");
        Console.ReadKey();
    }
}
```

Partial results are shown in Figure 20-11.

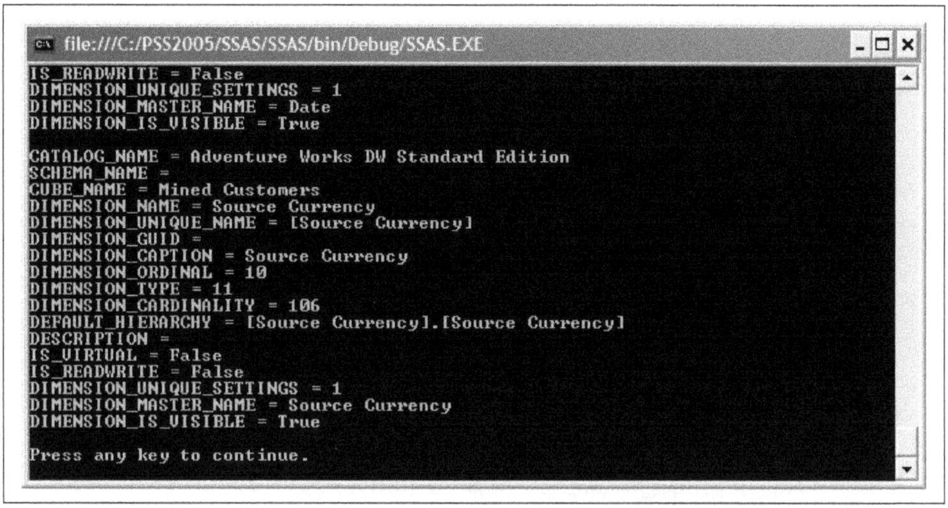

Figure 20-11. Partial results for retrieving schema information example

The GetSchemaDataSet() method of the AdomdConnection class returns schema information for the objects specified by the method arguments. The preceding example uses an overload of the GetSchemaDataSet() method that takes two arguments. The first argument identifies the object type by using its GUID as a static field from the AdomdSchemaGuid class. The second contains an array of restrictions used to return information for a subset of the objects.

Administering SSAS Objects

SSAS supports administration APIs that you can use to create or modify SSAS objects, process SSAS objects, and manage SSAS instances. This section describes Analysis Management Objects (AMO) and Decision Support Objects (DSO).

Analysis Management Objects (AMO)

AMO is a .NET Framework assembly containing a hierarchy of classes that lets you programmatically create, modify, and process SSAS objects and manage SSAS instances. The AMO namespace is Microsoft.AnalysisServices, implemented in the Microsoft.AnalysisServices.dll assembly, which is located by default in the *C:\ Program Files\Microsoft SQL Server\90\SDK\Assemblies* directory.

This example shows how to use AMO objects to retrieve information about key collections in an SSAS database—in this case, the Adventure Works DW database. You need a reference to the Microsoft.AnalysisServices assembly to compile and run the example.

```
using System;
using System.Data;

using Microsoft.AnalysisServices;

class Program
{
    static void Main(string[] args)
    {
        Server server = new Server();
        server.Connect(
          "Data Source=localhost;Catalog=Adventure Works DW Standard Edition");
        Database db = server.Databases["Adventure Works DW Standard Edition"];

        Console.WriteLine("DATA SOURCES:");
        foreach (DataSource ds in db.DataSources)
            Console.WriteLine(ds.Name);

        Console.WriteLine(Environment.NewLine + "DATA SOURCE VIEWS:");
        foreach (DataSourceView dsv in db.DataSourceViews)
            Console.WriteLine(dsv.Name);

        Console.WriteLine(Environment.NewLine + "CUBES:");
        foreach (Cube c in db.Cubes)
            Console.WriteLine(c.Name);

        Console.WriteLine(Environment.NewLine + "DIMENSIONS:");
        foreach (Dimension d in db.Dimensions)
            Console.WriteLine(d.Name);

        Console.WriteLine(Environment.NewLine + "MINING STRUCTURES:");
        foreach (MiningStructure ms in db.MiningStructures)
            Console.WriteLine(ms.Name);

        Console.WriteLine(Environment.NewLine + "ROLES:");
        foreach (Role r in db.Roles)
            Console.WriteLine(r.Name);

        Console.WriteLine(Environment.NewLine + "ASSEMBLIES:");
        foreach (Assembly a in db.Assemblies)
            Console.WriteLine(a.Name);

        Console.WriteLine(Environment.NewLine + "Press any key to continue.");
        Console.ReadKey();
    }
}
```

Results are shown in Figure 20-12.

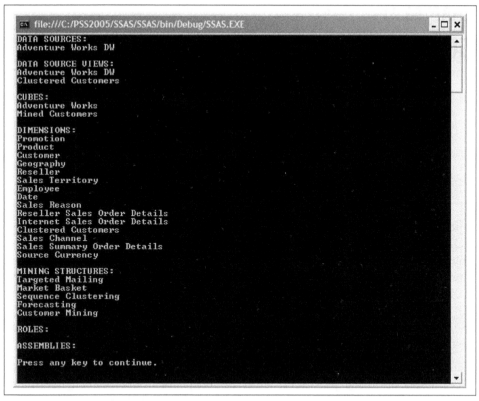

```
cx  file:///C:/PSS2005/SSAS/SSAS/bin/Debug/SSAS.EXE            - □ x
DATA SOURCES:
Adventure Works DW

DATA SOURCE VIEWS:
Adventure Works DW
Clustered Customers

CUBES:
Adventure Works
Mined Customers

DIMENSIONS:
Promotion
Product
Customer
Geography
Reseller
Sales Territory
Employee
Date
Sales Reason
Reseller Sales Order Details
Internet Sales Order Details
Clustered Customers
Sales Channel
Sales Summary Order Details
Source Currency

MINING STRUCTURES:
Targeted Mailing
Market Basket
Sequence Clustering
Forecasting
Customer Mining

ROLES:

ASSEMBLIES:

Press any key to continue.
```

Figure 20-12. Results for AMO example

The Server class is the top-level class in the AMO class hierarchy and represents the implementation of SSAS. Call the Connect( ) method of the Server class to connect to an SSAS instance. The Databases property of the Server class contains a collection of databases in the SSAS instance as Database objects. The Database class exposes a collection of properties that provides access to collections of objects in the database, including data sources, data-source views, cubes, dimensions, mining structures, roles, and assemblies. These collections and their objects have methods and properties used to query and manipulate the database objects.

Decision Support Objects (DSO)

DSO is a COM library that you can use to create applications that programmatically administer SSAS objects. You should use AMO instead of DSO in new applications and migrate existing applications to AMO, because DSO will be removed in the next version of SQL Server. For more information about DSO, see Microsoft SQL Server 2005 Books Online.

CHAPTER 21

SQL Server Mobile Edition

Microsoft SQL Server Mobile Edition (SQL Server Mobile) is the update to Microsoft SQL Server 2000 Windows CE Edition 2.0 (SQL Server CE). It extends enterprise solutions to applications running on a device by delivering relational database functionality in a compact footprint and by providing a consistent programming model. SQL Server Mobile is typically used on devices that run Windows CE 5.0, Windows XP Tablet PC Edition, Mobile Pocket PC, or Mobile Smartphone. You can also run SQL Server Mobile on a desktop Windows operating system for development and testing purposes.

SQL Server Mobile is integrated with the *.NET Compact Framework*—a subset of the .NET Framework that provides a hardware-independent environment for running applications on resource-constrained computing devices. SQL Server Mobile can be deployed as part of a Microsoft .NET Compact Framework application or independently on a smart device. The .NET Compact Framework Data Provider for SQL Server Mobile in the namespace System.Data.SqlServerCe provides access to data from .NET Compact Framework applications.

Remote data access and merge replication deliver data from SQL Server to SQL Server Mobile on supported devices. This data can be manipulated offline and later synchronized to the server when a connection is available.

A SQL Server Mobile database is stored in a file with a *.sdf* extension. A SQL Server Mobile database can be up to 4GB in size. Devices running SQL Server Mobile can access and modify the data, as can desktop computers running SQL Server Management Studio. SQL Server Mobile supports multiuser database access.

You can use SQL Server Management Studio to administer a SQL Server Mobile database. SQL Server Mobile management functionality in SQL Server Management Studio is limited to a subset of the capabilities for managing a SQL Server 2005 database. Many tasks cannot be performed using graphical tools but must instead be accomplished using T-SQL commands. SQL Server Management Objects (SMO) is not supported by SQL Server Mobile.

Environments

SQL Server Mobile includes both a client environment, where the application is hosted and offline data is stored, and a server environment, which serves as a central repository for data. Connectivity technologies provide periodic data synchronization between client and server environments. The following subsections describe the client and server environments.

Client

The client environment includes the SQL Server Mobile instance and the client application developed using the .NET Compact Framework.

The SQL Server Mobile client environment includes the following:

- Tools for setup, configuration, data access, and data modification.
- APIs to develop applications that access SQL Server Mobile data.
- The query processor, which parses, compiles, optimizes, and executes SQL expressions, queries, and commands. The SQL grammar supported by SQL Server Mobile is a subset of T-SQL supported by SQL Server 2005.
- SQL Server Mobile Database Engine, which manages the data store and tracks inserted, deleted, and modified records to support replication or remote data access (RDA) connectivity.
- SQL Server Mobile Client Agent, which supports connectivity by implementing the `Replication`, `RemoteDataAccess`, and `Engine` objects and lets you programmatically control connections to SQL Server.

Server

The server environment includes the following:

- SQL Server 2005, which provides server-side storage, management, and analysis of data.
- SQL Server Mobile Server Agent, which handles HTTP data and schema transfer requests made by SQL Server Mobile Client Agent.
- Internet Information Services (IIS), which provides the protocol that client devices use to connect to servers to transfer and exchange data using replication or RDA.

Prerequisites

The following are prerequisites for developing SQL Server Mobile applications:

- Windows 2000 SP4 or later, Windows XP SP1 or later, or Windows Server 2003.
- Visual Studio 2005 in the development environment.

- .NET Framework 2.0 in the server environment.
- Microsoft ActiveSync 3.7.1 or later in the development and server environments. ActiveSync is available as a free download from Microsoft.

If you are using Windows XP SP2, you need to configure the Windows Firewall to allow HTTP access. Follow these steps:

1. Select Control Panel → Windows Firewall.
2. Select the Advanced tab in the Windows Firewall dialog box.
3. Click the Settings button in the Network Connection Settings frame.
4. Select the Services tab.
5. Check the Web Server (HTTP) checkbox.
6. Click the OK button on both dialog boxes to make the changes.

Programming SQL Server Mobile

The SQL Server Mobile data provider classes in the `Microsoft.Data.SqlServerCe` namespace provide programmatic access to SQL Server Mobile databases from a managed application running on a supported device. The classes are similar to the classes in the .NET data provider for SQL Server. They let you connect to a SQL Server Mobile database, execute commands, retrieve result sets, refresh result sets, work with data offline, and synchronize local updates with the database. The data provider for SQL Server Mobile does not support batch queries or nested transactions.

The following subsections provide examples that show how to use the SQL Server Mobile classes and include descriptions of the classes. You need a reference to the `System.Data.SqlServerCe` assembly to compile and run the examples. To add the reference, select Microsoft SQL Mobile from the .NET tab of the Add Reference dialog box in Visual Studio 2005.

Creating a Database

This example creates a database named `TestDb.sdf`:

```
using System;

using System.Data.SqlServerCe;

class Program
{
    static void Main(string[] args)
    {
        SqlCeEngine engine = new SqlCeEngine(
            "data source=TestDb.sdf; database password=password;");
        engine.CreateDatabase( );
        engine.Dispose( );
```

```
            Console.WriteLine("Press any key to continue.");
            Console.ReadKey();
        }
    }
```

Running the example creates the mobile database (*.sdf* file) in the bin\Debug folder (if you compile a debug version of the example).

 You can connect to this database in SQL Server Management Studio. From the main menu, select View → Registered Server Types → SQL Server Mobile. Right-click SQL Server Mobile Edition Databases in the Registered Servers window and select Server Registration from the context menu to open the New Server Registration dialog box. Complete the Database file field with the full path to the TestDb.sdf file and the Password field with the password. Click the Save button to register the mobile database.

The local connection string that can be specified either in the SqlCeEngine class constructor or using the LocalConnectionString property has properties described in Table 21-1.

Table 21-1. SQL Server Mobile connection string properties

Property	Description
autoshrink threshold	Percent of free space allowed in the database before autoshrink starts. The default value is 60. A value of 100 disables autoshrink.
data source	Name of the SQL Server Mobile database file (*.sdf*) and, optionally, specifies the absolute path.
database password	Database password up to 40 characters long. If not specified, the default is no password.
	A database password cannot be recovered if lost.
default lock timeout	Length of time, in milliseconds, that a transaction will wait for a lock. The default value is 2000.
default lock escalation	Number of locks a transaction will acquire before escalating from row to page or from page to table. The default value is 100.
encrypt database	Boolean value specifying whether the database is encrypted. You must specify a password to enable database encryption. The default value is false.
	If the database password is lost, the data cannot be retrieved.
flush interval	Interval before all committed transactions are committed to disk, in seconds. The default value is 10.
locale identifier	Locale ID (LCID) to use with the database.
max buffer size	Largest amount of memory, in kilobytes, that SQL Server Mobile can use before it starts flushing data changes to disk. The default value is 640.
max database size	Maximum size of the database file, in megabytes. The default value is 128.

Table 21-1. SQL Server Mobile connection string properties (continued)

Property	Description
mode	Specifies how the database is opened. The options are:
	Read Write
	Opens the database so that other processes can open and modify the database
	Read Only
	Opens a read-only copy of the database
	Exclusive
	Opens the database so that other processes cannot open or modify the database
	Shared Read
	Opens the database so that other processes are allowed read-only access to the database
	The default mode is Read Write.
temp file directory	Location of the temporary database. The data source is used for temporary storage if a temporary database is not specified.
temp file max size	Maximum size of the temporary database file, in megabytes. The default value is 128.

The classes used to manage SQL Server Mobile databases and access data in a SQL Server Mobile database are described in Table 21-2. The data access classes are similar to those for the SQL Server data provider. Corresponding classes are prefixed by SqlCe instead of Sql—for example, SqlCeConnection instead of SqlConnection.

Table 21-2. SQL Server Mobile data provider classes

Class	Description
SqlCeCommand	T-SQL statement to execute against a database.
SqlCeCommandBuilder	Automatically creates single-table commands based on a SELECT query. Also used to update a database with changes made to a DataTable or DataSet object using a data adapter.
SqlCeConnection	Connection to the SQL Server Mobile database.
SqlCeDataAdapter	Used to fill a DataTable or DataSet object and subsequently update the database with changes made offline.
SqlCeDataReader	Provides access to a result set as a forward-only stream of data rows.
SqlCeEngine	Represents the SQL Server Mobile Database Engine. Used to create, modify, and manage a SQL Server Mobile database.
SqlCeError	Information about a specific SqlCeException object returned by the SQL Server Mobile data provider.
SqlCeErrorCollection	Collection of all errors generated by the SQL Server Mobile data provider.
SqlCeException	The exception raised when the provider returns a warning or error from the SQL Server Mobile database.
SqlCeFlushFailureEventArgs	Data for a flush failure (FlushFailure) event.
SqlCeFlushFailureEventHandler	The method that handles the FlushFailure event.
SqlCeInfoMessageEventArgs	Data for a warning (InfoMessage) event from the database.

Table 21-2. SQL Server Mobile data provider classes (continued)

Class	Description
SqlCeInfoMessageEventHandler	The method that handles the InfoMessage event.
SqlCeLockTimeoutException	The exception raised when a lock timeout occurs.
SqlCeParameter	A parameter to a SQL command (SqlCeCommand).
SqlCeParameterCollection	A collection of parameter (SqlCeParameter) objects and their mappings to columns.
SqlCeRemoteDataAccess	A remote data access instance.
SqlCeReplication	A replication instance.
SqlCeResultSet	An updateable, bindable, scrollable cursor.
SqlCeRowUpdatedEventArgs	Data for the row updated (RowUpdated) event that occurs when a row in the database is updated using a data adapter.
SqlCeRowUpdatedEventHandler	The method that handles the RowUpdated event.
SqlCeRowUpdatingEventArgs	Data for the row updating (RowUpdating) event that occurs before a row in the database is updated using a data adapter.
SqlCeRowUpdatingEventHandler	The method that handles the RowUpdating event.
SqlCeTransaction	A SQL transaction.
SqlCeTransactionInProgressException	The exception raised when an attempt is made to modify a database while a transaction is in progress.
SqlCeUpdatableRecord	A row of updateable data from the database. The SqlCeResult set contains a collection of SqlCeUpdatableRecord objects.

Maintaining a Database

The SqlCeEngine class public properties and methods used to create and manage SQL Server Mobile databases are described in Table 21-3.

Table 21-3. SqlCeEngine class properties and methods

Constructor	Description
SqlCeEngine	Takes an optional argument specifying the connection string to the SQL Server Mobile database.
Property	
LocalConnectionString	The connection string to the SQL Server Mobile database. The connection string properties are described in Table 21-1.
Methods	
Compact()	Reclaims space in the database file and changes properties of the database specified in the local connection string.
CreateDatabase()	Creates a new database.
Repair()	Attempts to repair a corrupted database.
Shrink()	Reclaims space in the database file.
Verify()	Verifies that the database is not corrupted.

The examples in this section show how to maintain a SQL Server Mobile database using the SqlCeEngine class.

Verifying and repairing

This example verifies that a database is not corrupted. If the database is corrupted, it is repaired.

```
using System;

using System.Data.SqlServerCe;

class Program
{
    static void Main(string[] args)
    {
        // connect to the database
        SqlCeEngine engine = new SqlCeEngine(
            "data source=TestDb.sdf; database password=password;");

        // check if the database is corrupted and repair if it is
        if (!engine.Verify())
        {
            engine.Repair(null, RepairOption.RecoverCorruptedRows);
            Console.WriteLine("Database repaired.");
        }

        Console.WriteLine("Press any key to continue.");
        Console.ReadKey();
    }
}
```

This example connects to the SQL Server Mobile database created in the preceding example. The Verify() method of the SqlCeEngine class checks the checksum for each database page to determine whether the database file is corrupt. A corrupt database file returns false and should be repaired using the Repair() method of the SqlCeEngine class. Repair() takes a single argument from the RepairOption enumeration—either DeleteCorruptedRows or RecoverCorruptedRows. The RecoverCorruptedRows option causes the engine to try to recover data from corrupted pages. However, the data is not guaranteed to be free of corruption. The DeleteCorruptedRows option results in data that is free of corruption, but because corrupt data is discarded, significant data can be lost.

Reclaiming space

The internal structure of a SQL Server Mobile database can become fragmented over time, resulting in wasted space. You can use the Shrink() or Compact() method of the Engine class to reclaim the space:

```
engine.Shrink();
```

The Shrink( ) method of the SqlCeEngine class is used to reclaim wasted space in the *.sdf* file. The Compact( ) method is described in the following subsection.

You can configure the database to automatically shrink when a fragmentation threshold is exceeded by setting the autoshrink threshold property (described in Table 21-1) in the LocalConnectionString property of the SqlCeEngine object.

Modifying properties

The Compact( ) method of the SqlCeEngine class reclaims space in the database just as the Shrink( ) method does, but also lets you change database connection settings by specifying them in an optional argument. For example, the following statement changes the database password to newPassword:

```
engine.Compact("database password=newPassword;");
```

Backing up and restoring

SQL Server Mobile is file based, so you can perform some common database tasks using the filesystem. You can back up a database by closing all open connections to it and copying the *.sdf* database file. Similarly, you can restore the database by copying the backup *.sdf* file to its original location.

You drop a database by closing all connections to it and deleting the *.sdf* file using the filesystem APIs. For example, the following statement deletes the database named TestDb.sdf created at the beginning of this section:

```
System.IO.File.Delete("TestDb.sdf");
```

Creating, Altering, and Dropping Database Objects

Because SQL Server Mobile does not support SMO, you create a table by executing T-SQL DDL commands using the ExecuteNonQuery( ) method of the SqlCeCommand class. This example creates a table named TestTable containing two columns:

```
using System;

using System.Data.SqlServerCe;

class Program
{
    static void Main(string[] args)
    {
        SqlCeConnection conn = new SqlCeConnection(
            "data source=TestDb.sdf; database password=password;");
        conn.Open();

        SqlCeCommand cmd = new SqlCeCommand(
            "CREATE TABLE TestTable(ID int, Description nvarchar(100))",
            conn);
        cmd.ExecuteNonQuery();
```

```
            conn.Close( );

            Console.WriteLine("Press any key to continue.");
            Console.ReadKey( );
        }
    }
```

The example uses SqlCeConnection and SqlCeCommand objects to execute the CREATE
TABLE T-SQL command against the SQL Server Mobile database. This is similar to
how you would accomplish the same task in SQL Server using SqlConnection and
SqlCommand objects.

Reading and Updating Data

This example adds two rows to the SQL Server Mobile table named TestTable created in the preceding example. The example then reads the new rows from the database and outputs them to the console.

You execute queries against a SQL Server Mobile database by using the SQL Server
Mobile database classes similarly to using the SQL Server data provider against a
SQL Server 2005 database. This example uses a SqlCeDataAdapter object to do the
following:

- Retrieve the contents of the table named TestTable into a DataTable object.
  Because TestTable has no rows, the DataTable object will have no rows.
- Add two rows to the DataTable object.
- Update the SQL Server Mobile database with the new rows.

The example then uses a SqlCeDataReader object to display the rows added to the
table from the database.

```
using System;
using System.Data;

using System.Data.SqlServerCe;

class Program
{
    static void Main(string[] args)
    {
        // create a data adapter and configure a command builder
        // to update the database
        SqlCeDataAdapter da = new SqlCeDataAdapter(
            "SELECT * FROM TestTable",
            "data source=TestDb.sdf; database password=password;");
        SqlCeCommandBuilder cb = new SqlCeCommandBuilder(da);

        // retrieve the results from the database into a DataTable
        DataTable dt = new DataTable( );
        da.Fill(dt);
```

```
        // add two rows to the DataTable
        dt.Rows.Add(new object[] { 1, "Row 1 description" });
        dt.Rows.Add(new object[] { 2, "Row 2 description" });

        // update the database with the new rows
        da.Update(dt);

        // create a connection for the data reader
        SqlCeConnection conn = new SqlCeConnection(
            "data source=TestDb.sdf; database password=password;");
        conn.Open();

        // create the data reader
        SqlCeCommand cmd = new SqlCeCommand(
            "SELECT * FROM TestTable", conn);
        SqlCeDataReader dr = cmd.ExecuteReader();

        // output the rows to the console
        while (dr.Read())
            Console.WriteLine(dr["ID"] + ", " + dr["Description"]);

        // clean up
        dr.Close();
        conn.Close();

        Console.WriteLine(Environment.NewLine + "Press any key to continue.");
        Console.ReadKey();
    }
}
```

The console output is shown in Figure 21-1.

Figure 21-1. Results from reading and updating data example

Error Handling

A SqlCeException object is created when a data provider for SQL Server mobile encounters an error. These exceptions are handled in a typical manner. The following example catches a SqlCeException object, raised because a nonexistent table is queried, and returns details about the exception:

```
using System;

using System.Data.SqlServerCe;

class Program
```

```
{
    static void Main(string[] args)
    {
        SqlCeConnection conn = new SqlCeConnection(
            "data source=TestDb.sdf; database password=password;");
        conn.Open();
        SqlCeCommand cmd = new SqlCeCommand("SELECT * FROM Table1", conn);

        try
        {
            SqlCeDataReader dr = cmd.ExecuteReader();
        }
        catch (SqlCeException ex)
        {
            foreach (SqlCeError sce in ex.Errors)
            {
                Console.WriteLine("HResult = {0:X}", sce.HResult);
                Console.WriteLine("Message = {0}", sce.Message);
                Console.WriteLine("NativeError = {0:X}", sce.NativeError);
                Console.WriteLine("Source = {0}", sce.Source);
                Console.WriteLine();
            }
        }
        finally
        {
            conn.Close();
        }

        Console.WriteLine("Press any key to continue.");
        Console.ReadKey();
    }
}
```

The console output is shown in Figure 21-2.

Figure 21-2. Results from error handling example

The SqlCeException class inherits from the Exception class and adds the several properties described in Table 21-4.

Table 21-4. SqlCeException class properties

Property	Description
Errors	A collection of SqlCeError objects, each containing details about an exception generated by the SQL Server Mobile data provider.
HResult	The HRESULT—a numeric value that corresponds to a specific exception. This corresponds to the value of the HResult property for the first SqlCeError object in the SqlCeError-Collection collection returned by the Errors property.
InnerException	Inherited from Exception class.
Message	The description for the first SqlCeError object in the SqlCeErrorCollection collection returned by the Errors property.
NativeError	The native error number for the first SqlCeError object in the SqlCeErrorCollection collection returned by the Errors property.
Source	The name of the provider that caused the exception. This corresponds to the value of the Source property for the first SqlCeError object in the SqlCeErrorCollection collection returned by the Errors property.
StackTrace	Inherited from Exception class.

ADO.NET 2.0

ADO.NET is a set of classes that gives .NET applications access to relational, XML, and application data. The classes let you connect to data sources such as SQL Server and Oracle, as well as to data sources exposed through OLE DB and ODBC, and XML data. After you connect to these data sources, the ADO.NET classes let you retrieve, manipulate, and update data.

This appendix describes the new functionality, support, and features in ADO.NET 2.0.

Data Provider Enumeration and Factories

Data providers in ADO.NET 1.0 and 1.1 are a set of provider-specific classes that implemented generic interfaces. These interfaces can be used to write code that is data provider independent. For example, the data connection classes in the Microsoft SQL Server data provider (SqlConnection) and the Microsoft Oracle data provider (OracleConnection) both implement the IDbConnection interface. Code based on the IDbConnection interface that is common to both classes, rather than a database-specific instance of a data provider, is independent of the data provider and therefore not dependent on the underlying database. The disadvantage of the interface approach is that you cannot use the interface to access any database-specific features implemented as members of the data provider class but not defined as part of the interface—the ChangeDatabase( ) method of the Oracle data provider, for example.

ADO.NET 2.0 introduces the *Common Model,* based on the *Factory* design pattern, which uses a single API to access databases having different providers. Data provider factories let your code work with multiple data providers without choosing a specific provider. The factory class creates and returns a strongly typed, provider-specific object based on information in the request. This lets you write data provider–independent code and select the provider at runtime. Using the Common Model, it becomes easier to write an application to support multiple databases.

The DbProviderFactories class in the System.Data.Common namespace lets you retrieve information about installed .NET data providers. The static GetFactoryClasses() method returns a DataTable object containing information about the installed data providers that implement the abstract base class DbProviderFactory, with the schema described in Table A-1.

Table A-1. DataTable schema for GetFactoryClasses() method results

Column name	Description
Name	Data provider name.
Description	Data provider description.
InvariantName	A unique identifier for a data provider registered in machine.config in the <system.data><DbProviderFactories> element. For example, the invariant name for SQL Server is System.Data.SqlClient.
	The invariant name is used to programmatically refer to the data provider.
AssemblyQualifiedName	Fully qualified name of the data provider factory class—enough information to instantiate the object.

The following console application uses the DbProviderFactories class to get information about the installed data providers:

```
using System;
using System.Data;
using System.Data.Common;

class Program
{
    static void Main(string[] args)
    {
        DataTable dt = DbProviderFactories.GetFactoryClasses();
        foreach (DataRow row in dt.Rows)
            Console.WriteLine("{0}\n\r  {1}\n\r  {2}\n\r  {3}\n\r",
            row["Name"], row["Description"], row["InvariantName"],
            row["AssemblyQualifiedName"]);

        Console.WriteLine("Press any key to continue.");
        Console.ReadKey();
    }
}
```

The output is similar to that shown in Figure A-1.

The providers listed in Figure A-1 correspond to the DbProviderFactories element in machine.config, shown in the following excerpt:

```
<system.data>
  <DbProviderFactories>
    <add name="Odbc Data Provider" invariant="System.Data.Odbc"
      description=".Net Framework Data Provider for Odbc"
      type="System.Data.Odbc.OdbcFactory, System.Data, Version=2.0.0.0,
      Culture=neutral, PublicKeyToken=b77a5c561934e089" />
```

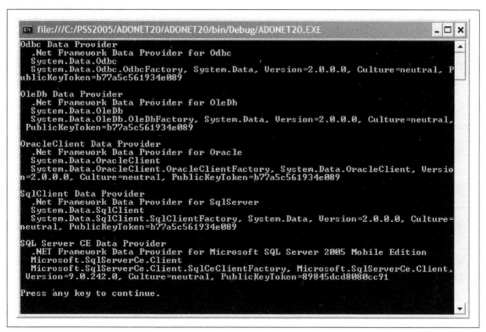

Figure A-1. Information about installed data providers

```
  <add name="OleDb Data Provider" invariant="System.Data.OleDb"
    description=".Net Framework Data Provider for OleDb"
    type="System.Data.OleDb.OleDbFactory, System.Data, Version=2.0.0.0,
    Culture=neutral, PublicKeyToken=b77a5c561934e089" />
  <add name="OracleClient Data Provider" invariant="System.Data.OracleClient"
    description=".Net Framework Data Provider for Oracle"
    type="System.Data.OracleClient.OracleClientFactory, System.Data.OracleClient,
    Version=2.0.0.0, Culture=neutral, PublicKeyToken=b77a5c561934e089" />
  <add name="SqlClient Data Provider" invariant="System.Data.SqlClient"
    description=".Net Framework Data Provider for SqlServer"
    type="System.Data.SqlClient.SqlClientFactory, System.Data, Version=2.0.0.0,
    Culture=neutral, PublicKeyToken=b77a5c561934e089" />
  <add name="SQL Server CE Data Provider"
    invariant="Microsoft.SqlServerCe.Client" support="3F7"
    description=".NET Framework Data Provider for Microsoft SQL Server 2005
    Mobile Edition" type="Microsoft.SqlServerCe.Client.SqlCeClientFactory,
    Microsoft.SqlServerCe.Client, Version=9.0.242.0, Culture=neutral,
    PublicKeyToken=89845dcd8080cc91" />
  </DbProviderFactories>
</system.data>
```

The static GetFactory( ) method of the DbProviderFactories class takes a single argument—either a DataRow object from the table returned by the GetFactoryClasses( ) method or a string containing the invariant name of the provider—and returns a DbProviderFactory instance for that data provider.

The `DbProviderFactory` class is an abstract base class that every ADO.NET 2.0 data provider must implement. `DbProviderFactory` is a data provider–independent class that provides a strongly typed object based on information supplied at runtime. The provider-specific classes derived from `DbProviderFactory` installed with .NET Framework 2.0 are listed in Table A-2.

Table A-2. Provider-specific classes derived from DbProviderFactory installed with .NET Framework 2.0

Factory class	Description
System.Data.Odbc.OdbcFactory	Used to create instances of ODBC provider classes
System.Data.OleDb.OleDbFactory	Used to create instances of OLE DB provider classes
System.Data.OracleClient.OracleClientFactory	Used to create instances of Oracle provider classes
System.Data.SqlClient.SqlClientFactory	Use to create instances of SQL Server provider classes

The `DbProviderFactory` class has public methods, listed in Table A-3, that are used to create the provider-specific class instances.

Table A-3. DbProviderFactory class public methods

Method	Description
CreateCommand	Returns a DbCommand instance—the base class for strongly typed command objects
CreateCommandBuilder	Returns a DbCommandBuilder instance—the base class for strongly typed command builder objects
CreateConnection	Returns a DbConnection instance—the base class for strongly typed connection objects
CreateConnectionStringBuilder	Returns a DbConnectionStringBuilder instance—the base class for strongly typed connection string builder objects
CreateDataAdapter	Returns a DbDataAdapter instance—the base class for strongly typed data adapter objects
CreateDataSourceEnumerator	Returns a DbDataSourceEnumerator instance—the base class for strongly typed data source enumerator objects
CreateParameter	Returns a DbParameter instance—the base class for strongly typed parameter objects
CreatePermission	Returns a CodeAccessPermission instance—the base class for strongly typed code access permission objects

The following console application shows how to create an instance of the `SqlClientFactory` class and use it to output the top 10 rows from the `Person.Contact` table in `AdventureWorks`:

```
using System;
using System.Data;
using System.Data.Common;
```

```
class Program
{
    static void Main(string[] args)
    {
        // create factory using the invariant name
        DbProviderFactory f =
            DbProviderFactories.GetFactory("System.Data.SqlClient");

        DbConnection conn = f.CreateConnection( );
        conn.ConnectionString = "Data Source=localhost;" +
            "Integrated Security=SSPI;Initial Catalog=AdventureWorks";

        DbCommand selectCommand = conn.CreateCommand( );
        selectCommand.CommandText = "SELECT TOP 10 " +
            "FirstName, LastName, EmailAddress " +
            "FROM Person.Contact ORDER BY LastName";

        DataTable dt = new DataTable( );

        DbDataAdapter da = f.CreateDataAdapter( );
        da.SelectCommand = selectCommand;
        da.Fill(dt);

        foreach (DataRow row in dt.Rows)
            Console.WriteLine(row[0] + ", " + row[1] + ", " + row[2]);

        Console.WriteLine(Environment.NewLine + "Press any key to continue.");
        Console.ReadKey( );
    }
}
```

Results are shown in Figure A-2.

Figure A-2. Results for SqlClientFactory example

The code is database-independent, with the exception of the invariant name of the provider and the connection string, highlighted in the preceding example. These arguments would normally be retrieved from a configuration file or similar mechanism rather than hardcoded, to make the application truly database-independent.

The ConfigurationManager class in the System.Configuration namespace provides access to application configuration information. The ConnectionStrings() method returns a ConnectionStringSettingsCollection instance containing the connection strings for the application, each one corresponding to a named connection string in the <connectionStrings> section of the application configuration file.

This example shows how to retrieve a connection string from the configuration file. First create a new console application project in Visual Studio .NET. Select Add → New Item → Application Configuration File to add a new application configuration file named *App.config*. Add a connection string to the file—the following snippet shows the completed configuration file with the connection string named MyConnection highlighted:

```
<?xml version="1.0" encoding="utf-8" ?>
<configuration>
  <connectionStrings>
    <add name="MyConnection" connectionString="Data Source=localhost;
      Integrated Security=SSPI;Initial Catalog=AdventureWorks"
      providerName="System.Data.SqlClient" />
  </connectionStrings>
</configuration>
```

The following code retrieves the connection string from the configuration file. You need to add a reference to the System.Configuration assembly to compile and execute this example.

```
using System;
using System.Collections;
using System.Data.SqlClient;

using System.Configuration;

class Program
{
    static void Main(string[] args)
    {
        //// get the configuration string from the config file
        Configuration c =
            ConfigurationManager.OpenExeConfiguration(ConfigurationUserLevel.None);

        ConnectionStringsSection css = c.ConnectionStrings;
        for (int i = 0; i < css.ConnectionStrings.Count; i++)
        {
            Console.WriteLine(css.ConnectionStrings[i].Name);
            Console.WriteLine("  " + css.ConnectionStrings[i]);
            Console.WriteLine();
        }

        Console.WriteLine("Press any key to continue.");
        Console.ReadKey();
    }
}
```

Results are shown in Figure A-3.

Figure A-3. Results for retrieving configuration strings from application configuration file example

Two connection strings are retrieved. The first is the default string defined in the *Machine.config* file, as shown in the excerpt that follows:

```
<connectionStrings>
  <add name="LocalSqlServer" connectionString="data source=.\SQLEXPRESS;
    Integrated Security=SSPI;
    AttachDBFilename=|DataDirectory|aspnetdb.mdf;
    User Instance=true" providerName="System.Data.SqlClient" />
</connectionStrings>
```

DbConnectionStringBuilder is a helper class used to construct provider-specific connection strings. You supply the connection string name-value pairs to the Add( ) method and retrieve the connection string using the ConnectionString property. You could change the previous example so that it constructs the connection string using the connection string builder, and then assign it to the ConnectionString property of the connection with the following code:

```
using System;
using System.Data;
using System.Data.Common;
using System.Data.SqlClient;

class Program
{
    static void Main(string[] args)
    {
        // build the connection string
        DbConnectionStringBuilder csb = new DbConnectionStringBuilder( );
        csb["Data Source"] = "localhost";
        csb["Integrated Security"] = "SSPI";
        csb["Initial Catalog"] = "AdventureWorks";

        // create a connection using the connection string
        SqlConnection conn = new SqlConnection( );
        conn.ConnectionString = csb.ConnectionString;

        // output the connection string
        Console.WriteLine(csb.ConnectionString);
```

```
            Console.WriteLine("Press any key to continue.");
            Console.ReadKey();
        }
    }
```

Results are shown in Figure A-4.

Figure A-4. Results for DbConnectionStringBuilder example

Data Provider Enhancements

ADO.NET 2.0 introduces new features and enhancements to .NET Framework data providers, which are used to connect to data sources, execute commands, retrieve data, and update data. The following subsections describe the key changes.

Asynchronous Processing

ADO.NET 2.0 supports asynchronous programming for data retrieval. This lets you delegate long-running data-processing tasks to a background thread while allowing the user interface to remain responsive. Standard asynchronous processing techniques include callbacks, wait handles, and polling. The SqlCommand class has six methods that support asynchronous processing, described in Table A-4.

Table A-4. SqlCommand class methods for asynchronous processing

Asynchronous method	Description
BeginExecuteNonQuery	Starts the asynchronous execution of the T-SQL statement or stored procedure for the SqlCommand object. The method returns an IAsyncResult object that can be used to poll for or wait for results, or to invoke the EndExecuteNonQuery( ) method.
	Each call to a BeginExecuteNonQuery( ) method must be paired with the EndExecuteNonQuery( ) method that completes the operation.
EndExecuteNonQuery	Completes the asynchronous execution of the T-SQL statement or stored procedure started using the BeginExecuteNonQuery( ) method of the SqlCommand object. The command returns the number of rows affected by the command.
BeginExecuteReader	Starts the asynchronous execution of the T-SQL statement or stored procedure for the SqlCommand object. The method returns an IAsyncResult object that can be used to poll for or wait for results, or to invoke the EndExecuteReader( ) method.
	Each call to a BeginExecuteReader( ) method must be paired with the EndExecuteReader( ) method that completes the operation.
EndExecuteReader	Completes the asynchronous execution of the T-SQL statement or stored procedure started using the BeginExecuteReader( ) method of the SqlCommand object. The command returns a SqlDataReader object containing one or more result sets.

Asynchronous method	Description
BeginExecuteXmlReader	Starts the asynchronous execution of the T-SQL statement or stored procedure for the SqlCommand object. The method returns an IAsyncResult object that can be used to poll for or wait for results, or to invoke the EndExecuteXmlReader( ) method.
	Each call to a BeginExecuteXmlReader( ) method must be paired with the EndExecuteXmlReader( ) method that completes the operation.
EndExecuteXmlReader	Completes the asynchronous execution of the T-SQL statement or stored procedure started using the BeginExecuteXmlReader( ) method of the SqlCommand object. The command returns an XmlReader object.

The asynchronous command Begin/End pairs for the SqlCommand object work similarly to each other. The examples in this section that use one of the pairs can be transferred easily to one of the other pairs.

You must add the Asynchronous Processing=true attribute to the SQL Server connection string to use any of the asynchronous methods.

The IAsyncResult interface stores state information about the asynchronous operation and provides a synchronization object that lets threads get signaled when the operation completes. Table A-5 lists the public properties exposed by the IAsyncResult interface.

Table A-5. Public properties of IAsyncResult interface

Property	Description
AsyncState	Returns a user-defined object that contains information about or qualifies an asynchronous operation
AsyncWaitHandle	Returns a WaitHandle object used to wait for an asynchronous operation to complete
CompletedSynchronously	A bool indicating whether the asynchronous operation completed synchronously
IsCompleted	A bool indicating whether the asynchronous operation has completed

The following Windows application uses an asynchronous data reader to get a result set containing all rows in the Person.Contact table in the AdventureWorks database. A WAITFOR T-SQL statement is used to delay the processing of the SELECT statement for five seconds to demonstrate the background processing of the query. After five seconds, the program executes the T-SQL statement to retrieve all rows into a DataReader object, and then calls the HandleCallback( ) callback to display the number of rows in a message box.

Create a new .NET Windows project. Replace the code in *Form1.cs* with the following code. There are no other user interface elements to this sample.

```
using System;
using System.Windows.Forms;
using System.Data;
using System.Data.SqlClient;
```

```
namespace ADONET2OWin
{
    public partial class Form1 : Form
    {
        public Form1()
        {
            InitializeComponent();
        }

        // use a delegate to display the results from the
        // async read since it is likely on a different thread and
        // cannot interact with the form
        private delegate void DisplayResultsDelegate(string results);

        // delegate to display results
        private void DisplayResults(string results)
        {
            MessageBox.Show(results);
        }

        private void Form1_Load(object sender, EventArgs e)
        {
            SqlConnection conn = new SqlConnection();
            conn.ConnectionString = "Data Source=localhost;" +
                "Integrated Security=SSPI;" +
                "Initial Catalog=AdventureWorks;" +
                "Asynchronous Processing=true";

            string cmdText = "WAITFOR DELAY '00:00:05';" +
                "SELECT * FROM Person.Contact;";
            SqlCommand cmd = new SqlCommand(cmdText, conn);

            conn.Open();
            // start the async operation. The HandleCallback() method
            // is called when the operation completes in 5 seconds.
            cmd.BeginExecuteReader(
                new AsyncCallback(HandleCallback), cmd);
        }

        private void HandleCallback(IAsyncResult asyncResult)
        {
            // get the original object
            SqlCommand cmd = (SqlCommand)asyncResult.AsyncState;

            int rowCount = 0;
            // get the data reader returned from the async call
            using (SqlDataReader dr = cmd.EndExecuteReader(asyncResult))
            {
                // iterate over the reader
                while (dr.Read())
                {
                    // do some work with the reader

                    rowCount++;
```

```
                    }
                }

                cmd.Connection.Close( );

                string results = "Rows in Person.Contact: " + rowCount;

                // output the number of rows using the delegate described
                // earlier in this sample
                DisplayResultsDelegate del =
                    new DisplayResultsDelegate(DisplayResults);
                this.Invoke(del, results);
            }
        }
    }
```

The next example is a Windows application that polls the IAsyncResult interface using its IsComplete property to determine when the operation is complete. The example is similar to the previous example except that the user can click a button to check the status of the asynchronous operation. The status is displayed in a message box and is either false if the query is still running or true if it has completed. After completion, the number of rows in the data reader returned from the query is also displayed.

Create a new .NET Windows project. Open Form1 in the designer and add two buttons to the form: one with Name = getDataButton and Caption = Get Data, and the other with Name = checkStatusButton and Caption = Check Status. Replace the code in *Form1.cs* with the following code. Run the application and click the Get Data button. Click the Check Status button periodically to check whether the query has completed. The number of rows is returned when the query has completed.

```
using System;
using System.Windows.Forms;
using System.Data;
using System.Data.SqlClient;

namespace ADONET2OWin
{
    public partial class Form1 : Form
    {
        IAsyncResult asyncResult;
        SqlCommand cmd;

        public Form1( )
        {
            InitializeComponent( );
        }

        private void getDataButton_Click(object sender, EventArgs e)
        {
            SqlConnection conn = new SqlConnection( );
            conn.ConnectionString = "Data Source=localhost;" +
```

```
            "Integrated Security=SSPI;" +
            "Initial Catalog=AdventureWorks;" +
            "Asynchronous Processing=true";

        string cmdText = "WAITFOR DELAY '00:00:10';" +
            "SELECT * FROM Person.Contact;";
        cmd = new SqlCommand(cmdText, conn);

        conn.Open();
        // start the async operation. The HandleCallback method
        // will be called when it completes.
        asyncResult = cmd.BeginExecuteReader();
    }

    private void checkStatusButton_Click(object sender, EventArgs e)
    {
        string status = "Query complete: " + asyncResult.IsCompleted;

        if (asyncResult.IsCompleted)
        {
            int rowCount = 0;
            // get the data reader returned from the async call when
            // the operation is complete
            using (SqlDataReader dr = cmd.EndExecuteReader(asyncResult))
            {
                // iterate over the reader
                while (dr.Read())
                {
                    // do some work with the reader

                    rowCount++;
                }
            }

            cmd.Connection.Close();

            status += Environment.NewLine + "Rows returned: " + rowCount;
        }

        MessageBox.Show(status);
    }
  }
}
```

The callback and polling techniques shown in the preceding examples are useful when you are processing one asynchronous operation at a time. The *wait* model lets you process multiple simultaneous asynchronous operations. The wait model uses the AsyncWaitHandle property of the IAsyncResult instance returned from the BeginExecuteNonQuery(), BeginExecuteReader(), or BeginExecuteXmlReader() method of the SqlCommand object.

The WaitAny() and WaitAll() static methods of the WaitHandle class monitor and wait for the completion of asynchronous operations. The WaitAny() method waits for any of the asynchronous operations to complete or time out—you can process the results and continue to wait for the next operation to either complete or time out. The WaitAll( ) method waits for all of the processes in the array of WaitHandle instances to complete or time out before continuing.

The following console application demonstrates using the WaitAny( ) method for asynchronous command processing:

```
using System;
using System.Data.SqlClient;
using System.Threading;

class Program
{
    static void Main(string[] args)
    {
        string connectionString =
            "Data Source=localhost;" +
            "Integrated Security=SSPI;" +
            "Initial Catalog=AdventureWorks;" +
            "Asynchronous Processing=true";

        Random rnd = new Random((int)DateTime.Now.Ticks);

        // create an array of commands with "n" members
        int n = 10;
        SqlConnection[] conn = new SqlConnection[n];
        SqlCommand[] cmd = new SqlCommand[n];
        string[] cmdText = new string[n];
        IAsyncResult[] asyncResult = new IAsyncResult[n];
        WaitHandle[] wh = new WaitHandle[n];

        for (int i = 0; i < n; i++)
        {
            // each command waits randomly for between 1 and 10 seconds
            cmdText[i] = "WAITFOR DELAY '00:00:" +
                rnd.Next(1, 10) + "';";

            conn[i] = new SqlConnection(connectionString);
            conn[i].Open( );
            cmd[i] = new SqlCommand(cmdText[i], conn[i]);
            asyncResult[i] = cmd[i].BeginExecuteNonQuery( );

            wh[i] = asyncResult[i].AsyncWaitHandle;
        }

        // wait for all processes to complete, outputing completion
        for (int i = 0; i < n; i++)
        {
            int index = WaitHandle.WaitAny(wh);
            int result = cmd[index].EndExecuteNonQuery(asyncResult[index]);
            Console.WriteLine("Completed command " + index +
                ": " + cmd[index].CommandText);
```

```
            conn[index].Close();
        }

        Console.WriteLine("Press any key to continue.");
        Console.ReadKey();
    }
}
```

The preceding example creates an array of 10 WAITFOR T-SQL statements of random duration between 1 and 10 seconds and displays a line to the console as each of them completes. Figure A-5 shows sample output.

Figure A-5. Results for WaitAny() method example

The *wait all* model waits for the completion of all processes. The method returns true if every element in the WaitHandle array receives a signal within the timeout time span (in this example, 20000 milliseconds, or 20 seconds). Otherwise, false is returned.

The following console application demonstrates using the WaitAll() method for asynchronous command processing:

```
using System;
using System.Data.SqlClient;
using System.Threading;

class Program
{
    static void Main(string[] args)
    {
        string connectionString =
            "Data Source=localhost;" +
            "Integrated Security=SSPI;" +
            "Initial Catalog=AdventureWorks;" +
            "Asynchronous Processing=true";

        Random rnd = new Random((int)DateTime.Now.Ticks);

        // create an array of commands with "n" members
        int n = 10;
        SqlConnection[] conn = new SqlConnection[n];
```

```
SqlCommand[] cmd = new SqlCommand[n];
string[] cmdText = new string[n];
IAsyncResult[] asyncResult = new IAsyncResult[n];
WaitHandle[] wh = new WaitHandle[n];

for (int i = 0; i < n; i++)
{
    // each command waits for randomly between 1 and 10 seconds
    cmdText[i] = "WAITFOR DELAY '00:00:" +
        rnd.Next(1, 10) + "';";

    conn[i] = new SqlConnection(connectionString);
    conn[i].Open();
    cmd[i] = new SqlCommand(cmdText[i], conn[i]);
    asyncResult[i] = cmd[i].BeginExecuteNonQuery();

    wh[i] = asyncResult[i].AsyncWaitHandle;
}

// wait for all processes to complete and output results
bool result = WaitHandle.WaitAll(wh, 20000, false);
if (result)
{
    for (int i = 0; i < n; i++)
    {
        int recAff = cmd[i].EndExecuteNonQuery(asyncResult[i]);
        conn[i].Close();
    }
    Console.WriteLine("Completed all commands successfully.");
}
else
    Console.WriteLine("Timeout error.");

Console.WriteLine("Press any key to continue.");
Console.ReadKey();
    }
}
```

The preceding example creates an array of 10 WAITFOR T-SQL statements of random duration between 1 and 10 seconds and displays a line to the console indicating when all of them have completed, as shown in Figure A-6.

Figure A-6. Results for WaitAll() method example

See MSDN for more information about the WaitAny() and WaitAll() methods.

Support for SQL Server Notifications

SQL Server 2005 and ADO.NET 2.0 let you ask for a notification if executing the same command to retrieve data would generate a different result set. This happens, for example, if another user has changed the data since the current user fetched it. This capability is built on top of the new queuing functionality in SQL Server 2005. The two classes that support notifications are SqlDependency and SqlNotificationRequest. A discussion and example of each follows.

Both examples use a table called Contact. Create the table and add two records to it with the following query:

```
USE ProgrammingSqlServer2005

CREATE TABLE Contact(
    ID int NOT NULL,
    FirstName varchar(50) NOT NULL,
    LastName varchar(50) NOT NULL,
  CONSTRAINT [PK_Contact] PRIMARY KEY CLUSTERED
  (
    [ID] ASC
  ) ON [PRIMARY]
) ON [PRIMARY]
GO

INSERT INTO Contact (ID, FirstName, LastName) VALUES (1, 'John', 'Doe');
INSERT INTO Contact (ID, FirstName, LastName) VALUES (2, 'Jane', 'Smith');
```

SQL Server 2005 databases do not have Service Broker enabled by default, for security reasons. Enable Service Broker for the ProgrammingSqlServer2005 database by executing the following T-SQL statement:

```
ALTER DATABASE ProgrammingSqlServer2005 SET ENABLE_BROKER
```

You can confirm that Service Broker is now enabled for the database by using the DATABASEPROPERTYEX function, as shown in the following T-SQL statement:

```
SELECT DATABASEPROPERTYEX('ProgrammingSqlServer2005', 'IsBrokerEnabled')
```

The function returns 0 for false and 1 for true.

The SqlDependency class lets you create an object to detect changes in the query result. In this example, you create a SqlDependency instance. You then register to receive notifications of changes to the result set through the OnChanged event handler. Follow these steps:

1. Create a SqlConnection object and a SqlCommand object with the query that you want to monitor for changes.

2. Create a SqlDependency object and bind it to the SqlCommand object.

3. Subscribe an event handler to the OnChanged event of the SqlDependency object.

4. Execute the SqlCommand object using any Execute( ) method.

The following example shows how to monitor and handle notifications using the SqlDependency class. For notifications to work, you must specify the database owner as part of the table name and a list of columns in the query—specifying all columns using an asterisk (*) will not work.

```
using System;
using System.Data;
using System.Data.Common;
using System.Data.SqlClient;

class Program
{
    static void Main(string[] args)
    {
        string connString = "Data Source=localhost;Integrated Security=SSPI;" +
            "Initial Catalog=ProgrammingSqlServer2005;";

        // create the connection and the command to monitor for changes
        SqlConnection conn = new SqlConnection(connString);
        SqlCommand cmd = new SqlCommand(
            "SELECT ID, FirstName, LastName FROM dbo.Contact", conn);

        // create the SqlDependency object and bind it to the command
        SqlDependency d = new SqlDependency(cmd);
        d.OnChange += new DEFANGED_OnChangeEventHandler(d_OnChange);
        SqlDependency.Start(connString);
        Console.WriteLine("Notification handler configured.");

        // create the DataReader
        conn.Open();
        SqlDataReader dr = cmd.ExecuteReader();
        while (dr.Read())
        {
            // process the DataReader row
        }
        dr.Close();

        Console.WriteLine(Environment.NewLine + "Press any key to end.");
        Console.ReadKey();

        conn.Close();
    }

    static void d_OnChange(object sender, SqlNotificationEventArgs e)
    {
        Console.WriteLine(Environment.NewLine + "SqlDependency.OnChange event");
        Console.WriteLine("  Source = " + e.Source);
        Console.WriteLine("  Type =   " + e.Type);
        Console.WriteLine("  Info =   " + e.Info);
    }
}
```

Run the example and, while it is running, add a row to the Contact table. The results are shown in Figure A-7.

Figure A-7. Results for SqlDependency event example

The SqlNotificationRequest class lets you execute a command so that SQL Server generates a notification when query results change. Unlike the SqlDependency class, once the notification is created, you do not have to maintain the SqlNotificationRequest object. You simply query your queue for notifications as you need to. This model is particularly useful in a disconnected environment.

You must first create a queue and a service to receive the notification messages, as shown in the following T-SQL statement:

```
USE ProgrammingSqlServer2005
GO

CREATE QUEUE ContactQueue

CREATE SERVICE ContactNotification
  ON QUEUE ContactQueue
  ([http://schemas.microsoft.com/SQL/Notifications/PostQueryNotification]);

CREATE ROUTE ContactQueueRoute
  WITH SERVICE_NAME = 'ContactNotification', ADDRESS = 'LOCAL';
```

This T-SQL block does three things:

- Creates a queue named ContactQueue to hold Service Broker messages.
- Creates a service named ContactNotification used by Service Broker to deliver messages to the ContactQueue queue in the SQL Server database.
- Creates a route used by Service Broker to route messages to the correct SQL Server for the service.

After setting up the queue, service, and route, you need to bind a SqlNotificationRequest object to the SqlCommand object containing your query. This means that when a T-SQL statement is executed, SQL Server keeps track of the query and sends a notification to the SQL Server queue specified in the notification request if a change is detected.

To do this, build a console application to create the notification as follows:

```csharp
using System;
using System.Data;
using System.Data.Common;
using System.Data.SqlClient;
using System.Data.Sql;

class Program
{
    static void Main(string[] args)
    {
        SqlConnection conn = new SqlConnection("Data Source=localhost;" +
            "Integrated Security=SSPI;" +
            "Initial Catalog=ProgrammingSqlServer2005;");

        SqlCommand cmd = new SqlCommand(
            "SELECT ID, FirstName, LastName FROM dbo.Contact", conn);

        // create the SqlNotificationRequest and bind to the command
        SqlNotificationRequest nr = new SqlNotificationRequest();
        nr.UserData = Guid.NewGuid().ToString();
        nr.Options = "Service=ContactNotification; " +
            "Local Database = ProgrammingSqlServer2005";
        nr.Timeout = Int32.MaxValue;
        cmd.Notification = nr;
        Console.WriteLine("Notification handler configured.");

        // create a data reader
        conn.Open();
        SqlDataReader dr = cmd.ExecuteReader();
        while (dr.Read())
        {
            // ... do some work with the data reader
        }

        Console.WriteLine("Press any key to end.");
        Console.ReadKey();

        conn.Close();
    }
}
```

When you run the example, SQL Server creates a new query-notification subscription. Any changes to the data that affect the results of the query SELECT ID, FirstName, LastName FROM dbo.Contact produce a notification.

While the example is running, add a record to the contact table using SQL Management Studio. The notifications are delivered to the ContactNotification service. The ContactNotification service uses the queue ContactQueue to store the notifications. You can retrieve those messages by using the following T-SQL statement:

```sql
SELECT * FROM ContactQueue
```

As the example shows, you must specify three properties for the SqlNotifica-tionRequest object:

UserData
    The application-specific identifier for the notification

Options
    The Service Broker service name where the notification messages are posted

Timeout
    The length of time, in seconds, that SQL Server waits for a change to occur before timing out

Multiple Active Result Sets

Multiple Active Result Sets (MARS) allows multiple commands to be executed on a single connection against a SQL Server 2005 database. Each command requires its own SqlCommand object and adds an additional session to the connection. You must enable MARS by setting the MultipleActiveResultSets key in the connection string to true.

The following console application queries AdventureWorks and returns the top 10 sales order headers and the sales order details for each header. A single connection is used with two command objects to create the DataReader objects.

```
using System;
using System.Data.SqlClient;

class Program
{
    static void Main(string[] args)
    {
        // open a connection
        SqlConnection conn = new SqlConnection();
        conn.ConnectionString = "Data Source=localhost;" +
            "Integrated Security=SSPI;Initial Catalog=AdventureWorks;" +
            "MultipleActiveResultSets=true";
        conn.Open();

        // create a DataReader with the top 10 sales header records
        SqlCommand cmdHeader = conn.CreateCommand();
        cmdHeader.CommandText =
            "SELECT TOP 10 SalesOrderID, TotalDue FROM Sales.SalesOrderHeader";
        using (SqlDataReader drHeader = cmdHeader.ExecuteReader())
        {
            while (drHeader.Read())
            {
                int salesOrderID = (int)drHeader["SalesOrderID"];
                Console.WriteLine("{0}\t{1}",
                    salesOrderID, drHeader["TotalDue"]);

                // create a DataReader with detail for the sales order
```

```
                    SqlCommand cmdDetail = conn.CreateCommand( );
                    cmdDetail.CommandText = "SELECT ProductID, OrderQty FROM " +
                        "Sales.SalesOrderDetail WHERE SalesOrderID=" + salesOrderID;
                    using (SqlDataReader drDetail = cmdDetail.ExecuteReader( ))
                    {
                        while (drDetail.Read( ))
                            Console.WriteLine("\t{0}\t{1}",
                                drDetail["ProductID"], drDetail["OrderQty"]);
                        drDetail.Dispose( );
                    }
                    Console.WriteLine( );
                }
            }

            conn.Close( );

            Console.WriteLine("Press any key to continue.");
            Console.ReadKey( );
        }
    }
```

Partial results are shown in Figure A-8.

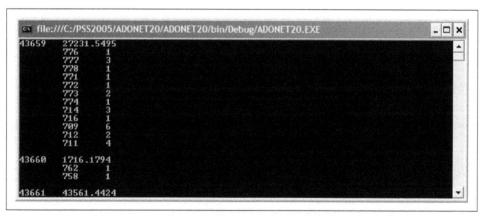

Figure A-8. Partial results for MARS example

Bulk Copy

Bulk copy is a high-performance mechanism for transferring large amounts of data into a database table or view. In ADO.NET 2.0, you can bulk copy data into SQL Server from either a DataTable or DataReader object using the new SqlBulkCopy class in the System.Data.SqlClient namespace. This class supports both single and multiple bulk copy operations within either dedicated (by default) or existing transactions.

Table A-6 describes the key methods and properties of the SqlBulkCopy class.

Table A-6. Key methods and properties of the SqlBulkCopy class

Constructors	Description

SqlBulkCopy(SqlConnection conn)
SqlBulkCopy(string connString)
SqlBulkCopy(string connString,
  SqlBulkCopyOptions options)
SqlBulkCopy(string connString,
  SqlBulkCopyOptions options,
  SqlTransaction, tx)
	Creates a new instance of the SqlBulkCopy class, where:
	
	conn
	  A SqlConnection instance.
	
	connString
	  A SQL Server connection string.
	
	options
	  Bitwise flag that specifies options for the SqlBulkCopy( ) method from the SqlBulkCopyOptions enumeration. See MSDN for more information.
	
	tx
	  An existing transaction (as a SqlTransaction object) in which the bulk copy takes place.

Properties	
BatchSize	The number of rows in each batch sent to the server. The default is 0, indicating that the rows are written in a single batch.
BulkCopyTimeout	Number of seconds for the bulk copy to complete before it times out.
ColumnMappings	A collection of SqlBulkCopyColumnMapping objects that defines the mapping of columns from the source data object to the destination table.
DestinationTableName	The name of the destination table on the server.
NotifyAfter	The number of rows to process before generating a notification event. The default is 0, indicating that notifications are not sent.
Methods	
Close( )	Closes the SqlBulkCopy instance.
WriteToServer( )	Copies all rows in the data source object (DataReader or DataTable) to the destination table.

In general, an application performs the following steps to bulk copy data:

1. Retrieve the data to copy into a DataTable or DataReader object.
2. Connect to the destination database server.
3. Create and configure the SqlBulkCopy object.
4. Call the WriteToServer( ) method of the SqlBulkCopy object.
5. Call the Close( ) method of the SqlBulkCopy object or dispose of the SqlBulkCopy object.

The following example copies all rows in the Person.Address table in the AdventureWorks database to a new table called Address (without a schema) in the ProgrammingSqlServer2005 database. Follow these steps:

1. Create a SQL Server 2005 database called ProgrammingSqlServer2005 if you haven't already created it.

2. Execute the following T-SQL command to create the Address table in the ProgrammingSqlServer2005 database:

```
USE ProgrammingSqlServer2005

CREATE TABLE [Address](
    [AddressID] [int] IDENTITY(1,1) NOT NULL,
    [AddressLine1] [nvarchar](60) NOT NULL,
    [AddressLine2] [nvarchar](60) NULL,
    [City] [nvarchar](30) NOT NULL,
    [StateProvinceID] [int] NOT NULL,
    [PostalCode] [nvarchar](15) NOT NULL,
    [rowguid] [uniqueidentifier] ROWGUIDCOL  NOT NULL,
    [ModifiedDate] [datetime] NOT NULL)
```

3. Create a Windows console application named BulkCopy.

4. Copy the following code into *Program.cs*. Change the highlighted connection strings if necessary.

```
using System;
using System.Data;
using System.Data.SqlClient;

class Program
{
    static void Main(string[] args)
    {
        // get data from the source server using a data reader
        SqlConnection srcConn = new SqlConnection();
        srcConn.ConnectionString = "Data Source=localhost;" +
            "Integrated Security=SSPI;" +
            "Initial Catalog=AdventureWorks;";
        srcConn.Open();

        SqlCommand cmd =
            new SqlCommand("SELECT * FROM Person.Address;", srcConn);
        IDataReader dr = cmd.ExecuteReader();

        // connection to the destination server
        SqlConnection dstConn = new SqlConnection();
        dstConn.ConnectionString = "Data Source=localhost;" +
            "Integrated Security=SSPI;" +
            "Initial Catalog=ProgrammingSqlServer2005;";
        dstConn.Open();

        // bulk copy the  data to the destination table
        using (SqlBulkCopy bcp = new SqlBulkCopy(dstConn))
        {
            bcp.DestinationTableName = "Address";
            bcp.WriteToServer(dr);
        }
        dstConn.Close();

        dr.Close();
```

```
        srcConn.Close( );

        Console.WriteLine("Press any key to continue.");
        Console.ReadKey( );
    }
}
```

5. Execute the application. The rows from the `Person.Address` table in the `AdventureWorks` database are bulk copied into the `Address` table in the `ProgrammingSqlServer2005` database.

If the column names in the source and destination table do not match, you need to map the columns by using the `SqlBulkCopyColumnMapping` class. Each `SqlBulkCopyColumnMapping` instance defines a map between a column in the bulk copy source and the destination. Add the mapping instances by using the `Add( )` method of the `ColumnMappings` property of the `SqlBulkCopy` object before calling the `WriteToServer( )` method.

For example, if you change the name of the address line fields from `AddressLine1` and `AddressLine2` to `AddressLine1a` and `AddressLine2a`, you must add the following mapping code before you call the `WriteToServer( )` method:

```
bcp.ColumnMappings.Add(
    new SqlBulkCopyColumnMapping("AddressID", "AddressID"));
bcp.ColumnMappings.Add(
    new SqlBulkCopyColumnMapping("AddressLine1", "AddressLine1a"));
bcp.ColumnMappings.Add(
    new SqlBulkCopyColumnMapping("AddressLine2", "AddressLine2a"));
bcp.ColumnMappings.Add(
    new SqlBulkCopyColumnMapping("City", "City"));
bcp.ColumnMappings.Add(
    new SqlBulkCopyColumnMapping("StateProvinceID", "StateProvinceID"));
bcp.ColumnMappings.Add(
    new SqlBulkCopyColumnMapping("PostalCode", "PostalCode"));
bcp.ColumnMappings.Add(
    new SqlBulkCopyColumnMapping("rowguid", "rowguid"));
bcp.ColumnMappings.Add(
    new SqlBulkCopyColumnMapping("ModifiedDate", "ModifiedDate"));
```

Mappings can be specified by ordinal or column name, but all mappings must be specified in the same way. If the `ColumnMapping` collection is not empty, every column must be mapped whether their names match or not.

The `SqlBulkCopy` class supports transactions that are dedicated to the bulk copy operation, and can also use existing transactions. Dedicated transactions are used by default, as shown in the preceding example. The bulk copy is committed or rolled back automatically.

You can perform a bulk copy within an existing transaction, making the bulk copy part of the transaction together with other operations. This Windows application is similar to the previous example. It performs a bulk copy within a transaction. It also uses a `DataTable` object as the data source instead of a `DataReader` object.

```csharp
using System;
using System.Data;
using System.Data.SqlClient;

class Program
{
    static void Main(string[] args)
    {
        SqlConnection srcConn = new SqlConnection();
        srcConn.ConnectionString = "Data Source=localhost;" +
            "Integrated Security=SSPI;" +
            "Initial Catalog=AdventureWorks;";

        SqlCommand cmd =
            new SqlCommand("SELECT * FROM Person.Address;", srcConn);
        SqlDataAdapter da = new SqlDataAdapter(cmd);
        DataTable dt = new DataTable();
        da.Fill(dt);

        // connection to the destination server
        SqlConnection dstConn = new SqlConnection();
        dstConn.ConnectionString = "Data Source=localhost;" +
            "Integrated Security=SSPI;" +
            "Initial Catalog=ProgrammingSqlServer2005;";
        dstConn.Open();

        // create the transaction on the destination connection
        SqlTransaction tx = dstConn.BeginTransaction();
        try
        {
            // ... do some work using the transaction (tx)

            // bulk copy the  data to the destination table within
            // the transaction (tx)
            using (SqlBulkCopy bcp =
                new SqlBulkCopy(dstConn, SqlBulkCopyOptions.Default, tx))
            {
                bcp.DestinationTableName = "Address";
                bcp.WriteToServer(dt);
            }

            tx.Commit();
        }
        catch
        {
            tx.Rollback();
        }

        dstConn.Close();

        Console.WriteLine("Press any key to continue.");
        Console.ReadKey();
    }
}
```

Support for New SQL Server Large-Value Data Types

SQL Server 2005 introduces *large-value data types*—varchar(max), nvarchar(max), and varbinary(max)—which allow storage of values up to 2^{32} bytes in size. These types simplify working with large object (LOB) data—working with large-value data types is the same as working with the smaller-value data types (varchar, nvarchar, and varbinary). Large-value data types can be used as column types and as variables, and they can be specified as input and output parameters without special handling. You can return a large-value data type in a SqlDataReader object or use a large-value data type to fill a DataTable object using a SqlDataAdapter object.

The limitations of the large-value data types are as follows:

- A sql_variant type cannot contain a large-value data type.
- A large-value data type cannot be specified as a key column in an index or used as a partitioning key column.

Support for SQL Server User-Defined Types

SQL Server 2005 introduces user-defined types (UDTs). These extend SQL Server data types by letting you define both custom data structures containing one or more data types and objects containing one or more data types together with behaviors. UDTs can be used everywhere that SQL Server system data types can be used, including as variables or arguments or in column definitions.

You can create a UDT by using any language supported by the .NET Common Language Runtime (CLR). UDTs are defined as a class or structure—data is exposed as fields or properties, whereas behaviors are defined by methods.

Once a UDT is compiled into a .NET assembly, you must register the assembly in SQL Server by using the CREATE ASSEMBLY T-SQL statement. You must then create the UDT in SQL Server by using the CREATE TYPE T-SQL statement before you can use the UDT.

Support for Snapshot Isolation in Transactions

SQL Server 2005 introduces support for snapshot isolation row locking. When snapshot isolation is enabled, updated row versions for each transaction are maintained in the tempdb system database. Each transaction is identified by a unique transaction sequence number, which is recorded together with the updated row versions. A transaction works with the most recent row versions having transaction sequence numbers prior to the sequence number of the current transaction—transaction sequence numbers that are greater than the current transaction sequence number indicate that the transactions occurred after the current transaction started, and thus are ignored. The result is that all queries in the transaction see a consistent view of the database at the moment the transaction started. No locks are acquired, which allows multiple simultaneous transactions to execute without blocking or waiting. This improves performance and significantly reduces the chance of a deadlock. Snapshot isolation uses optimistic concurrency—if an attempt is made to update data that has been modified since it was last read, the transaction will roll back and an error will be raised.

You can reduce the chance of update conflict by using locking hints in a T-SQL statement or at the beginning of a transaction. For example, the UPDLOCK hint locks rows selected in a statement and blocks attempts to update them before the statement completes. Hints should be used sparingly—excessive hints might suggest a problem with the application design.

Snapshot isolation is explicitly enabled for each database by setting the ALLOW_ TRANSACTION_ISOLATION option to ON. You also need to set the READ_COMMITTED_SNAPSHOT option to ON to allow access to versioned rows under the default READ_COMMITTED isolation level. If the READ_COMMITTED_SNAPSHOT option is set to OFF, you must explicitly set the isolation level when initiating a transaction, as shown in the following code snippet:

```
SqlTransaction tx = conn.BeginTransaction(IsolationLevel.Snapshot);
```

Database Mirroring Support

Database mirroring lets you keep an up-to-date copy of a database on a standby server. The two copies of the database provide high availability and redundancy—if the primary database fails, the mirror can quickly be promoted to take its place. The .NET Data Provider for SQL Server implicitly supports database mirroring—once the SQL Server 2005 database has been configured, database mirroring is automatic and is transparent to the developer.

SQL Server 2005 also supports explicit database mirroring. The SqlConnection object supports the Failover Partner parameter in the connection string. This lets the client application specify the name of the failover partner server. In this way, the client application can transparently attempt to establish a connection with the mirror database if the principal database is unavailable.

The name of the active server for the current connection is always available through the DataSource property of the SqlConnection instance—this property is updated when a connection is switched to the mirror server in response to a failover event.

 Microsoft does not support database mirroring in the November 7, 2005 release of SQL Server 2005. As a result, database mirroring should be used only for evaluation purposes and not in production. Database mirroring is disabled by default and can be enabled by using trace flag 1400 as a startup parameter.

Server Enumeration

The GetDataSources() method of the SqlDataSourceEnumerator class enumerates active instances of SQL Server 2000 and later that are installed on your local network. The results are returned in a DataTable object with the columns shown in Table A-7.

Table A-7. DataTable schema for GetDataSources() method results

Column name	Description
ServerName	Name of the SQL Server.
InstanceName	Name of the server instance. This value is blank if the server is running as the default instance.
IsClustered	Indicates whether the server is part of a cluster.
Version	The version number of the server.

The following console application uses the SqlDataSourceEnumerator object to enumerate SQL Server instances:

```
using System;
using System.Data;
using System.Data.Sql;

class Program
{
    static void Main(string[] args)
    {
        DataTable dt = SqlDataSourceEnumerator.Instance.GetDataSources();
        foreach (DataRow row in dt.Rows)
            Console.WriteLine("{0}\t{1}\t{2}\t{3}",
                row["ServerName"], row["InstanceName"],
                row["IsClustered"], row["Version"]);

        Console.WriteLine("Press any key to continue.");
        Console.ReadKey();
    }
}
```

The output looks similar to Figure A-9.

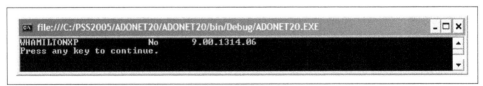

Figure A-9. Results for SqlDataSourceEnumerator example

The static Instance property of the SqlDataSourceEnumerator class returns an instance of the enumerator that is used to retrieve information about SQL Server instances.

Support for Retrieving Provider Statistics in SQL Server 2005

The .NET Framework Data Provider for SQL Server supports runtime statistics that expose information about processing queries in the database.

You must enable statistics by setting the StatisticsEnabled property of the SqlConnection object to true after the connection has been created. Once statistics are enabled, they can be retrieved into an IDictionary instance using the RetrieveStatistics( ) method of the SqlConnection object. The values in the dictionary are the statistic counter values, and are all of the long data type. The ResetStatistics( ) method of the SqlConnection object resets the counters. All statistics are gathered on a per-connection basis.

The following console application creates a connection, enables statistics, does a bit of work by filling a DataTable object using a data adapter, and iterates over the dictionary to output the name-value pair for each counter in the dictionary:

```
using System;
using System.Data;
using System.Collections;
using System.Data.SqlClient;

class Program
{
    static void Main(string[] args)
    {
        // open a connection and enable statistics
        using (SqlConnection conn = new SqlConnection( ))
        {
            conn.ConnectionString = "Data Source=localhost;" +
                "Integrated Security=SSPI;Initial Catalog=AdventureWorks";
            conn.StatisticsEnabled = true;

            // do some work with the connection
            SqlDataAdapter da =
                new SqlDataAdapter("SELECT * FROM Person.Contact", conn);
            DataTable dt = new DataTable( );
            da.Fill(dt);

            // get the statistics
            IDictionary d = conn.RetrieveStatistics( );
            // move the dictionary keys to an array
            string[] keys = new string[d.Count];
            d.Keys.CopyTo(keys, 0);

            // iterate over the dictionary displaying the key-value pair
            for (int i = 0; i < d.Count; i++)
                Console.WriteLine("{0}\t{1}",
                    keys[i], (long)d[keys[i]]);
        }

        Console.WriteLine(Environment.NewLine + "Press any key to continue.");
```

```
        Console.ReadKey();
    }
}
```

Results are shown in Figure A-10.

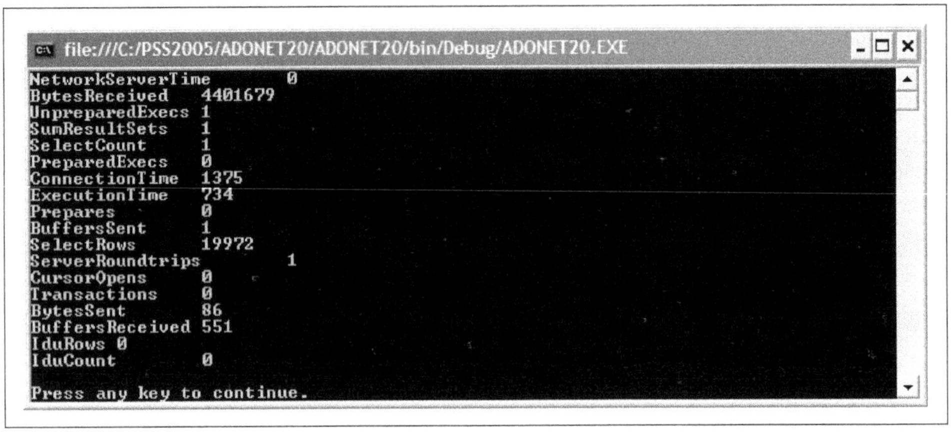

Figure A-10. Results for retrieving provider statistics example

See MSDN for a complete discussion of the available statistics.

Change Password Support

With SQL Server 2005 and Windows Server 2003 or later, you can programmati-cally change the existing password for the user specified in a connection string.

This example changes the password for a login named TestUser. First, create the user login in SQL Server Management Studio by right-clicking Security → Logins in Object Explorer and selecting New Login from the context menu. In the Login–New dialog box, do the following:

- Select the General page on the left side of the dialog box.
- Enter TestUser in the Login name listbox.
- Select the SQL Server Authentication radio button.
- Enter password in both the Password and Confirm Password listboxes.
- Uncheck the Enforce password policy checkbox.
- Select User Mapping on the left side of the dialog box.
- Check the AdventureWorks checkbox in the Users mapped to this login panel.
- Click the OK button to create the user.

Create a new console application, replace *Program.cs* with the following code, and execute the example:

```
using System;
using System.Data;
using System.Collections;
using System.Data.SqlClient;

class Program
{
    static void Main(string[] args)
    {
        string connStringOld = "Data Source=localhost;" +
            "uid=TestUser;pwd=password;Initial Catalog=AdventureWorks";
        SqlConnection.ChangePassword(connStringOld, "password2");
        Console.WriteLine("Password changed to 'password2'.");

        // open a connection
        string connStringNew = "Data Source=localhost;" +
            "uid=TestUser;pwd=password2;Initial Catalog=AdventureWorks";
        SqlConnection conn = new SqlConnection( );
        conn.ConnectionString = connStringNew;
        conn.Open( );
        Console.WriteLine("Connected with changed password.");

        conn.Close( );
        Console.WriteLine("Disconnected.");

        Console.WriteLine(Environment.NewLine + "Press any key to continue.");
        Console.ReadKey( );
    }
}
```

Results are shown in Figure A-11.

Figure A-11. Results for change password example

The ChangePassword( ) method of the SqlConnection class take two arguments:

- A connection string containing the user ID and password. An exception will be thrown if integrated security is specified in the connection string.
- The new password.

The ChangePassword( ) method can be used to change an expired user password without administrator intervention. If the password has expired, calling the Open( ) method of the SqlConnection object raises a SqlException exception. If the password needs to be reset, the Number property of the SqlException object will be either 18487 (password expired) or 18488 (password must be reset before logging in).

Schema Discovery

The new schema discovery API in ADO.NET 2.0 lets you programmatically find and return metadata about the database for a connection. The database-independent API exposes schema elements, including tables, columns, and stored procedures.

The data connection exposes five categories of metadata through the GetSchema( ) method of the DbConnection class. This returns a DataTable object containing the metadata. It takes one of the five metadata collection names from the DbMeta-DataCollectionNames class described in Table A-8.

Table A-8. DbMetaDataCollectionNames public fields

Collection name	Description
DataSourceInformation	Information about the database instance.
DataTypes	Information about data types that the database supports. This includes information about mapping data-source types to .NET Framework data types.
MetaDataCollections	List of metadata collections available.
ReservedWords	List of reserved words in the database.
Restrictions	Array of qualifiers for each metadata collection that can be used to restrict the scope of information returned. One value is returned per row with the position of the qualifier in the array specified by the RestrictionNumber column.

The following example retrieves and outputs the available metadata collections:

```
using System;
using System.Collections;
using System.Data.SqlClient;
using System.Data;
using System.Data.Common;

class Program
{
    static void Main(string[] args)
    {
        SqlConnection conn = new SqlConnection( );
        conn.ConnectionString = "Data Source=localhost;" +
            "Integrated Security=SSPI;Initial Catalog=AdventureWorks";

        conn.Open( );
        DataTable dt = conn.GetSchema(
            DbMetaDataCollectionNames.MetaDataCollections);
        conn.Close( );

        foreach (DataRow row in dt.Rows)
        {
            Console.WriteLine("{0}; {1}; {2}",
                row[0], row[1], row[2]);
        }
```

```
            Console.WriteLine("\n\rPress any key to continue.");
            Console.ReadKey();
        }
    }
```

Results are shown in Figure A-12.

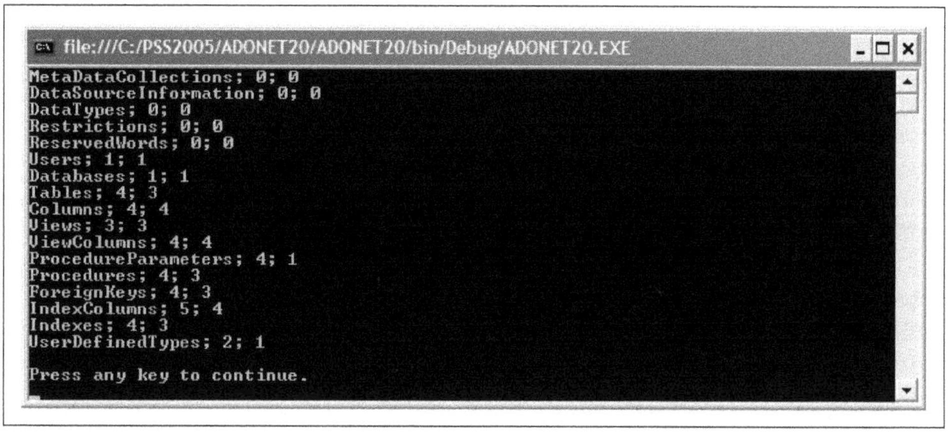

Figure A-12. Results for GetSchema() method example

The DataTable object returned from the GetSchema() method has three columns, as described in Table A-9.

Table A-9. Columns in DataTable object returned by GetSchema()

Column name	Description
CollectionName	The metadata collection name
NumberOfRestrictions	The maximum number of qualifiers for a metadata collection that can be used to restrict the scope of information returned
NumberOfIdentifierParts	The maximum number of identifier parts

An overload of the GetSchema() method takes the metadata collection name (one of the CollectionName values returned by the GetSchema() method) as an argument. For example, the following statement returns metadata about the tables in the database:

```
    DataTable dt = conn.GetSchema("Tables");
```

An extract from the result set follows:

TABLE_CATALOG	TABLE_SCHEMA	TABLE_NAME	TABLE_TYPE
AdventureWorks	dbo	AWBuildVersion	BASE TABLE
AdventureWorks	dbo	DatabaseLog	BASE TABLE
AdventureWorks	dbo	sysdiagrams	BASE TABLE
AdventureWorks	HumanResources	Department	BASE TABLE

...

TABLE_CATALOG	TABLE_SCHEMA	TABLE_NAME	TABLE_TYPE
AdventureWorks	Sales	vSalesPerson	VIEW
AdventureWorks	Sales	vSalesPersonSales ByFiscalYears	VIEW
AdventureWorks	Sales	vStoreWith Demographics	VIEW

Another overload of GetSchema() takes a string array of restrictions as a second argument. Call the GetSchema() method with the DbMetaDataCollectionNames.Restrictions argument to get a valid list of restrictions for a metadata collection. There is one row per restriction—each restriction has a unique RestrictionNumber value. For example, for the Tables metadata collection in SQL Server, there are four restrictions:

Restriction name	Restriction default	Restriction number
Catalog	TABLE_CATALOG	1
Owner	TABLE_SCHEMA	2
Table	TABLE_NAME	3
TableType	TABLE_TYPE	4

Continuing with the Tables metadata, the following code snippet uses restrictions to return information only for views in the Production schema:

```
string[] r = new string[] {null, "Production", null, "VIEW"};
DataTable dt = conn.GetSchema("Tables", r);
```

Support for DbConnection.GetSchema() is optional, so a data provider can choose to throw a NotSupportedException. There is no standard for the information returned when a metadata collection is queried—two providers can return different information (i.e., columns in the DataTable object) and support different restrictions.

Disconnected Class Enhancements

ADO.NET 2.0 introduces new features and enhancements for working with disconnected data. These changes affect both retrieving and updating data. The following subsections describe the key changes.

DataSet and DataTable Enhancements

The new DataTableReader class lets you iterate over the rows in a DataTable object in a read-only, forward-only manner much like a regular DataReader. The DataTableReader object returns the rows and columns in the same order as in the underlying DataTable object. The DataTableReader returns only the current version of the row in the DataTable object—rows marked for deletion are skipped over. The data in the underlying DataTable object can be modified or deleted while the

DataTableReader object is active, and the DataTableReader object will maintain its position and validity.

The DataTableReader object has an overloaded constructor—one takes a DataTable object as an argument and the other takes a DataTable[] object as an argument. The DataTableReader object can also be constructed by calling the CreateDataReader() method of the DataTable or DataSet class. For multiple tables, the tables appear in the same order in which they exist in the DataTable array or DataSet object. The NextResult() method of the DataTableReader object advances to the next result set if one exists.

The following console application creates a DataTable object containing all rows in the Person.Contact table in AdventureWorks, creates a DataTableReader object, and writes the first and last name for each person to the console window:

```
using System;
using System.Data;
using System.Data.SqlClient;

class Program
{
    static void Main(string[] args)
    {
        // open a connection
        SqlConnection conn = new SqlConnection();
        conn.ConnectionString = "Data Source=localhost;" +
            "Integrated Security=SSPI;Initial Catalog=AdventureWorks";

        // create a DataTable with the Person.Contact data
        SqlCommand selectCommand = conn.CreateCommand();
        selectCommand.CommandText = "SELECT * FROM Person.Contact";

        DataTable dt = new DataTable();

        SqlDataAdapter da = new SqlDataAdapter(selectCommand);
        da.Fill(dt);

        // create a DataTableReader
        DataTableReader dtr = dt.CreateDataReader();

        // iterate over the rows in the DataTableReader and output
        // the first name and last name for each person
        while (dtr.Read())
            Console.WriteLine("{0}\t{1}",
                dtr["FirstName"], dtr["LastName"]);

        Console.WriteLine("Press any key to continue.");
        Console.ReadKey();
    }
}
```

Results are shown in Figure A-13.

Figure A-13. Results for CreateDataReader() method example

Batch Processing with the DataAdapter

The DataAdapter class in ADO.NET 2.0 lets you group insert, update, and delete operations on a DataSet object or a DataTable object, instead of sending one row at a time to the server. This reduces round trips and typically results in performance gains. The SQL Server and Oracle providers support batch updates.

The UpdateBatchSize property of the DataAdapter object specifies the number of rows to be sent in each batch. If the UpdateBatchSize property is set to 0, the DataAdapter object uses the largest batch size that the database server can handle. Extremely large batches can negatively affect performance—the size of the batch should be tuned for your environment before deploying an application.

When batching updates, the UpdatedRowSource property of the DataAdapter object UpdateCommand, InsertCommand, and DeleteCommand properties must be set to the value UpdateRowSource.None or UpdateRowSource.OutputParameters. The values UpdateRowSource.FirstReturnedRecord and UpdateRowSource.Both are both invalid.

When updating rows using the DataAdapter object with batch processing disabled, the RowUpdating and RowUpdated events are raised for each row processed. When batch processing is enabled, the RowUpdating event occurs for each row processed, while the RowUpdated event is raised only once—after the batch is processed. Because the RowUpdated event is raised only once for all rows in the batch, its Row property is null. Instead, you can use the CopyToRows() method of the RowUpdatedEventArgs object to copy the processed rows to a DataRow array, where you can access them.

Index

We'd like to hear your suggestions for improving our indexes. Send email to *index@oreilly.com*.

classes *(continued)*
   events, 405
     creating, 424
   ExceptionMessageBox, 156–161
   HostedEventProvider, 431
   instance, instantiation, 239–241
   Job, 380
   JobSchedule, 381
   JobStep, 386
   LogProviders, 371
   ManagedComputer properties, 321
   MergeArticles, 458
   MergePullSubscription, 468
   notification, 405
     creating, 427–431
   Operator, 383
   PrecedenceConstraint, 363
   ProxyAccount, 386
   RegisteredSubscriber, 459
   Server, 275
   ServerAlias, 324
   ServerConnection, 241
   ServerPermission, 275
   ServerPermissionInfo, 275
   ServerPermissionSet, 275
   Service, 325
   ServiceBroker, 392
   SMO, 255–266
     backup/restore, 305–309
     object model, 235
     programming, 267–285
     programming WMI, 318–326
     RegisteredServer, 268
     scripting, 298–305
     SqlMail, 314–317
     trace/replay, 311–314
     Transfer, 309–311
   SmoException, 254
   SqlBilkCopyColumnMapping, 532
   SqlCeEngine, 499, 501
   SqlClientFactory, 512
   SqlCommand, 516
   SqlContext, 87
   SqlDataRecord, 89, 104
   SqlDependency, 526
   SqlMetaData, 104
   SqlNotificationRequest, 524
   SqlPipe, 88
   SqlSmoObject, 302
   SqlTriggerContext, 119, 124
   SQLXML 4.0, 130–142

   SqlXmlAdapter, 132
   SqlXmlCommand, 131
   SubscriberDevice, 435
   subscriptions, 405
   subscriptions, creating, 425
   UserDefinedFunctions, 99
   XmlReader, retrieving objects, 137
clauses
   AS SNAPSHOT, 13
   AUTHENTICATION, 230
   EXECUTE AS, 47
   FOR XML, 135, 201–208
   OUTPUT, 36
   TABLESAMPLE, 35
   TOP, 33
   WHERE, 482
     operators, 40
   .WRITE, 31
clients
   SQL Native Client,
     programming, 128–130
   SQL Server Mobile, 497
   SQLXML 4.0, 130
     annotated mapping schemas, 141–146
     DiffGrams, 153–156
     managed classes, 130–142
     template queries, 146–150
     UpdateGrams, 150–153
   XML result sets, processing, 137
CLR (Common Language Runtime), 1
   ADO.NET in-process extensions, 87–90
   assembly management, 73–76
   custom attributes, 90
   DDL, 68–73
   debugging/testing, 92
   design, 59–61
   enabling, 61
   Hello World example, 62–68
   .NET data types, 90
   required .NET namespaces, 61
   routines, 62
   stored procedures, 79–81
   triggers, 84–87
   UDA functions, 81–83
   UDFs, 76–79
   UDTs, 83–84
code access security (CAS), 59
CODEPAGE, 169
collections
   Database.Users, 271
   hierarchies, iterating, 319–323

OPENXML keyword, 176
    result sets, 179
operations
    BACKUP DATABASE, 307
    SMO, transacting, 248
Operator class, 383
operators
    ALL, 41
    ANY, 40
    APPLY, 45
    managing, 19
    OUTER APPLY, 46
    PIVOT, 42
    SOME, 40
    SQL Server Agent, creating, 382
    UNPIVOT, 42
    XQuery, 195
optimization
    data providers, 516–542
    disconnected class
        enhancements, 542–544
    FOR XML clause, 207
    T-SQL language enhancements, 32–48
        error handling, 51–53
        ranking functions, 48–51
    UDTs, 534
options
    AUTO_DREATE_STATISTICS
        database, 278
    BULK, 169
    flags, 176
    idoc, 176
    rowpatern, 176
Options property, 528
Options.WithDependencies property, 310
OUTER APPLY operator, 46
OUTPUT clause, 36

P

packages (SSIS)
    configuring, 349, 364
    creating, 351–371
    loading, 353
    logging, 370
    running, 357
    saving, 352
    tasks, adding, 354
    validating, 359
    variables, 350
    viewing, 353
PageAddress property, 383

parameters
    commands, values, 332
    Database_Name, 23
    queries, applying, 134
    servers, reports, 332
    URL, prefixes, 331
<Parameters> elements, 216
partitions
    functions, SMO classes, 288
    schemes, SMO classes, 289
passwords, modifying, 538
PATH, 202
PATH indexes, 180
Pause( ) method, 325
PercentCompleteEventHandler event
        handler, 309
performance, CLR integration design, 59
PerformanceQueryInterval property, 423
permissions
    configuring, 60
    CONNECT, 231
    creating, 232
    databases, SMO classes, 291
    endpoints, managing, 231
    objects, validating, 47
    servers
        managing, 275
        SMO classes, 290
    XML schema collections, managing, 190
PIVOT operator, 42
polling, 516
polygons, defining, 114
PrecedenceConstraint class, 363
precedent constraints, SSIS, 346
Precision property, 111
prefixes, URL parameters, 331
prerequisites, replication, 444
primary XML indexes, 180
processing
    asynchronous, 516–523
    batches, 544
    queries, DAT, 25
processing on clients, 137
profiles, Database Mail, 314
programmability enhancements, 2
programming
    asynchronous, 516–523
    control-flow, 351–371
    data-flow, 371
    Notification, 407–440
    replication, 442–477
    Service Broker, 389–401

R

ranking
    functions, 48–51
    rows, 50
RAW mode, 135
RDL (Report Definition Language), 328
Read( ) method, 488
reading databases, 504–505
RECEIVE T-SQL statement, 400
reclaiming database space, 502
records, DiffGrams, 153
recursive members, 39
references, adding databases, 64
Refresh( ) method, 326
Registered Servers window, 9
registered servers, SMO classes, 268, 286
RegisteredSubscriber class, 459
RegisterLocal( ) method, 422
registration
    assemblies, 73
    stored procedures, 101
    subscribers, 459–461
relational data
    binding, 195
    XML, 176–179
relational_schema, 186, 188
relationships
    creating, 13
    modifying, 16
reliability of CLR integration design, 59, 60
remote connectivity, SQL Server Surface Area
       Configuration, 25
remote service binding, 389, 395
RemoveReplicatedColumns( ) method, 458
removing
    assemblies, 75
    databases, SQL Server Mobile, 503
    endpoints, 229
    functions, 79
    indexes, 185
    stored procedures, 81
    triggers, 86
    types, 84
    UDA functions, 82
    XML schema collections, 188
Render button, 337
Render( ) method, 341
rendering reports, 329–335
repairing databases, 502
RepairType enumeration, 248
replace value of statement, 200
replay classes, SMO, 311–314

replaying trace results, 25
replication
    agents, 443
        managing, 472
    items
        enumerating, 455–457
        managing, 457
    monitoring, 474–477
    programming, 442–477
    schedules, 470–472
Replication Distribution Agent, 443
Replication Log Reader Agent, 443
Replication Management Objects (see
       RMOs)
Replication Merge Agent, 443
Replication node, 19
Replication Queue Reader Agent, 443
Replication Snapshot Agent, 443
ReplicationServer object, 443
ReplicationType property, 465
Report Definition Language (see RDL)
Report Manager, 329
Report Server web services, 336–341
Reporting Services, 9
    connecting, 10–20
reports
    server parameters, 332
    SSRS, 342
        installing, 328
        integrating into applications, 329–341
    URL access, 329–335
ReportViewer control, 335
requests, SOAP, 217
Reset( ) method, 97
ResetStatistics( ) method, 537
responses, SOAP, 217
restarting services, 325
restore classes, SMO, 305–309
RESTORE DATABASE event, 309
restoring SQL Server Mobile, 503
restrictions
    UDTs, 113
    XML DML, 201
result sets
    FOR XML clause, 201–208
    MARS, 528
    OPENXML, 179
    XML, 137
        applying XSLT transformations, 139
results, replaying trace, 25
Resume( ) method, 325
RETENTION property, 400

About the Author

Bill Hamilton is a software architect specializing in designing, developing, and implementing distributed applications using .NET and J2EE technologies. Over the last ten years, he has provided consulting services in B2B, B2C, B2E, data integration, and portal initiatives for banking, retail, accounting, manufacturing, and financial services. An early technology adopter, he frequently evaluates, recommends, and helps his clients use new technologies effectively. Bill has designed and helped build several award-winning software packages. He is the coauthor of *ADO.NET in a Nutshell* and the author of *ADO.NET Cookbook* and *NUnit Pocket Reference*, all from O'Reilly.

Colophon

The animal on the cover of *Programming SQL Server 2005* is an arctic cod. The arctic cod (*Boreogadus saida*) can be found living in the icy waters off northern Russia, Greenland, Canada, and Alaska. It is smaller and thinner than its cousin, the Atlantic cod, and characterized by a deeply forked tail, projecting lower jaw, and the presence of a small-sized "whisker" or barbel beneath its jaw.

Little is known about the life stages of young arctic cod as they are bred beneath layers of ice in autumn and winter off the coast of Canada, and from January to February off the coast of Russia. It is known that females can release between 9,000 to 21,000 eggs, which are then externally fertilized by the males with a milky substance called milt.

Arctic cod become mature at three years and can measure as long as 15 inches but usually not longer than a foot. Weight is related to length with a 4-inch fish weighing less than an ounce and an 11-inch fish weighing over six ounces. The body size of the species decreases from north to south so that Arctic cod in northern waters appear larger than their southern family members.

Arctic cod can be found near the surface waters or as deep as 2,953 feet. In open waters, arctic cod swim in schools, but closer to the surface, they tend to live in much smaller groups. They can be found living in narrow spaces of water called "water wedges" between layers of ice. The water wedges are inaccessible to larger predators such as seals.

Adults have small scales and are brown-colored along their sides and back, with black spots. Fins are dark and nearly black in color, with a pale edge and a long pale line that runs along the side of the fish from head to tail. The arctic cod can live up to six years, and scientists can determine their age by counting the rings that appear in the ear bones of the creatures.

Arctic cod consume mostly plankton, which are tiny marine plants and animals that float near the surface of ocean water. They are themselves an important part of the food chain, and narwhals, beluga whales, and seabirds such as murres depend on them as food.

The cover image is from *Wood's Animate Creation*. The cover font is Adobe ITC Garamond. The text font is Linotype Birka; the heading font is Adobe Myriad Condensed; and the code font is LucasFont's TheSans Mono Condensed.

Lightning Source UK Ltd.
Milton Keynes UK
UKHW052350101218
333807UK00005B/609/P

9 780596 004798